Facets of Russian Irrationalism between Art and Life

Studies in Slavic Literature and Poetics

Editors

O.F. Boele
S. Brouwer
J.M. Stelleman

Founding Editors

J.J. van Baak
R. Grübel
A.G.F. van Holk
W.G. Weststeijn

VOLUME 61

The titles published in this series are listed at *brill.com/sslp*

Facets of Russian Irrationalism between Art and Life

Mystery inside Enigma

Edited by

Olga Tabachnikova

Translation Editors

Elizabeth Harrison
Christopher Tooke

BRILL
RODOPI

LEIDEN | BOSTON

Cover illustration: Painting: Птица Гамаюн (Gamajun Bird), by artist Viktor Mikhailovich Vasnetsov. Printed on the cover of Russian artists of the 19th century, Lazuko A.K (1990). Leningrad: Khudozhnik RSFSR

Library of Congress Cataloging-in-Publication Data

Names: Tabachnikova, Olga, 1967- editor.
Title: Facets of Russian irrationalism between art and life : mystery inside
    enigma / edited by Olga Tabachnikova.
Description: Leiden ; Boston : Brill Rodopi, 2016. | Series: Studies in
    Slavic literature and poetics ; volume 61 | Includes bibliographical
    references and index. | Description based on print version record and CIP
    data provided by publisher; resource not viewed.
Identifiers: LCCN 2016010947 (print) | LCCN 2015047186 (ebook) | ISBN
    9789004311121 (E-book) | ISBN 9789004311114 (hardback : alk. paper)
Subjects: LCSH: Irrationalism (Philosophy) in literature. | Russian
    literature--History and criticism.
Classification: LCC PG2987.I73 (print) | LCC PG2987.I73 F33 2016 (ebook) |
    DDC 891.709--dc23
LC record available at http://lccn.loc.gov/2016010947

Want or need Open Access? Brill Open offers you the choice to make your research freely accessible online in exchange for a publication charge. Review your various options on brill.com/brill-open.

Typeface for the Latin, Greek, and Cyrillic scripts: "Brill". See and download: brill.com/brill-typeface.

ISSN 0169-0175
ISBN 978-90-04-31111-4 (hardback)
ISBN 978-90-04-31112-1 (e-book)

Copyright 2016 by Koninklijke Brill NV, Leiden, The Netherlands.
Koninklijke Brill NV incorporates the imprints Brill, Brill Hes & De Graaf, Brill Nijhoff, Brill Rodopi and Hotei Publishing.
All rights reserved. No part of this publication may be reproduced, translated, stored in a retrieval system, or transmitted in any form or by any means, electronic, mechanical, photocopying, recording or otherwise, without prior written permission from the publisher.
Authorization to photocopy items for internal or personal use is granted by Koninklijke Brill NV provided that the appropriate fees are paid directly to The Copyright Clearance Center, 222 Rosewood Drive, Suite 910, Danvers, MA 01923, USA.
Fees are subject to change.

This book is printed on acid-free paper and produced in a sustainable manner.

To the memory of
Alexander Ivashkin (1948–2014)
and
Oliver Smith (1979–2013)

Contents

Acknowledgements XI
List of Illustrations XII
Notes on Contributors XIII

Introduction: Rationalising Russian Irrationalism 1
Olga Tabachnikova

PART 1
On the Place of Irrationalism in the Russian History of Ideas

1 The Traditions of Rationalism in Russian Culture of the Pre-Soviet Period 51
   Barbara Olaszek

2 Irrationalism in Ancient Russia 72
   Tatiana Chumakova

3 Ethos Versus Pathos. The Ontologisation of Knowledge in Russian Philosophy 94
   Oliver Smith

4 Irrationalism and Antisemitism in Late-Tsarist Literature 115
   Christopher John Tooke

5 Russian Semiotics of Behaviour, or Can a Russian Person be Regarded as 'Homo Economicus'? 134
   Natalia Vinokurova

6 Fides et ratio: Catholicism, Rationalism and Mysticism in Russian Literary Culture of the Mid-Nineteenth Century 160
   Elizabeth Harrison

PART 2
Russian Classics and Their Influence in Space and Time

7 The Irrational Basis of Gogol's Mythopoetics 193
   Arkadii Goldenberg

8   On the Philosophical Sources and Nature of Dostoevskii's
        Anti-Rationalism   203
           Sergei Kibal'nik

9   Shifting French Perspectives on Dostoevskian
        Anti-Rationalism   222
           Alexander McCabe

10   The Concept of Love and Beauty in the Works of Turgenev   241
           Margarita Odesskaia

11   Patterns of European Irrationalism, from Source to Estuary: Johann
        Georg Hamann, Lev Shestov and Anton Chekhov – on Both Sides of
        Reason   258
           Olga Tabachnikova

12   Lev Tolstoi and Vasilii Rozanov: Two Fundamental(ist) Types of
        Russian Irrationalism   313
           Rainer Grübel

        PART 3
The Silver Age

13   From Neo-Kantian Theory of Cognition to Christian Intellectual
        Mysticism: Logical Voluntarism in Vladimir Solov'ev and Andrei
        Belyi   339
           Henrieke Stahl

14   Aleksei Remizov's *Pliashushchii demon – tanets i slovo*: Cultural
        Memory, Dreams and Demons   352
           Marilyn Schwinn Smith

15   Irrational Elements in Ivan Bunin's Short Story 'The Grammar of
        Love'   370
           Ildikó Mária Rácz

PART 4
Russian Culture into the 20th Century and Beyond

16 Viewing Askance: Irrationalist Aspects in Russian Art from Fedotov to Malevich and into the Beyond   387
   Jeremy Howard

17 Symbols, Metaphors and Irrationalities in Twentieth-Century Music   415
   Alexander Ivashkin

18 The Irrational in Russian Cinema: A Short Course   433
   Oleg Kovalov

19 The Rational and Irrational Standard: Russian Architecture as a Facet of Culture   455
   Elena Kabkova and Olga Stukalova

PART 5
Soviet and Post-Soviet Literature

20 The Irrational in the Perception of Andrei Platonov's Characters   469
   Kira Gordovich

21 The Metaphysics of Numbers in the Eurasian Artistic Mentality: Viktor Pelevin's *The Dialectics of the Transition Period* (*From Nowhere to No Place*)   475
   Liudmila Safronova

22 "Questions to Which Reason Has No Answer": Iurii Mamleev's Irrationalism in European Context   496
   Oliver Ready

23 Vladimir Sorokin and the Return of History   519
   David Gillespie

   Index   531

Acknowledgements

Personal

I am grateful to all the contributors for their forbearance and continuing faith in this project. My most heartfelt thanks go to the volume's translation editors Elizabeth Harrison and Christopher Tooke whose help in preparation of the manuscript has been invaluable. I am also truly grateful to all those who contributed to the proofreading stage, but especially to David Gillespie (Bath) and Jeremy Howard (St Andrews) for giving their time so generously, and to Elizabeth Burns (Lancaster, 1957–2015), who provided vital help in finalising the text, and who was a true joy to be around and to work with.

Two distinguished contributors, Oliver Smith and Alexander Ivashkin, tragically did not live to see the completion of this project, and it is to their lasting memory that this volume is dedicated.

Institutional

The editor acknowledges the financial support of the Leverhulme Trust and the University of Bristol (Russian Department) during the years 2009–2011 (Leverhulme Early Career Fellowship). The conference 'Russian Irrationalism in the Global Context: Sources and Influences' of March 2010, at the university of Bristol, organised as part of my fellowship, eventually gave rise to this book.

List of Illustrations

14.1 'Dancing Demon' by Aleksei Mikhailovich Remizov   354
16.1 Montage of Kazimir Malevich, Quadrilateral [The Black Square], 1914–15, oil on canvas, 80.1 × 80.1   388
16.2 Pavel Fedotov, The Gamblers, 1852, oil on canvas, 60.5 × 70.2   390
16.3 Anon., Paramoshka and Savoska playing Cards, c. 1760s, coloured woodcut, 29 × 33.1   393
16.4 Ilia Repin, Ivan the Terrible and his Son Ivan, 16 November 1581, 1882–85, oil on canvas, 199.5 × 254   395
16.5 Abram Balashov and Ilia Repin. Fragment of slashed Ivan the Terrible and his Son Ivan, as reproduced in Niva, 5, 1913   396
16.6 Ilia Repin, Poprishchin. 'I'm really astonished the deputation's so slow in coming. Whatever could have held them up...', 1882, oil on canvas, 98 × 69   403
16.7 Mikhail Vrubel, Demon Downcast, 1902, oil on canvas, 139 × 387   404
16.8 Nikolai Kulbin, Self-Portrait, c. 1913–14   408
16.9 Aleksandr Gorodetskii, Illustration to Sergei Gorodetskii poem, Intense Heat, 1906   411

Notes on Contributors

Tatiana Chumakova
is a Professor at the Department of Philosophy of Religion and Religious Studies at St Petersburg State University. Her teaching and scholarship focus on Russian philosophy, religious anthropology, the social history of science and the anthropology of religion. Professor Chumakova specialises in the intersection of religion and culture in pre-modern and modern Russia. She is the author of the monographs *V chelovecheskom zhitel'stve mnozi obrazy zriatsia: Obraz cheloveka v kul'ture Drevnei Rusi* (*The Image of the Person in Old Russian culture*, St Petersburg, 2001) and *Pravoslavie* (*Orthodoxy*) (St Petersburg, 2007, 2nd ed., 2009), and book chapters on a wide variety of subjects, ranging from the social history of science in Russia to philosophical anthropology.

David Gillespie
has been teaching and researching at the University of Bath since 1985. He has also taught at the Free University of Berlin, the University of Navarre (Pamplona), and the state universities of Tomsk, Krasnodar and Magnitogorsk in Russia. He has published extensively on modern Russian literature and film, including on Vladimir Sorokin, and is currently working on a book-length study of the history of Russian literature screen adaptations.

Arkadii Goldenberg
is full Professor at the Department of Literature at Volgograd State Socio-Pedagogical University. His research interests include cultural archetypes, mythopoetics of Russian literature, works by Nikolai Gogol, the history of Volga-Don literature of the Silver Age and folklore studies. He is the author of over 150 articles and books. His monograph *The Archetypes in the poetics of Nikolai Gogol* has won wide recognition and has been nominated as the all-Russian contest winner "The best scientific book of 2007" (the fifth edition, Moscow, 2014).

Kira Gordovich
has been teaching Russian literature since 1956. She has been Professor at the Northwestern Printing Institute for the past 27 years, and has taken part in preparing future editors and publishers. She has published around 200 articles and ten books on various issues of poetics. Her latest works include *Russian Writers of the XIX–XX Centuries*, as well as *N.G. Garin-Mihailovski. Personality and works*, St Petersburg: Petronivs 2014, and a collection of articles.

Rainer Grübel
was full Professor of Slavic Literature at Oldenburg University (Germany) from 1986 until 2008; he previously taught at the Universities of Utrecht (1976–1984) and Leiden (1984–1986). His main fields of interest are: the semiotics and axiology of literature, literature and the media, and the relation of literature and philosophy. His most important publications include: *Russischer Konstruktivismus. Künstlerische Konzeptionen, literarische Theorie und kultureller Kontext.* (=Opera Slavica NF 1) (Russian Constructivism. Artistic Conceptions, Literary Theory and Cultural Context), Wiesbaden, 1981; *Literaturaxiologie. Zur Theorie und Geschichte des ästhetischen Wertes in slavischen Literaturen.* (=Opera Slavica NF 40) (The Axiology of Literature. On the Theory and History of Aesthetic Value in Slavic Literatures), Wiesbaden: Harrassowitz, 2001; and *An den Grenzen der Moderne. Das Denken und Schreiben Vasilij Rozanovs* (At the Borders of Modernism. The Thinking and Writing of Vasily Rozanov), Munich: Fink-Verlag 2003.

Elizabeth Harrison
has recently been awarded her PhD from SSEES UCL in 'The Development of the Image of Catholicism in Russian Literary Tradition: 1820–1949', supervised by Pamela Davidson. She continues to work on Russian literary culture more broadly and on Russian literary tradition. Her current projects include a study of Vasilii Rozanov's *Ital'ianskie vpechatleniia* and Catholicism in Nikolai Berdiaev's *Russkaia ideia*. She is also preparing her thesis for publication.

Jeremy Howard
is Senior Lecturer in Art History at the University of St Andrews, Scotland and is a renowned authority on Russian art. He received his PhD from St Andrews in 1991 and the same year began his teaching and research career there. His books include *The Union of Youth: An Artists' Society of the Russian Avant-Garde* (Manchester, 1992) and *East European Art* (Oxford, 2006). He is also co-author, co-editor and translator of *Vladimir Markov and Russian Primitivism: A Charter for the Avant-Garde* (Farnham, 2015). In 2012 he was Henry Moore Institute Senior Research Fellow and the following year co-curated the exhibition 'Vladimir Markov: Displays and Fictions' held at the institute's galleries in Leeds. Besides specialising in Russian, east and central European art, architecture and design of the modern period, as well as the regional variations of Art Nouveau, Howard also works on the relationships between art and education. Lecturing and publishing widely on the latter, he recently co-authored and edited *The Decorated School: Essays on the Visual Culture of Schooling* (London, 2013).

Alexander Ivashkin

(1948–2014), a cellist, conductor and writer, was Director of Classical Performance and Head of the Centre for Russian Music at Goldsmiths (University of London). He also played the electric cello, viola da gamba, sitar and piano. His recitals, radio and TV recordings, and appearances with world-leading orchestras included performances in more than 40 countries. Alexander Ivashkin was a regular guest at important music festivals in Europe, Britain, the United States, Japan, Australia and New Zealand. He appeared regularly as a soloist with some of the world's leading orchestras. Ivashkin published twenty books, on Schnittke, Ives, Penderecki, Rostropovich and others, and more than 200 articles in Russia, Germany, Italy, the US, the UK and Japan.

Elena Kabkova

has a higher doctorate in Pedagogy, and is Professor at the Department of History and Theory of Music of Moscow City Pedagogical University. She is the author of numerous articles and monographs dedicated to the problems of artistic education, and an academic editor of the series 'Mirovaia khudozhestvennaia kultura' ('Piter' Publishing house, 2006–2008).

Sergei A. Kibal'nik

is Leading Researcher at the Institute of Russian Literature, Pushkin House and Full Professor at St Petersburg State University. He received his PhD from the Institute of Russian Literature in 1984 and defended his post-doctoral dissertation there in 2001. His books include *Russian Anthological Poetry of the First Third of the 19th Century* (Leningrad, 1989), *Pushkin's Creative Consciousness* (St. Petersburg, 1998), *Gayto Gazdanov and the Existentialist Tradition in Russian Literature* (St. Petersburg, 2011), *Classical Antiquity in Russian Literature of the 18th–the First Half of the 19th Centuries. Essays* (St. Petersburg, 2012). He co-edited *Chekhov's Image and the Image of Chekhov's Russia in the Contemporary World* (St Petersburg, 2010) and *Dostoevsky. Research and Materials. Vol. 19* (St. Petersburg, 2010). As a Fulbright scholar he taught at the University of Pittsburg (1994) and in 1995 he was the Kennan Institute for Advanced Russian Studies Scholar (Washington, D.C.). Besides specialising in classical and Russian emigré literature, he also works on contemporary Russian literature and theory of literature. He recently co-authored and edited *Victor Pelevin's Literary Strategy* (St Petersburg, 2008) and *Aleksandr Panchenko and Russian Culture* (St. Petersburg, 2010). His most recent book is *The Issues of Dostoevskii's Poetics of Intertextuality* (St Petersburg, 2013).

Oleg Kovalov
is a film studies specialist, historian of cinema and film director. He is the author of "Ostrov mertvykh" ("Gran-pris" in the Avtorskoe kino competition at Kinotavr film festival, 1993); "Sergei Eizenshtein. Avtobiografiia" (Nika prize for the best documentary film of 1996) and "Sergei Eizenshtein. Meksikanskaia fantaziia" (Laureate of the "Forum" programme at the Berlin International Film Festival in 1998). He has published widely in leading Russian film studies journals such as *Iskusstvo kino*, *Seans* and *Kinovedcheskie zapiski*. He is the author of the anthology *Sergei Eizenshtein in Russian reflections* (2014). Since 2005, he has been conducting masterclasses on film criticism at St Petersburg State University of Cinema and Television. Kovalov is also a member of the film academy Nika.

Alexander McCabe
holds a doctorate from the University of Glasgow, where he has been an award-winning teacher of French, Russian and Comparative Literature for four years. His doctoral project, "Dostoevsky's French Reception: Vogüé, Gide, Shestov, Berdyaev, Marcel, Sartre, Camus (1880–1960)", funded by the Carnegie Trust, was completed in 2013 and will soon be published. In addition to Franco-Russian intercultural exchange and European intellectual history, his research interests include theories of perception, the body and landscape. Alex also works as a contemporary dance artist.

Margarita Odesskaia
PhD, Professor, Russian State University for the Humanities, is the author of *Chekhov and the Problem of the Ideal* (Moscow: RGGU, 2011), *Chekov, Ibsen, Strindberg*, ed. by Margarita Odesskaia (Moscow: RGGU, 2007), *At the Centuries Edge. Russian-Scandinavian Literary Dialogue*, ed. by Margarita Odesskaia, Tatyana Chesnokova (Moscow: RGGU, 2001), *Among the Greats: Literary Meetings* (Moscow: RGGU, 2001), *Russia and USA: Forms of Literary dialogues*, ed. by Margarita Odesskaia, Irene Masing-Delic (Moscow: RGGU, 2000), *Russian Hunting Stories* (Moscow: Soviet Russia, 1991), among other works.

Barbara Olaszek
is Professor at the Russian literature department of the University of Łódź. Her areas of specialism include the idea in literature and the poetics of Russian drama. She is the author of the monographs *Dymitr Pisariew. Wokół problemów pozytywizmu w Rosji* (Dmitrii Pisarev. On the Problems of Positivism in Russia), University of Łódź, 1997 and *Russkii pozitivizm. Idei v zerkale literatury* (Russian

Positivism. Ideas in the Mirror of Literature), University of Łódź, 2005. Most recently, she has published a number of articles on the theme of dispute in Russian literature: "The situation with dialogue/debate in the novels of Ivan Turgenev", "The socio-cultural role of dispute in artistic discourse (on the basis on some selected Russian classical novels)", "*Belle-lettres* in the space of political debate", and others.

Ildiko Maria Racz
is nearing a completion of her doctorate at the Eötvös Lorand University in Budapest, Hungary, where she earned her MA degree in Hungarian, Russian and English literature and linguistics. She won a National Students' Competition on 20th-century Russian Literature with a paper discussing the literary craft of Ivan Bunin. Her interest in the author has extended to her PhD project, wherein she aims to find the characteristic features that have identified Ivan Bunin as a predecessor of the artistry of Vladimir Nabokov.

Oliver Ready
is Research Fellow in Russian Society and Culture at St Antony's College, Oxford. He is completing a book on folly and wisdom in Russian prose since the 1960s, and is the translator of works by Fedor Dostoevskii, Iurii Buida and Vladimir Sharov.

Liudmila Safronova
is Professor at the Department of Philology, Institute of Master's and PhD Programmes, Abai Kazakh National Pedagogical University (Almaty, Kazakhstan). Her main research interests are postmodernism, literary psychoanalysis and cognitive literature. She has published more than 200 works, including several monographs such as *The Author and Hero in Postmodern Prose* (St Petersburg, 2007), *The Literary Strategies of Viktor Pelevin* (St Petersburg, 2008, in collaboration with A. Bogdanova and S. Kibal'nik), *Psychoanalysis in Literature and Literary Criticism* (Almaty, 2008), *The Postmodern Text: Poetics of Manipulation* (St Petersburg, 2009) and *Postfolklore and Metadiscourse in the Prose of S. Dovlatov* (Saarbrücken, 2013, in collaboration with N. Bannikova). She has published about 50 works abroad, in Russia, the USA, Spain, Hungary, Finland, Germany, Bulgaria, Lithuania, Ukraine, Poland and South Korea.

Marilyn Schwinn Smith
is an independent scholar affiliated with Five Colleges, Inc. in Amherst, MA. Her publications include work on Jane Harrison and other English-language

translators of Remizov, as well as on Virginia Woolf and the Russian poet Marina Tsvetaeva. Her current research focuses on Anglo-American and Russian modernism, specifically on the Russian-Jewish-American writer, John Cournos, an early translator of Remizov, Fedor Sologub and Andrei Belyi.

Oliver Smith
(1979–2013) was a Lecturer in Russian Studies at the School of Modern Languages of the University of St Andrews. His research was focused on the Russian religious and intellectual tradition from the beginning of the 19th century, and particularly on the thought of Vladimir Solov'ev. His study, *Vladimir Solov'ev and the Spiritualization of Matter*, was published by the Academic Studies Press in 2011 and was reviewed by his peers as 'one of the best recent works in English about Soloviev, indeed about Russian philosophy in general'. Oliver also published several pieces on Russian environmental thought, and was working on questions of biblical exegesis and the influence of the prophetic tradition on Russian thought.

Henrieke Stahl
has been Professor of Slavonic Literature at the University of Trier, Germany, since 2003. She received her PhD from the University of Trier in 2001. She began her teaching and research career in Münster in 1996 and continued it in Trier (1996–2001) and Heidelberg (2001–2003). Her main interests are Russian and Polish literature and philosophy, especially the works of Andrei Belyi, Vladimir Solov'ev, Aleksei Losev, the reception of Nicolaus Cusanus in Russia, and contemporary poetry. She has written *Renaissance des Rosenkreuzertums. Initiation in Andrej Belyjs Romanen „Serebrjanyj golub'" und „Peterburg"* (Frankfurt/M. et al. 2002) and edited *Andrej Belyj – filosof. "Istorija stanovlenija samosoznajuščej duši i ee konteksty"* (Special Issue of Russian Literature, LXX (2011) I/II) and *Imidž – dialog – ėksperiment: polja sovremennoj russkoj poėzii* (co-editor: Marion Rutz. Munich/Berlin, 2013).

Olga Stukalova
has a higher doctorate in Pedagogy, and is a Reader and Senior Researcher at the Federal Scientific Institute of Artistic Education of the Russian Academy of Education. She is the author of numerous articles and monographs dedicated to the problems of higher education in the field of art and culture, and an academic editor of the series 'Mirovaia khudozhestvennaia kultura' ('Piter' Publishing house, 2006–2008). Stukalova is also a columnist for the section 'Chelovek. Kultura. Obshchestvo' of the scientific and social-educational journal *Initsiativy XXI veka*.

Olga Tabachnikova

is a Lecturer in Russian Studies at the University of Central Lancashire and a Visiting Research Fellow at the University of Bath. She has a twin background in science and the humanities, with two doctorates from the University of Bath – in Franco-Russian Studies (2007) and in Mathematics (1995). She has worked at the universities of Bath and Bristol, as both lecturer and researcher, and published widely in the field of Russian as well as Russian Jewish Studies, with a special focus on cultural continuity. Her recent books include *Russian Irrationalism from Pushkin to Brodsky: seven essays in literature and thought* (Bloomsbury Academic, 2015), *Russian Jewish Diaspora and European Culture (1917–1937)* (co-edited with Peter Wagstaff and Jorg Schulte) (BRILL, 2012), *Correspondence between Lev Shestov and Boris de Schloezer*, fully annotated edition (YMCA Press, 2011) and *Anton Chekhov through the eyes of Russian thinkers: Vasilii Rozanov, Dmitrii Merezhkovsky and Lev Shestov* (editor) (Anthem Press, 2010). Olga also authored two collections of poetry, published by Folio (2002) and Helicon-Plus (2012).

Christopher Tooke

holds a doctorate in Russian literature on the representation of Jewish women in pre-revolutionary Russian literature from University College London's School of Slavonic and East European Studies. His research interests include nationalism, antisemitism and the depiction of Jewish characters in Russian literature. He is also interested in linguistics. He currently works in political and economic analysis and forecasting, and as a freelance Russian-English translator.

Natalia Vinokurova

is a Senior Researcher at the Central Economics and Mathematics Institute of Russian Academy of Sciences, Moscow, Russia. She has published numerous articles and book chapters in the field of gender studies: "Russian Women in Science and Education: Gender Equality, Gender Inequality" in *Post-Communist Transition and Women's Agency in Eastern Europe*, Republic of Letters Publishing, the Netherlands, 2013; "Reprivatizing Women's Lives from Khrushchev to Brezhnev" in *Gender, Equality and Difference During and After State Socialism*, Palgrave, 2007; *Brauchen Frauen Helden? Russische Frauen zwischen Tradition und Moderne* (with H.K. Herold), Bremen, 2001; "Zhenshchiny i Muzhchiny v nauke: Dvoinoi Portret" in *Sotsiologicheskie issledovaniia*, Moscow, 1999. Currently Dr Vinokurova is researching the theme of Russian irrationalism from an economic perspective. She has published an article on economic behaviour, "Russkii Idealist vs Homo Economicus", in *Global'nye tendentsii razvitiia mira*, Moscow, 2013. Dr Vinokurova is a Member of the Board of the All Russian Association of Women in Science and Education.

INTRODUCTION

Rationalising Russian Irrationalism

Olga Tabachnikova

A real mystery by its very nature cannot be solved
LEV SHESTOV, On Job's Scales

The perception of Russia as an enigmatic, mysterious country, situated between East and West not only spatially, but also mentally, is traditional in Western Europe and the Anglophone world at large. Whatever the attitude to this enigma, whatever emotional charge the cliché of the 'mysterious Russian soul' carries, the difference between Russian and Western ways is understood as undeniable. Whether it is the acknowledged grandeur of Russian literature or weird Russian messianism and exceptionalism – at best raising an eyebrow, at worst taken as an insult – the attraction of the Other remains, and supplies an inexhaustible field for inquiry. That is why the topic of Russian irrationalism, neatly wrapped in Tiutchev's by now hackneyed lines "Russia cannot be understood with the mind, // She cannot be measured by the normal yardstick, // She has a special quality, // One can only believe in Russia",[1] and sealed by the brutal history of the nation which on the outside looks indistinguishably European, evokes immediate and never-ceasing interest. Russian irrationalism revealed itself diversely in literature and thought, taking shape in the archpriest Avvakum's autobiography in the seventeenth century and the teachings of Grigorii Skovoroda a century later, evolving into Fedor Dostoevskii's messianic irrationalism and Lev Shestov's critique of speculative philosophy and, through various modernist and post-modernist intellectual and cultural movements, has survived to the present day. The topic is obviously bottomless, openly provocative and challenging the norms of political correctness; and, using Pasternak's words from a different context, "is equal to [resolving] the mystery of life".[2] But, as with any insoluble riddle, it has an everlasting appeal, and is potentially constructive, not only in academic terms, but also for bridging cultural and political gaps, thus facilitating inter-cultural dialogue.

---

[1] Fedor Tiutchev, "Umom Rossiiu ne poniat..." (1866), in *Stikhotvoreniia F.I. Tiutcheva*, 1868, Moscow, 230, (transl. by the volume translation editor Elizabeth Harrison).

[2] (*razgadke zhizni ravnosilen*), Boris Pasternak, "Liubit' inykh tiazhelyi krest...", 1931; see http://max.mmlc.northwestern.edu/~mdenner/Demo/texts/love_some_cross.html (consulted 07.03.2014).

In one way or another, many scholarly works on Russia touch on its irrationalism, but no systematic, integral approach, which would treat it as a dominant rather than a theme, exists. The current volume is an attempt at such an approach, and launches the study of Russian irrationalism in philosophy, theology, and the arts – most notably in literature – of the last two hundred years, i.e. from the start of the 19th century to the present day. However, the volume also has to allow for the fact that this task is impossible to tackle without putting things in historical perspective, that is, without taking, even if sketchily and briefly, historical tours back in time, to Russian (and world) antiquity, since the past always conceals the roots of modernity.

The difficulty, however, begins even earlier – with the very definition of the concept. For it is clear that between an academic understanding of philosophical irrationalism, as a stance which "stressed the dimensions of instinct, feeling, and will as over and against reason",[3] and the opposite – rationalist – sensibility and way of cognition in which reason plays a crucial and dominant role, there is a whole range of possibilities where the role of reason varies in scale. Also, apart from a strictly philosophical interpretation of irrationalism, one can talk of its numerous other manifestations – from political and social life through to a semiotics of individual behaviour and, generally, a particular mind-set. Our primary interest in this book is to study the ways in which irrationalism manifests itself in Russian art and, inevitably, in Russian philosophy and theology – because Russian thought, including religious thought, is inseparable from its literature. Moreover, as Richard Peace once wrote, in Russia "art has more power over life than life has over art".[4] But the difficulties do not stop here, as, apart from irrationalism (which may be seen as a way of merely suppressing or downplaying the role of reason), one can talk about anti-rationalism: a radical crusade against reason, its outright denial. Or, for that matter, one can distinguish between irrationalism and a-rationalism, in the same way as one delineates between immoralism and amoralism.

It is clear, however, that a national culture, just as an individual mind, has a place for both rationalist and irrationalist modes of perception and existence, and, most likely, this is not a discrete combination, but an inseparable blend. Our aim is thus to distil and analyse manifestations of the irrational in Russian art and thought, bearing in mind the aforementioned varieties and the elusive nature of our understanding of the concept as such.

---

[3] Britannica Online Encyclopedia. See http://www.britannica.com/EBchecked/topic/294716/irrationalism (consulted 31.07.2012).

[4] Richard Peace, *Russian Literature and the Fictionalisation of Life*, Hull: The University of Hull, 1976, 16.

Although the principal rise of the irrationalist trend in world history can be measured from the time of the Enlightenment, as a radical reaction against it, the origins of the irrationalist approach to the world in the form of mysticism, intuition, instinct and so forth are evident from the time of antiquity, together with a continuous wrestling of two opposing traditions. As this volume demonstrates,[5] whether we talk, along the lines of Nietzsche, of the elemental and passionate Dionysian tradition as opposed to the Apollonian principle of classical ordered beauty, or, following Erich Auerbach, divide culture into two fundamental branches – arising either from the symbolism of the Old Testament or the ratio-based ancient Greek philosophy; or, like Lev Shestov, radically confront reason and faith, as epitomised by Athens and Jerusalem respectively, or consider Aristotelian versus Platonic philosophical heritages, or any further variations of a rationalist and irrationalist variety, there is little doubt that both constitute an intrinsic part of human history and human nature itself. Furthermore, emotion-driven romanticism in contrast to order-based classicism does not necessarily represent irrationalism in its pure form and is distinct from idealism, just as realism can be disjointed from rationalism, as we shall later see. Faith and reason, mind and soul, ethics and aesthetics do not inevitably mean a rationalist-irrationalist dichotomy, yet it is at their border that the painful conflict seems to live, hence the continuous strivings to polarise them.

The most obvious source of irrationalism in human existence appears to be our finiteness, the fact that we are "forever cut off from the sources and beginnings of life", from the mystery of death, that "we live surrounded by an endless multitude of mysteries".[6] However, man is equipped with reason in order to deal with universal chaos, as positivists (and not only them), thought. Yet, as many centuries of human history witnessed, as well as being a tool for self-management, a powerful instrument for constructive development on a cosmic scale, reason can be equally used for causing distraction – moreover, it is perceived as poisonous, potentially egotistic, in many philosophies. Is this because it is reason which helps us to use logic to our own ends, to rationalise our personal interests, implying in particular that those unable to do that and acting against themselves for the interests of others are perceived as idiots, as in Dostoevskii's novel?[7] But it is also with reason that mankind's

---

5   For further discussions of these ideas see the chapters by Odesskaia, Ivashkin, Olaszek and McCabe.

6   Lev Shestov, "Parmenides in chains, On the Sources of the Metaphysical Truths" in *Athens and Jerusalem*; see http://shestov.phonoarchive.org/aaj/aj1_1.html (consulted 27.07.2012).

7   For a further discussion on this see Fazil Iskander, "Ponemnogu o mnogom. Sluchainye zapiski", *Novyi Mir*, 10 (2000) (see http://magazines.russ.ru/novyi_mi/2000/10/iskan.html (consulted 01.06.2012)).

hopes lie for attaining universal harmony. Thus, starting from the New Age, associated with the names of Descartes, Spinoza and Leibniz, and especially from the Enlightenment era, classical philosophy began most decisively to identify the world with rationality per se, cleansing the mind of any irrational elements. This provoked a powerful opposing wave, creating an influential anti-Enlightenment irrationalist front.

Isaiah Berlin traces the origins of modern European irrationalism to Johann Georg Hamann, "the pioneer of anti-rationalism in every sphere", who launched a frontal attack against European Enlightenment and gave rise to "a movement that in the end engulfed the whole of European culture".[8] Within this movement, from the German Hamann, to the Russian-Jewish Shestov and beyond, scientific knowledge was denigrated as dry, calculating and mortifying, while art was exalted as inspirational and divine. This misconception of science (challenged by the famous words of the mathematician David Hilbert about one of his former students who dropped mathematics to study poetry: "Good. He did not have enough imagination to become a mathematician")[9] proved to be very long lived, apparently born in minds totally unfamiliar with the nature of science. Without going far for examples, an authoritative source referred to in one of the chapters of this volume opposes "complex figurative ideas to *discrete scientific ideas*" (italics mine – O.T.). Reason dissects and kills, the representatives of this stance believed, while art revives – "God was a poet, not a geometer".[10] A contemporary Russian philosopher A.V. Akhutin has written the following perceptive lines about Shestov's *idée fixe* centred around the fatal role of reason in human history – lines which can be equally applied to Shestov's fellow thinkers of all times and cultures who upheld to the last the radical anti-rationalist stance:

> There is a disturbing boundary which separates an ultimate knowledge from infinite ignorance, does not delineate between Hellenistic Reason and Biblical Faith, but goes instead to the very heart of that Reason. It is at this boundary – in the midst of the mythologised metaphysics which Shestov has in mind when he talks of the kingdom of Reason – that philosophy is born. [...] Philosophy takes thought to nothingness of thought and of being, where what may happen does not yet exist. Philosophy

---

8   Isaiah Berlin, *The Magus of the North: J.G. Hamann and the Origins of Modern Irrationalism*, London: Fontana Press, 1994, 4.
9   See, for example, David J. Darling, *The Universal Book of Mathematics: From Abracadabra to Zeno's Paradoxes,* Hoboken, New Jersey: John Wiley and Sons, 2004, 151.
10 Johann Georg Hamann, *Briefwechsel,* Arthur Henkel (ed.), Wiesbaden/ Frankfurt: Insel Verlag, 1955–1975, vol. 5, p. 164. Cited in Isaiah Berlin, *The Magus of the North*, 40.

deals not with eternal truths, but with how they are possible – with assumptions of eternal existence. Shestov himself is sometimes close to such an understanding of the 'second dimension of thought', but all this intense paradoxicality of philosophical thinking is immediately lost when it is split into two quite unambiguous poles – of reason and of faith.[11]

Equally ambiguous is the situation with other human faculties and activities. While true scientists know what genuinely poetic, divine inspirations scientific discoveries hold, interpretations of the nature of artistic activity are, in fact, similarly multi-dimensional. Not only the strict principles of classicism, but also quite a calculated character of Russian symbolism, testify to this. One can see, however, the temptation to declare art an intrinsically, *par excellence*, irrational activity.

As Jeremy Howard argues in the current volume, "art, for all its being a sign of things, frequently involves the suspension of the cerebral and engages instead with superstition, faith, emotion and illusion". Iurii Lotman wrote thus of the irrational nature of poetry: "The starting point in studying poetry is an understanding that poetry is paradoxical par excellence. If the existence of poetry were not an undoubtedly established fact one could have shown persuasively that it cannot be".[12] And Joseph Brodsky, contemplating the differences between art and reality, found that

> in art, owing to the properties of the material itself, it is possible to attain a degree of lyricism that has no physical equivalent in the real world. Nor, in the same way, does there exist in the real world an equivalent of the tragic in art, which (the tragic) is the reverse of lyricism – or the stage that follows it.[13]

However, it seems that the truly irrational is born out of discrepancy, out of a conflict that exposes the limitations of a purely rationalist enquiry – be it a tragic conflict of human finiteness and divine infinity or of a fantasy genre delivered through the rationalist discourse incompatible with it. In other

---

11   A.V. Akhutin, "Antichnost' v filosofii L'va Shestova"– the Introduction to Lev Shestov, *Lektsii po istorii grecheskoi filosofii*, Moscow-Paris: Russky Put'-YMCA-Press, 2001, 5–19 (13 and 17–18).

12   Yu.M. Lotman, *O poetakh i poezii (Analiz poeticheskogo teksta, statii, issledovaniia, zametki)*, St Petersburg: Iskusstvo-SPB, 1996, 45.

13   Joseph Brodsky, "A Poet and Prose" in *Less than One: Selected Essays*, Harmondsworth: Penguin Books, 1986, 176–194 (183).

words, irrationalism arises from the inability of its observer to construct a model for a given phenomenon, to explain it algorithmically, that is, to inscribe it into an existing causal chain and to find its place in a familiar context. Or, to put differently, to find a suitable vantage point, a system of coordinates in which the given phenomenon would start making sense, would reveal its inner logic, which otherwise remains obscure to an outsider. Thus rather than defying or ignoring the voice of reason, irrationalism encompasses those actions and phenomena whose logic we, as observers, cannot grasp.

This implies the relativity, or subjectivity, of the very concept of irrationalism. At the same time some connection of the inexplicable happenings with empirical reality should stay intact in order to sustain the inner contradiction conducive to the irrational. Otherwise everything slips into pure fantasy, into the realm of a fairy tale, thus losing its contradictory nature. Indeed, in contrast to the purely fantastic, the essence of the irrational is in the behaviour of familiar objects (or objects expected in the specific narrative, genre or situation) in an unexpected, unfamiliar way, incompatible with their nature. In this connection, Lotman's words on the sources of science sound both paradoxical and instructive:

> Science begins from peering hard into things which are customary and apparently clear, and suddenly discovering in them something uncanny and inexplicable. This gives rise to a question which, in order to be answered, needs a new theory or concept to be developed.[14]

The irrational thus seems to be based on duality, ambiguity, contradiction, on the misalignment of forces or strivings. It is concealed in the violation of expectations and proportions, causes and consequences. If and when the mismatch is present – as a function of our perception – the irrational is able to emerge.

On the ethical and religious plane, reason as such, although capable (and possibly inclined) to process one's own interests, is not necessarily to be perceived as a source of pure rationality, inevitably at odds with the heart (i.e. feelings, emotions). Interestingly, passions can be equally viewed as constitutive of egoism and sin – and are indeed regarded as such in many cultures, including that of the ancient Slavs, as we shall see below. Yet the contradiction between mind and soul, reason and faith, was not characteristic for Russian thought – hence, in particular, the ancient concept, explained in the sequel, of 'suffering reason'. While Western Christianity was influenced by Ancient Greek

---

14   Yu.M. Lotman, *O poetakh i poezii*, 45.

philosophy, based on the primacy of reason and rationality, Russian Orthodox tradition, by contrast, understood the soul as a sum total of all spiritual activity. It perceived Original Sin as having caused the division within human nature into three independent abilities: mind, emotions and free will. The human task thus became to reunite them again into one Divine whole. The ability of the soul to be holistic is called Faith, and is summarised by Maxim Ispovednik (St Maxim the Confessor) as follows: "Faith is the highest kind of cognition – it exceeds the mind, but does not contradict it".[15]

The contradiction that misinterpreted reason as a purely rationalist faculty, apparently, arose from a misconception started by the early Slavophiles, most notably Khomiakov and Kireevskii, who, as the Russian religious-philosophical historian Vasilii Zenkovskii remarks, ironically borrowed it from Western Europe. Indeed, the (derogatory) association of Western culture with rationalism originated in the 'pre-Romantic' period of the eighteenth century in the West itself, and only then was taken for granted by Russian thinkers.

> The fundamental epistemological distinction between reason and mind (*rassudok/razum*, Verstand/Vernunft) of Kant, Fichte, Hegel, Schelling and others got distorted on Russian soil, resulting in the identification of rationalism as a phenomenon of general-cultural character with reasoned cognition.[16]

Zenkovskii points to the crucial role of Kant's epistemology in this process, whereby *Verstand* was a function of purely logical operations, while *Vernunft* was a source of ideas.[17] This view of Western Europe as a shallow rationalist culture facilitated Russian opposition to it and revived the well-known Russian messianism. Together with the Westernisers' tendency to learn from the West which resulted more in a creative appropriation of Western cultural products than in adopting ready-made models, the Slavophiles' striving to serve more as a corrective than an apprentice to Western Europe gained momentum and expressed itself in propagating a special Russian way, based on the anti-rationalist sentiments of communal brotherhood and love, arising from the ideas about old pre-Petrine Russia and patristic teachings. Moreover, as Dmitrii Galkovskii rightly notes, even in the strange fascination of Russian

---

15　See Maxim Ispovednik prep., *Tvoreniia*, Moscow, 1993, vol. 1, 216, as well as A.I. Brilliantov, *Vliianie vostochnogo bogosloviia na zapadnoe v proizvedeniiakh Ioanna Skota Erigeny*, Moscow, 1998, 218.
16　Vasilii Zenkovskii, *Istoriia russkoi filosofii*, Rostov-on-Don: Fenix, 2004, vol. 1, 226.
17　*Ibid.*

thinkers with Western rationality, in conjunction with their inner psychological rejection of it, a great deal of irrationalism is concealed.[18]

But the roots of the difference between Russia and Western Europe seem to go deep into the difference in religious sensibilities, which exalted respectively the spiritual and material side of life, the heavenly and earthly, ideal and real, disproportionately focusing either on sublime ideas or on their practical implications. Such a vision has recently been expressed by V.N. Argunova and S.N. Tiapkov:

> The birth of Christ is the main event in the religion of Western Christians, which stresses the meaningfulness of earthly life. The arrangement of earthly life as well as the human relationship with God is based on quite understandable pragmatic foundations. A judicial conception of expiation, according to which Christ's sacrifice was predicated on the need to facilitate Divine punishment for Adam's sin, is dominant. Expiation is interpreted as due justice, which is more appropriate for the secular world.
>
> In Russian culture an individual is connected to the perishable world by special transcendental relationships. God is separated from the world by His will. God's ideas of creation are separated from creation itself, just as the will of an artist is separated from the work of art in which it is manifested. For this reason the material world loses its validity. The genuine world is the world of spiritual grace, the kingdom of genuine freedom and equality. In order to become united with God one must dismiss the surrounding world, which exists outside God.[19]

At the same time, as Reiner Grübel argues in his contribution to this volume, Russian irrationalism has to a considerable degree manifested itself through sectarianism and heresies being a counter-reaction to the rigidity of Russian Orthodoxy.

To what extent are the above cultural stereotypes and scholarly hypotheses true? How much are the conjectures of Russian thinkers about Russia in relation to Western Europe valid? After all, this theme, and in particular Russia's self-perception through literature and philosophy, is one of the central themes

---

18 See Dmitrii Galkovskii, *Beskonechnyi tupik* at http://www.samisdat.com/3/312-bt-p.htm (consulted 23.12.2015).

19 V.N. Argunova and S.N. Tiapkov, *Innovatsionnoe razvitie regiona: potentsial, instituty, mekhanizmy*, Ivanovo: IGU, 2011.

in Russian culture and constitutes a vital ingredient for a discussion of Russian irrationalism. Who (if anybody) is ultimately right in the on-going debate between Russia and the West? Maybe sceptical and condescending Western travellers, such as Marquis de Custine and the like, who regarded Russia as the Empire of lies, a fictitious self-promoting country based on illusions, incapable of constructive life-building, of any useful practical outcomes, but full of destructive power which ruins itself as well as others around it? After all, this criticism came from within as well: Petr Chaadaev was declared mad for expressing such views, which permeated, in fact, the whole of Russian cultural history and survived into the present. The eschatological character of the Russian idea was noted by many more Russian philosophers than Nikolai Berdiaev. "The Russian nation is not interested in any conscious historical activity because it has a different programme – passionate, sado-masochistic self-destructiveness under any pretext", exclaims Dmitrii Bykov.[20] "What did Russian history bring about in one thousand years – a great deal in order to aid understanding the world, but very little that helps us live in it", says a character in Zakhar Prilepin's novel, *San'ka* (2006).[21]

> The formula of Western logic (starting as early as Aristotle) is 'this is that and that' ('Socrates is a person', 'some swans are white'), whereas the Russian mind reasons according to the logic: 'not this, but that': 'No, I am not Byron, I am another', 'I do not love you so ardently...', 'Nature is not what you imagine it to be...'., 'It is not the wind that blows over the forest...', 'No, I do not cherish rebellious enjoyment',

provocatively wrote the contemporary Russian philosopher Georgii Gachev,[22] grounding his idea more in the Russian linguistic mode of expression than, necessarily, in the national mentality (although the connection between the two seems sufficiently subtle to merit investigation).[23]

---

20   Dmitrii Bykov, "Dvesti let vmesto", see http://berkovich-zametki.com/Nomer24/Bykov1.htm (consulted 23.11.2013).
21   See Zakhar Prilepin. *San'kia*, Chapter 8 at http://sankya.ru/chapters/8.html (consulted 23.11.2013).
22   See Georgii Gachev, *Natsional'nye obrazy mira* at http://lib.co.ua/history/gatchev/gatchev.txt_with-big-pictures.html (consulted 26.11.2013).
23   More generally, the topic of a possible link between Russian irrationalism and Russian language seems rich and intriguing. One of the chapters in my monograph *Russian Irrationalism from Pushkin to Brodsky: Seven Essays in Literature and Thought* (Bloomsbury Academic, 2015) is dedicated to it.

Or, perhaps, it is the Slavophile stance that is closer to the truth – whether it emerged as a compensatory mechanism to redress Russia's socio-political disharmony and backwardness, or as a genuine result of peculiarities of national identity. It has probably been more dominant, and equally long-lasting, representing a trend in Russia's self-perception that held firmly the belief in a superior Russian spirituality, in the dominance of an aesthetic principle, in the ideal, divine sphere underlying and sanctifying everyday occurrences, without which life degenerates into a hollow pragmatic existence and is not worth living. This unworthy boring existence, as previously mentioned, was associated in Russia mainly with Western pragmatism, positivism and materialism; with abstraction detached from reality, from "living life", labelled thus by Dostoevskii; with "economy, temperance and industry" of Pushkin's Herman – the protagonist of German descent of 'The Queen of Spades' epitomising the Western way of life. The perceived difference was sufficient to make its way into most xenophobic proverbs, such as "what is good for a Russian, is deadly for a German" (*"chto russkomu khorosho – nemtsu smert"*), as well as to evolve to more civilised formulas, akin to the one uttered by Turgenev in a conversation with Flaubert and his friends: "vous êtes des homes de la loi, de l'honneur; nous...nous sommes des homes de l'humanité!".[24] These sweeping generalisations, of course, should be treated with caution, but they do take us back to the persistent questions of stereotypes and ongoing cultural debates.

Yet, paradoxically, the Russian dislike of abstractions, of philosophical ideas divorced from reality, Russian striving to 'animate' reason, to deal with it only in the context of "living life", were combined with the (also Russian) propensity to displace love of man as an individual with love of mankind as a whole – which led to a total loss, not only of love, but also of basic respect of human rights. Thus such a peculiar, domestically grown abstraction of sorts co-existed in Russia with the rejection of a scholastic Western abstraction. And hence Russian reason is, in Russian eyes at least, always different from Western reason: Kireevskii, for instance, argued that a Russian Orthodox believer can arrive at atheism, but not (in contrast to a Western Christian) through a natural evolution of mind.[25] Russian reason is never detached from feeling, from faith as such, hence the aforementioned notion of suffering reason. For Pushkin, for

---

24   Edmond and Jules de Goncourt, Journal, under 5 March 1876. Cited in Frank Seeley, *Turgenev: A Reading of his Fiction*, Cambridge: Cambridge University Press, 1991, 30.
25   I. Kireevskii, "O neobkhodimosti i vozmozhnosti novykh nachal dlia filosofii" (1856), in I.V. Kireevskii, *Polnoe sobranie sochinenii v dvukh tomakh*, ed. M. Gershenzon, Moscow, 1911, reprinted by Gregg International, Hampshire, 1970, 250. (The actual quotation can be found in the chapter by Elizabeth Harrison in the current volume.).

example, it is his reason which is searching for Deity, and it is the heart which cannot find it! ("*Um ishchet Bozhestva, a serdtse ne nakhodit*").[26] In other words, in the Russian case we may be dealing with a different kind of reason, one which is inseparable from feelings and which craves the heavenly truth, the ideal, but within the shell of the "living life".

It would be natural to suppose that it is Russia's turbulent history, its delayed development – connected to the country having to serve for more than two centuries as a shield to Western Europe from the wild Tatar-Mongolian hordes – that can be regarded as responsible for its original national mentality, bold and fearless with respect to metaphysics, to the famous cursed questions of existence, for the Russians' ability to look tragedy straight in the eye instead of turning away from it by means of civilisation and material prosperity. "Our courage is drawn from our quite uncultured confidence in our own powers",[27] wrote Lev Shestov at the start of the twentieth century looking back at classical Russian literature. He elaborated that in the typical Russian rejection of earthly life with its tragedy and injustices, there lies in fact "a lingering belief in the possibility of a final triumph over evil".[28] Thus the disadvantage of belatedness brought with it is, in Shestov's view, a great spiritual advantage.

> Our simplicity and truthfulness are due to our relatively scanty culture. Whilst European thinkers have for centuries been beating their brains over insoluble problems, we have only just begun to try our powers. We have no failures behind us. [...] We admit no traditions. [...] We have wanted to re-examine everything, restate everything.[29]

Russian irrationalism, exemplified for Shestov by a completely distorted interpretation of Western ideas, is also derived from the same historical source:

> With few exceptions Russian writers really despise the pettiness of the West. Even those who have admired Europe most have done so because they failed most completely to understand her. They did not want to understand her. That is why we have always taken over European ideas in such fantastic forms. Take the sixties for example. With its loud ideas of

---

26 Aleksandr Pushkin, 'Bezverie' (1817), in A.S. Pushkin, *Sobranie sochinenii v 10 tomakh*, vol. 1, Moscow: Gosudarstvennoe izdatelstvo khudozhestvennoi literatury, 1959, 423–425.
27 Lev Shestov, *Apofeoz bespochvennosti* (*All things are possible*), translated by S.S. Koteliansky; see http://shestov.phonoarchive.org/all/all_23.html (consulted 10.03.2014).
28 *Ibid.*
29 *Ibid.*

sobriety and modest outlook, it was a most drunken period. Those who awaited the New Messiah and the Second Advent read Darwin and dissected frogs. It is the same today. We allow ourselves the greatest luxury that man can dream of – sincerity, truthfulness – as if we were spiritual Croesuses, as if we had plenty of everything, could afford to let everything be seen, ashamed of nothing [...] A European uses all his powers of intellect and talent, all his knowledge and his art for the purpose of concealing his real self and all that really affects him – for that the natural is ugly and repulsive, no one in Europe will dispute for a moment.[30]

At the same time, it would seem that a focus on the earthly, on practical needs, concentration on the physical rather than metaphysical, characteristic of the West in the Russian eyes, is an imprint of the hardship of life which leaves no room for dreaming about an unattainable ideal. However, perhaps Russian reality, for centuries on end full of destitution, hunger, slavery, blood and the tormented conscience of its intellectual elite, was even more brutal, if the constant search for the ideal, escape into the world of fantasy, into perpetual utopia became the Russian way of life.

Of course, the geo-political peculiarities of the Russian case are all well known and researched. Their manifestations in the country's ruthless totalitarian history have always served as a constant source of contemplation by artistic means:

> You had better not live in the Kremlin, the
> Preobrazhensky Guard was right;
> The germs of the ancient frenzy are still swarming here:
> Boris Godunov's wild fear, and all the Ivans' evil spite,
> And the Pretender's arrogance – instead of the
> People's rights.[31]

Russia's delayed development (marked, in particular, by a very late abolition of serfdom – much later than in the rest of Europe) was distinguished by the silent period, marked by icon-painting and known as the hesychasm, which preceded a sudden explosion of Russian literature, music, philosophy and other forms of arts and thought in the nineteenth century. The country's vast

---

30   *Ibid.*
31   Anna Akhmatova, "Stanzas" in *The Complete Poems of Anna Akhmatova. Expanded Edition*, transl. by Judith Nemschemeyer, ed. Roberta Reeder, Smerville and Edinburgh: Zephyr Press and Canongate Press, 1983, 669.

natural resources, huge spaces and the four marked seasons of its climate also had a significant role to play in forming what is understood as the Russian national spirit.

> The suicide of your Russian youngster is, in my opinion, a specific phenomenon unfamiliar in Europe. It results from a horrific struggle possible in Russia only. All the energy of an artist must be directed towards two forces: man and nature. On the one hand, physical weakness, nervousness, early sexual development, passionate thirst for life and for truth, dreams about activities as broad as a steppe, restless analysis, poverty of knowledge together with the broad span of thought; on the other hand, an endless plain, severe climate, grey and stern people with its heavy, cold history, Tatar invasions, bureaucracy, indigence, ignorance, dampness of the capitals, Slavic apathy and so on and so forth. Russian life smashes a Russian man so much that no trace is left; smashes like a rock of a thousand poods. In Western Europe people perish because it is crowded and suffocating to live; in Russia they die because there is too much space…So much space that a little man has no strength to find his way,

wrote Chekhov in 1888 in a letter to Grigorovich.[32] The question nevertheless remains as to why it is that even the era of globalisation, rapid scientific and technological progress and the succession of political regimes are still unable to change the course of Russia's development, as if constantly tripping over the ephemeral entities of Russian national mentality and cultural identity:

> You failed to realize that Russia sees her salvation not in mysticism or asceticism or pietism, but in the successes of civilization, enlightenment, and humanity. What she needs is not sermons (she has heard enough of them!) or prayers (she has repeated them too often!), but the awakening in the people of a sense of their human dignity lost for so many centuries amid dirt and refuse; she needs rights and laws conforming not to the preaching of the church but to common sense and justice, and their strictest possible observance. Instead of which she presents the dire spectacle of a country [...] where there are not only no guarantees for individuality, honour and property, but even no police order, and where there is nothing but vast corporations of official thieves and robbers of various descriptions. The most vital national problems in Russia today

---

32   Anton Chekhov's letter to D.V. Grigorovich of 05.02.1888, see A.P. Chekhov, *PSSP v 30 tomakh*, vol. 2, Moscow: Nauka, 1975, 190.

are [...] the strictest possible observance of at least those laws that already exist. This is even realised by the government itself [...] as is proved by its timid and abortive half-measures for the relief of the white Negroes'.[33]

These words, which sound extremely timely, as if written in a Russian newspaper of today, in fact were addressed by Belinskii to Gogol' almost two hundred years ago.

That is why this volume which attempts to get to the roots of the Russian phenomenon and its irrational underpinnings, and tackle the questions outlined above, seems as timely as ever, and will remain thematically engaging for the Western reader for as long as Russia continues to be the Western European Other.

However, this book only marks the beginning of a journey that, as is clear in historical perspective, does not have an end. The diverse views and approaches of scholars from seven different countries collected here, are structured both thematically and chronologically, and united by the quest to reach deep into the phenomenon of Russian irrationalism. Ultimately though, and perhaps inevitably so for a scholarly publication, they result in the attempts to rationalise it, highlighting at the same time its multifaceted (essentially all-pervasive!) nature, its rich complexity and its inseparability from rationalism – in fact, a mutual reversibility of rationalism and irrationalism which depends largely on your perspective. The range of perspectives stretches from the arguments for a fictitious nature and inflated perception of Russian irrationalism, advanced, somewhat ironically, by the Russian scholar Sergei Kibal'nik to the comments by the English academic David Gillespie on the archetypical enigma of the Russian soul, and includes the philosophical idea of his fellow countryman Oliver Smith of Russian 'pathos' rather than irrationalism per se. Importantly, the represented range of views incorporates literary, historical, philosophical, artistic, psychological and even socio-economic approaches.

Although the chapters of the volume embrace topics and names that go beyond the targeted period of the last two hundred years, and encompass several centuries of modern Russian cultural history, there are obvious gaps that further studies will hopefully address. These should undoubtedly include Russian poetry from the Golden Age onwards, starting from Pushkin and Griboedov, and many prominent prose writers, including Leskov and

---

33   V.G. Belinskii, Letter to Nikolai Gogol' of 15/3 July 1847 in N.V. Gogol', *PSS v 14 tomakh*, Moscow-Leningrad: Izd-vo AN SSSR, 1937–1952, vol. 8, 501–502; for the English version see http://www.marxists.org/subject/art/lit_crit/works/belinsky/gogol.htm (consulted 25.02.2014).

Saltykov-Shchedrin, as well as the activities of various literary groups, journals and societies, most notably of the early twentieth century, such as OBERIU, and a whole variety of the twentieth and twenty-first century Russian literary names such as Vasilii Shukshin and Aleksandr Vampilov, Liudmila Petrushevskaia and Fridrikh Gorenshtein. The same wish list can be easily extended with respect to other art forms. My aforementioned monograph on *Russian Irrationalism from Pushkin to Brodsky: Seven Essays in Literature and Thought* attempts to explore some of the above, thus opening – together with the present volume – the avenue for further studies. A few existing works (exemplifying more a rare exception than a rule) have already covered ground that needs no commentary in terms of its high relevance to the irrationalist and/or absurdist trends, by examining the works of Pilniak, Zamiatin and Bulgakov, as well as Daniil Kharms.[34]

A brief overview, below, of the chapters in order of their appearance in the volume should help readers to navigate through these ground-breaking studies, which provide us with the opportunity of travelling across the mysterious land of Russian cultural idiosyncrasies – a journey which should be as illuminating as it is exciting.

The volume is organised in five parts. The first tackles the theme of Russian irrationalism conceptually, as a general historical-cultural phenomenon. The chapters of the first section serve as a point of departure for the rest of the volume in their generalised approach to the theme of Russian Iirrationalism, providing a useful critical overview of the subject in different cultural areas. The second and third parts offer a study of individual authors and works of classical Russian literature respectively of the nineteenth century and of the Silver Age, which is traditionally regarded as the pinnacle of Russian irrationalism. The fourth part deals with other art forms such as painting, music, cinema and architecture. The fifth and final part addresses Soviet and post-Soviet Russian literature.

***

A study of Russian irrationalism would be incomplete without an understanding of the counter-tradition, as the two always develop in conjunction with one another. Thus Barbara Olaszek's chapter, which opens the volume, gives an extremely useful outline of the history of rationalism in Russia. Drawing on

---

34   See T.R.N. Edwards *Three Russian Writers and the Irrational: Zamyatin, Pil'nyak, and Bulgakov*, Cambridge: Cambridge University Press, 1982, and Neil Cornwell, *The Absurd in Literature*, Manchester and New York: University of Manchester Press, 2006.

existing research, Olaszek traces – behind the traditional self-perception of Russia (as spiritual) versus the Russian perception of Western Europe (as rationalist) – a dynamic interplay between two fundamental philosophical traditions, arising from Aristotle and Plato respectively, and associated, crudely speaking, with rationalism and irrationalism. Observing that, in the New Time, Western culture was mythologised as a source of reason, Olaszek turns inevitably to the aforementioned difference between *rassudok* (*Verstand*) and *razum* (*Vernunft*), and notes that cognitive processes were separated into these two different channels, for understanding respectively the earthly and the heavenly. The latter integral reason, compatible with religious faith, was considered in Russia as characteristic for its national culture and superior to the former, dry and abstract, restricted reason of the West. Olaszek sketches the cultural dynamics of both currents – Aristotelian and neo-Platonic – in Russian history, with a focus on the development of the rationalist tradition, attempting to redeem its – often discredited – role in Russian culture. To this end she treats rationalism more as a cast of mind than a strictly philosophical concept based on reason as a sole means of cognition. Starting with the seventeenth century with its shift from the 'soul' to the 'mind' as the organising principle of understanding the world, Olaszek follows the evolution of the rationalist trend in Russian culture through to the early twentieth century. She argues that rationalist tendencies intensified during turbulent periods when the need to rationalise and explain historical events was pressing.

Interestingly, although rather expectedly, as we shall see from other chapters, the same periods of turmoil evoked the rise of irrationalist elements in the national consciousness essentially for the same reason, because of growing ideological disorientation.

After being carried away with Enlightenment ideas, manifested in the activities of empress Catherine II and such Russian cultural figures as M.V. Lomonosov, Ia.P. Kozelskii, D.S. Anichkov, A.N. Radishchev and others, when the St Petersburg Academy of Sciences was founded, followed by the Russian Academy of Sciences, Moscow university and various other institutions, there came in Russia a period of disenchantment with rationalist aspirations. Russia of the early nineteenth century saw an emergence of irrationalist strivings, of mysticism and romanticism, and the origins of the two fundamental schools of thought in Russian culture – Westernisers and Slavophiles, oriented respectively towards the *ratio* of the West and the spiritual heritage of Russia. However, both movements were ambivalent in that Westernisers displayed some clear irrationalist traits, while Slavophiles did not consistently reject reason. This mixed stance characterises the works of Odoevskii, Chaadaev, Khomiakov and Kireevskii, followed by later generations of Russian thinkers where the rational-irrational dichotomy became more marked. Thus the waves of change from the romantics of the 1830s to the disillusionment of the 1840s, and the emergence of utopian socialism, materialist natural sciences and positivism facilitated a change of the basis of the cultural paradigm from art to science in the 1860s. The radical rationalism of Chernyshevskii, Dobroliubov and Pisarev in turn gave rise to a counter-current of the generation of the 1880s which saw another major shift in cultural consciousness at the turn of the nineteenth century, with the rise of symbolism and a new religious search, when the utopian character of Enlightenment aspirations became apparent. Vladimir Solov'ev's synthesis of science and religion, rationalist and metaphysical traditions symbolised a response to the crisis of rationalism and nihilism and marked the beginning of the Silver Age in Russian culture.

Having sketched the history of rationalist tradition in Russian thought, its ambivalence and creative wrestling with both Western rationalism and Russian irrationalism, Olaszek then examines the rational-irrational interplay in Russian literary culture, discussing classical poets and prose writers from the early nineteenth century right to the end of Imperial Russia.

Thus, *in nuce*, Olaszek identifies various manifestations of rationalism in Russian culture demonstrating how, fed on Western influence, it was at the same time creatively appropriated on Russian soil. She thus redresses the downplaying of the rationalist tradition in Russian cultural history.

A more radical view, which insists on the diminished or even distorted character of Russian rationalist tradition, is exemplified by Dmitrii Galkovskii (already quoted above, even if briefly, but to the same effect), who speaks of the intrinsic irrationalism inherent in the very rationalism of Russians:

> In all probability, somewhere in the subconscious of every Russian there is a barbaric aspiration to Western learning, rationality. Moreover, rationality itself is perceived by Russians as something extremely irrational, incapable of being grasped by the mind, and as something that provides secret knowledge. Amongst the schismatics there was a superstition that he who reads the whole Bible and understands it completely, would go mad. Stankiewicz read Schelling, Kant and Hegel with the same feeling.[35]

At the same time, Semen Frank, whose words are quoted in Kibal'nik's chapter, argued that

---

35 Dmitrii Galkovskii, "Beskonechnyi tupik", List 3 at http://www.samisdat.com/3/312-bt-p.htm (consulted 23.12.2015).

The Russian way of thinking is absolutely anti-rationalist. This anti-rationalism, however, is not identical with irrationalism, that is, some kind of romantic and lyrical vagueness, a logical disorder of spiritual life. It does not involve either a tendency to deny science or inability to carry out scientific research.[36]

In general, the schematic divisions within Russian literature and philosophy suggested in Olaszek's chapter, may be challenged by more intricate classifications, but they undoubtedly serve as a valuable background for other chapters of the volume with a more narrow focus on specific aspects of Russian culture which are thus given a more detailed analysis. In other words, Olaszek's contribution with its historical perspective and a clear – and thus inevitably simplified – model of evolution and interaction of both rationalist and irrationalist trends provides a most helpful framework for further discussion, as it throws into relief other authors' views on the routes and nature of irrationalism in Russian cultural history.

The next chapter, by Tatiana Chumakova, offers another invaluable historical discussion by taking a tour into the ancient Russian past, where one must seek the sources of Russia's irrationalism. In ancient Russian thought, Chumakova argues, it is irrationalism that dominated. The connection between the Mind/Reason (*um*) and the Heart was often discussed: the mind/reason was responsible for the spiritual (rather than the rational) life of man, and the heart for wisdom. This understanding is close to the Middle-Eastern tradition, but also converges with the New Testament. The Apostle Paul used reason as the intermediate faculty between conscience (*sovest'*) and intellect. According to the sixteenth century treatise 'On human substance, on the visible and invisible' ('*O chelovechestem estestve, o vidimem i nevidimem*') only interaction between the heart and mind was thought to achieve harmony and, in particular, to achieve reason (*um*). This understanding of reason as a result of joint work between heart and mind gave rise to the concept of the aforementioned 'suffering reason' (*stradaiushchii razum*), used by Ivan IV (the Terrible).

Chumakova notes that a holistic understanding of the world, where man and universe are united under God's blessing, was characteristic for eastern Christianity. God is incognisable, but penetrates everything in life – from the sublime to the mundane. He sends his divine light to humankind and everyone should receive and develop this spark of God within him/herself. Hence

---

36   S.L. Frank, *Russkoe mirovozzrenie*, Saint Petersburg: Nauka, 1996, 165. Cited in Kibal'nik's chapter.

He cannot be experienced without active practice. An ascetic practice of approaching God is a struggle against passions, and is regimented by various famous treatises, discussed in the chapter.

In particular, Nil Sorskii's '*Ustav*', as Chumakova explains, stipulated that man was conceived as pure and whole, and passions are simply an accidental disease. They are located in the heart and prevent reason, which reflects a divine image, to be reunited with other faculties into one divine whole. After the Fall both the soul and body became damaged – the previously pure man merged with the 'visible world' on the route of physicality and slavery. To restore the harmony of human nature, man has to restore and unite body and soul. The '*Ustav*' gives a detailed description of the aetiology and evolution of passions, and points to the ways of overcoming them, through praying and other activities during which mind should manage the heart in order to reunite them. In the writings of Nil Sorskii and others, Chumakova, importantly, distinguishes the following key existential concepts: love, joy, fear and death, and sketches the meaning of these in the pre-Petrine Russian tradition.

A philosophical approach taken by Oliver Smith in his chapter offers a productive and illuminating way to delineate between the two philosophical traditions – Western European and Russian. His contribution provides

> a phenomenological genealogy of the Russian envisioning of reason, not in the sense of an historical enumeration of the sources on which it drew, but rather the tracing of its energies back to the consciousness (collective and individual) from which it derived.

Without losing sight either of the rich spectrum of different philosophical persuasions, or the intricate distinctions within one tradition, Smith finds the overarching perspective that enables him to inscribe the diversity of Russian thinkers of the last two hundred years into the phenomenon of Russian philosophy. More precisely, he suggests that the heart of Russian thought be sought in the concept of 'pathos' (developed substantially beyond its application in Hegelian aesthetics), not as a passion that denies or negates reason, but as the rejection of all disembodied forms of reason and rationality.

Building on the distinction between ethos and pathos in classical rhetoric, Oliver Smith begins by examining the reaction to Kantian ethics (as filtered through Hegel) in early Russian literary criticism and *publitsistika*. In doing so, Smith is acutely aware of the need for a careful handling of philosophical terminology in view of the profound conceptual, and hence linguistic, differences between Russian and Western traditions. Importantly, Smith reminds us that:

Aleksei Losev's characterisation of the Russian tradition as a form of truth-seeking not 'via its reduction to logical concepts but always through the symbol or the image, by means of the power of imagination and a living, inner dynamism'[37] doubtlessly captures something of the distinctive spirit of Russian thought.

Here again we are forced to recollect a peculiar irrationalist character of Russian rationalism, mentioned previously in Galkovskii's quotation. It is essentially what Smith refers to as "a fascination with, and repulsion from, modes of rationality forged over centuries of intellectual history". As a perfect illustration of the above characterisation from Losev one could recall Berdiaev's words: "My thinking is intuitive and aphoristic, in it there is no discursive development of thought. I cannot develop or prove anything fully".[38]

In this connection Smith considers various ways of reconciling reason with faith in Russian intellectual tradition, leading to the integrality of consciousness. He thus evokes Vissarion Belinskii's concept of pathos, borrowed from Hegelian *Aesthetics*, as a guiding principle of artistic consciousness where neither reason nor feeling is dominant. Smith then traces the evolution of this approach in the ideas of Vladimir Solov'ev, for whom reason and feeling were balanced in the pathos of love that served as a meeting point between the ideal and the real. However, the central question arises as to whether the Russian synthesis between reason and feeling is to be realised in the realm of being or of knowledge. In answering this question, Smith finds points of commonality between the ideas of Russian thinkers and the "ontologisation of knowledge" that Henry Corbin regarded as Heidegger's highest achievement, at the same time illustrating significant points of departure by Russians from the abiding rationalism of much continental phenomenology. Smith concludes that

> the spirit that lives in much Russian thought is not a fixed pattern (an 'ethos' that is passed on through a given canon) but a pathos that perpetually treads water between the unordered irrationality of individual experience and the concordant rationality of absolute comprehension. And the history of Russian thought is one not of ideas but of persons.

---

37 A.F. Losev, 'Russkaia filosofiia', in *Filosofiia, mifologiia, kul'tura*, Moscow, 1991, 209–236 (213). Cited in Smith's chapter.

38 N.A. Berdiaev, *Samopoznanie*, Chapter 3. See http://www.vehi.net/berdyaev/samopoznanie/003.html (consulted 15.12.2013).

The next chapter, by Elizabeth Harrison, continues a comparative analysis of Russian and West European cultures, but changes the angle, focusing on the theological aspect of Russian thought and literature, and its role in shaping Russian identity. In her contribution to the volume she examines Russian tendencies to oppose Western European theological and intellectual traditions to Russian Orthodoxy as a means to highlight the mysticism of Russian faith against the rationalism of Western European Christianity. She argues that reality was more complex than these attempts suggest, and explores more generally the role in Russian culture – both philosophical and literary – of Catholicism, and Protestantism, with their own, often overlooked, mystical component.

Harrison traces the roots of mysticism in Russian culture not only to Orthodoxy itself, but also to Catholic and Protestant ideas, and influences from Freemasonry, Pantheism and Gnosticism. She demonstrates how, in the aftermath of Chaadaev's subversive stance, the early Slavophiles criticised Western churches for rationalism and saw them only as institutions where believers were not mystically united with each other. In their eyes, by contrast with Catholicism and Protestantism, which were mere religions, Russian Orthodoxy represented a faith, and as such it mystically united its members – under the concept of *sobornost'* – into one spiritual community without loss of individuality.

Notably, these ideas reinforce the previously mentioned difference in the very understanding of the faculty of reason in Russia and Western Europe. Harrison argues that the Slavophiles' philosophical discourse at the time was biased in its criticism of Western Europe in that the realities of the latter were compared (unfavourably) to the ideals of the former. Harrison concludes her analysis of the Slavophiles by saying that "positive evaluations of the influence of reason or scholasticism on Catholic theology and examples of Catholic mysticism were therefore excluded from their works". She then proceeds to juxtapose with these ideas a similar discussion arising from a purely literary discourse, drawing on the works of Pushkin, Gogol' and Tiutchev, which reveal a more complex picture, with the influence of mystical and aesthetic aspects of Western religion being more ambiguous, multifunctional and multidimensional.

Christopher Tooke's chapter raises the topic of Russian antisemitism – a huge and separate theme in its own right – and treats it from the point of view of a rationalist-irrationalist dichotomy. Tooke examines the ways in which antisemitic writers in late tsarist Russia engaged with irrational ideas proclaiming the existence of a Jewish conspiracy to take over the world. The texts studied in depth are the trilogy *The Yid is Coming* (1888–92) by the conservative journalist, war correspondent and fiction-writer Vsevolod Vladimirovich

Krestovskii (1839–95) and the short story 'On the Moscow River: An Autumn Night's Dream' (1906) by the spiritualist prose-writer Vera Ivanovna Kryzhanovskaia (1857–1924). Tooke argues that Russian concepts of rationalism and irrationalism are important aspects of Krestovskii's contrasting portrayal of the Jews and Russians. While Krestovskii presents Jews as human beings who wield great power because they are a strong race united by faith and a common goal, Kryzhanovskaia presents them as actual demons. A further contrast is that, while Krestovskii ostensibly gives documentary evidence for the conspiracy, Kryzhanovskaia resorts to an entirely irrational means of 'evidence', a vision. Yet both writers ultimately demand from their readers an irrational belief in Jews as an all-powerful force, a conviction prevalent in late tsarist Russia.

The ideas that underlie the antisemitic works studied by Tooke involve a contrasting opposition between the ostensibly selfless irrationalism of Russian Orthodox faith and the self-centred rationality of Judaism, which is supposed to be inherent in Russian Jewry in particular. These ideas smuggle in a deliberately distorted, yet primitive, and thus convenient antisemitic stereotype. The reality, on the contrary, appears to conceal a striking proximity between Russian and Jewish (or, more precisely, Russian Jewish) irrationalism – a theme deserving a separate major study. This proximity might be due to the mutual influence caused by the historical circumstances of the two nations living alongside one another.

Fazil Iskander's trickster-hero voices a humorous parallel of a broader nature (irrespective of the specificity of Russian Jewry) between Russian and Jewish nations:

> They are two spiritually related peoples. Only these two peoples over many centuries have spoken about their special historical mission on earth. It has ended up that the Jews captured time. Officially five thousand years, and how many they have in store no-one knows. Perhaps another ten thousand years. But, having been distracted by this captivity of time, Jews lost space. And we, Russians, were distracted by the capture of space, and fell out of time.[39]

Despite the light-heartedness and idiosyncrasy of this narrative, the cross-fertilisation of Russian and Jewish cultures in the Russian national space seems undeniable and profound.

---

[39] F. Iskander, "Dumaiushii o Rossii i amerikanets", in *Rasskazy, povest', skazka, dialog, esse, stikhi*. Series "Zerkalo XX vek", Ekaterinburg: U-Faktoriia, 1999, 580–581.

Another prominent idea which, ironically, permeates Krestovskii's antisemitic trilogy is that, as Tooke puts it, "it is the Jews [...] who prove themselves worthy of the status of a great nation" against the Russian "national weakness". Interestingly, the aforementioned Dmitrii Bykov, a prominent contemporary literary scholar, discerns the same undercurrent in Solzhenitsyn's controversial work *Dvesti let vmeste* on the coexistence of Russians with Jews in Russia:

> Jews in Russia have had to become publicists, thinkers, revolutionaries, counter-revolutionaries, commissars, dissidents, patriots, creators of official culture and the over-turners of that culture, because for some reason Russians did not have the strength to do this.[40]

Of course, there is an obvious historical explanation – that Lenin's and Stalin's Purges literally stripped the country of its best intellectual and cultural potential, and Russian Jews who strove for the freedom and equality at first offered to them by Bolshevism tended to remain in Russia in larger proportions. However, Bykov ventures to express a deeper and more polemical conjecture, already touched upon above, of a certain self-destructive tendency of the Russian nation – analogous, as indicated, to that discerned by Tooke in Krestovskii's novel:

> Perhaps Russians want someone else to blame, and therefore they don't bother to do anything, but instead lay all the blame on the Jews. [...] Or perhaps, and this is a more complex case – the Russian nation is not interested in any conscious historical activity because it has a different programme – passionate, sado-masochistic self-destructiveness under any pretext.[41]

In other words, "Jews played this role, and not a different role in Russian history because owing to a particularity of the local indigenous population they had to become Russians. The Russians for some secret reason abstained from this".[42] As a corollary, Bykov states that Russians cannot be called a nation if the concept is understood not in the ethnic but in the philosophical sense, and draws attention to similar conclusions by a young sociologist Iurii Amosov.

This set of ideas borders on the problem of Russian national consciousness and traditions of distrust, if not an outright hostility, towards outsiders.

---

40   Dmitrii Bykov, "Dvesti let vmesto".
41   *Ibid.*
42   *Ibid.*

Amongst a complexity of reasons for the antisemitic world-view, an inferiority complex plays a significant role, highlighted in the famous response attributed to Winston Churchill to the question of why it is that there is virtually no anti-semitism in England: "This is because we do not consider Jews cleverer than ourselves".[43] Similarly, Vasilii Grossman writes on the issue in his epic work *Zhizn' i sud'ba*:

> Anti-Semitism is always a means rather than an end; it is a measure of the contradictions yet to be resolved. It is a mirror for the failings of individuals, social structures and State systems. Tell me what you accuse the Jews of – I'll tell you what you're guilty of.
>
> [...] Anti-Semitism is also an expression of a lack of talent, an inability to win a contest on equal terms – in science or in commerce, in craftsmanship or in painting. States look to the imaginary intrigues of World Jewry for explanations of their own failure.
>
> [...] Historical epochs, unsuccessful and reactionary governments, and individuals hoping to better their lot all turn to anti-Semitism as a last resort, in an attempt to escape an inevitable doom.[44]

As Tooke concedes, there is a close proximity between the antisemitic beliefs and slogans of both Krestovskii and Kryzhanovskaia, even though the former attempts a rational discourse, while the latter engages in maximally irrational antisemitic propaganda; however,

> one must not lose sight of the fact that such ideas could gain acceptance only in the presence of amenability not only to irrational ideas, but also to ideologies of intolerance and hatred, and that no matter how prevalent themes of rationalism and irrationalism are in the works [...] discussed, what is primary is animosity towards outsiders.

In conjunction with his main theme of Russian antisemitism, Tooke derives from the works studied, especially from Krestovskii's novel, a stratification of Russian irrationalism into negative and positive strands. Alongside the "capacity for love, faith and self-sacrifice" the Russian nation also "has a tendency towards vice and dejection". Thus, "the people's irrationalism is both its

---

43 See, for instance, http://www.thejc.com/news/uk-news/25549/pianist-kissin-protests-against-bbc-anti-israel-bias (25.06.2012).
44 Vasilii Grossman, *Life and Fate*, translated by Robert Chandler, London: Vintage Books, 2006, 468–470.

moral and spiritual core under ideal conditions, and the cause of its downfall when times are bad", that is when there is no superior guidance and no idea to fight for. Although this classification is, unavoidably, simplified, it nevertheless captures some recurrent ideas, fundamental for the study of Russian irrationalism.

Some major areas of human existence, such as economics, which on the surface may not seem directly related to the cultural sphere, in reality prove inseparable from it. As specialists well know, the concepts of national mentality and cultural identity play an important role in a country's economic development. In her chapter Natalia Vinokurova addresses this elusive but vital connection between cultural values and economic behaviour in the Russian context, and argues for a fundamentally irrational stance which traditionally underpins Russian economic consciousness – even at times such as the modern era, when the actual semiotics of behaviour heavily gravitates towards rationalism. She poses the question of to what extent the basis of modern economic theory – the abstract concept of a homo economicus who behaves in a rational manner and aspires to maximise his gains within given social, political, moral and other constraints – can be applied in the Russian context. In order to answer it, Vinokurova traces the history of development of political-economic theories in Russia and Western Europe as ultimately rooted in ethical and religious spheres, and arrives at the ideological opposition inherent in contemporary Russian society between two types of economic behaviour: that of a Western-oriented homo economicus on the one hand, and of a traditional Russian Idealist on the other. This somewhat ironically and rather expectedly resonates with the typically Russian opposition of Westernisers and Slavophiles, but Vinokurova at the same time demonstrates how factitious this opposition, in fact, is, and shows that actual reality is more complex and ambiguous.

In her analysis Vinokurova convincingly uses extensive material drawn from academic as well as popular sources, including internet bloggers, national folklore and state-of-the-art social and economic theories, and examines how these correlate. She singles out a variety of distinguishing features common to a specifically Russian polemic on the extent to which homo economicus is present in the country. Amongst these features is a striving for an ideal disconnected from consumerism, and based instead on traditional Russian Orthodox values and the idea of Russian spirituality. Personally refraining from falling into dangerous comparisons between stereotypical Russian and Western European modes of thought and existence, Vinokurova cites Russian academician Dmitrii Likhachev who stresses that "one must differentiate the national ideal from the national character. The ideal does not always coincide with reality. But the national ideal is nonetheless very important", for "the people who are creating this ideal, in the end give birth to their heroes, their geniuses, getting closer to that ideal and the latter gives the tone to national culture as a whole".[45] Vinokurova thus expresses hope that "in Russian irrationalism there is something rational after all", as it is possible that "a new and healthy balance between two types of values – Western rational-liberal and Russian traditional – will allow a transition to a more just and stable economic order".

The study of individual authors, which characterises the next part of the volume, opens with Arkadii Goldenberg's chapter dedicated to Gogol' – one of the most obvious examples and sources of irrationalism and the absurd in Russian literary culture and beyond. Vasilii Rozanov famously contrasted Gogol' with Pushkin, arguing that the two gave rise to the tendencies that proved instrumental for the subsequent development of the entire Russian literature: diseased and healthy respectively. Gogol's "laughter through tears" is an intrinsic part of this "unhealthy" tradition where the grotesque, fantastic, supernatural all play a major role. Goldenberg in his study of the irrational element in Gogol's mythopoetics approaches the theme from a different angle – by focusing on the archaic rites and rituals, and the most ancient archetypes in K.G. Jung's "collective unconscious", which, through their strong presence in national folklore, feed into Gogol's world as its semantically and aesthetically meaningful components.

Goldenberg distinguishes as one of the most important ontological problems for Gogol the opposition between the world of the living and the world of the dead. The border between the two is constantly crossed, which enables Gogol's heroes to sustain the connection with their ancestors, vital for their sense of self. It is worth noting that a mythological conception of cyclical time, characteristic of this phenomenon, is described also in Chumakova's contribution, where it is juxtaposed to a Western European linear model. In his chapter Goldenberg conducts a close examination of how the relations between the two worlds, which were strongly regulated in Slavic culture, have a direct bearing on the irrational behaviour of Gogol's characters. He discloses the major cultural significance of the rituals surrounding the exchange between existence and non-existence, such as funerals, weddings and various other festivals, as well as of some important archetypes such as orphans and ritual guests. In demonstrating how all these archetypes of the "collective unconscious" are actualised in Gogol's oeuvre, Goldenberg throws into relief "the deep mythological intuition of the writer" and reveals that "the most important irrational aspects of his poetics can hardly be adequately comprehended outside of a

---

45   D.S. Likhachev, *Izbrannoe. Mysli o zhizni, istorii, kulture,* Moscow: PIK, 2006, 270. Cited in Vinokurova's chapter.

mythological and ritual context". Thus, in a sense, Goldenberg traces certain rational foundations, concealed in ancient Slavic cultural beliefs, which underpin the apparent irrationality of Gogol's literary world.

Sergei Kibal'nik, in his contribution, strives to recover Russian philosophical tradition from the radically irrationalist image it has been assigned in the West. To this end he makes an important conceptual distinction between irrationalism and anti-rationalism, insisting that it is the latter rather than the former that characterises the world of Dostoevskii's writings and, for that matter, Russian culture more generally. He refers to Semen Frank's similar distinction with respect to the archetypical Russian character, and makes the provocative (and rather controversial) implication that a great deal of the irrationalist reputation of Russian culture, especially literature, in Western Europe was promoted by peculiar (and covertly rationalist) thinkers like Lev Shestov. Kibal'nik explains the source of Dostoevskii's anti-rationalism as a perfectly rational reaction against the excessive rationalism of the French utopian socialist variety. Reading the Russian novelist's tale 'Stepanchikovo Village' as cryptic parody and polemics against his old ideals and former friends from Petrashevskii's circle, Kibal'nik deciphers its references to the utopian novel *Voyage en Icarie* by Etienne Cabet, which popularised the ideas of the French socialists.

Similarly, Kibal'nik traces Max Stirner's influence on Dostoevskii, most profoundly reflected in 'Notes from Underground', and sides with those scholars who saw in the Russian writer not only the traits of Stirner's philosophy, but also a rebellion against the latter's rationalist nihilism. Kibal'nik then examines the differences as well as similarities between Dostoevskii and Stirner, exemplified by extensive literary material, and demonstrates the complex role that reason plays in Dostoevskii world. In particular, Kibal'nik shows how, through the polemical engagement of both thinkers with Feuerbach, Dostoevskii's anti-rationalism is revealed.

Drawing on various sources and his own discussion of Dostoevskii, Kibal'nik reaches the conclusion that "Russian philosophy, even religious philosophy, in general, is not something absolutely irrational [...]. It is, rather, antirational [...] and at the same time has a significant rational pattern. This dialectical symbiosis to a great extent goes back to Dostoevskii". Instructively, similar ideas are present later in the volume, in Oliver Ready's study of Iurii Mamleev, whose oeuvre was substantially informed by Dostoevskii's writings.

Alexander McCabe's chapter continues the study of Dostoevskii's engagement with irrationalism by examining the reception of his 'Underground Man' in France, and thus reveals, more generally, how the anti-rationalist polemics of the novelist contributed to the post-Enlightenment epistemological reassessment of non-rational modes of thought in the European context. In particular, it explores the extent to which French philosophies of existence assimilated aspects of Russian irrationalism, and traces historical connections between Russian and French existential movements which have hitherto been widely ignored.

Starting with an outline of the initial exclusion of Dostoevskian 'underground philosophy' from French cultural discourse of the nineteenth century, McCabe follows the development of the French readings of Dostoevskii to the first half of the twentieth century when the influx of Russian émigré culture significantly fed into French intellectual life. Most notably, the chapter draws on the role of Lev Shestov's interpretation of Dostoevskii and Boris de Schloezer's 'subtly existential' translation which shaped the later reception of the Russian novelist in France and informed the treatment of the writer by Gide, Camus and Sartre.

McCabe shows the incongruence of Dostoevskii's anti-rationalist inquiry with the cultural agenda of France at the turn of the twentieth century, and highlights the initial attempts to rationalise the Russian narrative for the French readership fashioned as alien to the intrinsically enigmatic and mystic 'Russian soul'. The emphasis on morality inherent in these early interpretations was then shifted, as McCabe demonstrates, towards more 'immoralist' readings by cosmopolitan critics such as Gide and Faure. However, the real challenge to the primacy of reason began only with the emergence on the French intellectual scene of Shestov's writings on Dostoevskii and Schloezer's re-translation of 'The Notes'. At the same time, the existentialist and absurdist philosophies of Sartre and Camus, McCabe argues, while sharing with the Russian tradition an acute awareness of the irrational, still fell short of a sustained anti-rationalist stance. Notwithstanding these differences, as McCabe's engaging analysis illuminates, the irrationalist trend facilitated an inter-cultural dialogue, leading ultimately to a productive cross-fertilisation of cultures.

Margarita Odesskaia's chapter focuses on one of the 'most European' Russian writers, Ivan Turgenev, whom Lev Shestov in many ways opposed to the anti-rationalist Dostoevskii. Yet it was also Shestov who, in line with his own paradigm, uncovered the irrational rift in Turgenev's sensibility, and applied to the writer the famous Russian saying "scratch a Russian, and you will find a Tatar". Odesskaia takes an alternative, but equally revealing (and ultimately related) approach to the irrational in Turgenev, which subtly aligns him with Dostoevskii. By contrast to Kibal'nik's thesis of Russian cultural anti-rationalism being largely a reaction to the excessive rationalism of the West and its home-grown modifications, she offers an entirely different vision through her study of Turgenev's oeuvre. Focusing on the themes of love and beauty, Odesskaia traces the origins of Turgenev's creative imagination to antiquity, and reveals a conflict hidden in Turgenev's writings not as that between a Russian and a European in a direct sense, but between two incompatible traditions: classicist and Christian, as well as a dialectical unity between the two sides of the Greek spirit: Apollonian and Dionysian, as discerned by Nietzsche. In line with Jung's theory of the collective unconscious leading to a disintegration of the individual 'I', and Gilles Deleuze's analysis of Sacher-Masoch's female characters, Odesskaia examines Turgenev's treatment of love as a slave–master relationship and a burdening chain, as well as nostalgia for the lost ideal, attainable only through art rather than reality.

Drawing on existing scholarship, Odesskaia explains Sacher-Masoch's fascination with the Russian writer by tracing the roots of this new aesthetics of erotic cruelty to the specifically Russian social conditions of serfdom and associated personal brutality, which left a deep imprint in Turgenev's own biography, having undoubtedly affected his perception of love and the fatal character of his own passion for Pauline Viardot. The image of Turgenev presented in Odesskaia's chapter is based on a painful and inescapable conflict between man's ability for a sober rational assessment of his feelings and the irrational chaos of unruly passions to which his reason has no choice but to submit. Two types of women portrayed in Turgenev's fiction embody good and evil, Apollonian and Dionysian spirits respectively, and Turgenev, while showing the dark power of the latter, ultimately strives to reconcile his male heroes with the former, who represent the harmonious trinity of truth, good and beauty.

This rational-irrational dichotomy is, in a sense, a sophisticated development of Lev Shestov's perception of Turgenev as intrinsically torn between his wild and irrational Russian side on the one hand and his rational and balanced European education and convictions on the other. Thus, interestingly, this chapter by Odesskaia as well as the earlier one, by Kibal'nik, can be regarded as covert engagement with Lev Shestov, where Kibal'nik polemicises with the philosopher, while Odesskaia builds on Shestov's interpretation.

Olga Tabachnikova attempts to trace some continuities and breaks in the apparently distant, but actually not disjointed, cases of European irrationalism which represent its different phases and cultural traditions, by comparing the radical thought of "the father of modern European irrationalism"[46] Johann Georg Hamann (1730–1788) and the equally non-compromising opponent of reason in his battle against Western speculative philosophy, a precursor of

---

46 This is a perception of J.G. Hamann by Isaiah Berlin. See the editorial text by Henry Hardy in Isaiah Berlin, *The Magus of the North: J.G. Hamann and the Origins of Modern Irrationalism*.

Sartrean existentialism, Lev Shestov (1866–1938). She then juxtaposes with these anti-rationalist thinkers, whose stance is marked by a perception of reason as repression and whose "God is a poet, not a geometer",[47] the artistic world of Anton Chekhov where the irrationalist is of a much subtler kind, concealed under the veneer of rationalism, and helpful for throwing into relief these radical cases.

This, so to speak, more intelligent type of irrationalism embraces reason, while acknowledging both its constraints and its inseparability from other forms of perception. Through constant distrust of verbal communications, ultimately overcome by intense lyricism, and through multiple subversions of semantic layers which reflect the limitations of human ability for understanding themselves and the world, Chekhov, despite the age of faithlessness whose advance he witnesses and mirrors, represents, interestingly, a somewhat Biblical stance in that he assumes the deviousness of human nature as given, but based on the acceptance of its intrinsic evil his writings point us to the good.

For the same historical-religious reasons the tragic in Hamann is less acute than in Shestov and Chekhov, although all three are united by their emphasis on the individual path to truth which cannot be replicated, and the primacy of experience over theory. Of the same root is also Chekhov's insistence on ultimate personal freedom and personal responsibility requiring a constant spiritual effort in order to sustain and to give meaning to eternal values eroded by the loss of religious faith. This tradition, which treads water between moral relativism and an understanding that no category is absolute, equally absorbs rationalism and irrationalism as two inseparable parts of the same whole, and exalts human dignity and personal choice, made a strong impact on the Russian literary consciousness of the twentieth century and proved vital for the very survival of the national culture in brutal historical circumstances.

The chapter also argues that, while Shestov and Hamann share a radical opposition to reason, and Shestov and Chekhov with their chronological proximity reflect the crisis of nihilism, marked by the tragic consciousness and convulsions of morality outside religion, it is Hamann and Chekhov who turn out to be aligned in their attitude to life as communication and their focus on dialogue as opposed to Shestov's idiosyncratically monological world.

Rainer Grübel's chapter (like Odesskaia's) revisits, if only briefly, the Dionysian and Apollonian spirit in relation to rationalism and irrationalism, but with a different aim – in the course of demonstrating the complex character of their interaction and the inevitable synthesis of the two in world culture. By the same

---

47   Ibid., p. 40.

token, while tracing the history of European irrationalism from the perspective of ethics, Grübel disavows the idea of the ethical superiority of reason, and also dismisses as primitive, in the modern age of cognitive psychology and neuroscience, the traditional way of divorcing the rational and irrational faculties to the activities of the brain and heart respectively. Furthermore, he makes a useful observation of the rational-irrational dichotomy being a special case of the normal-abnormal one, and then points to, in the context of a specifically Russian irrationalism encompassing anti-Enlightenment and anti-positivist tendencies, a conflict between the normative idea of life and the reality that does not conform to this idea.

In connection to Tolstoi and Rozanov, Grübel provides an informative tour around the history of Russian sectarianism and finds the roots of the Russian criticism of normality, embodied by irrationalism, in the sectarian and heretical attitudes that emerged as a reaction against the inflexible ways of the Russian Orthodox church. Grübel then analyses both protagonists as representing two different types of Russian irrationalism: didactic and existential fundamentalism respectively, which he sees arising in Tolstoy's case by and large more from his biography, and in Rozanov's from his psychology.

Drawing on factual material, Grübel refutes the perception of Tolstoi as rationalist, and argues for his ambivalence in this respect, and the proximity of his stance to the early Slavophiles and various irrationalist philosophical schools as a result of a painful personal search which tested the limits of reason. By contrast, Rozanov, as Grübel explains, was never fascinated by reason, but oriented instead towards the irrational spirit of the universe. Without losing sight of the rational Rozanov nevertheless believed that God is not universal reason, but a universal soul. The continuity of this belief lies at the core of Russian culture, the author concludes. Thus Grübel's chapter not only offers a useful and elaborate historical and ideological framework for the study of modern Russian irrationalism, but also provides a bridge from nineteenth century Russian culture to the Silver Age – a cultural phase treated in the next part of the volume.

It is clear that the problematic of rationalism and irrationalism is closely connected to the theory of cognition. Moving forward in chronological terms and delving deeper into philosophy from the more historical-literary path engagingly walked by Grübel, in her chapter Henrieke Stahl provides comparative characteristics of two respective epistemologies – those of Vladimir Solov'ev and Andrei Belyi. She draws on their seminal works – Solov'ev's well-known 'Theoretical Philosophy' (1897–1899) and Belyi's previously unpublished 'History of Development of the Self-consciousness-soul' (1926–1931), only recently recovered and introduced by Professor Stahl to a wider scholarly community.[48]

In these works both authors develop a theory of cognition which is based on the critical reception of key-concepts of the Metaphysical (Johannes Volkelt) and the South-Western school of neo-Kantianism (Heinrich Rickert, Wilhelm Windelband). As Stahl explains, both Solov'ev and Belyi start with the idea of presuppositionlessness playing a central role in the epistemology of Volkelt and, based on corrections of it, try to inaugurate a third "Copernican turn" by showing scientifically that man's cognition is rooted in spiritual being. Stahl then shows that each of them in his own way arrives at a "logical voluntarism" (a term by which Belyi labelled his epistemology), based on the primacy of practical reason, typical for the South-Western school. But in opposition to neo-Kantianism, as Stahl argues, the Russian philosophers aim at the transformation of epistemological *theory* into spiritual *practice*, which can be characterised as Christian intellectual mysticism culminating in communion with Christ through the intellect.

This uneven but fascinating interplay between theory and practice fits well with the basic framework of Russian philosophical thought, characterised more by its pathos than its ethos, as suggested earlier in the volume by Oliver Smith, and more generally by the existing scholarship that emphasises the inseparable character of Russian philosophising and the "living life", to use Dostoevskii's term. Despite the above common denominator, as Stahl further demonstrates, Belyi differs from Solov'ev: in contrast to Solov'ev's modernising the Orthodox tradition of the Jesus prayer, Belyi opts for the esoteric path, founded by Rudolf Steiner in his anthroposophy.

The focus of the next chapter, by Marilyn Schwinn Smith, is 'The Dancing Demon – Dance and the Word' (1949) by Aleksei Remizov, one of the writers inseparable from the Russian Silver Age. The chapter provides a detailed analysis of the work and its cultural-historical roots, exploring more generally Remizov's affinity to the world of the irrational and his place within the Russian cultural milieu of the time. In her analysis, Smith reinforces the point made earlier in the volume by Rainer Grübel in the context of the turn of two centuries, the 19th and 20th: the new age has outgrown realist writing and required new literary devices. Drawing on rich scholarly material Smith thus traces in Remizov's prose specific modernist traits subversive of the rationalist discourse of realism, including his cosmology (or 'cosmo-centricity'). At the same time, as

---

48 See the proceedings of the international conference 'Andrei Belyi filosof – *Istoriia stanovleniia samosoznaiushchei dushi* i eio konteksty' (Trier, November 2010) in the special issue of *Russian Literature* LXX-I/II, 1 July – 15 August 2011, guest editor Henrieke Stahl.

is clear from Smith's chapter, Remizov's oeuvre can be read as a perfect example of Russian cultural continuity. Indeed, as Smith explains, cultural memory is the principal ethos of Remizov's writing. Dreams constitute its thematic focus, while demons serve as a metaphor for the creative impulse of earthly life; all together – demons, dreams and cultural memory – are categories pertaining to, or verging on, the irrational.

Smith demonstrates how 'The Dancing Demon' provides a cultural-historical tour around pre-Christian Russia with its pagan rituals and ancient practices, reconstructing the evolution of the culture of *skomorokhi* (medieval East Slavic harlequins, dancing, singing and performing, to whose culture Remizov ascribed himself) into modern arts. She examines the work's background encompassed by the Russian ritual practice grouped by Remizov under the umbrella term of *rusaliia*, emphasising first of all its performative aspect, and shows how through reconstructing the history of dance and word, Remizov retrieves something lost from the native consciousness.

Smith's exploration of Remizov's rootedness in Slavic folklore, of his tracing pagan imprints in modern culture through various marginalised cultural artefacts and performative art, is akin to Goldenberg's study of Gogol's poetics by revealing its intimate connection to Slavic folk culture and ancient religious rituals. Smith examines the route by which Remizov might have arrived at his perception, contrary to the accepted one, of *skomorokhi* culture as Russia's native cultural product rather than a derivative of foreign influence. Her research thus illuminates how Remizov's oeuvre anticipates and develops modern anthropological theories and a ritual theory of art, and how it dissolves the rationalist hypostases of such concepts as identity and time as stable and/or delineating categories. She further conjectures that 'The Dancing Demon' is a generative text for Remizov's later works of memoiristic prose combining fantastic genre with memoirs. As a result, the chapter situates Remizov within the culture of the Silver Age, with its distinct interest toward the irrational, as its true representative, both in spirit and in technique. At the same time it lays bare Remizov's role as an author who sustains Russian cultural continuity – a cultural conductor between the ancient Russian past (with its profound irrationalist element) and Russian modernity.

Ildikó Mária Rácz continues the study of irrationalism by offering her analysis of Bunin's short story 'The Grammar of Love'. Thus, similarly to the previous chapter, this contribution focuses not only on a specific author but also on his specific work, and gives equal emphasis to the vital role of the categories of space, time, imagination and memory in the construction of an irrationalist ethos. Throughout her piece, Rácz uncovers and explores the rational-irrational dichotomy that appears at various levels in the plot of the story, whose theme (just as that of Odesskaia's chapter on Turgenev) – the human ability to love – provides rich material for a discussion of irrationalism. As these chapters demonstrate, love is perceived as a devastating force in both Bunin's and Turgenev's worlds. However, if in Turgenev's oeuvre it is considered more from ethical, moral, existential or aesthetic perspectives in terms of the injustice of slavery and freedom, mental disease and fatal curse, in Bunin's universe love is above all a cosmic force, irrational and incomprehensible, which like nature itself transcends moral categories and rises above them. Human tragedy in Bunin's interpretation, as Rácz explains, is in the incongruence of the infinite and finite, in the human inability to accommodate the infinity of love.

The chapter demonstrates how Bunin's main character starts out with the intention to find a rational explanation for his neighbour's life history, but, during his travels, becomes captive to the same irrational forces that ruled the landowner's fate. Bunin's short story, as Rácz argues, leads us into an esoteric world through literary reference to superstitions and the interpretation of dreams. The work starts from real space, but moves towards the ever more bleak and schematic outer regions, since, in reality, travels are in the inner areas of consciousness, in memories and in the imaginary world.

The groundings of Bunin's narrative in Russian mythology connect this study with Marilyn Smith's study of Remizov's tale, where Russian pagan beliefs and superstitions were of high significance. More generally, in her detailed analysis of the story's construction, Rácz uncovers multiple parallels with fairy-tale structure and functionality, supported by an existing theoretical framework, as well as important differences that help to achieve a deeper understanding of Bunin's work, including its interplay between the rational and irrational. By providing an inter-textual analysis, with a meaningful reference to Baratynskii, whose lines are quoted in the story, Rácz concludes that clear understanding "cannot be attained either through a simple rational search for reasons, or by means of irrational identification only. It happens, namely, between the state of dreaming and of being awake, at the fine line bordering rational and irrational modes of cognition".

Jeremy Howard's chapter leads the way to the study of Russian irrationalism beyond literature – in visual arts and music – in his case, painting, but also involving some photography, graphic art, performance and cotton wool. Offering an exciting, thought-provoking and informative discussion on selected artists of a selected period, Howard also charts the way for future studies. He begins by raising a fundamental question (as we saw above) of art itself being an intrinsically irrational human activity, and moves into a discussion of visual representations of *supra*-phenomenal, intuitive and 'spiritual' or 'inner' realms. His focus is on the period c. 1850–1914, which can be regarded as the heyday of irrationalism in Russian art, in many ways continuing the Gothic tradition while serving also as a bridge to the new stage of Russian culture.

Howard examines the work of those artists who were deemed to have had some psychological or physical flaw as well as by others with an agenda to probe beyond reason such as Fedotov's final pieces, Vrubel's Demons, images of Poprishchin, Kulbin's promotion of 'psychological' art, Balashov's iconoclastic act and Malevich's 'zaum' painting. This analysis reveals continuity and parallels within and beyond the irrationalist trend, and throws into relief a striking proximity between visual arts and literature of the same period in their propensity to question the authority of reason, to examine the state of folly as part of inscrutable human striving to act against self-interest and the role of chance, uncertainty and risk in wrestling with fate – reflected most notably in Pushkin's 'The Queen of Spades', Gogol's examination of folly, Lermontov's romantic poems and Dostoevskii's major novels.

In his analysis of individual works and artists, Howard unravels a fascinating kinship between Fedotov's *Gamblers* and, against rationalist moralistic and derogatory interpretations, Repin's *Ivan the Terrible and his son Ivan 16 Nov 1581* by reading both as a study in anguish and agony, and simultaneously a response to Russia's brutal history, with Repin's painting also providing a warning call to Russia's rulers against further bloodshed, which, like Tolstoi's pacific sermon, went unheeded. By the same token, as Howard's analysis reveals, Vrubel's symbolist obsession with the fallen 'superhuman' spirit bears much in common with Repin's aforementioned realist depiction of the (existentially) 'fallen' tsar, in their portrayal of suffering and ultimately powerless human predicament. Howard also provides an interesting reading of a famous case of barbaric rebellion against Repin's painting (by an icon painter Balashov), and of its consequences in Russian art, as iconoclasm, and further – as an artistic phenomenon in itself which entailed heated controversy and debate. This turmoil is symptomatic of new times which required a new art, as earlier chapters also demonstrated. Thus, as Howard argues, quoting A.S. Byatt, the appearance of Kulbin on the art scene and the activities of his group *Treugolnik* (Triangle) encapsulated the pan-European age when "the irrational bubbled up, and met the rational, which fastened on it with glee…"[49] Reproductions of visual imagination and memory by the blind Nechaev were part of this phenomenon and required an inner (rather than standard external) sight to be adequately appreciated. Thus, Howard concludes, "through the exposure of artists like Gorodetskii, Nechaev and Ferdinandov to the Russian public Kulbin surpassed

---

49 A.S. Byatt, *The Children's Book*, London: Vintage, 2009, 484–485. Cited in Howard's chapter.

the irrationalist expressivity of Fedotov, Repin and Vrubel, taking visual art on a new stage of its journey into non-reason". This, in turn, evoked a new wave of highly innovative art in Russia in the years to come, continuing to blend together rationalist and irrationalist tendencies in the most interesting and captivating ways.

Most instructively, Aleksandr Ivashkin's chapter, which focuses on Russian twentieth century music, reinforces the points made by Jeremy Howard in relation to Russian (and not only Russian) visual arts in that their irrationalism represents a complex blend of logical reasoning and *supra*-phenomenal intuitive visions. In his discussion of irrationalism in Russian music, Ivashkin usefully places it in the broader context of world culture, revealing the unifying symbolist root of the Old Testament as opposed to the ancient Greek rationalist tradition – the division suggested by Erich Auerbach's *Mimesis*. This division, in fact, is closely connected to Lev Shestov's idiosyncratic dichotomy of Athens and Jerusalem, reason and faith, mentioned earlier in the volume. Ivashkin traces manifestations of the above irrationalist tradition in the music of both Russian and non-Russian composers of the twentieth century and highlights the striking parallels between them. Starting with Scriabin's theosophical ideas and his use of the so called 'mystical chord', he argues further that Shostakovich and some younger Russian composers of the irrationalist variety drew many of their ideas from the mentality of the Silver Age as well as the doctrines of Christian faith. Indeed, as Ivashkin explains, Shostakovich built in particular on Mussorgskii's music inspired by the Old Believers, and the repetitive character of Shostakovich's oeuvre, devoid of direct religious content, nevertheless owes much to Russian religious music with its radical spiritual might. Ivashkin then provides a fascinating historical analysis of Shostakovich's propensity for regular rhythmical structures and traces the origins of the composer's ritualistic principles, which, curiously, share much with communist rhetoric and Soviet mass-culture, to the so-called Church *Azbukas* (syllabaries) of the eighteenth century as well as Russian pagan beliefs, fairy tales, rituals and prayers. It is perhaps not surprising that this enlightening analysis in the musical-historical sphere is highly resonant of Katerina Clark's ground-breaking study of Soviet history as mythology.

From Shostakovich's use of the 'magic number' three, Ivashkin moves on to a more extended engagement with numerology as part of symbolist technique, rooted in number alphabets and cabalistic tradition. This is exemplified by the music of such composers as Alfred Schnittke and Sofia Gubaidulina in their connections to Bach as well as other composers whose musical texts often need to be deciphered. In their use of numbers as symbols and principles of natural proportion, these composers display a blend of strict logic and irrationalist sensibility – the phenomenon occurring not only in the visual arts, as we saw above, but also in Russian literature, and even more broadly – in the Eurasian mentality, as Liudmila Safronova's chapter demonstrates in the last section of the volume.

Thus part of the common denominator uniting separate studies represented in the volume is that the roots of irrationalism are concealed not only in the mystical, intuitive realm, in pure faith unaccountable to reason, but equally in a belief in some higher universal order which leads us to supernatural, divine spheres.

Ivashkin claims, in conclusion, that oppressive historical circumstances were conducive to creativity in Russia, while periods of relative liberties on the contrary diminished its creative impulse. However, he then observes that the nature of non-liberty is diverse and not restricted to political or social oppression, and suggests that the roots of hidden meanings and metaphoric language initiate from deeper and older cultural and spiritual sources – those situated essentially beyond reason. Furthermore, our acceptance of the absurd and irrational guarantees our spiritual continuity and cultural survival.

Oleg Kovalov's chapter on irrationalism in Russian film is ambitious in scope. Not only does it give a historical overview of the subject, but also conceptualises the phenomenon of Russian cinematic irrationalism, drawing on diverse scholarly sources and extensive cinematic material. Adopting this challenging bird's eye view perspective allows us to see more clearly some patterns of irrationalism in Russia that are generic and not restricted to cinematic genre alone.

Kovalov begins at the chronological start of cinema in Russia and the range of philosophical and artistic questions this new genre incurred. He stresses a metaphysical rather than purely technocratic aspect in its interpretation by the leading Russian intellectuals: an intuitive understanding of some magical powers of cinema, its intrinsic link to the very substance of existence. By the same token, a complex relationship between cinematic genre and time has always been fundamental (as it has been in other forms of art – for instance, in poetry where, most notably, the function and role of time were contemplated by Joseph Brodsky) and received a variety of interpretations. However, the central premise of Kovalov's investigation of cinematic irrationalism is based on Tsvetan Todorov's definition of the fantastic in art which, somewhat paradoxically, is determined above all by its perception: 'the fantastic exists while the reader remains unsure in which key – mystical or positivist – he is to interpret the narrative'. That is to say, it is the exciting ambivalence of interpretation of the original plot by the reader that creates the effect of the fantastic.

Thus true irrationalism is concealed in the peculiarities that contradict the film's very nature, be it in relation to its genre or theme. In other words, the fantastic world has to be internal rather than external, that is, it cannot be predetermined and opens up in an unexpected, unregulated, self-contradictory way. This conclusion determines the principle for distinguishing the irrational in Russian cinema: it has to be sought not in the films where the very plot allows for a fantastic element (science fiction, fairy tales, etc.), but in those where the cinematic subtext subverts the actual 'text' (whether it concerns the plot, genre or theme) which appears 'ordinary' and realistic.

This is why Kovalov begins his examination with the films of Evgenii Bauer – an ingenious film director who liked to shatter the accepted canons and stereotypes. In particular, Bauer overturned the archetypical melodramatic plot of early Russian cinema – that of seduction and retribution – based on Karamzin's 'Bednaia Liza', and, more generally, introduced an altogether different aesthetics – illogical and metaphysical, where life and death essentially swapped places. Kovalov shows how this rejection and distortion of reality was continued by the Soviet avant-garde cinema which developed the utopian Russian idea of the golden future for which the present must be sacrificed. He skilfully uncovers the means by which this line was developed by such renowned film directors as Eisenstein, Pudovkin, Dovzhenko and Vertov in whose works, under ideologically sound themes, a profound exploration of fundamental existential categories is concealed.

Kovalov further traces the evolution of the irrational element in Soviet films, distinguishing its gradual shift towards the uncanny, as well as revealing the emergence of neoclassical, religious, neoromantic and even surrealist tendencies often concealed under a most rationalist veneer. To this end, he examines diverse cinematic production from different Soviet and post-Soviet phases and by numerous directors, extending his considerations up to the present. In the course of this captivating analysis which lays bare the irrational in most unexpected quarters, Kovalov draws parallels with literature and painting, and emphasises the profound influences of foreign cinema and the global processes in world culture as a whole.

The chapter on Russian architecture, by Olga Stukalova and Elena Kabkova, begins by looking at the concept of a building as an object for dwelling as well as a process, and traces the etymology of this word in Russian (*zdanie*) to the old name for 'clay' (*z'd*). However, the very phonetics of it, which resonates with destruction, subverts the stable semantics of the word, thus providing a basis for ambivalence within the concept itself. This duality or even multi-meaningfulness, the authors argue, is inherent in the architecture of Moscow as its intrinsic feature. They remark on the wheel-like shape of Moscow and observe that the city almost continued this metaphoric image by absorbing and subjugating every new part to the organic whole. Thus some buildings which came to be seeming memorials of a certain political phase, more reminiscent of sculpture (space and volume) than architecture (space and construction), gradually became part of a specifically architectural landscape, harmoniously inscribed into the rest of the city.

The irrationalist tendencies of the end of the nineteenth century manifested themselves in architecture, through the symbolist style enriched with mystical features of ancient Russian culture. The authors explore how the emerging modernism developed artistic interest to national cultural heritage and expressed itself in architecture which best accommodated the modernist striving for synthesis of different artistic forms. Moreover, architecture also best reflected various utopian ideas of the universal character, typical of the time. Stukalova and Kabkova further sketch the evolution of Soviet architecture in a broader framework of the development of national Soviet culture and note how the mythologically oriented consciousness inhibited the formation of a more rationalist type of culture. The authors then devote much attention to the general cultural development of the Russian national mentality, psychology, identity, social habits, etc. in conjunction with the changing historical phases, up to the present day. They remark that while Russian modernity substantially preserved traditional national cultural values, the complicated dynamic processes of modernisation and globalisation are conducive to the uncontrollable and somewhat aggressive flow of cultural information streaming into the cultural void which resulted from the collapse of the previous ideologies in the country. As a consequence, one mass culture is replacing another, becoming simplistic, and gradually losing its national cultural flavour. In this connection the authors delineate between cultural monuments and works of art, exemplifying the distinction by the primitive architecture of 1959–1963 which at the same time is a symbol of a whole cultural epoch. The irrational here is, in a sense, a product of excessive rationalism. The authors distinguish the same tendency in the subsequent styles, in which reason based on calculation is ultimately unable to defeat the irrational human nature.

Kira Gordovich's chapter is the first in the section that continues the study of irrationalism in Russian literature of later years: in the Soviet and post-Soviet period, to the present. Gordovich focuses on one of the most fascinating and enigmatic Russian writers of the twentieth century – Andrei Platonov. The relationship in Platonov's literary universe between reality and the world of dreams, between the conscious and unconscious, between literature and life has been the object of intense scholarly attention, and Gordovich continues this line of investigation. She builds on the premise of Platonov scholars that in the opposition of "conscious and unconscious" in his fictional writings, it is the unconscious, intuitive and natural which are always above the rational and reasonable. Gordovich first singles out a distinct presence of the irrational in the sensibility of Platonov's literary characters, a peculiar balance between the real and unreal in the characters' imagination and the mutual reversibility of the rational and irrational. As the world of dreams in Platonov's writings occupies a major place and attracted a variety of interpretations, Gordovich pays special attention to it, analysing in detail, with reference to the text, the characteristics of dreams in the novel *Chevengur*.

She takes issue with the idea that everything in the novel is happening in a dream, and claims instead that sleeping is the state of everything and everyone in Chevengur at certain moments. As Gordovich argues, not only do the dreams form an important element of plot construction, but moreover, it is also in the dreams that insights take place and revelations are pronounced. The mind is often portrayed as a prohibiting mechanism which hinders emotional impulses and strivings, but the role of the bodily state, in turn, can easily exceed that of a mental state. This is especially evident for non-intellectual characters, and at the same time human knowledge and memories resist the power of the mind, as they do not imply the ability to control them.

In her study of the irrational, Gordovich demonstrates Platonov's propensity for investing inanimate objects with humane features, his portrayal of an almost schizophrenic duality of people, as well as a delirious state of mind which is not necessarily associated with illness or dreaming, but rather with life itself, and turns off the ability for rational thinking. In Platonov's depictions, people are often unable to understand themselves, their rational faculty is inactive, giving way to unconscious feelings and instincts. Thus, importantly, Gordovich's analysis exposes the irrational as a major force in Platonov's literary world which works more effectively than direct satirical descriptions in depicting the failure of communism in Chevengur, and, more generally, helps to expand and deepen the narrative.

Liudmila Safronova's chapter, while focusing on one of the leading writers of contemporary Russia, Viktor Pelevin, and his 2003 novel *The Dialectics of the Transition Period (From Nowhere to No Place)*, at the same time offers a generic analysis of postmodern literary characters in the framework of a study of Eurasian mentality. Emphasising modern escapist tendencies in the face of the ever more complex and fast changing world, Safronova explores the psychological defence mechanisms which characterise contemporary man, and by extension, a postmodern literary character, and the artistic means by which these characteristics are depicted. Safronova stresses the obsessive type of behaviour of such neurotic personalities, as well as the therapeutic effect of both their escapist strategies and their reception by the readers who can displace their own anxiety into the text, simultaneously transferring this process from the unconscious to the conscious.

Based on existing scholarship, Safronova gives a character description of such obsessive-compulsive personalities (a so-called anankastic literary character) suffering from neuroses of obsessive conditions, and notes their propensity for big numbers, collecting things and people, staying in control, ritualising their own life, and their distorted perception of reality. She then gives a number of examples of anankastic literary characters and their authors who exercised this obsessive therapeutic psycho-technique, which in a literary piece is reflected by a system of repetitions, a poetics of persisting patterns. The sources of this phenomenon can be traced back to the anti-historical and neo-mythological pre-postmodernist artistic paradigm of the 1920s European culture influenced by the obsessive philosophies of Nietzsche and Spengler with their idea of the eternal return.

A defining formal characteristic of this obsessive discourse, Safronova notes, is a fixation on numbers. Being representations of the world image in archaic cultures, numbers as symbolic entities help such neurotic characters to find order and stability from within and to protect themselves against the potentially destructive intrusion of the Other, especially against a destabilising feminine threat.

Drawing on multiple sources, philosophical, psycho-analytic and linguistic alike, Safronova examines the dependence of obsessive anankastic characters, and their authors, on numerology. In other words, she studies the dynamic process of the protective illusory world shaping, and ultimately replacing, reality, and traces manifestations of this phenomenon in Pelevin's work at various levels of the narrative. Safronova shows, on the one hand, how, through the example of an obsessive character, the postmodern author teaches his reader a pragmatic and conscious relationship to various forms of religion, which in turn constitute mechanisms that allow one to work with one's own consciousness and subconscious. On the other hand, her analysis demonstrates how an apparently rational underpinning of one's psyche, its numerical organising principle, is in fact highly irrational, as it is growing from the depths of the unconscious and is closely associated with the feeling of fear. Her original perspective facilitates a deeper understanding of Pelevin's novel and helps to throw into relief its symbolism and multiple allegories.

In particular, Safronova exposes the novel's agenda as revolving around a competition between the national sub-consciences, continental mentalities and physiological resources of Russia and the West. Based on existing theories, she offers interesting, albeit controversial, interpretations of the interplay between ethnicities, cultural identities and national mentalities.

Thus one of the hypotheses Safronova mentions belongs to Auezhan Kodar, who regards Russian philosophical thought, by and large, as part of the Oriental tradition, which does not transform reality, but adjusts to it, becoming an integral part of it. At the same time, the main drawback of the Russian character, since it is a Eurasian one, lies in its mixed hysterical-neurotic nature, with hysterics contributing to personal weakness. The same mixed nature characterises the Eurasian irrationalism which grows from a combination of mysticism and excessive (pragmatic) rationalism. Safronova claims that if in Pelevin's previous novel, *Generation 'Π'* people were driven by their own passion for money, then in *The Dialectics of the Transition Period (From Nowhere To No Place)*, man is manipulated by his own fears, with money-obsession being merely a psychological derivative of these fears.

The novel ends with a transition to a new level of fears as well as a new numerical combination as a defensive mechanism against them. Since material reality does not exhaust Pelevin's universe, the victory of the materialistic European mentality over Eurasian looks superficial and illusory. In this sense the writer portrays Oriental philosophy as more promising and multi-dimensional, while literary creativity itself overcomes universal chaos.

In his chapter Oliver Ready explores the 'metaphysical realism' of Iurii Mamleev, another contemporary Russian writer, but of the generation preceding Pelevin's. Ready stresses the central role of the irrational in Mamleev's fiction, where characters with distorted psyches, feeble-minded or altogether deprived of reason, have privileged access to ultimate existential truth that cannot be attained through rational means. The exaltation of folly is a trait also of Lev Shestov's philosophical anti-rationalism, and, as is clear from Ready's treatment of Mamleev, this Russian writer (1931–2015), who travelled the world and returned to Moscow in the post-Soviet era, represents a branch of the same anti-Enlightenment irrationalist tradition to which a number of Russian and Western thinkers alike can be ascribed. This tradition disavows any rationalist analysis or experience, and ultimately attacks reason *per se*. Such continuity, especially in its modern Russian phase, does not escape Ready's attention, as he stresses the unofficial reaction of the 1960s and early 70s to Soviet scientific atheism as a continuation of a major strand in Russian culture, and it is precisely Mamleev's short stories of that period which constitute the main focus of Ready's analysis. At the same time Ready traces some distinctly Western sources of Mamleev's ideas, most notably and directly the oeuvre of the French philosopher René Guénon, but also, indirectly, Michel Foucault and R.D. Laing, who all reacted strongly against the propensity of modern civilisation to simplification, and saw in folly a response to this cultural degradation.

Examining the biographical and intellectual context from which Mamleev's fiction first developed, Ready notes the writer's persistent urge to transcend the socio-political and ideological agenda, which should not, however, be disregarded, since the very irrationalism of Soviet existence facilitated the inversions and anti-images of Mamleev's writings, especially the central one: of madness replacing reason.

Giving an informative analysis of René Guénon's influence on Mamleev, Ready also comments on his specifically Russian literary roots, especially Dostoevskii and Platonov, but singles out an important difference which sets Mamleev apart from his native predecessors. This is in the recoiling from Christian compassion and humility, so characteristic of the Russian literary tradition. Instead, as Ready explains, Mamleev adheres to the "elitist principles and doctrine of his Guenonian mysticism, which affirms a hierarchy of spiritual knowledge and enlightenment" and posits against widespread ignorance of humans about themselves "a mystical plane of consciousness from which suffering and conflict appear as secondary, even negligible". Closely reading Mamleev's stories, Ready discovers further parallels: between Mamleev's apocalyptic visions of madness and death, and the imagery of the late-medieval West, most notably Hieronymus Bosch, and proceeds to place such imagery in the context of Foucault's explorations of the ancient link between water and madness. A contrast to that imagery is Mamleev's use of very modern language which draws on the professional terminology of the sciences of the mind, such as psychiatry, psychology and psychoanalysis. At the same time, Mamleev's agenda, as Ready observes, is strikingly similar to that of the American nonconformist psychiatrist R.D. Laing, who represents a tendency to challenge, in Foucault's words, "the monologue of reason about madness"[50] and to react by a psychological and mental disorder to the emptiness and inauthenticity of modernity where existence had been suffocated by stifling reason.

Thus, despite Mamleev's preoccupation in his later years with traditional Russian exceptionalism and his distinctly (although not exclusively) Russian, especially Dostoevskian, literary roots, Mamleev's irrationalism, as Ready concludes, forms part of a broader European tendency by which it is also informed. His anti-modernism, mysticism and anti-scientism, his embrace of death (in line again, we note, with Shestov's embrace of Plato's sentiments that "philosophy is a contemplation of dying and death"[51] and Euripides's belief that, maybe, "death is life and life is death"),[52] his omission of some distinctly Russian themes and ideas, and even his interest in Hinduism, all testify to this. What

---

50 Michel Foucault, *Madness and Civilization*, trans. Richard Howard, London and New York, 2001, xii. Cited in Ready's chapter.
51 Plato, *Phaedo*.
52 Euripides, *Phrixus*, Frag. 830.

remains so far unanswered, as Ready remarks, is the question of what Mamleev contributed to this tradition; as well as the means by which he succeeds along the lines of Dostoevskii "to drive the reader crazy", using the words of Malcolm Jones.[53]

Further breaks with Russian literary tradition are explored by David Gillespie in his chapter which, perhaps allegorically, concludes the volume. In his study of Russian irrationalism Gillespie focuses on one of the most controversial (if not the most controversial) figures on the contemporary Russian literary scene – Vladimir Sorokin, notorious for his graphic depictions of violence, sex, cannibalism, sado-masochism, coprophagy and other forms of deviance.

Gillespie examines the conceptualist Sorokin's writing which subverts traditional human values and where "Russian life and literature become not just parodies, but travesties of their former selves". He points to the irrationalist core of Sorokin's early fiction in the contradiction between, on the one hand, dismantling 'the ethical identity' of Russian literary tradition and denying the importance of literature altogether, and on the other, the author's perception of his own status as writer. Despite Sorokin's evident apolitical stance and proclaimed ethical detachment whereby he has defined his writings as simply "words on paper", in his later period, Gillespie argues, Sorokin became heavily engaged with Russian history and politics. Although working "within a clearly-defined Russian eschatological tradition which declares the end of all things, without delineating a beginning of anything new", Sorokin's "trajectory in post-Soviet Russia can be seen as a synecdoche of the passage of cultural history over twenty years or so" with his "evolution from 'paper' to 'politics'". Gillespie's central claim is that in his recent works Sorokin does not merely return to history, but rejects his initial irrational rejection of tradition by affirming "the role of literature and the writer in resisting tyranny and, rejecting his own past, accepts the 'rationality' of defiance".

An interesting fact that an author like this, who started by violently challenging "the reader's sensibilities – aesthetic, moral, linguistic and cultural – at the same time throwing down the gauntlet to the hallowed status of Russian literature itself", can be exalted to the status of a major writer in the contemporary literary landscape in Russia and beyond, or, at any rate, does not cease to evoke intense interest on the part of some Russian and much of Western scholarship, has perhaps something to tell us about the alignment of forces in modern culture. Of similar significance may be the fact that Mamleev with his apocalyptic Boschian universe and distinct lack of Christian humility and

---

53 Malcolm Jones, *Dostoyevsky after Bakhtin: Readings in Dostoyevsky's Fantastic Realism*, Cambridge, 1990, 113–146. Cited in Ready's chapter.

compassion is a magnet of post-Soviet culture, as Ready's contribution elaborates. Gillespie's chapter, which explores the dynamics of Sorokin's career and argues, from the rationalist versus irrationalist perspective, for the merits of his latest writings, might help to elucidate this peculiar, and in many ways irrational, phenomenon. Ultimately, of course, the reader's aesthetic and ethical choice is strictly personal.

With this sentiment in mind the book is now open to judgement (irrational or rational alike), and the discussion of Russian irrationalism – to continuation.

Bibliography

Akhmatova, Anna. 1983. "Stanzas", in *The Complete Poems of Anna Akhmatova. Expanded Edition*, transl. by Judith Nemschemeyer, ed. Roberta Reeder, Smerville and Edinburgh: Zephyr Press and Canongate Press, 669.

Akhutin, Anatolii. 2001. 'Antichnost v filosofii Lva Shestova", in Lev Shestov, *Lektsii po istorii grecheskoi filosofii*, Moscow-Paris: Russky Put'-YMCA-Press, 5–19.

Argunova, V.N. and S.N. Tiapkov. 2011. *Innovatsionnoe razvitie regiona: potentsial, instituty, mekhanizmy*, Ivanovo: IGU.

Belinskii, Vissarion. 1937–1952. Letter to Nikolai Gogol of 15/3 July 1847 in N.V. Gogol, *PSS v 14 tomakh*, Moscow-Leningrad: Izd-vo AN SSSR, vol. 8, 501–502; for the English version see http://www.marxists.org/subject/art/lit_crit/works/belinsky/gogol.htm.

Berdiaev, Nikolai. 1949. *Samopoznanie*, Chapter 3, http://www.vehi.net/berdyaev/samopoznanie/003.html.

Berlin, Isaiah. 1994. *The Magus of the North: J.G. Hamann and the Origins of Modern Irrationalism*, London: Fontana Press.

Brilliantov, A.I. 1998. *Vliianie vostochnogo bogosloviia na zapadnoe v proizvedeniiakh Ioanna Skota Erigeny*, Moscow.

Britannica Online Encyclopaedia. 2015. http://www.britannica.com/EBchecked/topic/294716/irrationalism.

Brodsky, Joseph. 1986. 'A Poet and Prose" in *Less than One: Selected Essays*, Harmondsworth: Penguin Books, 176–194.

Byatt, A.S. 2009. *The Children's Book*, London: Vintage.

Bykov, Dmitrii. 2003. "Dvesti let vmesto", http://berkovich-zametki.com/Nomer24/Bykov1.htm.

Chekhov, Anton. 1975. Letter to D.V. Grigorovich of 05.02.1888, in A.P. Chekhov, *PSSP v 30 tomakh*, vol. 2, Moscow: Nauka, 190.

Cornwell, Neil. 2006. *The Absurd in Literature*, Manchester and New York: University of Manchester Press.

Darling, David. 2004. *The Universal Book of Mathematics: From Abracadabra to Zeno's Paradoxes,* Hoboken, New Jersey: John Wiley and Sons.

Edwards, T.R.N. 1982. *Three Russian Writers and the Irrational: Zamyatin, Pil'nyak, and Bulgakov,* Cambridge: Cambridge University Press.

Frank, Semen. 1996. *Russkoe mirovozzrenie,* Saint Petersburg: Nauka.

Gachev, Georgii. 1995. *Natsionalnye obrazy mira,* http://lib.co.ua/history/gatchev/gatchev.txt_with-big-pictures.html.

Galkovskii, Dmitrii. 1994. *Beskonechnyi tupik,* http://www.samisdat.com/3/312-bt-p.htm.

Goncourt de, Edmond and Jules. 1956. *Journal: Mémoires de la vie littéraire, 1864–1878,* under 5 March 1876, Paris.

Grossman, Vasilii. 2006. *Life and Fate,* translated by Robert Chandler, London: Vintage Books.

Hamann, Johann Georg. 1955–1975. *Briefwechsel,* Arthur Henkel (ed.), vol. 5, Wiesbaden/Frankfurt: Insel Verlag.

Hardy, Henry. 1994. The Editorial, in Isaiah Berlin: *The Magus of the North. J.G. Hamann and the Origins of Modern Irrationalism,* London: Fontana Press.

Iskander, Fazil. 1999. "Dumaiushii o Rossii i amerikanets", in *Rasskazy, povest, skazka, dialog, esse, stikhi.* Series "Zerkalo XX vek", Ekaterinburg: U-Faktoriia, 544–585.

———. 2000. "Ponemnogu o mnogom. Sluchainye zapiski", *Novyi Mir,* 10 (2000) (see http://magazines.russ.ru/novyi_mi/2000/10/iskan.html).

Jones, Malcolm. 1990. *Dostoyevsky after Bakhtin: Readings in Dostoyevsky's Fantastic Realism,* Cambridge: University of Cambridge Press.

Kireevskii, Ivan. 1970. *Polnoe sobranie sochinenii v dvukh tomakh,* ed. by M. Gershenzon, Moscow, 1911, reprinted by Gregg International, Hampshire.

Likhachev, Dmitrii. 2006. *Izbrannoe. Mysli o zhizni, istorii, kulture,* Moscow: PIK.

Losev, Aleksei. 1991. "Russkaia filosofiia", in *Filosofiia, mifologiia, kul'tura,* Moscow, 209–236.

Lotman, Iurii. 1996. *O poetakh i poezii (Analiz poeticheskogo teksta, statii, issledovaniia, zametki),* St Petersburg: Iskusstvo-SPB.

Maxim Ispovednik prep. 1993. *Tvoreniia,* vol. 1, Moscow.

Pasternak, Boris. 1931. "Liubit' inykh tiazhelyi krest…", http://max.mmlc.northwestern.edu/~mdenner/Demo/texts/love_some_cross.html.

Prilepin, Zakhar. 2006. *San'kia,* Chapter 8, http://sankya.ru/chapters/8.html.

Pushkin, A.S. 1959. "Bezverie", in *Sobranie sochinenii v 10 tomakh,* vol. 1, Moscow: Gosudarstvennoe izdatelstvo khudozhestvennoi literatury, 423–425.

Richard Peace, Richard. 1976. *Russian Literature and the Fictionalisation of Life,* Hull: The University of Hull.

Shestov, Lev. 1920. *Apofeoz bespochvennosti (All things are possible),* translated by S.S. Koteliansky, http://shestov.phonoarchive.org/all/all_23.html.

―――. 1930. "Parmenides in chains: On the Sources of the Metaphysical Truths" in *Athens and Jerusalem*, http://shestov.phonoarchive.org/aaj/aj1_1.html.

Stahl, Henrieke (ed.). 2011. The proceedings of the international conference 'Andrei Belyi filosof – *Istoriia stanovleniia samosoznaiushchei dushi* i eio konteksty' (Trier, November 2010) in the special issue of *Russian Literature* LXX-I/II, 1 July–15 August 2011.

Tabachnikova, Olga. 2015. *Russian Irrationalism from Pushkin to Brodsky: Seven Essays in Literature and Thought*, London-New Delhi-New York-Sydney: Bloomsbury Academic.

Tiutchev, Fedor. 1868. 'Umom Rossiiu ne poniat...", in *Stikhotvoreniia F.I. Tiutcheva*, 1868, Moscow, 230.

Zenkovskii, Vasilii. 2004. *Istoriia russkoi filosofii*, vol. 1, Rostov-on-Don: Fenix, 2004. The popular phrases used, traditionally attributed to: Churchill, Winston. 2009. http://www.thejc.com/news/uk-news/25549/pianist-kissin-protests-against-bbc-anti-israel-bias.

PART 1

On the Place of Irrationalism in the Russian History of Ideas

CHAPTER 1

The Traditions of Rationalism in Russian Culture of the Pre-Soviet Period

Barbara Olaszek

In the context of the theme of irrationalism, it is impossible to avoid the notion of rationalism in the specific sense with which it has taken root in Russian culture. This sense is expressed in the identification, or synonymity, of rationalism with the West (that is, Western civilisation, founded on reason)[1] and the finding of its opposite in the spirituality of Russia. The meaning of rationalism is connected with the absence in the Russian tradition of Aristotelian thought (understood in its broadest sense), posited as the kernel of thought in the West, and the dominance of neo-Platonism in the Russian tradition.[2] In the works of one Polish scholar, these trends correspond to the rational and irrational methods of the perception and conceptualisation of reality. According to the American cultural theorist P. Tarnas, the Platonic and Aristotelian traditions complement each other. In the depths of this dual inheritance a tradition of critical thought was born. "And simultaneously with the birth of this tradition...", Tarnas states, "Western thought appeared".[3] The scholar attentively followed the philosophical reception of Platonic-Aristotelian thought in the medieval era, the Renaissance and the Enlightenment, and came to the conclusion that both traditions act together with different strengths, forming two cultures: one that emphasises rationality, empirical science and sceptical secularism, and another that expresses those aspects of human experience that were silenced or rejected by the enlightened spirit of militant rationalism.'[4] In Russia, they both either balanced or dominated each other, and so it is worth examining both traditions.

In Russian public consciousness of the New Era, the West was perceived as a source of reason and was mythologised.[5] The cause of this lies in the philosophical difference between two types of cognitive activity that have taken on

---

1   *Idei v Rossii. Leksykon rosyjsko-polsko-angielski*. 3. ed. A. de Lazari. Łódź: «Idem» 2000, 332.
2   I. Ia. Leviash, *Russkie voprosi o Rossii*. Moscow. 2005, 162.
3   S. Tarnas, *Istoriia zapadnogo myshleniia*, 1995, 62, cited from Leviash, *Russkie voprosi o Rossii. Diskurs s Marianom Brodoi*, 15.
4   *Ibid.,* 310.
5   Broda M. *„Zrozumieć Rosję"? O rosyjskiej zagadce tajemnicy*. «Ibidem». Łódź 2011, 322.

a specific meaning in Russia: *rassudok* and *razum*.[6] It is thought that *rassudok* can know that which is relative, earthly and finite. On the other hand, *razum* can know the absolute, divine, and infinite. *Rassudok* is attributed to Europe and is judged as 'dry', abstract, 'analytical'. *Razum* is attributed to Russia and is perceived as social, deep, intuitive and capable of being aligned to religious faith.[7] This 'holistic' or, to put it another way, 'integral' *razum* of Russia was opposed to the *rassudok* of the West and stood higher than it. Dostoevskii discerned the cause for the definition of reason in its subjugation to higher will: "not most importantly the mind, but rather that which directs it – nature, the heart, noble characteristics, development".[8]

The opposition of *rassudok* and *razum* as cognitive instruments in Russia accrued other ethical, social and historiosophical meanings. In summary, *rassudok* and the 'rationality' that was formed on its basis came to be perceived as both the cause and the demonstration of the Fall (that is, the loss by Western societies of the ideals of life), amorality and secularism. *Razum* is able to penetrate all non-empirical, higher reality, to discover and express the Divine, and was perceived as a means of being saved from the Fall.

Rationalism itself (derived from the Latin word *ratio* – reason, *razum*) is "a totality of philosophical movements, making the central point the analysis of *razum*, thought, *rassudok* – from the subjective perspective, and reasonableness, the logical order of things, from the objective [...] Rationalism, a method of thinking from the Enlightenment era, shares the optimism of this thinking, since it believes in the limitless power of human knowledge, which to some degree rules spiritually above all that exists".[9] It was understood in Russia as the hypertrophy of *rassudok* and was ascribed to the West. It was expressed in such traits as formalism, fragmentation, superficiality, rootlessness and lack of genuine contact with the Absolute.[10] The 'reasonable' rationalism of the West was mythologised by some Russian thinkers and treated as an object that needed to be overcome; many such thinkers saw their calling in this pursuit. Despite the aspiration of Russians to be free from rationalism, it nevertheless penetrated Russian thought.

The attitude to rationalism and the reception of its ideas by Russian thinkers became one of the platforms of ideological differentiation which it was

---

[6] In most contexts both best translate into English (which lacks true equivalents) as 'reason' [trans. ed. EH].
[7] M. Broda, *'Rassudok i razum'*, in *Idei v Rossii*, 330.
[8] F.M. Dostoevskii, *Polnoe sobranie sochinenii*, Leningrad: Nauka, 1988, III, 309.
[9] *Kratkaia filosofskaia entsyklopediia*, Moscow: «Progress», 1994, 386.
[10] M. Broda, *'Rassudok i razum'*, in *Idei v Rossii*, 332.

necessary to discover for the sake of the refinement of the character and image of Russian culture since, as T. Saburova writes, "alongside the tendency to mythologise the 'rational West' existed a different approach, which postulates its understanding as a reality which needs to be researched and understood".[11]

In the extract above, rationalism is understood not as a movement in philosophy that admits reason as the only source of knowledge, but more as an intellectual tradition, a style of thinking, an attitude to life, based on reason.[12] Our research is directed at the replication in Russian philosophical thought and literature (which, according to Sergii Bulgakov, was "the most philosophically refined literature" in Europe) of the traditions of rationalism and thus of the opposing tendency to discredit the role of rationalism in Russian culture. As the Polish scholar M. Broda notes, 'On the one hand, Russia's culture and intellectual traditions remain open, although not always teleologically and consciously, to Western influence, taking from there a series of concepts, ideas, values etc., and on the other hand, they cram them into their own intellectual and cultural schemas, rethink their meaning, frequently considering, moreover, that Western ideas are a point of negative correlation.'[13]

Within the theme of the dominance of irrationalism in Russian culture, the tradition of rationalism plays the role of a negative point of correlation. Observing the dynamics of the reception of rationalist ideas in Russia, one can formulate a theory about its intensification in transitional periods, that is, in historical situations where it becomes necessary to comprehend what is occurring through reason and to evaluate the causes of crises. The rationalist West became at such times a measure of how civilised Russia had become, and reason acquired the role of an organising principle, a basis of actions, without which it was impossible to manage. L.A Chernaia writes that, in the search for a point of support for the 'Century of Insurrection' (the seventeenth century), people began to seek support in human reason.[14] She notes that in the journalism of the seventeenth century people of the New Era attempted to understand the causal link of events. For example, 'Chronograph' (1617) contains two plans of events: the eternal and the present. The latter is directed by earthly

---

11 T. Saburova, *Prostranstvo 'svoe' i 'chuzhoe' v modeli mira russkoi intelligentsii*, *Kul'tura svoia i chuzhaia*, ed. by I.M. Bykhovskaia, O.I. Goriainova, Moscow: Fond niezavisimogo radioveshchaniia: 2003, 143.

12 *Bol'shoi tolkovyi slovar' russkogo iazyka*, S.A. Kuznetsov, Sankt-Peterburg: Norint, 2003, 1106.

13 Broda M. „*Zrozumieć Rosję*"? *O rosyjskiej zagadce tajemnicy*..Łódź: «Ibidem».2011, 19. My translation [B.O.].

14 L.A. Chernaia, *Antropologicheskiii kod drevnerusskoi literatury*, Moscow: Iazyki slavianskikh kul'tur, 2008, 178.

people and requires rational assessments. The 1630s to 1650s, according to Chernaia, reflect "the process of the change from the man of 'The Soul' to the man of 'Reason', and it is not soul but reason that begins to define a man. Man must aspire to be prudent, because prudence is equal to Divine Reason. [...] In the seventeenth century the definition 'prudential reason' appears".[15]

In the second half of the seventeenth century the educational activity of the Latinists – thinkers and teachers of the Slavonic-Greco-Latin Academy, founded in 1687 by the brothers I. and S. Likhudy – strengthened the position of *ratio* in Russia. In their teaching, the subjects of theology and philosophy were separated out into the divine and the real and, accordingly, there was a division of methods: theology was based on grace, and philosophy on explanation and understanding. The preferences of the Latinists' ideas aided the beginning of the Petersburg period of the Russian Enlightenment of the eighteenth century. The Petersburg Academy of Sciences (which later became the Russian Academy of Sciences) helped the spread of scholarly ideas, which glorified scientific and educational activity and achievements.

Moscow University, which was founded by the Empress Elizaveta Petrovna in 1755 on the initiative of I.I. Shuvalov and M.V. Lomonosov, facilitated the strengthening of a rational style of thought, as did the creative and scholarly activities of Lomonosov himself.

A period of intense assimilation of the ideas of French educational philosophy began in the eighteenth century, the epoch of the Enlightenment. St Petersburg became the centre of the Enlightenment, which was linked with the activity of the Empress Catherine herself, and her correspondence with the Encyclopaedists. Catherine II, wishing to pass for an 'enlightened monarch', took their advice on the creation of a Legislative Commission (1767) and the 'Nakaz' (Instruction). It is well known that she suggested the transfer of the printing of the forbidden 'Encyclopaedia' from Paris to Petersburg.

The influence of Enlightenment ideas appeared in the academic works of the outstanding representatives of the era: Ia. P Kozel'skii's 'Philosophical Proposals' (1768) and D.S. Anichkov's lecture course on Philosophy 'A Word about the Properties of Cognition' (1770), which underlined the ideas of Voltaire, Helvétius, Montesquieu, and Rousseau. They also appear in the works of a representative of sentimentalism, A.N. Radishchev, who during his five-year studies in Leipzig (1766–1771) became acquainted with the works of figures of the French Enlightenment, and, as he said himself, learnt to think by them. The results were displayed in his philosophical work 'On Man, on his Mortality and Immortality' (1792–1796), in which the author,

---

15   *Ibid.,* 180.

drawing conclusions about the immortality of the soul, presented the reader with a choice of systems of views from which they should choose the most plausible. In this way Radishchev followed the enlightened conception of man as a free being endowed with reason.

Enthusiasm for the ideas of rationalism changed to disenchantment with them in the first decades of the nineteenth century. It was displayed in 'Alexandrine mysticism', when arguments against the extreme certainty of reason appeared, an example of which was the fall of the vain Napoleon, and the Romantic Era. Moscow, where a centre for the study of German Idealist philosophy was located called the Society of Wisdom-Lovers, became the cradle of irrational ideas. In the early philosophical articles of the main founder of the Society, V.F. Odoevskii, the judgement of "the philosophy of Voltaire and Helvétius" and support for Schelling's philosophy of identity was accompanied by doubt in the stormy flourishing of mathematics, which 'counts digits, and the internal number of objects remains for it unobtainable'.[16] In *Russian Nights* (1844), in the excerpt 'Desiderata', the author disputed the role of mathematical truths in cognition, but, polemicising with the classification of sciences by A. Comte, the author of the *Russian Nights* fully posed the rational question 'what exactly is science'? and concentrated on the role of empirical knowledge. In the opinion of P.N. Sakulin, the evolution of Odoevskii's views went in the direction of confirming the scientific worldview,[17] which testifies to the presence of the ideas of rationalism in the worldview of the Moscow Idealist.

In the 'Philosophical Letters' of P.I. Chaadaev, which reflected the worldview of the thinker that had been intellectually formed in Moscow University and from the ideas of French and German Catholicism, and also the mystical essays of Schelling, we find thoughts about the reflection of objective reason in the subjective, about freedom and the subordinate nature of human reason, and its inability to know the spiritual order of existence. In the spirit of Kant's *Critique of Pure Reason*, the Russian thinker preferred objective reason. However, the Polish scholar A. Walicki thinks that "Chaadaev did not reject rationalism, he saw in reason not a destructive, but rather, an integrating force, and he prized highly 'Western syllogism' and 'logical analysis', too".[18]

---

16   V.F. Odoevskii, *Russkie nochi*, ed. by B. Egorov, E. Maimin, M. Medovoi, Leningrad: Nauka 1975, 20.
17   P.N. Sakulin, *Iz istori russkogo idealizma, Kniaz' V.F. Odoevskii, Myslitel'i pisatel'* Book 1, Chapters 1–2, Moscow: 1913, 313.
18   Walicki A. *W kręgu konserwatywnej utopii. Struktura i przemiany rosyjskiego słowianofilstwa*. Warszawa: PWN 1964, 78.

Representatives of the idealist movement among the Slavophiles continued the ideas of the Russian mystics. I.V. Kireevskii in his work 'O kharaktere prosveshcheniia Evropy i ee otnoshenii k prosveshcheniiu Rossii' ('On the Character of the European Enlightenment and its Attitude to the Enlightenment of Russia', 1832) argued that rationalism was an incurable ailment affecting European thought. In his assessment, rationalism caused the inner disintegration of the personality, which only faith could overcome. It is noteworthy that the thinker did not deny reason as a means to know the world, but denied it as a means of suppressing faith, an ideal he perceived in the union of knowledge and faith. I.V. Kireevskii and A.S. Khomiakov shared the Hegelian critique of educational reason [*rassudok*] but Hegelian dialectic reason [*razum*] they thought no less rationalistic than enlightened Reason [*rassudok*] and they discerned its failure in the predominance of pure logical thinking.

The thought of the Westernisers was inspired by Hegelian dialectical reason. The Westernisers were adherents of the assimilation of European science and the fruits of enlightenment. They pointed their contemporaries along the path of enlightened science and reason. For example, N.V. Stankievich perceived the eternal laws of life in reason and will.

The category of reason was predominant in the legacy of the representative of the Westerniser movement V.G. Belinskii. At the stage of reconciliation with reality he subscribed to the Hegelian formula: 'what is reasonable, is real, what is real, is reasonable', refuting enlightened reason (*rassudok*) in the name of rationalist dialectics. The critic aspired to create the ideal of the 'reasonable reality' by denying existing reality. After the refutation of the ideas of conservative Hegelianism, Belinskii returned to the ideals of Voltaire and the Encyclopaedists.

Also, as Shchukin writes, "in Herzen's intellectual development the naturalist-enlightened principle is present, inherited from the French Encyclopaedists and which had taken deep root thanks to the Voltairean atmosphere of the house...".[19]

The presence of elements of rationalism in the worldview of Romantic thinkers can be explained by the enlightened type of upbringing[20] they had undergone; a Western education requiring language learning, to which they had become accustomed in youth. The enthusiasm of the Russian Romantics in the 1830s for Goethe's 'Wonderful dream' (*dahin*) changed in the 1840s to disappointment with the possibility of its realisation. This disenchantment

---

19 V. Shchukin, *Russkoe zapadnichestvo. Genezis, sushchnost'*, *istoricheskaia rol'*. Łódź: «Ibidem» 2001, 108.
20 *Ibid.*, 92.

manifested itself in an aspiration to a realist attitude to the world, to the rationalisation of consciousness. New philosophical movements accompanied this process, such as utopian socialism, materialist natural science and positivism.

Without going into detail about the philosophical works of individual thinkers, we note the special interest in them among the *Petrashevtsy*, revealed in their attitude to the exact sciences, their aspiration to liberation from any type of illusion and prejudice by means of the rationalisation of thought and the permanent correlation of knowledge about man with findings from the natural sciences. Thus the *Petrashevtsy* were predecessors of the enlighteners of the 1860s: N.G. Chernyshevskii and D.I. Pisarev. The latter influenced a cultural paradigm shift, from a basis in art to a basis in science. A catalyst for this change was the fierce development of natural sciences. Russian natural scientists, such as I.M. Sechenov, K.A. Timiriazev, I.I. Mechnikov, D.I. Mendeleev, identified philosophy with metaphysics, and their worldview, formed on the basis of the data of the empirical sciences, was defined by the term 'realism'.

Enlightened thinkers such as N.G. Chernyshevskii and N.A. Dobroliubov in their views emerged from the rationalist, enlightened tradition. Chernyshevskii considered himself a disciple of the French Encyclopaedists, whose works he knew, and of Feuerbach. Chernyshevskii's ethical theory of 'rational egoism' contains in its name a reference to reason as a criterion for judging the usefulness of acts. It is characteristic that Chernyshevskii linked progress not with moral perfection, but rather with the development of science and knowledge: "only the fertile aspirations of man through knowledge have a character which serves the combined general and private good".[21] From the perspective of modernity, a scholar researching the legacy of Chernyshevskii, G. Przebinda, called him "the socialist grandson of the Enlightenment", convincingly stating that in Chernyshevskii's legacy the Enlightenment took central place, whereas the West was only considered a model for Russia when it had been infused with rational enlightened ideals.[22]

In the legacy of Chernyshevskii's followers N.A. Dobroliubov and D.I. Pisarev, the rationalist point of view on the world also dominated. The former was a representative of rationalist enlightenment, while the latter was an exponent of enlightened Scientism.[23] Dobroliubov was notable for his sober view of the world and thought that the reasonable man could build social projects only for

---

21 N.G. Chernyshevskii, *Izbrannye esteticheskie proizvedeniia*, Moscow: Iskusstvo 1978, 336.
22 See Przebinda G., *Od Czaadajewa do Bierdiajewa. Spór o Boga i człowieka w myśli rosyjskiej (1832–1922)*. Kraków: PAU 1998, 270, 256.
23 For more on this, see Olaszek, *Dymitr Pisariew. Wokół problemów pozytywizmu w Rosii...* Łódź: Wyd.Uniwersytetu Lodzkiego 1997.

the immediate future and only on the basis of concrete data. The philosophical views of Pisarev were formed on the back of a refutation of idealism, understood as "a daydream of a non-existent infinity", metaphysics, (*The Scholastics of the Nineteenth Century*, 1861) and arguments for the role of science. He placed materialism higher than idealism, relying on evidence and sensory perception. The author of the article 'The Process of Life' highly valued scientific methodology based on facts and the inductive method ('words and illusions die, facts remain') and also experience ('the absolute truth will cease to exist, because the test becomes impossible') and on statistics. Aspiring to the synthesis of scientific methods, he postulated the application of the methods of natural sciences in the humanities. An indisposition to discussion about essences and a preference for empirical conclusions provide further evidence for the a-philosophical and scientistic character of his thought.

At the basis of Pisarev's ideas on progress and the shifting forces of the historical process lay an enlightened theory about the meaning of changes in consciousness, combined with a conviction in the leading role of science in the movement of social processes. In his attempts to create a pattern of 'the thinking realist' and 'developed woman' the publicist postulated a rationalisation of awareness through refuting metaphysics and relying on knowledge. He warned people about getting lost in daydreams and called for a sober attitude to reality. Involved in the arguments of the Slavophiles (I. Kireevskii) on the theme of the Russian national character, Pisarev stated: "Common sense consists also of a significant share of humour and scepticism [...] the most noticeable character of the purely Russian mind".[24] As this stance demonstrates, Pisarev was close to the representative of rationalism, B.G. Belinskii, on the character of the Russian people, which Belinskii expressed in his letter to N.V. Gogol' (1847). Belinskii considered common sense a trait of the Russian national character: "the Russian people is not like this: mystical exaltation is not at all in its nature; it has too much common sense, cogency and positivity of mind, and in this, perhaps, lies the magnitude of its historical fate in the future".[25]

Pisarev linked progress with ideas of self-improvement of the person, which he understood as the "provision of freedom by the natural direction of man". At the centre of his conception was the idea of perfectibility, based on an irreligious preference for optimism, the source of which was the enlightened tradition of

---

[24] D.I. Pisarev, *Sobranie sochinenii v chetyrekh tomakh*, Moscow: «Khudozhestvennaia literatura» 1955. V., 118.

[25] B.G. Belinskii, *Polnoe sobranie sochinenii v 13 tomakh*, V. X, Moskva: Izdatel'stvo Akademii nauk SSSR 1956, 215.

philosophers of the eighteenth century: Cabanis, Voltaire and the modern positivists H. T Buckle and J.S. Mill.

In the judgement of types of literary character, especially the 'superfluous men', Pisarev emerged from the common sense position, which accused the 'superfluous men' of distance from life's practicalities. The critic compared the Romantic attitude to life with the sober attitude, formed by a reliance on reason and knowledge. The requirement to manage life by reason relates also to women. The critic noted the influence, fatal for women, of the hypertrophic fantasy: "Do not daydream, do not in any circumstances daydream".[26] He called upon contemporary young women to take part in practical actions. The reference of the publicist to reason as a regulator of the behaviour of the person points to a link with the conceptions of the Western European positivists, whose systems of thought departed genetically from the enlightened position.[27]

A positive attitude to the West accompanied the enlightened direction of the views of the men of the 1860s, who attributed their achievements to a rationalistic arrangement of political and social life. The rhetoric of the men of the 1860s displays this dominance of the enlightened tradition in their intellectual discourse. In articles and artistic works, the first place is occupied by the theme of science and scientific rigour, determinism, "rational egoism" and "vital life", which were opposed to "metaphysical waffle", "idealism" "scholastics" and "seminary scholastics". One can observe a similar differentiation of definitions in the leading desired type of personality: the realist, empiricist, utilitarian, "people of business and vital thinking", "clever people" "today's vanguard" and "progressives". Accordingly, the negative types are called Romantics, aesthetes, Byronists, "Onegin types" and "shades of Pechorin types".

It is possible to say that the generation of the 1860s was rationally inclined to have full confidence in science. Their intellectual formulae occurred in an atmosphere of a cult of science and growing secularisation. D.N. Ovsianiko-Kulikovskii, the author of *The History of the Russian Intelligentsia* admitted: "I've lost faith in God, but my faith in science has remained indestructible. [...] My naive [...] faith in science now takes a rational position and has turned into a type of a *conviction* or *philosophical dogma* that is unshakeable."[28] According to the men of the 1860s, idealist philosophy had outlived its time and its place had been taken by 'scientific philosophy' and 'practical philosophy'. Scientific philosophy was characterised by a "belief in the singularity of

---

26 D.I. Pisarev, ss. I: 267.
27 See, Olaszek B., *Dymitr Pisariew. Wokół...*, 170.
28 D.N. Ovsianiko-Kulikovskii, Literaturno-kriticheskie raboty v dvukh tomakh, v. II. Moscow: 322.

scientific methods in knowing existence, the worship of scientific means of thought, and naive rationalism...".[29]

The philosophical works of the main representative of 'scientific philosophy', V.V. Lesevich, declared a refutation of apriorism and reliance on fact, and philosophy itself was understood not in a literal sense, but rather as a scientific worldview, the basis of the behavioural spheres. "In the final analysis, then, science tries to come to a doctrine that embraces everything that can regulate life and the development of humanity".[30]

The unconditional faith of the men of the 1860s in the power of science as a cure for all the ailments of the age was shaken in the 1870s. The aforementioned Lesevich in the works 'An Experiment in the Critical Investigation of the Foundations of Critical Philosophy' (1877) and 'Letter on Philosophy of Science' (1878) critically assessed the epistemological possibilities of science.

Another philosopher, V.S. Solov'ev, in his defence of his doctoral thesis 'The Crisis of Western Philosophy (Against the Positivists)' (1874), criticised the opposition of 'abstract principles', i.e. empiricism and idealist rationalism, as outdated, and proposed the idea of all-unity, that is, the joining of scientific, philosophical and theological cognition. In his *Critique of Abstract Principles* (1880) he turned his attention to religion, which, in his words 'by placing Divinity in the first place, without any kind of living relationship to man, nature or society, is also a rationalist principle'.[31] In this comment the thinker preferred the approach to religious ideas based on pure reasoning, on *Verstand* to the rationalist approach, based on *Vernunft*. In 'Lectures on Godmanhood' (1881) Solov'ev openly postulated the synthesis of science and religion. One can say that his conception contains what is called "integral reason" which is what makes the Russian person different from the Western European.

Ivan Goncharov, in his letter, responding to 'Lectures on Godmanhood' assessed the meaning of all-unity as an attempt to join together the rationalist and metaphysical traditions:

...развившееся человеческое общество откинуло все так называемое метафизическое, мистическое, сверхъестественное. [...]

---

29   V.V. Zen'kovskii, *Istoriia russkoi filosofii. v. II. Part II.* 'Ego' Leningrad: Ego 1991, 6.

30   V.V. Lesevich, *'Filosofiia istorii na nauchnoi pochve (Ocherk iz istorii kul'tury XIX veka)'*. In *'Otechestvennye zapiski,* 1869, No. 1 № 1, 168.

31   Losev A.F., *'Tvorcheskii put' Vladimira Solov'eva* in Solov'ev V.S. *Sochineniia v dvukh tomakh,* Moscow: Mysl' 1990, I: 9.

И вот опора науки легла в незыблемое основание религии и повела бы человечество надежным путем к обетованному Откровением бытию.³²

(Developed human society had abandoned everything that is so-called metaphysical, mystical or supernatural. [...] And here the support of science lies at the unshakable foundation of religion and would take humanity by a reliable oath to the promised Revelation of existence).

The scientific rationalist approach of Vladimir Solov'ev was expressed also in the language of his philosophical discourse. In an article by the contemporary historian of philosophy we read:

By mysticism he [V.S. Solov'ev – B.O] understands, in reality, only holistic knowledge, always attempting to identify mystical knowledge with natural sciences, or sciences with most average nature. That which he calls 'free theosophy' does not have anything in common with theosophical teachings, which in Europe had spread widely over the nineteenth century, and which have not died out even now. He needed the term 'theosophy' in order to differentiate it from traditional theology, which seemed to him to be too rational and restrictive. His 'free' theosophy is a teaching about all-unity, formulated by us earlier, which included religious teaching. By the term 'theurgy' Solov'ev does not mean the trend for some type of magic or miracles which was developing and so popular at that time. Theurgy for him was free, universal creation, in which humanity embodies its higher ideals in material reality, in nature. Solov'ev calls his theurgy 'art', admitting that his art goes far outside the framework of traditional art with its extremely defined aims and possibilities.'³³

Towards the end of the century in thinkers' philosophical ideas, a crisis of science appeared that was linked with a conviction regarding the limitations of the possibilities of science in the insight of the spiritual world of the human and the impossibility of resolving social problems. The renaissance of Russian philosophy accompanied this crisis. This renaissance manifested itself in the dominance of irrational ideas, but the language of the epoch also contained the characteristics of rational study.

At the turn of the nineteenth and twentieth centuries, a change of generations occurred: the "fathers" of the sixties were replaced by the "children", who, having received an education in natural and physics-mathematical faculties,

---

32   Cited from V.I. Mel'nik *Eticheskii ideal I.A. Goncharova*, Kiev: Lybed' 1991, 79–80.
33   A.F. Losev, *'Tvorcheskii put' Vladimira Solov'eva*, 9–10.

became Symbolist artists. The "children" who had been brought up on words against science and the education of the "fathers" became adherents of science. Dmitrii Merezhkovskii in his article 'The Mystical Movement of our Age' (1893) agreed that the culture of the nineteenth century developed under the banner of science, the struggle of material civilisation and spiritual culture, but as well as that, he noted the negative consequences of the expansion of science in culture. In his opinion the stormy development of empirical knowledge gave birth to an instinctive mistrust of the creative abilities of the spirit. He recognised in the culture of the nineteenth century the coexistence of a scientific worldview with artistic mysticism.

Valerii Briusov turned out to be a writer with traits of 'academia', with a tendency towards scientific method. In his article 'The Keys of the Secret' (1904) he examined the limitation of science in questions of cognition. In his opinion the damage of positive sciences was that they refrained from penetrating the essence of matters, knowing only the relation between phenomena, knowing only how to compare and contrast them, and, in addition, remaining powerless in the study of aesthetic phenomena.

'The children of the fin-de-siècle', who constituted a group of 'members of the underground', denied the culture of the previous generation, but did not have a concrete idea about their own culture. Andrei Belyi wrote:

> ...мы были в те годы – заряд динамизма; отцы наши, будучи аналитиками, превратили анализ в догму; мы, отдаваясь текучему процессу, были скорей диалектиками, ища единства противоположностей, как целого, не адекватного только сумме частей.[34]

> (In those years we were charged with dynamism. Our fathers, as analytic types, transformed analysis into dogma; we allowed ourselves to be subjected to the developments of the time and were closer to the dialectical type. We sought the unity of oppositions as a whole, rather than a unity that was appropriate only for the sum of its parts.)

Apart from science, the Achilles heel of the relations between the older and younger generations of the turn of the century was religion. Being brought up in the families of believing 'fathers', many of the 'children' went through a stage of atheism. In questions of religion the 'children' were brought up not in the spirit of mysticism and irrationalism but rather of rational agnosticism. The 'fathers' understood that it was not possible to rely on a naive faith in

---

34 A. Belyi, *Na rubezhe dvukh stoletii*, Moscow: "Khudozhestvennaia literatura" 1989, I: 200.

explaining certain phenomena of life without contradicting science. They therefore deferentially answered the complex questions of the 'children'. They were not blind adherents of Orthodoxy, but people who believed reasonably, that is, a special type of agnostics who understood that sometimes it is better not to probe into the heart of a matter, rather than to give answers that contradict the facts of science. The 'children' understood that the existence of man as a part of nature consisted of two spheres, everyday life (*byt*) and existence (*bytie*), which are felt by a person, but that cannot be fully joined together. Only with the appearance of Solov'ev, wrote Blok, "the empty flowers of positivism wilted and fell, and the old tree of perpetually restless thought came into flower and blossomed with metaphysics and mysticism".[35] Thus, attempts to unite the religious and the academic were characteristic of the 'fathers' since the scientific principle was dominant in them, and in the 'children' the religious, irrational element dominated.

The next question to which we must turn our attention is the attitude of the "fathers" and "children' to art. Appealing to art as an alternative to science was a result of the disenchantment of the children in the cognitive possibilities of science and the conviction that only by means of art can we reach the heart of things. This brought them to the identification of art with religion. Briusov thought that the only purpose of art was "knowledge of the world, outside rational forms, outside thinking based on causality".[36] However, these methods of cognition themselves were at times scientific. For example, A. Belyi professed the dialectic character of thought and preferred the inductive method in Symbolist cognition:

> And when over a few years I think about the symbol, then it is clear to me, that the symbol is a triad, where the symbolic form is a concrete synthesis, where the thesis is a subject of nature, and the antithesis, is the narrative meaning: I do not need to 'compose' Symbolism, when I have many years' experience of playing with symbols, and a whole series of exercise in symbolisation. This symbolisation is induction from the facts of life.[37]

The statements of the famous poets of the Silver Age confirm the ambitiousness of searching for the manifestations of cohesion between rational and irrational thought not only in academic tracts, but also in the artistic image of

---

35   A.A. Blok, *Sobranie sochinenii v vos'mi tomakh,* Moscow, Leningrad: «Khudozhestviennaia literatura» 1963, VII: 23.
36   V. Ia. Briusov, 'Kliuchi tain', *Kritika russkogo simbolizma,* Moscow: I, Olimp, AST 2002, 130.
37   Belyi, 'Na rubezhe dvukh...', 227.

the world and of man, which was created by leading writers. In the first place, we will examine the image of the world. In classicist aesthetics, the rational underpinning of the picture of the world was programmatic, but by the Romantic era this became undesirable. The Romantic and the realistic attitude to life, based on rational principles, is characteristic of the turning point of eras.

In the Decembrist movement of the Romantic era, the heroes' perception of the world was formed on the basis of the political and civil values of the present, which were derived from the Enlightenment, but their behaviour shows that the convictions abandon the basis of reason and are transformed into civic exaltation (the poem 'Volynskii', the ode 'Will I be at the fatal time...'). At the same time, A. Griboedov in the title to his comedy warned his contemporaries: "Woe from wit"! Although in the play the faults of Moscow society are rationally analysed (the world of fools), the main hero, in spite of being armed with European Enlightenment ideals, is defined by criticism of his Moscow circles, does not seek out allies, acts alone and, ruled by emotions, abandons Moscow. For the Romantics the mind is not a reliable governing force for life. Their attitude to the mind changes under the influence of a feeling of the usefulness of scientific discoveries to everyday life.

In late Romantic poetry a picture was drawn of a world equipped with modern technology such as the telegraph, microscope, steam engines and gaslights.[38] The primary task was not the discovery of the mysteries of nature, as it had been for the real Romantics, but her subjugation, which was aided by the wonder of new technological inventions. As on the eve of the Enlightenment, the need arose for a man of Reason. Reason and Science gradually became the principles which united a generation of late Romantics. A trait of their worldview was not detachment from life, but rather a desire to perfect life. However, individual poets, such as P.A. Viazemskii, N.A. Nekrasov, F.I. Tiutchev, raised the question of negative consequences for a civilisation that is based on the principles of reason, which is accompanied by doubt in the cognitive abilities of reason. F.I. Tiutchev's poem "Umom Rossiiu ne poniat" testifies to this.

Russian writers were convinced of the necessity of the process of perfection and the advantage of the rational approach to life thanks to the experience of travelling in Western Europe. They shared this experience by publishing 'letters from overseas' and descriptions of their travels. One such example is I. A Goncharov, who became convinced of the advantages of the rational type of thought when he went on his trip around the world, and communicated this

---

[38] See, N.A. Nekrasov, *'Nash vek'* (1840) and P.A. Viazemskii, *'Nash vek nas osveshchaet gazom...'*, (1841).

experience to his readers in the descriptions of his travels in *Fregat 'Pallada'* (*The Frigate 'Pallas'*).[39]

Russian Europeans contrasted the 'dream', i.e. the Romantic, irrational worldview, with a sober, realistic attitude to life. I.S. Turgenev in his early work, *Perepiska* (1845) (*Correspondence*, 1845) noted the moment of the transfer "from a life of daydream to a real life". Goncharov had done this in his *Obyknovennaia istoriia* (*An Ordinary Story*) and *Oblomov*, comparing the idyllic-romantic chronotope of the provinces to life in the capital, organised on rational principles.

The opposition of irrational and rational attitudes to life became a structurally informing principle of building a model of the world in the novels of Goncharov *Oblomov* and *Obryv* (*The Precipice*). The plot and the endings of both novels convince the reader of the advantage of the rational organisation of the world. This organisation was natural for the epoch of awakening with its ambition for the 'repair of Russia' in the period of the Great Reforms and intensive industrialisation, and the rearrangement of the economy in accordance with a new plan.

The ideas of rationalism were also laid by other writers as the foundation of the artistic model of the world. Turgenev depicted attempts to reorganise the bases of life in both towns and country estates rationally. His landowner characters strive to improve the everyday lives of the peasants, penetrating into the secrets of the household. In the novel *Nov'* (*Virgin Soil*) the image of a well-organised factory appears, the brain-child of a Russian engineer, Solomin, who has learned from practices in England, and manages to transform Russian chaos into harmony. The mentality of the worker also becomes an object of transformation through education.

Dostoevskii was concerned with the question of the ideal organisation of the world. In his depiction of the world he emerged from Russian reality. In *Prestuplenie i nakazanie* (*Crime and Punishment*) the idea of the rational organisation of the world suffers disaster (the fourth dream of Raskol'nikov in the prison camp). The concept of the destruction of a world based on the principles of reason and science conserves its relevance in subsequent novels by the writer. The unceasing argument about the organisational basis for the world, whether it is rational or irrational, its turbulent course, testifies to the fact that Dostoevskii valued ideological and social meaning and moreover, the danger of ideas based on rationalism. We have duly noted that the image of the world's destruction, based on scientific principles is not identified with the denial by

---

[39] For more on this, see, B. Olaszek, *Russkii pozitivizm, Idei v zerkale literatury*, Lodz: Wyd. Uniwersytetu Lodzkiego 2005, 132–136.

the writer of the role of reason and science as a whole. Rather, they show that science and reason cannot be considered as the only basis of the world.[40]

It is possible to say that L.N. Tolstoi drew a similar conclusion. In the novel *Anna Karenina*, a special barometer of the mood of the 1870s, he attempts a rational rebuilding of landowner's lives in the conditions of the post Reform era. Konstantin Levin, attempting to perfect his estate management skills, turns to agronomical science and uses technological innovations, but is convinced that this is only a halfway house. Levin arrives at the conclusion that the condition of success in Russian estate management is not the owning of technology, but the invention of new models of relations between different classes on the basis of conscience. The solution of problems does not occur as the result of scientific arguments, but under the influence of the truth, discovered by the simple peasant. One can say that the rational principle permeates the everyday sphere of the novel, and the irrational, the spiritual, the way to the truth itself is torn away from rational soil, appearing as a result of the irrational epiphany of personality.

The crisis of the artistic picture of the world based on rational principles can also be discovered at the end of the century. In the picture of life that A.P. Chekhov drew in his works, the present is not attractive because it is not rationally organised. Strictly rational principles, linked with plans of transformation, are not approved, and meet mental obstacles. However, in spite of them, the building of railways, ('Ogni', 'Flames'), bridges ('Novaia dacha','The New Dacha'), brick factories (*Tri sestry*, *Three Sisters*) reveal the facts of the rational activity of man, with which hope for the future is linked.

On the basis of the novel *Zhar-Tsvet* (*Fire-Flower*) (1895) by A.V. Amfiteatrov, a writer who, like the poets-symbolists, called himself a disciple of 'the fathers' – "a descendent of Bazarov, a disciple of N.K. Mikhailovskii and a contemporary of Chekhov", one can draw different conclusions. The characters who have a rational inclination of mind, one a traveller (a typical rationalist, enthused by the ideas of the subordination of nature, and who has seen the path to truth in observations and experience), the other a financier, a pragmatic man, under the influence of the spirit of his times, who abandons his convictions and his post. They are both placed by the author in a situation in which their faith in the power of reason is shaken and the worship of irrationalism wins.

The meaning of reason and science in the rebuilding of Russian life is especially noticeable in the genre of science-fantasy utopia and novels, which arose on the wave of interest in science (V.F. Odoevskii, *4338-i god* (1840) (*The Year 4338*) and *Russkie nochi* (1844) (*Russian Nights*); N.G. Chernyshevskii's *Chto delat'?* (1864) (*What is to be done?*)). These works contain images of the future of

---

40 Ibid., 116.

Russia, using in practice the achievements of technological progress, rationalising the organisation of life. In V.F. Odoevskii's depiction, these achievements are not enough for the creation of Icarus; moral bases are also necessary.

In the novel *Chto delat'?*, a project is drawn for the ideal organisation of the world in the image of the Crystal Palace (the Fourth Dream of Vera Pavlovna). The Palace is built using scientific technology, the brain-children of thinking people. The organisation of the everyday life of the inhabitants of the palace was based on rational and scientific foundations. Their life is accompanied by social experiments. It is thought that in spite of the utopian character, the way of life in the Crystal Palace reflects the link of the hopes of the author for the future with its rational principle.

In a utopia from the end of the nineteenth century by K. Sluchevskii, *Kapitan Nemo v Rossii* (1898) (*Captain Nemo in Russia*), signals emerge of doubts about the possibilities of science and the scientific organisation of life. They are reflected in the utopias of the beginning of the twentieth century. In his story 'Respublika Iuzhnogo Kresta' (1905) ('The Republic of the Southern Cross'), V. Ia. Briusov depicted the Star City, in which everything is calculated and consistent, but, in spite of the forethought of the system, it falls apart as a result of an illness called by its scientific term *mania contradicens*: mania of contradictions. As a result of contradictory desires, the rationally organised order of life is destroyed.

It is obvious that a necessary condition for the success of rationalised life is the part played by personality. The leading classics created a model for the positive character, emerging from the framework marked out by Turgenev in his article, 'Hamlet and Don Quixote' (1860). These were 'prosaic characters' aspiring to transform the environment around them. The image of the rationalistic type of behaviour created by Turgenev can be found typically in such characters as Lezhnev (*Rudin*), Nikolai Kirsanov (*Ottsy i deti*), Litvinov (*Dym*), who found their field in the work of a landowner, or Solomin, who preferred "little matters" to revolutionary movement. Such characters were ruled in everyday practice by prudence, soberly assessing their possibilities to transform the world and their energy to manage the present tasks.

Goncharov's hero, the Romantic dreamer Aleksandr Aduev, gradually, and not without the pain of loss of ideas, comes to a sober and illusion-free attitude to life, which he is taught by his pragmatist uncle, and concentrates only on solving real tasks. In the next pair of characters, Oblomov and Shtol'ts, formed by a Rousseauian education,[41] but with detours from the system, only Shtol'ts is rationalist. However, the writer named not him, but Ivan Tushin, the hero of

---

41 See E. Krasnoshchekova, *I.A. Goncharov, Mir tvorchestva*, St Petersburg: Pushkinskii fond, 1997, 270.

the novel *Obryv*, as the representative of "our party of action", which was fulfilling a programme for the modernisation of Russia.

The transformation of Romantic ideals into sober life management is typical of the heroes of A.F. Pisemskii (*Tysiacha dush*; *A Thousand Souls*, 1857) and N.G. Pomialovskii (*Meshchanskoe schast'e*; *Bourgeois happiness*, 1861). It takes place on a rational foundation. The heroes – those who have left the class of *raznochintsy*[42] – value education as a path to social mobility and cultural improvement, but, having become convinced that their expectations are unachievable, soberly assess the situation and approach different methods, revealing in this an enterprising spirit. Their ambitions are close to the pragmatism of the liberals. They emphasise the significance of the personal principle, free from moral judgements. The image of the *raznochintsy* becoming *petit bourgeoisie* can be found in the works of representatives of popular literature such as I.A. Kushchevskii's *Nikolai Negor'ev, ili blagopoluchnyi rossiianin*; *Nikolai Negor'ev or the Prosperous Russian*, 1870) and K.M. Staniukovich's *Pokhozhdeniia odnogo blagonamerennogo molodogo cheloveka*; *The Adventures of a Well-meaning Young Man*, 1871).

The behavioural system of heroes in prose works by the *raznochintsy* in the 1860s was based on rational principles. In eighteenth-century Russia the rationalist underpinning of behavioural ethics clashed with idealistically orientated moral philosophy.[43] The 'Vanguard' heroes – 'the new people'– programatically refuted *a priori* truths and relied on facts and the indestructible results of arithmetical formulae such as '2+2 = 4'. A quest amongst youth arose for realist education and an education in natural sciences and certain professions, such as law, railway engineering and medicine were seen as more prestigious. The behaviour of the characters in the novel *Chto delat'?* by Chernyshevskii was governed purely by personal gain, the criterion of which was reason. Chernyshevskii's 'new people' were perceived by their readers as models for imitation. Admirers of Chernyshevskii's heroes attempted to follow the ethic of 'rational egoism' in their own lives.[44] Writers who imitated Chernyshevskii based the behaviour of their heroes on reason. A.K. Sheller-Mikhailov in his novel *Gnilye bolota*; *The Rotten Swamps*,1864) created the image of a teacher

---

42 *Raznochintsy* is a term indicating a specific part of the Tsarist class system, to which many members of the intelligentsia belonged, basically those of the middle class, non-nobility or impoverished nobility, often mercantile class.

43 See B. Zheimo, *Problemy etyczne we współczesnej prozie i publicystyce rosyjskiej*. Łódź: «Ibidem» 2000, 11–12.

44 See. I. Paperno, *Semiotika povedeniia, Nikolai Chernyshevskii, Chelovek epokhi realizma*, Moscow: Novoie Literaturnoie Obozrenie 1996, 12.

who aspired to educate his pupils as reasonable, practical people, who in their behaviour would act reasonably according to circumstances.

After the publication of the novel *Chto delat'?* Dostoevskii entered into a polemic with the concept of the determinism in human behaviour. In *Zapiski iz podpol'ia* (*Notes from Underground*), the hero-paradoxalist refutes reason as a basis for behaviour, comparing it to the caprice and to capricious desire. In *Prestuplenie i nakazanie* (*Crime and Punishment*), the main character excludes the influence of external circumstances in the roots of his action, pointing to the desire to test the idea of the imperative of action.

The characters of Dostoevskii's novels constantly cite reason, science, the incontrovertibility of arithmetic, Euclidean geometry, the necessity for scientific, precise and monovalent laws as foundations for the world order, but at the same time they feel their insufficiency. Dostoevskii's characters were modelled by their author on people who had found the truth as a result of mystical transformation. The departure point for the construction of the model is the rational man, who reacts adequately to circumstance, but such a man becomes helpless in the face of the power of all-pervasive evil, born from the passion for external ideas, for example, Western individualism, socialism etc., and searches for a way out from the trap of rational thought through faith in God. Despite the conviction of progressive types such as Luzhin, Lebeziatnikov, members of the Burdovskii company, Shigalev, Ivan Karamazov in the universality of mathematically exact laws, the truth turns out to be on the side of irrationally thinking characters – Sonia Marmeladov, Prince Myshkin, Shatov, Alesha Karamazov or those such as Dmitrii Karamazov, who saw the will of Providence and became a different man.

Lev Tolstoi in *Voina i mir* (*War and Peace*) also depicted characters who were formed in the sphere of influence of the individualist enlightened concept of personality, but when they live under the influence of existential experience of death, they are disenchanted by individualism (mystical foresight occurs in the mind of Andrei Bolkonskii). The change from a rational style of thought to religious asceticism became the experience of the characters in *Anna Karenina*, *Smert' Ivan Il'icha* (*The Death of Ivan Il'ich*) and *Otets Sergii* (*Father Sergii*). It must be noted that the new religiosity of the characters of the later works of Tolstoi has a rationalistic character.[45]

In Chekhov's universe those who transform life on the basis of rational principles are 'giants', or prisoners of the idea, like Professor Nikolai Stepanovich or Liza Volchaninova, but workers, such as the gardener Pesotskiii or the doctor Astrov, choose behaviour based on common sense.

---

45 E. Savinova, *'Tolstoi Lev Nikolaevich'* in *Idei v Rossii*, 550.

One can conclude that the rational aspect in the picture of the world and in the behaviour of people is most fully reflected in the output of writers of the Westernising orientation, such as Turgenev, Goncharov, the *raznochintsy* of the 1860s, and Chekhov, even though it was accompanied by a feeling of the insufficiency of purely rationalist principles. For the Russophile type, such as Dostoevskii, Tolstoi and the Symbolists, the dominant feeling was of the irrational basis of existence.

In the period following the Revolution, rationalism, understood in a Marxist manner as reasonable and grounded in necessity, was used for the organisation, regulation and direction of processes which took place within and without a person. In this role rationalism became the basis of the Communist utopia.

Modern culture is orientated towards rationalism, but the kind of rationalism that assumes the intelligent use of reason. Science has not lost its role. Once again in its long history, Russia has set out on the road of modernisation, but the impatient expectation of palpable results and an unwillingness to pay the price of modernisation give birth to disenchantment and, with it, a shift towards an irrationalist stance.

Translated by Elizabeth Harrison

Bibliography

Belinskii, Visarion. 1956. *Polnoe sobranie sochinenii v 13 tomakh*. V., X. Moscow: Izdatielstvo Akademii nauk SSSR.

Bol'shoi tolkovyi slovar' russkogo iazyka. 2003. S.A. Kuznetsov (eds). St Peterburg: Norint: 1106.

Belyi, Andrei. 1989. *Na rubezhe dvukh stoletii*. Moscow: Khudozhestviennaia litieratura.

Blok, Aleksandr A. 1963. *Sobranie sochinenii v vos'mi tomakh*, Moscow, Leningrad: Khudozhestviennaia litieratura.

Briusov Valerii. 2002. *'Kliuchi tain'. Kritika russkogo simbolizma*. Moscow: I, Olimp, AST.

Broda, Marian. 2000. *Rassudok i razum* in *Idei v Rossii*. 3, ed. A. de Lazari. Łódź: Ibidem: 330 – 332.

―――― 2000. *Racjonalizm* in *Idei v Rossii*. 3, ed. A de Lazari, Łódź: Ibidem: 332–334.

―――― 2005. *Russkie voprosi o Rossii*. Moscow: MAKS Пресс.

―――― 2011. *Zrozumieć Rosję? O rosyjskiej zagadce tajemnicy*. Łódź: Ibidem.

Chernaia, Liudmila. 2008. *Antropologicheskiii kod drevnerusskoi literatury*. Moscow: Iazyki slavianskikh kul'tur.

Chernyshevskii, Nikolai. 1978. *Izbrannye esteticheskie proizvedeniia*. Moscow: Iskusstvo.

Dostoevskii, Fiodor. 1988. *Polnoe sobranie sochinenii*. III. Leningrad: Nauka.

Leviash, Ilia. 2007. *Russkie voprosi o Rossii. Diskurs s Marianom Brodoi*. Moskwa: Labirynt.

Krasnoshchekova, Elena. 1997. *I.A. Goncharov, Mir tvorchestva*. St Petersburg: Pushkinskii fond.

Kratkaia filosofskaia entsyklopediia. 1994. Gubskii Je., Korableva G., Lutchenko V. (eds). Moscow: Progress.

Lesevich, Vladimir. 1869. *Filosofiia istorii na nauchnoi pochve (Ocherk iz istorii kultury XIX veka)* in *Otechestvennye zapiski*. No. 1.

Losev, Aleksei. 1990. *Tvorcheskii put' Vladimir Solov'ev* in Solov'ev V.S. *Sochineniia v dvukh tomakh*, 1. Moscow: Mysl: 3–32.

Mel'nik, Vladimir. 1991. *Eticheskii ideal I. A. Goncharova*. Kiev: Lybid.

Odoevskii, Vladimir. 1975. *Russkie nochi*. Egorov B., Maimin E., M. Medovoi (eds). Leningrad: Nauka.

Olaszek, Barbara. 1997. *Dymitr Pisariew. Wokół problemów pozytywizmu w Rosii*. Łódź: Wyd. Uniwersytetu Lodzkiego.

––––––– 2005. *Russkii pozitivizm, Idei v zerkale literatury*, Łódź: Wyd. Uniwersytetu Lodzkiego.

Ovsianiko-Kulikovskii, Dmitrii. 1989. *Literaturno-kriticheskie raboty v dvukh tomach*. II. Moscow.

Paperno, Irina. 1996. *Semiotika povedeniia: Nikolai Chernyshevskii – chelovek epokhi realizma*. Moscow: Novoie Literaturnoie Obozrenie.

Pisarev, Dmitrii. 1955. *Sobranie sochinenii v chetyrekh tomakh*, Moscow: Khudozhestviennaia literatura.

Przebinda, Grzegorz.1998. *Od Czaadajewa do Bierdiajewa. Spór o Boga i człowieka w myśli rosyjskiej (1832 – 1922)*. Krakov: PAU.

Saburova, Tatiana. 2003. *Prostranstvo 'svoe' i 'chuzhoe' v modeli mira russkoi intelligentsii*. In. *Kul'tura svoia i chuzhaia*. Bykhovskaia I.M. O.I. Goriainova (eds.). Moscow: Fond niezavisimogo radiovieshchaniia.

Sakulin, Pavel. 1913. *Iz istorii irusskogo idealizma, Kniaz' V.F. Odoevskii. Myslitel' i pisatel'.*. Book 1, Chapters 1–2. Moscow.

Shchukin, Vasilii. 2001. *Russkoe zapadnichestvo. Genezis, sushchnost', istoricheskaia rol'*. Łódź: Ibidem.

Savinova, Elena. 2001. *Tolstoi Lev Nikolaevich* in *Idei v Rossii* 4, ed. A. de Lazari. Łódź: Ibidem 546–556.

Tarnas, Richard. 1995. *Istoriia zapadnogo myshleniia* (tr. T.A. Azarkovich). Moskva: KRON-PRESS.

Walicki, Andrzei. 1964. *W kręgu konserwatywnej utopii. Struktura i przemiany rosyjskiego słowianofilstwa*. Warszawa: PWN.

Zen'kovskii, Vasilii. 1991. *Istoriia russkoi filosofii*. V. II. Part II. Leningrad: Ego.

Zheimo, Bozhena. 2000. *Problemy etyczne we współczesnej prozie i publicystyce rosyjskiej*. Łódź: Ibidem.

CHAPTER 2

Irrationalism in Ancient Russia

Tatiana Chumakova

Old Russian sources linked, as Gregory of Nyssa once did, one's mind with one's heart. The "mind" is the centre of a person's spiritual, rather than his rational, life, whereas the heart is the centre of wisdom. It can help a person to find a spiritual perspective, but can also hinder the process. The motif of the heart as a repository of wisdom is characteristic of the Middle Eastern tradition. One can find this conceptualisation of mind in the New Testament, too, where the notion of the 'mind' appears in the Bible for the first time. For Paul, this idea stands close to what we might now identify as 'conscience'. With a certain epistemological bias it is quite close to the definition of 'intellect', but does not fully coincide with it. Those who are free from the "bondage of corruption" (Romans 8:21 KJV) or "bondage to decay" (NRSV) are considered "light in heart". By contrast, the "heavy of heart" are deprived of spiritual freedom and cannot rise over earthly passions. The Old Russian miniaturist who illustrated Psalm 4 in the Kiev Psalter of 1397 depicted the "heavy hearted" as motionless, pressed down to the earth, indifferent to the call of the angel bending down to them. According to the Old Russian twentieth century treatise 'On human nature, the seen and unseen', it is only the interaction of heart and reason (literally, "of heart with thought") that permits one to attain spiritual and corporeal harmony, which, in its turn, brings forth the "mind"; the latter, for the author of this treatise, is a consequence of reason and the heart working in alliance. This sort of ontological epistemology dominates not only in Old Russian thought, but also in later Russian religious philosophy, and one of its most evident manifestations is the image of "suffering reason", so clearly demonstrated in the letters of Tsar Ivan IV (Ivan the Terrible).

The contradiction between the human understanding of the 'visible' and 'invisible' worlds is sublated at the level of the essentially Eastern Christian holistic worldview, which connects the human being and the Universe in communion within the Divine Grace. There are many media by which the pious may encounter the presence of God, not only in worship and reading of the Holy Scriptures, but also by mere observation of sunrays shining through the summer foliage, or an infant smiling, or by following any everyday human activity. It is impossible to know God since he remains outside the boundaries of existence, that is, time and space of His own creation. The only way of coming nearer to God is by means of theosis, which brings humans into their original state of unity with God. By receiving mysterious signs from God, those sparks of heavenly fire, a human soul ignites itself with "the light of Mount Tabor", and then the same light is perceived as gleaming everywhere. The doctrine of the world's divine nature became deeply perpetuated in the Russian culture, and from written tradition it came down to oral lore. This is well-illustrated by the folktale about the peasant hut (*izba*) published by F.I. Buslayev. The story says that once upon a time people began to freeze in the winter, and they hadn't yet learned how to put up a hut. So they turned to the Evil One, who taught them. "They timbered a blockhouse of four walls, with no gaps at all. Then they hacked a door and entered the hut – it was warm inside, but not suitable to live in such darkness. The people again turned to the Evil One. He tried and tried, but all in vain – it was still dark in the hut. The people then prayed to the Lord. And the Lord said to them – hack out a window! They chopped a window and it became light. You know it! How silly it is to ask for light from the Devil!"[1] This way of getting to know God is impossible without practice.

Ascetic practice is based upon the doctrine of passions. In Eastern Christian tradition, it was elaborated by John the Sinaite, alias John Climacus or John of the Ladder after his ascetic treatise, 'The Ladder of Divine Ascent' ('Climax' in the original Greek). This 'Ladder' consists of thirty homilies or exhortations according to the number of hidden years of Jesus' preparation for his earthly ministry. These homilies (named "steps" or "rungs") were addressed to monastics who strained after spiritual self-perfection, and on that way were to come up against the formidable obstacle of so-called "passions". According to John of the Ladder, the means necessary to struggle against them are provided by "remembrance of death", "joy-making mourning", which brings meekness, "stillness of body and soul", dispassion and perfection. In Rus' the 'Ladder' became known in the twelfth century or even earlier. Its advance was encouraged by the fact that portions of the text on certain occasions were read in churches. This work also influenced the way Nil Sorsky (otherwise known as Nilus of Sora) taught on passions and the way to approach God (theosis). He was tonsured in the Russian monastery of St Cyril of Beloozero (Kirillo-Belozerskii monastery) but spent many years on Mount Athos and in the monastery of Stoudios. After his return to Russia, Nil founded a *skete*, or an isolated cloister, on the River Sora. At first those who lived in the Sora cloister followed the monastic Rule of Cyril of Beloozero, but soon Nil composed his

---

1 Buslaev F.I., "Volot Volotovich" in *Istorichskie Ocherki Russkoi Narodnoi Poezii i Iskusstva*. St Petersburg: Tipogr. Tovarishchestva "Obshchestvennaia Pol'sa", 1861. Vol. I, *Russkaia Narodnaia Poeziia*, 457.

own manual, or 'Predanie' (literally, the 'Tradition'), better known by the first line: 'On the lives of the Holy Fathers, this tradition of the Elder (*starets*) Nil of the Desert to his disciples'. The ideas of this 'Tradition' were then developed in the longer 'Rule' (*Ustav*) of Nil Sorsky, who formulated the main point of his doctrine in the preface to this 'Rule'. It is based on the principle that the human mind as the image of God can be transformed by avoidance of "multiplicity". Passions hinder the unity of different parts of the soul. An ascetic whose aim is to create true reason must therefore subdue the passions, which are located in a particular organ of the body, namely the heart, from whence they come as evil thoughts. It is futile to rely on more conventional prayer in order to wrestle with them, since it does not interfere with the mind. Consequently, "what is done within one's heart" should come along with "mental observation" and "preservation of one's mind by means of various conversations". For Nil the conflict of good and evil within one's soul is a "mental battle". Right from the very opening of 'Ustav' Nil contemplates on the results of sinful thoughts and recommends how to avoid sin. Nil Sorsky shares the opinion previously expressed by Gregory of Sinai and other Orthodox mystics that the passions were some accidental affliction foreign to human nature. Thus the ultimate aim of an ascetic who strives to achieve personal holiness (the latter being synonymous with "transfiguration") is to be liberated from passions and to restore the condition of original purity.

Nil's anthropological intentions are clear from the very beginning of the preface, for he strives for a holistic vision of man. He considers the contemporary, or "fallen", human state to be not fully human, the latter being represented by Adam as he had existed before eating the fruit of the tree of Knowledge of Good and Evil. When Adam broke God's commandment, not only his soul but also his body were corrupted, and physical immortality lost. When the forbidden fruit was consumed, and Adam and Eve were exiled from Paradise, humans merged within the "visible world", with which they were brought together by corporality and slavery. This new existence is dominated and determined by flesh. However, the need to fulfil the Creator's violated design requires that true human nature is restored. And, since both the soul and the body in this world are equally flawed, this calls for both corporeal transformation and spiritual transfiguration, according to Nil's teaching. The main prerequisite of this harmonic coexistence demands that body and spirit should be united peacefully rather than by means of force and violation of the former.

The first chapter (literally, the first "word") explores "mental battles" which impede or block this sort of peaceful union are examined. In the original Russian their name is *prilog* – the first stage whereby sin penetrates the soul, "combination" and "captivity". Nil's means of obtaining inner and outer unity is to renounce all things external, all "certain ways and traces of the world", not, however, because the world is bad but because man is weak. "Vision of worldly things" (that is, sensual images), as distorted by human's "sick", "darkened" reason, would develop into passionate thoughts. Contrary to any further ethical or psychological developments brought by passion, thoughts are subconscious and are not controlled by reason. Thoughts are "laid over" upon the soul and thus, for a weak man, they would become that very *prilog* which can easily result in the development of passion. A soul approaches the outside world through an initially unconscious amalgamation of sensual things with spiritual ones. But when the soul begins to approach the world consciously, by its own will, it "grows into it". Nil Sorsky calls this stage in the development of passion "combination". Then comes the last stage, known as "captivity", which results in the collapse of spiritual unity: "reason" and "heart" are now separated. Passions find no obstacle now; they take hold of a human soul and ruin it. Unlike thoughts, passions are perennial, they persist and take root in the soul of an individual, they mould one's character or "temper" (*norov*).

In the second chapter Nil analyses the psychosomatic method of prayer. "Mental" or "tacit" prayer (or 'The Jesus Prayer') restores the unity of heart and mind (or reason). It is designated as "mental" due to the demand "to gather one's mind towards God". This practice is based upon the idea that mind, being an "image of God", rules over all physical affectations and passions ("the king of passions"), while the heart is the focus of personal life with all its sufferings, experiences and thoughts ("the treasury of thoughts"). Therefore, in order to cleanse the heart and the entire person, of all those too human minutiae, it is necessary that the mind rule over the heart:

> to make your mind deaf and numb during prayer...and to have the heart closed to any sinful thought...speak diligently, either while standing up, or when seated, or lying down, and confine reason to the heart in order to guard it from within, and hold your breath as much as possible...When calling the Lord Jesus...turn away from any thoughts.

It is extremely significant to control one's breathing during this prayer, as breath would very much "facilitate a clever composure". This is linked to the physiological idea, traced back to Galen, that air comes to the heart via the lungs, that is, to the centre of the person's psychic and emotional life, and the heart then spreads the air through the whole body. According to medieval treatises on natural philosophy, and partly to the treatise 'Galinovo na Ipokrata' (Galen's commentaries on Hippocrates's works), which Nil could have come across during his stay in the Kirillo-Belozerskii monastery, for a manuscript of

'Galinovo' belonged to the personal library of Kirill Belozerskii, the heart produces blood and blood was considered the medium to contain the living soul. The same concept occurs in the Bible, too (Lev.17:11–14; Deut.12:16, 23). Thus by regulating the way the heart works, it is possible to change the entire "contents" of a human body. "Evil spirits" may interfere with the practice of such "intelligent prayer" by "arousing sinful thoughts in your mind". One is advised not to pay any attention to them, but rather to "hold your breath as much as possible, and confine reason within the heart, and in your prayer, instead of a weapon, call the name of Lord Jesus to your help". Nil Sorsky considered this psychosomatic practice to be the first level of monasticism, and recommended beginners to combine it with handicraft.

In the third chapter, which explains "how and by what one should strengthen oneself through a mental tour-de-force", Nil Sorsky suggests that these spirits should be defeated through "constant repentance and unceasing prayer" and by "not weakening one's mental struggle". This is extremely hard for human beings, whose nature was distorted by and whose primordial purity was lost through the Fall. In the fourth chapter Nil Sorsky proceeds to consider the timing of daily works, emphasising the need for a personal confession of a monk before God: "praise God immediately upon awakening, confess to Him, and then start the deeds of prayer, singing, reading, hand-craft and other deeds". As Nil was more inclined towards an older, pre-Palamite version of hesychasm, he favoured personal confession of faith in particular. Unlike Gregory Palamas, Nil is rather inhibited about prayer techniques and psychophysical method in particular. Avoiding the Palamite sophistication of his age, Nil would rather opt for the older monastic tradition which centred on "ascetic behavior" (lit. "soberness") and "self-attention". From the issue of confession Nil Sorsky moves on to contemplate on death, which, in his opinion, is "only a (night) dream, while dream is almost death"; a dream is a "fleeting image" of death. The image of death as a dream is hardly new; it had already emerged in the Christian tradition during the patristic period. Christian writers believed that because life does not stop with one's death; the latter is not a real termination of existence, but only a temporary falling asleep (Dormition).

In the fifth chapter Nil proceeds to study eight passionate thoughts (gluttony, debauchery, avarice, anger, sadness, despair, vanity and pride) one by one. Of those, the first is the beginning of all thoughts not only within an individual's life, but also over the entire course of human history, as it was the 'insatiable' thought which had once caused the Original sin. However, in restraint from food, as well as in everything else, an individualised approach is necessary. Nil does not overlook the "variety of human faces" as he discusses various ways of self-improvement. In his opinion, the fact that human bodies differ significantly in strength and stamina should never be neglected in the monastic routine. Each monk should consume food "taking for oneself according to what one needs each day". In the discourse on the second thought, Nil follows the idea of John Cassian the Roman, who emphasised the need not only for chastity of the body, but also for that of the soul, and demanded that the 'internal' and 'external' person should be merged: in Nil's words, "chastity and purity are not only external sides of life, but also its inner sides, hidden in the very heart of man". Then, having considered "avaricious" and "angry" thoughts as well as those of "sadness" (i.e. despondency) and "vanity", Nil concludes the fifth chapter by exhorting "pride". The "proud thought" completes the catalogue of "passionate thoughts". Although it is the last on the list, it is far from being the least among them. In Christian tradition pride is the mother of all sins because it makes humans fully confident of their ethical and religious autonomy, of their ability to sustain themselves without divine help. Proud people would never be able to see their faults and vices. The sixth chapter of the Rule provides the reader with a number of general observations and analysis of passionate thoughts, along with advice on how to fight against those using the prayer of Theodore the Studite.

Chapter seven is a separate treatise on "The memory of death and ultimate Judgement". Here Nil says: "it is impossible for the hungry to eat without thinking about bread; in the same way it is impossible for those wishing for salvation to avoid remembering death". In order to achieve the distinctively prayerful state of mind one should always remember that human life is short, and it is recommended for a monk to "gather in his mind all the stories from the writings of the saints about various horrible demises…It is also useful to remember various deaths which he saw or heard of, or which happened in modernity". Nil understands death as a "horrible mystery", where the "soul is forced to part with the body and their natural union is broken by God's will". In the opinion of the ascetics, "thoughts about death" are rendered more realistic by physical sufferings, which are considered "useful for the soul". Nil Sorsky believed that it is necessary to be tolerant with respect to any illnesses, because "in all the parts of the body an illness can be turned into bliss". This reasoning suggests even a little bias towards a rejection of the patristic "natural man" concept, which presupposed physical integrity and health. On the other hand, such an attitude to physical illness became a literary commonplace of that time. Nil's practice of repentance and disdain of the physical comes to the extreme of self-denigration as embodied in his request of non-burial. In his will he asked: "Leave my body in the desert so that it will be eaten by animals and birds, for it has sinned a lot before God and is unworthy of burial". "Thinking about death" in ancient Russian thought is directly connected to eschatology, for death is the borderline of human existence. Beyond it nothing can be repaired, and retribution awaits everyone at the time of the Last Judgement to come at the end of times. The "memory of death" and "gift of tears" makes a soul contrite and repentant, while the doctrine of death remembrance and memory of God is particularly significant for Nil's anthropology. It was linked to the idea of transformation of mind and heart. Inasmuch as "contriteness", is a part of "intelligent doing", it helps to fight against "passionate thoughts" and to make "intelligent prayer" vivid. It brings the gift of tears as well. Contriteness is impossible without the remembrance of death and memory of God. Therefore it is based on repentance. The eigth and ninth chapters of the 'Rule' deal with the "gift of tears". Here Nil Sorskii explains how to attain a particular state of mind which induces tears, for "they give a lot of strength for overcoming sins and passions, more than diligence alone can provide". In the tenth chapter Nil recommends that monks should renounce the world totally; for them verbal communication is prohibited ("silence", rejection of "human conversations"), and replaced with the instruction by means of book reading which also has to be treated "with caution", as not all books are 'divine'. In the final chapter Nil Sorskii contemplates the ways and ultimate goal of the monastic "labour", which is based on achieving personal perfection, and opts for "internal strength" as opposed to external ritualism. Nil Sorskii saw salvation and personal holiness as the ultimate purpose of monasticism. Thus, in the works of Nil Sorskii, as well as in those by other ancient Russian authors, one can distinguish several pivotal existential concepts: love, joy, fear, and death.

Since a human being is both spiritual and physical in its essence, the human soul encased in the body would see the world through its glass, darkly. Therefore no spiritual change is possible without a physical one. By means of spiritual experience the glow of divine glory becomes permeable for a human soul, and transforms into fire which encompasses both the body and soul. This is the state of unification and love on which the Byzantine mystic Symeon the New Theologian wrote: "Numerous are its [i.e. love's] names, numerous its actions, even more numerous are its signs, divine and endless are its traits, but its nature is one and concealed equally from everybody by a mystery...Its meaning is unfathomable, love is eternal".[2] The doctrine of love has always been crucial for the Russian spiritual tradition. In general, its manifestations were so diversified owing to the idea that the flow of life is uniform and one, which was important for the formation of the national moral philosophy. The Byzantine expression "justification of life" happened to be very dear to a young nation

---

2 *Pamiatniki Vizantiiskoi Literatury IX–XIV Vekov*, ed. L.I. Freiberg, transl. T.A. Miller. Moscow: Nauka, 1968, 130.

whose entire pre-Christian experience pointed to the inseparable connection between macrocosm and microcosm, to the unity of spiritual and physical life. In no sense was this rejected by Christianity, as Christian asceticism is essentially free from any hostility to the lay and mundane life. This attitude was even more enhanced within Byzantine culture, which would strongly approve of a holistic perception of all the kinds of human activity as elements of the unified spiritual and material experience. By this it was possible to overcome a notable Graeco-Roman opposition between nature (*physis*) and the fruits of human activity (*techne*). Thus it was so distinctive for the ancient Russian perception of human nature to feel its connection with the cosmic nature of the Universe, bound neither by time or space. This is manifested most prominently in the descriptions of man prior to the Fall. By his "nature", or essence, this human being was considered isomorphic to the nature of the world, since he would not insulate himself from the rest of the "miraculous" and perfect world as created by God. This condition of primordial harmony also presupposes the unity of body and spirit within a human being: "God created man pure, without spite, simple, strong, grateful, free of sadness, embellished with various virtues and gifted with good of all sorts". Love is thus a prerequisite of human nature. The unity of body and spirit is most distinctively reflected in the doctrine of heart as a centre of psychosomatic and spiritual life of man. This doctrine, based on ancient pneumatology, was said to be fathered by Aristotle and later developed by the stoics. It received its scientific shape from Galen of Pergamon (second century AD), whose works came into common use in medieval medical tradition. Pneumatology turned out to be close to ancient Russian tradition, which borrowed its theoretical foundations from the Church Fathers.

The ancient Russian compilation 'Izmaragd' (fourteenth century) provides a classification of love. According to it, three "faces" of love exist. The first one is given by God; it converts love into the "mother of good deeds". The second one is a human love "bodily and assuaging thirst and hunger – pleasing for the body, impure and destined for fornication, it is repellent in God's eyes". The third face of love is the gloomiest – it is love caused by sorcery and by a pact with the Devil.

The first type of love is discussed in the 'Homily on love', a work attributed to Kliment Smoliatich. In this treatise, which is based mainly on quotations from the Gospel of John and the Epistles, love is described as a corollary of divine unity. God's love permeates the entire world and saves it. The gift of love distinguishes man from the "subhuman creatures, devoid of reason". Without it no salvation is possible because "God is love. The one who lives in love, lives in the union with God and God lives within him" (1 John 4:16). Within the medieval mind love is seen as a harmonic category, connected to the concepts of measure, harmony and concordance. In ancient Russian thought love is most frequently linked to the image of Sophia the Divine Wisdom, who through love and beauty renders the universe harmonious and creates *mir*. The semantics of this Old Church Slavonic term are very concise. It meant peace, tranquility, quietude and a union of people united by a common goal. Aesthetically love manifests itself as beauty, and ethically as mercy. Through "spiritual love", human will ("the lustful part of mind") is healed: Artemii Troitsky, following Nil Sorsky, regards the love towards one's fellow human being which overcomes anger as the most important of all virtues. Since Artemii Troitsky would follow the principles of his teaching throughout his entire lifespan, his acknowledgement of love's primary role in human relationships resulted in his tolerant attitude to heretics. Ancient Russian literature had no Shakespeare of its own, but ancient Russian legal books and penitentials abound in Shakespearean passions; the rustling of human feelings is audible through birch-bark manuscript letters. And since the Eastern Christian tradition was characterised by the convergence rather than divergence of two levels of consciousness as represented in the medieval dichotomy of "earthly and heavenly", it was natural that the routine mundane phenomena (including, of course, physical love) should be taken as sacred. Physical love was to be consecrated in religious marriage and was unthinkable outside wedlock. 'Nest-sharing', or matrimonial love, was deemed necessary for building an individual human life and for the life of the entire world as well. For an ordinary layperson to care for his nearest and dearest was regarded as so important that numerous "Teachings" condemned those who abandoned their family members for monastic vows. And thus, although sensuality was generally held suspect, it was not considered as being an evil fruit by definition, and earthly love was not opposed to heavenly love as it had sparks of the heavenly flame flashing through it. This fire emanating from the divine throne was supposed to thaw human hearts, so that, once warmed and softened, they would transform fear into love and joy.

The profession of joy is a characteristic feature of Christianity. Despondency and even spiteful dismay, sometimes excessively focused on one's own and more often on someone else's sins, were rather a hallmark of marginal groups. Christianity viewed itself as a religion of hope and joy. The Bible frequently mentions joy, the Acts of the Apostles and Epistles are full of it, and this joy is explained as belief in Jesus Christ as the Saviour of the human race who gave hope for eternal life to the people, which is why 'joy' is a key concept for a Christian. Similarly, the Old Testament too treats joy as an integral part of the fullness of religious life: "You show me the path of life: in your presence there is fullness of joy, in your right hand are pleasures forever" (Ps.16:11 NRSV).

Clement of Alexandria, contemplating in 'Stromata' on the ways of cognising God, writes:

> Let us then receive knowledge, not desiring its results, but embracing itself for the sake of knowing. For the first advantage is the habit of knowledge (γνωστική), which furnishes harmless pleasures and exultation both for the present and the future. And exultation is said to be gladness, being a reflection of the virtue which is according to truth, through a kind of exhilaration and relaxation of soul.[3]

The word joy in New Testament texts is often connected to the mention of Jesus Christ. In the Gospel of Luke his coming birth is heralded as a joy: "Do not be afraid; for see – I am bringing you good news of great joy for all the people: to you is born this day in the city of David a Saviour, who is the Messiah, the Lord" (Luke 2:10 NRSV). Why? The answer is obvious: joy is the opposite of despondency; the latter entered this world after the Fall, accompanied by the companion of death which was then atoned for by Christ.

Ancient Russian writers regarded joy (alongside reason, wisdom, pity and truth) as a 'natural' positive trait, given to man from birth.[4] In the 'Legend of the examination of faith', which is the part of the 'Primary Chronicle', joy also plays an important role. The chronicler explains that the envoys of the great prince Vladimir rejected Islam after visiting a mosque. Their impression was that "there is no happiness among them, but instead only sorrow".[5] The earliest Russian homily, 'Sermon on Law and Grace' by Hilarion, Metropolitan of Kiev, is virtually filled with joy. Paraphrasing the Psalter, Hilarion exclaims: "Let the nations rejoice and exult. Clap your hands, all ye nations; shout to God with a voice of exultation. For the Lord most High is terrible; He is a great king over all the earth".[6] This is a correct rendering of the inspiration one finds in ancient Russian booklore over the first centuries after the adoption of Christianity. It was characterised by an optimistic vision of the world, and even death was not

---

[3] *Strom.* VI, 99, 3 – 5. *Ante-Nicene Fathers.* New York: Christian Literature Publishing Co., 1885. Vol. II, *Fathers of the Second Century: Hermes, Tatian, Athenagoras, Theophilus, and Clement of Alexandria (Entire)* eds. Alexander Roberts and James Donaldson. Revised and chronologically arranged with brief prefaces and occasional notes by A. Cleveland Coxe, 503.

[4] See Gavriushin N.K., "Drevnerusskii Traktat "O Chelovechestem Estestve", in *Estestvennonauchnye Predstavleniia Drevnei Rusi*, ed. R.A. Simonov. Moscow: Nauka, 1988, 220–228.

[5] *The Russian Primary Chronicle, Laurentian Text.* Transl. and ed. by Samuel Hazzard Cross and Olgerd P. Sherbowitz-Wetzor. Cambridge, MA: The Mediaeval Academy of America, 1953, 10.

[6] *Sermons and Rhetoric of Kievan Rus'*, transl. by Simon Franklin. Cambridge, MA: Harvard Ukrainian Research Institute, 1991, 16.

to be feared. Indeed, death for a Christian is just the thinnest membrane between bodily existence and the afterlife (*pakibytie*, or, in the words of the Nicene Creed "the life of the world to come"). The motif of victory over death ("trampling down death by death", as Paschal Troparion says) manifests itself in the iconography, especially in the icons 'Descent into Hell' (or 'Harrowing of Hell'), which depict Christ rescuing the righteous and the progenitors of the human race from hell. And it is not by mere accident that these icons are perceived not only as one of the images of the festival of Easter Sunday, but also as a symbol that even the darkest soul, sunk in the infernal depths, may be transformed and brought to light. It appears that this particular theme was most important for Kirill of Turov (otherwise known as Kirill Turovsky). His sermons do not always speak of joy, but they give hope. The theology of joy, in my view, was also dominant in his sermons. Even the 'Homily on the Deposition from the Cross' is in fact a short treatise on joy. Kirill makes the Virgin Mary say that joy departed from this world at the moment when Christ died on the cross: "now my hope, joy and merriment, my son and god, is taken from me",[7] but then the joy comes back at his resurrection, turning weeping into joy. V.V. Kolesov notes that "in the Russian language of the twelfth century the word 'joy' alongside its Old Church Slavonic meaning of 'rejoice' acquired an additional meaning which later on became the main one: "a feeling of satisfaction". Therefore one may suppose that the passage from Kirill quoted above can have both meanings and point at "rejoice", and intrinsically, at "satisfaction" as well".[8] It can be thus concluded that in the Easter sermons of Kirill of Turov the idea of joy reaches its climax.

Alexander Schmemann wrote about this joy in particular. In the very first lines of his famous work 'The Eucharist: Sacrament of the Kingdom' he speaks of joy as an indispensable feature of a Christian:

> Thus those who believe in Christ and who accepted Him as the 'The Way, Truth and Life' live by hope for the future century. He no longer has here an 'abiding hail, but craves the future' (Euch. 13, 14). However, the whole joy of Christianity, an Easter essence of its faith, is in the fact that this future century' – future with respect to 'this world' – has already come, already been granted, is already 'amongst us'.[9]

---

7   Eremin I.P. "Literaturnoe Nasledie Kirilla Turovskogo", in *Trudy Otdela Drevnerusskoi Literatury*. Vol. XIII, ed. by D.S. Likhachev. Moscow, Leningrad: Izdatel'stvo AN SSSR: 1957, 420.
8   Kolesov V.V., "K Kharakteristike Poeticheskogo Stilia Kirilla Turovskogo", in *Trudy Otdela Drevnerusskoi Literatury*. Leningrad: Nauka, Leningr. Otdelenie, 1981. Vol. XXXVI, 46.
9   Shmeman A.D., *Evkharistiia. Tainstvo Tsarstva*. Moscow: Palomnik, 1992, 15.

Here spiritual joy reaches a climax and fills man up completely, which is akin to man's entire transformation – both physical and spiritual – in the sacrament of the Eucharist. Those who are sincerely devoted should behave like children; they should not reflect on their joy, nor separate one kind of it from another. Their aim is to be simply living and rejoicing both in body and spirit, thus surrendering to this joy completely. In this state of mind human beings return to their 'natural', or Paradisiacal, state; joy completely transforms them. As the service hymns to the saints of the calendar emphasise, it is already possible in this world to become a "citizen of the Heavenly Jerusalem" and it is this in particular that make a person holy. The *Zhitie* (Vita) of Uliania Osor'ina (died 2 January 1604) tells us about the life of an average, plain woman who sensed, ever since her childhood, a desire for a nun's life, but devoted herself to the world. Day and night she took care of her family and of all those who needed her care and support, and as regular and frequent churchgoing would demand her distraction from home duties, she was unable to attend church frequently. She lived an incredibly hard life, full of labours, worries, illnesses and suffering. And at the threshold of death she "although exhausted by destitution, was still more cheerful than in her young years".[10]

Another characteristic feature of ancient Russian thought was the idea that fear should form one of the most important themes of philosophical contemplation: fear of God and fear of death. According to Troitsky, it is precisely owing to the "fear of God" that man follows the "Saviour's Commandments" (the commandments of Jesus Christ), which, in turn, give rise to "spiritual reason". The first reasoning ("reason of the flesh") is given to a human being from birth and it expresses all *menschliches, zu menschliches* that lies inside him; at this stage man is completely at one with the world and can hardly detach his essence from it. He is radiant and proud of himself, for he cannot rise above the earth and see his pettiness and vanity. The second reason ("reason of the soul") develops as the human soul is instructed. It helps to understand one's own nature which is sometimes shielded off by corporeality ("pre-essence"). Perfection is gained at the stage of the "spiritual" reason; this is a moment when a person would fully realise their true predestination, and their authentic 'I', when it already ceases to be an 'Ego'. At this stage everything human gets absorbed by faith. The 'inner person' completely subjugates the 'outer person', and then nothing is to be feared of. However, the majority of humans cannot attain this ideal, and their destiny is to be scared of death, beyond the threshold of which one's earthly doings are to be reckoned.

---

10   "Povest ob Ulianii Osor'inoi", ed. T.R. Rudi, in *Pamiatniki Literatury Drevnei Rusi, XVII c.* Moscow: Khudozhestvennaia Literatura, 1988. Vol. I, 103.

The fear of death, this permanent human companion, permeates the 'Prayer to the Angel the Terrible', created by the Tsar Ivan the Terrible (Ivan IV Vasilievich, 'Groznyi'). It was characteristic of medieval descriptions of corporeality to emphasise gloomy and naturalistic details, at times even to the point of shock. In the description of a sinful soul, epithets such as 'filled with stench' and 'full of sin' were used, in order to stress its fusion with the body. Even the terrible angel – the archangel Mikhail – cannot cleanse the soul from the 'bodily trash' and thus rescue it. All he does is bring death – and what is after lies terrible and unknown.

Meditations on death and immortality are inevitable for any culture. Normally merged deep into their context, they move to the forefront during turbulent times, but never disappear completely. In the Middle Ages the themes of death and immortality came to occupy the central place in culture, and were distinctly pronounced from the latter half of the fourteenth until the sixteenth century, a period marred by various disasters. Earthly life was now devoid of its own meaning, and seen as a mere transition time to prepare oneself for death. This ultimately led to the creation of the most coherent conceptions of death and immortality of all those known to humankind. A vast number of ancient Russian sources, both literary, e.g. lives of saints, "visions", commemoration books (*sinodik*), "contemplations of death", religious verses, etc., and visual (icons or folk paintings) discuss the image of death and governing forces, the connection of this world with the afterworld, human perceptions of death, whether it is viewed as the end or just as a temporary sleep ("dormition").

It was normal for archaic Russian culture to see death in terms of transformation or even (re)incarnation, which was connected to a circular model of time:

> Come, appear, my darling dear baby,
> Come at least to my doorstep as a strong fine fellow,
> Or as a stranger, wandering singer,
> Or as a merchant come, from Moscow travelling.[11]

This image remained topical also for a medieval culture which perceived time as a "solidarity of human generations that change and return as seasons do",[12] and death as a transition from one state of existence to another: "For man is created from four elements which are infinite, but change. The soul goes back

---

11   Barsov E.V., *Prichitaniia Severnogo Kraia*. Moscow: Tipogr. "Sovremen. Izv"., 1872. Part 1, 103.
12   Gurevich A.Ia., *Kategorii Srednevekovoi Kultury*. Moscow: Iskusstvo, 1984, 110.

to God, while the body becomes earth, from which man was created in the beginning".[13] Such an image of time remained in the Russian language, where the word for time (*vremia*) derives from the Old Church Slavonic *veremia*, which is cognate with the words *vereteno* (spindle) and *votot'* (winch), which originally referred to a circular motion. This image of time substantially differs from the Western European one, where time appears as either 'stretching' and 'spreading' (in Latin and Greek) or a 'segment' (in German), which is related to the Christian linear model. In the Orthodox perception, the creation of time (as well as space) starts with the beginning of the world, and time is an expanse associated with the state of the world, for example, *Shestodnev*

('Hexaemeron', or 'Six Days of Creation') by Basil of Caesarea. Both ends of this stretch of space and time are bumping up into eternity. The seeming roundabout of the Christian liturgical year is in fact a distorted perception, for the liturgical year is a projection of the events of Sacred History which, once God takes his part in it, itself becomes timeless and spaceless. Annual repetition of all its events is demanded by the striving to get rid of the bonds of space and time here and now. With the end of the world, time is to end as well, it is extinguished on the Day of Judgement. The ancient Russian icon 'The Judgement' depicts angels convolving the scroll of time. God Himself exists outside time and space, as does everything associated with Him in Glory: the saints and angels in front of His throne are also timeless.

It is possible that coupling a 'pagan' model of time, as reflected in the national mentality and language, with the Christian one, which came to Rus' at the end of the tenth century, caused some duality in the perception of time and hence of human existence. On the one hand, a model was rooted in human consciousness whereby the end of time and space was inevitable, but on the other hand, as early as in the eleventh century, we find a new belief. According to this, certain procedures (such as Baptism and the Eucharist) and faith in Christ who came down to Hell and saved mankind from death (on this, see the apocryphal 'Gospel of Nicodemus' and the icons of the 'Descent into Hell') can provide both spirit and flesh, ideal and real, with an opportunity to enter into a new Covenant. By that they would be liberated from time-the-executioner, they would participate in eternity and destroy the difference between "now" and the time of "afterlife" (*pakibytie*): "Baptised into Christ, in Christ he clothed himself and he departed the font in the image of whiteness a son of incorruption, a son of the resurrection. Now he was named the eternal name of Vasilij, a name

---

13   Porfiriev I.Ia., "Apokrificheskie Skazaniia o Novozavetnykh Litsakh i Sobytiiakh po Rukopisiam Solovetskoi Biblioteki" in *Sbornik Otdeleniia Russkogo Iazyka i Slovesnosti Imperatorskoi Akademii Nauk*. Vol. LII, No.4, № 4. St Petersburg, 1890, 451.

which is famed from generation to generation".[14] This is what the metropolitan of Kiev, Hilarion, wrote about the baptism of the great Kievan prince Vladimir Sviatoslavich. In this connection death becomes no more than a thin membrane between the worldly existence and the afterlife ('*pakibytie*'). Those who were christened and took up faith are members of eternity, and death simply does not exist for them. As Maximus the Confessor wrote: "they are destined to be gods and to be called gods, because God filled them up totally, without leaving anything that would be devoid of His presence".[15]

The situation was gradually changing, and in fourteenth-century sources we already see an existential fear of death, from which one cannot be saved, either by baptism nor by faith, which are no longer sufficient. Kirill Belozerskii wrote:

> Here I am, sinful and humble hegumen Kirill, who sees old age catching up with me. I am now prone to various and frequent diseases, which possess me now too, but this is a manifestation of God's love for man which I still experience and see, and which forces me to think about death and the forthcoming Judgment. And for this reason my heart is trembling because of this terrible outcome, and the fear of death envelops me. I feel the dread of Judgment will come to me and cover me with darkness of the unknown. But what is to be done, I do not know.[16]

This change in the perception of death was due to many reasons. Firstly, at that time the orthodox view of death gained a foothold. The ethical element strengthened, and death was perceived as a disease, a difficult path by which one is to recover from evil and to exterminate sin. In this case life has no end except for true Christians who can be "healed" and gain immortality. Meanwhile, eternal torment and oblivion is prepared for all those who are unrepentant and marred by sin. Secondly, it was at that particular time that the inevitability of death, in all its ugly and repulsive detail, became apparent for the first time both for ancient Russian and for Western European culture. This might have been a reflection of the European mood at the time when traditional culture was breaking down.[17] In Western European art of the end of the fourteenth

---

14 *Sermons and Rhetoric of Kievan Rus'*, 19.
15 *Tvoreniia Prepodobnogo Maksima Ispovednika*, Vol. 1, Bogoslovskie i Asketicheskie Traktaty. Moscow: Martis, 1993, 83.
16 *Prepodobnye Kirill, Ferapont i Martinian Belozerskie*, ed. by Ie. G. Vodolazkin. St Petersburg: Glagol, 1993, 55.
17 See Delumeau J., *La Peur en Occident (XIV – XVIII siecles). Une Cite Assiegee*. Paris: Fayard, 1978.

century when, as it seemed, "the world is immersed into night and darkness and forsaken by God",[18] images of disintegrating flesh became popular on tombstones; in mural paintings cheerful cavalcades froze in front of open coffins; on engravings and paintings the 'Dance of death' started to reel.[19] In ancient Russian icon painting this emerged later, for Russian iconography was customarily based on the works of literature, and the literary explorations of the subject appeared only in the later half of the fifteenth century. Firstly, these were 'Penitential verses' (otherwise known as 'tenderly touching', 'additional' and 'supplementary', since they were not part of the church service). These penitential verses, composed in the monasteries, contemplated the frailty of life and the sinfulness of man. And secondly, it was 'Dialogue of life and death, that is a struggle between life and death',[20] translated at the end of the fifteenth century from the German. The translator is most likely to have been close to the archbishop Gennady of Novgorod, who substantially abridged the work and twisted its emotional colouring, turning it from satire into moral preaching. Since then, the 'Dialogue' has been re-edited on numerous occasions. Almost all surviving manuscripts of this text originated in the monastery of Volokolamsk. This cloister was the place where translation work started by Gennadii's circle had been developing over the entire sixteenth century. It is the Iosifo-Volokolamsk monastery that produced the majority of texts on "death memory". The first of these was the aforementioned 'Dialogue of life and death', also referred to by scholars as 'Disputation on life and death' (the full title being 'The most horrendous to all is death. Aristotle's third book: *Ethicorum* Dialogue of life and death. That is, a struggle between life and death'),[21] whereas the last was 'The Tale of Death of some Master, that is, a Philosopher', which was loosely translated from the sixteenth-century Polish work 'The Conversation of Master Polikarp with Death'.[22]

---

18 "Into the night and darkness is the world immersed, forsaken by God", Sebastian Brant wrote at the time (see S. Brant, *Korabl Durakov*, Moscow: Khudozhestvennaia Literatura, 1965, 23).

19 See Borts A. *Medieval Worlds. Barbarians, Heritics, and Artists in the Middle Ages*. Cambridge, 1991; Tristram Ph.. *Figures of Life and Death in Medieval English Literature*. New York: New York University Press, 1976.

20 See Dmitrieva R.P., "Prenie Zhivota i Smertiiu" in *Slovar Knizhnikov i Knizhnosti Drevnei Rusi*. Leningrad, 1988. Vol. II, Second Half of the XIV-XVI Centuries, part 2, ed. by D.S. Likhachev., 303–305.

21 Dmitrieva R.P., *Povesti o Spore Zhizni i Smerti*. Moscow, Leningrad: Nauka, 1964, 141–142.

22 On this translation, see Dmitrieva R.P. "Russkii Perevod XVI c. Polskogo Sochineniia XV c. "Razgovor Magistra Polikarpa so Smertiu"", in *Trudy Otdela Drevnerusskoi Literatury*. Moscow, Leningrad: Izdatel'stvo AN SSSR, 1963. Vol. XIX, 313.

Despite all the diversity of texts and manuscript versions, the general idea persisted. The ethical meaning of death, first referred to in the third book of Aristotle's 'Nicomachean ethics', is emphasised by all sorts of means. Besides, all such works lay stress on the ontological meaning of death, namely human caducity and frailty. In the style of the medieval macabre these texts make every use of repulsive details of decay, which in later works turn superlative: "Where is human beauty? Instead of beauty there is a stench emerging from the coffin [...] great is the grief, great is the sadness, great is the human sorrow in this world". In the later works Platonic motifs are strengthened, such as that life is only a dream: "What is our life in this world – it passes by like a dream".[23] This inescapable gloom is somewhat mitigated by the interpolation in one of the copies from Pogodin's collection.[24] This insertion is undoubtedly of Russian origin, and its main purpose is not to scare the reader, but instead to explain the everyday meaning of death, to bring forth reconciliation and consolation ("...And indeed made of stone is the heart of that man who does not cry about his fatal hour of dying"). It is interesting how this copy alters the meaning of death. While the other manuscripts would emphasise the general meaning of death as being universal and common for all, this one goes on to particularise: "death for the righteous is peace, for children it is delight, for the labouring folk it is rest, death means a relief for the needy, and liberation for those living in hardship, and concession for the sick, and propitiation for those sailing in the sea". The meaning of death is thus ontological, because without it there is no salvation: "Oh, brothers, if there were no death, we would have to punish ourselves, and it would be in vain to wait for judgement and there would be no hope for salvation". By this death turns into a stage of initiation *en route* to the transformation of the consecrated.

It is possible that to some extent these works appeared due to the activity of would-be metropolitan Daniil (latter half of the 15th century.-1547). Daniil succeeded Iosif Volotski (or, Joseph of Volotsk/Volokolamsk) as the hegumen of the Volokolams monastery, and later obtained the Metropolitan see. As he was editing the definition of philosophy of John Damascene, Daniil listed 'Thoughts on Death' first among the subjects of philosophy. 'Thoughts on Death' provided icon-painting with an appropriate subject not later than the sixteenth century. From that time we have some icons and book miniatures that visualise the human route to death. A little later, "folk pictures" (*lubok,* pl. *lubki*) on the same subject emerged. Two such icons were described by A.S. Uvarov, in whose collection they were kept. He names these two icons 'The Image of the Guardian

---

23 *Ibid.* 194.
24 *Ibid.* 196.

Angel and his Travels'.[25] The iconographic foundation of these icons is provided by 'The Tale of the Vision of the Apostle Paul', church prayers for the Feast of Assumption and some other texts on "death memory". At the top of the icon, in the centre, there is the Holy Trinity. The middle part is occupied by scenes of the life of man at daytime and at night. Below, a grave is depicted containing a human skeleton at which two people are gazing, one of whom is pinching his nose in disgust; the inscription below says "human faeces rotten".

As mentioned above, in the 16th and 17th centuries similar macabre themes were widespread. It is sufficient to recall the well-known headstone of Valentine Balbiani (between 1572 and 1583, Paris, Louvre) by the French sculptor Germain Pilon. The lid shows the deceased person, lying, dressed-up in exquisite manner; her little pet dog is frolicking nearby; below, on the sarcophagus wall there is a relief styled as a window into another reality. Here the repulsive remains of what used to be Valentine Balbiani are scattered between the rags of once-costly clothing. This is not the only parallel between Western European and Russian images. The icon depicts allegorical figures of Day and Night standing on both sides of the grave. These figures would also frame the sarcophagus of Giuliano Medici in the Medici Chapel by Michelangelo Buonarroti. The semantics of Day and Night images is very profound. In Greek mythology Nyx (Night) and Hemera (Day) are primary world-generating potencies which give rise to death, sleep, revenge, etc.; that is, everything that is related to the cycle of life and death. The dwelling of Night is supposed to be in the opened-up abyss Tartar which in Christian consciousness is associated with hell. These are also the natural images of time, since before the mechanical clock was invented, time had been measured by the alternation of light and darkness, by the motion of the moon and the sun. This is the reason why some old clocks are decorated by the figures of Day and Night. Such meaning is also present in the icon, for it designates here the time of the earthly human life, which during the period was already beginning to be considered an inseparable part of the making of an individual. Day and Night also served as images of light and darkness. The sun which Day is holding on the icon is a symbol of the Holy Trinity and that of light. For a mediaeval mind any visible light (produced by the sun's rays, flames, burning candles, etc.) symbolised God. The moon resting in the hands of Night is an antipode of the sun; it is an attribute of the night, that is, of the time when the dark sides of nature are triumphant and the body wins over the spirit. Moreover, these are also images of life and death; as we read in the prayer at Assumption Day: "My light is fading and night is covering me", and so on.

---

25   Uvarov A.S., "Obraz Angela-khranitelia s Pokhozhdeniiami", in *Sbornik Melkikh Trudov*. Moscow: Tip. G. Lissnera i D. Sovko, 1910. Vol. I, 133.

This confirms that the images of Day and Night in the mediaeval world-view are perceived as symbols of all that exists, i.e. things created and uncreated. On the icon from A.S. Uvarov's collection, Day is depicted in the bottom left part of the icon. It holds the sun and stands on the many-eyed wheels with wings. This is the symbol of the ophanim (Ezek. 1:15–20; 10:12–13), an angelic rank that symbolises the idea of God's Providence. The figure of Night, which is Day's twin, is standing on the right. It is wrapped in a starry veil and is holding the moon, while its feet rest on the wheel of Fortune, which is rotated by devils. A mechanical motion of the Wheel of Fortune is opposed here to the eternal and living rotation of the Wheel of Providence. Such understanding of Fortuna is distinctive for the 15th–16th centuries, when this concept gains an increasingly one-sided interpretation as a destructive, fatal force, saturated with mortal danger, "'non-destiny",[26] and it is no accident that Maksim Grek (Maximus the Greek) should say about the Wheel of Fortune that it is "invented by the devils".[27] Fortuna and Providence are totally different. The latter belongs unreservedly to the divine realm and impacts little on the course of our earthly corporeal life, although it sometimes influences the outcome of one's actions by allowing one's intentions to be fulfilled. What convinced people of the existence of Providence was the strict order of things, their expediency, and in particular the harmonious order of the motion of the stars, as well as retribution for sins and the torments of conscience which torture villains: "Vengeance comes at once from the Lord of the Commandments and not from the planets and zodiacs".[28] Fortuna, on the other hand, is earthly luck, blind chance, and it is not by chance that we see a wheel on the icon – a symbol of the volatility of happiness. A good Christian must not think much about the earthly pleasures that Fortuna brings. The figures of both Providence and Fortuna remind the observer that the afterlife of the soul was determined by the soul's earthly actions. A Christian soul that was appropriately treated departs to heaven, and all the other souls decay into hell. As we know, aspiration for salvation and fear of not attaining it were key concerns for a medieval person.

It has already been mentioned that life in medieval times was directly aimed at the death to come. In preparing himself for it, man had to live

---

26 Gurevich A.Ia., "Srednevekovyi Kupets", in *Odissei. Chelovek v Istorii*. Moscow: Nauka, 1990, 122. Providence (destiny) in Rus' was perceived as divine judgment (the Russian word *sud'ba* contains the root *sud* which means judgment, trial), while Fortuna is an accidental luck or happiness (similarly: shchastie – 'happiness' in Russian – contains chast', which means part, or share, i.e. a piece of the pie intended for more that one person).

27 *Sochineniia Prepodobnogo Maksima Greka*. Kazan: Tip. Gub. Pravleniia, 1862. Part 1, 441.

28 *Ibid.*

appropriately and to be a member of the church. Considerations were focused, first of all, on one's own individual death. Christianity made everyone responsible for their choice between good and evil. The individual approach to death is reflected in the cultural phenomena of that time, namely texts about death-contemplation, book miniatures or icons. Their task was one and the same: to show that the character of death depends not on physical conditions, but on spiritual connections. Although death was perceived as a natural process, many believed that this natural process was administered in a supernatural way (note, for example, the figure of Divine Providence on the icon). Death was believed in the Middle Ages to have emerged as a direct consequence of the Original Sin, and similarly, individual death was partly dependent on individual sins. Salvation from death and eternal life also became possible because of death: the main death in the Christian history of mankind is the death of Christ on the cross. Death on Golgotha, which was believed to be Adam's tomb, or even a mound over Adam's vast skull (which is reflected in the iconography of the Crucifixion where Adam's skull lies at the bottom of the cross), saved humanity from death by giving it the true eternal afterlife: "you have destroyed death by death" (as the Orthodox *Book of Hours* addresses Jesus). The theme of Golgotha and the subsequent descent into hell were popular in literature and folklore, where Christ acted as a cultural hero defeating death in its infernal lair. Human immortality was inseparable from human mortality. A human being was mortal in his temporal existence, but immortal from the perspective of eternity. Temporal existence is part of eternity, but no automatic transition from time to eternity is possible; its price is atonement (both personal and collective for all mankind). Its stages comprise the life of mankind full of suffering and revelations, Crucifixion and the Last Judgment. According to medieval beliefs, those who have come through all these tests will cease to be mortal: their 'essence' will be transformed and become immortal. This closes the circle, a typical outcome in ancient Russian philosophy, where everything is 'closed' in ethical and anthropological interpretations centred around the ideas of God's image and likeness, which will only be attained completely at the later time of *pakibytie* (afterlife, 'the life of the future'). And this incompleteness of a human being, his perpetual location on the border, is also a typical feature of the Russian Middle Ages, where man, whether he is righteous or dishonest, is constantly in a state of "already, but not yet" (S.S. Averintsev).

Many concepts of ancient Russian irrationalism became so ingrained in Russian culture that even after Peter the Great's reforms they remained current and dominated the culture, as was later manifested by the Russian writers and philosophers of the 19th and 20th centuries.

Bibliography

Barsov E.V. 1872. *Prichitaniia Severnogo Kraia*. Part 1. Moscow: Tipogr. "Sovremen. Izv".
Borts A. 1991. *Medieval Worlds. Barbarians, Heretics, and Artists in the Middle Ages*. Cambridge M.A.: Harvard Univeristy Press.
Brant S. 1965. *Korabl Durakov*. Moscow: Khudozhestvennaia Literatura.
Buslaev F. I. 1861 'Volot Volotovich' in *Istoricheskie Ocherki Russkoi Narodnoi Poezii i Iskusstva*. Vol. I, Russkaia Narodnaia Poeziia. St Petersburg: Tipogr. Tovarishchestva "Obshchestvennaia Pol'sa": 455–469.
Delumeau J. 1978. *La Peur en Occident (XIV – XVIII siecles). Une Cite Assiegee*. Paris: Fayard.
Dmitrieva R.P. 1964. *Povesti o Spore Zhizni i Smerti*. Moscow, Leningrad: Nauka.
—— 1988. 'Prenie Zhivota i Smertiiu' in Likhachev D.S. (ed.) *Slovar Knizhnikov i Knizhnosti Drevnei Rusi*. Vol. II, Second Half of the XIV–XVI Centuries, part 2. Leningrad: s.n.: 303–305.
—— 1963. 'Russkii Perevod XVI c. Polskogo Sochineniia XV c. 'Razgovor Magistra Polikarpa so Smertiu', in *Trudy Otdela Drevnerusskoi Literatury*. Vol. XIX. Moscow, Leningrad: Izdatel'stvo AN SSSR: 303–317.
Eremin I.P. 1957. 'Literaturnoe Nasledie Kirilla Turovskogo' in Likhachev D.S. (ed.) *Trudy Otdela Drevnerusskoi Literatury*. Vol. XIII. Moscow, Leningrad: Izdatel'stvo AN SSSR: 409–426.
Freiberg L.I. (ed.) 1968. *Pamiatniki Vizantiiskoi Literatury IX–XIV Vekov* (tr. T.A. Miller). Moscow: Nauka.
Gavriushin N.K. 1988. 'Drevnerusskii Traktat 'O Chelovechestem Estestve' in Simonov R.A. (ed.) *Estestvennonauchnye Predstavleniia Drevnei Rusi*. Moscow: Nauka: 220–228.
Gurevich A.Ia. 1984. *Kategorii Srednevekovoi Kultury*. Moscow: Iskusstvo.
—— 1990. 'Srednevekovyi Kupets' in *Odissei. Chelovek v Istorii*. Moscow: Nauka: 117–131.
Hazzard Cross, Samuel and Sherbowitz-Wetzor, Olgerd P. (eds). 1953. *The Russian Primary Chronicle, Laurentian Text* (tr. Samuel Hazzard Cross and Olgerd P. Sherbowitz-Wetzor). Cambridge, MA: The Mediaeval Academy of America.
Kolesov V.V. 1981. 'K Kharakteristike Poeticheskogo Stilia Kirilla Turovskogo' in *Trudy Otdela Drevnerusskoi Literatury*, Vol. XXXVI. Leningrad: Nauka, Leningrad. Otdelenie: 37–49.
Porfiriev I.Ia. 1890. 'Apokrificheskie Skazaniia o Novozavetnykh Litsakh i Sobytiiakh po Rukopisiam Solovetskoi Biblioteki' in *Sbornik Otdeleniia Pusskogo Iazyka i Slovesnosti Imperatorskoi Akademii Nauk*. Vol. LII, №4. St Petersburg: s.n.
Roberts, Alexander and Donaldson, James. (eds). 1885. *Ante-Nicene Fathers*. Vol. II, *Fathers of the Second Century: Hermes, Tatian, Athenagoras, Theophilus, and Clement of Alexandria (Entire)*. New York: Christian Literature Publishing Co.

Rudi T.R. (ed.) 1988. 'Povest ob Ulianii Osor'inoi' in *Pamiatniki Literatury Drevnei Rusi, XVII c.* Vol. I. Moscow: Khudozhestvennaia Literatura: 98–104.

Sermons and Rhetoric of Kievan Rus' 1991. (tr. Simon Franklin). Cambridge, MA: Harvard Ukrainian Research Institute.

Shmeman A.D. 1992. *Evkharistiia. Tainstvo Tsarstva.* Moscow: Palomnik.

Sochineniia Prepodobnogo Maksima Greka. 1862. Part 1. Kazan: Tip. Gub. Pravleniia.

Tristram Ph. 1976. *Figures of Life and Death in Medieval English Literature.* New York: New York University Press.

Tvoreniia Prepodobnogo Maksima Ispovednika. 1993. Vol. I, Bogoslovskie i Asketicheskie Traktaty. Moscow: Martis.

Uvarov A.S. 1910. 'Obraz Angela-khranitelia s Pokhozhdeniiami' in *Sbornik Melkikh Trudov*. Vol. I, Moscow: Tip. G. Lissnera i D. Sovko: 127–133.

Vodolazkin Ie.G. (ed.) 1993. *Prepodobnye Kirill, Ferapont i Martinian Belozerskie.* St Petersburg: Glagol.

CHAPTER 3

Ethos Versus Pathos. The Ontologisation of Knowledge in Russian Philosophy

Oliver Smith

The peculiar evolution of Russian thought from its earliest days to the present betrays both a fascination with, and repulsion from, modes of rationality forged over centuries of intellectual history. Typical of this dual response was the Russian reception of the father of critical philosophy, Immanuel Kant. From implacable enemy of Christianity and authentic philosophy in thinkers such as Nikolai Fedorov and Pavel Florenskii (who both associated the German thinker with the devil himself),[1] to any number of quasi-hagiographic interpretations,[2] for the Russians Kant was both hero and anti-hero, sometimes appearing in such contrary aspects within a single tradition or body of thought.

The present essay, however, will be concerned not so much with the traditional divisions that opened up after Kant, and which moved Russian philosophers to creativity: the rational vs. the irrational, or the division within reason itself between *rassudok* and *razum* (a division, of course, in many ways echoing, though not coinciding with, the German *Verstand* and *Vernunft* of Kantian epistemology). Instead, it will attempt a phenomenological genealogy of the Russian envisioning of reason, not in the sense of an historical enumeration of the sources on which it drew, but rather the tracing of its energies back to the consciousness (collective and individual) from which it derived. It aims to chart not how Russians modified or developed Kantian paradigms or discourse, but which structures of consciousness lay behind their thought, and how these differed from Western models. Viewing philosophy, not as indifferent conjecture on universal properties or values, but as always deriving from a position which in turn positions itself *vis-à-vis* its intended audience, the consciousness that enlivens Russian philosophy will be defined as one governed by 'pathos', which will be juxtaposed with the 'ethos' of the Western tradition. Such pathos can, in its most basic aspect,

---

1 See A.V. Akhutin, 'Sofiia i chert (Kant pered litsom russkoi religioznoi metafiziki)', in *Rossiia i Germaniia*, Moscow, 1993, 207–247.
2 For Lev Lopatin, for example, Kant was the 'first in philosophy to set out on the authentic path, finally solving the task that had evaded resolution for millennia.' L.M. Lopatin, 'Uchenie Kanta o poznanii', in *Filosofskie kharakteristiki i rechi*, Minsk, 2000, 65–81 (66).

be understood as the 'space' where the individual experience of the thinker steps into contact with the world outside, where it seeks to be heard, recognised and, perhaps, comprehended.[3] Defined in such a way as the art of representing an individual truth that seeks to exceed itself in the attainment of universality – an attainment realised only in its acceptance by the reader/hearer[4] – philosophy here becomes not a one-sided appeal to the rationality (or otherwise) of its attendee on the basis of postulated universal norms, but an integral constellation of consciousness which includes not just the philosophising subject but the philosophised-upon, as well as the historical (temporal) and material (spaciotemporal) conditions of its operation. The timespan covered by the essay ranges from 1800 to the present day, and includes philosophers of many persuasions. By drawing together a number of different thinkers, the intention is not to reduce the differences between them but rather to illustrate one way in which they may be understood as part of the phenomenon of Russian philosophy. Nor does the essay seek to perpetuate binary oppositions – the West vs. Russia – analysis vs. intuition; integrity and communality vs. atomisation and individual rights, and so on – so beloved by the generalist who adheres to one or the other camp as a leech to a syphilitic. Any typological account will necessarily lose sight of the wealth of attenuations that exist within any given tradition, as well as the fluid borders that enable cross-pollination between them.

Nevertheless, Aleksei Losev's characterisation of the Russian tradition as a form of truth-seeking not "via its reduction to logical concepts but always through the symbol or the image, by means of the power of imagination and a living, inner dynamism"[5] doubtlessly captures something of the distinctive

---

3 This directedness toward the other as the *prius* of cognition is rejected by the contrarian thinker Vasilii Rozanov. "'What business have you in *precisely what I think*," "in what way am I *obliged* to articulate my actual thoughts"? My most profound subjectivity (the pathos of subjectivity) has allowed me to live my whole life behind a *curtain*, which will not be taken down or torn to pieces.' V.V. Rozanov, 'Uedinennoe', in *Metafizika khristianstva*, Moscow, 2000, 383–451 (428). Even Rozanov's 'pathos of subjectivity' (*pafos sub'ektivnosti*) must of necessity, though, communicate with a domain outside the self, for his words, while deriving from subjectivity, can never coincide with it spatially or temporally. Even a statement of self-hiddenness appeals to an acceptance by an imagined other.
4 We leave aside for the moment the question of whether it is legitimate to consider philosophy an 'art' or a 'science', a question which has exercised Russian philosophers no less than those in the West. For two contradictory articulations, see Nikolai Berdiaev's *Smysl tvorchestva* (1914), and Shpet's *Mudrost' i razum* (1917).
5 A.F. Losev, 'Russkaia filosofiia', in *Filosofiia, mifologiia, kul'tura*, Moscow, 1991, 209–236 (213).

spirit of Russian thought, which is today in need of further elaboration. Unlike the workings of reason in the Western tradition, the particular functioning of reason in Russia suffers not so much from a deficit of investigation (although many of its aspects still await future research) as a deficit of appropriately responsive terminological figurations. Its researcher is thus forced to describe the character of its beast via an alien taxonomy, putting to use concepts such as *a priori* and *a posteriori*, potentiality or dialectics, in service of a species that may or may not prefer to be regarded from such a perspective. Or else the critic falls back on an appeal to the intuitivity of the tradition, its lack of systematisation, thinking by this that she has put an end to all talk of conceptual expressibility. Yet if the Russian contribution to poetics and philosophy of language has anything to teach us at all, it is that the human word contains within itself multiple nuances and levels, and that it can be wielded, even at the conceptual level, without a reduction of truth to a monological plane. An uttered thought is not necessarily, *pace* Tiutchev, a lie.[6]

While it is true that several words from the Russian tradition have entered common philosophical parlance – *sobornost'* being perhaps the best-known example – and that Bakhtin studies in particular has forged a compelling vocabulary of English-rooted words to render that particular thinker, there is still much work to be done. It is crucial here, especially when involved not in direct translation but rather in the broad typologisation of connected phenomena, to choose terms and conceptual clusters that are axiologically neutral, in such a way avoiding the temptation of sitting in judgment on one or the other tradition, instead aiming at the dispassionate study of distinct constellations of consciousness in the pursuit of thought. This is not to say that Russians were unconcerned with questions of value – great weight is placed by many Russian thinkers on their tradition's opposition to Western philosophy as residing outside the fullness of Truth – but that the typological terms we use to categorise the tradition should be divested, insofar as possible, of any axiological residue. The terms used here – 'pathos' and 'ethos' – are of ancient philosophical origin and, though the essay relies heavily on a Belinskian reading of pathos in distinguishing the Russian use of reason from that of Western 'ethos', it is not the intention to elevate one above the other. They are instead meant to add another tool to our potential for understanding the rich phenomenon of Russian thought in its perpetual continuities with, and divergences from, the philosophical canon of the West.

---

6   See F.I. Tiutchev's poem 'Silentium' in *Polnoe sobranie sochinenii*, Leningrad, 1957, 126.

The Condition and the Contradiction

The distinction between pathos and ethos goes back to classical rhetorics, according to which a poet or orator had a choice of two modes of presentation: "either he can appeal to his audience to view his figures in an 'ethical' way, as characterised agents, whose moral or personal qualities are presented for calm and rational assessment. Or he can aim at a more intuitive response, inducing his audience to share his figures' emotions, or to respond to the pathos of their situation, with very limited critical or ethical detachment".[7] In ethical terms, pathos was foreign to Kant's practical philosophy (not to mention his theoretical works), centred as it was around the categorical imperative, which made human feelings and desires wholly redundant in the face of the absolute duty of the moral law. Hegel was to cast a great shadow over such theories, arguing instead that "duties are drawn not from abstract moral reflection but from the concrete relations of a living social order".[8]

Even before the Hegelian philosophy became known in Russia, however, Russian thinkers were subjecting Kant to critique from a similar perspective. At the very beginning of the 1800s, Aleksandr Lubkin wrote that "it is impossible by a simple abstract concept of moral good or evil to decide what is good or evil, without penetrating into the nature of man and his natural relations in the world for which empirical knowledge of man is necessary".[9] For Lubkin, as later for Hegel, sensuality was not the enemy of reason but its necessary correlative and partner. In a similar vein, the Kantian Aleksandr Vvedenskii would at the end of the century call the "disjunction of mind and heart" the fundamental characteristic of the "intellectual climate of our age", pointing to the intractability of the problem in the Russian intellectual milieu.[10]

---

7   C. Gill, 'The Ēthos/Pathos Distinction in Rhetorical and Literary Criticism', *The Classical Quarterly*, 34, 1984, 1, 149–166 (165–166).

8   Allen W. Wood, 'Hegel's Ethics', in *Cambridge Companion to Hegel*, Cambridge, 1998, 211–233 (215). Hegel's critique of Kantian ethics was cited approvingly in Vladimir Solov'ev's encyclopaedic article on Hegel. See V.S. Solov'ev, *Filosofskii slovar'*, Rostov-na-Donu, 2000, 57–79.

9   Cited in T. Nemeth, 'Kant in Russia: the Initial Phase', *Studies in East European Thought*, 36 (1/2), 1988, 79–110 (99–100).

10 A.I. Vvedenskii, 'O vidakh very v ee otnosheniiakh k znaniiu', in *Filosofkie ocherki*, Prague, 1924, 161. For an enlightening discussion of Vvedenskii in this context, see J. West, 'Art as Cognition in Russian Neo-Kantianism', *Studies in East European Thought*, 47, 3/4, 195–223.

The rights of faith, and a Christianity of the heart, to an equal share in philosophy with reason were firmly declared by Ivan Kireevskii in *O neobkhodimosti novykh nachal v filosofii* (1856), and later developed in the Slavophile ideal of 'integral knowledge' (*tsel'noe znanie*). Kireevskii's thought on reason is far from the obscurantist position it was later to be portrayed as. Consider, for example, the following rather dense section from near the end of his article which contains the seeds of the corrective he wished to introduce to Western-style rationalism:

> Although reason is one, and its nature is one, its forms of action are different, just as its deductions are different depending on the level on which it finds itself, and on the force which impels and guides it. For this impelling and animating force derives not from thought confronting reason but from the inner condition of reason itself, and moves towards thought, in which this force finds its rest and through which it is communicated to other rational beings.[11]

Like so many Russian thinkers, Kireevskii strove to express both the unity of reason (its existence as a certain matrix, as relatedness, or the possibility of relation per se) alongside its boundless variety of manifestations. Reason is never pure, i.e. absolutely undirected or non-conformed; it is never the indifferent holder of *a priori* preconditions for cognition before all experience. It is, instead, informed and enervated by the 'level' on which it finds itself, and the 'force' that guides it. While there is but one reason, there are thus as many actualisations of it as there are individual bearers. Most crucially, according to Kireevskii, the force that animates reason is found not in thought confronting reason, i.e. in the mind's activity on itself, whereby a bifurcation emerges within consciousness – consciousness in pursuit of itself – but in its *inner condition*. Reason is revealed in its authentic aspect not through the study of itself, but rather in the living out of its movement towards rational, i.e. comprehensible, articulation. That is to say, its very being (its 'inner condition') is predicated on its self-discovery in otherness. Paradoxically, perhaps, reason is only actualised when it finds outside itself the conditions for its movement toward concrete expression ('the force that impels it', the 'level' of its operation), yet these conditions are at the same time revealed as nothing other than the law of its own *internal* movement toward this actualisation. Here, the purely internal movement of reason toward possession of absolute knowledge in the Hegelian system – in many ways the

---

11   I.V. Kireevskii, 'O neobkhodimosti novykh nachal v filosofii', in *Polnoe sobranie sochinenii*, 4 vols, Kaluga, 2006, vol I, 200–248 (246).

culmination of post-Cartesian Western systematic thought[12] – is supplemented by a particular kind of vitalism that posits the source of its drive (its 'force') somewhere 'out there'. Yet these constitute not a dual movement on the part of reason, but an integral whole; its internal condition is precisely the conjunction of internal and external causation.

To understand this more fully before progressing to a study of later Russian thought, it is instructive to cite another critic of the Western envisioning of reason, Søren Kierkegaard, who was writing during the same period as Kireevskii. In an unfinished work, fragments of which have been gathered under the title of *Johannes Climacus*, Kierkegaard explores the notion of doubt in philosophy. Opposing the immediacy of experience to the mediatedness that comes through exposing such experience to concrete expression, the Danish writer develops his argument:

> Immediacy is reality; language is ideality; consciousness is contradiction. The moment I make a statement about reality, contradiction is present, for what I say is ideality. The possibility of doubt, then, lies in consciousness, whose nature is a contradiction that is produced by a duplexity and that itself produces a duplexity [...] Reality is not consciousness, ideality no more so. Yet consciousness does not exist without both, and this contradiction is the coming into existence of consciousness and is its nature.[13]

At the core of this terse yet compelling passage is a rather novel conception of consciousness that shares much with the Russian tradition. Kierkegaard underlines, against the empiricists, that reality is never unmediated, for as soon as consciousness approaches it in the form of the word it becomes mediated through ideality. Neither, however – against the idealists – does there exist a fully autonomous sphere within consciousness (Enlightenment reason) conditioned solely by ideality, for this latter feeds off reality. Instead, human consciousness is precisely the contradiction between these two – ideality and reality – or their relation in contrariness. Importantly, Kierkegaard points to the same puzzling constellation of internal and external causation that

---

12   The principle of the autonomy of human reason, which many have seen as culminating in Hegel (the descriptor 'Panlogism' was widely used by Russian thinkers for the Hegelian system), is the distinguishing characteristic of so-called modern Enlightenment rationalism.

13   S. Kierkegaard, Philosophical Fragments. Johannes Climacus. Kierkegaard's Writings, VII, Princeton NJ, 1985, 168.

Kireevskii posits in reason: consciousness is both productive of, yet at the same time is itself produced, by the duplexity between reality and its emergence into expression. It subsists on both while itself being the relation which constellates each one. In *Philosophical Fragments*, which the author attributes to Climacus with himself as the editor, Kierkegaard develops, just as Kireevskii does, the notion of a 'condition' for all authentic truth-seeking. This condition, which he seeks to differentiate from the Socratic principle that the "truth is not introduced into [the human being] but was [already] in him" becoming actualised by a process of recollection facilitated by the teacher, can only be *given* by "the God" or "teacher".[14] Yet once this condition has been given from the "outside", Kierkegaard writes, "that which was valid for the Socratic is again valid".[15] In other words, once the condition is given, the human being moves toward truth *as if* as a discovery of its own interior yet theretofore dormant knowledge.[16] In a journal entry, Kierkegaard directly states that "faith is the condition",[17] though by "faith" he intends a meaning not wholly consonant with its conventional usage. Faith for him is "as paradoxical as the paradox"; although it is "given" in the sense of a capacity endowed by the God or teacher, it is at the same time an opening up of the interior self to truth from within.[18] Faith in this sense is a certain space, a constellation of consciousness that Kierkegaard calls a "happy passion", in which the "understanding and the paradox happily encounter each other", and the understanding, having no resources on which to draw, "steps aside" to reveal the fullness of the paradox (one of whose expressions is the contradiction between reality and ideality) which can never be possessed but only heeded.[19] The movement from the real to the ideal, the earthly to the heavenly, thus unfolds in human consciousness on the premise that the very law of this unfolding is gifted yet never owned.

It is here that we see important parallels between what Kireevskii called "believing reason" (*veruiushchii razum*), which he believed to have been approached by Schelling yet never definitively achieved, and Kierkegaardian

---

14   *Ibid.*, 9–18.
15   *Ibid.*, 63.
16   There has been much debate on whether the Kierkegaardian 'condition' is the Incarnation itself (a universal provision of the condition) or something given to each individual. See V.S. Harrison, 'Kierkegaard's "Philosophical Fragments": A Clarification', *Religious Studies*, 33, 4, 1997, 455–472 (463–67).
17   Kiekegaard, *Philosophical Fragments*, 197.
18   For an article that develops this paradoxical understanding of faith as both passive (in the sense of received) and active, see M.J. Ferreira, 'Kierkegaardian faith: the condition and the "response"', *International Journal for the Philosophy of Religion*, 28, 2, 1990, 63–79.
19   Kierkegaard, *Philosophical Fragments*, 59.

faith.[20] "To believe," wrote Kireevskii in explicitly Christian terms, "is to receive from one's heart that witness which God himself gave to His Son",[21] positing the same paradoxical convergence of faith's condition in the gift of God in the person of the Son with its issuing forth from the human heart.[22] Kireevskii contended that not only was faith compatible with reason, but that the very nature of human reason contained within itself a gravitational pull toward faith as its very ground.[23] Kireevskii is scornful of the type of reason promoted by Cartesian philosophy, with its universal *cogito* that holds equally for every individual. Believing reason, as the "concatenation of all cognitive faculties into one power, the inner integrality of mind",[24] is for him a deeply personal operation, precisely because it has its provenance in the whole human person, not merely its one faculty of logical thinking.

It was this integrality of consciousness that a thinker often regarded as belonging to the opposite camp in Russian intellectual history – Vissarion Belinskii – develops in the concept of pathos, which he borrows from Hegel's *Aesthetics*. For Hegel, pathos was "an inherently justified power over the heart, an essential content of rationality and freedom of will [...] the essential rational content which is present in man's self and fills and penetrates his whole heart".[25] An Hegelian commentator has further described it as "a passionate

---

20   Both Kierkegaard and Kireevskii are known to have attended Schelling's Lectures on the philosophy of revelation in early 1840s Berlin, both coming away with an overall negative impression (though Kierkegaard certainly the more so).

21   I.V. Kireevskii, 'Otryvki', in *Polnoe sobranie sochinenii*, 1, 181–199 (199).

22   The other convergence, which will not concern us here, is that between historical/universal revelation (the Incarnation) and personal/particular.

23   'In the fundamental depths of human reason, in its very nature, lies the possibility of consciousness of one's essential relation to God'. Kireevskii, 'O neobkhodimosti novykh nachal,' 244. The conviction, not only that some kind of accommodation between faith and reason could be found, but that the very actualisation of reason in its authentic aspect was dependent on faith, can be found in several Russian critiques of Western rationalism of this period. In a work of 1862–63, Bishop Sil'vestr (Malevanskii) writes that reason 'in its inner unity with Christian faith lost none of the legitimate rights of its rational nature. On the contrary, it acquired more, since it found in this faith that which, on its own, it had been unable to discover [...]: the fullest possible satisfaction of the demands of its own rational nature. It was not thereby demeaned, but on the contrary elevated and fulfilled.' Sil'vestr, 'Kratkii istoricheskii ocherk ratsionalizma v ego otnoshenii k vere', *Trudy Kievskoi dukhovnoi akademii*, 4, 1862, 388–432 (430). The continuation to this work was published in issues 5 (1862), 11 and 12 (1863) of the same periodical.

24   *Ibid.*, 208.

25   Hegel, *Aesthetics: Lectures on Fine Art*, vol I, Oxford, 1988, 232.

absorption in fulfilling a one-sided ethical purpose".[26] What Belinskii tries to do is free Hegel's understanding of pathos from what he saw as its one-sided rationalism. No longer is it a 'power' exercised by rationality over the heart, but the integral constellation of the entire human person in its pursuit of the ideal. Pathos, for Belinskii, is not merely an artistic *approach* whereby rationality transitions into passion (the mind of the artist 'becoming', or transitioning into, feeling) while remaining within its own domain (i.e. the universal here only offering up the *appearance* of the particular), but the guiding principle of the inner life of the artist, in which neither reason nor feeling is dominant. "In pathos," he wrote, "the poet is in love with the idea as a beautiful, living creature; he is passionately suffused with it, and he contemplates it not with reason or the intellect, not with feeling and not with any one ability of the soul, but with the entire fullness and integrity of his moral being".[27] In Belinskii's handling, pathos becomes something that possesses the artist as much as her audience, something through whose medium the meaning of a work of art appears "not as an abstract idea, not as a dead form, but as a living creation in which the living beauty of the form witnesses to the presence in it of a divine idea".[28] Like Kireevskii, Belinskii intends by his development of pathos to articulate a force that neither possesses nor is possessed, that is both rational and emotional, universal and individual. The heart is not penetrated by rationality as a one-sided diktat; rather, reason is itself transfigured in its union with the entire human person. And in such pathos, the artist confronts the idea not as a foreign object or ideal, but is suffused with it in love. This is not, as Belinskii writes in relation to Shakespeare's *Romeo and Juliet*, "merely a mutual admiring of one another" but a locatedness in the "pathos of love" which involves an "exultant, proud, ecstatic recognition of love as a divine feeling".[29] That is to say, it is a passion whose intensity is predicated on the experiential recognition of its transcendent source. To draw again on Kierkegaard, we are not talking here of a classical conception of passion as that which opposes, or even obstructs, reason, but a state of consciousness that is "its own guarantee that there is something sacred".[30] Since it refers to an external determinant, it is far from the unruly source of instability and chaos with which earlier philosophers associated the so-called 'passions', instead existing within a structure

---

26 G.R.G. Mure, *The Philosophy of Hegel*, London, 1965, 192.
27 V.G. Belinskii, *Sochineniia Aleksandra Pushkina*, Moscow, 1995, 231.
28 Belinskii, *ibid.*, 233.
29 Belinskii, *ibid.*, 232.
30 S. Kierkegaard, *Two Ages: The Age of Revolution and the Present Age, A Literary Review*, Princeton, 1978, 65.

that "integrates the personality because the self, as a synthesis of the finite and the infinite, the temporal and the eternal, is *designed* to be actualised in such a passion".[31]

It was this sense of the "pathos of love" as the meeting-place of the ideal and the real that was to be taken on several decades later by Vladimir Solov'ev, who would look to Belinskii as its originator,[32] and built into his Philosophy of All-Unity. Solov'ev took his predecessor's work on pathos in aesthetic practice and applied it more broadly to philosophy and human life itself. In some of the last words he wrote, he contended that:

> The life of the soul is not exhausted by the interplay between ideal-theoretical strivings, raising it into the intelligible realm of pure forms, and material-practical stimuli, sinking it into the dark stream of deceptive 'flux' (*byvanie*). There is in man a fact and a factor, which cannot be reduced to the material or the spiritual principle alone, but contains both indivisibly. Anyone who has experienced the quintessentially human pathos of personal love knows that one cannot attribute it in essence either to spiritual or to carnal needs, for both of these can be satisfied without this love, and that here we have to do with something particular, independent and intermediate, relating exactly neither to the one nor the other aspect of our nature, but to its wholeness, or fullness.[33]

In the pathos of love, according to Solov'ev, reason and feeling – those elements that the Russians traditionally argued Western thought had placed within a relationship of subservience and hierarchy – were balanced, neither one ascendant over the other. Reason, the domain of the universal, or the all, here enjoys an equal relationship with feeling, the realm of the particular and individual.[34]

Yet the crux of the problem, which Solov'ev himself never fully resolved, revolves around the precise nature of the Russian interpretation of 'wholeness' or All-Unity. How can the one, i.e. the particular, be included within the many

---

31 R.C. Roberts, 'Existence, emotion and virtue: Classical themes in Kierkegaard', in *The Cambridge Companion to Kierkegaard*, A. Hannay and G.D. Marino (eds.), Cambridge, 1998, 177–206 (181–182).

32 See the account of Solov'ev's 1898 speech on Belinskii in 'V filosofskom obshchestve', *Novoe vremia*, 13 Oct 1898, no. 8126, 3.

33 V.S. Solov'ev, *Sobranie sochinenii*, ed. E.L. Radlov and S.M. Solov'ev, 12 vols, Brussels, 1966–70, vol XII, 390.

34 For more on Solov'ev's elaboration of love as equality, see O. Smith, *Vladimir Soloviev and the Spiritualization of Matter*, Boston, 2011, 251–253.

without being swallowed up in the latter by the very force of its newly actualised relatedness? Will not such a synthesis be the result of concrete reasoning, a mere product of the human mind? We recall that Kireevskii spoke of the force that animates reason 'finding its rest' in concrete thought, yet how can the paradoxical convergence of the ideal and the real find 'rest' without transforming itself into a possession? Moreover, if, following Kireevskii, we are to accept a certain stratification of 'levels' of reason, will it then be possible to avoid a hierarchalisation of these levels, with the top rung occupied by what he calls 'absolute' (we might say, 'mystical') perception? If so, can we escape a gnostic model of cognition where its ideal forms are accessible only to initiates?[35]

But what if there is a way of imagining a synthesis that is less result than experience, less a static conception of actualised wholeness than a dynamic matrix of relation? And, if there is, must we admit that there will always remain a component outside the control of universal reason (or wholeness); that, in the words of the first issue of the journal *Logos* in 1910, "chaos, dark and irrational, has been set by the dark will of fate to watch everlastingly over the Russian synthesis"?[36]

The question, then, is this: is the Russian synthesis between reason and feeling to be realised in the realm of being or knowledge? Aleksei Losev once remarked that Russian philosophy is markedly and unequivocally ontological.[37] Indeed, Russians would repeatedly criticise Kant and the critical philosophy for turning being into a methodology, and reducing ontology to epistemology.[38] Instead, they sought to reforge epistemology on the ground of ontology. While for Kant, the antinomies were proof of a fundamental contradiction between the empirical and the rational, in Pavel Florenskii's thought such proof, as a product of knowledge, is itself ontologised: no longer do we have the static confrontation of thesis and antithesis but the "experience of antinomy", an experience in which the poles are given simultaneously, experiences that are "'yes' and 'no' at the same time".[39] Reason here does not confront the antinomic

---

35   From a typological perspective, an envisioning of reason that is based on hierarchy, even a hierarchy of holiness through ascesis, would seem to exclude the important strand in Russian thought that prioritises the simplicity of faith (for example, in Tolstoi or Rozanov).

36   Cited in West, 'Art as Cognition', 218.

37   See Losev, 'Russkaia filosofiia', 216–217.

38   See M.A. Meerson, '*Put*' against *Logos*: the Critique of Kant and Neo-Kantianism by Russian Religious Philosophers in the Beginning of the Twentieth Century', 47, 3–4, 1995, 225–243.

39   P.A. Florenskii, *The Pillar and Ground of Truth*, 1997, Princeton NJ, 117. The word Florenskii uses in the original is not *antinomiia* but *antinomichnost'*, stressing again the experiential

split as a division provided, or created, by knowledge. Rather, the antinomy is given as ontic foundation before it can be heeded as such by knowledge. Its givenness is thus evidence of the incapacity of rational perception to overcome it, in opposition to the Hegelian system, and calls into being a capacity to which Florenskii, like Kireevskii, gives the name 'faith'. Echoing Kierkegaard, Florenskii writes that "the ascesis of reason is faith, i.e. self-renunciation" and that this very act is the "expression of the antinomy [...] for only an antinomy can be believed".[40]

For another follower of Solov'ev, Evgenii Trubetskoi, "perception is in essence ontological: it is possible only as a result of the completely real effect of what is perceived on the mind of the perceiving subject".[41] Florenskii, too, claimed that reason never functions in an identical way since "it itself, its 'how' is defined by its object, its 'what'. The properties of reason are flexible." The object of gnoseology, then, is not to discover the nature of reason outside experience (for this is impossible) but to discover "under which conditions reason really becomes reason, where it finds its highest manifestation, where it flourishes and gives off a fragrant scent".[42]

There is therefore an immutability to individual perception in the Russian handling precisely as individual, as perception of *something*. And this 'something', moreover, presents itself as individual both in its reception (by the subject), and in its absolute reality as object.[43] Yet, as Trubetskoi argues after Kant, such perception necessarily presupposes the universal as the common ground

---

basis of antinomic being. Kierkegaard's elaboration of consciousness as contradiction again come to mind here, as does what one critic has called his 'existential transformation of Cartesian epistemology'. See A.M. Rasmussen, 'Rene Descartes: Kierkegaard's Understanding of Doubt and Certainty', *Kierkegaard and the Renaissance and Modern Traditions*, 3 vols., Farnham, 2009, I (Philosophy), 11–17 (17).

40   Florenskii, *The Pillar and Ground of Truth*, 109. Compare to Kierkegaard's description of faith: 'the understanding steps aside and the paradox gives itself'. Kierkegaard, *Philosophical Fragments*, 59.
41   E.N. Trubetskoi, *Smysl zhizni*, Moscow, 2005, 165.
42   Florenskii, 'Razum i dialektika', in *Sochineniia v 4-kh tomakh*, Moscow, 1999, vol II, 131–142 (136).
43   There are parallels here with Sartre's attempted corrective of Heidegger's *Dasein* as 'a being such that in its being, its being is in question' to 'a being such that in its being, its being is in question in so far as this being implies a being *other than itself* [my italics].' Being, in this conception, is not merely conditioned by consciousness; being itself is the conditioner, so that consciousness 'must produce itself as a revealed-revelation of a being which is not it and which gives itself as already existing when consciousness reveals it'. See Sartre, *Being and Nothingness*, London, 1996, xxxviii.

of all human perception for otherwise the world would collapse into a multiplicity of independently cognising centres.[44] Where Kant fails, for Trubetskoi, is in the insufficient distinction he draws between the self and the absolute in his theory of transcendental apperception, that act which allows the constellation of self (ideal) and world (real) with which we have thus far been concerned. For Trubetskoi, the human subject should "perceive itself *as other in relation* to the Absolute", while at the very same time "understanding the unity of the Absolute and its other in perception".[45] In other words, Trubetskoi invites us once more to inhabit the paradox: to experience oneself as separate from the absolute, yet at the same time to understand the unity of self and absolute given in cognitive experience. Here, truth judgments are still the products of consciousness, only "not the self-consciousness of the absolute in the Hegelian sense, but the self-consciousness of a cognising subject *vis-à-vis* the absolute".[46] As Meerson demonstrates, Trubetskoi is essentially here personalising Kantian epistemology: in every act of thought, it is not only the representation of the object that proceeds from the self, it is also 'my knowledge of myself', which in turn conditions the object of cognition just as much as the representation.[47] In this particular harnessing of individual perception to the universal in the realm of ontology, the connecting bridge between the two becomes not a sublimated unity of consciousness (Kant's "transcendental consciousness") but a meeting-place of non-identity in *personal* consciousness. The contradiction lies, therefore, not in the distinction between the ideal and the real, which is thereafter subsumed in identity, but in the very reaffirmation of the contradiction in the experiential evidence of its apparent removal.

The Word

In their insistence on the ontologisation of knowledge (perhaps the principal corrective they wished to introduce to the Western tradition), Russian thinkers prefigure in a number of important ways the development of continental phenomenology. For the philosopher and theologian Henry Corbin, Heidegger's

---

44 'The very act of cognition as the search for the absolute, i.e. authentic, definition of the perceived, presupposes that this perceived is defined by thinking within the Absolute.' E.N. Trubetskoi, *Metafizicheskie predpolozheniia poznaniia: Opyt preodoleniia Kanta i kantianstva*, Moscow, 1917, 20.
45 *Ibid.*, 83.
46 Meerson, '*Put*' against *Logos*', 239.
47 *Ibid.*, 239–240.

great merit was that he "centred the very act of philosophizing on hermeneutics": "what we truly understand," Corbin wrote, "is never anything but what we experience and undergo, what we suffer in our very being".[48] Corbin goes on:

> Hermeneutics does not consist in deliberating upon concepts, it is essentially the unveiling or revelation of that which is happening within us, the unveiling of that which causes us to emit such or such concept, vision, projection, when our passion becomes action, it is an active undergoing, a prophetic-*poetic* undertaking.[49]

This understanding of cognition as hermeneutics – both passive (as in the reception of the causes of experience) and active (the point where this transitions into consciousness) – leads Corbin to posit the location of such transition – the point at which, perhaps, Kireevskii's animating force of reason finds its "rest" – in the human word. In this context, he calls language an "absolutely primal act, not the decipherment of an already given and imposed text" but "the very apparition of things, their revelation by their being named".[50] This rest-revelation preserved in the word can operate, however, in different ways for different thinkers, and can be grounded, particularly in the Russian case, on the most divergent of ontologies.

For Gustav Shpet, much influenced by the German phenomenologists, the human word embodied just that non-sublimatory synthesis between the individual and universal that previous Russian thinkers had been pursuing: "Experience stops being simply 'experience' and our attention comes to rest on it as a source of knowledge, we interact with it not as a 'naked' given, but as a given necessarily clothed in the word".[51] Understood in this sense, the word for Shpet becomes the "*principium cognoscendi* of our knowledge": no longer purely subjective-individual, pure given, yet also not entirely given over to objectivity-universality. The word hovers between the subjective and objective domains while maintaining its citizenry in both. Yet, once again, we must ask ourselves what the nature of this principle is, and how it is that it becomes an

---

48   Cited in C. Bamford, 'Introduction', in H. Corbin, *The Voyage and the Messenger: Iran and Philosophy*, 1998, Berkeley CA, xiv–lx (xxxix).

49   H. Corbin, 'From Heidegger to Suhrawardi: An Interview with Phillipe Nemo,' <http://www.amiscorbin.com/textes/anglais/interviewnemo.htm> *From Heidegger to Suhrawardi* [para 12 of 56].

50   Cited in Bamford, 'Introduction', xxxviii.

51   G. Shpet, 'Mudrost' ili razum', in *Filosofkie etiudy*, Moscow, 1994, 295. See also V.N. Porus, 'Spor o ratsionalizme: Filosofiia i kul'tura (E. Gusserl', L. Shestov i G. Shpet)', in *U kraia kul'tury*, Moscow, 2008, 149–175.

object of *shared* knowledge and guarantor of a transcendental unity of experience? Must the rest at which thought arrives in the word be understood as static, a frozen form of a reason that has brought itself to a certain terminus? While he adopts the Platonic concept of *eidos* (form), Shpet seems to move away from such a conclusion when he separates the term from its belonging in the purely ideal world. For him, the eidetic world is qualified neither by ideality nor reality, but contains both in their pre-distinction:

> The form bears the characteristics of an individual, accidental thing as well as the characteristics of the idea [...] It is a materialised idea and an idealised thing, *ens fictum* [...] It is sometimes possible to fix a form, to 'stop' it, bringing it to the possibility of graphic representation and reproduction, but if in so doing we individualise it, it is destroyed as a form.[52]

Shpet argues that the eidetic aspect of the perceptible world is accessed through a particular form of "intelligible intuition" (which he distinguishes from "intellectual" and "empirical/sensual"), which in turn grounds all cognition and without which there would be only "madness". Intelligible intuition is thus the initial step in the transition toward the communicability of knowledge, or the actualisation of reason. However, crucial to understanding of Shpet's position is his argument that, although the word stands at this junction between immediate experience and its transition into knowledge, this process itself is not mediated through the word as such. "The word" does not directly relate to the object, relating to it instead only through its objective "content", which contains in itself the "meaning".[53] In this way, "ideation penetrates through experiential givenness to the eidetic object",[54] creating a superstructure of meaning that, though dynamic, is ultitmately objectified and suprapersonal.[55] Human societies then enter into interaction with the

---

52   G.G. Shpet, *Sochineniia*, Moscow, 1989, 445.
53   G.G.Shpet, 'Iazyk i smysl', <http://anthropology.rinet.ru/old/kniga1/SPETSM1.htm>, para 51 of 60.
54   G.G. Shpet, *Iavlenie i smysl*, Tomsk, 1996, 34.
55   This is why Shpet retains such a negative perspective on *mudrost'*-wisdom, which continues to direct and sustain itself in empirical reality, as opposed to *razum*-reason. See Porus, 'Spor o ratsionalizme', 171–72. A similar distaste for an abiding link with the contingencies of the empirium in the absolute realm can be observed in Evgenii Trubetskoi. In a review of Florenskii's *Stolp i utverzhdenie Istiny*, he writes: 'Antinomy and antinomism [*antinomia i antinomizm*, not *antinomichnost'* – os] are rooted in a rational (*rassudochnyi*) understanding of the world's mysteries. When we are elevated above the rational, the antinomies are resolved and the contradictions transformed into the union of opposites

'objective structure of the word', which, 'like the atmosphere of the earth, shrouds everything subjective and personal',[56] and actualises a semasiological mediation of meaning through history. The word in Shpet's understanding, then, is more aptly described as a vehicle carrying the subjective impulses of human reason through to the eidetic realm than as a bearer of these energies itself.

In Pavel Florenskii, we find something rather different. In his *U vodorazdelov mysli*, he presents the word itself as the place where the antinomic thrust of being reveals itself in its most intense aspect. The word, in his understanding, possesses both "monumentality" (*monumental'nost'*) and "susceptibility" (*vospriimchivost'*).[57] That is to say, it represents both an absolute identity with itself across all its manifestations (its universal aspect), allowing it to become comprehensible to all, but also absorbs all the attenuations, passions and characteristics of its individual practitioner. It thus displays the antinomic properties of "hardness and buoyancy, both qualities being worked over by the human spirit".[58] Otherwise put, in the word, experience is captured but not petrified: it moves with the antinomic energies of the very experience it names. The act of philosophising, which Florenskii understood as a form of art, should not therefore be defined as a "poetry of concepts" but rather as "the sculpture of the typical subjects of dialectics",[59] each word of which enters into interrelation with others, changing and modifying, ever grinding away at the hardness of the concept.

Two questions here arise: first, how can the word exhibit such contrary qualities in practical terms; and, secondly, why is it *important* that it do so? The contemporary philosopher Vladimir Bibler, whose work was geared toward the construction of a dialogics of human culture, offers intriguing answers to these questions, which resound with those of Florenskii and earlier thinkers. In one of his later works, Bibler develops his concept of the "possible" (*vozmozhnost-nost'*) as a kind of guarantor of the non-sublimation of the individual principle in the universal, forging a *via media* between the opposing poles of the rational and irrational.

   (*coincidentia oppositorum*).' See E.N. Trubetskoi, 'Svet Favorskii i preobrazhenie uma', *Voprosy filosofii*, 12, 1989, 112–29 (118). These two trends in post-Solovievian Russian thought may be understood as the bifurcation of Solov'ev's own vacillation between the poles of resolved and antinomic unity. See Smith, *Vladimir Soloviev*, 278–282.

56 G.G. Shpet, *Esteticheskie fragmenty. Svoevremennye napominaniia. Struktura slova in usum aestheticae*, Moscow, 2010, 130.

57 Florenskii, *Sochineniia*, 212–213.

58 *Ibid.*, 213.

59 Florenskii, 'Razum i dialektika', 141.

The hardness of the concept destroys individuality by regulating it. The element of the irrational destroys individuality by melting it. Only in the context of a possible concept, in the context of the pathos of understanding, the human being preserves itself and constantly strives toward the other. Mutual understanding should preserve and intensify the non-understandability (for me) of the other person (and her ideas), sharpen her mysteriousness, her personhood, her irreducibility to me and – in so doing – should preserve (in me) the thirst for full comprehension, my striving toward her.[60]

Bibler not only identifies the point where, as he writes, thought is always "on the eve of thought" (*nakunune mysli*)[61] – the possible concept – not yet a universal, but neither merely an individual possession or experience. He also adds an ethical dimension to the mix. The word for Bibler, in its on-the-eveness, its possibility, contains within itself the primacy of an appeal, a "striving toward the other", and performs a similar function to the face of the other in Levinas.[62] And it is this appeal that constitutes the specific environment of human communication through the word, what he calls the "pathos of understanding" (*pafos ponimaniia*). This pathos contains the moment of my passage into comprehensibility while never dissolving into the anonymity of universal reason, or melting away in the chaos of the irrational. Such pathos pulls in two contrary directions: towards an intuitive admission of the non-exhaustability of the other by any rational concept and at the same time towards a desire for an *absolute* comprehension of the same. In this sense, Bibler's "pathos of understanding" shares the dual aspectual wholeness of Solov'ev's "pathos of love" without reconciling the antinomic potentialities of its opposing terms into an overarching unity.

Conclusion: Pathos and the Person

It is no coincidence that, at the end of the twentieth century, Bibler was among a number of Russian philosophers who preferred to talk not of *filosofiia* (philosophy) but of *filosofstvovanie* (philosophising). Philosophy, as the concretisation of thought through language, becomes, in *filosofstvovanie*, charged with the pathos of understanding, reaching out to its attended

---

60 V. Bibler, *Vek prosveshcheniia i kritika sposobnosti suzhdeniia. Didro i Kant*, Moscow, 1997, 32.
61 V. Bibler, *Ot naukoucheniia k logike kul'ture*, Moscow, 1991, 10.
62 See E. Levinas, 'The Trace of the Other' in Taylor, M.C. (ed.) *Deconstruction in Context*, Chicago & London, 1986, 345–359.

recipient and involving them in a dialogue where thought is nothing other than the intuitive experience of a thinking-with-others in an ever-mobile historical and cultural landscape.[63] Just as the role of philosophy changes, so the role of the interpreter of philosophy (or the historian of ideas) changes with it. Bakhtin, perhaps Bibler's most prominent influence, becomes in the latter's treatment not so much the originator of the idea of dialogue as himself a dialogic partner in an everlasting hermeneutics of culture. The task for us, then, is, as Bibler writes, initiation into "the unitary *pathos* of [Bakhtin's] thought throughout his entire life".[64] This is something very different from deriving a thinker's ideas from the psychological backdrop of his or her biography. It is reading them in the pathos where their individual experience seeks universal articulation. In precisely the same way, Solov'ev would recommend that his listeners look not primarily at Belinskii's ideas but at the "pathos of his life: that which animated him and by which he lived".[65]

When Vladimir Ern contrasted Western philosophy, as defined by "rationalism and impersonalism", to the Russian tradition, as defined by "ontologism and personalism",[66] he surely paints with too broad a brush. The recovery of the ontic-ontological in Ern's own time was as much a part of the mandate of thinkers such as Heidegger as it was of the Russians. Yet the difference, perhaps, is that the Russian tradition's ontologism and personalism must be understood as parts of the same edifice. Russian thought is ontological because it is personalist, just as it is personalist precisely because it is ontological. In the Western tradition's pursuit of being at all costs, it perhaps (and here we must again do with generalisations) loses sight of the fact that consciousness of being is a revelation given not to consciousness per se, nor to consciousness as the primary matrix of being, but to a consciousness that lives only through personality. Being *is* personal. If all thought, then, emerges from the personal

---

63 'For Bibler, the essence of thinking is captured in and through an indefinite, unending cycle of questions and answers patterned now one way, now another, according to distinct 'logics' at the heart of past and present cultures, the constants of which can be brought to reflexive self-awareness in the practice of dia-logue [...] For him, philosophizing is intrinsic to what is dramatic, passionate in human engagement with the world, and is thus, by virtue of its uncompromising commitment to truth, morally charged.' Swiderski, Edward M. 'Culture, Contexts, and Directions in Russian Post-Soviet Philosophy', *Studies in East European Thought*, 50 (1998), 283–328 (289).

64 V.S. Bibler, *Mikhail Mikhailovich Bakhtin ili poetika kul'tury*, <http://www.bibler.ru/bim_bakhtin.htm#nachalo>.

65 See 'V filosofskom obshchestve', *Novoe vremia*, 1898.

66 V. Ern, *Grigorii Savich Skovoroda: Zhizn' i uchenie,* Moscow, 1912, 22.

as its ontic ground, the only way into an understanding of such thought, according to the Russians, is through the inhabiting of the pathos where such personality reaches out towards potential comprehension, while never becoming fixed in its result. It is to open ourselves as enquirers to a hermeneutics that is itself a participation in the dialogic structure of human culture. In this way, the spirit that lives in much Russian thought is not a fixed pattern (an 'ethos' that is passed on through a given canon) but a 'pathos' that perpetually treads water between the unordered irrationality of individual experience and the concordant rationality of absolute comprehension. And the history of Russian thought is one not of ideas but of persons.

Bibliography

Akhutin, Anatolii V. 1993. 'Sofiia i chert (Kant pered litsom russkoi religioznoi metafiziki)', in *Rossiia i Germaniia*, Moscow: 207–247.

Belinskii, Vissarion G. 1995: *Sochineniia Aleksandra Pushkina*, Moscow.

Bibler, V. 1991. *Ot naukoucheniia k logike kul'ture*, Moscow.

––––––1997. *Vek prosveshcheniia i kritika sposobnosti suzhdeniia. Didro i Kant*, Moscow.

–––––– Date not given by article's author. *Mikhail Mikhailovich Bakhtin ili poetika kul'tury*, http://www.bibler.ru/bim_bakhtin.htm#nachalo.

Bamford, C. 1998. 'Introduction', in H. Corbin, *The Voyage and the Messenger: Iran and Philosophy*, Berkeley CA: YaHaqq.

Corbin, H. 'From Heidegger to Suhrawardi: An Interview with Phillipe Nemo,' http://www.amiscorbin.com/textes/anglais/interviewnemo.htm *From Heidegger to Suhrawardi* [para 12 of 56].

Ern, V. 1912: *Grigorii Savich Skovoroda: Zhizn' i uchenie*, Moscow.

Ferreira, M.J. 1990: 'Kierkegaardian faith: the condition and the "response"', *International Journal for the Philosophy of Religion*, 28, 2, 63–79.

Florenskii, P.A. 1997: *The Pillar and Ground of Truth*, Princeton NJ; Princeton Univesity Press.

––––––1999. *Sochineniia v 4-kh tomakh*, Moscow.

Gill, C.: 1984. 'The Ēthos/Pathos Distinction in Rhetorical and Literary Criticism', *The Classical Quarterly*, 34, 1984, 1, 149–166.

Harrison, V.S., 1997. 'Kierkegaard's "Philosophical Fragments": A Clarification', *Religious Studies*, 33, 4, 455–472.

Hegel, G. 1988. *Aesthetics: Lectures on Fine Art*, vol i, Oxford.

Kierkegaard, S. 1978. *Two Ages: The Age of Revolution and the Present Age, A Literary Review*, Princeton: Princeton Univesrsity Press.

―― 1985. *Philosophical Fragments. Johannes Climacus. Kierkegaard's Writings*, VII, Princeton NJ. Kireevskii, I.V., 2006. *Polnoe sobranie sochinenii*, 4 vols, Kalu-ga.

Levinas, E. 1986. 'The Trace of the Other' in Taylor, M.C. (ed.) *Deconstruction in Context*, Chicago & London: University of Chicago Press. 345–359.

Lopatin, L.M. 2000. 'Uchenie Kanta o poznanii', in *Filosofskie kharakteristiki i rechi*, Minsk, 65–81.

Losev, A.F. 1991. 'Russkaia filosofiia', in *Filosofiia, mifologiia, kul'tura*, Moscow, 209–236.

Meerson, M.A. 1995. *Put'* against *Logos*: the Critique of Kant and Neo-Kantianism by Russian Religious Philosophers in the Beginning of the Twentieth Century', *Studies in East European Thought*, 47, 3/4, 1995, 225–243.

Mure, G.R.G. 1965. *The Philosophy of Hegel*, London: Oxford University Press.

Nemeth, T. 1988. 'Kant in Russia: the Initial Phase', *Studies in East European Thought*, 36 (1/2), 79–110.

Porus, V.N. 2008. 'Spor o ratsionalizme: Filosofiia i kul'tura (E. Gusserl', L. Shestov i G. Shpet)', in *U kraia kul'tury*, Moscow, 149–175.

Rasmussen, A.M. 2009. 'Rene Descartes: Kierkegaard's Understanding of Doubt and Certainty', *Kierkegaard and the Renaissance and Modern Traditions*, 3 vols., Farnham, 2009, i (Philosophy), 11–17.

Roberts, R.C. 1998. 'Existence, emotion and virtue: Classical themes in Kierkegaard', in *The Cambridge Companion to Kierkegaard*, A. Hannay and G.D. Marino (eds.), Cambridge: Cambridge University Press, 1998, 177–206.

Sartre, J-P. 1996. *Being and Nothingness*, London: Routledge and Kegan Paul.

Shpet, G.G. 1989. *Sochineniia*, Moscow.

―― 1994. 'Mudrost' ili razum', in *Filosofkie etiudy*, Moscow.

―― 1996. *Iavlenie i smysl*, Tomsk.

―― 2010. *Esteticheskie fragmenty. Svoevremennye napominaniia. Struktura slova in usum aestheticae*, Moscow.

Sil'vestr. 1862. 'Kratkii istoricheskii ocherk ratsionalizma v ego otnoshenii k vere', *Trudy Kievskoi dukhovnoi akademii*, 4, 1862, 388–432.

Smith, Oliver. 2011. *Vladimir Soloviev and the Spiritualization of Matter*, Boston: Academic Studies Press.

Solov'ev, V.S. 1966–1970. *Sobranie sochinenii*, ed. E.L. Radlov and S.M. Solov'ev, 12 vols, Brussels.

Swiderski, Edward M. 1998. 'Culture, Contexts, and Directions in Russian Post-Soviet Philosophy', *Studies in East European Thought*, 50 (1998), 283–328.

Tiutchev, F.I. 1957. *Polnoe sobranie sochinenii*, Leningrad.

Trubetskoi, E.N. 1917. *Metafizicheskie predpolozheniia poznania: Opyt preodoleniia Kanta i kantianstva*, Moscow.

―― 1989. 'Svet Favorskii i preobrazhenie uma', *Voprosy filosofii*, 12, 112–129.

———— 2005. *Smysl zhizni*, Moscow, 165.

V.V. Rozanov, 2000. *Metafizika khristianstva*, Moscow.

Vvedenskii, A.I., 1924. 'O vidakh very v ee otnosheniiakh k znaniiu', in *Filosofkie ocherki*, Prague.

West, J., 1995. 'Art as Cognition in Russian Neo-Kantianism', *Studies in East European Thought*, 47, 3/4, 195–223.

Wood, Allen W. 1998. 'Hegel's Ethics', in *Cambridge Companion to Hegel*, Cambridge: Cambridge University Press, 211–233.

CHAPTER 4

Irrationalism and Antisemitism in Late-Tsarist Literature

Christopher John Tooke

Early and mid-nineteenth century Russian literature and thought exhibited largely derivative antisemitic prejudices common to Europe as a whole. The principal Russian accusations against Jews were that they were religious fanatics who hated and considered themselves superior to non-Jews, whom they mercilessly exploited. However, from the mid-1860s and particularly the mid-1870s Russians incorporated more native elements into antisemitic strains by marrying hostility to Jews with the nationalistic-chauvinistic doctrines that were also gaining ascendancy during the period, such as pan-Slavism.[1]

A direct impetus for the development of Russian antisemitic thought was provided by the publication in 1869 of a work, *Kniga kagala* (*The Book of the Kahal*), by a Jewish renegade and convert to Russian Orthodoxy, Iakov Aleksandrovich Brafman. Brafman purported to provide evidence that the Jewish community in Russia constituted a state within a state that recognised only Talmudic law, exploiting non-Jews in accordance with its prescriptions and subverting the Russian state.[2] In fact, the ancient system of Jewish self-government to which Brafman refers, the *kahal*, had been abolished in 1844. Nonetheless, the book was so influential and its calumnies so trusted that it was even used in official state circles,[3] and it has been described as "the most successful and influential work of Judeophobia in Russian history".[4] Russian literature, including the works examined in this article, drew on and developed its accusations. Klier links Brafman's work and the furore it provoked with the rise of occult antisemitism that began in the 1870s and encompassed manifestations of antisemitism that relied not on reason and evidence, but on beliefs in "charges [that] were often fantastic, esoteric or even supernatural", such as ritual murder, the notion of the Talmud as anti-Christian, and Jewish

---

1   S. Iu. Dudakov, *Istoriia odnogo mifa*, Moscow: Nauka, 1993, 103.
2   David I. Goldstein, *Dostoyevsky and the Jews*, Austin, TX: University of Texas Press, 1981, 96.
3   *Ibid.*, 97.
4   John Klier, *Imperial Russia's Jewish Question, 1855–1881*, Cambridge: University of Cambridge Press, 1995, 281.

fanaticism.[5] He contrasts these with criticisms of Jews based on objective realities such as their concentration in tavern-keeping and petty trade.[6]

Rosenthal links the rise of occultism in Russia with the reaction against rationalism.[7] Despite the fact that the very term 'antisemitism' was invented (in 1879) to denote scientific reasons for hostility towards Jews, many leading proponents of Jew-hatred informed partly by racial 'science' in the late nineteenth century in both Western Europe and Russia adopted occultist beliefs.[8] An antisemitic myth that encompassed the occult antisemitic beliefs outlined above but was even more irrational, to the extent that it defied the whole possibility of evidence being adduced or reason being called upon to support it, developed in the last tsarist era: the notion that Jews are taking over the world and planning to enslave and destroy Gentile nations through secret international networks that are pursuing the control of political parties and governments, financial domination, the establishment of radical political groups to undermine state and society, and the moral and spiritual corruption of Gentiles.[9] Brafman had laid the groundwork for the development of this myth by portraying the *kahal* as "a manifestation of a gigantic, united, international Jewish movement", but it was only after the original publication of his book that the conspiracy took on its elaborate forms in Russia, partly inspired also by Western antisemitic publications.[10]

One can trace the world-conspiracy to ancient beliefs that Jews possess "uncanny, sinister powers" and to medieval beliefs that Jews are following a command from Satan to combat Christianity and harm Christians.[11] Yet the incorporation into anti-Jewish hostility of a belief in their manipulation of governments and infiltration of political groups was only possible in the nineteenth century. In this connection, Cohn therefore concludes that "The myth of the Jewish world-conspiracy represents a modern adaptation of [the] ancient demonological tradition".[12] In the wake of the 1905 Revolution, this perception of Jews culminated in a situation whereby "every catastrophe that

---

5   *Ibid.*, 417–18.
6   John Doyle Klier, *Russians, Jews, and the Pogroms of 1881–1882*, Cambridge: University of Cambridge Press, 2011, 6.
7   Bernice Glatzer Rosenthal, "Introduction", in *The Occult in Russian and Soviet Culture*, ed. Bernice Glatzer Rosenthal, Ithaca, NY: Cornell University Press, 1997, 1–32 (10–12).
8   Rosenthal, "Introduction", 16.
9   Klier, *Imperial Russia's Jewish Question*, 417.
10 *Ibid.*, 417, 440.
11 Norman Cohn, *Warrant for Genocide*, London: Serif, 1996, 25–26.
12 *Ibid.*, p. 26.

had befallen Russia, including the Russo-Japanese War and the Revolution of 1905, was blamed on the Satanic or demonic Jews and their henchmen".[13] *The Protocols of the Elders of Zion* (*Protokoly sionskikh mudretsov*, 1903) and the texts examined in this article draw on an age-old apocalyptic belief in the coming of the Antichrist, represented by the Jews, and an ensuing conflict between the forces of good and evil. Kellogg writes:

> The Imperial Russian radical right in general tended to view the Orthodox Christian struggle against Jewry and Freemasonry as the final battle between Christ and Anti-Christ along the lines of the last book of the Bible, Revelation. Apocalyptic anti-Semitism formed an integral component of the Imperial Russian far right.[14]

Nationalistic Russian antisemites, inspired by the messianic pretensions of pan-Slavism and related doctrines, perceived their nation as predestined to lead the battle against the Jewish threat.

Dudakov examines how the myth of the world-conspiracy was nurtured in *belles-lettres* and official circles, culminating in the publication of forged documents ostensibly constituting evidence of Jews' plans to take over the world and destroy Christian civilisation, *The Protocols of the Elders of Zion*, in the St Petersburg newspaper *Znamia* (Banner) in 1903. The *Protocols*, which were first fabricated in France at the end of the nineteenth century but were carried to and first published in Russia in a translated and modified form, were subsequently republished in various versions and translations throughout the world, winning millions of believing readers throughout the world in 1920s and 1930s. Cohn demonstrates that the *Protocols* were crucial to Nazi propaganda, and therefore to the ideology behind the Shoah.

On the one hand, the documents were intended to serve as evidence for the conspiracy to which they referred. On the other hand, the original disseminator of the *Protocols*, Sergei Aleksandrovich Nilus (1862–1929), conceded that the documents could justly be dismissed as "apocryphal". Although he pointed to the situation with Jews in the modern world as evidence for the authenticity of the *Protocols*, his principal argument for their authenticity is a circular one based on superstition. Nilus, who was a pseudo-mystic, asserted that attempting to adduce evidence such as the identity of the leaders of the conspiracy

---

13   Rosenthal, "Political Implications of the Occult Revival", in *The Occult in Russian and Soviet Culture*, 379–418 (382).

14   Michael Kellogg, *The Russian Roots of Nazism: White Émigrés and the Making of National Socialism, 1917–1945*, Cambridge: Cambridge University Press, 2005, 33–34.

would violate the "mystery of iniquity",[15] which is essential to the advent of the Antichrist and therefore, Dudakov infers, to the Second Coming. Reason thus proves inadequate to the task of understanding the conspiracy, and is denied by the pre-ordained apocalyptic plan. Nilus was therefore able to claim that it was not the documents but the teachings of the Church that constituted the most compelling attestation to the existence of the anti-Christian activity and the coming battle between good and evil. In reality, of course, the emphasis on demons and Satan takes the *Protocols* beyond church doctrine.[16] Dudakov concludes that what is at stake here is a form of "mystical-messianic" antisemitism.[17] Its adherents need not legal or other documentary evidence but only belief in a distorted interpretation of Christian teachings coupled with age-old superstitious prejudices, and in Russia's leading role in the ensuing battle with the Antichrist. In effect, not only do the *Protocols* and other texts making similar claims not appeal to reason: they require their readers to already believe in the essentials of the myth, even if the documents do flesh out those essentials. Like all conspiracies of such a scale, the Jewish world-conspiracy can be seen as ultimately immune to rational arguments against its existence; it purports to be extrarational. Thus, while rationalists in Russia were calling for all to be subsumed to reason and Russian Marxists were trying to employ reason to convince their fellow subjects of the existence of a law determining the inevitable trajectory of history, right-wing Russian antisemites were asserting that the exact nature of the most important phenomena in the world was at the present moment not meant to be known at all, whether by reason or other methods, and that revolutionary stirrings were the result not of processes that could be explained by science, but of hidden demonic forces. Antisemites were attempting to convince their countrymen that the power of reason is insufficient and inappropriate to understand a phenomenon that higher powers, including God Himself, have shrouded in secrets. While rationalists sought means to explain and order the world according to reason, antisemites resorted to pre-Enlightenment conceptions of events as preordained and beyond human will, advocating not the weighing up of evidence in order to adopt or reject beliefs based on reason but blind faith. Such antisemitism can therefore be seen as part of the discourse around rational, anti-rational and irrational modes of thought of the time, advocating the value of the *extra*rational. In this connection, Klier comments:

---

15 See 2 Thessalonians 2:7.
16 Walter Laqueur, *Black Hundred: The Rise of the Extreme Right in Russia*, New York: HarperPerennial, 1993, 150.
17 Dudakov, *Istoriia odnogo mifa*, 144–45.

Since occult phenomena are not susceptible to rational investigation, their widespread acceptance revealed a new psychological orientation as Russian society moved away from practical attempts to solve the Jewish Question.[18]

The key elements of the world-conspiracy are propagated by and developed in Vsevolod Vladimirovich Krestovskii's trilogy *Zhid idet* (*The Yid is Coming*), which has the distinction of being the longest text in Russian literature, and possibly in European literature, to feature a Jewess as its protagonist. The titles of the three novels within the trilogy are: *T'ma egipetskaia* (*Egyptian Darkness*, 1888), *Tamara Bendavid* (*Tamara Bendavid*, 1890) and *Torzhestvo Vaala* (*The Triumph of Baal*, 1891).[19] Despite the trilogy's virulent antisemitism, it portrays its heroine Tamara Bendavid, who converts to Orthodoxy in the first novel of the trilogy and escapes her family home and the Jewish community in which she has been raised, as able not only fully to take on Christian and Russian values, but also to embody these values to a far greater degree than the overwhelming majority of Russians. Her failure fully to assimilate into Russian society is a result of a combination of Russian national weakness and nefarious Jewish power: Russians fail to protect themselves and her from the Jews' pernicious influence, and as a result she falls into illness and poverty. At the very end of the trilogy she turns to her grandfather, whom she had left in the first part of the trilogy, for financial assistance. Krestovskii never finished the final part. Overwhelmed with work after being appointed editor and publisher of *Varshavskii dnevnik* (*Warsaw Journal*) in 1892, his plans to return to it were interrupted by his death.[20] Consequently, the reader is left wondering whether reconciliation between Tamara and her grandfather does indeed occur.

Krestovskii was born near Kiev into a family from the minor nobility.[21] He published both poetry and prose in the late 1850s and early 1860s, when Dostoevskii grew fond of him, impressed by his works' sympathy for the poor.

18 Klier, *Imperial Russia's Jewish Question*, 417.
19 Bibliographical details for the editions used are as follows: V.V. Krestovskii, *T'ma egipetskaia* (hereafter, *TE*), in Krestovskii, *T'ma egipetskaia. Tamara Bendavid. Torzhestvo Vaala. Dedy* (Moscow: Kameia, 1993), 2 vols, I (*T'ma egipetskaia. Tamara Bendavid*), 3–256 (29); *Tamara Bendavid* (hereafter, *TB*), in Ibid., 1, 257–589; *Torzhestvo Vaala* (hereafter, *TV*), in Ibid., II (*Torzhestvo Vaala. Dedy*), 3–224.
20 Iu.L. Elets, "Posleslovie", in V.V. Krestovskii, *Sobranie sochinenii*, ed. Elets, 8 vols, St Petersburg: Obshchestvennaia pol'za, 1899–1900, VIII, 488–89 (488).
21 Grazyna Lipska Kabat, "Vsevolod Vladimirovich Krestovsky", in *Dictionary of Literary Biography, Volume 238: Russian Novelists in the Age of Tolstoy and Dostoevsky*, ed. J. Alexander Ogden and Judith E. Kalb, Detroit, MI, and London: Gale Group, 2001, 144–53 (145).

Dostoevskii influenced Krestovskii's interest in *pochvennichestvo* (the conservative native-soil movement) and his treatment of subjects such as the mending of the rift between the intelligentsia and the people.[22] However, their relationship later cooled for non-ideological, personal reasons.[23] Krestovskii's blanket portrayal of all those Russians belonging to the upper classes in his best-known novel *Peterburgskie trushchoby* (*The Slums of St Petersburg*, 1864–66) as corrupt, depraved scoundrels (with the poor as their innocent victims) reveals a tendency towards gross generalisations and a scathing attitude towards his own kind. Other trends evident in both *Zhid idet* and the earlier novel are Krestovskii's pessimistic depiction of the evil characters' inevitable victory over the good ones, and his sympathetic portrayal of the plight of women. Until the early 1860s Krestovskii was moving principally in radical circles, but after the Polish Uprising of 1863 his alliance was firmly with the conservative camp.[24] Some of the components of his new position are evident in his novel *Krovavyi puf* (*The Bloody Bluff*, 1869–74), which he wrote in reaction to the Uprising, and in which he accuses Poles of Russophobia and of attempting, in collusion with Russian nihilists, to undermine Russian state and society. He also reproaches his former radical comrades for what he perceives as shame at their nationality in their sympathy for the Polish cause.

The Yid is Coming is the product of the growing antisemitism in the Russian Empire of the era, and also, more generally, of Russian nationalism and xenophobia following the Russo-Turkish war of 1877–78. While many found the work to be of low artistic merit and unrealistic, others, such as a critic for *Russkii vestnik*, found it to be an accurate representation of the reality of Jewish dominion and saw in it the writer's profound experience with and knowledge of Jews.[25] Krestovskii wrote the trilogy partly based on his impressions from his post as state war correspondent, which he gained following a distinguished career in the army that he had begun in 1868 as a non-commissioned officer.[26] Set in the late 1870s and early 1880s, the trilogy amounts to an anti-radicalist, antisemitic and Russian nationalist tract in the guise of a historical novel. Apart from Jews, Krestovskii inveighs against all the European nations that feature in the work, but particularly against Poles. One of the trilogy's main plotlines is the takeover of Russia by Jews, who manipulate all spheres of life

---

22 *Ibid.*, 147.
23 *Ibid.*, 149.
24 *Ibid.*, 148–49.
25 Anonymous, "Novosti literatury. Vs. Vl. Krestovskii. *T'ma egipetskaia. Tamara Bendavid*", *Russkii vestnik*, 10 (1890), 240–43.
26 Lipska Kabat, "Vsevolod Vladimirovich Krestovsky", 150.

to their own financial and political ends, ruthlessly exploiting and ruining Russians of every class in their attempts to weaken Russian state and society and wrest power for themselves. Krestovskii's trilogy reflects his own views on Jews, encapsulated in a letter of 1879 in which he describes Jewish economic and political dominance and the Jewish 'race's' attack on what he terms the Indo-European 'race' throughout Europe and America, which has led to the Indo-Europeans' degeneration while the Jews stand firm: "We have grown flabby, descended into dissipation, become some kind of milksops. And all the while the Yid stands strong – strong, first, through the power of his faith, and, second, through the physiological potency of his blood".[27] In the trilogy as in the letter, Krestovskii's attack on Jews combines long-established superstitious anti-Judaic myths with arguments from the discourse of modern, ostensibly scientific racial antisemitism.[28]

In *T'ma egipetskaia*, Krestovskii puts pronouncements about Jews' mission of world domination into a programmatic speech to an audience of eminent Jews by a prominent rabbi, Ionafan. He exhorts his audience to act on their convictions of racial superiority over and their racial hatred of Gentiles, spurring them on to continue their battle against Gentiles for Jewish world domination in accordance with the principle that "the task and final goal of Jewry is dominion over the entire world".[29] Jews are to achieve their goal of world domination principally through acquiring wealth, and through taking over journalism, the law and armies, following the principle "Not by iron but by gold; not by the sword, but by the pocket".[30]

Krestovskii bolsters the rabbi's venomous words with footnoted references to the Bible and the Talmud. The events of the trilogy, many of which are presented as actual occurrences in recent history, constitute the fulfilment of the plans promoted by the rabbi and other leading Jews. Krestovskii's approach therefore purports to represent actual Jewish beliefs and historical facts faithfully. He does not resort to the approach of writers such as Nilus of attributing the growing Jewish power to demonic forces, even though the actual manifestations of this growing power are more or less identical to those in the *Protocols*.

Krestovskii leaves no doubt that the reader is to trust his heroine's judgements as those of an intelligent, sensitive human being of tremendous

---

27   Quoted in Iu. L. Elets, "Biografiia Vsevoloda Vladimirovicha Krestovskogo", in Krestovskii, *Sobranie sochinenii*, I, iii–lv (xxxvii).

28   For an outline of Krestovskii's life discussing his views and works (including *Zhid idet*) from the perspective of his antisemitism, see Dudakov, *Istoriia odnogo mifa*, 118–30.

29   Krestovskii, TE, I, 29.

30   TE, 31.

willpower and valour with a profound capacity for love. Through her, the writer establishes Judaism as a religion that prescribes the tyranny of the upper classes and religious leaders over the lower classes through the kahal. Tamara's perception of the Jewish leadership's tyranny relates, first, to her conception of Judaism's oppressive, "dry" formalism,[31] and, second, to Jews' practical and rational prioritisation of the material over the spiritual, a stance that endorses their lust for enrichment. Just as the Jewish leadership dominates Jews through its self-interested rulings, so Judaism itself oppresses Jews with its excessive laws. Tamara complains to the Christian with whom she has fallen in love, Karzhol': "I'm suffocated by this Jewishness...I long for light and freedom!"[32] Jewish tyranny is associated with the rational prioritisation of the material because the community leaders, as well as successful Jews in Russia living outside Jewish communities, thrive through exploitation.

Tamara shows that Jewish rationality is a form of oppression in itself, working on an individual basis by subjugating not only Jewry as a whole, but also each individual Jew's mental processes and emotions. When Tamara is discussing with Karzhol' the reasons for and against her conversion, the narrator explains:

> Tamara's heart and soul had already long ago begun to incline towards her friend's side in the argument. Even earlier his arguments had been closer to her heart than those of her own reasoning, which were derived from the practical morality governing Jewish personal relations and customs, and which were built on the consciousness of the terrible oppression with which the *kahal* fetters the life, will and thoughts of every Jew.[33]

One reason for Tamara's conversion, then, is the desire to escape the stifling rationality of the Jewish mentality, which operates on the basis of venal, self-interested reason, as opposed to the faith and love central to Christianity.

Christianity represents the opposite of this way of thought, offering the chance for love for others to guide one's actions and thereby promising freedom and the capacity for moral choices rather than rational, practical decisions that put material considerations and the laws of one's faith above all others. Tamara explains that she came to the conclusion that Christianity was superior to Judaism not through logical reasoning, so anathema to the spirit of

---

31 Tamara asserts that Christianity is "in its idea broader, more loving, more human. In a word, it's higher than Judaism". See Krestovskii, TE, 39.
32 *Ibid.*, 40.
33 *Ibid.*, 38.

Christianity, but through her heart. She compares her discovery of her faith based on a reading of the Gospels to the experience of the women standing by the cross at Golgotha who came to believe through their hearts.[34] Krestovskii, having employed old anti-Judaic accusations that Judaism is a religion bound by laws and devoid of spiritual content, now enhances his criticism of Judaism by depicting genuine Christian faith as Judaism's maximal opposite.

A comparison with Dostoevskii is fruitful here. Krestovskii's representation of Jewry and Judaism contains the essential elements, blown up out of all proportion, of Dostoevskii's image of the Church in Western Europe using tyranny to force its adherents into unity with one another and with itself, and into obedience with its decrees.[35] While true Christianity for Dostoevskii and for Slavophiles involves the submission of reason to faith and love, the essence of Judaism according to Krestovskii consists in the destruction of true faith and love through demanding rigid adherence to laws and terrified obedience to what Krestovskii depicts as the Jews' equivalent of the Church, the *kahal*. Unlike Dostoevskii in his *Dnevnik pisatelia* (*Diary of a Writer*), Krestovskii delves deep into the psychology of Judaism as he sees it, rather than just offering an account from the outside. In this way, he relates Judaism to themes dear to Dostoevskii such as the idea of personal freedom. Tamara attains freedom as Dostoevskii might have liked her to: not through rational, external actions, but through instinct and faith; not through comfortable decisions protected by law, but through decisions that rob her of an easy life and the protection of her family, and for which she suffers. The sense of freedom with which Christianity endows Tamara is fundamentally irrational, depending as it does on faith rather than fiat, and on the renunciation of self-interest in pursuit of higher goals.

The quintessentially Russian element in the equation lies not in Krestovskii's depiction of Judaism, which is unoriginal from the European point of view, apart from in its incorporation of the *kahal*. Instead, it lies in Krestovskii's depiction of Judaism as the diametrical opposite of ideal Christian faith, as defined in terms of what Russian thinkers such as Dostoevskii had long ago established as quintessentially Russian: faith based not on reason and coercion, but on the spirit, love and instinct. A fundamental aspect of this faith is

---

34   *Ibid.*, 142.

35   Within *Dnevnik pisatelia* (*Diary of a Writer*), see, for example, F.M. Dostoevskii, *Polnoe sobranie sochinenii* (hereafter Dostoevskii, *PSS*), ed. G.M. Fridlender, 30 vols, Leningrad: Nauka, 1972–90, XXV, 7, where Dostoevskii compares Catholicism with French socialism. On this matter, see also Sarah Hudspith, *Dostoevsky and the Idea of Russianness: A new perspective on unity and brotherhood*, London: RoutledgeCurzon, 2004, 70–72.

its irrationality. Russian concepts of rationalism and irrationalism are therefore essential to Krestovskii's denigration of Judaism.

I shall now discuss how another cluster of related aspects of Dostoevskii and Krestovskii's conception of Russian irrationalism relates to Krestovskii's antisemitic ideology as expressed in his trilogy: the humility of the Russian people; its closeness to spiritual truth, unfettered by the constraints of reason; the need for unity between the people and other social classes; and the people's voluntary submission to the collective, the Church and the tsar. Krestovskii uses his semi-fictionalised account of the Russo-Turkish war – in which Tamara is serving as a sister of mercy – to show how the tsar can give courage to and unite the common Russian people, even when they are in a state of utter dejection from the physical and spiritual trials of the battlefield.[36] Tamara's observation of wounded soldiers' reactions to Alexander II's visit to their tent leads her to understand the power inherent in the unity between the people and the tsar. Dostoevskii in his *Diary of a Writer* lent this force historical significance by asserting that the historical decisions in Russia have always been based on such a unity.[37] Krestovskii follows the same ideology, demonstrating that unity between the people and the tsar is vital to the pursuit of Russian national goals. Krestovskii's insistence that it is Tamara's Christianity that allows her this insight completes her conversion both to Christianity and to Russian nationhood.

The tsar's infection of the soldiers with courage is irrational. Apart from religious faith, it relies on other notions that are hardly in keeping with West European rationalism, such as love for and absolute obedience to a patriarchal authority figure. It is the polar opposite of the rational pursuit of self-interest: in essence, it is self-sacrifice for the sake of one's leader and the group to which one belongs. This self-sacrifice is based on humility, specifically, on the idea that one has no worth as an individual, but only as part of a group and through one's capacity to serve others. Krestovskii codes the war as a battle between Russian high morality and irrationalism, and Jewish rational exploitativeness by accusing Jewish companies of exploiting Russian soldiers through selling them essential but poor-quality goods at inflated prices.[38] Jewish rational avariciousness therefore directly threatens Russians' pursuit of moral goals rooted in irrationality. However, while Dostoevskii posits Russians as the saviours of all humankind, Krestovskii demonstrates in his novel that all other nations, even supposedly brotherly ones like the Bulgarians, are at best indifferent to

---

36   Krestovskii, *TE*, 390–91.
37   Dostoevskii, *PSS*, XXV, 70.
38   Krestovskii, *TB*, 360.

and at worst enemies of Russia. What is presented at the beginning of the novel as a Jewish conspiracy against the whole world begins in the course of the novel to look more like a conspiracy led by the Jews in collusion with other nations against Russia alone.

Krestovskii also shows the negative side of Russian irrationalism. While the Russian people in Krestovskii's conception is immensely powerful through its capacity for love, faith and self-sacrifice, it is also fragile: it depends on the existence of an idea to fight for, and on the tsar's guiding fatherly hand. After the war, with the country at a low ebb, Tamara takes a job as a schoolteacher in a village. Together with his mainly Jewish cronies, the Polish-Jewish "magnate" Agronomskii has the whole region in his corrupting hands. He has in effect enslaved most of the region's inhabitants by turning them into drunkards, forcing them into debt, and impoverishing them to such a degree that disease is rife. He restricts Tamara's teaching of religious subjects and Russian history, and imposes a radical curriculum that promotes class resentment.

According to father Makarii, a character who is such a mentor to Tamara that she considers him her father,[39] it is the lack of unity in the Russian nation and the absence of an idea to fight for that have allowed Agronomskii to debauch the locals.[40] However, behind the people's dejection and apathy Tamara detects the very closeness to the spirit of Christianity that Dostoevskii believed the Russian *narod* (common people) had preserved to a greater extent than probably any other people (and certainly more than the Russian intelligentsia),[41] and which Dostoevskii asserted would ultimately save the *narod* from Jewish dominion.[42] Moreover, Tamara does find people of exceptional resolve and religious faith such as father Makarii and some peasant mothers, and there is some resistance among the locals to Agronomskii's atheist, anti-tsarist curriculum.

The problem with the bulk of the Russian people for Krestovskii is that, as Dostoevskii also conceded, it has a tendency towards vice and dejection. In the absence of unity and an ideal to work towards, the peasant's life lacks meaning: he has neither the sense of self-worth nor the rational, individualistic desire to pursue his own betterment, and therefore finds solace for his despondency in drink and depravity. In this sense, the people's irrationalism is both its moral and spiritual core under ideal conditions, and the cause of its downfall when times are bad. The fact that irrationalism makes the people vulnerable partly

---

39 Krestovskii, *TV*, 93.
40 *Ibid.*, 67.
41 Dostoevskii, *PSS*, XXV, 68–69.
42 Dostoevskii, *PSS*, XXI, 95.

explains the need for an autocratic regime in Russia. On the one hand, the people's irrationalism allows it to unite with the tsar and reach a consensus, giving it the qualities it needs to fight for Russia. On the other hand, in times where there is a lack of unity within the Russian nation as a whole, and specifically between the people and the tsar, the people's irrationalism works against it and it actually needs the tsar to guide it away from the dark paths its irrationalism is prone to lead it down.

The very rational thinking that characterises the Jewish religion as conceived in the first part of the novel is the ideal that lies behind the radical political belief that Jews propagandise in the last part. Such thinking transfers easily from the sphere of religious thought to that of political thought. It is now that the reader sees the true extent of the destructive power of Jewish rationalism, regardless of whether it is a cover for religious fanaticism and an obsessive sense of racial superiority. The reader also comes to understand how this rationalism is able to bring down the people so thoroughly – through attacking those qualities that derive from its greatest weakness in times of disunity, its irrationalism. It is telling that Krestovskii's Jews have won over the higher classes, especially the bourgeoisie, through pandering to their more rational, self-seeking and materialistic ideals. Such an approach is far less successful with the people, but the people's moral stultification and their authorities' corruption by the Jews means that it matters little whether the people resists political indoctrination. While it is the Russian bourgeoisie and the authorities whom Krestovskii presents as the most depraved, his trilogy leaves little hope that the people, for all its irrational and powerful spiritual strength, can fight off Jewish dominion without unity with right-thinking higher classes and authority. It is the Jews in Krestovskii's trilogy who prove themselves worthy of the status of a great nation, and, ironically, this may be one of the reasons why Krestovskii makes his heroine Jewish – although even her attempts to combat Jewish domination ultimately fail.

While Krestovskii can be considered to have used modes of writing and of providing evidence for his accusations that at least claimed to be based on reason and objective observation, Kryzhanovskaia was such a convinced adherent of spiritualism and the irrational that she claimed that many of her works were dictated to her by the spirit of the English poet Count J.W. Rochester (1647–80).[43] Her works, variously written in French and Russian, consisted principally of historical and occult novels. Many of the latter presaged apocalyptic

---

43   See A.I. Reitblat, "Kryzhanovskaia, Vera Ivanovna", in P.A. Nikolaev, *Russkie pisateli 1800–1917: bibliograficheskii slovar'*, 5 vols, Moscow: Bol'shaia Rossiiskaia Entsiklopediia, 1989–2007, III (1994), 173–74 (173–74).

battles between good and evil as a result of the decline of faith and morality among Europeans and the rise to power of Masons, Jews and other "foreigners" and advocates of liberalism and capitalism. Although her historical novels won her the title of officer of the French Academy,[44] Kryzhanovskaia was ignored or ridiculed by "serious" Russian critics, and she published most of her works in right-wing journals and newspapers.[45] Occult journals typically commended and trusted her occult insight and the chauvinistic views for which they frequently served as a vessel.

In her short story 'Na Moskve: Son v oseniuiu noch'' ('On the Moscow River: An Autumn Night's Dream', 1906), Kryzhanovskaia, appalled by the revolutionary upheaval of 1905 and the resulting October Manifesto, gives a similarly scathing indictment of the Russian nation's present state to Krestovskii, while attesting to her people's being chosen by God and to the demonic exterminatory power of Jewry. As in *The Yid is Coming*, what had originally been conceived by Russian antisemites as a world-conspiracy is presented in the story in narrower terms as a conspiracy against Russia. However, unlike Krestovskii's novel, the story explicitly portrays violence against Jews as the only way that Russians can counter the Jewish threat. Indeed, both Kryzhanovskaia's 'On the Moscow River' and her novel *Mertvaia petlia* (*Death Loop*), also published in 1906, constitute maximally antisemitic, reactionary tracts that equate the genocide of Jewry in Russia with ridding the country of the Antichrist and the only way that Russians can save themselves from obliteration. They support the worldview and promote the activities of state-supported antisemitic groups such as Soiuz russkogo naroda (SRN, Union of the Russian People). Established in November 1905, the SRN perceived the October Manifesto to constitute a "Judeo-Masonic constitution", and sets itself the goals of fighting reform and revolution and defending the monarchy, Russian Orthodoxy and the empire.[46] Among its supporters was Nicholas II.[47] While figures in the SRN called variously for severe restrictions on Jewish rights, internal exile, expulsion and extermination, Kryzhanovskaia sees the only solution in the last of these measures.[48] 'On the Moscow River' constitutes propaganda for the pogroms

---

44   Dudakov, *Istoriia odnogo mifa*, 175.
45   *Ibid.*, 174.
46   Hans Rogger, *Jewish Policies and Right-Wing Politics in Imperial Russia*, Berkeley and Los Angeles: University of California Press, 1986, 200. William Korey, *Russian Antisemitism, Pamyat, and the Demonology of Zionism*, Chur: Harwood Academic Publishers, 1995, p. 1.
47   Jonathan Frankel, *Crisis, Revolution, and Russian Jews*, Cambridge: Cambridge University Press, 2009, 60.
48   Rogger, *Jewish Policies*, 227.

that had reached unprecedented levels of bloodshed in 1905. It is telling to contrast the context of the publication of Kryzhanovskaia's work with that of Krestovskii's novel. The original publication of *The Yid is Coming* in the journal *Russkii vestnik* (*The Russian Herald*) had been broken off after a mere two instalments precisely because the journal's editor, M.N. Katkov, had feared provoking further violence following the assassination of Alexander II and the outbreak of pogroms in 1881.[49] Kryzhanovskaia's story therefore reflects the development of antisemitic propaganda from accusations of Jewish conspiracies in the late nineteenth century that held back from promoting agonistic measures to combat them, to the programmatic propaganda openly intended to provoke violence of the early 20th century. In this connection, Kellogg writes:

> At the height of their powers immediately following the 1905 Revolution, Imperial Russian far rightists, most notably members of the Soiuz Russkogo Naroda [...] disseminated their anti-Western, anti-socialist, and anti-Semitic message to the broad masses far more effectively than pre-World War I *völkisch* Germans ever did.[50]

Kryzhanovskaia depicts the conflict between Orthodox Russians and Jews in terms that Kellogg identifies as central to the radical right's worldview: as "the final battle between Christ and Anti-Christ".[51] While on the one hand, Kryzhanovskaia's story appears intended to provoke certain actions on the part of its readers, on the other hand, it also suggests that divine intervention will play a far greater role in the battle between good and evil than human agency.

Unlike Krestovskii, Kryzhanovskaia foresees a solution to what she portrays as the Jewish takeover of Russia, and, moreover, sees it in something that is probably more irrational than anything that either of the other two writers dreamt up: a miracle. The very form of the work attests to its irrational essence: it comprises a series of visions, presumably from a prophet, a role in which the spiritualist was prone to cast herself. In the tale, a beautiful Russian woman, representing "mother Russia", is about to be quartered in the Kremlin by an axe-wielding executioner. A crowd of Russians from both the high and low classes, all visibly patriotic devotees of Russian Orthodoxy and many of whom are fighters from battles fought centuries ago who have risen from the dead,

---

49 Dudakov, *Istoriia odnogo mifa*, 126.
50 Michael Kellogg, *The Russian Roots of Nazism: White Émigrés and the making of National Socialism 1917–1945*, Cambridge: Cambridge University Press, 2005, 19.
51 *Ibid.*, 33.

watch in horror, crossing themselves and praying. Another crowd arrives on the scene, swearing and blaspheming. Although presumably many of the members of the mob are Russians, they are led by "repulsive beings" identified as Jews by their "hooked noses and impudent, predatory eyes", who "intoxicate" their followers into shouting: "Down with the cross!...Down with faith!...Down with the Motherland, honour and duty! Let chaos and sedition reign! Our dominion has arrived..."[52] Suddenly, at what seems like the last moment for the Russian woman and therefore for Russia, a knell rings out across the city from the Tower of Ivan the Great, and the crowd of tearful Russian Orthodox martyrs rush to save the woman. Ivan IV rises from the dead and condemns those Russians who, "like Judas sold Christ", are selling their mother, "Holy Rus'". He is followed by armies of self-sacrificing fighters from Russian history and Peter I. The executioner, prompted by a Jew who continues to incite people against God and their land and into revolution, raises the axe, only to be disturbed by the appearance of Alexander Nevskii wielding a sword of fire. The Russian martyrs rush to pour healing ointment on the woman's wounds, and the traitors disperse. Kryzhanovskaia constitutes the ensuing battle between Russians and Jews as one between the forces of light and the forces of darkness, giving the final words in the story to Nevskii: "Our battle, my brothers, will be a battle between Light and Darkness. United and valiant we enter the fight for the salvation of the Motherland and the Orthodox faith..."[53] Kryzhanovskaia thus reverses imagery of the revolutionary period depicting state-sponsored violence against the Russian people: she portrays the state as the people's defenders, and places in the role of the perpetrators of violence a group widely considered to be victims of it – the Jews.

The emphasis on suffering and fighting for one's country is to be found probably in all mythologies of national mission and messianism. However, there are four main aspects of Kryzhanovskaia's conception of the Russian national mission in the work that make it specifically Russian. First, the glorification of Russian victories in battle; second, the professed need for unity between the tsars and the *narod*; and third, the depiction of Russia as an ethnically marked mother figure suffering and calling for suffering in her name: "Like a pack of hungry dogs they surrounded a woman of majestic, heavenly beauty. Her face was deathly pale, and in her large, calm grey eyes – humble

---

52 V.I. Kryzhanovskaia, "Na Moskve: Son v osenniuiu noch'", in I.V. Rochester (Kryzhanovskaia's pseudonym), *Spasenie. Trilogiia: roman, son v osenniuiu noch' i skaz*, compiled and ed. by V.P. Koval'kov, Moscow: Pravoslavnaia Russkaia Akademiia i VselaSvetnaia Gramota, 2004, 153–59 (155).

53 *Ibid.*, 159.

and clear *Slavonic* eyes – one saw spiritual torment..."[54] Fourth, sexual antisemitism, which draws on the notion of Jews as a predatory sexual threat, is used in the story to draw out the spiritual qualities of the Russians through contrasting them with the animal-like, materialistic, greedy Jews.[55] In this connection, Kellogg contends that this emphasis on Russian spirituality is a central feature of Russian nationalism, particularly those strains informed by antisemitism:

> In a manner similar to anti-Semitic *völkisch* German theorists who argued that the German possessed the heroic capability to achieve redemption by denying the will to live, Imperial Russian conservative revolutionaries used concepts of superior Russian or Slavic spirituality to further their anti-Western, anti-socialist, and anti-Semitic arguments. Russian far rightists also propagated apocalyptic notions of Europe's imminent demise largely through the agency of the Jews.[56]

The 'Russianness' of the national mission distinguishes it from national ideologies that locate a nation's mission in its benefit to other nations. One might expect a battle between light and darkness to have significance for the whole of humankind, given the belief of many leading Russian writers and thinkers that Russians had a universal mission.[57] However, no such national mission features in 'On the Moscow River' or in *Death Loop*. In 'On the Moscow River', by referring to the resurrected fighters and their battles, Kryzhanovskaia places the clash between Russians and Jews in the context of other more earthly battles fought for the sake of Russia and its people, rather than for the benefit of other nations.[58] Moreover, Russians are explicitly told by Nevskii to fight for the salvation of their motherland and Orthodoxy. Kryzhanovskaia's conception of Russia's national mission is therefore limited only to Russians. With

---

54   *Ibid.*, 156. See Joanna Hubbs, *Mother Russia: The Feminine Myth in Russian Culture*, Bloomington and Indianapolis, IN, 1988, xv: "as the Russia who calls for self-sacrificing champions, [Russia as motherland] also represents suffering and constraint".
55   On the role of sexuality in West European and Russian antisemitism, see Laura Engelstein's chapter 'Sex and the Anti-Semite: Vasilii Rozanov's Patriarchal Eroticism', in Engelstein, *The Keys to Happiness: Sex and the Search for Modernity in Fin-de-Siècle Russia*, Ithaca and London: Cornell University Press, 1992, 299–333.
56   Kellogg, *The Russian Roots of Nazism*, 30–31.
57   One recalls, for example, Dostoevskii's championing of Russians as pan-human and as destined to unite humankind in brotherhood in his "Pushkin Speech" of 1880. See Dostoevskii, *PSS*, XXVI, 129–49.
58   Kryzhanovskaia, "Na Moskve", 158.

Kryzhanovskaia we are clearly dealing with nationalist messianism, not universalist messianism.[59] She is concerned not with advocating the notion that Russians suffer for the salvation of all humankind, or even that Russians constitute a model nation that others should follow. Her paean to the ordinary people who have sacrificed their lives fighting for Russians fades into insignificance in the light of her demonstration of the power of the Russian state.

In context, the intervention of the two tsars and Nevskii heralding the salvation of Russia appears messianic, given that Russia's very existence is at stake. In this connection, Kryzhanovskaia's portrayal of Russians enslaved by Jews amounts to a Russian nationalist equivalent of Dostoevskii's image in his *Diary of a Writer* of the nations brought down by the Jewish Messiah's sword and sitting at Jews' feet.[60] The threat to Russia's existence gives one the impression that the country is at the edge of time itself, and the intervention appears both to rescue it from the abyss, and to herald a new, better era, even if this era constitutes a return to the country's glorious past rather than the consummation of Russian history. This aspect of the story, together with the rising of the dead, the judgments pronounced upon Russians, and the sense that there is a group of the elect, gives the work an eschatological dimension. By invoking a catastrophe of this scale and providing it with a transcendental resolution, Kryzhanovskaia uses irrational ideas, first, to bolster her antisemitism to the utmost degree by rendering Jewry an evil force, and, second, to firmly wrestle the mantle of messianic status from Jewish hands.

If one considers rationalism to refer to "the view that reason as opposed to, say, sense experience, divine revelation or reliance on institutional authority, plays a dominant role in our attempt to gain knowledge",[61] then Kryzhanovskaia's antisemitic tract may constitute a maximally irrational form of antisemitic propaganda, its contents being "revealed" in a vision. However, from the point of view of rational thinking there is little significant difference between the beliefs about Jews that Kryzhanovskaia and Krestovskii call on their readers to adopt. Krestovskii's Jews may be more earthly but they still effectively possess superhuman powers. Like many of their contemporaries, the two writers exploited society's growing interest in the irrational and the occult, as well as myths of Russian national 'irrationalism', to peddle antisemitic ideas. However, one must not lose sight of the fact that such ideas could gain acceptance only in the presence of amenability not only to irrational ideas, but also to ideologies of

---

59 On the distinction, see Duncan, *Russian Messianism*, 3.
60 Dostoevskii, PSS, XXV, 82.
61 Peter J. Markie, "Rationalism", in *Routledge Encyclopedia of Philosophy*, ed. Edward Craig, London: Routledge, 1998, 10 vols, VIII, 75–80 (75).

intolerance and hatred, and that no matter how prevalent themes of rationalism and irrationalism are in the works I have discussed, what is primary is animosity towards outsiders.

Bibliography

Anonymous. 1890. 'Novosti literatury. Vs. Vl. Krestovskii. T'ma egipetskaia. Tamara Bendavid', in *Russkii vestnik*, 10, 240–43.

Cohn, Norman. 1996. *Warrant for Genocide*. London: Serif.

Dostoevskii, F.M. 1972–90. *Polnoe sobranie sochinenii*, ed. G.M. Fridlender, 30 vols. Leningrad: Nauka.

Dudakov, S. Iu. 1993. *Istoriia odnogo mifa*. Moscow: Nauka.

Duncan, Peter J.S. 2000. *Russian Messianism*. London and New York: Routledge.

Elets, Iu.L. 1899–1900. 'Biografiia Vsevoloda Vladimirovicha Krestovskogo', in V.V. Krestovskii, *Sobranie sochinenii*, ed. Elets, 8 vols, I, iii–lv. St Petersburg: Obshchestvennaia pol'za.

—— 1899–1900. 'Posleslovie', in V.V. Krestovskii, *Sobranie sochinenii*, ed. Elets, 8 vols, VIII, 488–89. St Petersburg: Obshchestvennaia pol'za.

Engelstein, Laura. 1992. *The Keys to Happiness: Sex and the Search for Modernity in Fin-de-Siècle Russia*. Ithaca and London: Cornell University Press.

Frank, Joseph. 2002. *Dostoevsky: The Mantle of the Prophet, 1871–1881*. Princeton, NJ, and Oxford: Princeton University Press.

Frankel, Jonathan. 2009. *Crisis, Revolution, and Russian Jews*, Cambridge: Cambridge University Press.

Goldstein, David I. 1981. *Dostoyevsky and the Jews*. Austin, TX: University of Texas Press.

Hubbs, Joanna. 1988. *Mother Russia: The Feminine Myth in Russian Culture*. Bloomington and Indianapolis, IN: Indiana University Press.

Hudspith, Sarah. 2004. *Dostoevsky and the Idea of Russianness: A new perspective on unity and brotherhood*. London: Routledge.

Kellogg, Michael. 2005. *The Russian Roots of Nazism: White Émigrés and the Making of National Socialism, 1917–1945*. Cambridge: Cambridge University Press.

Klier, John. 1995. *Imperial Russia's Jewish Question, 1855–1881*. Cambridge: Cambridge University Press.

—— 2011. *Russians, Jews, and the Pogroms of 1881–1882*. Cambridge: Cambridge University Press.

Korey, William. 1995. *Russian Antisemitism, Pamyat, and the Demonology of Zionism*. Chur: Harwood Academic Publishers.

Krestovskii, V.V. 1993. *T'ma egipetskaia. Tamara Bendavid. Torzhestvo Vaala. Dedy*, 2 vols. Moscow: Kameia.

Kryzhanovskaia, V.I. 2004. 'Na Moskve: Son v osenniuiu noch'', in I.V. Rochester (pseudonym), *Spasenie. Trilogiia: roman, son v osenniuiu noch' i skaz*, compiled and ed. by V.P. Koval'kov, 153–59. Moscow: Pravoslavnaia Russkaia Akademiia i VselaSvetnaia Gramota.

Laqueur, Walter. 1993. *Black Hundred: The Rise of the Extreme Right in Russia*. New York: HarperPerennial.

Lipska Kabat, Grazyna. 2001. 'Vsevolod Vladimirovich Krestovsky', in *Dictionary of Literary Biography, Volume 238: Russian Novelists in the Age of Tolstoy and Dostoevsky*, ed. J. Alexander Ogden and Judith E. Kalb, 144–53. Detroit, MI, and London: Gale Group.

Markie, Peter J. 1998. 'Rationalism', in *Routledge Encyclopedia of Philosophy*, ed. Edward Craig. 10 vols, VIII, 75–80. London: Routledge.

Reitblat, A.I. 1989–2007. "Kryzhanovskaia, Vera Ivanovna", in P.A. Nikolaev (ed.), *Russkie pisateli 1800–1917: bibliograficheskii slovar'*, 5 vols, III, 173–74. Moscow: Bol'shaia Rossiiskaia Entsiklopediia.

Rogger, Hans. 1986. *Jewish Policies and Right-Wing Politics in Imperial Russia*. Berkeley and Los Angeles: University of California Press.

Rosenshield, Gary. 1997. 'Dostoevskii's "The Funeral of the Universal Man" and "An Isolated Case" and Chekhov's "Rothschild's Fiddle": The Jewish Question', in *Russian Review*, 56(4), 487–504.

Rosenthal, Bernice Glatzer (ed.). 1997. *The Occult in Russian and Soviet Culture*. Ithaca, NY, and London: Cornell University Press.

CHAPTER 5

Russian Semiotics of Behaviour, or Can a Russian Person be Regarded as 'Homo Economicus'?

Natalia Vinokurova

Homo Economicus – Who is He?

One of the main hypotheses of modern economic theory is based on the supposition that there exists an 'economic person' (homo economicus). This person behaves in a rational manner, is able to make well-thought-through decisions and to consider the various possible forms of action, and always aspires to receive the greater gain. This type of behaviour (the behaviour of the homo economicus) is the basis of modern economic models. All economic theory is based on the mechanism of rational choice, and the homo economicus can consistently be found in textbooks for this discipline. The concept of the homo economicus appeared in academic research even in the nineteenth century, although the idea itself is associated with economists of the eighteenth century such as Adam Smith and David Ricardo.

In economic theory the rationality of the behaviour of the homo economicus is viewed in a different way from rationality in everyday life. It is not simply reasonableness or common sense. Economic rationality is the ability to make an optimal choice, i.e. a choice that maximises one's own gains, while being constrained by certain conditions. Moreover, this supposition applies to the behaviour of any economic subject, whether an individual, enterprise, company or other: each of them aspires to receive maximum profits.

Karl Polani states that in economic science it goes without saying that "homo economicus is a true representative of nineteenth-century rationalism".[1] Over time, the concept of the homo economicus that was formulated in the West has been subjected to criticism from Western scholars of economics, sociology, psychology and biology. In particular, doubts have been expressed as to whether it is in principle possible to receive all the information necessary to make effective decisions – clearly, the lack of such information limits one's options for making an optimal choice out of the available alternatives. It has

---

1 Karl Polani, *Dva znacheniia termina 'ekonomicheskii'*, in: *Neformal'naia ekonomika* (ed. Teodor Shanin), Moscow: Logos, 1999, 19–27. (Reprinted from K. Polanyi, *Livelihood of Man*, New York: Academic Press, 1977).

been proven that in traditional societies a person taking a decision follows ethical norms, habits and traditions, which may be very different from economic motivations. Polani, who was one of the critics of the concept of the 'homo economicus', believed that "economists' mistake [...] lies in the tendency to identify one's economic activity with its market form", that is, with the world where tough competition and maximising profits are inseparably united.[2] Socio-economics, an academic discipline that has developed in the West in recent years, generally postulates the need for deliberate limitations on consumption. In a sense, the concept of the 'homo economicus' is an abstract academic one. Nevertheless, no one can deny that people's economic behaviour is to a significant extent defined by their economic interests, and the conclusions drawn on the basis of this abstract model give good practical results.

Economic rationalism historically appeared more developed under capitalism in Western Europe and in North America than in other regions and countries. Rationality permeates the whole sphere of material culture, economic ethics, accounting and economic rights there. The economic flourishing of the countries of the West confirms the fruitfulness of this movement. It is no coincidence that rationalism is seen as the route to historical progress.

The Russian Idea of the Homo Economicus

In Russia the idea of the homo economicus has long been a subject for discussion, and has been questioned not only by academics, but also by laypeople. The most distinctive example of criticism of the concept of 'homo economicus' can be found in the famous pre-revolutionary Russian political economic theory of Sergii Bulgakov. Russian economists of the end of the nineteenth and beginning of the twentieth century were characterised by universalism in their approach to the analysis of economic phenomena, the social orientation of their research, and the opening up the economic sphere to that of philosophy. This can all be noted in the works of Bulgakov, an economist, philosopher and religious thinker. Bulgakov tried to subject political economy to the ethical principles of Christianity. He reacted with great interest to the ideas of Weber, notably to his appraisal of the meaning of religion for the development of the economy, and to his proposition in his 'Protestant ethic' of moral justification for the aspiration to wealth. However, it was not personal, but national wealth that was important for Bulgakov. The Christian requirement for freedom from wealth in an individual's life becomes for Bulgakov a method to

---

2   *Ibid.*

direct individual efforts towards the development of material culture in society as a whole. For Bulgakov the rational homo economicus who seeks his own gain is not acceptable. He views rationality as something mechanic and inanimate. According to Bulgakov, 'homo economicus' is he "who does not eat, does not sleep, because he is busy counting his gains, striving for the greatest profit with the least effort, he is just a slide rule".[3]

The genius Vasilii Rozanov in his indignation at ideas concerning money-making became convinced of the desirability of the negation of economic progress generally, declaring that "normal" life is a life of "poverty and labour", of "prayer and heroism" and "without even thinking of becoming rich".[4] Ivan Il'in, another Russian philosopher, developed similar ideas. While he did not discuss the concept of 'homo economicus', as it lay outside his sphere of interests, he sharply condemned the excessive striving of people towards material goods, unceasing gains and material pleasures. The main thing for the philosopher was man's spiritual development, his striving "upwards". For Il'in, "the best" was spiritual, moral and social perfection. According to him, without spirituality any expediency, any manifestation of rationalism would not be conducive to the *rapprochement* between man and life's true values. As Il'in wrote in the 1930s:

> The disaster of modern humanity is in being no longer able to experience an act of conscience, to give itself to this act; all mankind's 'intelligence', all its 'education' are merely dead and abstract acts of mind which is well equipped to work out the 'expediency' of various means, but which is completely helpless in the question of the sacred purposes of life.[5]

The ideas of Russian religious philosophers continue to have an influence on the consciousness and views of our compatriots. To cite a modern example, a LiveJournal blogger recently produced a categorical criticism of homo economicus, saying that "in Russian religious Marxism" the economic man "has been given a whack on the head and has been exiled from the ideology of the masses".[6]

---

3   S.N. Bulgakov, *Narodnoe khoziaistvo i religioznaia lichnost'*, in: S.N. Bulgakov, *Sochineniia v 2 tomakh*, vol. 2, Moscow: Nauka, 1993.
4   V.V. Rozanov, *Sobranie sochinenii*, vol. 26 (ed. A.N. Nikoliukin), Moscow: Respublika, 2008, 89.
5   Ivan Il'in, *Put' dukhovnogo obnovleniia*, www.paraklit.org/sv.otcy/Iljin-Putj-duhovnogo-obnovlenija.htm (reproduced from the Munich edition of 1962; consulted 11.09.2012).
6   *Ekonomicheskii chelovek i Sovetskii Soiuz*, Newzz.in.ua/main/1148856221-yekonomicheskij-chelovek-i-sovetskij-soyuz.html (consulted 23.11.2011).

Russian Irrationalism in Everyday Life

One can say that Russian irrationality is widely acknowledged in the world. That does not mean that all Russian people are irrational, that no-one ever sets goals, ever achieves these goals, or that no one ever chooses the best means to these ends, and so on

From time to time we all behave irrationally, but we can use the term 'irrational people' only with respect to those who cross some boundary or norm accepted in society, those who differ from the average. Those whose behaviour is not defined by reason, but rather by emotions or errors are often called irrational. When the irrationality of a Russian person – the notorious 'Russian mentality' – is spoken about, and comparisons are made between Russians and representatives of Western civilisation, then that means only that among Russians there is a slightly greater proportion of such irrational people, than the proportion among people in the West.

Irrationalism is manifested in different spheres. Our irrationality in everyday life makes the strongest impression on foreigners who visit Russia, supporting their ideas about the uncivilised nature of Russians. Thus, for example, a PhD student from Germany visiting a Russian postgraduate halls of residence was amazed that in her friend's room the light switch for the bedside light was located on the wall opposite the bed. "This is not rational", she said in surprise. In fact I then remembered a room in a German hotel, where in a tiny space everything that was needed for life had been positioned. Nothing was lacking; everything was there, all the lights in their necessary places, everything convenient and functional. When one of this German postgraduate student's Russian colleagues invited her to tea, she was again surprised to find out that 'tea' consisted of a full lunch with alcohol, pies, etc. She liked this, but it seemed to her to be not at all rational and, I am afraid, somehow a little wild, not quite pleasant, but a rather 'primitive' habit. Obviously this story of being invited as a guest came to my mind not by coincidence, when referring to rational behaviour. Professor Andreeva in her book on economic psychology provides a similar example of hospitality:

> In the traditions of many Eastern peoples, it is normal to be generous in one's hospitality. Such peoples will rarely take money or goods for their hospitality. The whole family group takes part in this activity. It is usual to bring presents from distant lands for all the relatives. Russians, too, have always treated guests very generously. True, this took up the efforts of the greater part of a family. Amongst those European peoples brought up in the spirit of Protestantism and Lutheranism and in the tradition of

respect for labour and taking money for it, arrangements are made for the individual use of money: guests are modestly received, people eating together in restaurants pay for themselves, and so on.[7]

Andreeva explains this situation by the sociocultural peculiarities of Easterners' attitude towards money, which is manifested not only in the structure of spending or inclination to save, but also in their attitudes towards guests. Russian culture, in her opinion, is closer to the culture of traditional Eastern societies, in which economic motivations play a lesser role than in the West.

Attitude to Money and Wealth in Russia

One's attitude to money is one of the most important factors shaping economic behaviour. On the one hand, the rational desire to earn and receive the maximum material benefit is present in Russians just as in representatives of other nations. One can probably apply the definition of homo economicus as given by John Stuart Mill to Russians. Homo economicus wants to "obtain the greatest amount of necessaries, conveniences, and luxuries, with the smallest quantity of labour".[8] On the other hand, other characteristics of Russians – our sociocultural peculiarities – that occur nowadays and have been observed in the past as well are also evident:

- an inability or unwillingness to count money;
- a conscious lack of desire to earn money, a scornful attitude to money;
- irrational losses;
- sadness and boredom 'from having money', as it is experienced as something that does not bring happiness, but rather the reverse – it deprives life of something important;
- a fear of wealth.

The Director of the Russian Academy of Sciences' Institute of Sociological Research, Professor Gorshkov, states that research conducted by the institute

---

7   I.V. Andreeva, *Ekonomicheskaia psykhologiia*, St Petersburg: Piter, 2000.
8   John Stuart Mill, *On the Definition of Political Economy, and on the Method of Investigation Proper to It*, London and Westminster Review, October 1836, paragraphs 38 and 48, in: *Essays on Some Unsettled Questions of Political Economy*, 2nd ed. London: Longmans, Green, Reader & Dyer, 1874, essay 5.

in collaboration with the Ebert Fund demonstrates that up to now, an extremely 'calm' attitude to money has been preserved in Russian culture and daily life. One-third of the respondents said that generally they do not seek money and would not want to have a million dollars. Some 50% would not agree to make any kind of concession or sacrifice in order to receive that million.[9] At the same time, psychologists have proven that the level of the value of money for the inhabitants of a country is connected to signs of its economic growth, i.e. the importance of money in people's lives stimulates their economic activities and the economic progress of the country.[10]

It is easier to see the irrationality of Russians in relation to money and wealth by looking at real-life examples. One can argue that this method of argument is inadequate, but when analysing national character, habits and the semiotics of behaviour, practically every statement made in a scholarly discussion will be very relative.

Does Money Like to Be Counted? (Деньги счет любят)

In the early nineties, I worked with an American researcher. We did a survey of workers in Russian enterprises in order to use the data collected in a model of the work behaviour of workers. This model had been already tested in the USA, and could be called a classic model. We surveyed 1,000 people in four Russian businesses, and our colleague in Czechoslovakia asked another 200. One of the questions on the survey referred to wages. The question was absolutely simple – to name the sum of money they had earned in the last month (in Russia, to the nearest rouble). 80% of employees we asked could not answer this question or answered it with great effort (someone even went to the finance department to find out the answer). My American colleague could not believe that a person did not know how much money he earned. She even suggested that there was some sort of special point of secrecy or lack of development (stupidity!) in these people. In America, when asked this question, employees quickly gave an answer and were able to do so to the nearest cent. In Czechoslovakia, likewise, they had no difficulties.

---

9   Georgii Il'ichev, *Rol' blagosostoianiia grazhdan v ikh vzgliadakh na zhizn' obshchestva*, *Finansovye izvestia*, 20.05.2003.
10 R. Lynn, *The Secret of Miracle Economy: Different national attitudes to competitive money*, London, 1991, 55–69 (cited from O. Deineka, *Ekonomicheskaia psikhologiia: Uchebnoe posobie*, St Petersburg: Izdatel'stvo Sankt-Peterburgskogo universiteta, 2000).

The Rich in Russia: Making Money is Boring, Refusing Money is Easy

At the beginning of the nineties many young people in Russia ended up in business and quickly achieved success. My former PhD student went to work as an accountant for a famous commercial chain. The owners (two young mathematicians) were carried away by their work, constantly had new ideas and breakthroughs, and sometimes made adventurous moves and took risks. Over time the business did well and made money like a well-oiled machine. At this point the young owners got bored. They sold the business to a pragmatic foreigner, and went off to Goa. The new owner with his rational approach continuously developed the chain and has become a millionaire, while the creators of the business are still 'catching butterflies'. It is said that a whole Russian colony of such Russian businessmen has formed in Goa.

There is another example of a similar kind. In the mid-nineties I interviewed a businessman from Nizhnii Novgorod who had a few shops and a restaurant. During the conversation he complained that he wanted to go into politics. To my question as to the aims and reason for this (I suspected that he wanted to lobby for his business interests more easily) he replied: "Life's in full swing there, it's interesting". Pre-election passions in those years certainly were 'in full swing' – there were regular reports of people being imprisoned or shot.

The phenomenon of 'fatigue from business' (or 'burn-out') can be observed in other countries, too, but there it is connected with older businessmen, who prefer to retire from business in order to devote their time to hobbies. It should not apply to thirty-something bored young people. It must be noted here that many rich people in pre-revolutionary Russia also treated money with indifference. For example, Sergei Aleksandrovich Poliakov, the heir of the largest commercial dynasty, preferred not to earn, but to spend (he was the publisher of the journal *Vesy* and the patron of the Symbolists). Witnesses spoke of the fact that he accepted the loss of his wealth after the Revolution with "philosophical indifference".[11]

One of the most original contemporary Russian sociologists Kasianova (the pen-name of V. Chesnokova), who wrote a book on the Russian national character, believes that it is precisely the light-hearted attitude to money that is responsible for the peculiar Russian phenomenon whereby even huge sums are so easily spent, given as a gift, lost in gambling, and so on. Kasianova maintains that the following situation is standard for a Russian:

---

11   *Usad'ba Znamenskoe-Gubailovo. Kto zhe takoi Sergei Aleksandrovich Poliakov?*, http://www.imesta.info/places/show/182/ (consulted 07.02.2012).

when a person who earned substantial means through hard work, great hardship and abstinence and is able as a result to enjoy a peace of mind for years to come, suddenly wastes all these earnings in one evening in the most ridiculous, meaningless and impractical way. Not his son or grandson – who did not earn anything themselves and thus have no idea of hardship and stress, and of how difficult it is to live in poverty – but he himself, who knows everything, suddenly throws it all away and returns back on his old tracks.[12]

"He Saved up His Money, and Bought Something Stupid and Superfluous' (A Russian saying: Денег накопил, да дури накупил)

Many jokes have appeared about new Russians (the Russian nouveau riche) in raspberry-pink jackets. One of them concerns their irrational consumer behaviour. Here is a typical joke. Two Russians meet overseas. One asks the other "How much did your tie cost?" The second answers with pride: "Two hundred dollars". The first reacts "Well, you're a fool. I got the same one just round the corner for five hundred". In Russia expensive cars are sold in huge quantities; some of the most expensive boutiques in the world have opened up; and the most prestigious and highly paid performers are invited to private parties. Recent research has shown that one of the reasons that Russian tourists are not loved abroad is that they throw their money away too easily. The Russian newspaper *Komsomol'skaia pravda* quotes the words of a journalist from the *Daily Mirror* about such behaviour seen as characteristic for Russians on holiday as "throwing money away and constantly pestering hotel staff".[13] Russian merchants in their time were also known for their 'crazy' spending. Thus what we observe then and now is the extravagant financial behaviour of Russian merchants, traders, businessmen and the super-rich.

Extravagant Financial Behaviour? Existential Angst at the Roots...

This flashing of money, characteristic of commercial success, was a result of melancholy, boredom and dissatisfaction with life. Wealth by itself did not bring satisfaction and happiness. The melancholy of one of the merchants

---

12 K. Kasianova, *O russkom national'nom kharaktere*, Moscow: Institute of the national model of the economy, 1994, 183–184.

13 Nikita Krasnikov, *Russkie turisty stali razdrazhat'*, Komsomol'skaia Pravda, 31.08.2009.

would overflow into debauchery, drunkenness, the breaking of mirrors in restaurants. Reflections of this phenomenon can be found in literature, especially in Gor'kii's work. Another method of escaping the life of a 'rich man' was by extravagant love affairs. The rich men would give their lovers mansions, and not only in Moscow and Petersburg. In the provincial Viazniki one of the best houses was a gift of a local merchant to his beloved.

The best example of this is the life and fate of one of the richest merchants of the early twentieth century, Savva Morozov. He belonged to a well-known merchant Old Believer family. Morozov began his particular path into business as a totally 'rational capitalist': he purchased new modern equipment for the family factory in England, perfected the system of management, built new accommodation blocks for workers, and changed the system of fines. All this assisted the increase in the productivity of labour and the flourishing of the business. The Morozov factory took the third place in Russia for profitability. But it was difficult for Morozov to be a businessman and mix with his fellow manufacturers. He suspiciously called his colleagues "a pack of wolves". Morozov began to 'go off the rails'. He did not break any mirrors; after all, he had been brought up by a governess, and studied at Moscow and Cambridge Universities. But he headed for an outrageous scandal and a break-up with his relatives by going off with the wife of his nephew. This resulted in the nephew's divorce from his wife, and this is at a time when a divorce was a completely unthinkable action among the Old Believers. Morozov then married his nephew's wife, surrounded her with unbelievable luxuries and spent all his money in a provocative merchant manner. For example, at the opening of a market he once appeared with his wife like a royal couple. The train of his wife's dress was longer than the Tsarina's, which was considered shocking at the time. His subsequent love affair was no less scandalous. He fell in love with the MKhAT (Moscow Art Theatre) actress Maria Fedorovna Andreeva, whom we remember as a 'friend of Gor'kii'. Andreeva was linked with the Bolsheviks. For her sake, Morozov gave the Bolsheviks a significant part of his property. He helped to support Bolshevik newspapers, hid illegal literature and personally obtained agitational materials for his own factory. It is difficult to think of anything more irrational. As Mark Aldanov has written: "Savva subsidised the Bolsheviks because he had taken against people generally, and especially people in his own circle". In the end, Savva Morozov, tired of life and disenchanted by everything, committed suicide. He was only 44 years old. He remained faithful to Andreeva to the last, leaving her his insurance policy, from which she received 100,000 roubles. This money also ended up with the Bolsheviks.

The magazine *Profil'* published an article on Morozov, in which the author compares him with Dostoevskii's Rogozhin and explains his 'fatal passion' as a sense of ennui. The journalist writes:

> He had a passionate nature and was inclined to get carried away, he always wanted to take everything through to its finish, to the full demise. He took everything seriously. It is as if Dostoevskii when writing his novel *The Idiot* copied Rogozhin from Morozov word for word, or the great writer himself knew the "type" of a talented Russian businessman who becomes bored of all his money, goes out of his mind from the vulgarity and vanity that surrounds him and at the end of the day puts all his stakes on a woman, on love.[14]

The author of the article does not use the words 'rationalism' or 'irrationalism' but obviously he attempts to contrast Russian irrationalism with Western rationalism. He writes: "After all, in America there are no unresolved contradictions between capital and love. The capitalist Bill Gates, for example, will never fall for a communist and at any rate will never suffer for such a reason".[15]

Is Wealth a Sin?

Merchants built the majority of churches in Russia, donating a significant part of their property to do so. In our era, rich people continue this tradition, although the scope of it is not quite the same. Nevertheless, the new church on the central square of Pereslavl-Zalesskii was built by a member of the modern rich class, and in my native Zamoskvorechie in Moscow, several churches have been restored with the help of money from Moscow entrepreneurs.

However, motives for such charity are diverse. There is vanity, a desire to immortalise one's own name, and simply the following of traditions. In the past, parishioners were obliged by law to donate money to support the buildings of the church. The most widespread modern explanation is that rich people are trying to wash away their sins, their 'bloodsucking', through fear of God. But there is more here, in my opinion, than a mere question of fear – it is also a semi-aware 'feeling of shame' for their wealth. The building of churches

---

14 'Krasnyi fabricant' Savva Morozov, *Den'gi*, No 14–15 (63), August 2005; *Savva Morozov: Russkaia tragediia*, *Profil'*, 14 July 1997, No.26 (48).

15 Ibid.

can be viewed as a way of atoning not for concrete sins of a concrete person, but for the possession of 'money', which is sinful of itself. However, this is just a hypothesis. Yet Chekhov, an extremely observant author who penetrated to the core of Russian reality and can be deemed the best 'sociologist' of his time, confirms the idea of the contradictory emotions of the Russian rich, of their fusion of shame and pride:

> A rich man is by and large insolent, he thinks the world of himself, and yet he carries his wealth as a vice. If generals and wealthy ladies did not do their charity work at his expense, if impoverished students and the other destitute did not exist, he would feel angst and solitude. If the poor rebelled and agreed not to ask him for money, he would come to them himself.[16]

Nobility Syndrome (Дворянский синдром)

The Russian nobility of the period of serfdom was used to spending money without thinking about its origin. They were able to live in a disorderly and irresponsible way for more than a generation. It was almost dishonourable for an aristocrat to be calculating (or to be known as such). A modern-day historian, Semen Ekshtut,[17] demonstrates this by an excerpt from Lev Tolstoi's *War and Peace*. Tolstoi's favourite heroes are the Rostov family. Here is Ekshtut's account of the Rostovs' economic behaviour: "within four years, the financial situation of the family became hopelessly entangled due to the disorderly behaviour of the count Ilia Andreevich Rostov, the wasteful conduct of his wife, and Nikolai Rostov's loss at gambling". This is a typical situation for members of the nineteenth-century nobility. There is another character in the novel who is the opposite of the Rostovs in his behaviour and motivations, Berg from Lifliandia (a Baltic province of the Russian Empire). He works and earns money himself, is purposeful and calculating. In our terms Berg is a 'rational homo economicus'. However, Tolstoi's heroes, as well as the author himself, look at Berg with scepticism. And yet, it is precisely the fact that Berg managed to accumulate wealth that allowed him to marry the Rostovs' eldest daughter.

---

16 Anton Chekhov, *Zapisnye knizhki*, in: A.P. Chekhov, *Polnoe sobranie sochinenij i pisem v 30-ti tomakh*. Vol. 17, *Zapisnye knizhki. Zapiski na otlel'nykh listakh. Dnevniki*, Moscow: Nauka, 1987.

17 S.A. Ekshtut, *Zerkalo russkoi intelligentsii, ili apologia polkovnika Berga*, in: *Chastnoe i obshchestvennoe: gendernyi aspect*, vol. 2, Moscow: IEA RAN, 2011, 17–19.

Ekshtut argues that such sceptical views with respect to the 'economic' people, who were business- and career-oriented, had been common also amongst Russian intelligentsia of a later period, known as *raznochintsy*. "In the course of one and a half centuries, generations of Russian intelligentsia looked at Berg through the eyes of Tolstoi. [...] Someone who dared to articulate the idea of striving for a personal success would be submitted to moral condemnation. [...] A member of the Russian intelligentsia refuses to accept bourgeois values", Ekshtut writes. This is most surprising, since the intelligentsia, unlike the nobility of the 'Golden Age' was not wealthy at all, many literally had to live on a dime. Although Ekshtut does not extrapolate this situation onto a later period, but it would be fair to say that intelligentsia of the Soviet and post-Soviet time, brought up on classic Russian literature, in a sense also shared the same 'noble' syndrome. Thus the widow of the Russian actor, director and writer Leonid Filatov (1946–2003), the actress Nina Shatskaia, recalls:

> ...Once I told him: 'If only you had money, you could make your own film'. He didn't reply. Indeed, what can one say? He despised money. 'In Russia money never took centre stage, although money is not contraindicated for Russia, and there were people who knew how to make money and count it; but there was always something higher than money. Therefore in Russian literature too there are almost no passions based on money, and where there are, there will always appear some Nastasia Filippovna who will just throw it into the fire', Lionia liked to repeat.[18]

Russian Proverbs about Money

Proverbs reflect a certain historical experience, certain stereotypes imprinted into our consciousness. Of course, Russians have a lot of sayings which coincide with the sayings of other peoples or literally repeat them, for example, "Копейка рубль бережет" – "The kopeck takes care of the rouble" (which is equivalent to "Look after the pennies and the pounds will look after themselves"). There are many Russian proverbs that demonstrate the importance of money in everyday life. However, I wanted to look at those sayings rooted in our consciousness, which demonstrate a slightly 'suspicious' attitude to money. The most popular among them is probably "Не в деньгах счастье" – "Happiness is not in money" (or in other words, "Money can't buy you happiness"). Further, on the same theme: "Почет дороже денег" ("Respect is dearer than money"),

---

18   Nina Shatskaia, *Lionia*, http://www.kp.ru/daily/23761.4/56602/ (consulted 12.04.2011).

"Совет дороже денег" ("Advice is dearer than money"), "Не имей сто рублей, а имей сто друзей" ("Better to have a hundred friends than a hundred roubles"), "Денег ни гроша, да слава хороша" ("A good name is better than riches"). It is interesting that modern sociological research shows that even after "the reforms, which resulted in the mass impoverishment of the population of the country, the majority of its inhabitants are still convinced that "money can't buy you happiness"".[19]

Another theme to be found in proverbs is the impurity of wealth, the impossibility of earning money by honest means. For example, "Богатому черти деньги куют" ("It is devils who forge money for the rich") and "Трудом праведным не наживешь палат каменных" ("You won't make stone palaces by righteous work"). Money is linked with immorality, avarice and absence of conscience: "Когда деньги говорят, то правда молчит" ("When money talks, the truth is silent") and "У богатого зимой снега не допросишься" ("Don't ask a rich man for some snow in the winter", i.e. "A rich man would charge you for tap water"). Interestingly, some sayings link money not with intelligence, but with stupidity: "Умом туп, да кошелек туг" ("He's thick in the head, but his purse is full"), "Денег палата, да ума маловато" ("He's got a swathe of money but little brains"), "Денег много, да разума мало" ("He's got a lot of money, but no sense") and "Богатством ума не купишь" ("One can't buy brains with money").

Money is perceived as something burdensome: "Без денег сон крепче" ("A poor man sleeps better"), "Богачи едят калачи, да не спят ни днем, ни в ночи" ("Rich people eat bread rolls, but don't sleep by day or by night"), "Меньше денег – меньше хлопот" ("The less money, the less bother"). At this point it is impossible not to recall the aforementioned young businessmen who ended up going off to Goa.

The 'economic rationality' of Russians is reflected in our jokes. Here is an example: A band of men are being tried in court for robbing a shop. They stole a car full of vodka. The thieves are asked what they did with the vodka. They answer: "We sold it". "And where's the money?" "We spent it on drink". That is the 'homo economicus' Russian style.

An Ideological Comparison: Homo Economicus versus Russian Idealist. Attitudes to Money in the Era of the 'Building of Capitalism'

At the present time in Russia one can observe a dramatic contrast, a struggle between two tendencies: the liberal economic tendency oriented towards the

---

[19] Georgii Il'ichev, *Rol' blagosostoianiia grazhdan v ikh vzgliadakh na zhizn' obshchestva*, Finansovye izvestiia, 20.05.2003.

prosperity of people, and their material wellbeing, and the traditional approach to life with its orientation towards Christian values and ethical-moral categories. This reflects a profound conflict of values. Representatives of the liberal tendency believe that they fight against the archaic, anti-scientific ideas, and deem their outlook progressive. Representatives of the traditional tendency insist that their views are much more in line with the Russian mentality and that following their ideas through will lead more quickly to the well being of the country. It is possible that the acuteness of this ideological struggle is caused by the present crisis of the Russian economy, an immense thirst for wealth on the part of the 'new rich', and a widening gap between the prosperous minority and impoverished majority. Contemporary rich people are associated precisely with the concept of 'homo economicus'.

If, generally, around the country (as has already been noted), former values prevail, amongst which money does not take a leading role, then more of the young generation, primarily the youth in big cities, are orientated to a much larger extent towards material prosperity. In the middle of the last decade, sociological research was carried out on young Muscovites. The researchers conducted a comparative analysis with similar data taken from the pre-reform period. They came to the conclusion that:

> in the hierarchy of the dominating requirements (which define a person on the scale of status and position in society), in the judgements of graduates of the pre-reform period the first place was occupied by 'type of work', 'prestige of profession' and its 'positive impact on society', but for the same category of respondents in the market period the most important place was occupied by 'good pay', 'supplementary income' and guarantees of a 'profitable position in work'.[20]

Thus the choice of type of work with a dominating motivation of 'high pay' allows us to say that young people can be adequately characterised by the concept of homo economicus.

According to the materials of another piece of research, "the importance of material wellbeing" in 1987 was noted by 36% of respondents; in 2009, by 52%.[21] Based on the data from various sociological studies of this type, the sociologist Leontii Byzov came to the conclusion that in contemporary society there exists a "demand for the formation of a new-Russian nation based on the completely different social and ideological foundation" than the previously

---

20 G.M. Mkrtchian, *Stratifikatsiia molodezhi v sferakh obrazovaniia, zaniatosti i potrebleniia*, SOTsIS, №2, 2005 104.

21 *Nezavisimaia gazeta*. Appendix '*Politika*', №3, November 2009.

existing Russian nation.[22] However, the more people show leanings towards rational economic behaviour, the sharper become the arguments between them and their opponents, i.e. between people on both sides of the model 'homo economicus'. Evidence for this struggle can be found in the media, on the Internet and in the works of sociologists and economists of various schools.

Perhaps the clearest and most straightforward examples of this can be found on the Internet, most probably because people can post there anonymously. On the Internet there are more than 700,000 hits for the words "attitude to money". If one opens the first site that comes up on the search, then one finds that it is a site of an informational-analysts agency "Pomoshch' biznesu" (Help for Business – bishelp.ru), which was created by the authorities of St Petersburg. Their first project is called "How to get rich?" The first article is an attempt to change the attitude of people to money:

> For many years during the Soviet period we formed a negative attitude to money. Parents passed on this attitude to their children as though it was a relay baton. Conclusions were made from this negative opinion: big money was linked with criminals, and being rich was considered indecent and dangerous. This idea took root in the consciousness of the population. In order to orientate ourselves correctly in the modern climate, we must firstly get rid of these old-fashioned opinions.[23]

What sort of qualities, according to the authors, are the main (and necessary) ones for a businessman? "The main internal principle which unites all businessmen is their emotional attitude to money. They love money and money loves them back".[24] Another adviser on the Internet, a psychologist from an organisation with the meaningful name 'House of the Sun' says: "If your attitude to the world of money is disrespectful, negative or adverse, then even with the highest degree of professionalism it is hard to count on success. In the best-case scenario, the fruits of your labours will be used by others, the energy of their relationship with money is more powerful than yours".[25] The site offers services to "cleanse and lighten" money, etc. Often when trying to give an example of a correct attitude to money, the words of famous millionaires are quoted. For example, the words of Cornelius Vandebilt: "All my life I've gone

---

22   Aleksandr Kazin, *Srednen'kie evropeitsy?*, *Literaturnaia gazeta*, №3, 2012.
23   Leontii Byzov, *Literaturnaia gazeta*, №42, 2011.
24   *Kak stat' bogatym. Anatomiia bogatstva. Otnoshenie k den'gam kak sud'bonosnyi factor.* http://www.bishelp.ru (consulted 18.07.2011).
25   *Ibid.*

out of my mind because of money. The invention of new ways of making money simply left me no time for an education".[26] Or Aristotle Onassis: "The most important thing in life is money. The people who have it are the real kings of our times. You have to think about money night and day. You've got to dream of money, like I do, for example".[27] There is a large quantity of advisors and consultants of this sort, and all their advice is extremely similar. This similarity underlines my idea that Russian consciousness lacks something fundamental on the issue of money if such huge pressure is necessary in the attempt to put the national attitude to money on the right track.

Bloggers on Money

What kinds of questions are raised by the more serious arguments on the Internet? These are always the same: do we need to aspire to wealth, can wealth ever be honest, is it shameful to be rich, what is more important, material or spiritual wealth? There is an active process of comparing Russian and Western values. Bloggers often use clichés, but behind these clichés there clearly looms something important for them for which they cannot find their own words.

Defenders of the 'value' of money and material wellbeing accuse their opponents of envy, or adherence to the Soviet past, communist ideas, or even of stupidity. However, perhaps the majority of bloggers have a negative attitude to money and wealth, and especially, to the present-day oligarchs. The worldview of bloggers completely corresponds to the proverbs I have already cited, although they consider themselves advanced, modern people, and for the most part they are young people. From correspondence it is evident that the majority of them do not belong to the predominantly poor strata of the society who are paid from the government budget. I do not doubt that those people for whom money constitutes the ultimate value also condemn the aspiration to wealth. This is perhaps a sort of paradox, something similar to profligates condemning adultery.

The first thesis of the bloggers is: money and conscience (*sovest'*) are conflicting concepts. Here are some typical quotations: "They are not ashamed. Really not ashamed, because they have no conscience. And shame has got nowhere to take root", "They are not ashamed, but I'm ashamed for them. But

---

26 *Dom solntsa. Otnoshenie k den'gam.* http://www.sunhome.ru/journal/56367 (consulted 22.024.2012).

27 *Kak stat' bogatym. Anatomiia bogatstva. Chto govoriat milliardery o den'gakh.* http://www.bishelp.ru (consulted 18.07.2011).

they spit on that shame", "Decent money is rarely to be found among decent people", "To sum up what's been said, one can come to a single obvious conclusion, that the scale of one's wealth is in inverse proportion to the scale of one's conscience", etc. Moreover, the possession of a lot of money is not only considered shameful, but so too is thrift and miserliness in regard to money. A girl working in a bank who is already fully rational and even uses the software package 'personal finances' to organise her family budget, writes: "And I am still ashamed, really ashamed! So I don't waste money on the wedding magazines in Ashan [a hypermarket], I leaf through them there and read them there".

Making comparisons between material and spiritual types of wealth are also characteristic. A typical example of this sort is as follows: "I [...] never wanted to be wealthy (I only strove to be rich spiritually), the usual basics were enough for me". Those on the side of the idea that wealth is a burden are also obvious: "A motor-boat, a parachute, a yacht [...] there is everything in the West. But we don't have to tremble and shudder with fear that someone will steal your Mercedes".

The desire to compare Russia with the West constantly comes up in the discussion: "In the West they are preoccupied with money at work and at home, only money, money, money", "As far as money is concerned, we have aped the Americans", "'Well-wishers are trying to break the Russian mentality. They (including the president) are destroying the aspiration of Russian people towards collectivism", "I conclude that Russian 'capitalism' is falling apart at the seams'". Collectivism here is associated with the contempt to personal gain inherent in the homo economicus. An anonymous author expressed his indignation at the homo economicus in his LiveJournal blog:

> Considering that this homo economicus also received external support, being an inherent part of Western social thought, the extent to which he has "reformatted the brains" of a certain part of that class of the national intelligentsia becomes apparent. No sort of understanding between normal people who fully belong to Russian culture, the culture of "the enchanted wanderer", and this homo economicus can exist. The latter will with total sincerity regard a Russian as a slave by essence, because he cannot imagine how one could be so unfree (other ways of realising freedom – apart from enrichment – don't exist for him) and at the same time not to suffer from that lack of freedom. And the freedom of the national 'homo economicus' has not so much irritated our nostrils, as it has long since submitted to doubt the very existence of Russia and the Russian people. The main thing is that it is impossible to make an agreement with those who believe in the homo economicus, because for them

any restrictions placed on aspiration to material advantage constitute absolute and unbearable slavery.[28]

On the Internet, Professor Panfilova practically repeats the same sentiments:

> In the existing tendency in social life, we risk ending up with, instead of the Soviet person with his opposing aspirations, in the best-case scenario, an 'economic' man – a simple function of the self-developing economy which would constitute an unconditional step back in humanistic terms; in the worst and most probable case, we would end up with a degraded man, without any social foundations and therefore without a future.[29]

In April 2003 information appeared on the Communist Party of the Russian Federation website about a protest by the Union of Communist Youth, during which modern *komsomol'tsy* carried a coffin with a label on its lid saying 'homo economicus' through the centre of the city. There was commentary to the effect that those taking part in the protest made solemn speeches and merry jokes while saying their farewells to the 'financial scarecrow'. It is obvious that the homo economicus for all these people embodies all the sins of capitalism and, most importantly, all the sins of modern Russia's economic system.

Homo Economicus through the Eyes of Academics, Writers and Public Figures

An article by two professors from two of Russia's leading higher educational institutions, MGIMO (Moscow State Institute of International Relations) and MGU (Moscow State University), sharply criticises the view of Russians as irrational in the economic sphere. The authors insist that "Russians are an entirely bourgeois and standard European nation, whose dreams, hopes and aspirations are equally quite bourgeois and standard. In brief, this is a desire for a peaceful, prosperous and free life, an existence without any spiritually uplifting chimeras".[30] Having started with the economic motivations of people, the

---

28   *Ekonomicheskii chelovek i Sovetskii Soiuz*, Newzz, http://www.ua/main/1148856221-yekonomicheskij-chelovek-i-sovetskij-soyuz.html/ (consulted 23.11.2011).
29   T.V. Panfilova. *Sovetskii chelovek – voploshchenie obshchestvennykh protivorechii sovetskoi epokhi*, http://www.za-nauku.ru/index.php?option=com_content&task=view&id=2585 (consulted 20.12 2010).
30   T. Solovei, V. Solovei, *Chego ne khotiat russkie*, *Literaturnaia gazeta*, 12–18 October 2011, №49 (6341).

authors, just like the ordinary bloggers referred to above, move on to a more general discussion of the Russian national character, since this also constitutes a field of discussion within economics. They claim that it is a grave mistake and fantasy to describe the Russian national character in such terms as "ascetic, indifferent to material values, oriented towards brotherly love and community, dreaming of giving away your own shirt to your fellow human being…".[31] The authors insist that they *never* met in real life such individuals who would, for instance, be prepared to fight in order "to give the land in Grenada to the peasants" (a famous poem, made into a song, by Mikhail Svetlov about Russians and Ukrainians who were ready to risk their lives for the cause of the Spanish peasants). They deem Russians "especially insensitive to truth and justice", in contrast to those who hold the opposite view, regarding Russians as the people for whom these concepts are sacred and the very words are written with capital letters. They also insist that in the West "Christian brotherly love and the Christian order of life are encountered much more often than in Russia".[32] It appears that in this case the stance of the defenders of the idea that a Russian can be defined as homo economicus, a fully rational man, is reflected most prominently.

However, their opponents, who are also well-known and respectable people, are inclined to think that Russians are oriented above all towards the values of higher order than material well being. The Belorussian writer Svetlana Aleksievich speaks of a special mentality, of a particular attitude towards money: "Russia is an irrational country, just like Belorussia: money there, at the end of the day, is not always the ultimate solution".[33] The Russian Orthodox Church has also contributed to the discussion of this problem:

> Of course, the first and most important motive of development for the economy is the material interests of a person. The Church does not deny this motive, since at its heart there lies the aspiration of man to improve the conditions of his life for himself and his family. But the aspiration to increase one's personal wellbeing is not the only motive that must move economic relations. From the point of view of Orthodox ethics, another such motive is the aspiration to help those close to us, a desire to see that the results of our labour aid not just a concrete person, but the country

---

31 *Ibid.*
32 *Ibid.*
33 Vladimir Nuzov, *Vestnik*, http://www.allabout.ru/a15398.html, interview with Svetlana Aleksievich (consulted 20.12.2012).

and society in which a person lives. If one of these motives ceases to function, a crisis is unavoidable.[34]

The aforementioned sociologist Kasianova (V. Chesnokova) believes that a Russian person behaves in exactly the opposite manner to a Western rational 'homo economicus': "the Russian feels that the moment has arrived for him finally to complete the 'real deed', the deed from which he personally does not extract any gain". Kasianova argues that the Russian mentality in the realm of economics manifests itself in the fact that people behave not in the framework of a goal-rational model (when the result is aimed at and the means of achieving it are chosen), i.e. the model of homo economicus, but in the framework of the values-rational model. Such people are convinced that "a particular line of behaviour is highly valuable in itself, from aesthetic, ethical, religious and other viewpoints, completely regardless of the results". Just like Bulgakov, Kasianova draws here on the ideas of Weber about values-rational behaviour, but she also explains why exactly the Russian is inclined towards this type of behaviour: "not because he is too lazy to think, to calculate, unable to take risks, rigid or does not construct any plans, but because culture demands from him to behave in this way". According to Kasianova, in Russian culture achieving your personal goals is allowed to a lesser extent than in other cultures. She does not deny the need for consumption of material and cultural products, but it is not this which she deems the main purpose of human life:

> to have nourishing food, to rest fully, to read books, to consume art... – all this is necessary, without this life is hard, virtually impossible, but nevertheless this cannot constitute an *ideal*, it is not for this that a human being is born, and it is not for the sake of this that he lives. Indeed, all these are conditions, but where is the goal, where is the meaning of life?[35]

Another contemporary famous Russian economist, academician L'vov, underlines that such concepts as "conscience, moral principles and spirituality" have to stand out not as "limiters in economic models, but as criteria for the behaviour of economic agents", that there is no homo economicus, but rather homo socio-economicus. L'vov's ideas resonate with those of Bulgakov. Both think

---

34 Patriarch of Moscow and All Russia Kirill, Obshchestvo, ekonomika, etika v sluzhenii Russkoi Pravoslavnoi Tserkvi, in *Neekonomicheskie grani ekonomiki: nepoznannoe vzaimovliianie*, Moscow: INES, 2010, 104.

35 K. Kasianova, *O russkom national'nom kharaktere*, Moscow: Institute of the national model of the economy, 1994, 183–184.

that public interests should stand above individual interests and that people should choose the appropriate version of behaviour voluntarily. Moreover, L'vov, just like the bloggers, reminds us of typically Russian, in his view, features such as collectivism. He does not share the Soviet understanding of collectivism, but nevertheless regards collectivism a necessary condition of moral economics: "the only path which leads Russia to progress and prosperity is the path of moral economics. Its key aspect is a profoundly personal, individually chosen way towards the sense of the collective, of the community, for Russian collectivism is indeed based on a common task, common ideas and common goals".[36]

The academician, Makarov, one of the leading specialists in mathematical economics, says that, "profit maximisation and utility are suitable only for a simple market economy", only for a class of entrepreneurs. He suggests that the totally different motivations of people, not just material ones, should be accounted for among the criteria used in mathematical models – for example, a desire to go up the social ladder, to obtain a new rank.[37] Both L'vov and Makarov have many disciples and followers who are leading a serious discussion with economists representing mainstream economic theory.

A representative of the younger generation of economists, the academician Glaz'ev, shares their views: "Modern economic science obviously disregards the meaning of ethical values in the formation of economic behaviour. The dominating paradigm of market balance is based on an assumption of the rational behaviour of economic agents, directed at the single motive – maximisation of profits. This ignores the meaning of all other motives that influence economic behaviour and its moral limits".[38] His views are supported by those of Professor Dement'ev, for whom the homo economicus' rationality is primarily associated with a behaviour based on self-interest: "altruism and solidarity are clearly absent from the neoclassical portrait of homo economicus where the latter is presented as a hyper-rational, exclusively self-interested subject".[39]

---

[36] D.S. L'vov, *Nravstvennaia ekonomika*, Moscow: Institut ekonomicheskikh strategii, 2004, 38.

[37] V.L. Makarov, *Sotsialnyi klasterizm. Rossiiskii vyzov*, Moscow: Biznes Atlas, 2010, 191, 199.

[38] S.Yu. Glaz'ev, *Nravstvennye nachala v ekonomicheskom povedenii i razvitii – vazhneishii resurs vozrozhdeniia Rossii*, in *Ekonomika i obshchestvennaia sreda: neosoznannoe vzaimovliianie. Nauchnye zapiski i ocherki* (ed. O.T. Bogomolov), Moscow: INES, 2008, 406.

[39] V.E. Dement'ev, *Doverie – faktor funktsionirovaniia i razvitiia sovremennoi rynochnoi ekonomiki, Rossiiskii ekonomicheskii zhurnal*, №8, 2004, 46.

A recent textbook on economic history says that only such priorities about which L'vov and Glaz'ev speak "can cause a softening in existing social and political conflicts".[40] Modern Slavophiles exploit the ideas outlined above and try to extract from them a 'national idea', arguing that "the most important thing in Russian society in all periods was not money, but Morality, Truth and Justice" and that "this quality made and makes our culture not simply High, but supranational".[41]

We can therefore distinguish some characteristic features inherent in the Russian discussions of the concept of homo economicus:

Emotionalism and tendency to resort to personal comments
This relates first of all to internet discussions which often descend into gross rudeness, but at the same time it is also typical for journalistic discourse and for some scholarly works. This can be seen from the vocabulary used by the authors and from their desire to exaggerate the views of their opponents, thus bringing these views to the point of absurdity.

Emphasis on that part of the definition of the Homo Economicus that underlines his interest in material gain and the desire for wealth
The concept of rational economic behaviour, which even for academic analysis seems complicated, has, for the everyday awareness of a Russian person, acquired a simple, even vulgar meaning: the rational 'economic man' is a person who thinks only about money. His main aim is to get rich.

The comparison between Russia and the West
Western society is mainly presented as a consumer society, where people aim for personal riches, are calculating, grasping, etc. This is how the homo economicus is viewed by the average person. In spite of the fact that in our times, almost any information and sources are accessible, a mythical idea of the West often prevails over facts. Even scholars sometimes do not notice, it seems, that in the West many of the views which they criticise themselves, have also been long since submitted to criticism.

Attempts to link material wealth with soullessness and immorality.

Attempts to link the problem of economic behavior with a broader theme – behavior as moral or immoral, the issue of justice and injustice.

---

40   *Istoriia ekonomicheskikh uchenii* (ed. V. Avtonomov and others), Moscow: Infra-M, 2002, 78.

41   A.P. Bogatyrev, *My i Oni. Obshchestvo morali protiv obshchestva potrebleniia.* http://astreb.at.ua/biblioteka/cni_i_mi/bogatiryev_oni_i_mi.rar (consulted 27.10.2012).

What is morality? In essence it is here that the break of the logical chain and parting with rationality take place. Why 'do not steal', if in every separate case of 'economic behaviour' it may turn out to be most effective to steal?

Striving to search for an ideal which would not be connected to consumerism in any of its manifestations.

Conclusion

Can we thus regard a Russian person as 'homo economicus'? It follows from the above considerations that the concept of homo economicus is unacceptable for Russians because of ideological considerations, for it lacks such criteria as morality and spirituality. The ideas of Russian philosophers, who formulated these requirements most clearly and memorably, were obviously not born out of nothing. These Russian thinkers absorbed the moods and ideas characteristic of a Russian person and reflected in their works the Russian mentality. Even to this day the majority of Russians cannot and do not want to agree that rationality of economic behavior is determined by exclusively material factors. And, interestingly, this is what people think regardless of their actual behavior in real life. One can say that the hypothesis about the homo economicus appears to them irrational in its excessive rationalism.

Following the philosophers of the last century, modern idealists continue to speak about the priority of spiritual values, about selflessness, collectivism and justice, trying to prove the value of our civilisational matrix as opposed to the "civilisation of lucre", to use the words of the writer Iurii Mamleev.[42] For them it is important to believe in this, for it represents an ideal that warms the soul. It also reflects a desire to preserve Russian identity.

These peculiarities of the Russian mentality are perceived negatively by the Russian Westernisers and can annoy Westerners. It is difficult to give precise quotations, but it can be heard in everyday conversations nowadays that in Russia now there are two nations – large and small. The small nation consists of Westernisers, and they perceive the large nation as uncivilised, wild, full of complexes and not yet grown up sufficiently to understand Western values, in particular the concept of homo economicus.

I would not like, following various authors whom I quoted above, to oppose Russia and Western Europe. But I do think that 'Russian economic idealism'

---

[42] Elena Semenova, *Metafizicheskii realist Pushkin*, Interview with the writer Iurii Mamleev, http://litfest.ru/news/metafizicheskij_realist_pushkin/2011-02-18-924 (consulted 27.03.2011).

played its role in the creation of the all-European system of values. In the epoch labelled "financialism" by one Russian economist,[43] a so-called 'rational' financial policy leads to economic crises in Russia as well as in other countries. It is possible that a new healthy balance between the two types of values – Western rational-liberal and Russian traditional – represents the way to a new more just and stable economic order. May it not be the case then that in Russian irrationalism there is something rational after all?

I am far from idealising Russians, as I understand perfectly well that ideas and reality are two different things, and in their economic behaviour Russians can, of course, behave as populus economicus, forgetting the values of the higher order. However, I share the following thought of the academician Dmitrii Likhachev, who writes that "one must differentiate the national ideal from the national character. The ideal does not always coincide with reality. But the national ideal is nonetheless very important".[44] Likhachev thinks that "eventually, the people who are creating this ideal give birth to heroes and geniuses who come close to that ideal, and who give the tone to the national culture as a whole".[45]

Translated by Elizabeth Harrison and Olga Tabachnikova

Bibliography

Andreeva, I.V. 2000. *Ekonomicheskaia psyikhologiia*. St Petersburg: Piter.
Bogatyrev, A.P. 2012. *My i Oni. Obshchestvo morali protiv ob shchestva potrebleniia*. http://astreb.at.ua/biblioteka/oni_i_mi/bogatiryev_oni_i_mi.rar.
Bulgakov, S.N. 1993. *Narodnoe khoziaistvo i religioznaia lichnost'*. In: S.N. Bulgakov, *Sochineniia v 2 tomakh*, vol. 2. Moscow: Nauka.
Byzov, Leontii. 2011. *Literaturnaia gazeta*, №42.
Chekhov, Anton. 1987. *Zapisnye knizhki*. In: A.P. Chekhov, *Polnoe sobranie sochinenii i pisem v 30-ti tomakh*. Vol. 17, *Zapisnye knizhki. Zapiski na otdel'nykh listakh. Dnevniki*, Moscow: Nauka.
Dement'ev, V.E. 2004. *Doverie – faktor funktsionirovaniia i razvitiia sovremennoi rynochnoi ekonomiki. Rossiiskii ekonomicheskii zhurnal*, №8, 46.

---

43 V.A. Volkonskii, T.I. Koriagina and A.I. Kuzovkin. *Mozhno li schitat' krizisy rukotvornymi?, Bankovskoe delo*, 2009; V.A. Volkonskii, *Finansovyi krizis i smena ekonomicheskoi paradigmy*, Moscow: MAON, 2009.
44 D.S. Likhachev, *Izbrannoe. Mysli o zhizni, istorii, kul'ture*, Moscow: PIK, 2006, 270.
45 Ibid.

Dom solntsa. Otnoshenie k den'gam. http://www.sunhome.ru/journal/56367 (consulted 22.024.2012).

Ekonomicheskii chelovek i Sovetskii Soiuz. 2011. Newzz, http://www.ua/main/1148856221-yekonomicheskij-chelovek-i-sovetskij-soyuz.html/.

Ekshtut, S.A. 2011. *Zerkalo russkoi intelligentsii, ili apologia polkovnika Berga,* in *Chastnoe i obshchestvennoe: gendernyi aspect,* vol. 2. Moscow: IEA RAN, 17–19.

Glaz'ev S.Yu. 2008. *Nravstvennnye nachala v ekonomicheskom povedenii i razvitii – vazhneishii resurs vozrozhdeniia Rossii,* in *Ekonomika i obshchestvennaia sreda: neosoznannoe vzaimovliianie. Nauchnye zapiski i ocherki* (ed. O.T. Bogomolov). Moscow: INES, 406.

Il'ichev, Georgii. 2003. *Rol' blagosostoianiia grazhdan v ikh vzgliadakh na zhizn' obshchestva. Finansovye izvestiia,* 20.05.2003.

Il'in, Ivan. 2012. *Put' dukhovnogo obnovleniia.* www.paraklit.org/sv.otcy/Iljin-Putj-duhovnogo-obnovlenija.htm (reproduced from the Munich edition of 1962).

Istoriia ekonomicheskikh uchenii (ed. V. Avtonomov and others). 2002. Moscow: Infra-M, 78.

Kak stat' bogatym. Anatomiia bogatstva. Chto govoriat milliardery o den'gakh. http://www.bishelp.ru (consulted 18.07.2011).

Kak stat' bogatym. Anatomiia bogatstva. Otnoshenie k den'gam kak sud'bonosnyi factor. http://www.bishelp.ru (consulted 18.07.2011).

Kasianova, K. 1994. *O russkom national'nom kharaktere.* Moscow: Institute of the national model of the economy, 183–184.

Kazin, Aleksandr. 2012. *Srednen'kie evropeitsy?, Literaturnaia gazeta,* №3.

Krasnikov, Nikita. 2009. *Russkie turisty stali razdrazhat'. Komsomol'skaia Pravda,* 31.08.

'Krasnyi fabrikant' Savva Morozov. 2005. *Den'gi,* No 14–15 (63), August.

Likhachev, D.S. 2006. *Izbrannoe. Mysli o zhizni, istorii, cul'ture.* Moscow: PIK, 270.

Lynn, R. 1991. *The Secret of Miracle Economy: Different national attitudes to competitive money.* London, 55–69 (cited from O. Deineka, *Ekonomicheskaia psikhologiia: Uchebnoe posobie.* St Petersburg: Izdatelstvo Sankt-Peterburgskogo universiteta, 2000).

Lvov, D.S. 2004. *Nravstvennaia ekonomika.* Moscow: Institute konomicheskikh strategii, 38.

Makarov, V.L. 2010. *x. Rossiiskii vyzov,* Moscow: Biznes Atlas, 191, 199.

Mill, John Stuart. 1874. *On the Definition of Political Economy, and on the Method of Investigation Proper to It,* London and Westminster Review, October 1836, paragraphs 38 and 48, in: *Essays on Some Unsettled Questions of Political Economy,* 2nd ed. London: Longmans, Green, Reader & Dyer, essay 5.

Mkrtchian, G.M. 2005. *Stratifikatsiia molodezhi v sferakh obrazovaniia, zaniatosti i potrebleniia, SOTsIS,* №2, 104.

Nuzov, Vladimir. 2012. *Vestnik.* http://www.allabout.ru/a15398.html, interview with Svetlana Aleksievich.

Nezavisimaia gazeta. 2009. Appendix '*Politika*', №3, November.

Panfilova, T.V. 2010. *Sovetskii chelovek – voploshchenie obshchestvennykh protivorechii sovetskoi epokhi.* http://www.za-nauku.ru/index.php?option=com_content&task=view&id=2585.

Patriarch of Moscow and All Russia Kirill. 2010. *Obshchestvo, ekonomika, etika v sluzhenii Russkoi Pravoslavnoi Tserkvi,* in *Neekonomicheskie grani ekonomiki: nepoznannoe vzaimovliianie.* Moscow: INES, 104.

Polani, Karl. 1999. *Dva znacheniia termina 'ekonomicheskii',* in *Neformalnaia ekonomika* (ed. Teodor Shanin). Moscow: Logos, 19–27. (Reprinted from K. Polanyi. *Livelihood of Man.* New York: Academic Press, 1977).

Rozanov, V.V. 2008. *Sobranie sochinenii,* vol. 26 (ed. A.N. Nikoliukin). Moscow: Respublika, 89.

Savva Morozov: Russkaia tragediia. 1997. *Profil',* 14 July, No26 (48).

Semenova, Elena. 2011. *Metafizicheskii realist Pushkin.* Interview with the writer Iurii Mamleev, http://litfest.ru/news/metafizicheskij_realist_pushkin/2011-02-18-924.

Shatskaia, Nina. 2011. *Lionia.* http://www.kp.ru/daily/23761.4/56602/.

Solovei, T., Solovei, V. 2011. *Chego ne khotiat russkie. Literaturnaia gazeta,* 12–18 October, №49 (6341).

Usad'ba Znamenskoe-Gubailovo. Kto zhe takoi Sergei Aleksandrovich Poliakov? 2012. http://www.imesta.nfo/places/show/182/.

Volkonskii, V.A. 2009. *Finansovyi krizis i smena ekonomicheskoi paradigmy.* Moscow: MAON.

Volkonskii, V.A., Koriagina, T.I. and Kuzovkin. 2009. A.I. *Mozhno li schitat' krizisy rukotvornymi?, Bankovskoe delo.*

CHAPTER 6

Fides et ratio: Catholicism, Rationalism and Mysticism in Russian Literary Culture of the Mid-Nineteenth Century

Elizabeth Harrison

'Religious faith' is predicated on the value of religious experience and mystical contemplation of the Divine, although not necessarily to the detriment of reason.[1] In religious thought two main methods of gaining insight developed. These are the method by reason or intellect, which is that which rationalism uses and the scholastic method was founded on, and the second is mysticism, which seeks the same truths via intuition, religious experience and mystical contemplation. It is important to note that all Christians theoretically may give merit to both approaches in their proper balance and context. Eastern Christianity is usually viewed and defined as more mystically inclined, and as Kallistos Ware has put it 'all true Orthodox theology is mystical'.[2] However, Protestantism and Catholicism also have an often overlooked mystical tradition, as the popularity of praying with the rosary testifies. Modern Catholic teaching seeks to give priority to both reason and the mysticism of faith.[3]

Western Christian theologians used scholastic and rationalist methods to help explore faith and to make arguments for God's existence or to define teaching on doctrines such as the Eucharist. With time, rationalism became strongly associated with the Enlightenment and its proceeds: secularism, atheism and the French Revolution. By 1863, 'Rationalism' had been condemned by Pius IX in the *Syllabus of Errors*. This shows to what extent the over-prioritisation of reason had become repugnant to mainstream Catholicism by that point.[4] Fideism, which gives priority to faith, rather than reason, is a view mainly held

---

1   Article 156, *The Catechism of the Catholic Church* (Popular and Definitive Edition), London: Burns and Oates, 1974, (1999 ed.), 39.
2   T. Ware, *The Orthodox Church*, London: Penguin, 1997, 206.
3   Article 156, *The Catechism of the Catholic Church* (Popular and Definitive Edition), London: Burns and Oates, 1974, (1999 ed.), 39. See also the Encyclical Letter of John Paul II, 'Fides et ratio': http://www.vatican.va/holy_father/john_paul_ii/encyclicals/documents/hf_jp-ii-enc _15101998_fides-et-ratio_en.html, last accessed 24/08/2011.
4   On the Syllabus, see O. Chadwick, *A History of the Popes, 1830–1914*, Oxford: Oxford University Press, 1998, 175–76. The text of the Syllabus is available at: http://www.papalencyclicals.net/ Pius09/p9syll.htm, last accessed 24/08/2011.

by Protestants, and in its extreme forms has likewise been condemned by the Papacy on a number of occasions. However, there are also fideist currents in Catholic thought.

Russian Orthodoxy has an important mystical tradition, in particular, hesychasm and the use of the Jesus prayer.[5] In the late eighteenth and early nineteenth century, there were both rationalist and mystical strands in Freemasonry that influenced thought in Russia.[6] Even though the Catholic Church is against Freemasonry, some pro-Catholics such as Petr Chaadaev (1796–1856) and the convert and Decembrist Mikhail Lunin (1787–1845) had been associated with the Masons (as were many others such as the other Decembrists and Pushkin).[7] Joseph de Maistre, an influential figure in early nineteenth-century Russia, was involved in Freemasonry and rejected rationalism. He can be classified as a fideist. Maistre helped shape ideas about Catholicism in contemporary Russian culture.[8] Maistre's ideas influenced Chaadaev, although they did not concur in all areas.[9] Vaiskopf has written an informative article that discusses how in the Alexandrine epoch mysticism and pietism were popular. Writers such as Aleksandr Pushkin (1799–1837), and Nikolai Gogol' (1809–1852) read *Imitatio Christi* by the Catholic mystic Thomas à Kempis.[10] Other significant mystic influences on Russian mid-nineteenth century thought and literature include Protestant mystics such as Jakob Bohme and Schelling. In the mid-nineteenth century, the Slavophiles encouraged a revival of hesychasm, partly a result of their interest in Patristic theology.[11] One could therefore conclude that the idea of mysticism in Russian culture

---

5   Ware, *The Orthodox Church*, 62–70, 304–6.

6   J. Billington, The Icon and the Axe: An Interpretative History of Russian Culture, New York: Vintage, 1970, 258.

7   Lunin left the Masons before becoming a Catholic. G. Barratt, *M.S Lunin: Catholic Decembrist*, The Hague, Paris: Mouton, 1976, 6–7.

8   Billington, *The Icon and the Axe*, 271–276. See also, V. Miltchyna, "Joseph de Maistre in Russia: A Look at the Reception of his Work", in R. Lebrun, *Joseph de Maistre's Life, Thought, and Influence*, London, Montreal and Kingston: McGill University Press, 2001, 241–70.

9   R. McNally, Chaadayev and his Friends: an Intellectual History of Peter Chaadayev and his Russian contemporaries, Tallahassee, Fla.: Diplomatic Press, 1971, 191.

10 M. Vaiskopf, «'Vot evkharistiia drugaia': Religioznaia erotika v tvorchestve Pushkina,» *Novoe literaturnoe obozrenie*, 37, 3, 1999, 133–34. In Tolstoi's *Voina i mir*, Pierre Bolkonskii was given a copy of this book to read as part of his induction into the mysticism of Freemasonry. L. Tolstoi, *Voina i mir*, II: 2: III, *Polnoe sobranie sochinenii* (90 vols.), ed. by V. Chertkov, Moscow: Jubilee Edition, 1935–1964, X: 73.

11 P. Christoff, An Introduction to Nineteenth Century Russian Slavophilism: A Study in Ideas, I.V. Kireevskii, The Hague: Mouton, 1972, 126.

consists of a mixture of Orthodox, Catholic, Protestant ideas, and influences from Freemasonry, Pantheism and Gnosticism.

Rationalism versus Mysticism in Russian Thought

In his 'Lettre première' ('First Philosophical Letter') (1828/9, published 1836), Petr Chaadaev wrote that "Le syllogisme de l'Occident nous est inconnu"[12] ("The syllogism of the West is unknown to us"). In this work, he argued that Russian and Western Europe's intellectual paths had diverged in history. Some read his "Lettre" to mean that he lamented the lack of syllogism within Russia. Certainly, he continued with an appeal, "Or, je vous demande, où sont nos sages, où sont nos penseurs?"[13] ("I ask you, where are our sages, where are our thinkers?"). Those reading this work were given two apparent alternatives: to know 'Western syllogism' and take up the mantle of sage or thinker, or somehow come to terms with the idea that Russia lacked this syllogism. Crucially, Chaadaev was also thought to be pro-Catholic, and so his turn towards Western philosophy was associated with his supposed pro-Catholicism. One of the chief criticisms made by those who censored his letter was that its author had non-Orthodox, Catholic leanings. He was thought to be suffering from madness.[14] Chaadaev himself only underlined this view when he wrote his 'Apologie d'un fou' ('Apologia of a Madman'), which hovered somewhere between a retraction, development and explanation of his views. Chaadaev's ideas meant that on the one hand, Western syllogism and philosophising were connected with Catholicism, and on the other, Catholicism was connected with madness.

The publication of Chaadaev's 'Lettre' in the journal *Teleskop* led to a furious reaction not only from the censors, but also those such as the anonymous

---

12   P. Chaadaev, 'Lettre premiere', in P. Chaadaev, *Polnoe sobranie sochnenii i izbrannye pis'ma*, (2 vols.), Moscow: "Nauka", 1991, I: 93.

13   Ibid., 95.

14   R. Tempest, "Madman or Criminal: Government attitudes to Petr Chaadaev in 1836", *Slavic Review*, XLIII/ 2 (Summer 1984), 286. 'Postanovlenie tsenzurnogo komiteta o nedopushchenii k pechati dvukh statei Chaadaeva', Chaadaev, PSS, II: 531; Letter of F. Golubinskii A. Elagin, 1836, ibid., 527; Letter of S. Uvarov to Nikolai I, 20 Oct, 1836, ibid., 529; Letter of S. Uvarov to S. Stroganov, 1836, ibid., 531. Several later scholars have referred to Chaadaev's supposed 'monomania', see, W. Lednicki, *Russia, Poland and the West. Essays in Literary and Cultural History*, London: Hutchinson, 1952, 94; D. Budgen, "Pushkin and Chaadaev: The History of a Friendship", in *Ideology in Russian Literature*, ed. by R. Freeborn and J. Grayson, London: SSEES/Macmillan, 1990, 26.

writer of a rebuttal 'Neskol'ko slov o "Filosoficheckom pis'me"', who rejected what they regarded as a negative criticism of Russian culture and a suggestion that Russia turn towards Catholic Europe.[15] As scholars such as Walicki have suggested, Chaadaev's works presented a challenge to later writers and thinkers.[16] This was particularly the case with the Slavophiles, whose debates and writings developed in the period after the publication of the 'Lettre'. In his work, Ivan Kireevskii (1806–1856) confirmed that Western Europe had developed differently from Russia. Western Europe had fallen under the influence of the Roman Empire, and therefore of the Roman Church. Since Rome had been a conquering power, it had held sway by imposing its authority on Europe, latterly via the rule of the Church. The traces of this could be found in the rule of various types of logical system.

Kireevskii writes in his 'Answer to A.S. Khomiakov' (1838):

...Вся совокупность веры опиралась на силлогическую схоластику; инквизиция, иезуитизм, одним словом, все особенности католицизма развились силою того же формального процесса разума, так что и самый протестантизм, который католики так упрекают в рациональности, произошёл прямо из рациональности католицизма.[17]

(The whole totality of the [Catholic] faith relied on syllogistic scholastics; the Inquisition, Jesuitism, in a word, all the peculiarities of Catholicism developed by the force of that formal process of reason, so that Protestantism itself, which Catholics so reproach for rationalism, came straight from the rationalism of Catholicism.)

Kireevskii placed the blame for all the negatives of Western European history, right up to Napoleon, on the Catholic emphasis on reason. Furthermore,

---

15 Anonymous, "'Neskol'ko slov o Filosoficheckom pis'me' (*Teleskop* No. 15, Pis'mo k G-zhe N.)" in *Khomiakovskii sbornik*, ed. by N. Serebrennikov, 1998, 27. It has been suggested that the author of this article was Aleksei Khomiakov, see R. Tempest, "Neizdannaia stat'ia A.S. Khomiakova', *Simvol*, 1986, No. 16, 121–24, but this has been disputed by another scholar, see M. Medovyi, "A.S. Khomiakov? A.F. Vel'tman – avtor stat'i 'Neskol'ko slov o Filosoficheckom pis'me'" in *Khomiakovskii sbornik*, ed. by N. Serebrennikov, Tomsk: 'Vodolei', 1998, I: 20–32.

16 A. Walicki, *The Slavophile Controversy: History of a Conservative Utopia in Nineteenth century Russian Thought*, trans. by H. Andrews-Rusiecka, Notre Dame, Ind.: University of Notre Dame Press, 1989, 83.

17 Kireevskii, 'V otvet A.S. Khomiakovu', *PSS*, I: 112.

Kireevskii admitted that Russians can become atheists, but even then, by different paths from Westerners:

> Православно-верующий может заразиться неверием, и то только при недостатке внешней самобытной образованности, – но не может, как мыслящий других исповедований, естественным развитием *разума* прийти к неверию.[18]

(The Orthodox believer may become infected with atheism, but only because of a lack of some exterior original education, but he cannot, like a person of another confession, arrive at atheism by the development of *reason* alone.)

The Catholic love of syllogism had threatened the very roots of its religion, in short "...в отношении к Церкви вселенской, Рим в делах веры дает преимущество отвлеченному силлогизму перед святым преданием..."[19] ("...in relation to the Universal Church, Rome in matters of faith gives priority to abstract syllogism before holy tradition".) Kireevskii, Aleksei Khomiakov (1812–1860) and the other Slavophiles extended the principle of Chaadaev's "syllogisme de l'Occident" as a pervasive system, foreign to Russia, whose effects (scholasticism, rationalism, atheism) threatened the spirit of Russia. This fed into their conceptualisation of Russian nationality and Russian Orthodoxy.

Like Kireevskii, Khomiakov argued that rationalism emerged from scholasticism, and Protestantism and atheism resulted.[20] Khomiakov's work described how these alternative outlooks determine some differences between Orthodoxy and Catholicism, and analyses matters of doctrine in more detail.[21] In an essay polemic written in French, he wrote on the subject of the Eucharist:

> Mais aussi l'Eglise ne s'est jamais demandée quels sont les rapports du corps de notre Seigneur et des éléments terrestres de l'eucharistie; car elle sait l'action dans les sacrements ne s'arrête pas aux éléments, mais en

---

18   I. Kireevskii, 'O neobkhodimosti i vozmozhnosti novykh nachal dlia filosofii', (1856) I.V. Kireevskii, *Polnoe sobranie sochinenii v dvukh tomakh,* ed. by M. Gershenzon, Moscow, 1911, reprinted by Gregg International, Hampshire, 1970, 250. [My italics].

19   Ibid., 226.

20   A. Khomiakov, 'Po povodu stat'i I.V. Kireevskogo «O kharaktere prosveshcheniia Evropy i o ego otnoshenii k prosveshcheniiu Rossii»', (1852), A. Khomiakov, *Polnoe sobranie sochinenii,* Moscow: 1878, *PSS,* I: 209.

21   'Opyt Katekhiznogo izlozheniia ucheniia o tserkvi', ('Tserkov' odna'), Khomiakov, *PSS,* II: 14.

faire des intermediares entre le Christ et son Eglise, dont la foi (je parle de tout l'Eglise et non des individus) fait la réalité du sacrement. Evidemment c'est ce que ni les romains ni les protestants ne peuvent plus comprendre, car ils on perdu idée de la totalité de l'Eglise et ne voient plus que les individus qui, disséminés on agglomérés n'en restent pas moins isolés. De là viennent leur erreur et leurs doutes, et les exigences scolastiques de leurs catéchismes.[22]

(But the Church did not ever put the question about what relation exists between the Body of Our Lord and the earthly elements of the Eucharist, because it knows that the action of God in the sacraments is not based on elements, and uses them for means between Christ and the Church, the faith of which performs the sacrament (I am speaking about the Church as a whole, and not individuals). Neither the Romans [i.e. Catholics] nor the Protestants, obviously, can now understand this, because they have lost the idea about the wholeness of the Church, and see only individuals, scattered or crowded together, but always isolated. From here all their errors, doubts and the scholastic demands of their catechisms emerge.)

The Eucharist is a particularly interesting focal point for discussion because the Orthodox Church and Catholic Church do not have major differences of dogma on this particular sacrament, apart from on the use of azymes.[23] Yet Khomiakov manages to attack Catholics for what he nonetheless regards as their misunderstanding of it. He chooses to emphasise the mystical understanding of the Eucharist. He avers here that faith is more important to Orthodoxy than it is to other religions that seem to only want rational arguments, and accordingly, lack faith.

Furthermore, rationalism is viewed as emerging from a Catholic tendency to manipulate the believer, in order to ensure the power of the institution of the Church. For example, looking at the doctrine of Purgatory (a distinguishing point between Orthodox and Catholic beliefs):

Le rationalisme se développa sous la forme de décisions d'autorité; inventant le purgatoire pour expliquer la prière pour les morts; établissant entre l'homme et Dieu une balance de devoirs et de mérites; mesurant les

---

22   Khomiakov, 'Quelques mots par un chrétien orthodoxe sur les communions occidentales a l'occasion d'un Mandement de Mgr. L'Archeréque de Paris' (1855), in *L'Eglise Latine et le protestantisme au point de vue d'Eglise d'Orient*, ed. by B. Benda, Paris: Lausanne and Levey, 1872, 38–39.
23   See, Ware, *The Orthodox Church*, 283–85.

péchés et les prières, les fautes et les actes d'expiation; faisant des reports d'un homme sur un autre; sanctionnant des échanges d'actes nommés méritoires; introduisant enfin dans le sanctuaire de la foi tout le mécanisme d'une maison de banque. Pendant ce temps, l'Eglise-Etat établissant une langue d'Etat: le latin; puis se mettait en campagne d'abord les milices désordonnées des croisades, plus tard les armées permanentes des ordres de chevalerie et finalement, quand le glaive eut été arraché de ses mains, la troupe disciplinée des jésuites.[24]

(Rationalism developed in the form of ruling definitions. It invented Purgatory, to explain prayers for the dead. It placed between God and man a balance of responsibilities and rewards, it began to throw onto the scales sins and prayers, transgressions and expiatory acts, moved remittance from one person to another, legalised exchange of supposed rewards. In a word, it brought into the sanctuary of the faith the complete mechanism of a banker's house. At the same time the Church-State introduced a state language – Latin, then it took to its court secular matters, then it took up arms, and began to arm at first the disorderly horde of crusaders, next a standing army (the Knightly orders) and then finally, when the sword was removed from its hands, it promoted the formation of the trained militia of the Jesuits.)

Although points of dogma divide the two Churches, in the works of the Slavophiles, a pre-existing 'state of mind' seems to exist which then gives rise to differences of dogma. Khomiakov defines Orthodoxy as a faith, while Protestantism and Catholicism are merely religions:

Это Вера, Вера православная, которой, слава Богу, и по особенному чувству правды, никто еще не называл религией (ибо религия может соединять людей, но только Вера связует людей не только друг с другом, но еще и с Ангелами и с самим Творцом людей и Ангелов).[25]

(It is the Faith, the Orthodox Faith, which, Glory to God, and according to a particular feeling of truth, no-one has ever called a religion [because a religion can join together people, but only a Faith can connect people not only with each other, but also with the Angels and with the very Creator of humans and angels].)

---

24 Khomiakov, 'Quelques mots par un chrétien orthodoxe sur les communions occidentales à l'occasion d'une brochure de M. Laurentie' (1853), in *L'Eglise Latine*, 38–39.
25 Khomiakov, 'Po povodu stat'i I V Kireevskogo "O kharaktere prosveshcheniia Evropy i o ego otnoshenii k prosveshcheniiu Rossii"', 1852, *PSS*, I: 257.

The conceptualisation provided here of the Orthodox faith delineates it from the mere 'religions' of the Western Churches, which are united only as institutions and in which believers are not mystically united with each other. Khomiakov gave his concept of mystical unity in community of persons of faith the name *sobornost'*.[26] This was a concept he defined further in his 1855 polemic with the Russian Jesuit, Ivan Gagarin:

> Le mot qu'ils [Cyril and Methodius] ont choisi est celui de *sobornoi* [sic]. *Sobor* implique l'idée d'assemblée non pas nécessairement réunie dans un lieu quelconque mais existant virtuellement sans réunion formelle. C'est l'unité dans la pluralité [...] L'Eglise catholique c'est l'Eglise qui est selon tous, ou selon l'unité de tous, l'Eglise de l'unanimité parfaite, l'Eglise où il n y a plus de nationalités, plus de Grecs ni de barbares, où il n y a plus de différences de conditions, plus de maîtres ni d'esclaves, c'est l'eglise prophétisée par l'Ancien Testament et réalisée par le Nouveau; l'Eglise telle enfin que saint Paul l'a définie.[27]

> (The word which they [Saints Cyril and Methodius] chose was the word *sobornoi* [sic]. *Sobor* expresses the idea of assembly not only in the sense of an actual, visible gathering of many people in one place but also in a more general sense of the continual possibility of such a gathering. It is unity in multiplicity. [...] The catholic Church is the Church according to everyone, or according to the unanimity of all, complete unanimity, the Church in which nationalities have vanished, where there is neither Greek nor pagan, nor social differences, neither masters, nor slaves, it is that Church which was prophesied in the Old Testament and was fulfilled in the New Testament; the Church is finally as described by St. Paul.]).

It is worth noting that when writing about Orthodoxy and Russianness, the Slavophiles rarely referred to the problems of Russian Orthodoxy, but targeted all criticism at the Western Churches. They usually made appeals to a sense of the

---

26 Zernov defines sobornost' as 'gathering, collectivity, integrity; it denotes oneness, but without uniformity or loss of individuality'. N. Zernov, *Three Russian Prophets: Khomiakov, Dostoevsky, Solov'ev*, London: SCM Press Ltd, 1944, 22.

27 Khomiakov, 'Lettre au rédacteur de l'Union chrétienne a l'occasion d'un discours du Père Gagarine, Jésuite', in *L'Eglise Latine*, 398. [Italics in the original]. As Khoruzhii points out, the word 'sobornyi' was not in fact introduced by Cyril and Methodius, but much later in the fourteenth century. S. Khoruzhii, 'Bogoslovie sobornosti i bogoslovie lichnosti: Simfoniia dvukh putei pravoslavnogo bogomudriia', in *A.S. Khomiakov: Poet, Philosopher, Theologian*, ed. by V. Tsurikov, New York: Holy Trinity Seminary Press, 2004, 48.

'ideal' of Orthodoxy rather than its actualities. This meant that they were often comparing the incomparable. Their vision of Russia and indeed Russian Orthodoxy was principally constructed by making criticisms of Western Europe, especially Catholicism, and using these criticisms to imply what Russianness and Orthodoxy should consist in. This aspect of their approach means that it was impossible for them to give examples of anything positive in Catholicism that could liken it to Orthodoxy or suggest improvements to Orthodoxy. Positive evaluations of the influence of reason or scholasticism on Catholic theology and examples of Catholic mysticism were therefore excluded from their works.

Rationalism and Mysticism in Russian Literature

Vaiskopf points to religious eroticism inspired in part by Pushkin's reading of Catholic mysticism.[28] We can observe this phenomenon in narrative poems such as his *Gavriliada* (1821) as well as lyrics poems such as 'Madona' (1830), and in particular, the fascinating poem, 'Zhil na svete rytsar' bednyi...' (1829) ('There lived on the earth a poor knight...'):[29]

> Жил на свете рыцарь бедный
> Молчаливый и простой,
> С виду сумрачный и бледный,
> Духом смелый и прямой.
>
> Он имел одно виденье,
> Непостижное уму,
> И глубоко впечатленье
> В сердце врезалось ему.
>
> Путешествуя в Женеву,
> На дороге у креста
> Видел он Марию деву,
> Матерь господа Христа.
>
> С той поры, сгорев душою,
> Он на женщин не смотрел,

---

28 Vaiskopf, "Vot evkharistiia drugaia", 129–43.

29 'Madonna' (1830), A. Pushkin, *Polnoe sobranie sochinenii v deviatnadtsati tomakh*, Moscow: Voskresen'e, 1949: 1994, III: 224.

И до гроба ни с одною
Молвить слова не хотел.

С той поры стальной решетки
Он с лица не подымал
И себе на шею четки
Вместо шарфа привязал.

Несть мольбы Отцу, ни Сыну,
Ни святому Духу ввек
Не случилось паладину,
Странный был он человек.

Проводил он целы ночи
Перед ликом пресвятой
Устремив к ней скорбны очи,
Тихо слезы лья рекой.

Полон верой и любовью,
Верен набожной мечте,
Ave, Mater Dei кровью
Написал он на щите.

Между тем как паладины
Ввстречу трепетным врагам
По равнинам Палестины
Мчались, именуя дам,

Lumen coelum, sancta Rosa!
Восклицал в восторге он,
И гнала его угроза
Мусульман со всех сторон.

Возвратясь в свой замок дальный,
Жил он строго заключен,
Всё безмолвный, всё печальный,
Без причастья умер он.

Между тем как он кончался,
Дух лукавый подоспел,

Душу рыцаря сбирался
Бес тащить уж в свой предел:

Он-де Богу не молился,
Он не ведал-де поста,
Не путем-де волочился
Он за матушкой Христа.

Но пречистая, конечно,
Заступилась за него
И впустила в царство вечно
Паладина своего.[30]

[There lived on the earth a poor knight
Silent and simple,
He had a morose and pale look
But in spirit he was brave and straightforward.

He had a certain vision
That could not be understood with the mind.
It cut a deep impression
On his heart.

Travelling to Geneva,
On the road by a cross
He saw the Virgin Mary
The Mother of Our Lord.

From that time, his spirit burning,
He did not look at women
And until his death he
Would not exchange a word with one.

From that time he did not raise
His steel visor from his face.
He wound rosary beads
Instead of a scarf around his neck.

---

30   Pushkin, *PSS*, III: 161–2.

He did not raise his prayers
To the Father, nor Son
Nor Holy Spirit,
He was a strange man.

He spent whole nights
Before the Most Holy countenance,
Gazing at her with sorrowful eyes,
His tears quietly flowing like a river.

Full of faith and love
True to his devout dream
Ave, Mater Dei he wrote
In blood upon his shield.

While the Paladin rushed
Towards his trembling enemies
Along the ravines of Palestine
Calling the Lady's name,

Lumen coelum, sancta Rosa!
He cried out in delight
And his menace drove away
The Moors in all directions.

Returning to his distant castle
He lived strictly isolated.
Always silent, always sad,
He died excommunicate.

As was dying,
An evil spirit rushed
To get to the knight,
To drag the knight's soul to his domain.

'He did not pray to God', said he –
'He did not keep the fast,
And he courted the Mother of Christ
As an earthly woman'.

> But the Virgin, of course,
> Interceded for him
> And allowed into the eternal kingdom,
> Her paladin.]

The plot outline of this poem is a parody of a piece of Catholic hagiography or ballad with the Knight as the hero. The link to Catholicism is underlined by the Knight wearing a rosary, and by the fragments of Latin quoted. The first appears to be two citations from the "Hail Mary" ("Ave Maria [...] Mater dei..." ("Hail Mary [...] Mother of God...")). The line "lumen coelum, sancta rosa" ("light of heaven, holy rose"), although embedded as a single quotation, is two disjointed phrases, and is not a quotation at all. "Sancta rosa" evokes the rose as symbol of the Virgin Mary. The appearance of these Latin phrases helps give the text a Catholic hue without apparently adding anything much to the poem, and may have been chosen simply to fit the metre. In summary, the Knight's encounter with a mystical vision is seen to change his life. Two chief questions arise from this poem. Who is the Knight, and who or what, if anything, does his mystical vision represent?

Many scholars have sought to unlock the poem. For example, Slivkin's reading is inter-textual. He has argued that the poem may arise from Pushkin's interest in Freemasonry and the Knights Templar (a Catholic order). There is also the influence of Walter Scott, whose novel *Ivanhoe* (1819) was popular at the period in which Pushkin was writing. Slivkin has seen the Knight of the poem as perhaps based on the real story of Jehan de Luze.[31] The Knight may be identified as a knight of the Crusading Era, thanks to the references to the Holy Land and Moors; this would fit well with the setting of *Ivanhoe*.

The poem may also incorporate a parody of the life of Ignatius of Loyola, the founder of the Jesuit Order. It is quite likely that Pushkin would have known about the general shape of Loyola's life, even if he had not read the *Autobiography* itself. The Jesuits had been teaching in Russia in the earlier years of the poet's life, up to 1820. Pushkin had a friend who was an alumnus of a Jesuit school, and makes several references to the Jesuits in his work.[32] Loyola, having been a knight (from a rich family) saw a vision (of the Virgin

---

[31] Y. Slivkin, 'Was the Covetous Knight Poor and was the Poor Knight Covetous?', *Russian Literature* LV/4, (May 2004), 552–56.

[32] *Boris Godunov*, (Noch', sad. Fontan') Pushkin, PSS, VII:65; 'Table Talk', Pushkin, PSS, XII: 156; A. Pushkin to P.A. Viazemskii, 24 June, 1824, PSS. XIII: 99. P. Viazemskii went to a Jesuit school. W. Mills Todd III, *The Familiar Letter as a Literary Genre of the Age of Pushkin*, Evanston, Ill.: Northwestern University Press, 1976 (1999), 201.

Mary) and dedicated his life to Christ, laying his sword at the altar of Our Lady, living a life of extreme asceticism. He later travelled to the Holy Land, in order to convert the Muslims there, and having attempted to discern his path by using his mule to guide his decision,[33] he did not kill a Moor who had impugned the virginity of the Virgin Mary.[34] The Symbolist poet Elizaveta Dmitrieva (Cherubina de Gabriac), followed such a reading of 'Zhil na svete…' in her own poem about Ignatius of Loyola.[35] The Order Ignatius founded, the Society of Jesus, mixed mystical approaches, for example the use of mystical contemplation (most obviously *The Spiritual Exercises*) with intellectual academic rigour. However, the poem is not solely aimed at criticising or parodying Loyola – if this were the case, Pushkin would have made this explicit. Rather, he uses this story as a model.

Turning to cultural history, there is a general connection between Catholicism, knights and eccentric behaviour in Russian culture. This image was doubtless enhanced by figures such as Loyola and fictional characters like Cervantes' Don Quixote. In the early nineteenth century Catholic converts and those with pro-Catholic sympathies, such as Prince Petr Kozlovskii (1783–1840), Mikhail Lunin, Paul I (who became head of the Knights of Malta), or Chaadaev, were all considered eccentrics or madmen in their time.[36] Around the time the poem was written, Chaadaev, like the Knight, began to live a strange life, and ceased for periods to communicate with fellow human beings, to engage in romantic relationships with women, and to or (arguably) follow Orthodox religious practice. Pushkin's friendship with Chaadaev, Kozlovskii and Lunin, surely informs the exploration in the poem of conversion or similar life-changing experiences which seem to others to be completely irrational.[37] They may be blinkered by their faith, becoming single-minded and unaware of the rest of the

---

33　I.e. using the mule to reveal God's will or the Holy Spirit's influence on affairs.

34　J. Olin, (ed.), *The Autobiography of St Ignatius Loyola, with Related Documents*, trans. J.O'Callaghan, London: Harper and Row, 1974, 21, 22–25, 30–32, 45–51 *passim*.

35　N. Mednis, "Immenye ili personal'nye teksty. Pushkinskii tekst russkoi literatury", in *Sverkhteksty v russkoi literature: Uchebnoe posobie*, Novisibirsk: Izd. IGPU, 2003, 51–152. This article chronicles the use of Pushkin's themes in later poetry. The poem referred to is 'Sv. Ignatiiu' (1909), in *Sub rosa: Adelaida Gertsyk, Sofiia Parnok, Poliksena Solov'eva, Cherubina de Gabriac*, Moscow: Ellis Lak, 1999, 476.

36　On how the law discouraged conversion, see M. Fairweather, *Pilgrim Princess: A Life of Princess Zinaida Volkonsky*, London: Robinson, 1999, 254, see also O. Litsenburger, *Rimsko-katolicheskaia tserkov' v Rossii. Istoriia i pravovoe polozhenie*, Saratov: Povolzhskaia Akademiia gosudarstvennoi sluzhby, 2001, 89–91.

37　Pushkin addressed poems to three Catholic converts: *Evgenii Onegin*, in Pushkin, PSS, VI: 524, 'Kn. Kozlovskomu' Pushkin PSS, III: 430, 'Kniagine Z.A. Volkonskoi', Pushkin PSS, III: 354.

world by an idea of their own virtue. The poem's *topos*, the road, and the idea of a journey is very significant, because this is frequently seen as the space where encounters and changing experiences occur.[38] The topos of a road is significant in many stories of religious experience and conversion. One of the best-known conversion stories is that of St Paul on the Road to Damascus (Acts 9: 3–9). Pushkin therefore uses this outline to explore the motif of mystical experience and conversion.

'What' the Knight meets is a mystical vision ("Он имел одно виденье,/ Непостижное уму". ("He had a certain vision/That could not be understood with the mind"). This vision is of the Virgin Mary, and he appears to develop an inappropriate affection for her. Vaiskopf has pointed out that Pushkin not infrequently identifies earthly love with love for the Virgin Mary.[39] Scholarship has already investigated the biographical angle of Pushkin's view of women as depicted in his poetry. In particular, his relationship with Natalia Goncharova and his mother are thought to be significant.[40] It is certainly worth considering that one of the potential models for the Virgin in the poem is Natalia Goncharova, Pushkin's wife. Pushkin applied the epithet *"stabat mater dolorosa"* to Goncharova.[41] These words are taken from a Catholic hymn, which has the same metre as this poem (trochaic tetrametre). Although this metre is fairly common, Goncharova's connection to 'Madonna' figures in Pushkin's work seems to make it more likely that the choice was not coincidental. In finding a connection between earthly women and the Virgin Mary, Pushkin used Catholic (i.e. Western European) representations of Mary rather than

---

His relationship with Chaadaev was unquestionably significant, see Budgen, "Pushkin and Chaadaev", 1–46.

38 M. Bakhtin, 'Formy vremeni i khronotopa v romane', in M. Bakhtin, *Epos i roman*, Saint Petersburg: Azbuka, 2000, 23, 176.

39 Vaiskopf, "Vot evkharistiia drugaia", 141.

40 My thanks to Sergei Kibal'nik for pointing out this angle when I first gave this paper. S. Berezkina, "Motivy materi i materinstva v tvorchestva A.S. Pushkina", *Russkaia literatura*, 1, 2001, 167–86; M. Stroganov, "Pushkin i Madona", *A.S. Pushkin: Problemy Tvorchestva*, ed. by S. Fomichev, Kalinin, 1987, 15–35. For other examples of the pursuit of the feminine ideal, see 'K **' ('Ty bogomater', net somnen'ia...'), (1826), Pushkin, PSS, III: 45; Untitled ('Kto znaet krai, gde nebo bleshchet...') (1828), ibid., III: 96–98, and others. On the use of Raphael's Madonna, see also, I. Pearson, 'Raphael as seen by Russian writers from Zhukovsky to Turgenev', *Slavonic and East European Review*, LIX/3, (1981), 346–69, (350–52) on Pushkin.

41 *Al'bom Elizavety Ushakovoi*, ed. by T. Krasnoborod'ko, St. Petersburg: IRLI/ 'Logos': 1999, 208 (This shows a sketch by Pushkin – the signature is on the sleeve in the lace, forming the pattern of the lace) and commentary, 283. Cited in Berezkina, 'Motivy materi', 186.

icons, which may have helped this connection seen less 'profane' in contemporary Russian culture. Criticisms or references to Catholicism can therefore seem to help the poet distance his satirical comment from those subjects that are protected in his own culture and time.

If the Virgin figure is meant to represent Goncharova, and a biographical reading is considered relevant, then it is possible that the poem refers to Pushkin himself as the Knight. This gives the poem a new, more sympathetic feeling and an added irony: if Pushkin is the Knight, then the poet would himself go into battle with a desire to defend the honour of his own 'Madonna' and die as a result. At the same time the use of the medieval colour in the story gently distances us from such strict contemporary or purely biographical readings. The poem can be read to fit any person's life, not excluding the poet's. This may explain why the poem has intrigued scholars so much and been of such interest to other writers, such as Dostoevskii, Ivanov and Dmitrieva.

Religious experience, posited as something that cannot be understood with the mind, becomes a conversion experience. In the first thirteen stanzas this conversion is seen as absurd; because of the way it makes the Knight behave, Pushkin appears to discard the usefulness of such an experience for any person. Only in the very last stanza does the vision appear to be justified by the fact that the Knight is allowed into heaven, through the intercession of the Virgin. Ivanov read the poem as a reflection on the poet's regrets that he was unable to be moved by such visions.[42]

The poem represents what mystical experiences can mean and as such it is as intriguing and ambivalent as the experiences themselves. It leads the reader to question what motivates our decisions in life, and why it is that we can be so sure that we are pursuing the correct path, when others do not find our decisions rational. Catholicism and the 'foreignness' of the mysticism in the poem are very useful tools for the poet. The references to non-Russian religion and culture, such as knights, or the Latin phrases, allow the poet to apparently distance his ideas from Russia. This ironic distance helps the poet to explore issues that were in fact very relevant to Russian culture and perhaps his own life and friendships at the time when he was writing.

Gogol's novella *Taras Bul'ba* (written in 1835 and rewritten in 1842) also contains a meditation on religious experience and conversion. Andrii symbolically converts to Catholicism in the novella, by falling in love with a Polish girl and changing sides in the ethnic-religious conflict between Orthodox Cossacks and Catholic Poles. Catholicism's influence is so infectious that, as the text

---

42 V. Ivanov, "Dva Maiaka", in *Pushkin v russkoi filosofskoi kritike*, ed. by R. Haltsevoi, Moscow: 'Kniga', 1999, 250.

seems to suggest, the merest brush with it can cause a fatal change in a person. Andrii's encounter with Roman Catholicism, like Gogol's own, contains a strong aesthetic and mystical element. The description of Andrii's entry into the Polish Catholic town of Dubno contains a description of a church which scholars have long assumed to have been inspired by Gogol's experience of Rome's churches:

> Окно с цветными стеклами, бывшее над алтарем, озарилося розовым румянцем утра, и упали от него на пол голубые, желтые и других цветов кружки света, осветившие внезапно темную церковь. Весь алтарь в своем далеком углублении показался вдруг в сиянии; кадильный дым остановился на воздухе радужно освещенным облаком. Андрий не без изумления глядел из своего темного угла на чудо, произведенное светом. В это время величественный рев органа наполнил вдруг всю церковь. Он становился гуще и гуще, разрастался, перешел в тяжелые ропоты грома и потом вдруг, обратившись в небесную музыку, понесся высоко под сводами своими поющими звуками, напоминавшими тонкие девичьи голоса, и потом опять обратился он в густой рев и гром и затих. И долго еще громовые ропоты носились, дрожа, под сводами, и дивился Андрий с полуоткрытым ртом величественной музыке.[43]

(A stained-glass window above the altar was lit by the pink flush of the morning, and dapples of light in blue, yellow and other colours suddenly illuminated the dark church. The whole altar in the distant depths seemed suddenly to shine; the incense smoke hung in the air in a cloud of rainbow light. Andrii, with wonder, looked from the dark corner to the miracle performed by the light. At that moment, the grand roar of the organ suddenly filled the whole church. It became richer and richer, flowing outwards. It changed to heavy rumbling, like thunder, and then, suddenly, transformed into heavenly music which carried itself in melodic tones high up to the vaults, reminding one of the delicate voices of young girls. Then it again turned back into a deep roar and thunder, then grew silent. For a long time the thunderous rumbles carried up, quivering, to the vaulting, and Andrii continued to be surprised, his mouth half-open mouth at the majestic music.)

---

[43] *Taras Bul'ba,* N. Gogol', *Polnoe sobranie sochinenii* (14 vols.), Moscow: Akademia Nauk, 1937–1952, III: 96–97. See, E. Bojanowska, *Nikolai Gogol: Between Ukrainian and Russian Nationalism*, Cambridge, Mass.: Harvard University Press, 2007, 301.

It is interesting to compare this fictional extract of an encounter with unfamiliar Catholic architecture and music with that of the convert Vladimir Pecherin (1807–1885) in his memoirs:

> Мне пришлось идти мимо церкви. Из неё неслись звуки органа. Вхожу – церковь битком набита. Алтарь пылал разноцветными огнями, вазы с цветами распространяли благоухание, дым ладана вился голубою струею и терялся под готическим сводом. В то время я всё мерил республиканским масштабом. Что я, оборванный, небритый, нечесанный, запыленный, грязный, что я в этом нищенском образе мог выйти в этот великолепный храм, наполненный *изящным людом* (*beau monde*) и мог найти место между ними и наравне с ними имел право наслаждаться звуками очаровательной музыки – всё это в глазах моих обличало демократический характер католической церкви.[44]

> (I had to walk past a church. The sounds of an organ were coming from it. I went in. It was full of people. The altar was ablaze with many colours – vases with flowers spreading their fragrance, incense wafting in a blue stream and disappearing under the gothic vault. At that time, I was judging everything according to a Republican scale. The fact that, despite being ragged, unshaven, unkempt, dusty and dirty, I could enter this magnificent house of worship filled with *elegant people* (*beau monde*) in such an impoverished state, and that I could find a place among them and have the same right to revel in the sounds of the captivating music – all this revealed in my eyes the deeply democratic nature of the Catholic Church.)[45]

Both Gogol's and Pecherin's descriptions emphasise an aesthetic appreciation of the forms of Catholicism which turns into a mystical attraction to Catholicism. The *Primary Chronicle* had also underlined the factor of the beauty of form when recording how Vladimir's emissaries to Byzantium recommended Orthodoxy to him.[46] It is significant that Gogol' specifically uses

---

[44] V. Pecherin, 'Apologia pro vita mea', in *Russkoe obshchestvo 30-kh godov XIX v. Liudi i idei. Memuary sovremennikov*, ed. by I. Fedosov, Moscow: Moskovskii Universitet, 1989, 198. [Italics in the original].

[45] V. Pecherin, *The First Political Emmigre: Notes from Beyond the Grave, or Apologia pro vita mea*, trans. by M. Katz, Introduction by N. Pervukhina-Kamyshnikova, Dublin: University College Dublin Press, 2008, 63–4.

[46] 'И пришли мы к немцам [i.e. Catholics] и видели их службу, но красоты не видели никакой. И пришли мы в Греческую землю, и ввели нас туда, где служат они Богу своему, и не знали мы – на небе или на земле: ибо нет на земле такого зрелища и

the word "небесный" ("heavenly") in relation to the music, when the writers of the *Chronicle* had emphasised that the Byzantine rites were heavenly. The very aestheticism of this description divides readers and critics. While Bojanowska largely sees this as showing Gogol's sympathy for Catholic architecture and art, if not as a sign of the desire to convert *per se*, Yoon reverses this reading to argue that the passage deliberately makes the juxtaposition between Orthodoxy and Catholicism, but seeks to show that Orthodoxy is superior. This opinion basically assumes that aesthetic contemplation is viewed negatively in Russia. Taking into account the *Primary Chronicle* and its importance in Russian culture, this does not make sense. Certainly, an examination of Gogol's letters would suggest the reverse, that aesthetic appreciation was entwined with the spiritual aspect of Catholicism for him.[47]

Pecherin, having noted a spiritual reaction to aesthetic stimulus, interprets this by reference to the idea of Catholicism as an institution that allows everyone access to beauty. He therefore provides a rational explanation for what had led him in the direction of conversion. He turns a highly specific subjective experience into grounds for a making a broader, objective analysis about the genuinely universal nature of 'ideal Catholicism'. By contrast, these passages from *Taras Bul'ba* dismiss rational reasons for Andrii's change of heart in favour of non-rational reasons. The author makes no attempt to make a broader point about Catholicism; it is left to the reader to ask whether the aesthetic appeal of

---

красоты такой, и не знаем, как и рассказать об этом, – знаем мы только, что пребывает там Бог с людьми, и служба их лучше, чем во всех других странах. Не можем мы забыть красоты той, ибо каждый человек, если вкусит сладкого, не возьмет потом горького; так и мы не можем уже здесь жить'. [And we came to the Germans [i.e. the Catholics] and saw their service, but saw no kind of beauty. And we went to the Greek land, and they took us to the place where they do service to their God, and we did not know if we were in heaven or on earth: for there is not on earth such a sight and beauty as this, and we do not even know how to tell about this – we only know that in that place, God comes among people, and that their service is better than in all other countries. We cannot forget such beauty, for every man, once he has tasted something sweet, cannot then taste anything bitter; so we cannot live here'.] Quoted from this online text of the Primary Chronicle: http://www.pushkinskijdom.ru/Default.aspx?tabid=4869 IRLI RAN, last accessed 24/08/11. [My translation from the modern Russian text].

47 Bojanowska, *Nikolai Gogol*, 301–2, cf. S. Yoon, 'Transformation of a Ukrainian Cossack into a Russian Warrior: Gogol's 1842 *Taras Bul'ba*', *Slavonic and East European Journal*, XLIX/ 3, (2005), 435. See, N. Gogol' to E. and A. Gogol', 15 October 1838, *PSS*, XI: 177, N. Gogol' to M.I. Gogol', March 28 1837, *PSS*, XI: 89–90, N. Gogol' to N. Prokopovich, March 30 1837, *PSS*, XI: 93, N.V. Gogol' to E. and A. Gogol', April 28 1838, *PSS*, XI: 137–39. N. Gogol' to M.P. Balabina, April 1838, Gogol', *PSS*, XI: 140.

Catholic architecture is universal or not. Aesthetic appeal may be subjective and may give rise to mystical religious experience, but the subjectivity of that experience, recorded in literature and directed at the reader, does not make it invalid. Rather, the fact that this idea has not been dictated to the reader in a didactic way allows the reader to contemplate these ideas for themself. Such is the contribution that literature can make as opposed to memoirs and essays.

The novella contrasts the phenomenon of knighthood in Western (Catholic) Christendom with Cossacks who, as Orthodox 'knights', were meant to be celibate and not care about women.[48] The depiction of Andrii in the text therefore forms an interesting counterpoint to Pushkin's poem 'Zhil na svete rytsar' bednyi...' While we cannot be certain that Gogol had read the poem, he was certainly playing with the idea of knighthood in *Taras Bul'ba* and, as Mann argues, sometimes chose to parody as well as emulate Pushkin.[49] Andrii, who is referred to as a *rytsar'* on numerous occasions, like the Poor Knight meets a "lady"; in this case an earthly one, apparently. Yet in the text, Andrii encounters a "vision" of the "Madonna" as well:

> Они достигли небольшой площадки, где, казалось, была часовня; по крайней мере, к стене был приставлен узенький столик в виде алтарного престола, и над ним виден был почти совершенно изгладившийся, полинявший образ *католической Мадонны*. Небольшая серебряная лампадка, пред ним висевшая, чуть-чуть озаряла его.[50]

> (They reached a small landing where there seemed to be a chapel; at least, there was a narrow table affixed to the wall acting as an altar table and above it an almost totally faded and effaced image of a *Catholic Madonna*. A small silver lamp hanging before the image illuminated it a little.)

The fact that the narrator (somewhat unnecessarily in the context) specifies that the depiction of the Madonna is Catholic foregrounds the role of

---

48   A common possible inter-text is Walter Scott's *Ivanhoe*, see G. Rosenshield, *The Ridiculous Jew: The Exploitation and Transformation of a Stereotype in Gogol, Turgenev, and Dostoevsky*, Stanford, CA.: Stanford University Press, 2008, 61–69, and Slivkin, "Was the Covetous Knight Poor", 556–59.

49   The theme of knights has been briefly mentioned by, Iu. Mann, *Gogol': Trudy i Dni, 1809–1845*, Moscow: Aspekt Press, 2004, 514, I. Vinogradov, "Taras Bul'ba i otnoshenie Gogolia k katolitsizmu", in *Gogol': khudozhnik myslitel': khristianskie osnovy mirozertsaniia*, Moscow: IMLI RAN / 'Nasledie', 2000, 184. For Mann on Pushkin and Gogol, see Mann, *Gogol': Trudy i Dni*, 472–73.

50   Ibid., 95. [my italics].

Catholicism in the text. The narrator's remarks that the image is "faded" and "effaced" appears to link the Madonna to the Polish girl in the text. The girl, like every person in the town of Dubno, is starving and pale. Andrii, like the Knight, is also described as silent; in a number of points in the text he is unable to say anything.[51] Unlike Pushkin's knight, he carries a real scarf as a memento of his lady (not a rosary).[52] Andrii, too, is a convert inspired by a non-rational vision, whose conversion leads to him betray a 'normal' Orthodox lifestyle; in defence of his Lady he kills not Muslims but his own Orthodox kindred, which leads to his death. One wonders whether the manner of his death may mean that, like the Poor Knight, eternal salvation is his reward. The text leaves this unclear.

Gogol's literary work, like Pushkin's, contains an appeal to the reader to think about subjective experience in an open way. His essays in *Vybrannye mesta iz perepiski s druz'iami* (1847) (*Selected Passages from Correspondence with Friends*), by contrast, are far more didactic and dogmatic in the way they discuss Catholicism. It is worth noting that he, like other writers, compared the Orthodox Church and the Catholic Church through the story of Martha and Mary (Luke 10: 38–42).

> ... вижу всю мудрость Божью, повелевшую [...] одной [церкви] – подобно скромной Марии, отложивши все попеченья о земном, поместиться у ног самого Господа, затем, чтобы лучше наслушаться слов его, прежде чем применять и передавать их людям, другой же – подобно заботливой хозяйке Марфе, гостеприимно хлопотать около людей, передавая им еще *не взвешенные всем разумом* слова господни. Благую часть избрала первая [...] Полный и всесторонний взгляд на жизнь остался на ее восточной половине, видимо сбереженной для позднейшего и полнейшего образования человека. В ней простор не только душе и сердцу человека, *но и разуму, во всех его верховных силах*; в ней дорога и путь, как устремить всё в человеке в один согласный гимн верховному существу.[53]

(I see all the wisdom of God in making it so that [...] one [the Church], like the modest Mary, putting aside worldly cares, takes its place at the feet of the Lord himself, in order better to hear his words before adapting and transmitting them to men, and let the other, like the careful

---

51 'Андрий был безответен', [Andrii did not answer]. *Taras Bul'ba,* Gogol', PSS, III: 144, see also 102.
52 *Taras Bul'ba,* Gogol', PSS, III: 142–43.
53 'Prosveshchenie', in *Vybrannye mesta iz perepiski s druz'iami,* Gogol', PSS, VIII: 284 [My italics].

housekeeper Mary, hospitably fuss about with people, transmitting to them the word of the Lord *unsupported by reason*. The first one chose the good part [...] The full and total view of life remained in the eastern Church, manifestly kept in reserve for the later and more complete education of man. She has room not only for the *soul and heart* of man, but also for *his reason, in all its supreme powers;* in her is the way and the road by which everything in man will turn into an harmonious hymn to the supreme being.)[54]

Mary can be seen as representative of the contemplative principle in Christianity. Contemplation is closely aligned with mystical experience (although not solely). In this passage Gogol' chooses to emphasise that Russian Christianity is traditionally more contemplative. However, he also argues that reason is a supreme power, and Orthodoxy can use this power as well as emotion. Unlike the Slavophiles, Gogol' does not therefore choose to criticise Catholicism for its rationality. He in fact criticises the lack of reason in the Catholic Church's approach. The essay criticises Catholicism, but not by suggesting that Catholicism is less of a faith because it is more rational than mystical.

It is worth noting in support of Gogol's understanding of Catholicism as a mystical religion that he had sent copies of *Imitatio Christi* to some of his friends in 1844, telling them to read it and explaining how to use the mysticism of the book and how it could help them.[55] After the publication of *Vybrannye mesta,* Gogol' was accused of being drawn to Roman Catholicism and behaving like a Catholic.[56] This was despite his clear preference for Russian Orthodoxy within the work as a whole.[57] The fact that Gogol' was associated with both Catholicism and madness or mental illness added further fuel to existing perceptions that those who were pro-Catholic were suffering from some illness. The fact that madness is surely antithetical to the idea of 'reason' did not appear to be viewed as contradictory by those making accusations.

In some of his writings Gogol' is pro-Orthodox and a Russian nationalist. At the same time, as we have seen, Gogol' as a writer conveys some understanding

---

54 'Enlightenment' in N. Gogol, *Selected Passages from Correspondence with Friends,* trans. by J. Zeldin, Nashville: Vanderbilt University Press, 1969, 93–95.

55 N. Gogol to S. Aksakov, M. Pogodin and S. Shevyrev, January, 1844, *PSS,* XII: 249–250. See also, for example, N. Gogol to M. Pogodin, 20 December 1844, *PSS,* XII: 402.

56 S. Shevyrev to N. Gogol', 30 January 1847, in *N.V. Gogol': Perepiska v dvukh tomakh,* ed. by V.E. Vatsuro, et al., Moscow: Khudozhestvennaia literatura, 1988, II: 344.

57 'Neskol'ko slov o nashei tserkvi i o dukhovenstve', Gogol', *PSS,* VIII: 245; 'O tom zhe', Gogol', *PSS,* VIII: 247.

of the fact that Catholic religion could hold similarities to Orthodox believer's experience of their faith. In this he departs very much from the views of the Slavophiles. However, his reflections on the mystical element of Catholicism are most clearly expressed in his fiction (and his letters), not his essays. It is these texts that explore and best convey the fact that people can be drawn to change their lives as a result of a non-rational experience (emotional, mystical, religious visions), and subjective religious experiences on both sides of the denominational line.

Both Gogol' and Pushkin as writers of 'fiction' (we can see Pushkin's poem as fiction in poetry) allow different readings and their texts are open to some sympathy towards the mystical element of Catholicism. Fedor Tiutchev (1803–1873) is an interesting poet to compare with Pushkin because, like Gogol', he wrote in non-literary forms such as essays. Tiutchev was more closely linked with the Slavophiles than Pushkin, and the influence of mysticism on Tiutchev's poetry has been researched to a far greater extent, so this will not be repeated here. Influences on him include Schelling and Bohme (both Protestants) and Pascal, who was a Catholic.[58] Tiutchev allows Pascal a different treatment than other Catholics. His essays are highly critical of the Catholic Church, this moderation towards Pascal maybe because was a Jansenist and therefore disagreed with elements of Catholic doctrine. Tiutchev's essay 'La Question Romaine', the writer views Pascal as an ally in their shared dislike of the Jesuits.[59] In a remark quoted by Aksakov, he wrote very clearly:

> Une philosophie qui rejette le surnaturel, et qui veut tout prouver par la raison, doit fatalement dériver vers le materialisme pour se noyer dans l'athéisme. La seule philosophie compatible avec le Christianisme est contenu tout entière dans le Catéchisme. Il faut croire ce que croyait Saint Paul, et après lui Pascal, plier le genou devant La Folie de la Croix, on tout nier. Le surnaturel est au fond ce qu'il y a de plus naturel a l'homme.[60]

(A philosophy that rejects the supernatural, and wants to prove everything with reason, has no choice but to deviate towards materialism and

---

58 R. Gregg " 'Dream at Sea': Tiutchev and Pascal", *Slavic Review*, XXIII, 3, (September 1964), 526–63; A. Polonskii, "Mistika v zhizni i mistitsizm v tvorchestve Fedora Tiutcheva" *Russian Literature*, LIV (2003), 505–24, 508; S. Pratt, *Russian Metaphysical Romanticism: The Poetry of Tiutchev and Baratynskii*, Stanford CA: Stanford University Press, 1984.

59 'La Question Romaine', Tiutchev, *Polnoe sobranie sochinenie i pis'ma v shesti tomakh*, Moscow: Klassika, 2003, III: 66.

60 A. Aksakov, *Biografiia Fedora Ivanovicha Tiutcheva*, Moscow: 1886, 319, quoted in Gregg "'Dream at Sea'", 527.

end up drowning in atheism. The only philosophy compatible with Christianity is contained it its entirety in the contents of the Catechism. One must believe that which St Paul, and after him Pascal, believed – bend the knee before the Folly of the Cross, and one denies everything. The supernatural is at the foundation of what is most natural in man.)[61]

Tiutchev's mysticism in his poetry is highly syncretic, drawing on Western types of mysticism to describe Russian themes and universal themes. In respect to his understanding of Russia and the West, his lyrical poetry gives priority to instinct and mystical understanding over reason, but it shows an ambivalence towards Russia and Western Europe which is typical of Tiutchev's poetry. He not infrequently (especially in the first half of his life) reveals a deep attraction to Western Europe, and in the latter half of his life this moves generally towards a more straightforward attitude towards Russia. He attempts to adjust his posture towards Europe

One poem shows Tiutchev meditating on a turning point between two directions in which he is drawn. The poem relates to the period of Tiutchev's return to Russia after a long spell abroad. He was to remain in Russia, apart from short trips, for the rest of his life. In 'Gliadel ia, stoia nad Nevoi' (1844) ('Standing by the Neva, I gazed...') Tiutchev shows an instinctual, mystical and aesthetic attraction and appreciation for both East and West. He uses a poetic vision of Italy to perform the role of antithesis to St. Petersburg:

Глядел я, стоя над Невой,
Как Исаака-великана
Во мгле морозного тумана
Светился купол золотой.

Всходили робко облака
На небо зимнее, ночное,
Белела в мертвенном покое
Оледенелая река.

Я вспомнил, грустно-молчалив,
Как в тех странах, где солнце греет,
Теперь на солнце пламенеет
Роскошный Генуи залив...

---

61   My thanks to H. Colyer and S. Jivraj for their assistance with this translation.

О Север, Север-чародей,
Иль я тобою околдован?
Иль в самом деле я прикован
К гранитной полосе твоей?

О, если б мимолетный дух,
Во мгле вечерней тихо вея,
Меня унес скорей, скорее
Туда, туда, на теплый Юг...[62]

[Standing by the Neva, I gazed
At St. Isaac's – 'the Giant'
At how its golden dome
Shone through the gloom of the frosty fog.

Shyly the clouds rose up to float
In the wintery night sky
And the frozen river
Shone pale in the deathly stillness.

I recalled, sadly taciturn
How in those countries where the sun is warm
Now the splendid Gulf of Genoa
Is set aflame by the sun...

Oh North, Northern-Enchanter
Am I bewitched by you?
Am I really fettered
To your granite embankment?

Oh, if only a passing spirit
In the evening gloom should quietly waft by
And take me swiftly, all the sooner,
There, to the warm South...]

On a first reading, the poem appears to be simply a description of a real experience, and so the religious or national theme seems secondary to the imagery of

---

62   Tiutchev, *PSS*, I: 193.

the weather.[63] However, the images of the poem do reflect on Tiutchev's image of Russia and Europe. The dome serves as a linking symbol uniting different topoi, just as the poet compares the waters of Gulf of Genoa with the River Neva, which flows to the Gulf of Finland. Importantly, Petersburg was frequently compared to Italian cities such as Venice or Rome, and St Isaac's is a Cathedral based on Western models, like Petersburg the city. The most famous dome of this type in the world is St Peter's Basilica in Rome. Both Gogol', and later, Viacheslav Ivanov use the image of the dome as a symbol of the presence of Catholicism in Italy.[64] So although the architecture of St Isaac's owes more to European neo-Classicism as a general movement, rather than being a copy of a particular Roman Catholic Cathedral, the contribution of Catholic and Western architecture to this apparent symbol of Russian religious life would be obvious to most of Tiutchev's readers as well as to himself; it disrupts the image of Russia's religious culture as purely Orthodox, without reference to Western culture and religion. If the dome is meant to be a symbol of Russian religious identity, it is problematic also because it is shrouded in mist, so the poet apparently cannot see it clearly.

Mist, darkness and cloud, are clear traits of mysticism in poetry.[65] The mist in this poem emphasises the poet's mystical meanderings of spirit. Tiutchev is caught somehow between the North and the South, and as a poet he is listening to his intuition or his heart, not to his reason. The lyric poem of this period of return suggests that Tiutchev was struggling to feel at home in the 'North', which we can understand to mean Russia. The poem, unlike so many of Tiutchev's poems on national and Catholic themes, is a personal reflection and as such, leaves considerable room for doubt about his position in relation to Russia and Orthodoxy. Instead a mystical attachment to Europe is revealed.

By the 1860s, Tiutchev's attraction to Western Europe and European mysticism appears crushed. Instead, his anti-Catholicism has become vitriolic and there is no sympathy towards European or Catholic culture. He concentrates on criticising Western Europe and on using his lyric skills to write national poems for Russia. In his famous short poem 'Umom – Rossiiu ne poniat'...'

---

63   Dewey discusses this poem in the context of Tiutchev's dislike of the notorious Petersburg climate. J. Dewey, *Mirror of the Soul: A Life of the Poet Fyodor Tyutchev*, Shaftesbury: Brimstone Press, 2010, 291.

64   'Тот же вечный купол, так величественно круглящийся в воздухе...' ['That same eternal dome, so majestically turning in the air'], N.V. Gogol' to M.P. Balabina, April 1838, Gogol', *PSS*, XI: 14.. 'Один, На золоте круглится синий Купол'. ('Alone, in gold, the blue dome circles'.) from *Rimskie sonety*, IX, V. Ivanov, *Sobranie sochinenii*, ed. by D.V. Ivanov and O. Deshart, (4 vols.), Brussels: Foyer Oriental Chretien, 1971–1987, III: 582.

65   Pratt, Russian Metaphysical Romanticism, 146.

(1866) ('One cannot understand Russia with the mind...') he provides an overview in miniature of the Slavophiles' arguments about the West as rationalist and scholastic, seeking to define and to measure, whereas Russians have belief.

> Умом Россию не понять,
> Аршином общим не измерить.
> У ней особенная стать –
> В Россию можно только верить.⁶⁶

(One cannot understand Russia with the mind,
One cannot measure her with the general yardstick.
She has a special quality –
One can only believe in Russia.)

Conclusion

As we have seen, Chaadaev was prominent in formulating the idea that Western Europe and Catholicism were reliant on the 'syllogism' and lamenting the absence of both in Russia. He was also treated as mad as a result of his ideas. After him, the Slavophiles very clearly sought to define Western Catholic thought as rationalist and scholastic, and ignored or underplayed mysticism's role in Catholicism. Their arguments attempted to assert that Western religion was not a faith, but an institution. Russian Orthodoxy, meanwhile, was a real faith. The concept of reason was undervalued in their writing, even though they used some methods built on rationalist or scholastic foundations.

Pushkin's poem 'Zhil na svete rytsar' bednyi...' appears to show evidence that the poet found mystical experience problematic and difficult to grasp. He does not estrange mystical tendencies from Catholicism – in fact he links them together. Pushkin also uses the enigmatic nature of a mystical experience and the intractability of a person who has undergone such an experience in order to make his poem intriguing, and open to different readings. His use of Catholicism in this poem is highly instrumental in distancing the ideas of the poem from contemporary Russia, Russian Orthodoxy or the poet's life. Gogol's work, like Pushkin's, reveals an interest and even sympathy with mystical experience. *Taras Bul'ba* conveys very well the idea that other people cannot understand the reasons for a person's conversion even though for them it is a life-changing event. Despite the writer's need to convey Russian nationalist

---

66   Tiutchev, *PSS*, II: 165.

ideas in his *Vybrannye mesta,* he does not fall into line with the Slavophiles on this theme. Lastly, Tiutchev's work also reveals ambivalence about how mysticism may convey national-religious themes. In his essays his criticism of Catholicism and Western Europe is straightforward, but when his lyric voice initially turns to poetry he cannot abandon the idea that Western Europe is connected to mysticism and romance for him; only later in his career when he turns to writing on increasingly political and national themes does this ambivalence fade. Writers who wrote for the sake of nationalist or political programmes tended to underline the fact that Russia and Russian Orthodoxy were defined by mystical faith. Writers who wrote with other intentions, tended to be more open, or at least ambivalent, towards examples of the connection between Catholicism and mysticism. Their works allowed some space for Catholics having religious faith in the same way as the Orthodox. This helped their own works gain empathy, intrigue and depth.

Bibliography

Bakhtin, M. 2000. *Epos i roman*, Saint Petersburg: Azbuka.

Barratt, G. 1976. *M.S Lunin: Catholic Decembrist*, The Hague, Paris: Mouton.

Benda, B. (ed.), 1872. *L'Eglise Latine et le protestantisme au point de vue d'Eglise d'Orient*, Paris: Lausanne and Levey.

Berezkina, S. "Motivy materi i materinstva v tvorchestvea A.S. Pushkina", *Russkaia literatura*, 1, 2001, 167–86.

Billington, J. 1970. *The Icon and the Axe: An Interpretative History of Russian Culture*, New York: Vintage.

Bojanowska, E. *Nikolai Gogol: Between Ukrainian and Russian Nationalism*, Cambridge, Mass.: Harvard University Press, 2007.

Chaadaev, Petr 1991. *Polnoe sobranie sochinenii i izbrannye pis'ma*, (2 vols.), Moscow: "Nauka".

Chadwick, Owen 1998. *A History of the Popes, 1830–1914*, Oxford: Oxford University Press.

Christoff, P. 1972. *An Introduction to Nineteenth Century Russian Slavophilism: A Study in Ideas, I.V. Kireevski*, The Hague: Mouton.

Dewey, J. 2010. *Mirror of the Soul: A Life of the Poet Fyodor Tyutchev*, Shaftesbury: Brimstone Press.

Fairweather, M. 1999. *Pilgrim Princess: A Life of Princess Zinaida Volkonsky*, London: Robinson.

Fedosov, I. (ed.), 1989. *Russkoe obshchestvo 30-kh godov XIX v. Liudi i idei. Memuary sovremennikov*, Moscow: Moskovskii Universitet.

Fomichev, S. 1987. *A.S. Pushkin: Problemy Ttvorchestva*, Kalinin.
Freeborn, R., and J. Grayson, (eds.), 1990. *Ideology in Russian Literature*, London: SSEES/Macmillan.
Gogol', N. 1937–1952. *Polnoe sobranie sochinenii* (14 vols.), Moscow: Akademiia Nauk.
———. 1969. *Selected Passages from Correspondence with Friends*, trans. by J. Zeldin, Nashville: Vanderbilt University Press, 1969.
Gregg, R., "'Dream at Sea': Tiutchev and Pascal", *Slavic Review*, XXIII, 3, (September 1994), 526–63.
Haltsevaia, R. (ed.), 1999. *Pushkin v russkoi filosofskoi kritike*, Moscow: 'Kniga'.
Ivanov, V. 1971–1987. *Sobranie sochinenii*, ed. by D.V. Ivanov and O. Deshart, (4 vols.), Brussels: Foyer Oriental Chretien.
John Paul II. 1998. 'Fides et ratio': http://www.vatican.va/holy_father/john_paul_ii/encyclicals/documents/hf_jp-ii_enc_15101998_fides-et-ratio_en.html, last accessed 24/08/2011.
Khomiakov, Aleksei. 1878. *Polnoe sobranie sochinenii*, Moscow.
Kireevskii, I.V. 1970. *Polnoe sobranie sochinenii v dvukh tomakh*, ed. by M. Gershenzon, Moscow, 1911, reprinted by Gregg International, Hampshire.
Lebrun, R. 2001. *Joseph de Maistre's Life, Thought, and Influence*, London, Montreal and Kingston: McGill University Press.
Lednicki, W. 1952. *Russia, Poland and the West. Essays in Literary and Cultural History*, London: Hutchinson.
Litsenburger, O. 2001. *Rimsko-katolicheskaia tserkov' v Rossii. Istoriia i pravovoe polozhenie*, Saratov: Povolzhskaia Akademiia gosudarstvennoi sluzhby.
Mann, Iu. 2004. *Gogol': Trudy i Dni, 1809–1845*, Moscow: Aspekt Press.
McNally, Raymond. 1971. *Chaadayev and his Friends: an Intellectual History of Peter Chaadayev and his Russian contemporaries*, Tallahassee, Fla.: Diplomatic Press.
Olin, J. (ed.), 1974. *The Autobiography of St Ignatius Loyola, with Related Documents*, trans. J. O'Callaghan, London: Harper and Row.
Pearson, R. 1981. 'Raphael as seen by Russian writers from Zhukovsky to Turgenev', *Slavonic and East European Review*, LIX/3, (1981), 346–69.
Pecherin, V. 2008. *The First Political EmmigreÉmigré: Notes from Beyond the Grave, or Apologia pro vita mea*, trans. by M. Katz, Introduction by N. Pervukhina-Kamyshnikova, Dublin: University College Dublin Press.
Polonskii. 2003. "Mistika v zhizni i mistitsizm v tvorchestve Fedora Tiutcheva", *Russian Literature*, LIV, 505–24.
Pratt, S. 1984. *Russian Metaphysical Romanticism: The Poetry of Tiutchev and Baratynskii*, Stanford CA: Stanford University Press.
Pushkin, A.S. 1994. *Polnoe sobranie sochinenii v deviatnadtsati tomakh*, Moscow: Voskresen'e.

Rosenshield, G. 2008 *The Ridiculous Jew: The Exploitation and Transformation of a Stereotype in Gogol, Turgenev, and Dostoevsky*, Stanford, CA.: Stanford University Press.

Serebrennikov, N. 1998. *Khomiakovskii sbornik*, Tomsk: 'Vodolei'.

Tempest, Richard. 1984. "Madman or Criminal: Government attitudes to Petr Chaadaev in 1836", *Slavic Review*, XLIII/2, pp. 282–287.

———, 1986. "Neizdannaia stat'ia A.S. Khomiakova", *Simvol*, No. 16, 121–24.

The Catechism of the Catholic Church (Popular and Definitive Edition), 1999. London: Burns and Oates.

Tiutchev, Fedor. 2003. *Polnoe sobranie sochineniie i pis'maem v shesti tomakh*, Moscow: Klassika.

Todd III, William Mills. 1999. *The Familiar Letter as a Literary Genre of the Age of Pushkin*, Evanston, Ill.: Northwestern University Press.

Tolstoi, Lev. 1935–1964. *Voina i mir*, in *Polnoe sobranie sochinenii* (90 vols.), ed. by V. Chertkov, Moscow: Jubilee Edition.

Tsurikov, V. (ed.), 2004 *A.S. Khomiakov: Poet, Philosopher, Theologian*, New York: Holy Trinity Seminary Press.

Vaiskopf, M. 1999. '«"'Vot evkharistiia drugaia'": Religioznaia erotika v tvorchestve Pushkina',» *Novoe literaturnoe obozrenie*, 37, 3.

Vatsuro, V.E. (ed.). 1988. *N.V. Gogol': Perepiska v dvukh tomakh*, Moscow: Khudozhestvennaia literatura.

Vinogradov. 2000. "*Taras Bul'ba* i otnoshenie Gogolia k katolitsizmu", in *Gogol': khudozhnik i myslitel'. khristianskie osnovy mirosozertsaniia*, Moscow: IMLI RAN/ 'Nasledie'.

Walicki, A. 1989. *The Slavophile Controversy: History of a Conservative Utopia in Nineteenth century Russian Thought*, trans. by H. Andrews-Rusiecka, Notre Dame, Ind.: University of Notre Dame Press.

Ware, Timothy. 1997. *The Orthodox Church*, London: Penguin.

Y. Slivkin. 2004. "Was the Covetous Knight Poor and was the Poor Knight Covetous?",, *Russian Literature* LV/4, (May 2004), 549–57.

Yoon, S. 2005. 'Transformation of a Ukrainian Cossack into a Russian Warrior: Gogol's 1842 *Taras Bul'ba*', *Slavonic and East European Journal*, XLIX/ 3, (2005), pp. 430–44.

Zernov, N. 1944. *Three Russian Prophets: Khomiakov, Dostoevsky, Soloviev*, London: SCM Press Ltd.

PART 2

Russian Classics and Their Influence in Space and Time

∴

CHAPTER 7

The Irrational Basis of Gogol's Mythopoetics

Arkadii Goldenberg

Gogol' occupies a special place in twentieth- and twenty-first-century world culture as the writer who anticipated its irrational and absurdist tendencies. Franz Kafka, Daniil Kharms, Mikhail Bulgakov, Eugène Ionesco, Samuel Beckett, Venedikt Erofeev, Viktor Pelevin and many other writers concerned with the illogical and paradoxical in literature could sign their names under the phrase attributed to Dostoevskii: "We all came out of Gogol's 'Overcoat'."

When one speaks of the irrational basis of Gogol's poetics, one usually has in mind his treatment of the grotesque, which is one of the principal features of his style. Many of his works feature encounters between the real and the fantastic, the human and the demonic, and the living and the dead. Recall, for example, the totally unmotivated disappearance of Major Kovalev's nose and its autonomous existence in the Counsellor of State's uniform in 'The Nose'.

Many of the irrational features of Gogol's poetics can be traced back to ancient rites and rituals, and to archaic archetypes in Carl Jung's 'collective unconscious'. They enter the artist's creative conscious via the intermediary sphere of folklore, in which, as Propp showed in his studies of the fairy tale, the structures of primordial rites are reincarnated. The mythological concepts of Slavonic folklore underlying the archetypes of traditional ritual culture are essential to Gogol's artistic world, and influence his works' engagement with ontological questions.

The oppositions of existence and non-existence and of the living and the dead constitute key ontological problems for Gogol'. One of the ways in which his characters' irrational behaviour manifests itself is in their constant crossing of the border between the world of the living and that of the dead. As early as in his first collection of stories, *Evenings in a Village Near Dikanka*, the sense of a perpetually living connection with one's ancestors becomes one of the main archetypal features of his characters' behaviour and of their consciousness of their origin. It is not the conventional time of the fairy-tale that prevails here, but a mythological conception of time as a cycle regulating the resurrection of souls in their descendants. The narrator of 'The Lost Letter' ponders:

> And when some kinsman of one's own is mixed up in it, a grandfather or great-grandfather – then I'm done for: may I choke while praying to St. Varvara if I don't think that I'm doing it all myself, as though I had

crept into my great-grandfather's soul, or my great-grandfather's soul were playing tricks in me...[1]

In traditional Slavonic culture, relations between the living and the dead were regulated in strict accordance with mythological conceptions of ancestors' after-death existence.[2] The folk calendar designated days on which to honour and invite home the souls of one's ancestors. When an ancestor returned prematurely, his descendants would become frightened, try to protect themselves against him and tell him to leave. *Bylichki* (stories based on superstitions about evil spirits) and funeral lamentations reflected ideas that the death of a person occurs because a deceased relative who appears before the fortieth day after his death takes the person away with him to the 'other world'.[3] In calendar-regulated rites, patronage was requested from one's forefathers, while in family rites such as births, weddings and funerals, protective semantics played a major role. New-born children, fiancées and the recently deceased were considered liminal beings who had to undergo – to use Arnold van Gennep's terminology – a 'rite of passage' in order to become firmly established in their new statuses as people, married women or deceased ancestors. Any violation of the regulations governing the rite were fraught with dangerous consequences for its participants and for their entire family.

Orphans had a special status in folkloric conceptions of rites. They were perceived as defective people not only socially, but also ritually. Orphans were deprived of their share of their families' legacies, and consequently could not take part in family rites lest their deprived status spread to those around them and to the rites themselves. Orphans were not allowed to take part in the wedding rite, and also in some calendar-regulated rites that were performed in order to ensure fertility and that life took its proper course. Deprived of protection and patronage in their lives on earth, orphans could turn to the 'other world'

---

1 Nikolai Gogol', "The Lost Letter", in N. Gogol', *The Complete Tales of Nikolai Gogol'* (tr. Constance Garnett; revised and ed. by Leonard J. Kent). 2 vols. Chicago, IL, and London: University of Chicago Press, 1985, I, pp. 77–88 (p. 77). Location in Russian original: N.V. Gogol', *Polnoe sobranie sochinenii* (14 vols.), Moscow: Akademiia nauk, 1937–1952, I, 189. Hereafter all references to this publication are given in the text in parentheses, followed by the volume number in Roman numerals and the page numbers in Arabic numerals. Translations are the article translator's own apart from where otherwise indicated through the insertion of footnotes.

2 S.M. Tolstaia, "Mir zhivykh i mir mertvykh: formula sosushchestvovaniia", *Slavianovedenie*, 6 (2000), 14–20.

3 O.A. Cherepanova, "Ocherk traditsionnykh narodnykh verovanii Russkogo Severa", in *Mifologicheskie rasskazy i legendy Russkogo Severa*, St. Petersburg: St. Petersburg University, 1996, 116.

for help, since they enjoyed the status of mediators between that world and the world of people.[4]

Gogol' attributes to the protagonists of most of the stories of *Evenings...* features associated with full or partial orphanhood. This is why marriage is so problematic for them. Gritsko ('The Fair at Sorochintsy') and Petro ('St John's Eve') have lost both their parents; Levko ('A May Night'), Vakula ('Christmas Eve') and Katerina ('A Terrible Vengeance') have each lost a parent. And even Ivan Fedorovich Shpon'ka is an orphan under the patronage of his aunt. With the exception of the last story (which limits its treatment of marriage to a remark that the institution is capable of transforming "a child into a man"), all these works feature a wedding as a key plot motif and depict an evil spirit taking part in the ceremony. The characters' orphanhood taints these weddings with signs of 'pollution', transforming them into 'anti-weddings'. Even if the wedding ceremony is conducted in accordance with the rules governing the rite, as in 'St John's Eve' or 'A Terrible Vengeance', it does not bring the protagonists happiness. Orphanhood in Gogol's works has a metaphysical subtext: it is a sign of apostasy and of divine abandonment of the world inhabited by his characters, who easily fall victim to imaginary demonic forces.

Wedding and funeral rites are structurally isomorphic in Slavonic folklore.[5] The indissoluble connection of these rites reflects archaic conceptions of the isomorphism of death and birth. There are echoes of the series of semantic structures characteristic of the wedding and the funeral in *Evenings...*, *Mirgorod* and the Petersburg stories. For example, in the short story 'Vii' the relations between the complete orphan Khoma Brut and the young witch develop via a conflict between various plot elements. A number of Gogol' scholars have pointed out how the short story 'The Overcoat' travesties the romantic subject of the mystical marriage.[6] However, a more satisfactory interpretation of Bashmachkin's transformation into one of the 'walking dead' at the 'fantastical' end of the story can be found in mythological explanations for the appearance of a dead person in the world of the living, for example, that his death was untimely. The dead man's search for his overcoat "directly identifies him as a deceased person who wanders around, living out his time beyond the grave".[7]

---

4   E.E. Levkievskaia, "Sirota", in *Slavianskaia mifologiia: Entsiklopedicheskii slovar'*, ed. by S.M. Tolstaia, Moscow: Mezhdunarodnye otnosheniia, 2002, 433.

5   See, A.K. Baiburin and G.A. Levinton, "Pokhorony i svad'ba", in *Issledovaniia v oblasti balto-slavianskoi dukhovnoi kul'tury (Pogrebal'ny obriad)*, Moscow: Nauka, 1990, 64–99.

6   See for example, Iurii Mann, *Dialektika khudozhestvennogo obraza*, Moscow: Sovetskii pisatel', 1987, 77.

7   V. Sh. Krivonos, *Povesti Gogolia: Prostranstvo smysla,* Samara: Samarskii gosudarstvennyi pedagogicheskii universitet, 2006, 386.

The subject of after-death existence is a dominant semantic motif in the epic poem in prose 'Dead Souls'. It realises not only Christian, but also pagan concepts of living and dead souls. The archetypal features of funeral rites, which appear at different textual levels, are associated with the protagonist's preoccupation with an activity beyond the world of the living – the buying of dead souls. The compositional peculiarity of the first six chapters of the work can be accounted for by a concept from folklore and ethnography, *obkhod* (plural: *obkhody*). The term refers to the custom among some Slavs of paying successive visits to all the homes within a village for ritual or magical purposes during fixed folk festivals. Christmas-time carol-singing ceremonies consisted in entering each house to sing the hosts a carol, the text of which included well-wishing, such as for an abundant harvest, an increase in livestock, and health and prosperity for the entire family. In exchange, the hosts were to give the singers gifts, such as bread, sausages, biscuits and the like, and sometimes money. They thereby made a sacrifice to their ancestors' souls through the singers. The magical significance of the song and the ceremony itself lies in the fact that the proper conduct of the ritual would ensure the fulfilment of the wishes.

In 'Dead Souls', Chichikov initially visits the town's officials, or 'fathers', and then rides around town paying visits to nearby landowners who own dead souls. These visits are structured as ritual *obkhody* associated with fixed festivals within the folk calendar. At Christmas time, *obkhody* constitute the compositional core of house-to-house carol-singing. In 'Christmas Eve', Gogol' reproduces this tradition with ethnographic precision. The rite consisted of groups of carol-singers paying successive visits to houses and receiving gifts from the heads of the households. The mythological meaning of the rite dates back to archaic conceptions of carol-singers standing in for their deceased ancestors.[8] By giving gifts, they hoped to secure the patronage of those who had passed away during the new agricultural year and to thus guarantee economic security and health for their families. The rite was accompanied by the performance of conjuring songs known as *koliadki* (singular: *koliadka*), an inherent part of whose structure was offering one's well wishes to the heads of the households.[9] The carol-singers and the hosts also exchanged gifts, with the former receiving gifts in their roles as surrogates of the souls of dead people

---

8 See, L.N. Vinogradova, *Narodnaia demonologiia i mifo-ritual'naia traditsiia slavian*, Moscow: Indrik, 2000, 115.

9 See, T.A. Agapkina and L.N. Vinogradova, "Blagopozhelaniia: ritual i tekst", in *Slavianskii i balkanskii fol'klor: Verovaniia. Tekst. Ritual,* ed. by L.N. Vinogradova, Moscow: Indrik, 1994, 168–208.

returned home, a custom based on mythological ideas that deceased ancestors were capable "not only of predicting their fate, but also of influencing all spheres of life on earth. In this connection, funeral rites are nothing other than a sacrifice intended to gain the favour of the deceased, so that they might promote the well-being of their relatives in the future".[10]

With his ability to "flatter everybody very skilfully" (PSS, VI, 12), Chichikov conducts a typologically similar exchange of gifts during his visits to the landowners by offering his good wishes for dead souls. This ritual archetype is presented not as a direct hypostasis, but as a travestied one in all the dialogues with the landowners apart from in the chapter about Nozdrev. Manilov, who gave his dead to Chichikov, responds to Chichkov's expression of gratitude thus: "Manilov was embarrassed, blushed from head to toe and [...] expressed himself by saying that it really was a trifling matter, that he would actually like to give proper proof of his heartfelt affection, this magnetism of souls, but dead souls were something too trivial" (PSS, VI, 36.)[11] In other instances, the exchange of gifts occurs on a commodity-money basis.

The dialogue between Chichikov and Manilov amounts to an inversion of the rite of well-wishing that features in Christmas-time games with the deceased, in which funeral rites are parodied by 'playing dead'. A Ukrainian Gogol' scholar perceptively points out that "Chichikov plays his role under the cover of 'false modesty', and Manilov appears in the role of a generous 'singer of praise'".[12] Games with the deceased were closely connected with festivals, through which they expressed the idea of an eternal cycle of life and death. These games were special forms of light-hearted folk culture: parody 'dress-funerals' and burial services. They had an erotic undertone intended to stir into life the reproductive functions of the world of the living and influence the fertility of the land, animals and people.[13]

However, the most archaic forms in which they were preserved were found not in calendar-regulated rites, but in family rites. Until as late as the 1930s ethnographers investigating West Ukrainian funeral traditions observed cheerful games with actual dead bodies. Participants would tie a piece of string to the

---

10   L.N. Vinogradova, *Zimniaia kalendarnaia poeziia zapadnykh i vostochnykh slavian. Genezis i tipologiia koliadovaniia*, Moscow: Nauka, 1982, 148.

11   Nikolai Gogol', *Dead Souls*, trans. by Donald Rayfield, London: Garnett Press, 2008, 39.

12   A.I. Karpenko, "Cherty narodno-smekhovoi kharakterologii v mire Mertvykh dush N.V. Gogolia," in *Mysl', slovo i vremia v prostranstve kul'tury. Vyp. 1:Teoreticheskie i lingvodidakticheskie aspekty izucheniia russkogo iazyka i literatury*, Kiev: Agrarnaia kniga, 1996, 53.

13   For more detail, see I.A. Morozov, I.S. Sleptsova, *Krug igry. Prazdnik i igra v zhizni severnorusskogo krest'ianina (XIX–XX vv.)*, Moscow: Indrik, 2004, 559–572.

corpse's leg and tug at it, or tickle its heels in order to 'wake' him up and return him to life.[14] Such actions might appear blasphemous, but they were a part of a whole set of rituals intended to remove the fear of the harmfulness of death. Touching the deceased's heel was considered one of the most effective methods of protection against death. In the Russian North the heels of the departed were tickled, "because the heel is the part of the body that representatives of the Evil Spirit lack (cf. one of the appellations of the devil, *Antipka* the 'heelless')".[15] It is therefore telling that Chichikov first gets to know Korobochka when the hospitable widow offers to scratch his heels to help him fall asleep: "My late husband could never get to sleep without that" (VI, 47).[16] Within the mythological consciousness, a guest arriving by night at an inopportune moment from an unknown place was considered a representative of 'the other', or of the 'other world': he could be a demonic being, one of the 'walking dead'. It is no coincidence that Korobochka, who has an "unusually strong" fear of devils, "dreams all night of the cursed one" not long before her meeting with Chichikov (VI, 54). If one interprets Korobochka's offer of a heel-tickling, with its reference to "my dear departed who just couldn't get to sleep without it", from the point of view of ritual, one can see it as an attempt to identify whether the guest is "one's own" or "an Other", a "person" or an "evil spirit".

The belief that the souls of the deceased visit their former homes on funeral days and on Christmas Eve was widespread among Slavs. There was also an associated popular belief that anyone who came as a guest on Christmas Eve was a 'holy person'.[17] It was believed that 'namely through ritually significant individuals one can connect with the world of the dead'.[18] It is telling that the Eastern Slavs in their funeral lamentations call the deceased a 'guest'.[19] Rituals could be both collective and individual, and several departed relatives could communicate with the living through a single ritual guest. The first visitor to a house at the beginning of a series of autumn and winter folk festivals was taken to be a ritual guest and given the title *polaznik*.[20] A guest of this sort

---

14   P.G. Bogatyrev, "Igry v pokhoronnykh obriadakh Zakarpat'ia," in *Seks i erotika v russkoi traditsionnoi kul'ture,* Moscow: Ladomir, 1996, 490–491.
15   *Mifologicheskie rasskazy,* 115.
16   Rayfield, *Dead Souls,* 50.
17   Vinogradova, *Zimniaia kalendarnaia poeziia,* 195.
18   *Ibid.,* 144.
19   L.G. Nevskaia, "Kontsept gost' v kontekste perekhodnykh obriadov", in *Iz rabot moskovskogo semioticheskogo kruga,* Moscow: Iazyki russkoi kul'tury, 1997, 443.
20   For more detail see, P.G. Bogatyrev, "'Polaznik' u iuzhnykh slavian, mad'iarov, slovakov, poliakov i ukraintsev," in P.G. Bogatyrev, *Narodnaia kul'tura slavian,* Moscow: OGI, 2007, 131–214.

was accorded particular respect as a representative of the 'other world'. Within the same semantic field there is yet another meaning of the word 'guest' that was recorded in Vladimir Dal''s dictionary and has a direct relationship to the protagonist of *Dead Souls*: "a merchant from another land or another town living and trading in a different place to where he is registered".[21] The transformation of the 'other' into a 'guest' is associated with ritual forms of exchange, including feasts, the provision of refreshments and the holding of celebrations in his honour.

"You're our guest: we should treat you," the magistrate tells Chichikov after the deeds of purchase for the dead souls have been drawn up. In effect, it is here that the work establishes the model by which the relationship between the officials, the landowners and Chichikov will develop henceforth. The archetype of the ritual guest features in the work as part of a system of subtle allusions associated with the protagonist and his obsession with dead souls. It is not only that Chichikov is generously treated to the traditional dishes of the wake. The abundance of pancakes on Korobochka's table has been identified as an element of *Maslenitsa* (Shrovetide carnival) rituals,[22] when pancakes were cooked principally for deceased ancestors. The custom of making pancakes was popularly considered to be one of the surest means to connect with the 'other world': to make pancakes was "to pave the way for Christ to heaven".[23] Dishes on the table at the wake included *shchi* (cabbage soup), buckwheat porridge (the filling of the famous "niania" enjoyed at Sobakevich's house) and tarts "a lot larger than a plate". An abundant table indicated that ritual funeral activity was taking place to ensure that the souls entering the house were sated. There may be a ritual context to Sobakevich's comical phrase "I'd rather eat two courses and eat my fill of them, to my heart's content (literally 'to my soul's content')."[24] The rusk from the Easter cake with which Pliushkin intends to treat Chichikov is also associated with Christian funeral rites. Only Nozdrev does not take part in this tradition of ritually providing food for one's guest: "dishes did not play a big role" on his dinner table (*PSS*, VI, 75). It is therefore telling that Nozdrev is the only landowner with whom Chichikov does not manage to reach an agreement on the purchase of dead souls.

Korobochka's and Sobakevich's stories about their dead peasants are openly funereal, and can be compared with the poetics of funeral lamentations, a

---

21   V.I. Dal', *Tolkovyi slovar' zhivogo velikorusskogo iazyka, v chetyrekh tomakh*, Moscow: Izd-vo inostrannykh i natsional'nykh slovarei, 1955, I: 386.
22   E.A. Smirnova, *Poema Gogolia 'Mertvye dushi'*, Leningrad: Nauka, 1987, 48.
23   Quoted in Vinogradova, *Zimniaia kalendarnaia poeziia*, 188.
24   Rayfield, *Dead Souls*, 106.

central motif of which was praise of the dead. Korobochka tells Chichikov: "And the ones that died were such good people, all good workmen. [...] Last week my blacksmith burned to death, such a fine blacksmith and he was a master metal-worker, too."[25] Sobakevich speaks about his deceased peasants in picturesque panegyrics: "And how about Stepan the Cork, the carpenter? I'll bet my life you'd never find a man like him. The sheer strength of the man! If he'd served in the guards, God knows what they'd have made of him, he was nearly seven tall."[26] Typologically, Chichikov's meditations on the list of purchased souls and the symbolic 'inspection' he carries out recall the pagan custom of ritually 'calling' the dead on Maundy Thursday, which is recorded in the statutes of the major Church Council known as *Stoglav* that was summoned by Ivan IV in Moscow in 1551: "Early on Maundy Thursday people burn straw and call out the names of the dead."[27]

The theme of death enters 'Dead Souls' via Chichikov as early as in his first conversation with the servant in the hotel, when the guest "asked in detail about local conditions, prevalent diseases – epidemic fevers, lethal contagious diseases, such as smallpox" (*PSS*, VI, 10).[28] Within folk cultures, epidemics and illnesses were personified and perceived as invasions by elements from the 'other' into 'one's own' sphere.[29] In order to stave them off, people would make prophylactic *obkhody* of their 'own' territory, 'ploughing' and 'enclosing' it. The behaviour of Gogol's protagonist within the plot and the structure of his visits and peregrinations are characterised by an inversion of these apotropaic rites.

Chichikov's trade in dead souls violates the traditional regulations concerning relations between ancestors and descendants. According to popular belief, by trying to seize his share from the world of the dead, he is depriving the purchased souls of family connections and facilitating the unsanctioned invasion of the 'other' into the world of the living, thereby expanding the amount of space occupied by death.

In *On the Scales of Job: A Peripateia of Souls*, Lev Shestov compares the existential aspects of Gogol's and Lev Tolstoi's works, asserting: "this is how Gogol' thought: only death and the madness of death can awaken people from the

---

25 *Ibid.*, 56.
26 *Ibid.*, 112.
27 Quoted in B.A. Uspenskii, *Filologicheskie razyskaniia v oblasti slavianskikh drevnostei (Relikty iazychestva v vostochnoslavianksom kul'te Nikolaia Mirlikiiskogo)*, Moscow: Moscow University, 1982, 141.
28 Rayfield, *Dead Souls*, 12.
29 See V.V. Usacheva, "Kontakty cheloveka s demonami bolezni: sposoby zashchity i izbavleniia ot nikh", in *Mif v kul'ture: Chelovek – ne chelovek*, Moscow: Indrik, 2000, 58–67.

nightmare of life".[30] The failure of Chichikov's business signifies a victory over the entropic element that threatens the earthly world. After all, "the main task of funeral rites is fully to restore clear-cut boundaries between the world of the living and the world of the dead...",[31] thereby bringing about the victory of the cosmos of life over the irrationality and chaos of death. As Vladimir Nabokov perspicaciously observed, the comic in Gogol' is differentiated from the cosmic by a mere letter.

Within mythological thought – often described as 'pre-logical', to use Lucien Lévy-Brühl's terminology – the irrational serves a means of understanding the essence of things. The reification of funeral rite archetypes, that is, of the 'collective unconscious', in Gogol's works, testifies not only to the deep mythological intuition of the writer, but also to the fact that the most important irrational aspects of his poetics cannot be adequately comprehended outside a mythological and ritual context.

Translated by Christopher Tooke

Bibliography

Agapkina, Tatiana and Vinogradova, Liudmila. 1994. "Blagopozhelaniia: ritual i tekst", in *Slavianskii i balkanskii fol'klor: Verovaniia. Tekst. Ritual* (ed. by L.N. Vinogradova). Moscow: Indrik: 168–208.

Alekseevskii, Mihail. 2007. "Motiv ozhivleniia pokoinika v severnorusskikh pominal'nykh prichitaniiakh: tekst i obriadovyi kontekst", in *Antropologicheskii forum*, (2007) No 6: 227–262.

Baiburin, Al'bert and Levinton, Georgii. 1990. "Pokhorony i svad'ba", in *Issledovaniia v oblasti balto-slavianskoi dukhovnoi kul'tury (Pogrebal'ny obriad)*. Moscow: Nauka, 1990: 64–99.

Bogatyrev, Pyotr. 1996. "Igry v pokhoronnykh obriadakh Zakarpat'ia", in *Seks i erotika v russkoi traditsionnoi kul'ture*. Moscow: Ladomir, 1996: 484–508.

——— 2007. "'Polaznik' u iuzhnykh slavian, mad'iarov, slovakov, poliakov i ukraintsev", in Bogatyrev, P.G. *Narodnaia kul'tura slavian*. Moscow: OGI: 131–214.

Cherepanova, Ol'ga. 1996. "Ocherk traditsionnykh narodnykh verovanii Russkogo Severa (Kommentarii k tekstam)", in *Mifologicheskie rasskazy i legendy Russkogo Severa*. St Petersburg: St Petersburg University: 113–181.

---

30   L. Shestov, *Sochineniia v dvukh tomakh*, ed. by A.V. Akhutin, Moscow: Nauka, 1993, II: 107.
31   M.D. Alekseevskii, "Motiv ozhivleniia pokoinika v severnorusskikh pominal'nykh prichitaniiakh: tekst i obriadovyi kontekst", in *Antropologicheskii forum*, (2007) No. 6, 246.

Vladimir Dal', 1955. *Tolkovyi slovar' zhivogo velikorusskogo iazyka* (4 vols.). Moscow: Izd-vo inostrannykh i natsional'nykh slovarei.

Gogol', N. V. 1937–1952. *Polnoe sobranie sochinenii* (14 vols.). Moscow: Akademiia nauk.

——— 1985. *The Complete Tales of Nikolai Gogol'* (trans. Constance Garnett; revised and ed. by Leonard J. Kent). 2 vols. Chicago, IL, and London: University of Chicago Press.

——— 2008. *Dead Souls* (trans. by Donald Rayfield). London: Garnett Press.

Karpenko, Aleksandr. 1996. "Cherty narodno-smekhovoi kharakterologii v mire 'Mertvykh dush' N.V. Gogolia", in Mysl', slovo i vremia v prostranstve kul'tury. Vyp. 1: Teoreticheskie i lingvodidakticheskie aspekty izucheniia russkogo iazyka i literatury. Kiev: Agrarnaia nauka.

Krivonos, Vladislav. 2006. *Povesti Gogolia: Prostranstvo smysla*. Samara: Samarskii gosudarstvennyi pedagogicheskii universitet.

Levkievskaia, Elena. 2002. "Sirota", in *Slavianskaia mifologiia: Entsiklopedicheskii slovar'* (ed. by S.M. Tolstaia). Moscow: Mezhdunarodnye otnosheniia.

Mann, Iurii. 1987. *Dialektika khudozhestvennogo obraza*. Moscow: Sovetskii pisatel'.

Morozov, Igor' and Sleptsova, Irina. 2004. *Krug igry. Prazdnik i igra v zhizni severnorusskogo krest'ianina (XIX–XX vv.)*. Moscow: Indrik.

Nevskaia, Lidiia. 1997. "Kontsept 'gost' v kontekste perekhodnykh obriadov", in *Iz rabot moskovskogo semioticheskogo kruga*, Moscow: Iazyki russkoi kul'tury: 442–452.

Shestov, Lev. 1993. *Sochineniia v dvukh tomakh* (ed. by A.V. Akhutin). Moscow: Nauka, 1993.

Smirnova, Elena. 1987. *Poema Gogolia "Mertvye dushi"*. Leningrad: Nauka.

Tolstaia, Sofia. 2000. "Mir zhivykh i mir mertvykh: formula sosushchestvovaniia", in *Slavianovedenie*, No 6, 14–20.

Usacheva, Valeriia. 2000. "Kontakty cheloveka s demonami boleznei: sposoby zashchity i izbavleniia ot nikh", in *Mif v kul'ture: Chelovek – ne chelovek*, Moscow: Indrik: 58–67.

Uspenskii, Boris. 1982. *Filologicheskie razyskaniia v oblasti slavianskikh drevnostei (Relikty iazychestva v vostochnoslavianksom kul'te Nikolaia Mirlikiiskogo)*. Moscow: Moscow University, 1982.

Vinogradova, Liudmila. 1982. *Zimniaia kalendarnaia poeziia zapadnykh i vostochnykh slavian. Genezis i tipologiia koliadovaniia*. Moscow: Nauka, 1982.

——— 2000. *Narodnaia demonologiia i mifo-ritual'naia traditsiia slavian*. Moscow: Indrik, 2000.

CHAPTER 8

On the Philosophical Sources and Nature of Dostoevskii's Anti-Rationalism[1]

Sergei Kibal'nik

I am not certain that it is quite appropriate to apply the concept of "irrationalism" to Dostoevskii. I would rather speak of anti-rationalism. I share the approach to this issue offered by Semen Frank who in his work *Russische Weltanschauung* wrote:

> The Russian way of thinking is absolutely anti-rationalist. This anti-rationalism, however, is not identical with irrationalism, that is some kind of Romantic and lyrical vagueness, a logical disorder of spiritual life. It does not involve either a tendency to deny science or the inability to carry out scientific research.[2]

It is quite obvious that Russian anti-rationalism revealed itself in literature, and most clearly in Fedor Dostoevskii's works. Western scholars often speak of Dostoevskii's irrational messianism. I am not certain that Dostoevskii in his *A Writer's Diary* is trying to prove that Constantinople has to belong to Russia in an irrationalist way. On the contrary, developing Nikolai Danilevskii's theory of Pan-Slavism, Dostoevskii sounds quite rational; he constantly appeals to logic. That is why Tolstoi did not have to change his generally rather rational way of thinking to beat Dostoevskii's approach to the Balkan war in the last part of *Anna Karenina*.[3] Let us not forget that very soon Dostoevskii himself denied his own former Messianism in his Pushkin Speech of 1880. This makes rather problematic not only Dostoevskii's irrationalism but also his messianism.

Dostoevskii's anti-rationalism was obviously one of the main sources of Lev Shestov's critique of speculative philosophy, rationalism and ideology. Shestov actually borrowed the central idea of his very monotonous philosophical

---

1 This work was completed as part of the project RGNF No 15-34-01013.
2 S.L. Frank, *Russkoe mirovozzrenie*, Saint Petersburg: Nauka, 1996, 165.
3 See, S.A. Kibal'nik, "Spory o Balkanskoi voine na stranitsakh *Anna Karenina*," in *Russkaia literatura*, (No. 4, 2010), 39–44.

essays from literature, first of all from Dostoevskii and Chekhov.[4] He expressed his critique of rationalism in his first books, *Dostoevskii and Nietzsche* (1903) and *The Apotheosis of Groundlessness* (1905), which are mostly based on Chekhov's and Turgenev's literary works. As Sergei N. Bulgakov once noted: "Lev Shestov was himself a very rationalist author who did not have much to say except for his perpetual accusations of rationalism."[5] Apparently, Shestov, who lived abroad for almost half a century and published most of his works in French and Russian in well-known Western philosophical journals and publishing houses, contributed a great deal to the reputation of Russian literature in the West as an irrationalist one.

1

In order to understand the nature of Dostoevskii's anti-rationalism one should analyse his early works, that is, his short novels and short stories of the 1840s–1850s. Dostoevskii began his literary career with the novel *Poor Folk*, which was to a great extent based on ideas from French utopian socialism. Valentina Vetlovskaia has shown that Dostoevskii is very sympathetic in this work even to the communist ideas of Babeuf and his followers.[6] The ideological basis of Dostoevskii's first tale, which brought him great success, is therefore quite rationalist. However, his method of portraying the main characters' deep and genuinely expressed human feelings serves to counteract and even subvert this.

Resuming his literary career in the second half of the 1850s, Dostoevskii already had a very critical attitude to utopian socialism and to any rational formula for human happiness. But he could not express this openly: it would look like a betrayal of his former ideals and, most importantly, of his former friends who had attended Mikhail Petrashevskii's gatherings; many of them were still in Siberia. That is why he wrote his tale *The Village of Stepanchikovo* as a crypto-parody. In a concealed manner he parodies the ideas of utopian socialism as well as the personalities of some members of the Petrashevskii

---

4 See, S.A. Kibal'nik, "Khudozhestvennaia fenomenologiia Chekhova," in *Obraz Chekhova i chekhovskoi Rossii v sovremennom mire. K 150-letiiu so dnia rozhdeniia A.P. Chekhova*, (*Sbornik statei*), ed. By V.B. Kataev and S.A. Kibal'nik, St. Petersburg: Petropolis, 2010, 18–28, 18.

5 S.N. Bulgakov, "Nekotorye cherty religioznogo mirovozzreniia L. Shestova," in *Sovremennye zapiski*, (No 68, 1939) Paris, 305–323.

6 V.E. Vetlovskaia, "Ideia Velikoi frantsuzskoi revoliutsii v sotsial'nykh vozzreniiakh molodogo Dostoevskogo" in *Velikaia Frantsuzckaia revoliutsiia i russkaia literatura*, ed. By G.M. Fredlender, Leningrad: Nauka, 282–317.

circle and those of other Russian socialists like Vissarion Belinskii.[7] Dostoevskii once said that "life in Icar's commune or in a phalanstery seems to him more horrible and disgusting than any hard labour".[8] While using the term "phalanstery" Dostoevskii obviously referred to Charles Fourier's ideas, and by mentioning "Icar's commune" he meant the novel *Voyage en Icarie* by French utopian socialist Etienne Cabet. This utopian novel was quite a successful attempt to make the ideas of French socialists popular among the people. Its first edition came out in 1840 and its fifth edition, published in 1848, was very soon prohibited by censorship. In Russia this book was well known and read by most of the Petrashevts.[9] *Voyage en Icarie* is one of the main pretexts of Dostoevskii's *The Village of Stepanchikovo*. It is worth mentioning that the Russian name 'Stepan' has a direct equivalent in the French language, and this equivalent is 'Etienne'. Thus, the title of Dostoevskii's tale is a transformation of Pushkin's *The History of the Village of Gorokhino* (*Istoriia sela Gorokhina*), done in such a way that it conceals a discreet reference to a French bestseller by Etienne Cabet.[10]

The composition of both works is very similar. The protagonist appears in a different world where he does not understand anything and asks many questions in order to figure out what is going on around him. However, in *Voyage en Icarie*, where evil existed before but was eliminated by the kind supreme ruler Icar, the protagonist is delighted with everything. Now in Icaria, in full accordance with the ideas of Fourier and Saint-Simon, 'Reason reigns'.[11] In *The Village of Stepanchikovo* even the naïve and young narrator Sergei very soon understands that Rostanev's house is "something like bedlam". But the landlord of Stepanchikovo, Rostanev, a kind of ideal man as he was portrayed by French socialists ("his soul was as pure as a child's soul"), is willing to make everyone happy as well. And in this respect he resembles Icar "whose passion was love for humankind. Since his childhood he could not see another child without approaching and caressing him, embracing and sharing with him even

---

[7] S.A. Kibal'nik, "*Selo Stepanchikovo i ego obitateli* kak kriptoparodiia," in Dostoevskii: *Materialy i issledovaniia*, ed. by N.F. Budanova and S.A. Kibal'nik, St. Petersburg: Nauka, XIX, 108–142.

[8] A.P. Miliukov, *Literaturnye vstretchi i znakomstva*, St. Petersburg: Izd. A.S. Suvorina, 1890, 181; O.F. Miller, *Materialy dlia zhizneopisaniia F.M. Dostoevskogo: Biografiia, pis'ma i zametki iz zapisnoi knizhki F.M. Dostoevskogo*, St. Petersburg: Izd. A.S. Suvorina, 89.

[9] *Delo petrashev'sev*, Leningrad: Akademiia nauk SSSR, 1937, (I) 89, 370, 563. *Delo Petrashevtsev*, Leningrad: Akademiia nauk SSSR, 1951, (III) 143, etc.

[10] Pushkin's tale was at first mistakenly published under the title *Istoriia sela* Gorokhina.

[11] Etienne Cabet, *Voyage en Icarie*, Paris: 5me edition. Au Bureau du Populaire, 1848, 111.

the little that he owned".[12] Like "the kind Icar", Rostanev cannot understand why "man is such an evil. Why am I so often evil when it is so good to be kind?"[13] Rostanev is a Russian Icar but an unfortunate Icar who is trying to make everyone happy, not in the whole country, but in his own estate only, and nevertheless fails.

His last name, 'Rostanev', is almost a complete anagram of the Russian word *ravenstvo* (equality). He calls almost everyone, including his peasants, "brother". He is ready to make any concession and compromise with all inhabitants of his house. But he is treated by them as a nonentity and is even prohibited from marrying the woman he loves. The more he concedes to his dependent Opiskin, the worse he is treated by him. Rostanev is trying to give Opiskin good money on the condition that he moves out of his house. But it results only in increasing Opiskin's power, which makes Rostanev call him now "Your Highness". The kind Icar also "in his youth could not see an unhappy man without suffering himself from his misfortunes and without trying to console him. Once, meeting a poor man almost naked and dying of cold in the street he gave him his clothes, which he got only two days ago, and returned home full of joy, but almost naked".[14]

The last chapter of the tale is called 'Foma Fomich creates universal happiness' ('Foma Fomich sozidaet vseobshchee schist'e'). 'Vseobshchee schast'e' (universal happiness) is an obvious reference to the French Enlightenment and the revolutionaries' concept of 'bien-être general'. But the content of this chapter is rather sarcastic. Russian Icar Rostanev eventually forces Opiskin to let him marry Nasten'ka by kicking him out of his house (literally pushing him in his back). Only after such a shock does Opiskin slightly change and become more 'reasonable'. There are in the story plenty of other details that clearly indicate that *The Village of Stepanchikovo* is a crypto-parody of *Voyage en Icarie*. I will mention only one more: it appears to Opiskin that Rostanev looks like a Frenchman (and therefore has too little love for his country), and Opiskin orders him to shave off his side-whiskers.

Let us try to answer the question: why could Dostoevskii not accept people's happiness made by 'the kind Icar' who realised in his country the idea of communal property, 'brotherhood' and other socialist and communist ideas? Partly, of course, because of the main characteristics of this rational world: everyone is watching over everyone else, writers are appointed by a supreme ruler, books are censored, prohibited and even burned, and sexual partnership

---

12   *Ibid.*, 211.
13   Dostoevskii, *The Village of Stepanchikovo*, 111.
14   Cabet, *Voyage en Icarie*, 129.

is allowed by law only with spouses (just in case, men are only allowed to dance with men). This did not look to Dostoesvky like an ideal world. But there was another reason: it looked too rational for him. One thing was not taken into account in Icaria. It is the the complexity of human nature and psychological contradictions between people. Dostoevskii's anti-rationalism in *The Village of Stepanchikovo* is obviously a reaction against excessive rationalism.

In Icaria there are no lazy people "because work is so pleasant"; there is no "poisoning of a spouse, perfidious courting, destructive jealousy or duels!" However, there are passions and human attractions in Icaria. "When I compared him with Valmor, as Dinaîse confesses in her letter to his sister, Reason brought me to your brother; but a sort of irresistible force pushed me towards your friend."[15] Instead of fighting for the woman he loves, the narrator decides to leave. But Valmor beats his generosity and self-denial. All of a sudden, he decides to marry Dinaîse's cousine Alaé, and such a radical change of his feelings is far too easy for him. Thus, a love triangle is transformed into two couples who are going to marry on the same day.[16] What can we find in *The Village of Stepanchikovo* instead? We see that Opiskin constantly blames Rostanev for showing ambition and being an egoist, and appeals to him to restrain his passions. Rostanev accepts this and is trying to become "more kind". But in reality it is Opiskin who is possessed with an ambition to dominate Rostanev. And not even for the sake of money, as Tartuffe in Molière's famous play, but 'being tempted to pull faces, to act, to present himself', as Misinchikov put it.

Fourier was certain that "it is impossible to oppress human passions which are God's voice: facing an obstacle at one point they turn to another point and go to their purpose destroying everything instead of creating something".[17] He believed that one should create social and economic conditions that would satisfy everyone's passions, and this would result in a harmonious combination of human personalities. In *The Village of Stepanchikovo,* Dostoevskii creates a situation where everyone in Rostanev's house follows his own ambition and self-interest no matter whether he or she is oppressed by his or her economic conditions or not. The harmonious combination of human personalities does not take place there, and the characters are not capable of directing their

---

15   *Ibid.,* 329.
16   There is an analogous "rational" solution in Chernyshevskii's novel *What Is To Be Done?* obviously also dependent on Cabet's *Voyage en Icarie*.
17   See Charles Fourier, *Le Nouveau monde industriel et sociétaire*, in Charles Fourier, *Le Nouveau monde industriel et sociétaire Oeuvres complètes,* Paris: Troisième édition, A la librairie sociétaire, VI, 111.

passions to achieve some suitable purpose. Dostoevskii's discreet parody of Fourier's doctrine is aimed first of all at its rational character.

In criticising the rational happiness of the socialist utopia Dostoevskii nevertheless drew on some secondary elements of French socialists' doctrines. Thus Saint-Simon in *Lettres à un Americain* pointed out that "proletarians inspired with the passion to achieve equality after they had obtained power proved that something worse than the former regime is quite possible".[18] Does that not sound like one of the sources for Dostoevskii's *The Village of Stepanchikovo*?

2

As a a frequent visitor to Mikhail Petrashevskii's house, Dostoevskii once made a speech 'on personality and egoism' where 'he wanted to prove that there is among us more ambition than human dignity, and that we ourselves are inclined to self-denial and destroying of our own personality caused by egoism and absence of clear purposes'.[19] This idea was inspired by another influence. It has been already indicated that this speech was composed by Dostoevskii under the influence of a famous book *Der Einzelne und sein Eigenthum* (*The Ego and Its Own*) by Max Stirner which came out at the end of 1844;[20] Dostoevskii may have borrowed a copy of this book from Petrashevskii.[21] The only thing which was underestimated by Otverzhennyi is that the content of this speech as Dostoevskii later formulated it is not only permeated with the elements of Stirner's idea of egoism, but at the same time is directed against it.

It is clear that Stirner's book shaped to a great extent another of Dostoesvky's works, *Notes from Underground*.[22] This novella is the most remarkable and passionate manifesto of Dostoevskii's anti-rationalism. It is interesting to compare it with its German philosophical source and try to figure out to what extent Dostoesvkii's anti-rationalism was influenced by Stirner's book. Otverzhennyi thought that not only Dostoevskii's "extreme individualism, moments of the deep disbelief, a passionate hymn to the creative specificity of human personality", but also "the dominance of intuition over reason as well [...] closely

---

18   C.-H. Saint-Simon, *Oeuvres*, ed. by B.P. Enfantin, Paris, 1865–1878, Vol. 1–47 , V.XIII (1), 178.
19   F.M. Dostoevskii, *Polnoe sobranie sochinenii v tridtsati tomakh*, Leningrad: Akademiia nauk, 1979, XVIII: 129.
20   N. Otverzhennyi, *Shtirner i Dostoevskii*, Moscow: «Golos truda», 1925, 27–28.
21   A. Semevskii, *M.V. Butashevich-Petrashevskii i petrashevtsy*, Moscow: Zadruga, 168–170.
22   Otverzhennyi, *Shtirner i Dostoevskii*, 29.

resemble the central issues of Stirner's philosophy"[23] He shows that Stirner's rational and individualistic nihilism became the type of consciousness Dostoevskii fought throughout his whole life: in *Crime and Punishment, The Devils, The Adolescent,* and *The Brothers Karamazov*. But the author of the introduction to this work of scholarship, Borovoi, sounds quite reasonable when he points out that 'Stirner and everything Stirner's is only a part of Dostoevskii who fought *the rationalist nihilism* of Stirner'.[24]

Comparing the two books, we have to admit first of all that the discourse of Dostoevskii's Underground Man is broadly based on Stirner's philosophy of extreme individualism and nihilism. The very title of Dostoevskii's *Notes from Underground* has something in common with the title of Stirner's book. This title as compared to the title of Stirner's book has some polemic patterns. Stressing the loneliness and solipsism of his character, Dostoevskii underlines that 'the Ego's Own' can be only 'underground'. A critical approach to Stirner's doctrine is thus expressed in the very title of his literary masterpiece.

The Underground Man's passionate exclamation: "Is the world to go to pot, or am I to go without my tea? I say let the world go to pot as long as I get my tea every time"[25] reminds the reader of the introduction to Stirner's book: "*My business is* not the divine and not the human one, not the business of truth and kindness, justice, freedom and so forth. It's *exceptionally mine*, not common but the only one – as well as I am the only one. *To me there is nothing higher than me*".[26] Thus, Dostoevskii's anti-rationalism, partly directed against Western rationalism, has its origins in Western thought as well. The difference between these two phrases as well as between Stirner and Dostoevskii in general is as follows. Stirner's passionate and emotional discourse is mostly logical and rationalist. Revolting against Hegel's system, Stirner at the same time was very dependent on Hegel. His main idea is just an extreme conclusion from his metaphysical reasoning.[27] But the very passionate and at the same time logical

---

23   Ibid., 74. Unfortunately, this was not acknowledged and taken into account in the commentaries on *Notes from Underground* in the Dostoesvkii's *Complete Works* in 30 volumes, where the name of Stirner was only once mentioned along with the names of Kant and Schopenhauer. See: Dostoevskii, *PSS*, 1973, V: 380.
24   Borovoi's Introduction in Otverzhennyi, *Shtirner i Dostoevskii*, 6.
25   Dostoevskii, *Notes from Underground and The Grand Inquisitor*, 108.
26   http://www.df.lth.se/~triad/stirner/theego/theego.html, last accessed 12/09/11. All quotations below from the English translation follow this version. The German edition consulted by the author of this article is: Max Stirner, (Kaspar Schmidt). *Der Einzige und sein Eigenthum,* Leipzig: Drud und Werlag von Phikipp Reclam jun., 1892.
27   V. Savodnik, *Nitscheanets 40-kh godov, Maks Shtirner i ego filosofiia egoizma*, Moscow: I.N. Kuchnerev and Co, 1902, 72.

exclamations of the Underground Man are only a part of Dostoevskii's narrative. Dostoevskii's anti-rationalism in *Notes from Underground* seems to be partly directed against Stirner's contradiction between the mainly irrational spirit of his book and its rational form.[28]

However, within the Underground Man's passionate exclamations we paradoxically discover a sort of logical formula as well, an opposition of the 'real life' principle to the 'idea', the 'theory'. "Two times two makes four" in the Underground Man's discourse is identified with "the goal", "the thing to be attained" and with the "beginning of death", while "twice two makes five" is identified with the "incessant process of attaining" and with "real life".[29] Does it not sound more antirational than irrational? The Underground Man does not deny that "two times two makes four". He declares: "I admit that two times two makes four is an excellent thing" (although he considers it "a piece of insolence" at the same time). And he finds it insufficient to describe the complexity of real life: "...two times two makes five is sometimes also a very charming little thing".[30] Thus, in the essence of Dostoevskii's passionate advocacy of 'real life' against 'an idea' one can surprisingly notice a great deal of anti-rationalism as well as even some rationalism. He turns reason against reason. All this also partly explains why Dostoevskii's fiction is very often perceived as philosophy.

One can say perhaps that the Underground Man is a kind of Russian Stirner. But Stirner is equal to 'the Ego' while the Underground Man is not equal to Dostoevskii.[31] However, even the Underground Man himself sees in *reason* only one out of many human faculties:

---

28   Pavel Novgorodtsev saw in the philosophy of the early anarchists a mixture of rationalism and irrationalism: "Being irrationalist in its social perspectives, a philosophy of anarchy is combined with the most decisive rationalist optimism, with unconditional belief in life-saving strength of abstract dogmas. As in socialism, the extreme irrationalism is mixed up with the extreme rationalism" (627). But he regarded the early anarchists as mainly the irrationalists: "A utopian belief of anarchism is characteristic of the early anarchist, especially of Stirner and Bakunin. The later development of anarchism leads it to a change. The true element of anarchism was irrationalism. But as far as the revolutionary enthusiasm is weakening, anarchism is moving towards more concrete doctrines which could replace a decline in religious belief with a thorough elaborating of details. One can see this already in P.- J. Proudhon's works" (P.I. Novgorodtsev, "Ob obshchestvennom ideale, Chast' II: Krizis anarkhizma" in P.I. Novgorodtsev, *Ob obshchestvennom ideale,* Moscow: "Pressa", 1991, 628).

29   F. Dostoevskii, *Notes from Underground and The Grand Inquisitor* trans. by R. Matlaw, New York: Dutton, 1960, 108.

30   *Ibid.,* 30.

31   See, A.P. Skaftymov, "*Zapiski iz podpol'ia* sredi publitsistiki Dostoevskogo," in *Sobranie sochinenii v trekh tomakh,* Samara: Vek 21, 1972. Мщдю 3ю

> You see, gentlemen, reason is an excellent thing, there is no disputing that, but reason is only reason and can only satisfy man's rational faculty, while will is a manifestation of all life, that is, of all human life including reason as well as all impulses. <...> After all, here I, for instance, quite naturally want to live. In order to satisfy all my faculties for life, and not simply my rational faculty, that is, not simply one twentieth of my capacity for life. What does reason know? Reason only knows what it has succeeded in learning (some things it will perhaps never learn; while this is nevertheless no comfort, why not say so frankly?) and human nature acts as a whole, with everything that is in it, consciously or unconsciously, and, even if it goes wrong it lives.[32]

It means that *reason*, as Romain Nazirov comments on this, has to concede to 'will', that is, to the integral striving in which the rational element is one of the main parts.[33] I would add to this that in their attack on *reason*, the Underground Man as well as Dostoevskii himself in his journalism applies logic here and there. As Nikolai Trubetskoi points out:

> At this time he argued in his articles with rationalism and utilitarianism and, making the rationalist ideology absurd, often expressed ideas very close to the Underground Man's thoughts. He emphasised that the representatives of Russian intelligentsia who want to live according to the principles of rationalism are only dreaming and chatting, but are incapable of acting, that they are embittered and extremely proud.[34]

Very often he appeals to 'logic' in his journalism of that time.[35] The fact that one can find very close parallels to Dostoevskii's *Notes from Underground* in his journalism and literary criticism written for the journals *Time* and *Epoch* supports this idea.[36] To quote Mark Twain, one can say that rumours about Dostoevskii's irrationalism are 'slightly exaggerated'.

Otverzhennyi stresses the similarity between Dostoevskii and Stirner, but underestimates Dostoesvsky's transformation of Stirner's philosophy in his images of 'individualists'. At the same time he slightly exaggerates its similarities to the Underground Man's thinking:

---

32 F. Dostoevskii, *Notes from Underground*, 25.
33 R.G. Nazirov, "Ob eticheskoi problematike povesti *Zapiski iz podpol'ia*" in *Dostoevskii i ego vremia*, Leningrad: Nauka, 1971, 145.
34 N.S. Trubetskoi, "O *Zapiskakh iz podpol'ia*' i *Igroke*" in N.S. Trubetskoi, *Istoriia, Kul'tura*, Moscow: Progress, 1996, 695.
35 See e.g. Dostoevskii, *PSS*, XX: 54, 100.
36 See, Skaftymov, "*Zapiski iz podpol'ia* sredi publitsistiki Dostoevskogo," 161–184.

...the Ego is close to the Underground Man not only in his individualistic outlook but in a deep psychological sensation. We know what a sharp hatred the Underground Man has towards himself, how his dissatisfaction with himself torments him. This finding himself offensive, this internal drama burning 'the Ego' on the bonfire of his tragic introspection is similar in its psychological essence to the feelings of the Underground Man.[37]

But does 'the Ego' finds itself offensive? The Underground Man is not equal to 'the Ego', since Dostoevskii's narrative unmasks the Underground Man's confession.

Shimizu stresses the difference between 'the Ego' and Dostoevskii's individualists and adds some quite appropriate parallels with some of Dostoevskii's other characters: Raskolnikov, Rogozhin, Stavrogin, Kirillov and Ivan Karamazov; these ultra-egotist heroes have extreme egotism, while they also have the very strong motivation to become Imitatio di Christi. In this point, they differ fundamentally from the Stirnerian egotist. They make of the Stirnerian ultra ego not only a God in the Russian way, but also sacrifice themselves to him, at which point they have fallen and betrayed Stirner's thought. The Stirnerian egotist will always be free from the worship of any authority other than himself. Stirner condemns suicide. Needless to say, if one commits suicide, one shows oneself to kneel before an idea. But Stavrogin and Kirillov have realised their infinite freedom by ending their lives through suicide.[38]

But the scholar appears not to realise clearly that the differences between his characters and 'the Ego' are intentional. By means of these differences Dostoevskii formulates his own approach to Stirner's doctrine. In other cases Shimizu slightly exaggerates the critical attitude of Dostoevskii to Stirner. For example, *Notes from Underground* is hardly "a parody of Stirner's philosophy".

The parallels between Dostoevskii and Stirner can be expanded. For example, in the initial chapters of the second part *Ownness* and *The Owner*, this motif is developed in a way which recalls Raskolnikov's thinking:

> When the 'loyal' had exalted an unsubdued power to be their master and had adored it, when they had demanded adoration from all, then there came some such son of nature who would not loyally submit, and drove the adored power from its inaccessible Olympus, 'You long for freedom?

---

37   Otverzhennyi, *Shtirner and Dostoevskii*, 36–37.
38   Takayoshi Shimizu, "Dostoevskii and Max Stirner," Paper presented at 14th International Dostoevskii Symposium, Naples, 13–20th June 2010.

You fools! If you took might, freedom would come of itself.' See, he who has might 'stands above the law', 'Man' is the God of today, and fear of Man has taken the place of the old fear of God. [...] In consideration of right the question is always asked, 'What or who gives me the right to it?' Answer: God, love, reason, nature, humanity, etc. No, only *your might, your* power gives you the right (your reason, e. g., may give it to you). [...] This means nothing else than 'What you have the *power* to be you have the *right* to'.[39]

Stirner discusses further in *The Ego and Its Own* the issue of 'crime':

The State practices 'violence,' the individual must not do so. The State's behaviour is violence, and it calls its violence 'law'; that of the individual, 'crime.' Crime, then, is what the individual's violence is called; and only by crime does he overcome the State's violence when he thinks that the State is not above him, but he is above the State. [...] 'The criminal is in the utmost degree the State's own crime!' says Bettina. One may let this sentiment pass, even if Bettina herself does not understand it exactly so. [...] Every ego is from birth a criminal to begin with against the people, the State.[40]

Then he deals even with 'crime and punishment':

Punishment has a meaning only when it is to afford expiation for the injuring of a *sacred* thing. If something is sacred to any one, he certainly deserves punishment when he acts as its enemy. A man who lets a man's life continue in existence *because* to him it is sacred and he has a *dread* of touching it is simply a *religious* man. [...] 'Crime' or 'disease' are not either of them an *egotistic* view of the matter, i.e. a judgment *starting from me*, but starting from *another* – to wit, whether it injures *right*, general right, or the *health* partly of the individual (the sick one), partly of the generality (*society*). 'Crime' is treated inexorably, 'disease' with 'loving gentleness, compassion,' etc. [...] But it is exactly punishment that must make room for satisfaction, which, again, cannot aim at satisfying right or justice, but at procuring *us* a satisfactory outcome.[41]

---

39 Stirner, *The Ego and Its Own*.
40 *Ibid.*
41 *Ibid.*

Some of these formulae look like excerpts from Raskolnikov's article:

> It is said that punishment is the criminal's right. But impunity is just as much his right. If his undertaking succeeds, it serves him right, and, if it does not succeed, it likewise serves him right.[42] But let the individual man lay claim to ever so many rights because Man or the concept of man 'entitles' him to them, because his being man does it.[43]

To some extent Dostoevskii's arguments are based on Stirner's polemics with socialists and communists:

> Consequently one has a prospect of extirpating religion down to the ground only when one antiquates *society* and everything that flows from this principle. But it is precisely in Communism that this principle seeks to culminate, as in it everything is to become *common* for the establishment of 'equality'. If this 'equality' is won, 'liberty' too is not lacking. But whose liberty? *Society's*! Society is then all in all.[44]

Otverzhennyi found it "significant" that the former member of Petrashevskii's circle Dostoevskii borrows arguments and strength of thought from a thinker who considered liberals as well as socialists the enemies of human individuality.[45]

Criticising the inconsistency of the socialists' position, Stirner expressed ideas in which one can see, as well as in some Dostoevskii's works, a source of all anti-utopias:

> The Socialists, taking away *property* too, do not notice that this secures itself a continued existence in *self-ownership*. Is it only money and goods, then, that are a property, or is every opinion something of mine, something of my own? So every *opinion* must be abolished or made impersonal. The person is entitled to no opinion, but, as self-will was transferred to the State, property to society, so opinion too must be transferred to something *general*, 'Man', and thereby become a general human opinion.[46]

---

42 This parallel in a general way was made by Otverzhennyi, *Shtirner i Dostoevskii*, 44.
43 Stirner, *The Ego and its Own*.
44 Ibid.
45 Ibid.
46 Ibid.

3

In his characters' arguments Dostoevskii reproduces the arguments of Stirner and some other philosophers. Thus, at the very beginning of the second part of *The Ego and Its Own* we find Kirillov's motif of 'God-man'. This motif is known to go back first of all to Ludwig Feuerbach and to his *The Essence of Christianity*.[47] But Stirner opposes to God not just a Man, but 'the Ego', and therefore Kirillov's feeling that he is "bound to show *self-will*"[48] reminds one first of all of an intention of 'the Ego' to kill not only the God, but the Man in him as well:

> At the entrance of modern time stands the 'God-man'. At its exit will only the God in the God-man evaporate? And can the God-man really die if only the God in him dies? They did not think of this question, and thought they were through when in our days they brought to a victorious end the work of the Enlightenment, the vanquishing of God: they did not notice that Man has killed God in order to become now 'the sole God on high.' The *other world outside us* is indeed brushed away, and the great undertaking of the proponents of the Enlightenment completed; but the *other world in us* has become a new heaven and calls us forth to renewed heaven-storming: God has had to give way, yet not to us, but to Man. How can you believe that the God-man is dead before the Man in him, besides the God, is dead?[49]

Kirillov's idea of suicide in this context looks like the realisation of Stirner's metaphor in the last phrase: '…before *the Man in him*, besides the God, *is dead*'. Certainly, Kirillov differs from Stirner's *The Ego*, since he wants to commit suicide not for himself but because he sees in it "salvation for all".[50] Kirillov embodies not Stirner's idea itself but Dostoevskii's transformation of this idea, directed to show that it leads to Man's self-ruin.

In *The Possessed* the idea of 'no God' has given birth to a well-known Dostoevskian formula, "If there's no God, how can I be a captain then?":

> Ah, here's another anecdote. There's an infantry regiment here in the district. I was drinking last Friday evening with officers. We've three friends

---

47   Dostoevskii, *Besy*, in PSS, XII, 221–222.
48   F. Dostoyevsky, *The Possessed*, trans. by C. Garnette. New York, The Modern Library, 1963, 627.
49   Stirner, *The Ego and its Own*.
50   Dostoevskii, *The Possessed*, 629.

> among them, *vous comprenez?* They were discussing atheism and I need hardly say they made short work on God. They were squealing with delight. By the way, Shatov declares that if there's to be a rising in Russia we must begin with atheism. Maybe it's true. One grizzled old stager of a captain sat mum, not saying a word. All at once he stands up in the middle of the room and says aloud, as though speaking to himself: 'If there's no God, how can I be a captain then?' He took up his cap and went out, flinging up his hands.[51]

Here we find a sort of irrational reaction to a rational argument, and this reaction represents Dostoevskii's denial of Stirner's reply to Feuerbach's *The Essence of Christianity*. Dostoevskii opposes to it his own reaction to Feuerbach's denial of God. The rational sense of his *captain*'s irrational reaction could be formulated as follows: 'If there is no God, and God is just a human essence put in the sky, then a man not only does not become God but stops being a man'. One can also say that an apparently irrational reaction of the *captain* to a rational idea of the modern world has in the context of Dostoevskii's novel an antirational character.

In *The Brothers Karamazov* Ivan Karamazov's analogous formula "if there's no immortality of the soul, then there's no virtue, and everything is lawful" is a logical consequence which Stirner had derived from Feuerbach's centring on man instead of God. A denial of 'God-man' and the idea that 'everything is lawful' is the main idea of Stirner's book. Ivan Karamazov's idea is argued by a "divinity student" Rakitin, "a young man bent on a career".[52] Rakitin's defence of an atheist morality is as follows:

> His article is absurd and ridiculous. And did you hear his stupid theory just now: *if there's no immortality of the soul, then there's no virtue, and everything is lawful.* (And by the way, do you remember how your brother Mitia cried out: 'I will remember!') An attractive theory for scoundrels! (I'm being abusive, that's stupid). Nor for scoundrels, but for pedantic poseurs, 'haunted by profound, unsolved doubts. He's showing off, and what it all comes to is, 'on the one hand we cannot but admit' and 'on the other it must be confessed!' His whole theory is a fraud! Humanity will find in itself the power to live for virtue even without believing in immortality. It will find it in love for freedom, for equality, for fraternity.[53]

---

51 Dostoyevsky, *The Possessed*, 229.
52 F. Dostoevskii, *The Brothers Karamazov, A novel in four parts and an epilogue*, trans. by C. Garnette, London: William Heinemann, 1915, 38, 75.
53 *Ibid.*, 81.

This resembles Ludwig Feuerbach's position. 'The Ego' makes also some remarks which are similar to Ivan Karamazov's and the Grand Inquisitor's phrases:

> I am owner of humanity, am humanity, and do nothing for the good of another humanity. Fool, you who are a unique humanity, that you make a merit of wanting to live for another than you are. <...> The world belongs to 'Man,' and is to be respected by me as his property. Property is what is mine! Property in the civic sense means *sacred* property, such that I must *respect* your property. [...] Whoever knows how to take and to defend the thing, to him it belongs till it is again taken from him, as liberty belongs to him who *takes* it. [...] My intercourse with the world consists in my enjoying it, and so consuming it for my self-enjoyment. *Intercourse is the enjoyment of the world*, and belongs to my self-enjoyment. [...] Whether what I think and do is Christian, what do I care? Whether it is human, liberal, humane, whether unhuman, illiberal, inhuman, what do I ask about that? If only it accomplishes what I want, if only I satisfy myself in it, then overlay it with predicates as you will; it is all alike to me.[54]

Generally speaking, in Ivan Karamazov's poem 'The Grand Inquisitor' Stirner's impact is displayed here and there: "Then we shall give them the quiet humble *happiness of weak creatures such as they are by nature*. [...] Oh, we shall allow them even sin, they are weak and helpless, and they will love us like children because we allow them to sin".[55] Dostoevskii's conviction that an individualistic approach to life is doomed is perhaps partly based on the fact of Stirner's early death in 1856. Having been freed from hard labour, Dostoevskii definitely read about this.

Some Russian thinkers were aware of the affinity between the main Dostoevskian philosophical topic and Stirner's polemics with Feuerbach. For example, Semen Frank in his book *Ethics of Nihilism* wrote:

> The Russian intelligentsia's moralism is just an expression of its *nihilism*. However, speaking strictly logically, one can deduce from nihilism only nihilism that is immoralism, and it was not very difficult for Stirner to explain to Feuerbach and his disciples this logical consequence. If being is deprived of an internal meaning, if subjective human desires are the only reasonable criteria for a practical orientation of man in the world,

---

54   Stirner, *The Ego and its Own*.
55   Dostoevskii, *The Brothers Karamazov*, 273.

then why should I acknowledge any obligations and isn't my egoistic and natural enjoyment of life my legal right?[56]

Boris Vysheslavtsev in his *Ethics of the Transfigured Eros* formulated 'the idea of man-god' in the following way:

> If a man is a live concrete person then why not recognise man as the only God we know? This idea occurs by necessity and leads to 'a religion of mankind', to the only possible form of atheistic ethics, in other words, of an atheistic hierarchy of values. It is thought in two ways: either the only value and a sacred thing for me is my live and concrete 'I' – all the rest is subordinated to him (Max Stirner) – or the only value and sacred thing is 'mankind', collective, 'proletariat' (Feuerbach, Marx). And he concluded that 'dealing with this dialectic is shown by Dostoevskii, and it is still being dealt with by contemporary humankind...'[57]

In his novel *The Night Roads*, one of the followers and at the same time opponents of Dostoevskii in twentieth-century Russian prose, Gaito Gazdanov, makes a homeless French philosopher Plato say:

> I am very far from Cartesian ideas [...] I consider that they have caused great harm to our thinking. The possibility of a full and clear answer to a complex question seems attainable only to a limited imagination: this was Descartes' fundamental flaw. But in certain cases one highly significant and definitive aspect of a question seems to me irrefutable.[58]

It is quite natural that the Russian writer makes a Frenchman criticise Cartesian tradition. But let us not forget: he still acknowledges some rational reasoning "in certain cases", and the French character is doing this in full accordance with the Russian writer's creative will. According to 'the supplementary principle' of Niels Bohr, rationalism and irrationalism are two different sides of reality. Although the majority of contemporary intellectuals see in the basis of reality mostly irrational elements they consider them as only a part of their unity with the rational ones.

---

56 S.L. Frank, "Etika nigilizma," in S.L. Frank, *Sochineniia*, Moscow: Pravda, 1990, 84–85.
57 B.P. Vysheslavtsev, *Etikia preobrazhennogo Erosa*, Moscow: Respublika, 1994, 539.
58 Gayto Gazdanov, *Night Roads: A Novel*, trans. by Justin Doherty, Dublin (European classics). New Paper Back, 2006, 111.

Russian intellectual history includes phenomenological philosophy (Nikolai Gartman, Gustav Shpet, Semen Frank) which has obviously a very rationalist basis.[59] Even Russian intuitivism, developed by Nikolai Losskii, was formulated by him in a quite rational way. In general, Russian philosophy, even Russian religious philosophy, is not something absolutely irrational, as evinced by Lev Shestov's writings. It is, rather, anti-rational, as Frank put it, and at the same time has a significant rational pattern. This dialectical symbiosis to a great extent goes back to Dostoevskii.

Bibliography

Cabet E., *Voyage en Icarie*, Paris 1848.
Dostoevskii F., *Notes from Underground and The Grand Inquisitor*, trans. by R.E. Matlaw, New York 1960.
Dostoevskii F., *The Brothers Karamazov*, transl. by C. Garnette, London 1915.
Dostoevskii F., *The Village of Stepanchikovo*, New York, 1995.
Dostoyevsky F., *The Possessed*, transl. by C. Garnette, New York 1963.
Fourier Ch., *Le Nouveau monde industriel et sociétaire*, in idem, *Oeuvres complètes*, vol. 6, Paris 1848.
Gazdanov G., *Night Roads A Novel*, transl. by J. Doherty, Dublin 2006.
Saint-Simon, C.-H. de., Enfantin, B.-P, *Oeuvres, publiées par des membres du conseil institué par Enfantin...et précédés de deux notices historiques*. Vol. 1–47. Paris, 1865–1878.
Stirner M., *The Ego and Its Own*, trans, by S.T. Byington, <http://www.df.lth.se/~triad/stirner/theego/theego.html>.
Bulgakov S.N. Nekotorye cherty religioznogo mirovozzreniia L.Shestova, "Sovremennye zapiski", vol. 68 (1939), 305–323.

---

[59] See for example some research on Gustav Shpet's rational aspects of his phenomenology: V.N. Porus, "Spor o ratsionalizme: Filosofiia i kul'tura (E. Husserl', L. Shestov i G. Shpet)", in *Gustav Shpet i sovremennaia filosofiia gumanitarnogo znaniia*, ed. by V. Lektorskii et al, Moscow: Iazyki slavianskoi kul'tury, 2006, 146–168; E.A. Iurkshtkovich, "Vozmozhnosti germenetiki kak metoda ratsional'nogo myshleniia v filosofii G. Shpeta", in *Tvorcheskoe nasledie Gustava Gustavovicha Shpeta v kontekste filosofskikh problem formirovaniia istoriko-kul'turnogo soznaniia (mezhdictsiplinarnyi aspect)*, Tomsk: Tomsk University, 2003 124–132; L.A. Mikeshina, "Logika kak uslovie I osnovanie nauchnoi strogosti istoricheskogo znaniia (Pis'mo G.G. Shpeta D.M. Petrushevskomu 16 aprelia-6 maia 1928)", in *Gustav Shpet i ego filosofskoe nasledie: U istokov semiotiki i strukturalizma*, ed. by T. Shchedrina, Moscow: Rospen, 2010, 28–56.

Vetlovskaia V.E. Idei Velikoi frantsuzskoi revoliutsii v sotsial'nykh vozzreniiakh molodogo Dostoevskogo, in G.M.Fridlender (ed.). *Velikaia Frantsuzskaia revoliutsiia i russkaia literatura*. Leningrad, 1990, 282–317.

Vysheslavtsev B.P. *Etika preobrazhonnogo Erosa*. Moskva, 1994.

Desnitskii V. A. (ed.). *Delo petrashevtsev. Vol. 1. Moskva – Leningrad, 1937. Дело петрашевцев*, vol. 1, Москва – Ленинград 1937.

Desnitskii V. A. (ed.). *Delo petrashevtsev, vol. 3. Moskva – Leningrad, 1951. Дело петрашевцев*, vol. 3, Москва – Ленинград 1951.

Dostoevskii F.M. *Polnoe sobraniie sochinenii V 30 t*. Leningrad, 1972–1990.

Kibal'nik S.A. "Selo Stepanchikovo i ego obitateli" kak kriptoparodiya in N.F.Budanova, S.A.Kibalnik (eds), *Dostoevskii. Materiały i issledovaniya*, Sankt-Peterburg 2010, 108–142.

Kibal'nik S.A. O filosofskom podtekste formuly "Esli Boga net..." v tvorchestve Dostoevskogo, "Russkaia literatura" 3 (2012), 153–163.

Kibal'nik S.A. Spory o Balkanskoi voine na stranitsakh "Anny Kareninoi", Russkaia literatura 4 (2010), 39–44.

Kibal'nik S.A., Khudozhestvennaia fenimenologiia Chekhova, in V.B.Kataev, S.A. Kibalnik (eds), *Obraz Chekhova i chekhovskoi Rossii v sovremennom mire. K 150-letiiu so dnia rozhdeniia A.P.Chekhova. Sbornik statei*, Sankt-Peterburg 2010, 18–28.

Mikeshina L.A., Logika kak usloviie i osnovaniie nauchnoi strogosti istoricheskogo znaniia (Pis'mo G.G.Shpeta D.M.Petrashevskomu 16 aprelia – 6 maia 1928), in M.Denn et al. (eds), *Gustav Shpet i ego filosofskoie nasllediie. U istokov semiotiki i strukturalizma*, Moskva 2010, 28–56.

Miliukov A.P. *Literaturnyie vstrechi i znakomstva*, Sankt-Peterburg 1890, 167–249.

Miliukov A.P. *Materiały dlia zhizneopisaniia F.M.Dostoevskogo. Biographiia, pis'ma i zametki iz zapisnoi knizhki F.M.Dostoevskogo*, Sankt-Peterburg 1883, 3–178.

Nazirov R.G. Ob eticheskoi problematike povesti "Zapiski iz podpolia", in V.G.Bazanov, G.M.Fridlender (eds), *Dostoevskii i ego vremia*, Leningrad 1971.

Novgorodtsev P.I., *Ob obshchestvennom ideale*, Moskva, 1991.

Otvetzhennyi N., *Shtirner i Dostoevskii*, Moskva, 1925.

Porus V.N., Spor o ratsionalizme: filosofiia i kul'tura (E. Gusserl', L. Shestov i G. Shpet), in V.A.Lektorskii et al. (eds), *Gustav Shpet i sovremennaia filosofiia gumanitarnogo znaniia*, Moskva, 2006, 146–168.

Savodnik V., *Nitssheanets 40-kh godov. Maks Shtirner i ego filosofiya egoizma*, Moskva 1902.

Semevskii A., *M.V. Butashevich-Petrashevskii i petrashevtsy*, Moskva, 1922.

Skaftymov A.P. "Zapiski iz podpol'ia" sredi publitsistiki Dostoievskogo, in idem, *Sobraniie*.

Trubetskoi N.S. O "Zapiskakh iz podpol'ia" i "Igroke". In idem, Istoriia. Kul'tura, Moskva 1996.
Frank S.L., Russkoie mirovozzreniie, Sankt-Peterburg 1996.
Frank S.L., Etika nigilizma, in idem, Sochinenya, Moskva 1990.
Iurtkshtkovich E.A., Vozmozhnosti germenevtiki kak metoda ratsional'nogo myshkeniia v filosofii G.Shpeta, in G.V.Zabolotnova (ed), Tvorcheskoie nadlediie Gustava Gustavovicha Shpeta v kontekste filosofskikh problem formirovaniia istoriko-kul'turnogo soznaniia (mezhdistsiplinarnyi aspect), Tomsk, 2003, 124–132.

CHAPTER 9

Shifting French Perspectives on Dostoevskian Anti-Rationalism

Alexander McCabe

Introduction

The past two hundred years of European thought have often been interpreted in terms of mounting backlashes against the inheritance of the Enlightenment, resulting in a gradual and radical epistemological re-evaluation of non-rational modes of thought and non-scientific modes of discourse. This upheaval, one of the most critical in modern intellectual history, was brought about through successive waves of sceptical and subjectivist revolt against a rationalist intellectual mainstream geared towards objective knowledge. The anti-rationalist polemics of Dostoevskii represent a turning point of purport in this process; commentators have placed his novelistic critique of the thought of his contemporaries among the earliest and most forceful expressions of dissatisfaction with the nineteenth century's dominant schools of thought, combining romantic arguments against rationalism and positivism with a simultaneous rejection of idealism. His innovative fictional disentanglement of realism from rationalism and of romanticism from idealism had an enduring impact on Russia's intellectual landscape from the turn of the last century, feeding directly into the various anti-rationalist and proto-existential strands of religious thought that flourished in Russia's Silver Age. Of course, Dostoevskii's impact was not restricted to Russia. A degree of scholarly attention has also been attracted by numerous similarities between the outcry of the Dostoevskian 'Underground Man', the unnamed protagonist-narrator of his *Notes from Underground,* and later two-pronged critiques of the rationalist and idealist traditions associated with existential movements further afield, and strikingly so in the French context.[1] However, historical connections between Russian and French existential movements have been widely ignored.

---

1   The best comparative study to date of Dostoevskii's thought and French existentialism remains Erofeev's 1975 doctoral research, published as *Naiti v cheloveke cheloveka*, Moskva 2003. Latynina's 1972 article, in essence a defence of the humanist reading of Dostoevskii from association with anti-rationalist trends in bourgeois philosophy, has dated somewhat, but testifies nonetheless to the need to assess the question of reception historically.

The bulk of discussion to date has approached Dostoevskii's fiction either as an incidental parallel or else a 'prophecy' of twentieth-century trends in continental philosophy. This has left even innovative and influential ideas expressed through his characters doubly marginalised from mainstream histories of European thought insofar as their fictional mode of expression lay beyond the brink of traditional philosophical discourse and as they could not be straightforwardly attributed to an 'author', Dostoevskii often having been at odds with his own characters' conclusions. Nonetheless, overviews of Existentialism persevere in including discussion and excerpts of the Underground Man's attack on traditional philosophy[2]: whatever Dostoevskii's personal metaphysical bent (a persistently problematic issue in its own right) the increasing resonance of his sustained novelistic epistemological polemic against the limiting 'brick wall' of $2 + 2 = 4$ with readers across Europe throughout the first half of the twentieth century cannot be disputed. The present analysis thus responds to a need to consider historically the process through which these two intellectual movements, Russian anti-rationalism and French existential philosophies, reached a productive dialogue by the middle of the century.

The stakes of such inter-cultural reception history are never limited exclusively to literary philosophy and philosophical literature. Throughout the romantic period the territorialisation of the rationalist-irrationalist dichotomy along cultural frontiers fed into national myths which in turn interacted powerfully with the intercultural exchange of ideas. Many of the assumptions of French discourse with regards to the 'Orient' encompassed Russia up until World War I. Regardless of the fact that post-colonial cultural thought has fairly successfully deconstructed lingering *Volksgeists* and discarded them as a passing zeitgeist, the sway of national myths in nineteenth-century intellectual history cannot be easily shirked. *L'esprit français* ('the French mind') was a term broadly used throughout the nineteenth century in reference to a dominant notion of the French national character. It was an expressly rationalist self-conception, founded on a perceived direct inheritance of the Greco-Roman tradition, the advent of Descartes, along with Paris's self-defined position as the 'centre' of the Age of Reason. *L'âme russe* ('the Russian soul') was a contrary construct conceived as inherently mystic and as such in essential opposition to the cerebral *esprit français* and Enlightenment values. The role of such dichotomous national myths in the genesis and development of

---

A.N. Latynina, "Dostoevskii i Ekzistentsializsm" in *Dostoevskii: khudozhnik i myslitel'*, ed. K.N. Lomunov, Moskva.

2   Walter Kaufmann, *Existentialism from Dostoevskii to Sartre*, New York 1975; *Basic Writings of Existentialism*, ed. Gordon Morino, New York 2004.

Russian romantic thought and its anti-rationalist movements, from the Slavophils through Dostoevskii to the Silver Age, lies beyond the scope of the present analysis; however, the extent to which these myths interacted and often interfered with intercultural exchange up to the Great War and Russian Revolution is clearly brought into evidence by analysis of Dostoevskii criticism and translation, just as their subsequent steady decline emerges from analysis of the post-war period.

I propose here firstly to outline some of the obstacles Dostoevskian 'underground philosophy' encountered in a nineteenth-century France that affiliated itself with rationalism. Drawing on criticism, translation analysis and fictional reworkings, a line of development will be sketched from the initial exclusion of anti-rationalist motifs from nineteenth-century French readings of Dostoevskii to 'modern' rereadings of the *Belle Époque*. The arrival in France of Russian émigré thinkers, most notably Lev Shestov, will then be discussed as a factor in the significant deepening and broadening of the dialogue between Russia's anti-rationalist tradition and French literary thought, leading the way towards Sartre's early Existential fiction and Camusian philosophy's significant engagement with the fictional thought of Dostoevskii.

Initial Reception

The reception of Dostoevskii in France dates from the mid-1880s, with Vogüé's hugely influential critical introduction to the Russian novel. By this time the last vestiges of French romanticism had been quashed; positivism dominated firmly over the intellectual climate and a pessimistic naturalism over French literature. Vogüé, a diplomat and conservative Catholic moralist, discovered in Russia what he saw as an escape route from the impasse down which the excesses of positivism had led France's novelists. Judging by the reception of Vogüé's study, a generation had been thirsting for such an alternative. However, while Vogüé found in Tolstoi and the early works of Dostoevskii the humanity and spirituality that he deemed lacking from the cold naturalism of a Zola or a Flaubert, the mature works of Dostoevskii clearly went too far beyond Vogüé's vision. Rejecting naturalism in fiction was one thing; challenging the rational basis of moral interaction – whilst reasoning against reason – was quite another. Thus, while Vogüé spoke rapturously of *Poor Folk, Humiliated and Offended* and *Crime and Punishment* (reduced to conventional moralism) he wrote off all of Dostoevskii's subsequent fiction. *The Devils, The Idiot* and *The Brothers Karamazov* were all far too full of delirious philosophical diversions and moral ambiguity, not to mention far too long: in Vogüé's highly trusted opinion, best avoided.³ As for *Notes from Underground*, it was swept entirely under the carpet.

Vogüé was swiftly elected to the prestigious *Académie Française* in recognition of his intermediary contribution to French literature: '*les Russes*' were in fashion, and decadent circles began to work a Tolstoi and Dostoevskii-informed mysticism into their fiction.⁴ Of course, they were not without fierce protectionist opposition. Critics like Pontmartin condemned all those who drew from this "littérature d'épileptiques, de malades, de visionnaires".⁵ Pessard, in 1888, warned:

> L'imitation des Russes, et particulièrement celle de Dostoïevski, risque de nous amener à faire trop bon marché de nos qualités nationales de clarté, de bon sens, de droiture intellectuelle, de grâce et de charme. (In imitating the Russians, and in particular Dostoevskii, we risk being led to undercut our national qualities of clarity, good sense, intellectual rectitude, grace and charm.)⁶

Along with Vogüé and the critics of the period, those who proceeded to translate Dostoevskii deemed it necessary to 'protect' the public from the subversive – if not 'unseemly' – irrationalism of his post-exile writings. *Notes from Underground*, not surprisingly, suffered most gravely. An 1886 version by Harpéline-Kaminski and Maurice, entitled *L'Esprit souterrain*, was in fact an awkward synthesis of Dostoevskii's *The Landlady* (1847) and the *Notes* (1864) themselves. The two protagonists are rolled into one through a fabricated bridge section with cross-references added throughout. Ordynov's tale is essentially used as a *rationale* for the composite character's later 'underground' mind state, as the altered title and invented bridge section make explicit. Dostoevskii's original, however, had consciously done precisely the opposite: in reversing the chronology of the two halves of his *Notes*, Dostoevskii's original structure discouraged from approaching the Underground Man's polemics (the first half of the work) in terms of such psychological causality.

Perhaps even more consequential is that the content of Dostoevskii's anti-rationalist thesis was drastically reduced through gaping omissions in the

---

3   E.-M Vogüé, *Le roman russe* Montreux, 1971, 242–243.
4   Victor Charbonnel, *Les mystiques dans la littérature présente*, Paris 1897 20; F.W.J. Hemmings, *The Russian Novel in France (1884–1914)*, London 1950.
5   Armand de Pontmartin, *Souvenirs d'un vieux critique*, Paris, 1881–1889, VII 285.
6   Hector Pessard, "Chronique théatrale," *Revue bleue* (22 sep 1888) 380. Translations into English are my own throughout.

translation. Half of Chapter 9 and 11 were removed entirely, and all that remains of Chapter 10 is a single paragraph: the Underground Man's apology for his own subversive philosophising. Much of the mathematical imagery and philosophical terminology employed by Dostoevskii to attack positivism and utilitarianism are removed from the translation. The *desired* effect was clearly to reduce an anti-rationalist polemic to a far more accessible and far less subversive irrational 'outburst'. It is thus hardly surprising that so few readers of the period recognised any import in the text.

Nonetheless, even in this reductive and rather sloppy adaptation, *L'Esprit souterrain* did find at least one highly attentive reader on French soil, who saw through to the gravity of its implications. Friedrich Nietzsche, stumbling upon the curious adaptation in Nice, described it, alongside Schopenhauer, as one of the great discoveries of his intellectual life: "Der Instinkt der Verwandtschaft (oder wie soll ich's nennen?) sprach sofort, meine Freude war außerordentlich" (I instantly perceived a kindred instinct (or how to put it?) I was overjoyed).[7] If Dostoevskii's critique of rationalism had been lost on – or rather concealed from – a first generation of French readers, the next generation would delve significantly deeper into the subversive side of Dostoevskii's presentation of the human condition, thanks in part to a parallel reading with Nietzsche's oeuvre. Translations of *Thus Spoke Zarathustra* and *Beyond Good and Evil* appeared in 1899, emblematically accompanied by André Gide's 'Sixième lettre à Angèle': an essay comparing Nietzsche to Dostoevskii. This association, which would prove so enduring and influential in the French discourse on both thinkers, was thus established from the outset of Nietzsche's French reception. From the turn of the century, Gide and a quasi-mystic *Belle Époque* generation began to unearth in Dostoevskii a 'modern' conception of man as an irreducible paradox, reading him, alongside Nietzsche, as 'permission' to make a clean break at once from classicist aesthetics and the positivistic, deterministic psychologies that reigned over the naturalism of the previous generation.

Nonetheless, few commentators make explicit mention of Dostoevskii's anti-rationalist polemics at this time. Gide, seen in his influential circle as the leading authority on Dostoevskii, offers no analysis of the *Notes* in any of his three pre-war essays on his Russian predecessor. Dostoevskii is hailed as an aesthetic and psychological innovator in the complexity his fiction achieves, rather than the paradoxalism it fosters, and the vast majority of French commentators are at this stage still intent on settling for a straightforward ethnographic justification for any disparity between Dostoevskii's fiction and their own tradition

---

7 Letter to Overbeck, 23 feb 1887. *Briefwechsel: Friedrich Nietzsche, Franz und Ida Overbeck*, Suttgart; Weimar 2000, 354.

and appeasing themselves – whether rapturously or disparagingly – with the unfathomable Russian soul. Suarès, following Vogüé, overlooked the *Notes* entirely in his dichotomous *âme russe – esprit français* reading of Dostoevskii's fiction: "Ce que l'Occident connaît par mesure, le Russe le devine par le sentiment".(What the West knows by measure, the Russian guesses by emotion);[8] "Ils [les russes] ont cette faculté d'émotion, qui est si generale en Orient. Ils peuvent ne jamais rire, mais ils pleurent", (They [Russians] have this faculty of emotion that is so general to the Orient. They are capable of never laughing, but they weep).[9] Faure's *Les constructeurs*, in its rare mention of the *Notes* sees nothing in them beyond a Roussauian interrogation of the fundamental nobility of man "suis-je noble ou suis-je vil?" (am I noble or am I vile?).[10] The comparison is legitimate but telling: Faure homes in on a moral parity, ignoring the epistemological dimension of Dostoevskii's polemics.

Reassessment: Émigré Re-readings and Re-writings

The Great War was doubtlessly a key factor in the rapid re-evaluation of Dostoevskii's anti-rationalism. Once content with the rapturous orientalist intuitionism of a Suarès, from 1918 a sober if not jaded post-*Belle-Époque* youth began to see neo-romantic philosophies of life such as Bergson's as ever more insufficient expressions of the tragic absurdity of human existence. Nineteenth-century theories of rational historical progress were also looking tragically dubious. At the same time, the events of 1917 turned all eyes to Russia, and Dostoevskii attracted a second wave of interest, this time with the enhanced status of the 'prophet of the Revolution'. The interwar years were thus both a significant peak and turning point in Dostoevskii's French reception. French readers began to note an increased resonance with Russian literature; commentators began to recognise themselves in characters they had once deemed 'unfathomable': suspicion was rising that all along Dostoevskii had been depicting not 'Russian' but 'Modern' man.[11]

---

8   Andrè Suarès, *Dostoïevski*, Paris 1911, 18.
9   Ibid. 76.
10 Élie Faure, *Les constructeurs*, Paris 1914. 118–119.
11 See, for example, Robert Sébastien's inaugural presentation at the Studio Franco-Russe, 29 Oct 1929: 'L'Inquiétude dans la littérature' reprinted in *Le studio franco-russe*, ed. Leonid Livak, Toronto 2005, 49–58. Gide, an advocate of the view that political events have no impact on the history of thought, even went as far as to attribute the change in part to exposure to Dostoevskii: "Oui, vraiment, je crois que Dostoïevsky nous ouvre les yeux sur

A third significant factor was the arrival of much of Russia's exiled intelligentsia in Paris. Among them were several key representatives of the anti-rationalist, amoralistic religious and proto-existential strands of thought of the Silver Age: Shestov, Berdiaev, Merezhkovskii, who would each present his own conceptions of Dostoevskii's thought to the French elite. Each of these readings was steeped in the anti-rationalist climate of the Silver Age.

If Dostoevskii's critique of the post-enlightenment intellectual tradition was already a key source of inspiration to the Silver Age generation, it became it became so all the more in emigration. This curious phenomenon has duly attracted considerable attention in recent analyses of émigré thought, underlining the importance of Dostoevskii's fictional world to the émigré conception of Russianness.[12] What has generally been overlooked, however, in studying the diaspora in isolation from its 'host' cultures, is the great significance of Dostoevskii as a platform for intercultural discourse. Parisian salons were already abuzz with Dostoevskii, and it was principally as his authoritative interpreters that thinkers such as Shestov were invited into the high profile French journals through which they accessed the francophone readership.

It was through Dostoevskii that Shestov's existential revolt against reason first came into contact with rising existential currents in French literary thought from the early twenties. Shestov's main French publications on his predecessor, *Dostoïevsky et la lutte contre les évidences* (1922)[13] and *La Philosophie de la tragedie: Dostoïevsky et Nietzsche* (1926)[14] played a key role not only in establishing his own voice in the French intellectual milieu, but also in carving out a place for the Dostoevskian Underground Man in the history of European philosophical literature. *Dostoïevsky et la Lutte* is a radical existential reading of the yet little-discussed *Notes from Underground*, raised up by Shestov to no less than "une des œuvres les plus extraordinaires de la littérature universelle"

---

certains phénomènes, qui peut-être ne sont même pas rare – mais que simplement no n'avions pas su remarquer. " (Yes, truly, I believe that Dostoevskii opens our eyes to certain phenomena that perhaps are not even uncommon, but that we simply did not know how to recognise.) André Gide, *Dostoïevsky*, Paris 1923, 180.

12 See, for example, Zhan-Filipp Zhakkar (Jean Philippe Jaccard) and Ul'rikh Shmid (Ulrich Scmid), "Dostoevskii i russkaia zarubezhnaia kul'tura: k postanovke voprosa", in *Dostoevskii i russkoe zarubezh'e xx veka*, eds Zhan-Filipp Zhakkar and Ul'rikh Shmid Sankt-Peterburg 2008 7–26; Leonid Livak, *How it was done in Paris: Russian Emigré Literature and French Modernism*, Wisconsin 2003 16.

13 An extract from *Preodolenie samoochevidnostei* appearing in the NRF in Feb 1922, translated and prefaced by Schloezer. The article was translated and published in full in *Les révélations de la mort* in 1923.

14 Originally published in Russian in 1902.

(one of the most extraordinary works of universal literature).[15] This 'universalisation' of Dostoevskii's thought was critical to Shestov's success in France in comparison to other émigré commentators, many of whom persisted along nineteenth-century Volksgeist lines of interpretation.[16] In separating anti-rationalism likewise from Dostoevskii's ultimate Christian goals and analysing it in agnostic epistemological terms, Shestov's 'secularisation' of Dostoevskii's anti-rationalism thus also further broadened the scope of the work's impact. If Shestov's reading penetrated more deeply in France than that of any other Russian émigré thinker (even than the more widely read Berdiaev, as Mercadé has argued[17]) it is doubtlessly due to the cosmopolitanism and secularism of his method. In interpreting the work as an outburst of individual existential revelation, Shestov disentangles the anti-rationalist drive of Dostoevskii's thought from the 'Russian Soul' construct, from Slavophilia and from the religious fanaticism on which previous readings had hinged. By entirely removing any possible Christian moralistic motive from Dostoevskii's original and dealing almost exclusively with the first section of the *Notes* in isolation from the second, Shestov's representation of the work comes to resemble an anti-rationalist manifesto, which he explicitly refers to as European philosophy's first genuine "critique of pure reason".[18]

Thus setting underground philosophy in opposition to Kantian idealism's *praise* of pure reason, Shestov then extrapolates his argument back to Plato. In a creative use of metaphor, Shestov melds Dostoevskii's 'underground' with Plato's 'cave', using the former to subvert the latter.[19] By Shestov's inverted allegory, any philosophy (be it idealist, rationalist or indeed empiricist) dependent on universal laws is left in the cave with the idyllic transcendental 'shadows' Plato had inadvertently venerated. In confining universality to the cave, Shestov aims to debunk not only platonic idealism but rational thought *per se*. The result is not obligatorily an irrationalism: Shestov revolts not against the validity of rational processes but the presumption of the *authority* that truths obtained rationally claim over any conception of truth that lies outwith its boundaries, in this case, the existential revelation that he posits behind Dostoevskii's underground paradoxalist polemics.

15 Léon Schestov (Lev Shestov), "Dostoïevsky et la lutte contre les évidences", *Nouvelle Revue Française*, XVIII/101 (fév 1922) 142.
16 Livak, *How It Was Done in Paris*, 14–18.
17 Jean-Claude Marcadé, "Proniknovenie russkoi mysli vo frantsuzskuiu sredu: N.A. Berdiaev & L.I. Shestov", in *Russkaia religiozno-filosofskaia mysl' xx veka*, ed. N.T. Poltoratskii, Pittsburg 1975 150.
18 Schestov, "Dostoïevsky et la lutte contre les évidences", 150–151.
19 Ibid. 144.

In pitting the Underground Man against the entirety of the European philosophical mainstream from the Greeks to Kant, and from idealism to positivism, Shestov indulges in a fairly radical extrapolation of the Underground Man's original thesis: Dostoevskii's polemicist had focused his attack against various contemporary attempts to rationalise human interaction, employing psychological realism against assumptions as to the infallibility of human reason and human science with the ultimate end of reaffirming the preeminence of Christian anthropology over such doctrines as utilitarianism.[20] In Shestov's reading, however, Christian dogma is rejected as yet another universalism,[21] thus liberating both ethics and epistemology to a near anarchistic subjectivism.

Shestov's goal is no more gratuitous (and ultimately no less religious) than Dostoevskii's. It is to challenge what he sees as the despotic governance of rationalism over thought: the pretensions of science to exclusive rights to truth and the tendency of philosophy to accept them. His methodological recourse to literary criticism in revolt against the philosophical mainstream is a further means of undermining the authority of the objectivising rationalist mode (its language, methods, values) over individual will, caprice and creativity. Shestov is well aware that his critical method, like Dostoevskii's fictional method before him, implies an undermining of the structure of philosophical discourse:

> Vous n'êtes pas habitué à de tels arguments ; vous êtes même offensé peut-être qu'en parlant de la théorie de la connaissance je cite ces passages de Dostoïevsky. Vous auriez raison si Dostoïevsky n'avait pas soulevé la question de droit. Mais deux fois deux quatre, la raison avec toutes ses évidences ne veulent justement pas admettre qu'on discute la question de droit.
>
> (You are not accustomed to such arguments; you are perhaps even offended that I cite passages from Dostoevskii in relation to the theory of knowledge. You would be correct were it not that Dostoevskii had raised

---

[20] See Dostoevskii's 26 Mar 1864 letter to Mikhail Dostoevskii: "Свиньи цензора, там, где я глумился над всем и инода богохульствовал *для виду*, – то пропущено, а где из всего этого я вывел потребность веры и Христа – то запрещено". (The censors are swine: wherever I sneered at everyone and even blasphemed *for show*, they permitted it, but when I deduced from this the need for faith and Christ – they disallowed it.) F.M. Dostoevskii, *Polnoe sobranie sochinienii v tridtsati tomakh*, Leningrad 1973 XXVIII II 73.

[21] For Shestov, only an adogmatic, absurd faith – "unfounded" faith (to employ Piron's term) is admitted. Geneviève Piron, *Léon Chestov: philosophe du déracinement*, Lausanne 2010 75.

the question of rights. But twice two is four, reason with all its evidences, refuses precisely to admit discussion of the question of rights).[22]

Shestov's inventive philosophical approach to Dostoevskii is thus perhaps a less significant innovation than his 'literary' approach to philosophy, which, rooted in Russia's non-academic tradition and informed by Nietzsche, represents a challenge to disciplinary boundaries that were arguably more institutionally entrenched in French than Russian discourse.

Shestov's anti-rationalist, existential reading of Dostoevskii quickly began to make waves. Gide, having published alongside Shestov in the NRF, would subsequently describe the *Notes* as the philosophical 'key' to Dostoevskii's oeuvre.[23] Shestov, along with his translator, close friend and philosophical disciple Boris de Schloezer were both invited to Desjardin's 'Décade' at Pontigny in 1923, an elitist ten-day conference on the question "Y a-t-il dans la poésie d'un peuple un trésor réservé, [sic] impénétrable aux étrangers ?" (Does the poetry of a people contain a reserved treasure inaccessible to foreigners?)[24] Dostoevskii was naturally high on the agenda. Schloezer would soon undertake to re-translate *Notes from Underground,* under the title *La Voix Souterraine (The Underground Voice),* published in 1926. Having translated and clearly assimilated Shestov's philosophical-critical writings (his translation of *The Philosophy of Tragedy: Dostoevskii and Nietzsche* appeared in the same year), Schloezer's 'underground voice', as the title might suggest, proves distinctly more philosophical and confident in tone than had Harpéline-Kaminski and Maurice's 'underground mind' – indeed, slightly more so even than Dostoevskii's original. Where the initial translation/adaptation had emphasised (through the altered title, edited content and disjointed format) the deranged aspect of the protagonist's state of mind and the incoherence of his monologue, Schloezer's more subtle linguistic alterations veer it towards the philosophical treatise that Shestov had extrapolated from the text. Given that Schoezer's translation was to become the canonic version of the Edition de la Pléiade, it warrants close consideration. A few examples with literal English back translations, from the original, the initial translation and from Schloezer's canonic version, must here suffice to illustrate the means by which Schloezer bends the text towards his and Shestov's anti-rationalist existential philosophy.

22 Schestov, "Dostoïevsky et la lutte contre les évidences", 156.
23 Gide, *Dostoïevsky*, 237.
24 N. Baranova-Shestova, *Zhizn' L'va Shestova: po perepiske i vospominamiam sovremenikov*, Paris 1983 256.

Shestov's understanding of the *Notes* hinged on an equation, which permeates his philosophical writings, of moralists, 'men of action' and rationalist thinkers, in that they are each "convinced in advance that they know what truth is".[25] The same equation is written into Schloezer's translation:

Original	1886 translation	1926 translation
Известно, многие из этих **любителей [человеческого рода]**, рано ли, поздно ли, под конец жизни **изменяли себе**, произведя какой-нибудь анекдот, иногда даже из самых неприличнейших. (As is known, many of these philanthropists sooner or later, towards the end of their lives, betrayed themselves, producing some ridiculous incident, even of the least respectable kinds.)[26]	(Entirely omitted)[27]	On sait que nombre de ces **amateurs de sagesse** finissent tôt ou tard par **trahir leurs idées** et se compromettent dans de scandaleuses histoires. (As is known, many of these lovers of wisdom end sooner or later in betraying their ideas and compromise themselves in scandalous incidents.)[28]

Here Dostoevskii's image of lovers of mankind letting themselves down has been replaced by philosophers betraying their doctrines. The suggestion of such a comparison was not entirely absent from the original, however; Schloezer's liberal rendering is clearly informed by Shestov's reading. Where Dostoevskii had thus placed equal stress on the ethical consequences of the fundamental irrationality of man, Schloezer follows Shestov in homing in on the epistemological stakes.

With regard to anti-rationalist revolt the original and the two translations clearly operate within disparate ideological frameworks:

---

25   Lev Shestov, *Sochinenia v dvukh tomax*, Moscow 1993 379.
26   Dostoevskii, *Polnoe sobranie sochinienii*, v 116.
27   F.M. Dostoevskii, *L'esprit souterrain*, (tr. Halpérine-Kaminsky and Maurice) Paris 1886 185.
28   F.M. Dostoïevski, *Carnets du sous-sol*, (tr. Boris de Schloezer) Paris 1995 89 (References to Schloezer's translation use the recent reprint in Folio Bilingue for ease of comparison. The re translated title differs from the 1926 edtion).

…вполне понимая свои настоящие выгоды, отставляли их на второй план и **бросались на другую дорогу, на риск, на авось,** никем и ничем не принуждаемые к тому, а как будто именно только не желая указанной дороги, и **упрямо, своевольно пробивали другую, трудную, нелепую,** отыскивая ее чуть не в потемках. Ведь, значит, им действительно это **упрямство и своеволие** было приятнее всякой выгоды…

(…fully understanding their own interests, they set them aside and launched out on another path, on a risk, on a perhaps, obliged by nothing and no-one, but precisely as if they simply did not wish to the path indicated to them, and stubbornly, willfully ['self-willedly'], they beat out a different, difficult, absurd path, searching for it almost in the dark. Surely this means that this stubbornness and self-will was more pleasant to them than any interests)[29]

…sans le leurrer de leurs véritables intérêts, sans y être poussés par rien, pour **se détourner** *exprès*, dis-je, **de la voie droite,** en cherchant à tâtons, le **mauvais chemin, des actions absurdes et mauvaises.** C'est que cet **libertinage** leur convient mieux que toute considération d'intérêt réel…

(…without deluding themselves as to their genuine interests, without being forced by anything, in order, I tell you, to turn away from the proper road *on purpose*, groping their way along, they took the wrong path, of absurd and wrong actions. It is that this libertinage suited them better than any consideration of genuine interests.)[30]

…tout *en se rendant compte* de leur intérêt, le rejettent au seconde plan, et s'engagent dans une **tout autre voie, pleine de risques** et de hasards ? Ils n'y sont pourtant pas forcés ; mais il semble qu'ils veuillent précisément éviter la route qu'on leur indiquait, pour en **tracer librement, capricieusement, une autre, pleine de difficultés, absurde,** à peine reconnaissable, obscure. C'est donc que cette **liberté** possède à leurs yeux plus d'attraits que leurs propres intérêts…

(…*fully aware* of their interests, did they not set them aside and engage themselves in an entirely different path, full of risks and dangers? They were not forced, however, but it seems they wanted precisely to avoid the route indicated to them, in order to freely, capriciously trace another, absurd route full of difficulties, barely recognisable, obscure. It is that this freedom thus possessed more attraction than their own advantage.)[31]

---

29   Dostoevskii, *Polnoe sobranie sochinienii*, V 110.
30   Dostoïevski, *L'esprit souterrain*, (tr. Halpérine-Kaminsky and Maurice) 79.
31   Dostoïevski, *Carnets du sous-sol* (tr. Boris de Schloezer) 61.

Harpéline-Kaminsky and Maurice's rendering clearly slides the original in the direction of conventional romantic rebellion, which it in turn overtly condemns. Their underground speaker draws attention only to the fact that there have been cases when men have gone against the grain, choosing "the wrong path" (note their choice of definite article) of "libertinage" where the same section in the original had referred to a "different", "difficult" path, suspending moral judgement on either path. Schloezer's translation slides the text in the opposite direction. His rebels stray "freely and capriciously" from the beaten track (where Dostoevskii's had strayed stubbornly and "self-willedly") superimposing positive connotations on the original. Where Dostoevskii's rebels had "thrown themselves on a risk", Schloezer's "engaged themselves on a path full of risks", thus lexically implicating the rebels in a 'mission'; while Dostoevskii's throw themselves somewhat arbitrarily "at a perhaps" in self-affirmation, Schloezer's seem to have another, unspoken objective: they are not on "their own" paths of self-will, but rather engaged in a somewhat defined alternative path "full of risks".

Observe also Schloezer's consistently higher register and more confident expression than the voice Dostoevskii had consigned to the Underground Man, manifest in the above example through Schloezer's addition of a rhetorical question and a semi-colon (where Harpéline-Kaminsky and Maurice had lowered the tone, and consequently the content's gravity, with an interjected '*dis-je*'). This is another means by which Schloezer systematically raises the text to the philosophical manifesto of Shestov's reading. The Underground Man's famously idiosyncratic tone has been significantly refined throughout Schloezer's translation. Though the translator is even strikingly faithful to the original syntax in most aspects, time and again he freely omits an expression of uncertainty, a *kak by*, a *mozhet byt'*, a *tak skazat'*, or a *kak-to* even a whole "*nu, i...nu khot' by dazhe i*"[32] adding a causal *car*, or a *parce que*.[33] Commas are systematically upgraded to colons; ellipses to periods; periods to exclamation marks.[34] Subtle and indeed permissible alterations these may be, but they are not inconsequential. These subtle but systematic alterations serve to significantly polish the Underground Man's rhetoric, where Dostoevskii had taken pains to confer to his character a relatively grotesque linguistic persona. Just as Shestov had extended the character's argument towards philosophical discourse, so Schloezer has edged his language towards a philosophical register.

---

32   Ibid. 28–29, 38–39, 46–47, 80–81.
33   Ibid. 38–39 (three examples).
34   Ibid. 18–19, 22–23, 24–25 46–47.

Thus France's most authoritative translation of *Notes from Underground* was literally impregnated with Shestov's existential reading.

Towards Assimilation: Intertextual Existential Dialogues

Throughout the twenties and thirties Dostoevskii would continue to carry a great deal of weight in French intellectual life, and continue to function as a communicative platform for French and Russian émigré thinkers. The Studio Franco-Russe, established in 1929, brought together high-profile French and Russian intellectuals for heated debates, of which the full transcripts have been recently republished.[35] In the course of the first two (consecrated to post-war angst [*inquiétude*] and contemporary Franco-Russian intercultural literary influence) so abundant were references to Dostoevskii that the third was dedicated entirely to his thought and its French reception. The dialogue achieved at the Studio, as at Pontigny and the salons, went a long way to establishing contact between the intellectual tradition of the Silver Age and France's developing absurdist and existential movements, Dostoevskii and Shestov informing perhaps most notably Camus, Marcel and Ionesco's perceptions of the human condition.[36]

Several authors of French philosophical fiction would engage with Dostoevskii's *Notes from Underground* from this period onward, but doubtlessly the highest-profile cases were Sartre and Camus. However, despite both aesthetic and conceptual steps made by both authors in the direction of the underground, comparative analysis of *La nausée* and *La chute* with Dostoevskii's *Notes* reveals curious persisting tensions between the 'Cartesian' tradition and the anti-rationalist stance of Dostoevskii or Shestov. In *Nausea*, Sartre presents his own 'underground' hero, Roquentin, reminiscent of Dostoevskii's in his embodiment of the sickly experience of individual consciousness faced with an acute and paralysing perception of an irrational reality. In Sartre's case, the individual consciousness is literally engulfed by the absurdity of facticity until the distinction between object and perception disintegrates, taking with it the possibility of the Cartesian model of consciousness from which Sartre had departed. Roquentin further radically rejects any rational 'method'. In refusing to subjugate sensory data to the faculty of reason and remaining on the surface of perception, Sartre's early novel's modernist poetics express in practical terms what Dostoevskii and Shestov had performed on a conceptual level by

---

35   Livak, ed., *Le Studio Franco-Russe*.

36   See Marcadé, "Proniknovenie russkoi mysli vo frantsuzskuiu sredu", 158–160.

waging paradoxalist polemics against reason. Roquentin thus relates to underground philosophy through a willful rejection of the Socratic command to examine; the capricious fruits of consciousness, his estranged perceptions and disengaged actions, go unrationalised.

Both the *Notes* and *Nausea* present comparably unromanticised romanticisms: i.e. romantic paradigms dissociated from idealism. The extra-rational mental state is presented not as an alternative to reason but as a pathology that the individual can contract in extreme isolation from a 'rational' collective. This, however, does not lessen the challenge to Descartes: the individual reasoning reason is revealed to be dependent on collective consensus. Unlike Shestov, both Sartre and Dostoevskii were driven to present 'glimmers of hope', routes of potential reintegration for those minds that had embarked on a revolt against common sense. For Dostoevskii, the only possible return ticket was Christian ethics: the hope embodied by the downtrodden Lisa of the second half of the *Notes* (albeit, as in many of his works, represented in negative relief in keeping with his tragic mode). Sartre associates Roquentin's nauseating subjectivism to his detachment from the collective, from which his loss of all bearings for judgement springs, as his epigraph indicates: "C'est un garçon sans importance collective, c'est tout juste un individu". (It is a boy without collective importance, only just an individual.)[37]

In keeping with Sartre's later philosophical writings, the suggestion is that this very *disengagement*, Roquentin's unawareness of his being-for-others, leaves his existence meaningless. Thus, while Dostoevskii's anti-rational hero can emphatically find *no earthly* escape from his tormented irrational state of being,[38] Sartre proposes a course of treatment for the insular consciousness of a Roquentin, who allegedly could and supposedly 'should' be transformed through 'authentic' engagement with the collective, as explored in *Being and Nothingness* and later expounded in 'Existentialism is a humanism'. Though ostensibly more radically subjectivist than previous rationalistic approaches to ethics, Sartre's system nonetheless resorts to an *a priori* valuation of authenticity (even if the definition of the term remains relativistic), in order to reunite with systematic rationalist humanist traditions, and effectively to return from the underground to Kantian ethics. The author of the second half the *Notes from*

---

37   J.-P. Sartre, *Oeuvres Romanesques*, Paris 1981 1.
38   "Вру, потому что сам знаю, как дважды два, что вовсе не подполье лучше, а что-то другое, совсем другое, которого я жажду, но которого никак не найду!" ("I am lying because I myself know, like two times two, that it is not the underground that is better at all, but something else, something entirely different, that I thirst for but will never be able to find!") Dostoevskii, *Polnoe sobranie sochinienii*, V 121.

Underground (not to mention *Crime and Punishment*), however, had emphasised the impossibility of an ethics founded on relative concepts such as authenticity, thus concluding on the necessity of Christianity. However, Shestov had categorically rejected both Dostoevskii's and Sartre's escape routes from the Absurd to meaningful existence through ethics, a stance that Camus would pick up in his own Dostoevskii-informed critique of Sartrian existentialism.

Camus's *The Fall* (1957) represents in many ways a more significant interaction with Russian anti-rationalist thought, and a more direct intertextual dialogue with *Notes from Underground*. Camus had a lifelong infatuation with Dostoevskii, reaching from his youthful theatre role as Ivan Karamazov to his theatre adaptation of Schloezer's translation of *The Devils*, shortly prior to his death. *The Fall*, his last completed novel, has been discussed by Irina Kirk, among others, as a parodistic attack on Sartre's Existentialist humanism and its return from the 'underground' revelation of the absurd to neo-Kantian ethics. To wage this polemic, Camus goes back to its roots: to the Dostoevskian underground, and employs against Sartre, as Kirk has explored, the same techniques that Dostoevskii had pioneered against nineteenth-century rationalism.[39] Critically, Camus was not only an enthused reader of Dostoevskii but also of Shestov and Berdiaev. Atheist, anti-Gnostic and, in a sense, rationalist to the end, Camus was critical of Shestov and Dostoevskii's religious 'leaps of faith'.[40] However, he would nonetheless re-align himself in his maturity with the paradoxalist, anti-systematic philosophies of Shestov, Kierkegaard, and Pascal, in fierce opposition to Sartre's turn from the Absurd to a 'dogmatic' Existentialism.[41] In *The Fall* he presents Clamence: a charismatic Parisian humanist, 'fallen' suddenly into a radical cynicism, following an existential awakening to the Absurd. Clamence is subsequently disgusted by his own former humanist self-satisfaction, exactly as the underground man had been by the complacent positivistic humanism of his era. The setting, unlike all of Camus's previous 'Mediterranean' narratives, is a cold, canal-riddled, northern capital; more specifically its cramped living quarters and grimy taverns.[42] Significantly, however

---

39 Irina Kirk, *Dostoevskij and Camus: The Themes of Consciousness, Isolation, Freedom and Love*, München 1974 36.

40 Albert Camus, *Oeuvres complètes*, Paris 2008 I 242–243.

41 "If the premises of existentialism are to be found, as I believe they are, in Pascal, Nietzsche, Kierkegaard or Shestov, then I agree with them. If its conclusions are those of *our* existentialisms, then I no longer agree because they contradict their premises". From a late interview cited in Kirk, *Dostoevskij and Camus*, 33.

42 Davison has explored Camus's debt to Dostoevskii in his conceptualisation and fictional representation of urban space in relation to the decline of rationalism. See Ray Davison, *Camus: The Challenge of Dostoevskii*, Exeter 1997 162–163.

consonant in atmosphere, Camus has set his underground polemic not in St. Petersburg but in Amsterdam. In so doing he has expressly expatriated his underground protagonist to the land to which Descartes had fled France, symbolically bringing the father of the French rationalist tradition into conflict with underground polemics. Clamence, a clear parody of Sartre, defines himself as "a Cartesian Frenchman" ironically noting in passing, that Descartes' Dutch abode now serves as an insane asylum, thus drawing his analogy between reason and pathology.[43]

Camus's 'fallen' Cartesian narrator is doubtlessly a still more disturbing image than Dostoevskii's Underground Man, in that, emphatically, Clamence is not an inherently *bolnoi, zloi, neprivlekatelnyi* (sick, spiteful and unattractive) man,[44] but rather a healthy, handsome and successful humanitarian 'man of action', more akin in presentation to the strapping officer the Underground Man had so envied. Nonetheless, when faced with the tragic absurdity of human life and death, his fall to the underground is equally swift and irrevocable. Clamence, like Shestov before him, offers no escape route from the existential truths of the Absurd and no possible compromise between reason and an existence for which it cannot account. Unlike Dostoevskii's Orthodox preaching later expounded through Zossima, or Sartre's Existentialist moralising, Camus and Shestov both refute attempts to escape from the Absurd or to 'rebuild the crystal palace' on either dogmatic or rationalistic foundations.

Camus, however, did not venture down Dostoevskii and Shestov's road of paradoxalism, of turning reason against reason. While the anti-rationalist conclusions of his most 'underground' novel, *The Fall*, echoed Dostoevskii's and Shestov, Camus's philosophical essays were critical of his religious existential predecessors' "philosophical suicide"[45] and their ensuing 'leaps of faith'. Where Dostoevskii concluded his critique of reason ultimately with the necessity of Christianity, and Shestov with an anxious, agnostic leap into a religious unknown, Camus's (equally paradoxical) conclusion argued a need to continue reasoning rationally, cognisant of the incompatibility between reason and the experience of existing: to remain in an inescapably strained recognition of the Absurd.[46]

---

43   Camus, *Oeuvres complètes*, III 750.
44   Dostoevskii, *Polnoe sobranie sochinienii*, V 99.
45   Camus, *Oeuvres complètes*, I 241–247.
46   Ibid. III 316–324; I.303–304.

Conclusion

To speak of a direct appropriation, in any of the cases here explored, of Dostoevskii's attack on the rationalist tradition would be problematic, despite marked dialogues in existential, existentialist and absurdist writings that I have traced across the middle of the last century. As observed, initial interpretations by critics and translators at the turn of the century such as Vogüé, Harpéline-Kaminski and Maurice, clearly remained impervious to (whether oblivious of or hostile toward) the anti-rationalist polemics that permeate Dostoevskii's fiction. Early adaptations made active attempts to 'rationalise' Dostoevskii's narratives, and critics focused entirely on their moral enquiry, attributing any epistemological remonstrance to an innate oriental mysticism within the Russian soul, disregarded as inherently incomprehensible to the French mind. This interpretation was then challenged from the turn of the century by more cosmopolitan 'immoralist' readers such as Gide and Faure; however, the primacy of reason *per se* remained unchallenged. Existential commentary by Shestov was to launch this challenge, and together with Schloezer's re-translation, to present the *Notes from Underground* as a coherent anti-rationalist polemic launched from literature at the dominance of rationalism in European thought. Whilst Sartre's early existentialist literature was seen to be comparable to the *Notes* in form, thematics, and its staunch rejection of transcendentalism, he ultimately returned to the rationalist tradition on the plane of ethics, concluding with a rationalist conception of authenticity rendering life meaningful in a socialised world. Finally, Camusian Absurdism engaged profoundly with Dostoevskii and Shestov's revolt against rationalism, not, like Dostoevskii, to conclude from the absurd the necessity of the divine, nor, like Shestov, to associate the Absurd with the Divine itself, but nonetheless to share with his Russian predecessors an acute awareness of an ever-strained, irreconcilable recognition of the irrational.

Bibliography

Baranova-Shestova, N, 1983. *Zhizn' L'va Shestova: po perepiske i vospominamiiam sovremenikov*. Paris: La Presse Libre.

Camus, Albert. 2008. *Oeuvres complètes*. Paris: Gallimard.

Charbonnel, Victor. 1897. *Les mystiques dans la littérature présente*. Paris Mercure.

Davison, Ray. 1997. *Camus: The Challenge of Dostoevskii*. Exeter: University of Exeter Press.

Dostoevskii, F. M, 1973. *Polnoe sobranie sochinenii v tridtsati tomakh*. Leningrad: Nauka.

——— 1886. *L'Esprit souterrain* (tr. E. Halpérine-Kaminsky and Charles Maurice) Paris: Plon.

——— 1995. *Carnets du sous-sol* (tr. Boris de Schloezer) (Collection Folio Bilingue) Paris: Gallimard.

Erofeev, V. V, 2003. *Naiti v cheloveke cheloveka*. Moskva: Zebra E.

Faure, Élie. 1914. *Les constructeurs* (Collection Les Proses) Paris: George Crès.

Gide, André. 1923. *Dostoïevsky*. Paris: Plon.

Hemmings, F.W.J, 1950. *The Russian Novel in France (1884–1914)*. London: Oxford Univ. Press.

Kaufmann, Walter. 1975. *Existentialism from Dostoevskii to Sartre*. New York: New American Library.

Kirk, Irina. 1974. *Dostoevskij and Camus: The Themes of Consciousness, Isolation, Freedom and Love*. München: Wilhelm Fink Verlag.

Latynina, A. N, 1972. 'Dostoevskii i ekzistentsializsm', in Lomunov, K.N. (ed.) *Dostoevskii: khudozhnik i myslitel'* Moskva: Khudozhestvennaia Literatura: 210–259.

Livak, Leonid. 2003. *How it was done in Paris: Russian Emigré Literature and French Modernism*. Wisconsin: University of Wisconsin Press.

——— (ed.) 2005. *Le Studio Franco-Russe: Textes réunis et présenté par Léonid Livak sous la rédaction d Gervaise Tassiss* Toronto: Toronto Slavic Quarterly.

Marcadé, Jean-Claude. 1975. 'Proniknovenie russkoi mysli vo frantsuzskuiu sredu: N.A. Berdiaev i L.I. Shestov', in *Russkaia religiozno-filosofskaia mysl' xx veka*. Poltoratskii, N.T. (ed.) Pittsburg: Pittsburg Univ Press: 150–163.

Morino, Gordon. (ed.) 2004. *Basic Writings of Existentialism*. New York: Modern Library.

Nietzsche, Friedrich. 2000. *Briefwechsel: Friedrich Nietzsche, Franz und Ida Overbeck*. Suttgart and Weimar: Metzler.

Pessard, Hector. 1888. 'Chronique Théatrale' in *Revue Bleue* (22 sep 1888).

Piron, Geneviève. 2010. *Léon Chestov: Philosophe du déracinement*. Lausanne: Age de l'homme.

Pontmartin, Armand de. 1881–1889. *Souvenirs d'un vieux critique*. Paris: Calmann Lévy.

Sartre, Jean-Paul. 1981. *Oeuvres romanesques, Pléiade*. Paris: Gallimard.

Schestov, Léon. 1922. 'Dostoïevsky et la lutte contre les évidences', in *La Nouvelle Revue Française* 18(101) (fév 1922): 134–158.

Shestov, Lev. 1993. *Sochinieniia v dvukh tomax*. Moscow: Nauka.

Suarès, Andrè. 1911. *Dostoïevski* (*Cahiers de la Quainzaine* 13/8). Paris: Cahiers de la Quainzaine.

Vogüé, E.-M. 1971. *Le roman russe, Slavica*. Montreux: Ganguin et Laubscher.

Zhakkar, Zhan-Filipp, and Ul'rikh Shmid (eds) 2008. *Dostoevskii i russkoe zarubezh'e xx veka*. Sankt-Peterburg: Dmitrii Bulanin.

CHAPTER 10

The Concept of Love and Beauty in the Works of Turgenev[1]

Margarita Odesskaia

Dmitrii Merezhkovskii called Turgenev the poet of beauty and the state of being in love.[2] This characterisation of the writer is as undisputed as the fact that, as V. V Rozanov put it, there is no happy love in the works of the 'old knight'. Philosophers, psychologists, critics and literary scholars have interpreted the reason for Turgenev's poeticisation of unhappy love in various ways. Naturally, many search for an explanation in the writer's own romantic history, which did culminate in what conventional conceptions would deem to constitute happiness, that is, in marriage. In conceiving his characters' behaviour, Turgenev undoubtedly drew on his own experiences. Conversely, the idealist conception of beauty and love inculcated in him by many centuries of European culture influenced the course of his personal relationship with the "tsarina of tsarinas".[3] According to Rozanov, "he gave a wonderful Russian re-working to many European ideas". Iulii Aichenval'd has written of the idealism and bookish literariness of love as Turgenev depicts it, demonstrating how Turgenev uses quotations and allusions to link his characters to the cultural traditions of the world.

---

1 This work is a translated version of a chapter from the earlier published monograph (in Russian) by Margarita Odesskaia: *Chekhov i problema ideala*, Moscow, RGGU, 2011. The author is grateful to the Russian publisher (Publishing Centre of the Russian State Humanitites University: RGGU) and personally to its director S.S. Ippolitov for the permission to re-print the work in the current volume.
2 Dmitrii Merezhkovskii, *Lev Tolstoi i Dostoevskii. Vechnye sputniki. Turgenev*, Moscow: Respublika, 1995, 475. See also, Iulii Aikhenval'd, "Turgenev", in *Siluety russkikh pisatelei*, Moscow: Respublika, 1994, 255–262.
3 Turgenev called Pauline Viardot this before his death. See, B. Zaitsev, "Zhizn' Turgeneva", in B. Zaitsev, *Zhukovskii. Zhizn' Turgeneva. Chekhov*, Moscow: 'Druzhba narodov', 1999, 356. In his work on Turgenev, Lev Shestov highlights Turgenev's European education, which differentiated him from other Russian writers such as Dostoevskii and Tolstoi, and also Turgenev's consequent adherence to aesthetic and ethical categories that had developed in Europe. See, Lev Shestov, *Turgenev (Otryvki iz neokonchennoi knigi)*, ed. by B. Aleksandrova, Moscow: Literaturnaia ucheba, 2000, II: 187–202.

Turgenev's portraits of women are associated with antiquity. One of his first published poems, 'K Venere Meditseiskoi' ('To the Medici Venus', 1838), reflects the writer's meditations on classical culture. Being from another historical period, the poem's narrator maintains a distance from classical cultural heritage, thereby affording the opportunity for an analytical stance towards Venus as a cultural symbol of the Hellenic era. Turgenev shows that the cultural-historical reality of the classical world passed through two stages in the course of history: destruction and renaissance. The heroes and gods created in that era influenced the consciousness and emotions of the Greeks. Although they receded into the past together with the ancient era, they were preserved in myths and the classical canon. Turgenev alerts his readers to the fact that nineteenth-century man understands Venus through layers of cultural stratification, and through the artistic creations of other later eras, which made her mythological image immortal and divine. Man in the nineteenth century does not worship Venus as she really was, but rather, her embodiment in art, her image as carved by the sculptor Praxiteles.

In 'Turgenev's Novella *Spring Torrents*: The Problem of the Borders of the Text', G.S. Knabe shows that Turgenev's attitude to antiquity corresponds to a new conceptualisation of the culture of Ancient Greece and Rome that was formed in the second half of the nineteenth century. Turgenev's contemporaries noted another side to the classical world, its savagery.[4] This radical rethinking of classical culture found its most fully realised expression in Nietzsche's *The Birth of Tragedy* (1871). Nietzsche revealed two sides to the Greek spirit, the Apollonian and Dionysian principle, which are found in opposition to each other and yet also form a unity. It was Nietzsche who formulated these ideas, but Romanticism laid the ground for them, and they were fully in keeping with the mind set of Turgenev's time. Although neither Turgenev nor his contemporaries drew parallels between his novella *Veshnie Vody* (*Spring Torrents*, 1872) and Nietzsche's work, the novella reflects the following oppositions: night/day, Dionysian/Apollonian, and passionate, animal and chaotic versus rational and ordered according to civilised norms. Knabe finds that these oppositions lend a special significance to the contrast between the female characters in the novel. Gemma is respectable and calm, and has the classic beauty of a classical statue – the obvious embodiment of the Apollonian spirit. "The Ancient-Roman sculptural principle is constantly emphasised in Gemma, as though it grew through her 'Italianism', augmenting, darkening and deepening it", Knabe notes. "She has 'classically strict features', marble hands

---

4   G.S. Knabe,"Povest' Turgeneva *Veshnie vody*: problema granits teksta", *Vestnik RGGU*, 2, (1998), 243.

'similar to the hands of Olympic goddesses'. She is 'a goddess...virginal and pure marble', 'like a statue', and, more precisely, 'like an ancient statue'".[5] At the same time there is Polozova who, with her unbridled passions, the uncontrollability of her instincts and her wild will for power embodies the other features of the ancient spirit, the Dionysian principle. In his portrait of Maria Nikolaevna Polozova, Turgenev emphasises her grey, predatory, avaricious and wild eyes, her serpent-like locks and her greedy breathing. Her mischief, debauchery and lust are not even in keeping with the classical image of a female Amazon-warrior. As Turgenev ironically notes, her lack of restraint places her in the tradition of the masculine image of a centaur:

> Разыгрались удалые силы. Это уже не амазонка пускает коня в галоп – это скачет молодой женский кентавр, полузверь и полубог, и изумляется степенный, благовоспитанный край, попираемый ее буйным разгулом (8, 373).[6]

> Sporting strengths were running riot. This was no longer an Amazon releasing her stallion into a gallop – here gallops a young female centaur, half-animal and half-god, and the sedate, well-brought up provincial people were shocked and trampled underfoot by her riotous revelry. (8, 373).

There is an antinomical female pair in an earlier novel of Turgenev's, *Dym* (*Smoke*, 1862). The physical appearance of Litvinov's former fiancée Tat'iana is markedly calm, kind and meek. At the moment of her parting with her beloved, she stands before him in all her greatness, like a classical statue. It is not difficult to recognise in her the statue of the goddess Themis:

> Перед ним действительно стоял его судья. Татьяна показалась ему выше, стройнее; просиявшее небывалой красотой лицо величаво окаменело, как у статуи; грудь не поднималась, и платье, одноцветное и тесное, как хитон, падало прямыми длинными складками мраморных тканей к ее ногам, которые оно закрывало. Татьяна глядела прямо перед собой, не на одного только Литвинова, и взгляд ее, ровный и холодный, был также взглядом статуи.(S. 7: 382).

---

5 *Ibid.*, 243.
6 I.S. Turgenev, *Polnoe sobranie sochinenii i pisem v 30 tomakh*, Moscow: Nauka, 1978–1986, VIII: 373. Further citations are from this edition with the volume and page references after the quotation in round brackets.

> It really was his judge standing in front of him. Tat'iana seemed to him taller, more graceful; her magnificent face, which shone with unprecedented beauty, had turned to stone, like that of a statue; her breast did not quiver, and her dress, monochrome and close-fitting, like a chiton, fell in straight long folds of marble fabric to her feet, which it covered. Tat'iana looked straight ahead, not only at Litvinov, and her gaze, even and cold, was at once also the gaze of a statue. (7, 382)

The writer contrasts the Apollonian equanimity, spiritual equilibrium, that is associated with harmony and correctness of form in a classical statue, with the Dionysian spirit of Irina's character: impetuosity, unpredictable behaviour, chaos of feelings and will to power. In her relationship with Litvinov, coldness unexpectedly changes to passion and vice versa. The protagonist characterises the sudden appearance of Irina's feelings thus: her love 'словно вспыхнула пожаром, словно грозовою тучею налетела' (7, 382) ['as it were came alight, as if a thundercloud had descended' (7, 382)]. If in Tat'iana's figure, gestures and glance, it is sculptural perfection, coldness and stoniness of form that are brought to the fore, then every aspect of Irina's appearance, on the contrary, is characterised by inconstant, unpredictable movements. She is spontaneous, fickle and nervous:

> ...в медлительных наклонениях ее красивой шейки, в улыбке, не то рассеянной, не то усталой, сказывалась нервическая барышня, а в самом рисунке этих чуть улыбающихся тонких губ, этого небольшого, орлиного, несколько сжатого носа было что-то своевольное и страстное, что-то опасное и для других и для нее. (С.7, 281).

> ...in the slow inclination of her neck, in her somehow vague, somehow tired smile, one could read her nervous disposition, and in the drawing together of these slightly smiling, delicate lips, of this small, slightly short, eagle nose was something willful and passionate, something dangerous both for herself and for others. (S. 7, 281).

In his article 'Symbols of Beauty in Russian Writers', Innokentii Annenskii argues that female beauty in the works of Turgenev has a supernatural power, that beauty 'takes' a man:

> In Turgenev's works, beauty necessarily takes because it is the truest power. For Turgenev, if beauty does not lower man with the pleasure it promises, it removes his will and renders him powerless. This is not just a

simple promise to make him happy, as with Stendal: for Turgenev, beauty is aware of its own power, more than that, of the *audacity of powerful beauty*.[7]

It seems that Annenskii in his characterisation of Turgenev's idea of love came very close to implying the presence of the Dionysian complex, which is present in a certain type of Turgenevan women. Dionysianism seizes his characters, removing from them their individuality and forcing them to forget themselves. Jung used term 'collective consciousness' for this state of Dionysian inebriation, this subjection to instinctive, natural principles the destroy the individual 'I' and make a person dependent only on their drives.[8] The spontaneous, irrational and unconscious destroy the integrity of the 'I' of Turgenev's characters. In the poem-in-prose 'Liubov' ('Love'), Turgenev manages succinctly to capture the state of a person in love, his or her sense of the invasion of 'another I' as the death of their own ego. Turgenev therefore conceives of love as a tragic feeling for an earthly being of mortal flesh:

> Все говорят: любовь – самое высокое, самое неземное чувство. Чужое я внедрилось в твое: ты расширен – и ты нарушен; ты только теперь зажил [?] И твое я умерщвлено. Но человека с плотью и кровью возмущает даже такая смерть…Воскресают одни бессмертные боги… (C.10, 186).

> Everyone says that love is the highest, the most unearthly feeling. Another 'I' has taken root in yours: you are widened – and you are destroyed; only now have you begun to live [?]] And your 'I' is killed. But even a death of this kind is an outrage for a man of flesh and blood…Only the immortal gods are resurrected…(10, 186).

Endowed with this 'supernatural power', Turgenev's women do not just 'take' men, as Annenskii writes – they impoverish them. Aleksei Petrovich (*Perepiska*; *Correspondence*, 1856) having suffered the inexplicable power of love, which he conceives of as an illness such as cholera or fever, comes to the following conclusion:

---

7 Innokentii Annenskii, "Simvoly krasoty u russkikh pisatelei", in Innokentii Annenskii, *Kniga otrazhenii (II)*, Moscow: Nauka, 1979, 134.

8 Karl Gustav Jung, "Apollonicheskoe i dionisiiskoe nachalo", in Karl Gustav Jung, *Psikhologicheskie tipy*, trans. by S. Lorie, St. Petersburg: Azbuka, 2001, 224.

В любви нет равенства, нет так называемого свободного соединения душ и прочих идеальностей, придуманных на досуге немецкими профессорами...Нет, в любви одно лицо – раб, а другое – властелин, и недаром толкуют поэты о цепях, налагаемых любовью. Да, любовь – цепь, и самая тяжёлая. По крайней мере, я дошёл до этого убеждения, и дошёл до него путём опыта, купил это убеждение ценою жизни, потому что умираю рабом (С.5, 47).

In love there is no equality, no so-called free uniting of souls or other ideals invented in the spare time of some German professors...No, in love one is always a slave and the other – a master. Not without reason do poets refer to the chains imposed by love. Yes, love is a chain, and the heaviest chain at that. At least that was the conclusion I reached, and I did so by experience. I bought that conviction with the price of my life, because I die a slave. (5, 47).

Turgenev depicts the clearest example of slavery-in-love in *Spring Torrents*. Sanin 'threw himself at the feet' of his 'mistress', although he felt shame and disgust at himself for it. In the position of an 'enslaved man' he had to cosy up to and ingratiate himself with the husband and former love of his mistress, endure 'все унижения, все гадкие муки раба, которому не позволяется ни ревновать, ни жаловаться и которого бросают наконец, как изношенную одежду...'(С.8, 379) (all the humiliations, all the awful tortures of a slave, who is not permitted to be jealous, nor to complain, and who will be cast aside, in the end, like worn-out clothes) (8, 379).

Enslavement is Polozova's aim, and, having achieved it, having won the bet with her husband, she cynically celebrates victory:

...всеми десятью пальцами она схватила его за волосы. Она медленно перебирала и крутила эти безответные волосы, сама вся выпрямилась, на губах змеилось торжество – а глаза, широкие и светлые до белизны, выражали одну безжалостную тупость и сытость победы (С.8, 377).

She seized him by his hair with all ten of her fingers. She slowly went through and twisted these unresponsive hairs, herself all straightened up, the celebration of the moment curving her lips. Her eyes, wide and shining to whiteness, expressed only pitiless vacancy and the satiety of victory. (S.8, 377)

Women-mistresses are depicted as having similar attributes to conquerors. When Aleksei Petrovich, the hero of *Correspondence*, sees the dancer for the first time, she is wearing a costume of the Bacchae (Maenads), a vine wreath on her head (a Dionysian symbol) and a tiger-skin on her shoulders. Polozova had a whip in her hands. It is important to note that Turgenev's male characters, having fallen into slavery, realise that they are in a humiliating situation, are burdened by it. Although they soberly and critically assess the object of their adoration, they cannot free themselves from the yoke of love. An irrational force, invading the 'I' of the heroes, seizes them completely, removes their will and enslaves them:

> ...с той роковой минуты я принадлежал ей весь, вот как собака принадлежит своему хозяину; и если я и теперь, умирая, не принадлежу ей, так это только потому, что она меня бросила, [признается Алексей Петрович].
>
> Вы, может быть, думаете, что она была умна? Нисколько! Стоило взглянуть на её низкий лоб, стоило хоть раз подметить её ленивую и беспечную усмешку, чтобы тотчас убедиться в скудости её умственных способностей. И я никогда не воображал её необыкновенной женщиной. Я вообще ни одного мгновенья не ошибался на её счёт; но это ничему не помогало. Что б я ни думал о ней в её отсутствие – при ней я ощущал одно подобострастное обожание...(С.5, 46).

> ...from that fatal minute I entirely belonged to her, exactly as a dog belongs to its owner; and if now, dying, I do not belong to her any longer, it is only because she left me [Aleksei Petrovich confesses].
>
> You, maybe, think that she was clever? Not a bit of it! One only had to take a glance at her low forehead, one only had to just once notice her lazy and careless smirk, to at once be convinced of the miserliness of her intellectual abilities. I never once imagined her to be an unusual woman. I had taken full measure of her and was not even for a moment mistaken about her; but that did not help at all. Whatever I thought about her in her absence, when in her presence, I felt only an obsequious adoration... (5, 46).

Aleksei Petrovich's reflections on a love which has enslaved him and his critical remarks towards his beloved almost coincide with the contradictions of Turgenev's own experiences in connection with Pauline Viardot, shared with

Countess Lambert on the 10th (22nd) June 1856: 'Как оглянусь я на свою прошедшую жизнь, я, кажется, больше ничего не делал, как гонялся за глупостями. Дон-Кихот по крайней мере верил в красоту своей Дульцинеи, а нашего времени Дон-Кихоты и видят, что их Дульцинея – урод – а всё бегут за нею' (П.3, 107). (As I look at my past life, I, it seems, did nothing but chase after stupidities. Don Quixote at least believed in the beauty of his Dulcinea, while the Don Quixotes of our times see that their Dulcinea is a monster and they still run after her.) (P.3, 107). In the beginning of the letter Turgenev soberly assesses the lack of perspective in his relationship with Viardot. He admits that 'уехать за границу – значит: определить себя окончательно на цыганскую жизнь и бросить все помышленья о семейной жизни' (П.3, 106) ('to go abroad means to finally confine oneself to a gypsy life and to throw aside all thoughts of family life') (P. 3, 106). L.F. Nelidova, to whom Turgenev showed a photograph of the singer, shares Turgenev's impressions about the unusual power of the woman who had conquered the Russian writer, and at the same time of her plain looks:

> Портрет г-жи Виардо был и раньше знаком мне. Это – некрасивое в обычном смысле, но очень интересное лицо южного типа, с прекрасными черными глазами. На сцене, в костюме она должна была быть очень эффектной. В складе губ, в выражении глаз, в посадке головы чувствовалась энергичная, властная натура. Такою именно изображал ее в своих рассказах нам и сам Тургенев.[9]

> Ms Viardot's portrait was already familiar to me from before. Her face was not beautiful in the conventional sense, but it was a very interesting face of the southern type, with wonderful dark eyes. On the stage and in costume she must have had a great effect on people. One could sense her energetic, powerful character in the fold of her lips, the expression of her eyes and in the set of her head. This was exactly how Turgenev himself depicted her in his stories.

The commentary on the story 'Correspondence' notes:

> В первом варианте портрет танцовщицы, которую полюбил герой, ассоциировался с внешним обликом Полины Виардо. В первоначальном тексте у героини были вместо золотисто-пепельных – черные

---

[9] L.F. Nelidova, "Pamiati I.S. Turgenev", *Vestnik Evropy,* No. 9 (1909), 217.

волосы, вместо светлых – черные глаза и говорила она на ломаном испанско-французском наречии (намек на испанское происхождение П. Виардо) (С.5, 395).

In the first draft, the portrait of the dancer whom the hero loved was associated with the external appearance of Pauline Viardot. In the original text the heroine's hair was dark instead of golden ash-blonde, she had dark instead of fair eyes and she spoke in a broken Spanish-French dialect (a hint at the Spanish origin of P. Viardot) (S. 5, 395).

In his literary biography *The Life of Turgenev* Boris Zaitsev shows that Pauline Viardot loved the devices of theatre. She used embodiments of natural wildness and power, such as bearskin, in order to emphasise her victory over the numerous admirers lying at her feet:

Или же такая картина: огромная медвежья шкура в гостиной, распростертый русский зверь, с позолоченными когтями лап. На каждой из них по поклоннику, а королева на диване – это ее маленький двор, ручные преданные звери. Виардо смолоду взяла венценосную позу – очевидно, имела на то данные, да и характер подходил: не из смиренных же она была![10]

Or a picture like this: a huge bearskin in the drawing room, a Russian beast prostrate, its paws with gilded claws. One for each admirer, and the queen on the divan – this is her little court, her loyal, tame animals. Since her youth, Viardot had taken a crown-bearing pose – obviously she had the qualifications for it and it also suited her character. She was not one of the meek!

In discussing the theme of love-slavery in Turgenev's works, it is impossible to avoid recalling the resemblance with the Austrian writer Leopold von Sacher-Masoch. Contemporaries called Sacher-Masoch, who made love-slavery the main subject of his works, a follower of Turgenev, who had received worldwide recognition at that time. Consequently, Theodor Storm in a letter dated 30th May 1868 points to Sacher-Masoch's story 'Moon Night', which in his opinion could 'never have appeared' without Turgenev's 'Faust'. Although he names this story the "descendent" of Turgenev, he nevertheless stipulates that it is a

---

[10] Zaitsev, *Zhukovskii*, 224.

"wayward child".[11] Undoubtedly, one can find in Sacher-Masoch's work typological similarities with the works of Turgenev. This is evident in their methods of depicting nature, hunting scenes, the effect of music on the feelings of characters, and also an understanding of love as anirrational and timeless force for man. However, in the depiction of love-slavery, which is accompanied by the spiritual and physical sufferings of the hero – a weak male intellectual – Sacher-Masoch went further than his Russian contemporary. He focused attention on sensuality and cruelty as constituents of erotic pleasure, with the attendant theatrical effects. Sacher-Masoch's characters, unlike Turgenev's, experience pleasure in their romantic suffering. They create artificial conditions for torture, which strengthens their passion. The Austrian psychologist Krafft-Ebing named the clinical pathological reception of sexual enjoyment from pain and moral indignity 'masochism' after Sacher-Masoch. Sacher-Masoch's characters gain pleasure not just from moral humiliation but also from physical tortures. In a departure from Turgenev's characters, who critically assess their beloved and do not lose the ability to reflect after falling into the net, Sacher-Masoch's men willingly enslave themselves. In *Venus in Furs*, Severin concludes an agreement with Wanda concerning his own slavery. The chosen roles (mistress and slave), the sophisticated methods of punishment and the attendant entourage (whips, Wanda's fur jackets and fur coats) all create the atmosphere required to sharpen the sexual feelings of the characters and strengthen their pathological passions. They cannot experience love in any other circumstances.

Turgenev himself did not consider Sacher-Masoch his follower. In a letter to A.S. Suvorin from the 9th April 1876 he definitively drew a line between himself and the 'Austrian Turgenev':

Я с ним не знаком лично – и, признаюсь, не большой охотник до его романов. В них слишком много "литературы" и "клубнички" – две вещи хорошие – но при излишнем пережевывании нестерпимые. Я никогда не мог понять, с какой точки зрения меня сравнивали с ним. (П. 11,251)

I am not personally acquainted with him, and I admit, I am not a big fan of his novels. There is too much 'literature' and 'strawberries' in

---

11   *Turgenevskii sbornik. Materiały k polnomu sobraniiu sochinenii i pisem I.S. Turgeneva*, ed. by M.P. Alekseev et al., Moscow: Nauka, 1964, 436. In the commentary to the letter A. Granzhar writes that in the Leipzig magazine "Der Salon fur Literatur, Kunst und Gesellschaft" a few pages were devoted to L. Sacher-Masoch as an 'imitator' of Turgenev. More detail in the commentary to the letter referred to above, 437.

them – two good things, but intolerable in excessive doses. I could never understand from what perspective people compared me to him. (11, 251)

One can assume that by 'strawberries' Turgenev meant the depiction of romantic relations, accompanied by scenes of lustful torment (which were more explicit than was the norm in the Victorian era). Apparently, when referring to 'literature' Turgenev was hinting at the far-fetched, artificial world created by Sacher-Masoch's characters, in which romantic passions and sufferings are developed. Speaking of excessive 'doses' reveals that Turgenev felt that the Austrian writer had betrayed good taste.

In her article 'Sacher-Masoch and Russia', L.N. Poluboiarinova raises the question of how Turgenev's works, including his *Zapiski okhotnika* (*Huntsman's Sketches*, 1852), could have influenced Sacher-Masoch's 'dramatisation of sexual perversion'. The scholar thinks that Sacher-Masoch did not read *Huntsman's Sketches* as physiological sketches of the trend against serfdom, but gave special meaning to the 'non-verbalised', 'empty places' of Turgenev's text, and presented the 'unsaid as implied'.[12] Thus Turgenev's scenes of the punishment of serfs and images of cruel female landowners inspired Sacher-Masoch to create erotic pictures in which cruelty is united with lust.

The American scholar Michael Finke sees the mental slavery induced by serfdom in Russia as one of the reasons for the fact that Sacher-Masoch's cruel female lovers have Russian or at least Eastern Slav origins. Corporal punishment – an integral component of slavery – was prevalent in the relationships between man and woman in peasant families. The notion that if a man does not beat a woman it means that he does not love her enough held fast in the consciousness of the peasants. Consequently, the pathological eroticism, the roles chosen by Sacher-Masoch's characters and the combination of lust and cruelty in romantic relations arise from a centuries-old Russian tradition. Finke emphasises that he presents a Western view of Russian culture.[13] In the light of these judgements it becomes clear why Sacher-Masoch, a man of Western culture, 'reads' in *Hunstman's Sketches* a subtext that carries important social-psychological and cultural-historical information that is obvious to a foreign reader.

---

12 L.N. Poluboiarinova, "Zakher-Mazokh i Rossiia", in L. Fon Zakher-Mazokh, *Zhenshchina-sultan*, Moscow: Prosodiia, 2003, 3–45.

13 See Michael S. Finke, "Sacher-Masoch, Turgenev, and Other Russians", in *One Hundred Years of Masochism: Literary Texts, Social and Cultural Contexts*, ed. by Michael Finke and Carl Niekerk, Amsterdam: Rodopi, 2000, 120–121.

The writer's biography helps us understand why Turgenev may have unconsciously combined cruelty (an integral part of serfdom) and eroticism in his short stories. Turgenev grew up in a family where the mother – a typical serf-owning landowner – inflicted harsh punishments not only on her slaves but also on those close to her: she maintained her authority roughly and cruelly, attempting to subject her sons to her will. A love-hate relationship developed between the mother and her sons. Consequently, since his childhood the writer had observed corporal punishment, the behaviour of a strong woman who was obviously compensating for the lack of love from her husband with acts of cruelty. These impressions of childhood and youth are sublimated in the text of the *Huntsman's Sketches*, and are doubtless reflected in his other works. It is important to note that in the late novel *Spring Torrents* Turgenev consciously underlines the Russianness of dissolute despot Polozova, which he further strengthens through the low social origins of his heroine (the father of Maria Nikolaevna is a peasant who "сам едва разумел грамоте" ("could barely read")) and folklore motifs: for example, when she is seducing Sanin, she talks about love spells. Polozova does not like classical music, she prefers 'одни русские песни – и то в деревне, и то весной – с пляской' (С.8, 352) ('only Russian songs, and then only in the countryside and in the springtime at that, with a folk dance' (8, 352)). Turgenev does not accentuate the beauty of her appearance. Rather, he emphasises her allure, those things given to her by nature and her origins:

> И не то, чтобы она была отъявленная красавица: в ней даже довольно явственно сказывались следы ее плебейского происхождения. Лоб у ней был низкий, нос несколько мясистый и вздернутый; ни тонкостью кожи, ни изяществом рук и ног она похвалиться не могла [...] Не перед 'святыней красоты', говоря словами Пушкина, остановился бы всякий, кто бы встретился с нею, но перед обаянием мощного, не то русского, не то цыганского, цветущего женского тела (С.8, 344).

> [It was not that she was a noted beauty: one could even observe in her fairly obvious traces of her plebeian origins. Her forehead was low, her nose somewhat meaty and upturned; she did not have the delicateness of skin or elegant hands or feet that attract such praise in other girls [...] Any person who met her would stop not before a 'shrine of beauty', to use Pushkin's phrase, but rather before a half-Russian, half-gypsy, blossoming female body of alluring power...(8, 344)].

Her Russian lack of restraint combined with passionate cruelty become particularly pronounced when compared with the decent behaviour and way of life of the Italian woman, Gemma. Significantly, Polozova herself realised the reason for her provocative, uncontrolled behaviour and explains its motivation by saying that 'в детстве [...] очень много насмотрелась рабства и натерпелась от него' (C.8, 365). [In childhood [...] I saw slavery a lot and suffered a great deal from it' (S.8, 365)].

In his 'The Representation of Sacher-Masoch (The Cold and the Cruel)', Gilles Deleuze divides Masoch's women into three types. The first type is the pagan, Greek, Hetaera or Aphrodite, who brings about disorder. She lives – in her own words – for the sake of love and beauty, and for the moment. She is sensitive and loves the men to whom she takes a fancy; she gives herself to the person who loves her. She speaks about the independence of women and the transience of romantic relations. She insists on the equality of men and women. She is a hermaphrodite. [...] The other extreme, the third type, is a sadist. She likes to cause suffering, to torture. Remarkably, it is by a man that she is induced to act. She constantly risks becoming his victim herself. Everything happens as if the primitive Greek woman had found her Greek man, her Apollonian element, her male sadistic impulse [...] it is clear, however, that neither the woman-hermaphrodite nor the woman-sadist represent Masoch's ideal'.[14]

As Deleuze argues, the two types of women represented constitute "the borders between which this ideal hangs move like a swinging pendulum".[15] The second type (who, according to Deleuze, is the ideal of Sacher-Masoch's woman) is a trinity that unites coldness, sensitivity and cruelty in one person. "The function of Sacher-Masoch's ideal is to prepare the triumph of feeling 'on ice' and with the help of coldness".[16] Deleuze argues that Greek beauty and feeling have lost their integrity and unity in the Christian world. Nostalgic for the ideal, Sacher-Masoch's characters try to unite past and present by "wrapping up the stone Venus in heavy furs".[17]

Nostalgia for the lost Greek world with its wholeness and beauty is undoubtedly present in Turgenev's discourse as well. We recall that even in

---

14 Gilles Deleuze, 'Predstavlenie Leopolda fon Zakher-Mazokha, (Kholodnoe i zhestokoe)', *Venera v mekhakh. L. Fon Sacher-Masoch. Zhil' Delez. Zigmund Freid*, RIK Kul'tura, 1992, 225–227.
15 Ibid., 227.
16 Ibid., 230.
17 Ibid., 232.

the early poem dedicated to Venus, Turgenev writes that for the modern man Venus is a myth, and he does not worship Venus the Goddess but copies of her: he worships the beauty of a handmade marble icon of her carved by the artist.

The meeting with the perfection of classical beauty in real life is a dream, a poetic illusion. This theme is taken up in Turgenev's story *Tri vstrechi* (*Three Meetings*, 1852). The image of a woman whom the narrator met three times is woven with secrecy and mystery. She unexpectedly appears to him, then slips away like an hallucination. At the end of the story the narrator appears to be conversing with a real woman who has finally told him the secret of her love. However, reality is deceptive: the scene of declaration occurs at a masquerade, that is, in an atmosphere intended to be distant from real life, orientated towards games. The beautiful woman's face is hidden by a mask and her name remains unknown. In the world of the masquerade everything is possible: the mirage obtains real characteristics, the classical statue – flesh. 'Прекрасное сновидение, которое бы вдруг стало действительностью [...] статуя Галатеи, сходящая живой женщиной с своего пьедестала в глазах замирающего Пигмалиона. Я не верил себе, я едва мог дышать' (С.4, 241). ['A wonderful dream that suddenly became real...the statue of Galatea stepping down from her pedestal as a living woman in the eyes of the dying Pygmalion...I did not believe it; I could barely breathe' (4, 241)]. The sad realisation that in life there is no place for absolute beauty permeates the whole story. The narrator ironises the fact that talking in person to a classical statue, Ovid's Galatea, could only hapen in daydreams or at a masquerade, where the laws of genre allow for substitutions, falsehood and games of imagination. This is why the statue returns to its pedestal in the end:

> 'Неужели, – думал я, – эта женщина – та самая, которая явилась мне некогда в окне того далекого деревенского домика во всем блеске торжествующей красоты?... И между тем время, казалось, не коснулось ее. Нижняя часть ее лица, не скрытая кружевами маски, была почти младенчески нежна; но от нее веяло холодом, как от статуи... Возвратилась Галатея на свой пьедестал, и уже не сойти с него более' (С.4, 244).

['Surely', I thought, 'this is the same woman who appeared to me once at the window of that distant country cottage in all the splendour of victorious beauty?... And meanwhile it seemed that time had not touched her. The lower part of her face, which was not hidden by the lace of the mask, was almost childishly delicate; but from it wafted coldness, as from a statue... Galatea had returned to her pedestal, never to descend from it again'. (4, 244)].

Not wishing to become disenchanted, the narrator prefers to remain with his dream or mirage. Consequently, he does not try to find out the name of the woman whom he meets at the masquerade. It is not a real woman, a creation of nature, that he loves, but a dream, a myth, a statue, an ideal – an artistic image created by his imagination. He loves dream, myth, statue, ideal, the image that his imagination creates – art – and not a real woman, a creation of nature. Turgenev's philosophical meditations are similar to Schiller's. For example, they recall Schiller's idea that art is a game and that it returns us to our origins in nature, and to a golden age of knowledge, moral responsibility and freedom of choice. A cultured man can return to wholeness, according to Schiller, through the ideal.

Only in daydreams can one bring to life and recreate the classical world with its organic natural beauty and freedom of feelings, a world incompatible with Christian culture. The poem-in-prose 'Nimfy' ('Nymphs', 1878) is a poetic dream, the hallucination of an artist attending a Bacchanalian feast:

> Впереди несется богиня. Она выше и прекраснее всех, – колчан за плечами, в руках лук, на поднятых кудрях серебристый серп луны... [...] Но вдруг богиня остановилась... и тотчас, вслед за нею, остановились все нимфы. Звонкий смех замер. Я видел, как лицо внезапно онемевшей богини покрылось смертельной бледностью; я видел, как опустились и повисли ее руки, как онемели ноги, как невыразимый ужас разверз ее уста, расширил глаза, устремленные вдаль...Что она увидала? Куда глядела она? [...] На самом краю неба, за низкой чертою полей, горел огненной точкой золотой крест на белой колокольне христианской церкви...Этот крест увидала богиня (С. 10, 160).

> [The goddess rushed along before them. She was taller and more wonderful than all the others – a quiver on her shoulders, a bow in her hands, the silver sickle of the moon on her raised curls...[...] But suddenly the goddess stopped...and then, straight after her, all the nymphs halt. The loud laughter fell silent. I saw how the face of the goddess, suddenly still, was covered in a deathly paleness; I saw how her hands dropped and hung there, how her legs went numb, how an inexpressible horror opened her mouth, widened her eyes, staring into the distance...what had she seen? Where was she looking? [...] On the very edge of the sky, beyond the low line of the

fields, burning like a fiery point, the golden cross on the white belltower of a Christian church...The goddess had seen the cross. (S. 10, 160)].

In the above passage Turgenev metaphorically depicts the meeting of two cultures and the change from the pagan culture to the Christian one. In the eyes of the narrator the living becomes dead, the pagan goddess takes the form of a stone-cold statue. To repeat the words of Deleuze, "an ice age covered the Greek world in ice and made the existence of Greek woman impossible".

Turgenev shows that antiquity, like primitive art, exhausted itself. This is why classical Dionysianism in Turgenev's female Bacchae had taken on new characteristics and become interwoven with Russian spontaneity and despotism. As Knabe reveals, Turgenev parodies classical subjects and images. For example, the tragic story of the love of Dido and Aeneas, used by Polozova as an analogy for her relationship with Sanin, is nothing other than 'a rude and impudent defamation' of higher feelings.

Turgenev embodied the 'light-aesthetic' and 'darkly instinctive' principles in two types of women. Women who 'take' not so much by their beauty as by conquering through mysterious charms are destroyers; they possess a hidden, irrational power which knocks the weak male characters from their path. A woman who carries the light, Apollonian principle is the ideal; she embodies the trinity of truth, good and beauty, and resembles a classical statue. At the end of the novel, Turgenev tries to return to the Apollonian spirit some of his heroes who have been driven from the path and ended up in a whirlpool of passions. His characters seek forgiveness and make peace with their women-ideals. Before his death, Aleksei Petrovich explains his behaviour to Maria Aleksandrovna; Litvinov returns to Tat'iana; and Sanin tries to find Gemma and writes her a repentant letter. In Shestov's view, Turgenev revealed his European nature in his attempts to bring everything to a peaceful ending with all the rough edges smoothed over.[18] Good and evil stand in opposition to one another, like the two women who possess these qualities. Ultimately, Turgenev supports the good, embodied in an

---

18   Shestov explains the ends of Turgenev's works by connecting everything to the ideal, to the *Good*. He writes: '...a consoling end is necessary, one needs "faith in goodness" to be retained, come what may. "Why is this necessary?" ask readers. There will not an answer for that. This the reader himself must know. But how to "retain faith in goodness" Turgenev explains with a sincerity, which does not us to wish anything more from those who want to get to the final source of the understanding "about the Good"'. Further, as evidence the critic provides the ending of *The Gentry's Nest*. See, Shestov, *Turgenev*, 199.

ideal female nature that unites the harmonious trinity of truth, good and beauty.

Translated by Elizabeth Harrison

Bibliography

Annenskii, Innokentii. 1979. "Simvoly krasoty u russkikh pisatelei", in Innokentii Annenskii, *Kniga otrazhenii (II)*, Moscow: Nauka, 134.

Aikhenval'd, Iulii. 1995. "Turgenev", in *Siluety russkikh pisatelei*, Moscow: Respublika, 255–262.

Deleuze, Gilles. 1992. 'Predstavlenie Leopolda fon Zakher-Mazokha, (Kholodnoe i zhestokoe)', *Venera v mekhakh. L. Fon Sacher-Masoch. Zhil' Delez. Zigmund Freid*, RIK Kul'tura, 225–227.

Finke, Michael S. 2000. "Sacher-Masoch, Turgenev, and Other Russians", in *One Hundred Years of Masochism: Literary Texts, Social and Cultural Contexts*, ed. by Michael Finke and Carl Niekerk, Amsterdam: Rodopi, 120–121.

Jung, Karl Gustav. 2001. "Apollonicheskoe i dionisiiskoe nachalo", in Karl Gustav Jung, *Psikhologicheskie tipy*, trans. by S. Lorie, St. Petersburg: Azbuka, 224.

Knabe, G.S. 1998. "Povest' Turgeneva *Veshnie vody*: problema granits teksta", *Vestnik RGGU*, 2, (1998), 243.

Merezhkovskii, Dmitrii. 1994. *Lev Tolstoi i Dostoevskii. Vechnye sputniki. Turgenev*, Moscow: Respublika, 475.

Nelidova, L.F. 1909. "Pamiati I.S. Turgenev", *Vestnik Evropy*, No. 9 (1909), 217.

Poluboiarinova, N. 2003. "Zakher-Mazokh i Rossiia", in L. Fon Zakher-Mazokh, *Zhenshchina-sultan*, Moscow: Prosodiia, 3–45.

Shestov, Lev. 2000. *Turgenev (Otryvki iz neokonchennoi knigi)*, ed. by B. Aleksandrova, Moscow: Literaturnaia ucheba, 2000, II: 187–202.

Turgenev, I.S. 1978–1986. *Polnoe sobranie sochinenii i pisem v 30 tomakh*, Moscow: Nauka, VIII: 373. Further citations are from this edition with the volume and page references after the quotation in round brackets.

Turgenevskii sbornik. Materialy k polnomu sobraniiu sochinenii i pisem I.S. Turgeneva, ed. by M.P. Alekseev et al., Moscow: Nauka, 1964, 436.

Zaitsev, B. 1999. *Zhukovskii. Zhizn' Turgeneva. Chekhov*, Moscow: 'Druzhba narodov', 1999, 356.

CHAPTER 11

Patterns of European Irrationalism, from Source to Estuary: Johann Georg Hamann, Lev Shestov and Anton Chekhov – on Both Sides of Reason

Olga Tabachnikova

Russian culture is sometimes described as imitative – highly susceptible to outside influence and able to absorb the foreign with sensitivity.[1] A more conventional perception of Russian culture is that, having started with mimicry, it proceeds to transcend and transform the source into something unrecognisable, Russia's own. An opposite view insists on the independent originality of Russian culture: as the wife of the early Slavophile Kireevskii pointed out to him when they were learning together the latest achievements of Western European thought, the ideas of Schelling coincided with those long since expressed by the Russian Church Fathers.[2]

This remains, however, a matter of opinion, and the question of influence is always tricky. Of course ultimately everything is inter-connected: "No man is an island entire of itself; every man is a piece of the continent, a part of the main".[3] Nevertheless, the cases of 'disconnected' cultural parallels – when similar ideas occur in very different quarters without any immediate, direct link between them – are always fascinating, as they indicate a possibility of some anthropological universalities (or at least a susceptibility to the same cultural currents in different contexts).

---

1 See, for example, Dmitrii Galkovskii, "Beskonechnyi tupik", http://www.samisdat.com/3/312-bt-p.htm (consulted 25.01.2015): "The Russian soul is silent, wordless and shapeless. It is an absolute void; silence, hiatus. Similarly, Russia is fruitless. 'This world is superfluous'. But this very emptiness gives rise to immense sensitivity and the ability to illuminate in a remarkable, unequalled way the material that is being absorbed". Similar views are expressed by John Shemiakin in his conversation with A. Smirnova and T. Tolstaia in "Shkola zlosloviia" – see https://www.youtube.com/watch?v=U4nfTomWPmg (20.12.2015). In a way, Chekhov's "Little Darling" portrays the same type of mentality, only at a personal rather than national level.
2 See Vasilii Zenkovskii, *Istoriia russkoi filosofii* in two volumes, Rostov-on-Don: Fenix, 1999 (reprint of the first edition: Paris: YMCA Press, 1948), vol. 1, 248.
3 John Donne, "Devotions upon emergent occasions and several steps in my sickness", Meditation XVII, 1624.

For example, as Lev Shestov explains in his lectures on the history of Greek philosophy, the idea of mortality as divine punishment for disobedience of being occurred independently amongst the Jews and the Greeks. In the Old Testament it is Original Sin – man's daring, against God's will, to escape from the nest in which he was destined to live; in the teaching of Anaximander it is treacherously breaking away from the womb of the unified, eternal entity into existence. Shestov emphasises that no borrowing whatsoever was possible between ancient Greeks and Jews, and thus both nations, stunned by the horror of death, posed the same question and gave the same answer.[4]

The idea of the irrational is likely to be equally universal. Occurring largely (albeit not exclusively) as an (opposing) reaction to the advance of rationalism, it must be predicated on human nature itself. At the same time, in the case of European history, cultural continuity is inevitable, even if no direct influence can be traced. Singling out such unexpected parallels between 'disconnected' patterns of European irrationalism as represented, in varying degrees, by the three cultural figures in the title above, is the aim of this chapter, which should lay another stone on the path of comparative East–West cultural and intellectual characterisation.

The rebellion against radical rationalism can be inscribed into a broader framework whereby opposite cultural (or by the same token, economic, political, social, religious and other) currents wrestle with each other in a pendulum-like fashion or, even more subtly, in waves where each one replaces the other by bringing within itself the seeds of its own destruction. Thus Enlightenment, by becoming all-pervasive, was heading inevitably for the ultimate crisis, upon reaching its extremes. J.G. Hamann's merit is in anticipating (and speeding up) this crisis at a very early stage.

Johann Georg Hamann (1730–1788), or "The Magus of the North", as he called himself, a contemporary and friend of Kant, Herder and Goethe, but unlike them little known outside Germany, is "the forgotten source of a movement that in the end engulfed the whole of European culture",[5] "the father of modern European irrationalism, and a crucial forerunner of romanticism and existentialism".[6] In a similar way, Shestov is an equally radical and uncompromising opponent of rationalism (only in Russia, at the dawn of modernism) who in the same unacknowledged and eccentric manner paved the way for the

---

4 Lev Shestov, *Lektsii po istorii grecheskoi filosofii*, Moscow-Paris: Russkii Put' – YMCA-Press, 2001, 66–67.
5 Isaiah Berlin, *Magus of the North. J.G. Hamann and the Origins of Modern Irrationalism*, Fontana Press: London, 1994, 4.
6 See the editorial text by Henry Hardy, in Isaiah Berlin, *The Magus of the North*.

much more famous existentialism of Sartre and the ideas of Leo Strauss and Derrida,[7] and who "felt and transmitted with an extraordinary force the supernatural origin of faith".[8]

If both Hamann and Shestov can be viewed as representing different phases of radical irrationalism, the case with Chekhov is clearly different. However, chronologically, both Shestov and Chekhov in many ways faced the consequences of the extensive advance of rational thought, the Enlightenment heritage, which Hamann so acutely anticipated and against which he launched a fierce resistance. They both lived at a time when Hegelian tradition effectively led to a dead-end for speculative philosophy, when positivism and utilitarianism reached a radical degree and caused a front of opposition that resulted in modernism, most notably Symbolism, and irrationalism.

The revolt started by Hamann had a strong following and shaped such thinkers as Herder, Jacobi, Schelling and Kierkegaard, to name but a few. The latter is in many ways Shestov's spiritual twin, and their kinship, spotted first by Edmund Husserl who advised Shestov (by then in his 50s!) to read Kierkegaard, exemplifies precisely those 'independently' occurring cultural parallels described above. The inverted commas here reflect the relative character of any disconnectedness in European culture, and in this case, as indicated, we are dealing with an entire movement directed against advancing rationalism. Adherents of this movement, as we shall see in the cases of Hamann and Shestov, show a striking resemblance in their convictions. But, significantly, even the proponents of a rationalist method of enquiry and approach to the world – and Chekhov in many ways is amongst them – also arrive ultimately at the limitations of purely rational thought.

Chekhov is different in another way too – unlike Hamann and Shestov, who can both be, with some qualifications, labelled philosophers, or at any rate, philosophical thinkers, Chekhov is a writer. Moreover, unlike Dostoevskii and Tolstoi, he is not commonly associated with philosophical thought. However, this should not be misinterpreted.[9] Thus Vladimir Kataev argues that the "philosophical substance of his [Chekhov's] oeuvre is indisputable, but it is not

---

7 See this argument advanced by Savely Senderovich and Elena Shvarts, "Kto Kanta na golovu biet (K teme: Lev Shestov i literatura 20-go veka)", *Toronto Slavic Quaterly*, 12 (2005), http://www.utoronto.ca/tsq/12/senderovich12.shtml (consulted 12.08.2013).

8 Vasilii Zenkovskii, *Istoriia russkoi filosofii*, vol. 2, 376.

9 A major attempt to overcome this misconception was undertaken by an international conference organised in Irkutsk in 2006, which resulted in a scholarly volume with the unequivocal title "The Philosophy of A.P. Chekhov" (*Filosofiia A.P. Chekhova*), Anatolii Sobennikov (ed.), Irkutsk: ISU Publishers, 2008.

reducible to philosophical statements and logical theses; instead one should talk about a specific conceptual foundation of his artistic world".[10] An attentive reading of Chekhov's legacy reveals his thorough familiarity with the writings of many ancient and modern philosophers, including Marcus Aurelius, Schopenhauer, Goethe, Voltaire, Pascal, Spinoza, and Nietzsche, as well as various lesser-known names. However, Georg Hamann is never mentioned. The same is true in Shestov's case, where Hamann's name is absent from the extensive list of thinkers of the last three thousand years whom Shestov sorted in a binary division (very alien to Chekhov) between allies and opponents: those who, like Shestov himself, rebelled against Reason (Plotinus, Pascal, Luther, Nietzsche, Kierkegaard), and those who sided with it (Aristotle, Descartes, Spinoza, Leibnitz). Save for the indirect chain of impact concealed in some of the listed names, one has no grounds to suggest any direct 'Hamannian' influence on either Chekhov or Shestov. This makes the task of uncovering the parallels between these different patterns of irrationalism ever more fascinating.

Shestov and Hamann: Irrationalist Thought – A Meeting of Radical Minds

Shestov's similarity to Hamann is multifaceted. The core of it lies in the uncompromising radicalism of their anti-rationalist thought. The frontal attack on the Enlightenment launched by Hamann is very much continued in Shestov's crusade against the whole history of Western speculative philosophy. Certainly in Russia, where systematic anti-Enlightenment ideas can be noted from the early Slavophiles, Shestov was the most radical anti-rationalist for his century, as Hamann was for his.

At the centre of their concerns there was a living being, with his suffering and joy, and it is his private, finite (but ever more precious for this) existence, created and sustained only by the irrational, omnipotent God of the Bible, that they tried to protect from a variety of deadening factors promoted by rationalism.

Czeslaw Milosz's description of Shestov's philosophical stance neatly portrays it as a revolt in defence of the I, of a powerless being, a finite individual:

> What does a creature that calls itself 'I' want for itself? It wants to be. Quite a demand! Early in life it begins to discover, however, that its

---

[10] Vladimir Kataev, "Istinnyi mudrets", in *Filosofiia A.P. Chekhova*, ed. Anatolii Sobennikov, 68–75 (70).

demand is perhaps excessive. Objects behave in their own impassive manner and show a lack of concern for the central importance of 'I' [...] The 'I' is invaded by Necessity from the inside as well, but always feels it as an alien force. Nevertheless the 'I' must accept the inevitable order of the world. The wisdom of centuries consists precisely in advising acquiescence and resignation. Shestov simply refuses to play this game of chess, however, and overturns the table with a kick. For why should the 'I' accept 'wisdom', which obviously violates its most intense desire? Why respect 'the immutable laws'? Whence comes the certainty that what is presumably impossible is really impossible? And is a philosophy preoccupied with man in general of any use to a certain man who lives only once in space and time?[11]

Hence Shestov's attack upon universal necessity, in his eyes facilitated and validated by Reason, which he thus declares the main enemy of mankind. This is a direct corollary of Shestov's interpretation of the Fall – "a choice of an inferior faculty with its passion for a *distinguo* and for general ideas, with pairs of opposites: good, evil; true, untrue; possible, impossible".[12] In other words, Original Sin consisted of man's renunciation of faith in order to gain knowledge. But the fruits from the Tree of Knowledge which "could just as well be called synthetic judgments a priori"[13] bring only tragedy and death. Faith in the omnipotent, living God of the Bible – as opposed to the God of philosophers, who is no more than a syllogism, a schema – is the only alternative to reason and a second dimension of thought, able to bring salvation to tragic mankind.

Isaiah Berlin describes Georg Hamann's central stance in very similar terms. In his "New Apology of the Letter H" – a riposte to C.T. Damm, "an old Wolffian theologian much respected by the educated public in Berlin",[14] who suggested the abolition of the letter *h* in many German words as superfluous – Hamann identifies this "poor little useless *h*"[15] with individual existence and steps in to defend it from the rationalists. As Berlin writes, "the letter *h*, this parasitic letter, useless, a nuisance, embodies for Hamann the unpredictable element in

---

11   Czeslaw Milosz, "Shestov, or the Purity of Despair", *Emperor of the Earth. Modes of Eccentric Vision*, Berkeley-Los Angeles-London: University of California Press, 1977, 99–119 (103–104).
12   Czeslaw Milosz, "Shestov, or the Purity of Despair", 107.
13   Ibid.
14   Isaiah Berlin, *The Magus of the North*, 69.
15   Ibid, 70.

reality, the element of fantasy in God's direction of the world".[16] "Your life is what I am myself, a breath [ein Hauch]",[17] Hamann writes to Damm on behalf of letter *h*. "The tract grows into [...] a paean to irregularity and the beauty of the irrational. The human faculty of reason is a lamentable, poor, blind, naked thing".[18] In the universe where "the logician is evidently logically prior to God, [...] in such a universe I – *h* – could not survive, but thanks to the true God I do and shall",[19] Berlin explains Hamann's position.

This little treatise, although an apparent sidetrack, is nevertheless typical of Hamann's thought and elucidates, in nuce, his irrationalist outlook. More generally, reason for Hamann is as hostile as it is for Shestov, and in a strikingly similar manner: "All evil comes from the tree of science", whereas "wisdom is one of the fruits of the tree of life".[20] The worldly rootless intellect is the arch-deceiver,[21] as it can only dissect, "disrupt and fragment",[22] and forces a fatal disintegration of a human being into disconnected, lifeless fragments. No general proposition, no theory, Hamann maintains, can "catch [...] life",[23] and the world of *a priori* is a fiction.[24] Thus reason for Hamann is merely an arbitrary theoretical fancy,[25] and abstraction only captivates a living being, forcing man to exist in a strait-jacket of invented entities.[26] In other words, Hamann "rose in revolt against the entire structure of science, reason, analysis",[27] as distorting human nature. Systems, theories, abstractions were for him "at best useful fictions, at worst [...] – a form of escape from facing reality itself".[28] Thus philosophy itself is vacuous, as "philosophers are imprisoned in their own systems, which have become as dogmatic as those of the Church".[29] As a result, Hamann sees his main task in exposing "the deleterious influence of abstractions and the false knowledge which is built upon and out of them".[30]

---

16   *Ibid.*
17   *Ibid.*
18   *Ibid.*
19   *Ibid.*, 71.
20   *Ibid.*, 38.
21   *Ibid.*, 43.
22   *Ibid.*, 41.
23   *Ibid.*, 42.
24   *Ibid.* 38.
25   *Ibid.*
26   *Ibid.*, 83.
27   *Ibid.*, 23.
28   *Ibid.*
29   *Ibid.*, 40.
30   *Ibid.*, 42.

In a similar fashion, Shestov observes that "reality cannot be deduced from reason, reality is greater, much greater than reason",[31] and is convinced of the powerlessness of reason to solve human problems, of its inadequacy as a weapon for cognition. Reason for him is an impertinent imposter, which claims with outrageous self-assuredness to be the highest authority and has no doubts in its omnipotence, but instead of rescuing man it merely seals and approves his tragic destiny. Shestov ascertains the fact that amongst the multiplicity of mysteries which surround a human being the most horrifying is the thought that "we are somehow definitely and forever cut off from the sources and beginnings of life".[32] This leads one to presume that

> either there is something that is not right in the universe, or that the way in which we seek the truth and the demands that we place upon it are vitiated in their very roots. Whatever our definition of truth may be, we can never renounce Descartes' *clare et distincte* (clarity and distinctness). Now, reality here shows us only an eternal, impenetrable mystery – as if, even before the creation of the world, someone had once and for all forbidden man to attain that which is most necessary and most important to him. What we call the truth, what we obtain through thought, is found to be, in a certain sense, incommensurable not only with the external world into which we have been plunged since our birth but also with our own inner experience. [...] We know many things and our knowledge is a 'clear and distinct' knowledge. Science contemplates with legitimate pride its immense victories and has every right to expect that nothing will be able to stop its triumphant march.[33]

And yet, "the haze of the primordial mystery has not been dissipated. It has rather grown denser".[34] Speaking from a chronologically superior position, Shestov essentially exposes the defeat not only of the Enlightenment, but of the whole tradition of Western systematic philosophy. He points to the distorted nature of this tradition and raises the alarm: helpless to improve our

---

31   Lev Shestov, *Na vesakh Iova*, Moscow: Folio, 2001, 256. English version of the text in this and other quotations from *On Job's Balances* is taken from http://www.angelfire.com/nb/shestov/ijb/jb2_6.html (accessed 15.01.2013).
32   Lev Shestov, *Afiny i Ierusalim*, Moscow: Folio, 2001, 26. English version of the text in this and other quotations from *Athens and Jerusalem* is taken from http://www.angelfire.com/nb/shestov/aaj/aj1_1.html (consulted 23.02.2013).
33   *Ibid.*, 26–27.
34   *Ibid.*, 27.

inner life, to solve our eternal questions, scientific methods nevertheless continue their advance and encroach upon the areas which are completely outside their control. Thus, Shestov tolls the bell, "a man of science, a scientist by education and habits, by the very make-up of his soul, came out of the silence of his study and put his hand upon life. This is undoubtedly, the greatest fact of modern history".[35]

This distrust of science and of reason more generally is compensated in both Hamann and Shestov by their belief in art and artistic method, especially in poetry. The method of art is always individual, and as such it embodies a struggle of the private against the general. If reason is an oppressor, art, by contrast, liberates. Thus Hamann "loves the English poets, for 'they don't analyse, they don't dissect'".[36] Berlin draws a parallel between the views of Hamann and William Blake, because both, in their anti-rationalism, put an "emphasis on the fullness of life, and in particular on the importance of everything in man that is generative, creative, passionate".[37] Artistic or religious imagination for them is part of this creative power, while scientific investigation, in their eyes, is clearly denied creative impulse. Instead, rational enquiry, "the Reasoning power in man" is distinguished by "cold reason, arid, hard, with lust for domination, mad pride, ambitious, violent, hating, brutally and implacably egoistic, perverted, avid".[38] This is supported by Hume – one of the most important sources for Hamann (the other being the Bible) – who claimed that "reason taken by itself is impotent, and when it dictates it is an usurper and an impostor".[39]

These sentiments could not be closer to Shestov's heart, who had read Dostoevskii's oeuvre, especially his "Notes from Underground", in a Nietzschean light, as an uncompromising revolt against universal necessity validated by reason, and believed that it is Dostoevskii, not Kant, who has provided the real critique of pure reason. "Once they prove to you, for instance, that you are descended from apes there's no point frowning about it, you must accept it as a fact. [...] there's nothing else to do because twice two is mathematics. Try and refute it",[40] the Underground Man (and Shestov after him) exclaims bitterly. By the same token, Shestov cherished the words of Stavrogin addressed to

---

35   Lev Shestov, "Shekspir i ego kritik Brandes" in *Sochineniia v dvukh tomakh*, Tomsk: Vodolei, 1996, vol. 1, 3–212 (11).
36   Isaiah Berlin, *The Magus of the North*, 41.
37   *Ibid.*, 62.
38   *Ibid.*, 63.
39   *Ibid.*, 105.
40   Fyodor Dostoevsky, "Notes from the Underground", in *Notes from the Underground and the Gambler*, transl. by Jane Kentish, Oxford, New York: Oxford University Press, 1991, 15.

Shatov in Dostoevskii's *The Possessed* as revealing the helpless nature of the human mind in the moral sphere: "Reason has never been powerful enough to define good and evil or to demarcate good from evil, even approximately; on the contrary, it's always confused them shamefully and pitifully; science has always provided solutions by brute force".[41] The same charge against reason is expressed by Hamann, who claims that "God is a poet, not a geometer",[42] and, following in his footsteps, by Goethe: "mathematics [...] can achieve nothing in the moral sphere".[43]

For Shestov reason equates necessity because – despite its intrinsic inadequacy – it claims universal authority, an absolute power, it claims to lay hold of the truth. Necessity for him is multifaceted: it is both physical and metaphysical. Hamann differs little: his "great enemy is necessity – metaphysical and scientific", which turns "living life" (as Dostoevskii was later to call it), an individual experience and specific human vision into "a pseudo-objective source of authority – [...] a world of necessary truths, mathematics, theology, politics, physics, which man did not make and cannot alter, crystalline, pure, an object of divine worship for atheists".[44] Hamann "rejects this absolutely".[45] He is indignant that, effectively, "what the theory cannot embrace is mere expendable rubbish".[46] Shestov repeats the same charge: "if science at last managed to get rid of all remainders which hitherto did not fit into formulas it would have celebrated its ultimate victory",[47] and defends "the interior impulse" – "the 'irrational residue' which is beyond the limits of possible experience".[48] On Job's scales, Shestov says, human grief outweighs the sand of the seas, just as for Dostoevskii's Ivan Karamazov, the tear of a child outweighs all the possible harmony of the universe. In other words, for both Shestov and Hamann, the value of an individual is supreme, one man with his private experience bursts out of all the theories and is more important than mankind as a

---

41   Fedor Dostoevskii, "Besy" in *Polnoe sobranie sochinenii v 30 tomakh*, Leningrad: Nauka, 1982, vol. 10, 199. Cited in Lev Shestov, "O 'pererozhdenii ubezhdenii' u Dostoevskogo" in *Umozrenie i otkrovenie*, Paris: YMCA-Press, 1964, 193. English version of the text Fyodor Dostoevsky, "Devils", translated by M. Katz, Oxford: Oxford University Press, 1992, 171–196 (264).
42   See Isaiah Berlin, *The Magus of the North*, 40.
43   Johann Wolfgang von Goethe, *Maximen und Reflexionen*, ed. Max Hecker, Weimar, 1907, No 608, p. 132, cited in Berlin, *The Magus of the North*, 40.
44   Isaiah Berlin, *The Magus of the North*, 45.
45   Ibid.
46   Ibid., 114.
47   Lev Shestov, "Dnevnik myslei", see *Kontinent*, 8 (1976), 235–252 (249).
48   Lev Shestov, "The Conquest of the Self-Evident" ("Preodolenie samoochevidnostei. K stoletiiu so dnia rozhdeniia F.M. Dostoevskogo"), see: http://www.angelfire.com/nb/shestov/ijb/jb1_5.html (consulted 20.12.2013).

general entity. What Berlin states about Hamann is valid with respect to Shestov with an even stronger force:

> Any doctrine that stresses the general, the impersonal, the conceptual, the universal, seems to him [Hamann] likely to flatten out all differences, peculiarities, quirks – to obstruct the soul's free flight by clipping its wings in the interests of comprehensive inclusiveness.[49]

Shestov hates the "universal and necessary", and follows with admiration Dostoevskii, who just

> like Kierkegaard 'withdrew from the general', or, as he himself expresses it, 'from the allness (*vsemstvo*)'. And he suddenly felt that it was impossible and unnecessary for him to return to the allness; that the allness – i.e., what everyone, in every time and place, considers to be the truth – is a fraud, is a terrible illusion; that all the horrors of existence have come into the world from the allness toward which our reason summons us.[50]

A struggle for the private against the general (and rationalism for them is the embodiment and celebration of the general) lies at the heart of both Hamann's and Shestov's thought.

> Hamann speaks for those who hear the cry of the toad beneath the harrow, even when it may be right to plough over him: since if men do not hear this cry, if they are deaf, if the toad is written off because he has been "condemned by history" – if the defeated are never worth attending to because history is the history of the victorious – then such victories will prove their own undoing, for they will tend to destroy the very values in the name of which the battle was undertaken.[51]

This stance of Hamann is strikingly reminiscent of Belinskii's in his famous letter to Botkin where he demands an account for every victim of history[52] – and which Shestov embraces passionately, commenting that speculative

---

49 Isaiah Berlin, *The Magus of the North*, 115.
50 Lev Shestov, *Kierkegaard and the Existential Philosophy*: http://www.angelfire.com/nb/shestov/sk/sk_01.html (30.11.2013) (*Kirgegard i ekzistentsial'naia filosofiia* (*Glas vopiiushchego v pustyne*), Moscow: Progress-Gnozis, 1992, 21).
51 Isaiah Berlin, *The Magus of the North*, 117.
52 See V.G. Belinskii, *Izbrannye filosofskie sochineniia*, vol. 1, Moscow: Gos. izd-vo politicheskoi literatury, 1948, 572–573.

philosophy considers such victims "in principle, worthy of no attention, since they are created and finite beings [...] whom no one in the world is able to help, as speculative philosophy well knows".[53] Shestov mocks with disdain the foundations of such a philosophy which justifies and promotes the superiority of the general over the private:

> All the hitherto invented 'consolations', including so-called metaphysical, are nothing but a comic mixture of social considerations with arithmetic, which can be exhausted in essence by the following principle: 'a person has given his life, but this does not matter, because he fell for a noble cause. A noble cause is a cause useful to society, and it will triumph sooner or later, and thousands of people will be happy at the expense of one person's misery. A thousand is, of course, larger than one – nobody can doubt that'. Thus the sacrifice is justified, isn't it?[54]

This bitter exposure by Shestov of the utilitarian underpinning of the lofty social rhetoric, on which most totalitarian regimes have been based – a product of subjugating the private to a general theory – is a direct legacy of Hamann. By the same token,

> when Herzen speaks of communism (of such writers as Cabet or the Babouvists) as simply tsarism stood on its head, an equally oppressive and individuality-ignoring system, and when Bakunin complains of Marx's authoritarianism, this is the tradition they continue – the terror of any establishment that hems in the individual and destroys his deepest values.[55]

Theory, abstraction, general ideas subsume and swallow an individual life, as soon as "a compassion for a fairy-tale, understood as a new truth, replaces a compassion for an individual".[56] Then "a multifaceted and complex character of the duty with respect to concrete people is replaced by a unified and radiant duty with respect to an idea".[57] Such attempts to renounce one's conscience, to

---

53   Lev Shestov, *Kierkegaard and the Existential Philosophy* (see http://www.angelfire.com/nb/shestov/sk/sk_01.html (13.12.2013)).
54   Lev Shestov, *Turgenev*, Ann Arbor: Ardis, 1982, 31.
55   Isaiah Berlin, *The Magus of the North*, 115.
56   Fazil Iskander, *Rasskazy, povest', skazka, dialog, esse, stikhi*. Seriia "Zerkalo XX vek", Ekaterinburg: U-Faktoriia, 1999, 589–590.
57   *Ibid.*

turn away from the tragedy of existence, ending up with a hollow form from which the content has gone or being treacherously replaced, is a central premise of the oeuvre of Chekhov – the writer who represents the same era as Shestov, but whose irrationalism is of a much subtler kind and who can serve as the litmus paper which reveals not only the continuity of the irrationalist stance, but also the distinctions and divides within it.

Chekhov: 'Poetic Reason'; Freedom and Responsibility

The wave in European culture that brought about Schopenhauer, Nietzsche, Kierkegaard and to an extent Freud was engendered by polemics with rationalism that hugely overstepped its boundaries (the phenomenon which Hamann sensed right from the start). But the utopia of progress was still gaining momentum, and it took another century to see its ultimate collapse. At the same time the crisis of the great illusions of the 19th century was evident, "God was dead" and the profound change of the whole cultural paradigm was imminent. Both Shestov and Chekhov were amongst the first to sense that change. "…There ends for man the thousand-year reign of 'reason and conscience'; a new era begins – that of 'psychology'",[58] Shestov wrote in 1903. While still a passionate and pure youngster in the desolate 80s, he dreamt to "utter a new word and to start a new endeavour".[59] As a result, he did not so much pronounce a new word as sensed where the new winds were blowing, because his key words, which determined his whole outlook, apparently became "individualism" and "tragedy" – concepts which turned out to be seminal also for the cultural consciousness of modernity. Shestov

> showed that a genuine consciousness, not trimmed for the Procrustean bed of rationalism, together with the profound thought that awakens in it, lives on the territory of tragedy. This understanding is very close to Chekhov's, who, in his own intuitive fashion, moved in the same direction.[60]

---

58   Lev Shestov, *Dostoevsky and Nietzsche: The Philosophy of Tragedy* (see http://www.angelfire.com/nb/shestov/dtn/dn_7.html (05.06.2013)).

59   See an extract from Shestov's youthful writings, quoted in Natalie Baranova-Shestova, *Zhizn L'va Shestova*, Paris: La Presse Libre, 1983, vol. 1, 14.

60   Savely Senderovich, "Shestov-Chekhov, Chekhov-Shestov", in *Anton Chekhov Through The Eyes Of Russian Thinkers: Vasilii Rozanov, Dmitrii Merezhkovskii and Lev Shestov*, ed. Olga Tabachnikova, Anthem Press: London-New York-Delhi, 2010, (199–218) 201.

That is why Shestov wrote about Chekhov – with the passion of a spiritual twin. He obviously saw his resemblance to the writer in their common steadfast focus on tragic individuals, on people who find themselves in existential crisis, without firm ground under their feet and have to create from the void (hence the title of Shestov's piece on Chekhov: 'Creation from the void', 1905). The loss of inner orientation was very much in tune with the disintegration of external structures, with the crumbling of old beliefs and re-evaluation of values. However, what distinguishes both Shestov and Chekhov is an acute realisation that the roots of tragic consciousness lie intrinsically within man and are much more (or at least as much!) to do with his relationship with himself than with any external conditions – economic, social or political. This existential discovery was subversive to the highly socially charged climate of Russia at the end of the 19th century, although it was not long before existentialism came to dominate European thought. Both Shestov and Chekhov were precursors of it. While Chekhov worked by artistic means, Shestov fought his war using polemical intellectual essays with a strong literary flavour.

The crisis of speculative philosophy was mirrored by the crisis of literary genres, and a shift from realism to modernism. Chekhov provided the required bridge in literature, while Shestov joined together the old and new cultural eras in philosophical terms, and became, as Albert Camus once described him, one of the few philosophers most important to the new "Man of the Absurd".[61] Given Chekhov's medical background and apparently rational method of inquiry, his sober, disillusioned outlook, he seems far from irrationalism. This, however, is only a superficial – and deceptive – view.[62] In fact, Chekhov undermined the rationalist tendency and subverted the very foundations of realism. By his characteristically quiet, implicit means, he combatted the primitive utilitarian view of literature dominant amongst his contemporaries, and opened a new stage infusing poetry back into prose, bringing the dramatic element from the external plot inwards, inside the psyche of the protagonists, and uncovered the spiritual within the mundane thus marking (as Andrei Belyi labelled it assigning Chekhov to Symbolism), a "gateway into eternity".[63] The

---

61 See Albert Camus, "The Myth of Sisyphus (Le Mythe de Sisyphe)", in *Essais* (Paris: NRF/Gallimard, 1965).

62 For a detailed analysis of Chekhov's irrationalism concealed under a deceptive rationalist veneer see Olga Tabachnikova, "Chekhov and Brodsky: behind the veneer of rationalism...", in *Russian Irrationalism from Pushkin to Brodsky: Seven Essays in Literature and Thought* (Bloomsbury Academic, 2015).

63 Andrei Belyi, "Chekhov" in *A.P. Chekhov: Pro et Contra. Tvorchestvo A.P. Chekhova v russkoi mysli kontsa XIX – nachala XX v. (1887–1914)*, Anthology, eds. I.N. Sukhikh and A.D. Stepanov, St Petersburg: Izdatel'stvo Russkogo Khristianskogo gumanitarnogo Instituta, 2002, 839.

primacy of the aesthetic for Chekhov, the profound poetic texture of his writings, their lyrical intensity, are already sufficient pointers to the irrational underpinning of his vision and his texts. Most importantly though, Chekhov demonstrated the limitations of pure rationalism, which, in his oeuvre, is constantly undermined. This is manifested in particular by subtext subverting the text. Thus, as Father Shmeman wrote about Chekhov's story 'Arkhierei' ('The Bishop'):

> I understand Chekhov's hero with all my being. [...] All this is such sublime, pure art which tells us more about the essence of Christianity and Russian Orthodoxy than theological triumphalist definitions do. [...] Everything in this Christianity is a defeat and yet the whole story radiates some inexplicable, mysterious victory.[64]

In the same vein, life in Chekhov's universe is always broader than any idea of life, and the complexity of the human psyche resists rationalist explanations. As Aleksandr Chudakov remarked, "Chekhov is a greater irrationalist and mystagogue than Merezhkovskii",[65] while the literary critic Liubov Gurevich noted as early as 1912 that "Chekhov is the first of our artists who consciously opposed the rational activity of man to that organic thinking which takes its origins in the irrational depths of our spirit, and rejects the validity of any purely rational thought".[66]

Shestov aptly noticed Chekhov's discontent with any ideology, be it essentialist or reductionist. He correctly claimed that both "crude materialism" and "humanising idealism" were deeply unsatisfying for Chekhov. While placing his trust in scientific method even in the artistic domain (by admitting the possibility of constructing a philosophy of art), Chekhov at the same time envisaged a misconception and misapplication of it (through attempts to construct a physiology of art):

> It's always good to think scientifically; the trouble is that thinking scientifically about art will inevitably end up by degenerating into a search for the "cells" or "centres" in charge of creative ability, whereupon some

---

64 Aleksandr Shmeman, *Dnevniki*, see entries of Tuesday, 04.11.1975 and Monday, 24.04.1978, Moscow: Russkii Put, 2005, 220 and 428.

65 Aleksandr Chudakov, "Chekhov and Merezhkovskii: Two Types of Artistic-Philosophical Consciousness", in *Anton Chekhov Through The Eyes Of Russian Thinkers*, ed. Olga Tabachnikova, 2010, (93–112) 101.

66 Liubov Gurevich, *Literatura i estetika*, Moscow, 1912, 47; quoted by Chudakov (see *Ibid.*).

dull-witted German will discover them somewhere in the temporal lobes, another will disagree, a third German will agree, and a Russian will skim through an article on cells and dash off a study for the *Northern Herald*, and the *Herald of Europe* will take to analyzing the study, and for three years an epidemic of utter nonsense will hover in the Russian air, providing dullards with earnings and popularity and engendering nothing but irritation among intelligent people.[67]

Notably, Chekhov's mockery of shallow rationalist tendencies in the treatment of art, of attempts to reduce the complexity of the creative process to crude materialism resonate with Dostoevskii's distrust (unequivocally shared by Shestov) towards rationalisation of the human psyche:

> Ugh, these Bernards! They are all over the place. [...] Imagine: [...] in the brain... (damn them!) there are sort of [...] little tails of those nerves, and [...] you see, I look at something with my eyes and then they begin quivering, those little tails...and [...] then an image appears... [...] that is, an object, or an action, damn it! That's why I see and then think, because of those tails, not at all because I've got a soul, and that I am some sort of image and likeness. All that is nonsense! Rakitin explained it all to me yesterday, brother, and it simply bowled me over. It's magnificent, Alyosha, this science! A new man's arising – that I understand... And yet I am sorry to lose God! [...] It's chemistry, brother, chemistry! There's no help for it, your reverence, you must make way for chemistry.[68]

But unlike Dostoevskii and Shestov, Chekhov does not oppose reason and faith to each other, and does not see any threat to the divine in science per se. Instead he reconciles the two, as if marrying ethics and aesthetics in a poetic type of reason, and calls a genuine wizard someone who is able to walk, invariably with great difficulty, the huge field that lies "between 'there is God' and 'there is no God'".[69] Hamann's aforementioned formula "God is a poet, not a geometer", which is very much akin to Shestov, is completely alien to Chekhov

---

67 From Chekhov's letter to Aleksei Suvorin, See *Anton Chekhov's Life and Thought. Selected Letters and Commentary*, selection, introduction and commentary by Simon Karlinsky, University of California Press: Berkeley, Los Angeles, London, 1973, 122.
68 Fedor Dostoevskii, *The Brothers Karamazov*, Chapter 73; see http://www.online-literature.com/dostoevsky/brothers_karamazov/73/ (25.07.2012).
69 Anton Chekhov, "Dnevnikovye zapisi", 1897, in A.P. Chekhov, *PSSP v 30 tomakh*, Vol. 17, Moscow: Nauka, 1980, 224.

who unites the scientific and artistic, and believes in the unity of science and poetry. As he wrote in a letter to Dmitrii Grigorovich, "an artist's intuition is sometimes worthy of a scientist's brain, [...] both have the same goals and the same nature"[70] and continued in a letter to Aleksei Suvorin,

> Both anatomy and belles-lettres are of equally noble descent; they have identical goals and an identical enemy – the devil – and there is absolutely no reason for them to fight. [...] It is for this reason that geniuses never fought among themselves and Goethe the poet coexisted splendidly with Goethe the naturalist.[71]

Yet, Chekhov's and Dostoevskii's types of irrationalism, while coming from different directions, especially in their attitude to reason, still meet – on the ethical plane.

Thus Dostoevskii's Ridiculous Man corrupted the people of an unknown planet, happy in their innocence, by teaching them to lie. For Shestov, who views this novella as a metaphor of the metaphysical state of mankind before the Fall, it is Reason that lies at the root of this corruption. In Chekhov's universe, lies (and above all self-deception) are often born of cowardice and force man not to dare (in contrast to Dostoevskii's daring characters striving to overstep existing boundaries). Reason in this (notably irrational) process is subjugated to cowardice, and thus an insufficient moral (or spiritual) effort leads to a disintegration of personality. This of course only concerns a certain type of Chekhov's heroes, and does not include those of them who are situated at the animal level – both in terms of their reason and their morality. Interestingly, Shestov's statement that the strongest human feature is a fear of truth penetrates to the very core of Chekhov's world-view. In Dostoevskii's oeuvre reason is exalted to the ruling position, but only to disclose its ultimate impotence: once it is separated from moral sense it becomes a slave to naked ambition. Thus, in both Chekhov's and Dostoevskii's writings reason is often enslaved: in Dostoevskii's – by egotistic ambition, in Chekhov's – by pusillanimity. More importantly, both Dostoevskii and Chekhov tell us, in a somewhat Hamannian way, about a disharmony between the two faculties – of conscience (*sovest'*) and of reason. However, while Dostoevskii (and following him, Shestov) shows the impotence of 'pure reason' with righteous satisfaction, Chekhov states this

---

70   From the draft of Chekhov's letter to Grigorovich of 12.02.1887, see *PSSP v 30 tomakh*, Vol. 2, Moscow: Nauka, 1975, 28–31.

71   Chekhov's letter to Suvorin of 15.05.1889. See Karlinsky, *Anton Chekhov's Life and Thought*, 145.

with sad dissatisfaction. In fact, Shestov goes further than Dostoevskii in his disdainful treatment of reason. For him it is detached from other human faculties par excellence, and alone is responsible for man's tragic fate.

With regard to Chekhov's attitude to "humanising idealism" – the other side of the coin, according to Shestov, of "crude materialism" – it has been interpreted in a number of ways. Shestov ascribed to the writer a hatred of any general idea and 'accused' him of "killing human hopes".[72] This charge has been relieved in subsequent scholarship by replacing it with the claim that Chekhov, in fact, killed illusions rather than hopes. In my view this requires yet further qualification, for in Chekhov's world there are no absolute categories, and it is an individual who invests them with meaning depending on the concrete situation. In this sense illusion as well as ideal by themselves are neutral entities, and it is only man's treatment of his illusion, his conduct in relation to it, which changes the nature of this illusion turning it either into self-deception or into Pushkin's "sublime delusion" (*nas vozvyshaiushchii obman*) – discussed in detail below.

Chekhov himself would probably reject both concepts – of materialism and idealism – as mere words, hollow meaningless entities. "...Idealism and all the rest of those incomprehensible words", he wrote to Viktor Miroliubov in 1901.[73] Indeed, Chekhov was convinced of the primacy of experience over theory – a conviction which allows one to treat him as existentialist and which brings him surprisingly close to the irrationalist trend.

As Evdokimova notes, "as most other existential thinkers and phenomenologists, Chekhov regarded traditional systematic or academic philosophy as too abstract and remote from concrete human experience".[74] She then makes a most important observation that Chekhov's

> most cherished thought is [...] the utter impenetrability of the world; not the exaltation of folly, as in the case of Shestov, but a sober acknowledgement of our inability to know the truth and yet at the same time the realization that 'there is nothing beyond reason', to use Camus's words.[75]

Her conclusion is that Chekhov is opposite to Shestov in his epistemology – while the philosopher believes that mankind's doomed fate originates from

---

72 See Lev Shestov, "Tvorchestvo iz nichego", in *Sochineniia v dvukh tomakh*, Tomsk: Vodolei, 1996, vol. 2, 184–213.

73 Letter of 17.12.1901. See Simon Karlinsky, *Anton Chekhov's Life and Thought*, 414.

74 Svetlana Evdokimova, "Philosophy's Enemies: Chekhov and Shestov", in *Anton Chekhov Through The Eyes Of Russian Thinkers*, ed. Olga Tabachnikova, 219–245 (226).

75 *Ibid.*, 230.

eating of the tree of knowledge, the writer laments on the contrary that human tragedy is in never having tasted from the tree of knowledge. However, both voiced the resulting sense of meaninglessness and disorientation, the feeling, expressed above by Shestov's words that "we are somehow definitely and forever cut off from the sources and beginnings of life".[76]

One of the best illustrations of the scary meaninglessness and disarming unknowability of the world is Chekhov's story 'Terror', where human reason is unable to accommodate such a state of affairs.

> When I lie on the grass and watch a little beetle which was born yesterday and understands nothing, it seems to me that its life consists of nothing else but fear, and in it I see myself. [...] I looked at the rooks, and it seemed so strange and terrible that they were flying.[77]

This reflects the unblinkered quality of Chekhov's vision, his ability (with which he invests his characters) to see ordinary and familiar things in the extraordinary light. A little beetle or a rook in the sky suddenly become enigmatic, railway lights (in the novella 'Lights') are associated in the characters' imagination with mankind's remote past or with a human attempt at cognition: a mysterious world lives not just next to the everyday one, but within it too. Not only for the hero of 'Black Monk', whose visions and daydreams are part of his world, but for the characters unaffected by psychiatric illness, the realm of the supernatural moves freely into the natural, is interwoven with it – thus the sound of the breaking string in *The Cherry Orchard* is simultaneously a mystical symbol and a real sound of a bucket fallen into a shaft or a bird's screech.

This is not so much about the irrational having a rational explanation, as it is about their relative nature and mutual reversibility. Thus, as Andrei Stepanov remarks, in Chekhov's writings often "what makes sense from one point of view, is meaningless from another viewpoint...".[78] The following entries in Chekhov's notebooks can serve as an illustration of his ability to view reality

---

76   Lev Shestov, *Athens and Jerusalem*. http://www.angelfire.com/nb/shestov/aaj/aj1_1.html (consulted 20.05.2013).

77   Anton Chekhov, "Terror", see http://www.online-literature.com/anton_chekhov/1267/ (consulted 12.06.2013).

78   Stepanov aptly observes that while Chekhov understands the reciprocal relationship between the rational and irrational, Shestov fails to spot their mutual reversibility. See Andrei Stepanov. "Lev Shestov on Chekhov", in *Anton Chekhov Through The Eyes Of Russian Thinkers*, ed. Olga Tabachnikova, 169–174 (171).

from diverse vantage points: "From the diary of an old dog: people do not eat the slop and bones which the kitchen-maid throws away – what fools!"; "Our entire universe may be just a crumb in a tooth of a beast".[79] The mutual penetrability, interconnectedness of both worlds: of the rational and irrational, of the natural and transcendental is a marked feature of Chekhov's universe.

The terror experienced by Silin (from the story 'Terror') is more scary than the fear of death – it is a fear of life, of the eternal enigma of existence – and widens the standard range of contemplations of man's tragic predicament, his position of a speck of dust easily blown away from a smooth surface of eternity, which have always been part of human thought. These ponderings became particularly prominent in the disoriented tottering world consumed by the crisis of nihilism, which in Russia manifested itself in the disillusioned generation of the 1880s. Chekhov recognises the universal character of this pessimistic stance, in particular through his literary hero Ananiev in the story 'Lights':

> Thoughts of the aimlessness of life, of the insignificance and transitoriness of the visible world, Solomon's 'vanity of vanities' have been, and are to this day, the highest and final stage in the realm of thought. The thinker reaches that stage and – comes to a halt! There is nowhere further to go. The activity of the normal brain is completed with this, and that is natural and in the order of things.[80]

At this point the human psyche leaps into extreme pessimism unable to find an exit from this existential dead-end. Chekhov's generation of writers, who came of age in the era of *bezvremenie*, were characterised by this despondency. By the same token, Dostoevskii's Kirillov reacted to this crucial necessity by suicide as proof of the ultimate possibility of free will in a godless world,[81] and Lev Tolstoi perceived such a suicidal solution as a way of strength, as his 'Confession' explains.[82] An alternative offered by Shestov is an *a priori* doomed, but nevertheless perpetual, state of rebellion against the immutable world order and an ultimate breaking away from impotent rationalism through an irrational act of faith.

---

79 Anton Chekhov, Notebook IV, in *PSSP v 30 tomakh*, vol. 17, 1980, 154.
80 Anton Chekhov, "Lights" ("*Ogni*"): http://www.online-literature.com/anton_chekhov/1250/ (consulted 21.02.2014).
81 See Fedor Dostoevsky's novel "The Possessed".
82 Lev Tolstoi, "Confession" (*Ispoved'*), in *Sobranie sochinenii v 22 tomakh*, Moscow: Khuddozhestvennaia literatura, 1983, vol. 16, 106–165. (For the English translation see *The Cambridge Companion to Tolstoi*, ed. Donna T. Orwin, Cambridge University Press, 2002).

Chekhov's response is different and carefully concealed. James Wood, in a sense, sees it in the opposition of man's intrinsic inner freedom to the external pressure of the universe:

> In Chekhov's world, our inner lives run at their own speed. They are laxly calendared. They live in their own gentle almanac, and in his stories the free inner life bumps against the outer life like two different time systems, like the Julian calendar against the Gregorian. This was what Chekhov meant by 'life'. This was his revolution.[83]

Alternatively, one can see Chekhov's reaction to the ultimate necessity in a distinctly stoic stance, in the perpetual Sisyphean effort by which its very meaninglessness may eventually be transcended into meaning.[84] But there is more than this in Chekhov, it seems to me. The quotation from Camus, given by Evdokimova to illustrate a common existentialist stance of confronting the impossibility of knowing, does not, in my view, fully reflect Chekhov's position:

> This heart within me I can feel, and I judge that it exists. This world I can touch, and I likewise judge that it exists. There ends all my knowledge, and the rest is construction. [...] Between the certainty I have of my existence and the content I try to give to that assurance, the gap will never be filled.[85]

"A carrot is a carrot, according to Chekhov", Evdokimova comments, referring to Chekhov's famous response to Olga Knipper's question of what is life ("This is the same as to ask: what is a carrot? The carrot is a carrot, we know nothing else"), "We know nothing else, or, in Camus's terms 'the rest is construction'".[86]

In the rest of this section I shall argue that it is indeed a construction for Chekhov too, but, unlike Camus – for whom the gap will never be filled – Chekhov does fill the gap, even despite his own references to the contrary. And he fills it, as we shall see, in a way similar to Pushkin's (in general, the parallel

---

83   James Wood, *The Broken Estate. Essays on Literature and Belief*, London: Jonathan Cape, 1999, 89.
84   See, for example, Sobennikov, "Chekhov i stoiki" (in *Filosofiia A.P. Chekhova*, ed. Anatolii Sobennikov, 168–180) or Evdokimova ("Philosophy's Enemies: Chekhov and Shestov", 229): "When faced with 'absurd walls', Chekhov ultimately chooses the path of Sisyphus".
85   Svetlana Evdokimova, "Philosophy's Enemies: Chekhov and Shestov", 226.
86   *Ibid.*

between the two, drawn by some scholars, is not accidental).[87] As Aleksei Mashevskii explains,

> Not only was Pushkin a pioneer of the realist method, but he was also the first who realised a threat concealed in such an absolutely 'real' view of the world. This threat could be labelled a Machiavellian syndrome. Indeed, the famous Florentinean thinker just strove to show that the actions of a politician should be based on an authentic reality which has no place for our moral principles and our ideas of justice.[88]

In Search of an Ideal (Reading both the Lines and between them)

At first sight, it seems that Chekhov strives for the same Machiavellian reality in literature, free from our judgements about it. Hence his famous credo of the writer's task being merely the depiction of life, or, more precisely, the most important aspects of it: "The artist is not meant to be a judge of his characters and what they say; his only job is to be an impartial witness"; his business is merely "to be talented, that is to know how to distinguish important testimony from unimportant, to place [...] characters in the proper light and speak their language".[89] Yet, Chekhov speaks with clear nostalgia about the writers of previous generations whose work, while staying faithful to realism was at the same time saturated with the juices of their striving for an ideal:

> the writers we call eternal or simply good, the writers who intoxicate us, have one highly important trait in common: they're moving toward something definite and beckon you to follow, and you feel with your entire being, not only with your mind, that they have a certain goal [...]. The best of them are realistic and describe life as it is, but because each line is saturated with the consciousness of its goal, you feel life as it should be in addition to life as it is, and you are captivated by it.[90]

---

87   See, for instance, Andrei Bitov, "Moi dedushka Chekhov i pradedushka Pushkin", (http://lit.1september.ru/article.php?ID=200403603 (consulted 08.03.2012)).
88   Aleksei Mashevskii, "Nas vozvyshaiushchii obman", *Zvezda*, 1999, No 6.
89   Anton Chekhov's letter to Suvorin of 30.05.1888. See Karlinsky, *Anton Chekhov's Life and Thought*, 104.
90   Anton Chekhov, Letter to Suvorin of 25.11.1892. See Karlinsky, *Anton Chekhov's Life and Thought*, 243.

In the very same letter to Suvorin, Chekhov simultaneously testifies to the changing times by saying (words which are often cited) that he and his generation of writers are ill with emptiness and disbelief:

> We describe life as it is and stop dead right there. We wouldn't lift a hoof if you hit into us with a whip. We have neither immediate, nor remote goals, and there is emptiness in our souls. We have no politics, we don't believe in revolution, there is no God, we're not afraid of ghosts, and I personally am not even afraid of death or blindness. No one who wants nothing, hopes for nothing and fears nothing can be an artist.[91]

And later on: "Yes, I am intelligent enough at least to refuse to hide my malady from myself and lie to myself and cover up my emptiness with other people's rags like the ideas of the sixties, etc.".[92] Another of Chekhov's confessions, also frequently quoted (written also to Suvorin only four years earlier), is of similar character: concerning not being able to understand the world and not having answers to eternal questions:

> It's about time that everyone who writes – especially genuine literary artists – admitted that in this world you can't figure anything out. Socrates admitted it once upon a time, and Voltaire was wont to admit it. The crowd thinks it knows and understands everything; the stupider it is, the broader it imagines its outlook. But, if a writer whom the crowd believes takes it upon himself to declare he understands nothing of what he sees, that alone will constitute a major gain in the realm of thought and a major step forward.[93]

Thus on the one hand Chekhov unambiguously confesses his inner emptiness, typical for his entire generation; on the other he states that this is incompatible

---

91 *Ibid.*
92 *Ibid.*, 243–244.
93 *Ibid.*, 104 (from Chekhov's letter to Suvorin of 30.05.1888). Interestingly, Shestov too perceived writers in the same light – as not possessing any answers to eternal questions, but having to pretend otherwise, in order to please the public which believes them and expects definite and consoling answers from them: "it needs ideals, and whoever wishes to serve it must furnish it with ideals at any cost. An old story! The writer is like a wounded tigress that rushes to her young in her lair. The arrow is in her back, but she must nurse with her milk the helpless creatures who know nothing of her mortal wound". (From the preface to "The Good in the Teaching of Tolstoy and Nietzsche: Philosophy and Preaching"; see http://www.angelfire.com/nb/shestov/dtn/tn_01.html (consulted 11.08. 2013)).

with being an artist and admires those writers of the past who saw meaning and had ideals; also: honest acknowledgement of your own lack of answers, à la Socrates or Voltaire, he deems a virtue. Are we, then, to take these confessions at face value and conclude from them that (as a logical corollary) Chekhov is not a true artist, he really has no beliefs and knows nothing about the world; and that, by the same token, Socrates and Voltaire are not true wizards?!

Only a week later Chekhov writes to Suvorin – who had shown his alarming letter about emptiness to S.I. Smirnova-Sazonova, the journalist friend, and then revealed to Chekhov her response – a disambiguation of his stance:

> I write that there are no goals, and you understand, I hope, that I consider those goals necessary and would be only too happy to set out in search of them, while Sazonova writes that it is wrong to tantalize men with advantages they will never know. 'Value what already exists'; in her opinion all our troubles boil down to the fact that we all seek lofty, remote goals. If that's not female logic, it certainly must be a philosophy of despair. Anyone who sincerely thinks that man has no more need of lofty remote goals than do cows and that those goals cause 'all our troubles' can do nothing more than eat, drink and sleep, or when he's had his fill, take a flying leap and bash his head against the corner of a trunk.[94]

It is therefore clear that when Chekhov speaks of the disease of his generation, aligning himself to this brotherhood (notably: without attempts to be raised above it, without any claims to exceptionalism),[95] he realises acutely the need for a search for meaning and faith, for the sublime goal. In 1901 Chekhov wrote to Viktor Miroliubov, "One should either believe in God, or if faith is lacking, one should do something other than fill the void with sensationalism, one must seek, seek on one's own, all alone with one's conscience...".[96]

---

[94] Anton Chekhov, Letter to Suvorin of 03.12.1892, see Karlinsky, *Anton Chekhov's Life and Thought*, 246 (I have changed "you assume" for "you understand, I hope", which I deem more precise).

[95] Recall, for example, Chekhov's famous words from his letter to V.A. Tikhonov of 7.03.1889, "...we can prevail only through the efforts of our entire generation, and not otherwise. Instead of being known as Chekhov, Tikhonov, Korolenko, Shcheglov, Barantsevich or Bezhetsky, we will be called 'the eighties' or 'the end of the nineteenth century'. A guild, so to speak". (see Karlinsky, *Anton Chekhov's Life and Thought*, 131).

[96] Chekhov's letter to Miroliubov of 17.12.1901. See Karlinsky, *Anton Chekhov's Life and Thought*, 414. This, again, resonates highly with Shestov's own lonely search for God thus described by Viktor Erofeev: "In the meantime N. Berdiaev and S. Bulgakov as well as other God-seekers have become Christians with a greater or lesser degree of orthodoxy,

Veniamin Albov, whose detailed analysis of Chekhov's oeuvre was accepted by Chekhov with rare approval, discerns as a specifically Chekhovian perspective the striving to evaluate phenomena "not from the point of view of cause and consequence or some moral viewpoint, but from the point of view of meaning and purpose".[97] He singles out at the initial stage of Chekhov's search for meaning a rather disillusioned portrayal of humans as being a continuation of fauna, a vision of the incredible instability and ephemeral character of the cultural side of human nature:

> How quickly does this cultural coating slip off a human being under the influence of such petty circumstances as illness, fear of death and so on, and what a disgusting animal base becomes exposed even under such a flower of life as the old professor. [...] More generally, what an animal any man really is – a pitiful, helpless animal, lost amongst the boundless incomprehensible world.[98]

However, afterwards Albov observes "a new and very important rift"[99] in Chekhov's creativity. This is a change from seeing culture as a thin coating on the essentially animal foundation of a human being to discovering that this cultural dimension constitutes, in fact, the nucleus of personality and of life:

> A curious metamorphosis occurred with Mr Chekhov. That which, clearly, previously seemed to him as a volatile coating on a purely animal basis, existing on the surface of life, now found itself at the very bottom, in the deepest 'crypts' of life, and precisely as its eternal reality. [...] And it is from this moment on that his talent acquires more general significance.

---

and, one must say, without particular torments. Shestov thus resembled a hapless pupil twisting his brain over a school exercise, while his mates were running around the school-yard with merry shouts. But watching them through the window and gnawing at his pen, a miserable boy knows firmly that they had not solved the problem either, they merely 'fixed' the answer". (see Viktor Erofeev, "'Ostaetsa odno: proizvol' (Filosofiia odinochestva i literaturno-esteticheskoe kredo L'va Shestova)", *Voprosy literatury*, 10 (1975), 153–188).

97   V.P. Albov, "Dva momenta v razvitii tvorchestva Antona Pavlovicha Chekhova" (1903), *A.P. Chekhov: Pro et Contra. Tvorchestvo A.P. Chekhova v russkoi mysli kontsa XIX – nachala XX v. (1887–1914)*, Anthology, eds. I.N. Sukhikh and A.D. Stepanov, St. Petersburg: Izdatel'stvo Russkogo Khristianskogo gumanitarnogo Instituta, 2002, 373.

98   *Ibid.*, 377, 387.

99   *Ibid.*, 389.

The most 'necessary', 'most important' (Chekhov's favourite phrases of late) is necessary and important equally for everybody.[100]

Chekhov's route, from the very start, was in an uncompromising, bold refusal to accept common truths – or rather common lies – of consoling, idealistic self-deception, when the old ideals, now getting stripped of meaning and falsified, were being used as a convenient existential shield. "I hate lies and violence in all of their forms [...]. My holy of holies is [...] the most absolute freedom imaginable, freedom from violence and lies, no matter what form the latter two take".[101] It is therefore not moral or cultural ideals that Chekhov renounced, but man's hypocritical attempts to abuse these ideals by minting them into vacuous hollow clichés. "If it's insincerity you're after", he says to Suvorin referring to the aforementioned letter by Sazonova,

> there are tons of it in Sazonova's letter. 'The greatest wonder of all is man himself, and we shall never tire of studying him...' or 'The aim of life is life itself...' or 'I believe in life, for whose bright moments we not only can, but should live. I believe in man,[102] in the good side of his soul', etc. Can all that really be sincere and mean anything? That's no view of life; that's a lollipop. [...] She believes 'in life', but that means that she doesn't believe in anything if she's intelligent or else, if she's uneducated, that she actually believes in the peasant God and crosses herself in the dark.[103]

Accused by Suvorin of insincerity and pessimism Chekhov rebuffs by saying that Sazonova's "cheerful letter is a thousand times more like a tomb"[104] than his own.

---

100   *Ibid.*, 402.
101   Anton Chekhov's letter to Aleksei Pleshcheev of 04.10.1888. See Karlinsky, *Anton Chekhov's Life and Thought*, 109.
102   When comparing this with Chekhov's own sentiments from the letter to Ivan Orlov of 22.02.1899 ("I have faith in individuals, I see salvation in individuals...", see Karlinsky, *Anton Chekhov's Life and Thought*, 341), it becomes clear that it is the aesthetic cliché which repels him, rather than the semantics per se. This interplay of ethics and aesthetics will be discussed in more detail below.
103   Anton Chekhov, Letter to Suvorin of 03.12.1892, see Karlinsky, *Anton Chekhov's Life and Thought*, 245–246.
104   *Ibid.*

From Objective to Subjective

Thus, on the one hand, at the core of Chekhov's attitudes, as Evdokimova penetratingly observes, lies

> a new sensibility of the modern man undergoing a crisis of traditional religious worldview [...]. Chekhov's oeuvre as a whole reflects the agony of modernization as culture changes from sacred paradigms to a new secular humanism.[105]

However, on the other hand, Chekhov expresses the vision of a man who – although trapped in a shift from the absolute truths of the Bible to the age of faithlessness and relativism, to one's own conscience (now cut off from its religious roots) becoming the only moral guidance – had been himself raised on those very same sacred paradigms. Hence his nostalgia for the departing age of high ideals, as well as his distrust of their abuse.

Hence also the fact that Chekhov effectively accomplishes more than can be expected from a proponent of the new secular humanism: while embodying a departure from religious truths he still reflects the ethical foundations of the Bible, and the difference can be formulated as follows:

> A humanist philosopher strives to teach good, grounding his teaching on morality (which is alien to human nature). The Bible teaches good grounding its teaching on human egoism, for, unlike humanists, it does not ignore the true nature of man. However, in contrast to virtuoso fascists who ground their teaching on evil and preach evil, the Bible teaches good, while grounding its teaching on evil human nature.[106]

In other words, Chekhov's oeuvre in fact follows a Biblical pattern in its basic principle that, while based on the merciless recognition of selfish and low human nature rather than on high morality, it still teaches good.

By the same token, with an almost medical necessity 'to be cruel in order to be kind', Chekhov realised that man's first task is to recognise the truth – and ways of treatment have to be sought only after the diagnosis has been established. Thus, in response to Sazonova's aforementioned letter he wrote, crucially, "She stresses 'can' and 'should' because she's afraid to talk about what

---

[105] Svetlana Evdokimova, "Philosophy's Enemies: Chekhov and Shestov", 220.
[106] Fridrikh Gorenshtein, *Psalom*, Moscow: Eksmo-Press, 2001, 292.

does exist and must be taken into account. If she first states what exists, I'll be willing to listen to what can be and what should be".[107]

Chekhov, with his sobriety and honesty, recoils from the falsity of commonplaces, sensing the danger of moral rhetoric used as a shield to cover up hypocrisy and to remove personal responsibility. In other words, he feels the danger of the dawning age of moral relativism. At best his characters are wandering in the dark, hiding from actions behind words like the three sisters with their cries "To Moscow!"; at worst – they are merciless hypocrites, like the Countess from the story of the same name – oblivious to the suffering of others, and the road between the two extremes passes through intrinsically deceptive idealistic abstractions. Fazil Iskander's fable of two passengers at the railway station reflects the nucleus of Chekhov's implicit warning: faced with homeless children, these two passengers act in opposite ways. The first gives them, bit by bit, his entire loaf of bread. The second gives away a bit, but then decides to solve the problem in general, puts his loaf away and starts drafting a plan of future happiness of the whole mankind. "The first passenger is [...] superior to the second one theoretically too. [...] he understands that the tragedy of existence is insurmountable, it can only be attenuated. [...] People who [...] shake off the tragedy of existence, simultaneously shake off their duties with respect to others". Then, as was quoted above, "the multifaceted and complex character of duty with respect to concrete people is replaced by a unified and radiant duty with respect to an idea".[108] In "The House with the Mezzanine" – and this is one of the central Chekhovian themes – Misius gives away 'the bread' of her soul, while her sister, behind grandiose humanitarian projects, loses sight of individual life and the need for personal kindness in her immediate surroundings.

This motif of personal responsibility and true involvement (as the other side of the coin of absolute freedom, of man always having a choice – being left alone in a godless universe) is crucial for Chekhov, and unites him with Pushkin, as we started saying above.

Filling the Gap: The Tangibility of the Metaphysical

Indeed, the danger of a realistic method, as Mashevskii explains, essentially re-applying Plato's ideas to the modern literary context, is in stripping off from

---

107 Anton Chekhov, Letter to Suvorin of 03.12.1892, see Karlinsky, *Anton Chekhov's Life and Thought*, 246.
108 Fazil Iskander, *Rasskazy, povest', skazka, dialog, esse, stikhi*, 589–590.

under the writer's feet firm ethical foundations.[109] For Chekhov's and Shestov's generation, when both speculative philosophy and traditional religion were being questioned, this ideological vacuum was most profoundly felt. This disillusionment penetrated to the most important depths of existence, shaking human faith in the subjective, ideal world of the spiritual which until then was perceived as objective and moral values as absolute:

> under close scrutiny, neither modernity nor historical perspective testified to the triumphant power of moral laws. It followed that, if the world is regarded as a laboratory desk containing certain objects, then a presence of such things, so important for our spiritual being, as conscience, honour, faith, love, heroism or justice is not confirmed [...] in the same way as, say, the presence of a table or the chair on which I can sit. I can then get up, get distracted, go for a walk and upon my return discover it in the same place. The chair surely exists, its existence is automatic and independent of me. However, if we now try to 'catch' in the same way something pertaining to the domain of spirit – for instance, heroism – we will be struck by disappointment. Having discovered in our soul repentance, love or faith, we cannot go for a walk and find them, upon our return, as if situated in the same place, unchanged.[110]

The implication of the highly subjective (essentially irrational!) nature of human spirituality, of the 'relativity' of moral concepts, is precisely our personal responsibility and personal engagement: these spiritual entities "exist only insofar as I sustain them. I love only as long as I perform a spiritual effort of loving".[111] Thus

> directly or indirectly realism presupposes the world existing as an object independent of the subject which observes it. What is analysed exists as a thing in itself, as it were automatically reproducing itself in time. These are natural and social processes which develop according to their own laws, or, in Pushkin's words, 'low truths'.[112]

Shestov calls them universal necessity and, as already noted, fights them by rebellion, by beating his head against this brick wall – as an individual spiritual

---

109   See Aleksei Mashevskii, "Nas vozvyshaiushchii obman".
110   Ibid.
111   Ibid.
112   Ibid.

effort resulting in a leap into true faith, away from reason. Pushkin and Chekhov choose a different path – by opting for an individual spiritual effort of personal responsibility able to transcend these "low truths".[113] This is because "conscience, good, heroism are concepts which acquire meaning only in the human (and not merely human, but personal) dimension".[114] And therefore

> they exist only as long as there is a subject which sustains and reproduces them. From the point of view of a natural or social process, heroism is only a 'sublime delusion'. But it is no coincidence that Pushkin stresses the words 'to me it is more precious' ('to me' rather than 'to us', although this phrase is often quoted in this latter form). 'To me' – because honesty, say, exists in this world not generally, not embodied by someone else, but only if I (precisely I) myself behave honestly.[115]

The above acceptance of the individual nature of moral reality is typically Chekhovian and was hard to accept by his contemporaries who simply accused him of having no ideals and moral norms.[116] By the same token, Mashevskii's conclusion thus is that

---

113 The difference is that Pushkin focuses mainly on the positive examples – as in his poem "Geroi", while Chekhov – on the negative, showing how without a required individual effort the "low truth" cannot be overcome, as in his "Mournful Story" where the old professor fails to rescue Katia precisely because he does not invest sufficient inner effort in his love for her: "My hero – and this is one of his principal character traits – is too careless with respect to the inner life of people around him: when they cry, make mistakes, deceive, he happily talks about theatre and literature. Had he been of a different type, Liza and Katia might not have perished" (from Chekhov's letter to A.N. Pleshcheev of 30.09.1889).

114 Aleksei Mashevskii, "Nas vozvyshaiushchii obman".

115 *Ibid.*

116 What they failed to see is that, while demonstrating the conditional and narrow-minded character of our judgements, Chekhov never oversteps the boundary that separates the conditional from the immutable and unconditional – as Albov sensed in the mature Chekhov. In response to Leontiev's (Shcheglov's) accusation of moral transgressions, Chekhov wrote (in a letter to him of 22.03.1890), "there is no such thing as low, high or medium morality; there is only one, the one which in days of old gave us Jesus Christ and which now prevents you, me and Barantsevich from stealing, calling names, lying, etc. As for me, if I can trust my clear conscience, never in my life have I ever in word, deed or thought, in my stories or farces coveted my neighbor's wife, nor his manservant, nor his ox, nor any of his cattle, nor have I ever stolen, or played the hypocrite, or flattered the strong, or sought any advantage from them, or engaged in blackmail, or lived at another's expense" (see Karlinsky, *Anton Chekhov's Life and Thought*, 163). Yet, the clash between objective and subjective, and testing the meaning and an interpretation of moral norms

the meaning of Pushkin's phrase is not that man will always prefer sweet delusion to bitter truth, but that a spiritual truth does not exist by itself – it is born only through my uplifting effort inside a deception of a certain kind. It is a deception from the point of view of a stranger, of an observer, who, in order to acquire faith in heroism and love, demands first a proof of their existence from others and only then turns towards his own self. No, this is not the way forward, it will lead nowhere. The only reliable method to prove the existence of good in this world is to start immediately creating it yourself.[117]

This is precisely what Chekhov accomplishes: he tests the commonly accepted, but largely discredited ideals and demonstrates that they are indeed vacuous by themselves – as long as we do not invest them with our personal spiritual effort. Otherwise they will be no more than lies, deception – "for love without good deeds is dead".[118] In other words, the main nerve of Chekhov's writings lies in the dynamic interplay between the 'objective' meaning of the eternal concepts as absolute values and the 'subjective' individual filling we invest them with. As this dynamic is based on the profound psychic intricacy of human nature, par excellence much broader than reason alone, what we have as a result can be expressed by Stepanov's words of Chekhov's fictional world where the writer strives "to commentate on as broad a range of material as possible, not so much a rational *Weltanschauung*, as an irrational sensibility".[119]

In this sense one can draw a parallel between Chekhov's sensibility that focuses on the danger of moral values regenerating into hollow abstractions and Shestov's "existential ethics of life, his critique of ethical rationalism that kills the living wholeness of our moral being".[120] By the same token, and with stronger force, Chekhov's view is resonant with Bakhtin's intention "to develop a moral philosophy which would fix directly the original reality of action as a

---

in concrete circumstances, which Chekhov's oeuvre displays, were taken as a sign of immorality.

117 Aleksei Mashevskii, "Nas vozvyshaiushchii obman".
118 This is part of the sentence "she won't be surprised by love, for love without good deeds is dead" from Chekhov's letter to his brother Aleksandr of 20.02.1883, where Chekhov encourages him to help their sister Maria by true involvement rather than by words alone. In his fiction Chekhov never permitted such direct statements – and here too it is covered up by a tinge of irony concealed in a deliberately old-fashioned linguistic discourse, paraphrasing the famous Biblical saying "faith is dead without deeds" – to muffle the didacticism.
119 Andrei Stepanov, "Shestov i Chekhov", 173.
120 A. Guseinov, *Istoriia eticheskikh uchenii*, Moscow: Gardariki, 2003, 863.

holistic form of our moral being", his "challenge to ethics as a fetish form of monological consciousness in conjunction with his attempts to replace it with a truly dialogical philosophy of action".[121]

More generally, although Chekhov strives to be merely documenting life, without passing judgements, without showing his authorial face, it is clear that this task is hardly accomplishable because of the inseparability of ethics and aesthetics. Brodsky in his Nobel lecture stresses the highly personal nature of our aesthetic choice; but this is equally true about our ethical choice – and precisely because the latter is concealed in the former. In other words, aesthetics will not tolerate the betrayal of ethics.[122] Or, putting it differently, "the truth of poetry is higher than the truth of history"[123] – which squares also with the above interpretation of the interplay between "sublime delusion" and "low truths". This means that in fact it is impossible for a writer to be an impartial reporter, because in his very choice of material and in his very style his whole outlook is concealed. He may attempt to hide and camouflage it, but he cannot exterminate it – precisely because our sensibility, our ethical choice is rooted in our aesthetic choice, and shining through it. And Chekhov who flees from any aesthetic cliché must be doing it with a clear feeling that behind it there is an ethical cliché, i.e. aesthetic falsity is intrinsically connected to ethical falsity, and it is precisely for this reason that the language of enchantment and hypnosis is dangerous. That is why Chekhov feels 'suffocated' by lofty words: "How all of you in Petersburg enjoy being stifled! Aren't you stifled by expressions like solidarity, the unity of young writers, a community of interests and so on?"[124] In this sense Chekhov – just like the irrationalist Hamann, as we shall see below – understands the inseparability of form and content in language. Shestov too is very susceptible to ideological (ethical) falsity, finding it behind lofty rhetoric[125] and demonstrating, just as Chekhov does, the degenerated character of abstract concepts of good – the common truths of 'allness'.

---

121   *Ibid.*
122   Indeed, even Brodsky, having stated in his Nobel Lecture that "aesthetics is the mother of ethics", then gives a further qualification, saying that it is not so much that a virtue guarantees a masterpiece as that evil is a bad stylist. That is to say that a highly ethical choice does not necessarily imply the appropriate aesthetic solution, but an unethical one will surely be impossible to mould into a beautiful aesthetic framing. The form will not be deceived by the content.
123   Fridrikh Gorenshtein, *Psalom*, 368.
124   Anton Chekhov, from the letter of 03.05.1888 to Leontiev (Shcheglov); see Karlinsky, *Anton Chekhov's Life and Thought*, 99.
125   See for example Shestov's disambiguation of the epilogue to "War and Peace", or his interpretation of Levin in Anna Karenina (in "Dostoevsky and Nietzsche: The Philosophy of Tragedy").

But their conclusions differ. For Shestov it is human reason that lulls us to sleep, separating us from the truth, inventing false consolations. For Chekhov reason is a necessary and highly valuable instrument of cognition, albeit not omnipotent. However, outside it we lose our orientation much more than we can within it. Importantly, reason cannot exterminate other faculties, it is not destructive in itself – it is only destructive when it is misused, which would testify to its insufficiency in a given individual. That is why Chekhov wrote to Suvorin: "If you tell me that X has taken to writing nonsense because his intelligence overpowered his talent or vice versa, then I would say that this means X had neither intelligence nor talent".[126] It is our cowardice, our spiritual laziness and apathy which manipulate our reason into inventing false, meaningless justifications (slogans), thus turning language into a mesmerising weapon. "For a lazy brain it is better to deny than to affirm", "where degeneration and apathy reign, [...] there is a decline of arts, indifference towards science and *injustice* to its full extent".[127] In not laying the blame for human misery on reason, Chekhov displays more intelligence than both Shestov and Hamann. Moreover, as mentioned, Chekhov accepts evil as an inevitable part of human nature, and hence of existence, and is thus not preoccupied by the question of theodicy, which for Shestov as well as for Dostoevskii, Tolstoi and the majority of the classical Russian writers by contrast remains at the forefront. Instead Chekhov understands that suffering and tragedy can only be mitigated, but cannot be removed. Shestov, on the contrary, hopes to remove them through an act of faith, whereby the omnipotent God can reverse the course of history and, presumably, return mankind to the Garden of Eden, to the state of happiness that preceded the Fall. Moreover, what for Shestov is a source of unceasing torment, of deepest suffering – the immutable indifference of nature towards humanity, of dead matter towards the live, can be for Chekhov's characters a source of inspiration:

> the monotonous hollow roar of the sea came up to them, speaking of peace, of the eternal sleep lying in wait for us all. The sea had roared like this long before there was any Yalta or Oreanda, it was roaring now, and it would go on roaring, just as indifferently and hollowly, when we had passed away. And it may be that in this continuity, this utter indifference to the life and death of each of us lies hidden the pledge of our eternal

---

[126] From Chekhov's letter to Suvorin, 25.11.1892; see Karlinsky, *Anton Chekhov's Life and Thought*, 244.

[127] From Chekhov's letter to Suvorin, 27.12.1889. See *PSSP v 30 tomakh*, vol. 3, 1976, 308–309.

salvation, of the continuous movement of life on earth, of the continuous movement toward perfection.[128]

Shying away from direct statements, almost distrusting a verbal way of expression per se – due to the social function of language: precisely because words are vulnerable to abuse and can so easily change their nature – Chekhov, like Antoine de Saint-Exupéry, believes in what cannot be seen by the eye, but can be sensed by the heart alone – in the truth concealed beneath appearances. His universe is irrational if only because it is atmospheric rather than logocentric. It is a 'feminine' type of literary reality where what matters is 'how' rather than 'what' (or rather – where 'what' is inseparable from 'how'), where 'irrational' subtext is superior to 'rational' text and constantly subverts it. Those who proclaim the ideas of humanism and perform acts of public good are often cruel to the people around them, as Lida Volchaninova is towards her younger sister Misius' in 'The House with the Mezzanine'; Ivan Ivanovich, who tells a highly moralistic story (in 'Gooseberry'), is careless with respect to his listeners by disturbing them with the heavy smoke of his pipe which keeps Burkin uneasily awake. A short line from Chekhov's diaries can be used as the poetic epitome to these subversions where a crucial detail undermines the grandeur of the whole: "In the editorial office of *Russkaia mysl'* there are bedbugs in the sofa".[129]

Presenting a multiplicity of personal truths in his fiction, their clashes and struggles, Chekhov himself remains elusive, but not invisible. Convinced that a good writer must "throw himself overboard all the time, avoid imposing himself as the main hero of his novel, forget himself for at least half an hour" and that it is "better to understate than to overdraw",[130] Chekhov at the same time creates his fiction in the hope that "the reader and the spectator would be attentive and not need a sign saying, 'This is a plum, not a pumpkin'".[131] As Simon Karlinsky writes, Chekhov "preferred his literary work to speak for itself" and stated his views and intentions in his oeuvre "precisely and clearly".[132] Even more telling are Chekhov's notebooks and correspondence. Strikingly,

---

128   Anton Chekhov, "The Lady with the Dog" (1899), translated by Ivy Litvinov, see http://www.ibiblio.org/eldritch/ac/lapdog.html (consulted 12.05.2012).
129   Anton Chekhov, Dnevnikovye zapisi in Chekhov A.P., *PSSP v 30 tomakh*, vol. 17, 1980, 226.
130   Anton Chekhov, Letter to Aleksandr Chekhov, February 1883. *PSSP v 30 tomakh*, vol. 13, 46–52.
131   Anton Chekhov, Letter to Suvorin, 30 December 1888, see Karlinsky, *Anton Chekhov's Life and Thought*, 81.
132   Simon Karlinsky, *Anton Chekhov's Life and Thought*, 10.

independence of mind leads to optimism: "If you want to become an optimist and to understand life, then stop believing in what others say and write, but instead watch and think for yourself".[133] Private space is sacred and its meaning impenetrable to others; it needs to be concealed rather than shared:

> It is your nest, your place of comfort, your woe and your joy, your poetry, and you are running around with this poetry as if with a stolen watermelon, you look at everything suspiciously (say, what does he think about it?) [...] You are interested in how I think, or Nikolai, or the father?! Why on earth should it bother you? They will not understand you [...] no matter how close they stand to you and anyway there's no point in understanding you. Live, and that's it.[134]

Rebellion, to be meaningful, has to be non-ingratiating: "You know that you are right, well then, stand by it [...] in an (uningratiating) sort of protest, that's the whole point of life, friend".[135] And freedom has a high price: "Man has to be prepared for anything and ought to carry on his duty as well as he can and nothing else...".[136] "You seem to be the first man I have ever seen who is free and worships nothing", wrote Maksim Gorkii to Chekhov in 1899.[137]

Indeed, for Chekhov, despite the external pressures of the world (or rather within the obvious constraints), the ultimate choice is still ours, as is the responsibility. It is, if you like, a literary tradition continued by Iuri Dombrovskii and Fazil Iskander, with the supremacy of personal dignity, where, against the most brutal predicaments, "a human being is ultimately free and not doomed by anything".[138] This, in my view, is how Chekhov "fills the gap" designated by Camus. The metaphysical which distinguishes us from the animal world is as tangible as physical matter: "He knew nothing of pain, had no conception of it, so he was not to blame, but his conscience, as inexorable and as rough as

---

133 Anton Chekhov, Dnevnikovye zapisi in Chekhov A.P., *PSSP v 30 tomakh*, Vol. 17, op. cit., 169.
134 Anton Chekhov, Letter to Aleksandr Chekhov, February of 1883. See http://az.lib.ru/c/chehow_aleksandr_pawlowich/text_0050.shtml (consulted 21.05.2012).
135 *Ibid.*
136 Anton Chekhov, Letter to Maria Chekhova of 13.11.1898, *PSSP v 30 tomakh*, vol. 25, 1974–1983.
137 Gorkii's letter to Chekhov of 22–23.04.1899, in *Polnoe sobranie sochinenii v 30 tomakh*, Moscow: Khudozhestvennaia literatura, 1949–1956, vol. 28, 73–74.
138 This is a formula derived by Dombrovskii from the works of William Shakespeare. See Iurii Dombrovskii, "Italiantsam o Shekspire – glavnye problemy ego zhizni", in *Roman. Pis'ma. Esse*, Ekaterinburg: U-Factoriia, 2000, 658.

Nikita, made him turn cold from the crown of his head to his heels";[139] the human soul and body are one, for "psychic phenomena are so strikingly similar to physical ones that it is almost impossible to figure out where the former start and the latter end"; and "There's no lack of faith. Everyone believes in something...".[140]

History itself is equally tangible and meaningful – as long as we, as individuals, invest it with our personal involvement, our own spiritual effort:

> The student thought again that if Vasilisa had shed tears, and her daughter had been troubled, it was evident that what he had just been telling them about, which had happened nineteen centuries ago, had a relation to the present – to both women, to the desolate village, to himself, to all people. The old woman had wept, not because he could tell the story touchingly, but because Peter was near to her, because her whole being was interested in what was passing in Peter's soul. And joy suddenly stirred in his soul, and he even stopped for a minute to take breath. 'The past', he thought, 'is linked with the present by an unbroken chain of events flowing one out of another'. And it seemed to him that he had just seen both ends of that chain; that when he touched one end the other quivered.[141]

Equally tangible and meaningful is nature: if for Shestov existence when it is "torn away by reason from its Creator" turns into a tragic nightmare,[142] and for Hamann the rationalistic approach dissects and destroys life, its spontaneity and joy, then for Chekhov's Gurov (and such a stance is sustained consistently throughout Chekhov's oeuvre) – who feels "soothed and enchanted by the sight of all this magical beauty – sea, mountains, clouds and the vast expanse of the sky" – "everything in the world is beautiful really, everything but our own thoughts and actions, when we lose sight of the higher aims of life, and of our dignity as human beings".[143]

---

139   Anton Chekhov, 'Ward No 6', see http://www.americanliterature.com/Chekhov/SS/WardNo6.html (consulted 11.04.2012).

140   Anton Chekhov's letter to Suvorin of 07.05.1889, see Karlinsky, *Anton Chekhov's Life and Thought*, 144.

141   Anton Chekhov, "The Student" (1894), translated by Constance Garnett, see http://www.ibiblio.org/eldritch/ac/student.html (consulted 17.06.2012).

142   This is, in nuce, how Shestov interprets (and shares) Dostoevskii's worldview. See Lev Shestov, "O 'pererozhdenii ubezhdenii' u Dostoevskogo", in *Umozrenie i otkrovenie*, Paris: YMCA, 1964, 171–196 (194).

143   Anton Chekhov, "The Lady with the Dog".

Life as Communication. Language as a Source of Irrationalism[144]

Chekhov's subtle ability to uncover the irrational within the rational and vice versa brings the radical irrationalism of Hamann and Shestov into sharp relief. However, if we apply a Bakhtinian perspective this configuration will change – Hamann and Chekhov will become surprisingly aligned, forcing Shestov into the margins.

The catalyst for this stratification of views is the problem of communication and, by extension, of understanding – another significant source of irrationalism. Generally speaking, perception of life as communication – of an individual with another individual, with God, with nature, with the material world is inherent in many philosophical systems and often highlights their irrationalist features. For Chekhov the problem of communication is a principal problem of existence and the semantic core of his works. More precisely, the impossibility of effective dialogue, the doomed character of human interaction when the protagonists simply do not hear one another is characteristic for Chekhov's artistic universe, where "a description of human psychology is not accomplished individually, by the example of separate characters, but collectively, through portrayal of the relationship between people".[145]

Closely connected to the problem of communication is language. Interestingly, it is precisely in the domain of language that Hamann had some revolutionary insights which turn out to be closely related to Chekhov's perception of life. These insights are summarised thus by Isaiah Berlin:

> Every language is a way of life, and a way of life is based on a pattern of experience which cannot itself be subjected to criticism, since one cannot find an Archimedean point outside it from which to conduct such a critical examination.[146]

This Hamannian premise is linked to Chekhov's stance via the bridge provided by the ideas of Bakhtin. Namely, according to Bakhtin, to get to know your own self adequately is possible only through a dialogue with the Other, i. e. from outside. Indeed, Bakhtin conducts "a major revision of the Kantian

---

144   This section in a modified form was presented in Russian at the international conference "Philosophy of the Soviet era" (the Academy of European intellectual history, Bernkastel-Kues, Germany, November 2011).

145   Douglas Clayton. "'Zhenshchina kak ptitsa i loshad': k fenomenologii chelovecheskikh otnoshenii v hudozhestvennom mire Chekhova" in *Filosofiia A.P. Chekhova*, ed. Anatolii Sobennikov, 75–85 (75–76) (highlighting is mine, O.T.).

146   Isaiah Berlin, *The Magus of the North*, 130.

presumption" according to which "knowledge, being limited to personal experience, can never adequately penetrate another's soul – and thus information can be gathered only 'from the inside out', that is, by self-observation".[147] Bakhtin insists, by contrast to Kant, that "it is precisely our own selves that we cannot know, since the human psyche is specifically set up to work from the outside in, that is, to know others".[148]

For Chekhov the situation is almost identical, because in his world, as Andrew Durkin observes, "only the experience of feeling has true validity, especially empathy, and in order to understand your own self it is necessary *first* to understand others, their joy and their grief".[149]

According to Hamann, in order to understand a foreign language as another way of life and pattern of experience

> at most, all one can do is to examine the symbolism by which the pattern of experience is expressed. This is because to think is to use symbols, and as the symbols so thought. Above all, content and form cannot be divorced – there is an 'organic' connection between all the elements of a medium of communication, and the meaning lies in the individual, ultimately unanalysable whole.[150]

From this Hamann concluded the impossibility of an adequate translation between languages, since form and content are inseparable, and foreign language is a different pattern of experience and way of thinking. As a corollary, Hamann believed,

> one cannot truly understand what men are saying by merely applying grammatical or logical or any other kind of rules, but only by an act of 'entering into' – what Hereder called 'Einfühlung' – their symbolism, and for that reason only by the preservation of actual usage, past and present.[151]

---

147 See Caryl Emerson, "M.M. Bakhtin as philosopher", in *Russian Thought After Communism. The Recovery of a Philosophical Heritage*, ed. James P. Scanlan, New York-London: M.E. Sharpe, 1994, 206–226 (218). Emerson here quotes Natalia Bonetskaia's article "M.M. Bakhtin and traditions of Russian philosophy" published in *Voprosy filosofii*, 1 (1993), 83–93.
148 *Ibid.*
149 Andrew Durkin, "Modeli khudozhestvennogo slova v chekhovskikh rasskazakh 'V ssylke' i 'Student'" in *Filosofiia A.P. Chekhova*, ed. Anatolii Sobennikov, 44–59 (52) (highlighting is mine, O.T.).
150 Isaiah Berlin, *The Magus of the North*, 130.
151 See Isaiah Berlin, *The Magus of the North*, 130.

From this perspective, Hamann's irrational ideas of language turn out to be highly relevant to Chekhov's artistic world, and the link can be found in Bakhtin's theories as well as in the ideas of Martin Buber. Indeed, Hamann perceived language above all as a *Weltanschauung* which, in order to be understood, has to be 'entered into' and cognised through continuous use only. For him, since any thought or speech is communication, it has to be a communication between concrete individuals. Similarly for Bakhtin, language represents a continuous living interaction, "it is a living word exchanged between existing people, and can only be properly understood in the full range and richness of the moral and social meanings contained in discourse".[152] Moreover, Bakhtin's concept of *'vnenakhodimost'* (outsideness) in a sense generalises and extends Hamann's ideas. What Hamann in fact propagates is reminiscent of Stanislavsky's system of 'transfiguration into the Other', whereby the way to understand the Other is to 'become' him/her, to 'enter' his/her inner world. Bakhtin, on the other hand, stresses that the stance of *'vnenakhodimost'* implies for the subject the possibility not only to identify himself/herself with the Other (a possibility of *perevoploshchenie*, of 'entering into' the Other's psyche), but also to return subsequently to him/her-self, to his/her own position and system of relations with the world.[153] The result of such 'empathising' and 'disembodiment', of such understanding of the Other is a 'compassionate thinking', caring-attentive attitude to the Other, without naming your own self. It is selfless and impartial. It is the only way to see another person as the Other. Its opposite is passionate attachment, where at the forefront there is our own egotistic 'I' rather than the Other.[154]

These constructions are apparently related to Martin Buber's classification of relationships 'I-You' and 'I-It', where the former is a loving dialogue and living interpersonal communication, while the latter is an everyday utilitarian interaction, which is linked to Aristotlean logic. It is the relationship 'I-You' which corresponds to effective dialogue in the Bakhtinian sense and achieves understanding between people. According to Buber, a human being cannot be forever in the state of an 'I-You' relationship, but it is also inhuman to be permanently in the state 'I-It'. Andrei Platonov's story 'Return' ('Vozvrashchenie')

---

152   Joseph Frank, "The Voices of Mikhail Bakhtin", in *Through the Russian Prism*, Princeton: Princeton University Press, 1990, 25.

153   See Gennadii Diakonov, "Dialogiinaia kontseptsiia estetiki i literaturovedeniia M.M. Bakhtina" (see http://hpsy.ru/public/x3070.htm, consulted 13.04.2012). The (Ukrainian) original is published in *Sotsialna psykhologiia*, 6 (20), 2006, 35–46.

154   See Mikhail Bakhtin, *Literaturno-kriticheskie statii*, Moscow: Khudozhestvennaia literature, 1986, 54.

illustrates a break away from the egotistic 'I-It' to the loving 'I-You' with piercing power and artistic truth:

> Ivan closed his eyes, not wanting to see and feel the pain of the exhausted children now lying on the ground, and then felt a kind of heat in his chest, as if the heart imprisoned and pining within him had been beating long and in vain all his life and had only now beaten its way to freedom, filling his entire being with warmth and awe. He suddenly realised everything he had ever known before, but much more precisely and more truthfully. Previously, he had sensed the life of others through a barrier of pride and self-interest, but now, all of a sudden, he had touched another life with his naked heart.[155]

Rainer Grübel in his chapter in the current collection, when commenting on Chekhov's irrationalism – which in the eyes of Gorkii "destroyed the rationalism of realistic narration" – emphasises the need Chekhov felt for creating a new narrative technique, "no longer based on the model of an omniscient narrator".[156] It is quite possible that what Chekhov offered instead corresponds precisely to the Bakhtinian concept of *vnenakhodimost'*. Indeed, given Chekhov's elusiveness, this concept, it seems, adequately characterises his authorial stance – a deliberately impartial position of an observer and storyteller, who is at the same time able to understand every character, to 'feel' him/her, and yet to preserve his own authorial, detached vantage point. Bakhtin's *vnenakhodimost'* means precisely such an "aesthetic stance which allows to see and to create a holistic image of a character without introducing authorial subjectivity".[157] In this connection, Gennadii Diakonov comments:

> The more fully and profoundly the author tends to express his own self in his artistic work, the closer the position he has to take in relation to himself is to the concept of *vnenakhodimost'*, or, in other words, the more he has to 'dis-identify' with his own self, i.e. to decentre, distance and alienate himself from his own self. On the other hand, the more the author is fixated on expressing his own self, the less his work will correspond to the criteria of aesthetic artistry, moral value and ontological depth.[158]

---

155   Andrei Platonov, "The Return", in *The Return and other Stories*, transl. by R. Chandler, E. Chandler and A. Livingstone, London: Harvill Press, 1999, 203.
156   See Rainer Grübel's chapter in the present volume for detailed references.
157   Gennadii Diakonov, "Dialogiinaia kontseptsiia estetiki i literaturovedeniia M.M. Bakhtina".
158   *Ibid.*

Chekhov knew these truths extremely well, as can be seen from the literary advice he gave to others,[159] and from the state of disorientation in which he leaves the reader by a very intricate self-withdrawal – so that a century after his death critics are still arguing as to what his authorial stance actually was.

However, with respect to the positions of Chekhov's heroes as opposed to his own authorial stance, the situation is more complex. As a rule Chekhov depicts human lack of understanding, broken communications, inadequate interactions, ineffective dialogue. As Andrew Durkin has persuasively argued, analysing Chekhov's stories "In Exile" and "The Student", two opposite conceptions of the artistic word as well as their underlying philosophies prove equally inadequate: on the one hand, an authoritarian, monological proof, intolerant to objections, which does not give freedom either to the narrator or his listeners, and, on the other hand, emotive lyrics which does not find an effective way for establishing contact. The first conception is usually connected in Chekhov's world with defenders of a stoic outlook who like to quote Marcus Aurelius and for whom "a pain is a vivid idea of pain": "make an effort of will to change that idea, dismiss it, cease to complain, and the pain will disappear".[160] This 'stoicism', which could be labelled 'cold blood', as a rule, serves as a shield for a 'cemetery-like' philosophy that justifies inactivity and indifference. In fact, as Skaftymov aptly observes, it corrupts Marcus Aurelius's teaching which is much more selfless, directed outward and thus hostile to apathy[161] (tracing this kind of corruption is, of course, an usual Chekhovian theme). Such 'stoics' are Doctor Ragin from 'Ward No 6', and Semen from the story 'In exile'. Opposed to them are the 'hot blooded lyricists', who are passionate and alive, who are rebels agitating against indifference, for a stance of active involvement:

> Comprehension... – repeated Ivan Dmitritch frowning. – External, internal. ...Excuse me, but I don't understand it. I only know, – he said, getting up and looking angrily at the doctor – I only know that God has created me of warm blood and nerves, yes, indeed! If organic tissue is capable of life it must react to every stimulus. And I do! To pain I respond with tears

---

159 Recall, for instance, the lines given above from Chekhov's letter to his brother Aleksandr (footnote 130). In the same vein, see Chekhov's famous words from the letter to Lidiia Avilova of 19.03.1892: "when you depict the unfortunate and talentless, and wish to move the reader to pity, try to be colder – this, as it were, throws another's grief into relief. In your case, both your heroes cry and you sigh. Yes, be cold".

160 Anton Chekhov, "Ward No 6".

161 A.P. Skaftymov, *Nravstvennye iskaniia russkikh pisatelei. Statii i issledovaniia o russkikh klassikakh*, Moscow, 1972, 381–403.

and outcries, to baseness with indignation, to filth with loathing. To my mind, that is just what is called life. The lower the organism, the less sensitive it is, and the more feebly it reacts to stimulus; and the higher it is, the more responsively and vigorously it reacts to reality. How is it you don't know that? A doctor, and not know such trifles! To despise suffering, to be always contented, and to be surprised at nothing, one must reach this condition – and Ivan Dmitritch pointed to the peasant who was a mass of fat – or to harden oneself by suffering to such a point that one loses all sensibility to it – that is, in other words, to cease to live.[162]

As I argue elsewhere,[163] it is, paradoxically, the stance of 'cold blood' which is more irrational than the passionate 'hot blood', because of its more profound inner contradictions.

However, curiously, neither of these two routes leads to an effective dialogue, because both represent, even if with opposite signs, an existential and aesthetic stance directed above all inwards, at one's own self, unable to break out of the boundaries of one's 'I' and to establish proper contact with the Other, to hear the Other. Indeed, a monological stance strives to the Other via one's own 'I', from within it, and ends up imposing one's own authoritarian model; on the other hand – and this is less obvious – passion is equally ineffective, because it is opposite to Bakhtin's *vnenakhodimost'*, i.e. a caring-attentive attitude to the Other, without naming yourself, and thus instead of the Other it brings to the forefront one's own egotistic 'I'.

Hence the question: Is Bakhtin's *vnenakhodimost'* possible for Chekhov's heroes – that is, is warm impartiality – that very point of equilibrium – possible, or does it inevitably grow either into passion fixated on its own self or into 'stoic' indifference?

The answer is in fact positive, as Chekhov's stories 'The Student' and 'The Lady with the Dog' demonstrate. Adequate communication and true understanding are not illusory, they are possible in principle, although they happen very seldom in Chekhov's artistic world.[164] In 'The Lady with the Dog' it is

---

162 Anton Chekhov, "Ward No 6".
163 See Olga Tabachnikova, "Cases of Subversion: Chekhov and Brodsky: (Under the Veneer of Rationalism, or On the Concepts of Hot and Cold Blood as Philosophical Categories)" in *Russian Irrationalism from Pushkin to Brodsky: Seven Essays in Literature and Thought*, London-New Delhi-New York-Sydney: Bloomsbury Academic, 2015, 161–189.
164 Recall Chekhov's words to his brother, quoted above: "They will not understand you [...], no matter how close they stand to you". Yet, Chekhov created literary examples (described in the sequel) which transcend these alleged boundaries.

precisely this 'compassionate thinking', this 'caring-attentive attitude' which can be traced with distinct clarity:

> He moved over and took her by the shoulders, intending to caress her, to make a joke, but suddenly he caught sight of himself in the looking-glass. His hair was already beginning to turn grey. It struck him as strange that he should have aged so much in the last few years, have lost so much of his looks. The shoulders on which his hands lay were warm and quivering. He felt a pity for this life, still so warm and exquisite, but probably soon to fade and droop like his own.[165]

In the story 'The Student' the mechanism of attaining authentic contact between people is different – mutual understanding is achieved there on the basis of a common myth inscribed in a contemporary context: "through a mythical dimension of art the student achieves unity with his two listeners and creates a union in the same way as a narrator achieves unity with a reader using his narration (in particular, nested narration)".[166] Thus,

> the narration by Velikopolskii (a student of a clerical academy) is neither preaching moralism, nor symbolic lyricism; to a large extent it compensates the shortcomings of both. [...] Merging of the immutable with the transient frees Velikopolskii's narration from a pseudo-authorial tone, on the one hand, and from the purely subjective, on the other.[167]

This is yet another illustration of Chekhov's ability to portray the relativity of truths and viewpoints, or, more precisely, of their dependency on a given context.

Another implication of these considerations based on Chekhov's texts is the relevance of the concept of translation and Hamann's views on it. In essence, the student translates a famous mythical text into contemporary language, into the terminology of his own life and that of his listeners, thus simultaneously entering into the evangelical text and subjectivising it, returning to the everyday. In other words, he is actualising Bakhtin's concept of *vnenakhodimost'*.[168]

---

165   Anton Chekhov, "The Lady with the Dog".
166   Andrew Durkin, 'Modeli khudozhestvennogo slova v chekhovskikh rasskazakh 'V ssylke' i 'Student'', 56.
167   *Ibid.*
168   This also shows how much translation is a dialogical process, a creative act based on one's attempts to understand both one's own self and the Other. It is thus not surprising that in

At the psychological-religious level Bakhtin's *vnenakhodimost'*, is closest, perhaps, to Russian Orthodox humility, capable of compassion, of warm participation, which is selfless for the sake of the Other, but without losing one's own dignity. In Bakhtin's eyes, Christ accomplished a unique synthesis – by deepening individual self-consciousness, and simultaneously having supplied it with an infinitely kind attitude to the Other.[169] Such humility presupposes trust towards God and acceptance of the world He created. Chekhov's oeuvre reflects such humility in a multifaceted way – as an intrinsic attribute of Russian religiosity and as an existential feature. Moreover, Chekhov himself exercised such humility in his own life.[170] At the same time, Chekhov's own

the recent years Bakhtin's theory of dialogue is being successfully integrated into the theory of interpretative translation (see, for example, http://samlib.ru/w/wagapow_a_s/bodrova-gozhenmos.shtml, consulted 16.07.2013). Indeed, from a modern perspective Hamann's conviction of the impossibility of a perfect translation of texts seems obvious, due to profound cultural differences. However, Hamann overlooks a creative aspect of translation, connected not only with a transfiguration into the Other's sensibility and outlook, but also with transplanting these into one's own soil, i.e. with creative appropriation. From this point of view it is clear that, figuratively speaking, when God mixed languages at Babylon, He not only indemnified Himself, having moved away to Eternity, but also gave to humanity a powerful creative potential connected to the cross-fertilisation of cultures. Indeed, everything in the world is, in essence, just a translation from one language into another – and this is exemplified best by science, where a theory from one branch of knowledge expressed in terms of a neighbouring discipline reveals new meanings. This is because in a new system of coordinates the existing knowledge is seen under a different angle, is illuminated by a new light, exposing the hitherto concealed – and this facilitates a genuine semantic break through.

169   See Joseph Frank, "The Voices of Mikhail Bakhtin", 24. Further on this theme of humility and Christianity in Bakhtin's eyes, see: S.G. Bocharov (notes of the conversation with Bakhtin of 9 June 1970): "He spoke, and spoke seriously, of Christ depicted by Bulgakov – that this is Christ in the tradition of the spirituals, of the medieval mystics, followers of Ioakhim Florskii, who preached on the forthcoming era of the Holy Spirit and a new relationship between man and God, liberated from authoritarianism and submission. The theme of the spirituals was close to Bakhtin's heart, as he liked to repeat that truth and force are incompatible, that truth always exists in a humble image, while any power and triumph are fatal, and the very combination of words 'the triumph of the truth' is contradictio in adjecto. It is through this connection with the tradition of the spirituals that Bulgakov's Christ was interesting to him" (S.G. Bocharov, "Ob odnom razgovore i vokrug nego", *NLO*, 2 (1993), 72).

170   See, for instance, the incident of Chekhov's arrival in Yalta by sea when he stood up for a Tatar porter against his abuse by a brutal captain's assistant. This episode, described by Aleksandr Kuprin in "Pamiati Chekhova", exemplifies Chekhov's non-resistance to evil by force – or more precisely, his resistance to evil by spiritual rather than physical strength,

stoic stance co-existed with his striving to rejoice at life: "We are all to die sooner or later anyway, hence it is at any rate improvident to be despondent".[171]

What opposes such acceptance of God's world, is rebellion, Ivan Karamazov's will to 'return the ticket to the Creator' and Tsvetaeva's "To Your insane world my only response is refusal!", and, equally, Lev Shestov's struggle against Universal Necessity, his unwillingness to reconcile to the tragic reality (and it is no coincidence that he is regarded as a philosophical predecessor of the poet Tsvetaeva).[172] Indeed, constantly searching for the living omnipotent God, Shestov at the same time does not, in fact, accept the world created by this God – he rejects the necessity not only of natural or social laws, but even aesthetic necessity. Thus Shestov demands that God repairs the past, i.e. re-makes what He Himself created; equally, Shestov often imagines a writer as a substitute for a Demiurge, unrestrained in his liberty, and in particular unrestricted by the demands of artistic truth. In his struggle against Necessity for the sake of the completeness of Freedom Shestov essentially refutes the premise that freedom (in particular Divine freedom) is not unrestrained will. As Henri Poincare wrote in his treatise 'On science', "Mathematical truths [...] put up boundaries to the freedom of the Creator and allow Him to make a choice only between several, relatively non-numerous solutions. Then a few experiments will be enough to reveal to us which choice He had made".[173]

Thus, curiously, merging with Hamann almost literally with respect to many claims of irrationalism, Shestov drastically differs from the German thinker in his ideas of the human place in the world, human destiny and paths, precisely because Shestov's philosophical constructions are in essence monological. If Hamann, and following him Buber, and Chekhov, and Bakhtin are characterised by the perception of human life above all as communication, and thus the problem of understanding for them is central, and the idea of human interactions: communication, dialogue – is primary, then for Shestov it is tragedy which is primary, and genuine contact between people is impossible in principle. "Tragedies happen in the depth of the human soul where not a single eye can reach. That is why they are so horrendous, as crimes which happen

---

somewhat along the lines of Dostoevskii's Prince Myshkin (see Aleksandr Kuprin, "Pamiati Chekhova", in *Chekhov v vospominaniiakh sovremennikov*, eds. S.N. Golubeva et al., Moscow: Khudozhestvennaia literatura, 1960, 539–569).

171 Anton Chekhov, Letter to K.S. Barantsevich of 15.04.1890. See A.P. Chekhov, *PSSP*, vol. 4, 1975, 61.

172 See, for instance, Joseph Brodsky, "A Poet and Prose", in *Less Than One. Selected Essays*, Harmondsworth, Middlesex, England: Penguin Books, 1986, 188–189.

173 Henri Poincare, *O nauke* (*On science*), ed. by L.S. Pontriagin, Moscow: Nauka, 1983, 8 (highlighting is mine O.T.).

underground. A human voice cannot reach either in or out of there. It is torture in the dark...",[174] Shestov wrote already in his first book. In his philosophy, born out of despair, striving for a dialogue is absent, and, moreover, the condition of the search for the truth is a state of isolation and solitude. Thus philosophically justified for a human being is only "that fearful loneliness from which not even the most devoted and loving heart is able to deliver him".[175]

While declaring – in a rather Chekhovian way, it would seem – a multiplicity of truths and viewpoints, Shestov at the same time imposes on everybody the same existential paradigm, or, using Vladimir Papernyi's words, the same religious experience.[176] Man (in particular, the author) turns out to be hopelessly locked within his own self, and his only path is inwards (i.e. that very self-understanding that originates from within which Bakhtin rejects). Such a communication with his own self leads the author – in Shestov's literary-aesthetic system – either to self-denial (Dostoevskii) or to self-justification (Tolstoi), and basically means ultimate breakage of the author's contact with himself. Moreover, Shestov insists on the principle of inexpressibility, denying the possibility of the adequate transmission of human feelings and experience. For him it is beyond doubt that *"mysl izrechennaia est lozh"* ("a thought put into words is a lie").[177] The main message of Shestov's most peculiar book *Sola Fide (Tol'ko veroiu)* (his spiritual autobiography of sorts, published only posthumously, in 1966) – that truth is lost in transmission – implies in particular that neither human language, nor non-verbal communications can ensure adequate contact between people. "As a result", Viktor Erofeev observes, "rigidly limiting the extent of understanding between people, Shestov substantially devalues his own philosophical activity".[178] While Chekhov examines the faults and break-downs in human communications, Shestov denies the very possibility of human mutual understanding.

For Chekhov, as we saw, genuine interaction is possible, although any direct discourse, whether linguistic or non-verbal, is prone to falsification. The poetry

---

174 Lev Shestov, "Shekspir i ego kritik Brandes", in *Sochineniia v dvukh tomakh*, Tomsk: Vodolei, 1996, vol. 1, 30.

175 Shestov, "Dostoevsky and Nietzsche: The Philosophy of Tragedy": http://www.angelfire .com/nb/shestov/dtn/dn_11.html (consulted 07.05.2012).

176 See Vladimir Papernyi, "Lev Shestov: religioznaia filosofiia kak literaturnaia kritika i kak literature", *Toronto Slavic Quarterly*, 12 (2005), http://www.utoronto.ca/tsq/12/paperni12 .shtml (26.03.2012).

177 A famous line from Tiutchev's poem "Silentium!" (1830). See *F.I. Tiutchev, Polnoe sobranie stikhotvorenii*, Leningrad: Sovetskii pisatel, 1987, 105–106.

178 Viktor Erofeev, "'Ostaetsa odno: proizvol' (Filosofiia odinochestva i literaturno-esteticheskoe kredo L'va Shestova)", 181.

of the soul and the poetry of life, their volatile and subtle nature, can only be captured by the poetic spirit, by indirect expression. By the same token, true understanding originates first of all in the outward orientation of one's I – in one's sensitivity to the Other; it is dialogical *par excellence*.

At the same time, the dogmatism of Shestov's 'adogmatic' philosophy originates precisely in the monological, authoritarian nature of his discourse, when he hears in the Other only that which he strives to hear, i.e. puts his template over the Other's speech and thus extracts from it precisely those elements which confirm his own thoughts. As a result, the idea of fighting against the autonomy of reason and the enslaving power of ideologies turns itself into an ideology.

By contrast, for Chekhov no category is absolute, and no ideology is possible as a doctrine – which is directly resonant with Hamann's conclusion that

> while we cannot do without rules and principles, we must constantly distrust them and never be betrayed by them into rejecting or ignoring or riding rough-shod over the irregularities and peculiarities offered by concrete experience.[179]

Instructively, despite his monologism, Shestov nevertheless finds himself involved in a dialogue, because he "almost never formulates his ideas outside the ideas of others; instead he always builds his thought over the reconstruction of previous thinkers' achievements".[180] Yet, this dialogue bears the same monological features. Still, curiously, in spite of this tendency, Shestov has quite a number of meeting points with dialogical thinkers. Thus he, like Bakhtin, is involved with the carnivalesque – in that his treatment of thinkers is an attempt at unmasking them, at striving to penetrate the hidden, secret rift between pen and soul – between the writer's public persona and his naked and lost human soul – the rift which the writer's activity is basically designed to conceal. Chekhov's literary activity is akin to the same unmasking – when he strips his characters of every pretence forcing them to reveal their true faces, as if conducting an x-ray of their souls. At the same time the idea of 'unmasking' writers is alien to Chekhov, it violates his ethics, his respect for the work and privacy of others.

Notably, the problem of understanding, dialogical in its essence, is considered by Shestov more from the epistemological than ontological viewpoint: he

---

179 See Isaiah Berlin, *The Magus of the North*, 130.
180 Vladimir Papernyi, "Lev Shestov: religioznaia filosofiia kak literaturnaia kritika i kak literature".

is interested above all not in the possibility of effective human contact, but the possibilities and ways of cognition.

Here is Shestov's reaction to the complaint by his friend Adolf Lazarev that he does not understand Shestov's writings:

> One can understand Pythagoras's Theorem, Mendeleev's periodical system, Einstein's theory and even any philosophical construction. This is because the task in hand is in reducing the unknown to the known. However, [...] when the unknown wants to stand up for its independence and refuses to be captured by the known then the task changes. 'Understanding' becomes obsolete and to understand the unknown is then equivalent to losing it altogether. I believe that even indisputable scientific explanations ultimately do not lead us to understanding. It is agreed that we 'understand' water, when we say that it is a union of two gases taken in certain proportions. But is this in fact 'understanding'? Water remains as non-understood as it was. [...] A deaf person may perfectly well learn the theory of the sound waves, but he will still never know what sound is.[181]

Later in the letter Shestov explains that any substance that we attempt to include into the causal chain, is in fact trying to break away from that chain. Hence the conclusion: Lazarev's lack of understanding is due to his (wrongful, detrimental) striving to order Shestov's thought, to include it into the logical chain. This squares up with Shestov's motto taken from Pascal: "let people not blame us any more for our lack of clarity, since we practice this deliberately".[182] Despite his own "severe, unornamented style"[183] and the pungent force of his argument, clarity for Shestov, as we saw, represents first of all an Aristotlean rationalist logic and way of thinking – the deadening calm of scientific enquiry, as Shestov sees it. This calm is incompatible with the disturbing and mysterious reality in which we live. Hamann too professes obscurantism – likely for the same reason – as most suitable for reflecting the mystery of existence, its irrational and chaotic nature. Chekhov, of course, with his striving for brevity and clarity, is entirely the opposite in this respect. Yet, he was accused by the

---

[181] The letter (of 22.09.1927) is cited in Baranova-Shestova, *Zhizn' L'va Shestova*, vol. 1, 349–350.

[182] See, for instance, Lev Shestov, *Na vesakh Iova*, 287, where this quotation from Pascal's *Pensées* is given.

[183] Czeslaw Milosz, "Shestov, or the Purity of Despair", 110–111.

contemporary critics of breaking causal connections and exalting the random and accidental; by the same token, his clarity and brevity were in a sense excessive, so that many readers were lost as to the meaning behind them.[184] Nevertheless, all three, as we saw, approach the irrationality of existence from different directions.

Conclusions

We thus have three different patterns of European irrationalism, each offering its own philosophy. The anti-Enlightenment tradition uncompromisingly launched by Hamann enjoyed a great following within European culture. It strongly resonated in classical Russian literature which ultimately absorbed a good deal of this Western European rebellious anti-rationalist stance. Realisation of the intrinsic irrationality of the nature of man and the universe as a whole became an integral part of nineteenth-century Russian culture. Shestov, fed on Dostoevskii and reconsidering Nietzsche, came as a pinnacle, to an extent an exaggeration of Russian irrationalist stance, which has proved to be strikingly in demand to this day.

Shestov displays a profound continuity of Hamann's radical anti-rationalist position, but with qualifications brought about not only by a different cultural environment (or even by a different temperament), but largely by the change of eras – to Hamann's unquestioning faith and joyful feeling of universal unity and human indivisible wholeness, Shestov juxtaposes the tormenting search for that (by then disappearing) unquestioning faith as a way out from existential absurdity and alienation, from the tragic necessity which marked the modern 'age of faithlessness'.

Nevertheless, despite the somewhat sensual, almost hedonistic character of Hamann's ideas of man, as well as his emphasis on the communicative nature of existence and focus on the problem of language – in contrast to Shestov's orientation (bordering on solipsism) towards despair, solitude and tragedy – these two thinkers have more similarities than differences. Both are extremists, both passionately stand up for the private against the general, and reason for both means repression. Theory, science and ideology destroyed human wholeness and subjected man to the power of the abstractions which man himself

---

184   As Andrei Bitov aptly noted in connection to Chekhov's works, "even his idea is concealed in such a clear narration that it may easily escape you that it is indeed an idea, until you grow up sufficiently to be able to understand and appreciate it" (see Bitov, "Moi dedushka Chekhov i pradedushka Pushkin").

had created. True knowledge is possible only by means of revelation, for "God is a poet, not a geometer".

Chekhov decisively criticises such attacks against science which demonstrate a total unawareness of its nature. For him science is, like Caesar's wife, beyond reproach.[185] And yet, without opposing science and art, body and soul, and deeply respecting human reason and scientific method, Chekhov nevertheless never regards these as absolute and creates characters – especially in his plays – who are irrational, absurdist, who both talk and live irrationally, or, more precisely, where the rational and irrational are inseparably merged and mutually reversible.

Thus the irrationalist in Chekhov is hidden deeper, represented through multiple subversions of semantic layers which reflect the limitations of human ability for understanding the self and the world, the volatile character of moral judgement, and the overall shift from objective to subjective. This – subtler – type of irrationalism embraces reason, while acknowledging both its constraints and its inseparability from other ways of perception. Chekhov's 'poetic reason' in a sense continues the tradition of the 'suffering reason' of the ancient Slavs described by Chumakova in her chapter of this volume. It thus accepts the irrational underpinning of existence which Shestov calls the 'irrational remainder'. To the radical irrationalist reaction to the Enlightenment's dead-ends, as exemplified by Hamann's and Shestov's thought, Chekhov juxtaposes the quiet heroism of non-radicalism and a new type of individualism: not the tormented, self-obsessed individualism of a Romantic, but an exaltation of personal freedom and personal responsibility.

However, if Hamann lives within faith and Shestov in search for it, and their ultimate hope is based on God, then Chekhov is already in the vacuum of faithlessness, where man is alone and can only rely on his own self. Hence the feeling of tragedy is attenuated in Hamann and sensed much more acutely in Shestov and Chekhov. Still, all three are united by their insistence on the individual path to the truth which cannot be replicated, and the primacy of experience over theory.

The deeply individual and alienating nature of tragedy causes Shestov's refusal to recognise human unity – after the Fall, seduced by treacherous Reason, people turned into a hopelessly disjointed herd of mortals. By contrast, Hamann regards life as communication, and irrationalism as a way to restore the wholeness of man and his unity with himself, with others and with God. He rejoices in the fullness of life, where both soul and body are divine and not to be separated. Chekhov in effect adheres to the same vision, and views

---

185 See Chekhov's letter to Suvorin of 27.12.1889, *PSSP*, vol. 3, 308–309, where he states this idea.

Puritanism as hypocrisy. The aesthetic feeling which in the end underpins this type of attitude is largely absent in Shestov with his preference for the abstract beauty of ideas, and is more akin, perhaps, to Rozanov in the margins of Russian letters, and to D.H. Lawrence – in the margins of English ones. Yet Chekhov too is distinguished by a focus on the human inability for effective dialogue and on a fragile balance between the deceptive and redeeming nature of illusion. For him the search for individual truth, filling general concepts with personal meaning is an end in itself, which implies a search for dignity, a sudden sensation that "in his veins there is flowing at last real human blood and not any longer that of a slave".[186]

Shestov's ends are, as it were, more applied. If Chekhov, if you like, strives for beauty which will save the world because his aesthetic feeling is violated by ethical transgression, Shestov's Salvationism is, although abstract, still more practical. He disavows idealism in order to defeat Reason which, in his eyes, brought mankind to tragedy. Once humanity renounces reason it will be led to the truth of the Bible, it will return to the omnipotent living God and abandon suffering.

Arguably, it may also be aesthetic feeling which determines the (different) attitudes of all three to Nature. For Shestov this is always a hateful, unbearable, cruel indifference, the embodiment of universal necessity, of the general which defeats the private – thus he repeats after Dostoevskii with regard to Holbein's painting of the dead Christ:

> Nature appears to one, looking at this picture, as some huge, implacable, dumb monster; or still better – a stranger simile – some enormous mechanical engine of modern days which has seized and crushed and swallowed up a great and invaluable Being, a Being worth nature and all her laws, worth the whole earth, which was perhaps created merely for the sake of the advent of that Being. This blind, dumb, implacable, eternal, unreasoning force is well shown in the picture, and the absolute subordination of all men and things to it is so well expressed that the idea unconsciously arises in the mind of anyone who looks at it.[187]

For the believer Hamann nature is intrinsically linked to God's dialogue with the universe: "the world is God's language; [...] God thinks in trees [...], or rocks and seas".[188]

---

186 See Chekhov's letter to Suvorin of 7.01.1889, *PSSP*, vol. 3, 133.
187 F. Dostoevskii, *The Idiot*, transl. by Eva Martin (see http://www.planetpdf.com/planetpdf/pdfs/free_ebooks/The_Idiot_NT.pdf (12.04.2012)).
188 See Isaiah Berlin, *The Magus of the North*, 80.

In Chekhov's universe, nature comes forth as a multifaceted force – not just senseless and brutal, alienating and depressing, but also sacred and divine, beautiful and tender, or even itself worthy of compassion.[189] It is constancy, immutable and given, which, importantly, is always to be accepted just as life itself: with dignity, but without (pointless) rebellion. Although superior to human life in its power to absorb the latter easily, in its destructive might and its unruly indifference, nature also guarantees our immortality as a species, and even carries the idea of progress: "in this continuity, this utter indifference to the life and death of each of us lies hidden the pledge of our eternal salvation, of the continuous movement of life on earth, of the continuous movement toward perfection".[190]

It is beyond doubt that the followers of extreme irrationalism, fighters against reason are unceasing – whether they are of the Hamannian type ('hedonistic' and elevating the body to the level of the spirit; exalting and practising faith), or of the Shestovian type (ascetic and searching for faith in torment). They will, apparently, forever be compensated by the equally vehement rationalists who believe in reason only, without testing it by their conscience. As these are two sides of the same coin, the consequences are equally unconsoling. The dangers inherent in either of these approaches are evident. However, there will always exist a middle way – the much more difficult, Chekhovian road of personal responsibility and personal spiritual involvement, forever balancing between the rational and irrational, in the multitude of human experience, amidst this senseless world, impenetrable by humans; the road which, although starting from an acknowledgement of intrinsic human evil, still leads to the good. And there will always be those most intelligent and courageous people who "want to resemble only Chekhov".[191]

Bibliography

Albov V.P. 2002. "Dva momenta v razvitii tvorchestva Antona Pavlovicha Chekhova", in *A.P. Chekhov: Pro et Contra. Tvorchestvo A.P. Chekhova v russkoi mysli kontsa XIX – nachala XX v. (1887–1914)*, Anthology, eds. I.N. Sukhikh and A.D. Stepanov, St. Petersburg: Izdatel'stvo Russkogo Khristianskogo gumanitarnogo Instituta.

---

189 To see these differences compare, for instance, the descriptions of nature in the following stories: "Steppe", "The Lady with the Dog", "Gusev", "The House with an Attic", "The Student" and "Enemies".
190 This is part of a longer quotation, already given above. See footnote 128 for the source.
191 This is a quotation from Sergei Dovlatov's 'Solo na undervude'; see Dovlatov, *Sobranie prozy v 3 tomakh*, St Petersburg: Limbus Press, 1993, vol. 3, 237–338 (271).

Bakhtin, Mikhail. 1986. *Literaturno-kriticheskie statii*, Moscow: Khudozhestvennaia literatura.
Baranova-Shestova, Natalie. 1983. *Zhizn L'va Shestova*, Paris: La Presse Libre, vol. 1.
Belinskii, V.G. 1948. *Izbrannye filosofskie sochineniia*, vol. 1, Moscow: Gos. izd-vo politicheskoi literatury.
Belyi, Andrei. 2002. "Chekhov" in *A.P. Chekhov: Pro et Contra. Tvorchestvo A.P. Chekhova v russkoi mysli kontsa XIX – nachala XX v. (1887–1914)*, Anthology, eds. I.N. Sukhikh and A.D. Stepanov, St Petersburg: Izdatel'stvo Russkogo Khristianskogo gumanitarnogo Instituta.
Berlin, Isaiah. 1994. *The Magus of the North. J.G. Hamann and the Origins of Modern Irrationalism*, London: Fontana Press.
Bitov, Andrei. "Moi dedushka Chekhov i pradedushka Pushkin", http://lit.1september.ru/article.php?ID=200403603.
Bocharov, S. G. 1993. "Ob odnom razgovore i vokrug nego", *NLO*, 2 (1993), 70–89.
Bodrova-Gogenmos, Tatiana. 2009. "Kontseptsiia M.M. Bakhtina i interpretativnaia teoriia perevoda", http://samlib.ru/w/wagapow_a_s/bodrova-gozhenmos.shtml.
Bonetskaia, Natalia. 1993. "M.M. Bakhtin and traditions of Russian philosophy", *Voprosy filosofii*, 1 (1993), 83–93.
Brodsky, Joseph. 1986. "A Poet and Prose", in *Less Than One. Selected Essays*, Harmondsworth, Middlesex, England: Penguin Books, 1986, 176–194.
Camus, Albert. 1965. *Essais* Paris: NRF/Gallimard.
Chekhov, Anton. 1974–1983. *PSSP v 30 tomakh*, Moscow: Nauka.
——— 1979. "The Student", transl. by Constance Garnett, in *Anton Chekhov's Short Stories*, selected and edited by Ralph E. Matlaw, New York: W.W. Norton & Company, 106–109.
——— 1993. "Ward No 6", in *Longer Stories from the Last Decade*, transl. by Constance Garnett, London: Random House, 146–198.
——— "The Lady with the Dog", transl. by Ivy Litvinov, http://www.ibiblio.org/eldritch/ac/lapdog.html.
——— "Lights", http://www.online-literature.com/anton_chekhov/1250/.
——— "Terror", http://www.online-literature.com/anton_chekhov/1267/.
Chudakov, Aleksandr. 2010. "Chekhov and Merezhkovskii: Two Types of Artistic-Philosophical Consciousness", in *Anton Chekhov Through The Eyes Of Russian Thinkers: Vasilii Rozanov, Dmitrii Merezhkovskii and Lev Shestov*, ed. Olga Tabachnikova, London-New York-Delhi: Anthem Press, 93–112.
Clayton, Douglas. 2008. "'Zhenshchina kak ptitsa i loshad': k fenomenologii chelovecheskikh otnoshenii v hudozhestvennom mire Chekhova", in *Filosofiia A.P. Chekhova*, ed. Anatolii Sobennikov, Irkutsk: ISU Publishers, 75–85.
Diakonov, Gennadii. 2006. "Dialogiinaia kontseptsiia estetiki i literaturovedeniia M.M. Bakhtina", *Sotsialna psykhologiia*, 6 (20), 2006, 35–46.
Dombrovskii, Iurii. 2000. "Italiantsam o Shekspire – glavnye problemy ego zhizni", in *Roman. Pis'ma. Esse*, Ekateringburg: U-Factoriia.

Donne, John. 1624. "Devotions upon emergent occasions and several steps in my sickness", Meditation XVII.

Dostoevskii, Fedor. 1991. "Notes from the Underground", in *Notes from the Underground and the Gambler*, transl. by Jane Kentish, Oxford, New York: Oxford University Press.

———— 1992. *Devils,* translated by M. Katz, Oxford: Oxford University Press.

———— *The Idiot*, transl. by Eva Martin, http://www.planetpdf.com/planetpdf/pdfs/free_ebooks/The_Idiot_NT.pdf.

The Brothers Karamazov, Chapter 73, http://www.online-literature.com/dostoevsky/brothers_karamazov/73/.

Dovlatov, Sergei. 1993. 'Zapisnye knizhki', in *Sobranie prozy v 3 tomakh*, St Petersburg: Limbus Press, 1993, vol. 3, 237–338.

Durkin, Andrew. 2008. "Modeli khudozhestvennogo slova v chekhovskikh rasskazakh 'V ssylke' i 'Student'" in *Filosofiia A.P. Chekhova*, ed. Anatolii Sobennikov, Irkutsk: ISU Publishers, 44–59.

Emerson, Caryl. 1994. "M.M. Bakhtin as philosopher", in *Russian Thought After Communism. The Recovery of a Philosophical Heritage*, ed. James P. Scanlan, New York-London: M.E. Sharpe, 206–226.

Erofeev, Viktor. 1975. "'Ostaetsa odno: proizvol' (Filosofiia odinochestva i literaturno-esteticheskoe kredo L'va Shestova)", *Voprosy literatury*, 10 (1975), 153–188.

Evdokimova, Svetlana. 2010. "Philosophy's Enemies: Chekhov and Shestov", in *Anton Chekhov Through The Eyes Of Russian Thinkers*, ed. Olga Tabachnikova, 219–245.

Frank, Joseph. 1990. "The Voices of Mikhail Bakhtin", in *Through the Russian Prism*, Princeton: Princeton University Press.

Galkovskii, Dmitrii. 1997. *Beskonechnyi tupik*, Moscow: Samizdat.

Goethe, Johann Wolfgang von. 1907. *Maximen und Reflexionen*, ed. Max Hecker, Weimar, 1907, No 608.

Gorenshtein, Fridrikh. 2001. *Psalom*, Moscow: Eksmo-Press.

Gorkii, Maksim. 1949–1956. *Polnoe sobranie sochinenii v 30 tomakh*, Moscow: Khudozhestvennaia literatura, vol. 28, 73–74.

Gurevich, Liubov. 1912. *Literatura i estetika*, Moscow.

Hardy, Henry. 1994. The Editorial, in Isaiah Berlin, *The Magus of the North. J.G. Hamann and the Origins of Modern Irrationalism,* London: Fontana Press.

Guseinov, Abdusalam. 2003. *Istoriia eticheskikh uchenii*, Moscow: Gardariki.

Iskander, Fazil. 1999. *Rasskazy, povest', skazka, dialog, esse, stikhi*. Seriia "Zerkalo XX vek", Ekaterinburg: U-Faktoriia.

Karlinsky, Simon. 1973. *Anton Chekhov's Life and Thought. Selected Letters and Commentary*, Berkeley, Los Angeles, London: University of California Press.

Kataev, Vladimir. 2008. "Istinnyi mudrets", in *Filosofiia A.P. Chekhova,* ed. Anatolii Sobennikov, Irkutsk: ISU Publishers, 68–75.

Kuprin, Aleksandr. 1960. "Pamiati Chekhova", in *Chekhov v vospominaniiakh sovremennikov*, eds. S.N. Golubeva et al., Moscow: Khudozhestvennaia literatura, 539–569.

Mashevskii, Aleksei. 1999. "Nas vozvyshaiushchii obman", *Zvezda*, 6 (1999).

Milosz, Czeslaw. 1977. "Shestov, or the Purity of Despair", in *Emperor of the Earth. Modes of Eccentric Vision*, Berkeley-Los Angeles-London: University of California Press, 99–119.

Papernyi, Vladimir. 2005. "Lev Shestov: religioznaia filosofiia kak literaturnaia kritika i kak literatura", *Toronto Slavic Quarterly*, 12 (2005).

Platonov, Andrei. 1999. "The Return", in *The Return and other Stories*, transl. by R. Chandler, E. Chandler and A. Livingstone, London: Harvill Press.

Poincare, Henri. 1983. *O nauke (On science)*, ed. L.S. Pontriagin, Moscow: Nauka, 1983.

Senderovich, Savely, and Shvarts, Elena. 2005. "Kto Kanta na golovu biet (K teme: Lev Shestov i literatura 20-go veka)", *Toronto Slavic Quaterly*, 12 (2005).

Senderovich, Savely. 2010. "Shestov-Chekhov, Chekhov-Shestov", in *Anton Chekhov Through The Eyes Of Russian Thinkers: Vasilii Rozanov, Dmitrii Merezhkovskii and Lev Shestov*, ed. Clga Tabachnikova, Anthem Press: London-New York-Delhi, 199–218.

Shestov, Lev. 1964. "O 'pererozhdenii ubezhdenii' u Dostoevskogo", in *Umozrenie i otkrovenie*, Paris: YMCA, 171–196.

—— 1976. "Dnevnik myslei", *Kontinent*, 8 (1976), 235–252.

—— 1982. *Turgenev*. Ann Arbor: Ardis.

—— 1992. *Kirgegard i ekzistentsial'naia filosofiia (Glas vopiiushchego v pustyne)*, Moscow: Progress-Gnozis. In English: *Kierkegaard and the Existential Philosophy*: http://www.angelfire.com/nb/shestov/sk/sk_01.html.

—— 1996. "Dobro v uchenii gr. Tolstogo i Nitsshe (filosofiia i propoved)", in *Sochineniia v dvukh tomakh*, Tomsk: Vodolei, vol. 1, 213–316. In English: *The Good in the Teaching of Tolstoy and Nietzsche: Philosophy and Preaching*: http://www.angelfire.com/nb/shestov/dtn/tn_01.html.

—— 1996. "Dostoevskii i Nitsshe (filosofiia tragedii)", in *Sochineniia v dvukh tomakh*, Tomsk: Vodolei, vol. 1, 317–464. In English: *Dostoevsky and Nietzsche: The Philosophy of Tragedy*: http://www.angelfire.com/nb/shestov/dtn/dn_7.html.

—— 1996. "Shekspir i ego kritik Brandes", in *Sochineniia v dvukh tomakh*, Tomsk: Vodolei, vol. 1, 3–212.

—— 1996. "Tvorchestvo iz nichego", in *Sochineniia v dvukh tomakh*, Tomsk: Vodolei, vol. 2, 184–213.

—— 2001. *Afiny i Ierusalim*, Moscow: Folio. In English: *Athens and Jerusalem*, http://www.angelfire.com/nb/shestov/aaj/aj1_1.html.

—— 2001. *Lektsii po istorii grecheskoi filosofii*, Moscow-Paris: Russkii Put' – YMCA-Press.

——— 2001. *Na vesakh Iova*, Moscow: Folio. In English: *On Job's Balances*, http://www.angelfire.com/nb/shestov/ijb/jb2_6.html.

——— "The Conquest of the Self-Evident", http://www.angelfire.com/nb/shestov/ijb/jb1_5.html.

Shmeman, Aleksandr. 2005. *Dnevniki*, Moscow: Russkii Put.

Skaftymov, A.P. 1972. *Nravstvennye iskaniia russkikh pisatelei. Statii i issledovaniia o russkikh klassikakh*, Moscow, 381–403.

Stepanov, Andrei. 2010. "Lev Shestov on Chekhov", in *Anton Chekhov Through The Eyes Of Russian Thinkers: Vasilii Rozanov, Dmitrii Merezhkovskii and Lev Shestov*, ed. Olga Tabachnikova, London-New York-Delhi: Anthem Press, 169–174.

Sobennikov Anatolii (ed.). 2008. *Filosofiia A. P. Chekhova*, Irkutsk: ISU Publishers.

——— *"Chekhov i stoiki"*, in *Filosofiia A.P. Chekhova. 2008*, 168–180.

Tabachnikova, Olga. 2015. "Cases of Subversion: Chekhov and Brodsky: (Under the Veneer of Rationalism, or On the Concepts of Hot and Cold Blood as Philosophical Categories)" in *Russian Irrationalism from Pushkin to Brodsky: Seven Essays in Literature and Thought*, London-New Delhi-New York-Sydney: Bloomsbury Academic, 2015, 161–189.

Tiutchev, Fedor. 1987. "Silentium!" in *Polnoe sobranie stikhotvorenii*, Leningrad: Sovetskii pisatel', 105–106.

Tolstoi, Lev. 1983. "Ispoved'", in *Sobranie sochinenii v 22 tomakh*, Moscow: Khudozhestvennaia literatura, vol. 16, 106–165.

Wood, James. 1999. *The Broken Estate. Essays on Literature and Belief*, London: Jonathan Cape.

Zenkovskii, Vasilii. 1999. *Istoriia russkoi filosofii* in two volumes, Rostov-on-Don: Fenix (reprint of the first edition: Paris: YMCA Press, 1948).

CHAPTER 12

Lev Tolstoi and Vasilii Rozanov: Two Fundamental(ist) Types of Russian Irrationalism

Rainer Grübel

> Видеть в иррациональности рациональность и в рациональности — иррациональное всегда было темой моей мысли и всей моей жизни.[1]
>
> (To see the rational in the irrational and the irrational in the rational has always been the theme of my thinking and my life).
>
> PAVEL FLORENSKII, in Rozanov, *Literaturnye izgnanniki*.

The Ethical Trap of Accusing Someone of Irrationalism: (ab)normality

> There are more things in heaven and earth, Horatio, than are dreamt of in your philosophy.
>
> WILLIAM SHAKESPEARE, *Hamlet*, Act 1, Scene 5.

Everyone who accuses someone else of irrationalism puts himself at risk of implying that his or her own position and argument are rational and, thus, that he or she is better at reasoning than the other. In European intellectual discourse rational thinking and behaviour are often considered to be of higher value than their irrational counterparts. It was on this basis that the philosopher György Lukács criticised all modern thought that does not belong to Marxism as bourgeois irrationalism. In *The Path of Irrationalism from Schelling to Hitler* he even proposed a direct development of irrationalism from German idealistic philosophy to National Socialism.[2] In this chapter we try to avoid this trap of superiority, firstly by admitting that in the behaviour of any person (and above all of Lukács himself) about which we have sufficient knowledge, we can find irrational thoughts and acts, and secondly, by asserting that rational acts

---

1 Vasilii Rozanov, *Literaturnye izgnanniki. P.A. Florenskii, S. A Rachinskii*, Moscow: Respublika, 2010, 24.
2 Georg Lukács: *Die Zerstörung der Vernunft: Der Weg des Irrationalismus von Schelling zu Hitler*, 4. Aufl. Berlin: Aufbau, 1988.

are not self-evidently better than irrational ones. Rationality and irrationality are much more interrelated than the average intellectual would like to admit.[3] The philosophical idea that rational ways of thinking and acting are ethically superior to irrational ones was one of the fundamental ideas of the European Enlightenment. It has survived as a way of thinking in Western trivial philosophy until our times. Even now, there is a branch of philosophy called 'moral rationalism'.[4] However, by 1755 the Lisbon earthquake gave rise to doubts about the universal validity of reason in the world, and in the period of Romanticism influential thinkers showed the basic shortcomings of the rationalist image of the human being.[5] Whereas Kant considered the irrational still in its original sphere of infinite numbers, Fichte marked in his epistemology the gap between the projection of the object and the object as an empty place, as *projectio per hiatum irrationalem*.[6] Hegel turned this upside down: now the irrational implied reasonableness (*Vernünftigkeit*) and the rational only calculability (*das Verständige*).[7] At the beginning of the twentieth century the sociologist Max Weber called an individual acting because of an act's meaningful interpretability "principally less irrational than the individual process in nature".[8] In the second half of the nineteenth century, when positivism, with its conviction that not only nature but also culture and society are founded on strict laws, was popular, it was Friedrich Nietzsche who balanced the so-called rational model of culture in Apollonianism with its irrational equivalent of Dionysianism.[9] Using the example of ancient Greek culture, the philosopher tried to show not only that all cultures are mixtures of rationalism and irrationalism,

---

3   Cf. Aleksandr Mikhailovich Abrochnov, *Sosushchestvovanie i vzaimoperekhody ratsional'nogo i irratsional'nogo*, Nizhnii Novgorod: Izdatelstvo NGU, 2006.
4   Cf. Marcus George Singer, The Ideal of a Rational Morality. *Philosophical Compositions*, Oxford: Clarendon Press, 2002, 2008.
5   Cf. Baudelaire's speech at the „Salon des curiosités Estethiques'. The German mystic and religious fanatic Beate Barbara Juliane von Krüdener was of great influence on the Russian Emperor Alexander i and influenced the Holy Alliance of 1815.
6   Johann Gottlieb Fichte, *Werke: Auswahl in VI Bänden*, ed. Fritz Medicus, Vol. 4, Leipzig: Fritz Eckardt, 1910, 288.
7   Georg Wilhelm Friedrich Hegel, Enzyklopädie des Geistes, § 231. In: *Werke*, hg. Glockner, Vol. 8, Stuttgart: Fromann, 1927, 442.
8   Max Weber: 'individuelles Handeln ist, seiner sinnvollen Deutbarkeit wegen – soweit diese reicht – prinzipiell weniger irrational als der individuelle Naturvorgang' Max Weber: *Gesammelte Aufsätze zur Wissenschaftslehre*, Tübingen: J.C.B. Mohr, 1951, 67. Strangely enough, in congruence with this statement, Rozanov's vote for the irrational takes nature as its starting point.
9   Bykov related the view of Volynskii on Tolstoi to his interest in Nietzsche's Apollonianism. (A.V Bykov, Nravstvennoe uchenie i tvorchestvo L.N. Tolstogo v interpretatsii A.L. Volynskogo. http://www.ksu.ru/miku/info/sob/konf_tolstoi/s22.htm [consulted 26.2.2010]).

but also that the highest achievements of world culture are grounded on a synthesis of rational and irrational cultural elements.[10]

We could list a lot of examples of acts where reason is considered by many as ethically good, but which are actually irrational, and we could note a sufficient number of acts, seen by the majority as bad, which from a certain point of view are rational. On the one hand, Christ's death on the cross, or the behaviour of the Polish doctor and pedagogue Janusz Korczak, who voluntarily accompanied his Jewish children to Treblinka, though he knew that he would be killed there by the German ss, were in some significant respects irrational acts. So too was the action of the young Czech student of philosophy Jan Palach, who burned himself to death in January 1969 in Prague as a sign of protest against the Warsaw Pact invasion of Czechoslovakia. On the other hand, in Lessing's play *Nathan the Wise* (1779) a rational way of thinking about the three monotheistic religions motivates the father in the famous parable, told by Nathan, to cheat his sons, which in itself is surely an unethical act. The rationalism of the German railway timetable, which made the transportation and killing of millions of Jews possible, was without any doubt a barbarian non-ethical phenomenon. It is a good example of system-rationality (Systemrationalität). If we define rational thinking as a type of thinking which follows the rules of formal logic, and if we consider the rules of formal logic as norms, the relationship between rational and irrational phenomena can be taken in a more general framework as a special case of the relationship between normality and abnormality.[1] At the present time, in philosophy and sociology there is a broad discussion on the discourses of normality and abnormality. Of course we do not have space here to go into depth about this discussion, but we should note that in our time we observe a clear tendency to go back to the dominance of normality, which has been abandoned in the period of post-modernism. Also we should not forget that in the framework of cognitive psychology and physiology of the brain the claim that human beings can take rational decisions is principally denied. Decisions, we are told, are taken by the brain before they become part of our consciousness.

---

10 The most famous example of an irrational model of the human world is presented in Albert Camus' *Le mythe de Sisyphe. Essai sur l'absurde*. Paris: Les Éditions Gallimard, 1942. Its Russian absurdistic counterpart is the work of the group Oberiu (Union of Real Art), founded in 1928 by Daniil Kharms and Alexander Vvedenskii.

11 Christine Korsgaard, *The Sources of Normativity*, New York: Cambridge University Press, 1996. Thomas Rolf, Normalität. Ein philosophischer Grundbegriff des 20. Jahrhunderts. München: Fink, 1999. Jürgen Link, *Versuch über den Normalismus, Wie Normalität produziert wird*, Göttingen: Vandenhoeck & Ruprecht 2006.

The simplistic solution to relate the rational to the mind ('brain') and the irrational to the feeling ('heart') is still present in the background and nevertheless destroyed by the predicate 'hot fire' (*pyl*), related to reason in Blok's verses:

О, сердце, сколько ты любило!
О, разум, сколько ты пылал![12]

[O heart, how much you were in love!
O, reason, how much you were on fire!]

This is no longer possible in an era of neuroscience and cognitive psychology.

Two Phases of Russian Irrationalism: The Nineteenth and Early Twentieth Centuries

Гегель иррационален в рационализме. Русский иррационализм глубже, он *под* рационализмом.[13]

Hegel is irrational in rationalism. Russian irrationalism is deeper, it is *beneath* rationalism. Galkovskii, *The Infinite Deadlock*.

The argument of irrationalism has not only been used in the mutual evaluation of individuals, and groups of human beings, but also in discourse about nations and cultures. It has affected even the shared vision of genders in culture.

In the development of modern Russian culture we distinguish two prominent phases of irrationalism. The first was quite congruent with the Western reaction to the Enlightenment in European Romanticism. So we observe in Russia not only the tendency towards unification in the Slavophile opposition to Western culture, which seemed to disintegrate, but also Gogol's early death by fasting because of (too) rigidly applied religious rules and measures. The history of the interpretation of Gogol's death can serve as a model for the tendency to interpret an evidently irrational act as a nevertheless rational

---

12   Aleksandr Blok, 'Blagoslovliaiu vse, chto bylo' in: idem, *Polnoe sobranie sochinenii i pisem v dvadtsati tomakh.* vol. 1, Moscow: Nauka 1997, 96.
13   Dmitrii Galkovskii, *Beskonechnyi tupik*, Moscow: Samizsdat, 1997, 12. Cf. also Dmitrii Galkovskii, Deviatnadtsatyi vek. Sviatochnyi rasskaz Nr. 13. In: *Novyi mir*, 3, 2004, 89–97.

one.[14] In Gogol's stories the dark aspect of night with its strange feelings, later synthesised by Freud under the name of *das Unheimliche* ('the Uncanny'), was contrasted to the light of the day and the real or only supposed clarity of scientific reasoning. This phenomenon was also present in Russian society, where researchers, who worked in their laboratories during the day, also took part in spiritualist séances at night: Occultism and Mesmerism interested a lot of people.[15]

A second wave of irrationalism in Russian culture can be traced as a reaction to philosophical positivism in the nineteenth century. To a certain degree, positivism was also an integral part of realism in Russian art and literature. The basic aesthetic model of 'mirroring reality', which (not only in Russia) still governs the superficial understanding of art, works with a metaphor taken from physics. It is not by chance that prose, with its art of visual perspective and narrative focalisation, was dominant in Russian realism. In Polish literature the corresponding epoch of literature with prose at its centre is even called Positivism. The Russian founder of the Theosophical society Elena Petrovna Blavatskaia/Helena Petrovna Blavatsky (1831–1891) was one of the most influential spiritualists in all of European culture.[16]

The disbelief in the possibility of giving an objective picture of reality motivated Chekhov to create a new manner of narration, which is no longer based on the model of an omniscient narrator who is able to reproduce reality by narration. Chekhov reduced the function of the narrator by introducing characters who give their own view on the world, a view, however, which is quiet uncertain. In the eyes of Gor'kii, Chekhov thus destroyed the rationalism of realistic narration. (A third wave of irrationalism came about with the epoch of Postmodernism. Some even consider Postmodernism itself as irrationalism.)

The two 'heroes' of our investigation into Russian irrationalism are both (along with the parts of their oeuvre relevant to this study) situated between the epoch of realism or positivism on the one hand and Modernism or what is called also the Silver Age of Russian culture, on the other. Going back to the medium of poetry, Russian symbolism weakened the rational perspectives and probabilism of Russian realism. V. Zen'kovskii has shown that the philosopher

---

14 Rainer Grübel, 'Gogoljeva glad – jelovnik dvadesetog stoleća. Gladovanie kao estetsko samouništenie' in: Jasmina Vojvodić (ed.), *Hrana od gladi do prejedanja*. Zagreb 2010, S. 59–84; idem, 'Gogol's Hunger(n) – Eine Speisekarte des 20. Jahrhunderts' in: *Zeitschrift für Kulturwissenschaften*, 2012, 1, 147–166.

15 Encyclopedia of Occultism & Parapsychology.

16 H.P. Blavatsky, *The Secret Doctrine: The Synthesis of Science, Religion, and Philosophy*, 2 vols., London ets.: The Theosophical Publishing Company, 1895.

and poet Vladimir Solov'ev integrated into his philosophy of all-unity (*vseedinstvo*) not only elements of unity from German Romantic philosophy (above all of Schelling), but also the idea of theurgy from occultism and mysticism.[17]

In the late prose of Tolstoi the common-sense-rationalism of the Russian nineteenth century is replaced by a conflict between the rationality of society and the irrationality of the individual in the eyes of this pseudo-rational society. So the central hero of Tolstoi's novel *Resurrection* (*Voskresenie*) opposes the rationalism inherent in the Russian judicial system. However, in fact this is not an opposition against the Russian system of jurisprudence, but against the system of jurisprudence in itself, and against all rational systems. Its foundation is the discord between the normative idea of life and the fact that it does not satisfy these norms in reality. Where does this critique of normality come from in Russia?

Irrationalism in Modern Russian Culture Expresses Heretic Attitudes

Этот воинственный иррационализм увёл его [Тертуллиана] из Церкви в секту монтанистов (примерно с 200 г.).[18]

(This warlike irrationalism drove him [Tertullian] out of the Church to the sect of Montanism.) c200AD]

In Russian culture, rationality is incorporated into Orthodox belief, as it is represented by the official Church. In Russia, heretical belief has always been one of the most influential phenomena corrupting the rationality of official religious doctrine. In eastern Slavic cultures these steadily blooming heresies were motivated by a rather immobile, mentally inflexible Orthodox Church.

One of the first sects that disseminated heresies in Russia was an offshoot of the so-called Bogomils. Coming in the tenth century from Bulgaria, they spread the belief that God had not one but two sons, Satanel and Logos, who was born of the Virgin Mary from her ear: norm and order (Logos) were counterbalanced by chaos and disorder (Satanel). This sect rejected all Holy Sacraments, demanded an ascetic lifestyle and disapproved of the owning of land by the Church. In the eighteenth century it divided into two sects called Khlysty

---

17   Vasilii Zen'kovskii, Aus der Geschichte der ästhetischen Ideen in Russland im 19. und 20. Jahrhundert. The Hague: Mouton, 1958, 37. Cf. about the import of Auguste Viatte, Les sources occultes du romantisme; 2 vol. Paris: H. Champion, 1928.

18   See, *wapedia.mobi/ru/История_христианства* (consulted 10.02.2010).

(Flagellants) and Skoptsy (Eunuchs, or castrati). Lev Tolstoi agreed with them in his disapproval of land-owning, his negation of the Sacraments and his propaganda for an ascetic lifestyle. In the fourteenth century the Strigol'niki formed in Novgorod and Pskov a religious movement that renounced all ecclesiastic hierarchy and monasticism, sacraments of priesthood, communion, repentance, and baptism.[19] Their negation of all social hierarchy and administration found its way also into Tolstoi's late vision of society that repeatedly has even been called Tolstoyan 'nihilism', for the first time (as far as I know) in 1918 by the philosopher Nikolai Berdiaev.[20]

The Dukhobortsy (Deniers of the Holy Ghost), a sect which in the Kharkov province in the beginning of the eighteenth century emerged from the Quakers, were at the end of the following century quite attractive to Russian intellectuals. They believed in the Divinity of Christ and acknowledged the transposition of souls. But hell and heaven they understood only allegorically, and they rejected Church hierarchy and rites, oaths and military service. Here again we see a source for Tolstoi's late belief.[21]

---

19   Boris A. Rybakov, *Strigol'niki: Russkie Gumanisty XIV stoletiia*, Moscow: Nauka, 1993.
20   Nikolai Berdiaev, 'Gibel' russkikh illiuzii'. In: *Dukhovnye osnovy russkoi revoliutsii. Opyty 1917–1918 gg.* St Petersburg: RGKhI, 1919, 173: «Л. Толстой должен быть признан величайшим русским нигилистом, истребителем всех ценностей и святынь, истребителем культуры.» ('Tolstoi should be acknowledged as the greatest Russian nihilist, an eradicator of all values and sanctuaries, an eradicator of culture') Cf. also: «Для спасения России и русской культуры каленым железом нужно выжечь из русской души толстовскую мораль, низкую и истребляющую.» ['In order to redeem Russia and Russian culture we need to burn out of the Russian soul with red-hot iron the mean and eradicating morality of Tolstoi'.] *Ibid.* «Мировая война проиграна Россией потому, что в ней возобладала толстовская моральная оценка войны. Русский народ в грозный час мировой борьбы обессилили кроме предательств и животного эгоизма толстовские моральные оценки. Толстовская мораль обезоружила Россию и отдала её в руки врага.» ['The First World War was lost by Russia because it was dominated by Tolstoi's moral estimation of war. The Russian people were weakened at the harsh time of the world struggle not only by treachery and animal egoism, but also by Tolstoi's moral judgements. Tolstoy's morality disarmed Russia and handed it over to the enemy'.] Nikolai Berdiaev, *Dukhi russkoi revolutsii,* Moscow: Izdatel'stvo Moskovskogo universiteta 1990, 83.
21   Cf. Peter Kropotkin in his article on Tolstoi in the *Encyclopædia Britannica*, London 1911: 'Without naming himself an anarchist, Leo Tolstoi, like his predecessors in the popular religious movements of the fifteenth and sixteenth centuries, Chojecki, Denk and many others, took the anarchist position as regards the state and property rights, deducing his conclusions from the general spirit of the teachings of Jesus and from the necessary dictates of reason'.

The members of the Piatoknizhniki sect (Pento-books) believed that there is only one God, and that the five books of Moses are the cornerstone of the Bible. For them Jesus Christ is not God. In this respect Tolstoi agreed with them.[22] Like them, he considered the Church to be only a community of the faithful. For the Piatoknizhniki all visible appearance is manmade and should be rejected. They took the building of a church as a pagan temple, icons as idols, hierarchy as pseudo-teachers, and priesthood as pagan office. For them there are no Sacraments at all. Communion is simply bread and wine. Repentance means self-delusion. In their beliefs, icons and the cross should be annihilated as idols. Fasting and monastic life should be discarded. Tolstoi also shared with them the belief that all people of different faiths are equal in God's eyes, that there should be no wars or governments. Here again we see relevant similarities with Tolstoi's late belief.[23]

Since the Middle Ages one can observe in Eastern Slavic culture various sects that mixed the principles of Judaism and Christian belief. During the middle period of his life, between 1898 and 1909, Vasilii Rozanov was very interested in these 'Judaising' heresies, for he thought the Old Testament had priority over the New Testament. The Old Testament stressed a crucial question for him at that time, that of family: Rozanov, whose first wife Apollinaria Suslova (18 years his elder) left him in 1886, lived unmarried in a relationship together with the widow of a teacher, because his first wife did not agree to a divorce. As they also had five children, who were born in legal terms out of wedlock, this created a rather precarious situation for him as a civil servant.

The Khlysty (Flagellants) lived in 'societies', which they called 'Ships' (singular: *korabl'*). These were headed by prophets, christs, theotokoses and prophetesses. They rejected sacraments, priesthood and the Church and believed in an 'improvised' Christ: that is, that anyone practising ascetic methods can become a Christ. Their services were called *rvenie* (zeal), and consisted of reading and interpretations of the Holy Scripture with singing, jumping, running and spinning, which culminated in loss of consciousness and hallucination, interpreted as prophetic inspiration. The Flagellants were wild fanatics and for Vasilii Rozanov they formed very attractive communities. He studied them ethnographically and provided a dense description of their belief in *The Apocalyptic*

---

22   One of the first to accuse Tolstoi of heresy was Annenkov.
23   Tolstoi, *Ispoved'.* (*A Confession*), in: idem, *Polnoe sobranie sochinenii*. Vol. 23, Moscow: Khudozhestvennaia literatura, 1957, 39: 'And I began to draw near to the believers among the poor, simple, unlettered folk: pilgrims, monks, sectarians, and peasants'. («И я стал сближаться с верующими из бедных, простых, неученых людей, со странниками, монахами, раскольниками, мужиками.»)

Sects. Khlysty and Skoptsy,[24] which shows their ethical and social priority above the Orthodox Church. Aleksandr Etkind's *Chlyst. Sects, Literature and Revolution* offers an interesting analysis and interpretation of their effect on Russian culture in the early twentieth century.[25]

Tolstoi's Irrationalism as a Didactic Type of Fundamentalism

'Трижды убили меня, трижды воскресал из мертвых'.

('Three times they killed me and three times I was resurrected'.)
Interlocutor of ROSTOPCHIN IN LEV TOLSTOI, *War and Peace, Vol 3, xxv.*

Non vi sed virtute, non armis sed arte paritur victoria.

('Not by force but by virtue, not with arms but with art is victory won'.)

We consider Tolstoi's and Rozanov's intellectual discourses to be two different types of Russian irrationalism during the last two decades of the nineteenth and the first two of the early twentieth century. Both were examples of reactions against the rationalism of the European Enlightenment (or what has been taken for it) and against nineteenth century's positivism. In both cases we observe a strange and fascinating combination of rational and irrational motives, habits and methods. In the case of Tolstoi this confrontation of reason and 'the unreasonable' is first of all one of his biographical development; in the case of Rozanov it seems to be rooted in his psychology.

Both authors show elements of Russian messianism, and are in different ways bound to the traditions of Russian heresy, but they differ in their aims and means. Both in a strange manner combine belief in the logic of everyday life with horror at the logic of calculation and belief in science with distrust of sociology, psychology and ethnology. In the footsteps of Rousseau, but in a contemporary, nineteenth century version of his thought, Tolstoi seeks a way back to nature or, better, to the human being as a phenomenon of nature, as represented in the peasant. He thus denies his aristocratic descent. The *raznochinets* Rozanov (his mother was the daughter of an impoverished aristocrat) looks for a better future in the way back to an ancient type of culture, which, in

---

24 Vasilii Rozanov, *Apokalipticheskaia sekta*, St Petersburg: Tipografiia Veisberga i Shunina, 1914.
25 Aleksandr Etkind. *Chlyst. Sekty, literatura i revoliutsiia*, Moscow: NLO, 1998.

his opinion, did not imply any difference between mind and body, between man and God. His syncretistic way of thinking comes across in his concept of love, which knows no difference between divine agape, human Eros and physical sex. In his irrational thinking the 'genuine' family should be the model for society.[26] Their appeals to cultural traditions were also different: Tolstoi modelled himself as a 'teacher of the people', Rozanov as the insane offspring of 'God's fool', as Ivan-durak.[27]

Comparing Dostoevskii and Tolstoi a century ago, the critic Akim Volynskii wrote, that, unlike Dostoevskii, Tolstoi expressed in a strictly logical way the 'right of the people' through the ideas of Andrei Bolkonskii. However, Volynskii admitted that the novelist found the people's rights by using an instinctive feeling for God, that is – in an irrational way.[28] Thus Volynskii combined Tolstoi's irrational method of finding the idea with the rational method of its expression in his prose. Even to this day, Tat'iana Zhikhareva is convinced that 'Tolstoi's rationalism'[29] was totally alien to Shestov, who denied it. Therefore in her view the philosopher was not at all capable of understanding the novelist.

Tolstoi was not at all a stable representative of reason. His ideology was not so far from Kireevskii's 'spiritual reason' and his idea about the struggle against the 'disintegration of the spirit', is (like Tolstoi's appeal to reinstall its 'integrity') close to the Slavophile position. When in his tract *On Life* Tolstoi declared 'rational consciousness' (*razumnoe soznanie*) to be his aim, this 'rationality' was far from the optimism and the belief in progress of the Enlightenment and positivism. Already in 1869, in a letter to Fet, Tolstoi wrote about his enthusiasm for Schopenhauer's philosophy, which with reason is considered as irrational:

> Знаете ли, что было для меня настоящее лето? – Непрестающий восторг перед Шопенгауэром и ряд духовных наслаждений, которых я никогда не испытывал. Я выписал все его сочинения, и читал, и читаю (прочел и Канта). […] теперь я уверен, что Шопенгауэр – гениальнейший из людей.[30]

---

26   It seems to be fully improbable that Rozanov's idea of family and society had anything in common with Engel's idea of the family as the original model for society.
27   Of course, this picture of himself was not free of irony.
28   Akim L. Volynskii, *Dostoevskii*, St Petersburg: Tipografiia Energiia, 1906, 498.
29   T. Iu. Zhikhareva, Irratsionalizm i problema dobra i zla v zapadnoevropeiskoi mysli 19–20 vv. http://frgf.utmn.ru/last/No4/text13.htm (consulted 26.02.2010).
30   L. Tolstoi in a letter to A.A. Fet on the 30th of August in 1869. Tolstoi started to translate Schopenhauer into Russian, and he even suggested that Fet should edit these translations together with him.

Do you know what the present summer has been for me? – I felt an endless enthusiasm for Schopenhauer and a number of spiritual pleasures that I have never experienced before. I have ordered all his works, and read, and am still reading (I also read Kant). [...] I am now convinced that Schopenhauer is the most ingenious of all people.

Considering Tolstoi's reception of Yoga's philosophy,[31] A.M. Piatigorskii wrote: "Tolstoi's interpretation, knowledge and reason melted together to a single rationalistic complex". We have reason to call this merging of different mental activities itself an irrational act. Tolstoi's monism (the absolutism of eternity) and the motion towards it stood on the edge of Buddhist dualism of the unearthly dharma and nirvana on the one hand and a phenomenal state of mind on the other.

In his *Confession*, which is a remarkable text because it transfers the intimate oral genre of repentance in the tradition of Augustine and Rousseau into a public printed exhibitionist discourse, Tolstoi, looking back at his own ideological biography, told how after a period dominated by reason, he found his new insight into life to be nonsense: "Rational knowledge brought me to the realisation that life is meaningless [...]".[32] This confession was first distributed in Russia in 1882 and first published in 1884. Here he tells of one of the fundamental consequences of this insight into himself: "[...] irrational knowledge is faith [...]".[33] As he lost his faith after his youth and gained it again around 1881, the development from

---

31 Svami Vivekananda, *Filosofkaia ioga. Lektsii o radzhi-ioge, ili Ovladenie vnutrennei pravdoi*, New York, 1896. Cf. Irina A. Belaia, Buddizm kak teoreticheskii istochnik ucheniia o soznanii zhizni L.N. Tolstogo, in: *Eticheskaia mysl'*. Vol. 2, Moscow: IF RAN, 2001.

32 «Разумное знание привело меня к признанию того, что жизнь бессмысленна [...].» Lev Tolstoi, *Ispoved'* 35. Cf. for the English translations of Tolstoi's *Confession*: Donna T. Orwin (ed.), *The Cambridge Companion to Tolstoi*, Cambridge University Press, 2002 or Lev Tolstoy, *A Confession and Other Religious Writings*, transl. by Jane Kentish, New York: Penguin Books, 1987.

33 «[...] неразумное знание есть вера [...]» Tolstoi, *Ispoved'*, 33. Cf.: 'The fourth way out is that of weakness. It consists in seeing the truth of the situation and yet clinging to life, knowing in advance that nothing can come of it. People of this kind know that death is better than life, but not having the strength to act rationally – to end the deception quickly and kill themselves – they seem to wait for something. This is the escape of weakness, for if I know what is best and it is within my power, why not yield to what is best?... I found myself in that category'. («Четвертый выход есть выход слабости. Он состоит в том, чтобы, понимая это и бессмысленность жизни, продолжать тянуть ее, зная вперед, что ничего из нее выйти не может. Люди этого разбора знают, что смерть лучше жизни, но, не имея сил поступить разумно – поскорее кончить обман и убить себя, чего-то как будто ждут. Это есть выход слабости, ибо если я знаю лучшее и оно

faith to lack of it and back to faith again in his own religious life formed a circle from irrational via rational back to irrational knowledge...[34]

In Tolstoi's retrospection, the period of reason was, however, defective from the very beginning. Though all the conclusions seemed to be reasonable, in reality (and this conclusion is due to his positivism) they did not lead to the act that should be the consequence of all reasoning – suicide:

> Все эти сомнения, которые теперь я в состоянии высказать более или менее связно, тогда я не мог бы высказать. Тогда я только чувствовал, что, как ни *логически* неизбежны были мои, подтверждаемые величайшими мыслителями, выводы о тщете жизни, в них было что-то неладно. В самом ли *рассуждении*, в постановке ли вопроса, я не знал; я чувствовал только, что убедительность *разумная* была совершенная, но что ее было мало. Все эти доводы не могли убедить меня так, чтоб я сделал то, что вытекало из моих *рассуждений*, т. е. чтоб я убил себя. И я бы сказал неправду, если бы сказал, что я *разумом* пришел к тому, к чему я пришел, и не убил себя. *Разум* работал, но работало и еще что-то другое, что я не могу назвать иначе, как сознанием жизни.[35]

> All these doubts, which I am now able to express more or less systematically, I could not have expressed at the time. I then only felt that however *logically* inevitable my conclusions were concerning the vanity of life, confirmed as they were by the greatest thinkers, there was something not right about them. Whether it was in the *reasoning* itself or in the statement of the question I did not know – I only felt that the conclusion was *rationally* convincing, but that that was insufficient. All these conclusions could not so convince me as to make me do what followed from my *reasoning*, that is to say, kill myself. And I should have told an untruth had I, without killing myself, said that *reason* had brought me to the point I had

---

в моей власти, почему не отдаться лучшему? Я находился в этом разряде.» Tolstoi, *Ispoved'*, 28–29.)

[34] In the case of Rozanov we find the opposite circle from disbelief at school via belief at the university back to disbelief in Jesus Christ from the turn of the century. It speaks for itself, that Tolstoi as the most condensed example of reasoning used the formula 'o = o': 'Together with the best brains of mankind I came to the conclusion, that o = o, and was very embarrassed, whereas nothing different could be the result'. («Вместе с лучшими умами человечества я пришел к тому, что о = о, и очень удивился, что получил такое решение, тогда как ничего иного и не могло выйти.» Tolstoi, *Ispoved'*, 36.)

[35] *Ibid.*, 31. (All italics in this and the following quotations are mine [RG.])

reached. *Reason* worked, but something else was also working which I can only call a consciousness of life.

Besides Reason, which had been crowned during the French Revolution as the new God, Tolstoi felt another force, which led him in a different direction. It is necessary here to quote such extended passages of his argument in order to show that Tolstoi carefully followed the rules of reason to show its bad results in reality as well as the good results of the unreasonable:[36]

> Работала еще та сила, которая заставляла меня обращать внимание на то, а не на это, и эта-то сила и вывела меня из моего отчаянного положения и совершенно иначе направила разум. Эта сила заставила меня обратить внимание на то, что я с сотнями подобных мне людей не есть все человечество, что жизни человечества я еще не знаю.[37]

A force was working which compelled me to turn my attention to this and not to that; and it was this force which extricated me from my desperate situation and turned my mind in quite another direction. This force compelled me to turn my attention to the fact that I and a few hundred similar

---

[36] Of course, this 'reasonable argumentation' has in itself something of a *contradictio in adjecto*: the consequent line of the bad leads to the good. It was Lev Shestov (*Dobro v uchenii gr. Tolstogo i F. Nitshe (Filosofiia i propoved')*. St. Petersburg, 1900) who first showed the absurdity of Tolstoi's 'good' concepts of God *and* of the human being. Cf. about the reception of Tolstoi in existentialism: Rainer Grübel, Existentialismus. In: Martin George a.o., eds., *Tolstoj als theologischer Denker und Kirchenkritiker*, Göttingen, 2013.

[37] Tolstoi, *Ispoved'*, 31. *A Confession*. It is interesting, that Tolstoi in this context applies and denies the predicate of irrationality with respect to the others: 'I saw that, with rare exceptions, all those billions who have lived and are living do not fit into my divisions, and that I could not class them as not understanding the question, for they themselves state it and reply to it with extraordinary clarity. Nor could I consider them epicureans, for their life consists more of privations and sufferings than of enjoyments. Still less could I consider them as *irrationally* dragging on a meaningless existence, for every act of their life, as well as death itself, is explained by them'. (Я увидал, что все эти миллиарды живших и живущих людей, все, за редкими исключениями, не подходят к моему делению, что признать их не понимающими вопроса я не могу, потому что они сами ставят его и с необыкновенной ясностью отвечают на него. Признать их эпикурейцами тоже не могу, потому что жизнь их слагается больше из лишений и страданий, чем наслаждений; признать же их *неразумно* доживающими бессмысленную жизнь могу еще меньше, так как всякий акт их жизни и самая смерть объясняются ими. *Ibid.*, 32.)

people are not the whole of mankind, and that I did not yet know the life of mankind.

Although Tolstoi never called the force of reason a diabolical force, it seems to be quite obvious that in his argumentation the unreasonable force is the force of the good, if not of God. The advantage of the unreasonable force was namely the fact that it brought him not to death but to life. Life – again in keeping with his belief in positivism – is in itself a positive phenomenon:

> Я знал, что я ничего не найду на пути *разумного* знания, кроме отрицания жизни [...] Выходило противоречие, из которого было только два выхода: или то, что я называл разумным, не было так разумно, как я думал; или то, что мне казалось неразумно, не было так *неразумно*, как я думал. И я стал проверять ход рассуждений моего *разумного* знания.[38]

> I knew I could find nothing along the path of *rational* knowledge except a denial of life. [...] A contradiction arose from which there were two exits. Either that which I called *reason* was not as *rational* as I supposed, or that which seemed to me *irrational* was not as irrational as I supposed. And I began to verify the line of argument of my *rational* knowledge.]

Here Tolstoi starts a *tour de raison* through rational knowledge, which goes back to that very relation between the finite and the infinite that in European history (as we have seen) stood at the beginning of all the ideas about the irrational:

> Поняв это, я понял, что и нельзя было искать в разумном знании ответа на мой вопрос и что ответ, даваемый разумным знанием, есть только указание на то, что ответ может быть получен только при иной постановке вопроса, только тогда, когда в рассуждение будет введен вопрос отношения конечного к бесконечному. Я понял и то, что, как ни *неразумны* и уродливы ответы, даваемые верою, они имеют то преимущество, что вводят в каждый ответ отношение *конечного* к *бесконечному*, без которого не может быть ответа.[39]

---

[38] *Ibid.*, 33.
[39] *Ibid.*, 34.

Having understood this [that philosophical knowledge denies nothing, but only replies that the question cannot be solved by it – that for it the solution remains indefinite], I understood that it was not possible to seek in *rational* knowledge a reply to my question, and that the answer given by *rational* knowledge is a mere indication that a reply can only be obtained by a different statement of the question and only when the relation of the finite to the infinite is included in the question. And I understood that, however *irrational* and distorted might be the replies given by faith, they have this advantage, that they introduce into every answer a relation between the *finite* and the *infinite, without which there can be no solution*.

Tolstoi admits that in the line of positivism he was looking for "an answer in the experimental sciences". And he considered himself "a part of the infinite".[40]

In Tolstoi's novel *Resurrection* (*Voskresenie*) Nekhliudov admits that it is not possible to influence the habits and behaviour of other people, and concludes: "but if the very opposite is proven and it is clear that it is beyond the power of people to change other people, then the only reasonable thing that you can do is to cease to do that which is not only useless, but even harmful and, moreover, immoral and cruel".[41] In the end, the hero of this novel understands, that "every human being cannot do anything else but follow the Commandments" of the *Sermon on the Mount* and "the only reasonable meaning of a human being's life consists in this, that every deviation from it is a mistake, which at once causes punishment".[42] In this ethical fundamentalism, often called also the 'ethical

---

40   His correspondent, the Moscow female student Vera Mordvinina wrote to him in a letter of 14th February 1915 showing the presence of the European origin of the nation of the irrational in Russian culture of the early 20th century: "That truth, my Truth is not composed of irrational numbers, but of something different". ("Та истина, моя Истина, не из иррациональных чисел составлена, а из другого"). Vasilii Rozanov, *Literaturnye izgnanniki. P.A. Florenskii, S. A Rachinskii,* Moscow: Respublika 2010, 903). In her opinion the truth of the world consists of the gentle behavoir of the male and the female turkey, breeding their eggs.

41   '[...] но когда доказано совершенно обратное, и явно, что не во власти одних людей исправлять других, то единственное разумное, что вы можете сделать, это то, чтобы перестать делать то, что не только бесполезно, но вредно и, кроме того, безнравственно и жестоко.' Lev Tolstoi, *Voskresenie,* in: idem, *Sobranie sochinenii v dvenadtsati tomakh*, vol. 11, Moscow 1959, 468.

42   «[...] что всякому человеку больше нечего делать, как исполнять эти заповеди, что в этом – единственный разумный смысл человеческой жизни, что всякое отступление

nihilism', of the late Tolstoi, which culminates in the advice not to resist evil, we notice the negation of law, of judiciary, of state and Church. However, all these objects of Tolstoi's negation were results of a development that has been called by sociologists the 'differentiation of culture, functions and values' in European societies. In this respect Tolstoi's way of thinking followed the line of Slavophile tradition, which posited a fundamental difference between the positive *inner* ethical rule of Christianity and the negative juridical *outer* law of ethical institutions. Thus 'good' Christian ethics was opposed to 'bad' Roman jurisprudence.[43]

When Tolstoi tried to reduce all possible evaluation of actions to the rules of Christ's *Sermon on the Mount*, he read the New Testament, like many members of Russian sects, literally; very often he read it even like a literary text. This reading culminated in the maxim "resist not him that is evil".[44] His reasoning about this text denied in a pseudo-rational way all the miracles, sacraments and mystic elements, but it ended in the self-dismissing doctrine that you should not follow any doctrine, and what was more provocative – that you should not hinder evil.[45] A victim of the Holocaust who did not fight against

от этого есть ошибка, тотчас же влекущая за собою наказание.» Lev Tolstoi, Voskresenie, in: idem, *Sobranie sochinenii v dvenadtsati tomakh*. Vol. 11, Moscow: Khudozhestvennaia literatura, 1959, 469.

[43] Cf. Pavel Novgorodtsev, *Krizis sovremennogo pravosoznaniia*. Moscow: Tipografiia I.N. Kušnera & Co. 1909. Anita Schlüchter, Zur Verteidigung des Rechts. Die Kritik an Tolstojs Rechtsnihilismus durch Juristen und Solov'ev. http://www.jfsl.de/publikationen/2004/Schluechter.htm (consulted 1.11.2009) Rainer Grübel, "'Gordoe slovo: spravedlivost'" – "Ein stolzes Wort: Gerechtigkeit". Der Gerechtigkeitsdiskurs in Tolstojs Roman Krieg und Frieden', in: Holger Kuße / Nikolaj Plotnikov (Ed.), *Pravda. Diskurse der Gerechtigkeit in der russischen Ideengeschichte*. München: Verlag Otto Sagner, 2011, 39–74.

[44] Cf. Matthew, v. 38, 39: 'Ye have heard that it was said, An eye for an eye and a tooth for a tooth: But I say unto you, Resist not him that is evil'.

[45] Gandhi found the principle of 'nonresistance to evil' in Tolstoi and Henry Thoreau. Cf. Peter Singer (ed.), *A Companion to Ethics*. Oxford: Blackwell, 1993, 54. There is an interesting case of congruence with the principle of Martin Luther 'non vi sed verbo' (Not through violence, but through the word alone). Cf. Max Josef Suda, *Die Ethik Martin Luthers*, Göttingen: Vandenhoeck & Ruprecht, 2006, 180. Cf. the same principle with respect to the administration of the church in Philipp Melanchthon: Walter Elliger (ed.), Philipp Melanchthon, Göttingen: Vandenhoeck & Ruprecht, 1961, 103. Hans-Marin Müller, Homiletik. In: Gerhard Krause, Gerhard Müller, Theologische Realenzyklopädie, Band 15, Berlin: Walter de Gruyter, 1986, 526–565, here 553. Cf. also Gunter Krusche, The Church between accommodation and refusal: The significance of the Lutheran doctrine of the 'two kingdoms' for the Churches of the German Democratic Republic, in: *Religion, State and Society*, vol. 22, 3, 1994, 323–332.

the deeds of the German SS therefore behaved in agreement with the ethical maxim of Tolstoi!

Rozanov's Irrationalism as an Existential Type of Fundamentalism

Отчего у меня всегда так глупо? Отчего вся моя жизнь 'без разума' и 'без закона'?[46]

Why is it with me always so foolish? Why is all my life 'without reason' and 'without law'?

Все было в высшей степени благоразумно.[47]

All was in the highest degree reasonable.
ROZANOV ON TOLSTOI in *Solitaria*.

Rozanov, who visited Tolstoi in 1903, wrote after the excommunication of the novelist in 1902: "Nature is always more inscrutable than the reason of the human being. Tolstoi is reason. And history and the Church are nature".[48] In this statement he pointed out the difference between the novelist and himself: Tolstoi tried to be reasonable, but did not succeed in it, whereas he himself was less orientated towards calculation than towards history, the Church (not the Orthodox one) and nature. Already in 1900 Rozanov, considering Tolstoi's writing, asked a provocative question: "How can the rationalism of the word be

---

46 V. Rozanov, Opavshie list'ia. Korob pervyi. In: idem, O sebe i o zhizni svoei. Moscow: Moskovskii rabochii, 1990, 307.
47 Rozanov, *O sebe i o zhizni svoei*, 86.
48 Rozanov, *Tolstoi i russkaia Tserkov'*, St Petersburg: Tipografiia A.S. Suvorina, 1912. «Nature is always a more unfathomable secret than human reason. Tolstoi was reason. And history and the church were nature'. («Природа всегда более неисповедимая тайна, чем разум человеческий. Толстой – был разум. И история и Церковь – это природа.») Cf. also: «Мне кажется, Толстого мало любили, и он это чувствовал. Около него не раздалось, при смерти, и даже при жизни, ни одного 'мучительного крика вдруг', ни того 'сумасшедшего поступка', по которым мы распознаем настоящую привязанность.» «It seems to me that they had little love for Tolstoi, and he felt it. Near him at his death, and even during his lifetime, there was not even one "sudden torturous cry", nor that "crazy act", from which we recognise a real affection'. Rozanov, *Uedinennoe* in: idem, *O sebe i o zhizni svoei*, 86.

adequate for the expression of the irrational?" ("Рационализм слова для выражения иррационального?"[49]).

Rozanov's religious fundamentalism, which was visible in his cult of Egypt, his cult of phallus and blood and in his philo- and antisemitism[50] can also be considered as a type of Russian irrationalism, which is based on fundamentalism. Already in his early article 'The Idea of Rational Science' he counterbalanced the rationality of exact knowledge about nature with the irrationality in and of society. The author of the reviewed book, Strakhov, is not supposed to tell his innermost belief: "Here we enter the sphere of the 'irrational': To be constantly only reasonable, to behave always correctly, with controlled virtue, is not at all the best thing for a human being".[51] Here Rozanov turns the reader's attention to Dostoevskii's short piece *The Golden Age in One's Pocket*. In his late essay 'The Grand Inquisitor of Dostoevskii' Rozanov used the *Notes from Underground* (1864) as the example for his certainty that the human being:

> [...] в цельности своей природы есть существо *иррациональное*; поэтому как полное его объяснение недоступно для разума, так недостижимо для него – его удовлетворение. Как бы ни была упорна работа мысли, она никогда не покроет всей действительности, будет отвечать мнимому человеку, а не действительному. В человеке скрыт акт творчества, и он-то именно и привлек в него жизнь, наградил его страданиями и радостями, ни понять, ни переделать которых не дано разуму.[52]

> [...] in its totality is an *irrational* being; therefore as its full explanation is inaccessible to reason, so too is its satisfaction unachievable. However forceful the work of the thinking might be, it will never extend to the

---

49 Vasilii Rozanov, Novaia rabota o Tolstom i Dostoevskom. In: idem, *Iudaizm. Stat'i i ocherki*, Moscow: Respublika, Saint Petersburg: Rostok, 2009, 492.

50 Genrietta Mondry, Vasilii Rozanov, Evrei i russkaia literatura, in: E. Kurganov/eadem, (ed.), *Rozanov i evrei*. Saint Petersburg: Akademicheskii proekt, 2000. Rainer Grübel, 'Judenfreund – Judenfeind: Vasilij Rozanovs Judenbild: eine problematische ästhetische Imagologie mit aporetischem Sprung aus der Theorie in die Praxis', in: S. Mierau/F. Mierau (ed.), *Werke in zehn Lieferungen / Pawel Florenski*. (Appendix 2) Berlin: Kontextverlag, 2001, 7–58.

51 Vasilii Rozanov, 'Ideia ratsional'nogo estetvoznania' in: *Russkii vestnik*, 1892, Nr. 8, 196–221. Reprinted in: idem, *Esteticheskoe ponimanie istorii*, Moscow: Respublika 2009, 114–132.

52 V. Rozanov, *Velikii inkvizitor Dostoevskogo*, Saint Petersburg: Tipografiia S.N. Nikolaeva, 1894/1902, 29. Reprinted in: idem, *Legenda o Velikom inkvizitore. Sochineniia*, vol. 7, Moscow: Respublika, 1990, 71.

whole of reality, it will answer only the transient human being, not the real one. An act of creation is concealed in the human being, and even it has pulled him into life, provided him with suffering and with pleasure, which reason is neither able to understand nor alter.

In the eyes of Rozanov the entire artistic world of Dostoevskii was a universe of the irrational. But even more fundamentally he considered the basis of society, the family, in itself as an irrational phenomenon: "The family is an institution that is essentially irrational, mystical".[53] The reason for the 'unreasonable' nature of the family, and consequently also of society, is love. Like Freud, Rozanov unfolded a detailed reasoning about love, but as opposed to Freud, it was not his aim to make reasonable something that he considered fundamentally unreasonable. Instead he considered it his duty to keep the incalculable nature of sex, Eros and agape (they all were the same for him) unchanged.

It would be a mistake to conclude that Rozanov was an irrational person throughout his life – he taught geography and history for ten years in a school and wrote a very reasonable philosophical book entitled *On Understanding*.[54] And he chose as his model the philologist Buslaev, giving an interesting reason for this choice: "My ideals are those of Peredol'skii[55] and Buslaev. Buslaev in his quiet rationality and high humanity".[56]

A good example for the relativity of reason in Rozanov's view can be found in a beautiful prose-miniature in his *Fallen Leaves*. Here the philosopher and

---

53   «Семья есть институт существенно иррациональный, мистический.»; Vasilii Rozanov, *Semeinyi vopros*, vol. 1, Saint Petersburg: Tipografiia M. Merkuševa, 1903, 75, 78.
54   Vasilij Rozanov, *O ponimanii. Opyt issledovaniia prirody, granits i vnutrennego stroeniia nauki kak tsel'nogo znaniia*, Moscow: Tipografiia E. Lissnera i Iu. Romana, 1886. Reprint Moscow: Tanais 1994.
55   Vladimir Vasil'evich Peredol'skii (1869–1936) was an ethnographer, historian, teacher and journalist, who worked at the Geographic institute of the University of St Petersburg, before in 1921 he became a professor of anthropology.
56   Rozanov, 'Opavshie list'ia. Korob pervyj', in: idem, *O sebe i o zhizni svoei*, 289. He added, however: 'On the sheet of paper where this was written, little Vera from the 7th class of Stoiunina has added, full of Pathos and Romanticism: "This is not true, is not the truth, your literature is *you*, all *you*, with your wild, pathetic and tired soul. Nobody could do this, in such a clear (form?) and so fully reflect each of his motions"'. ('Мой идеал – Передольский и Буслаев. Буслаев в спокойной разумности и высокой человечности. На клочке бумаги где это было записано, Верунька -VII кл. Стоюниной, вся в пафосе и романтизме, приписала: «Неверно, неправда, ибо ты был первый, что смог так ярко и полно выразить то, что хотел. Твоя литература есть *ты*, весь ты, с твоей душой мятежной, страстной и усталой. Никто этого не смог сделать в такой яркой (форме?) и так полно отразить каждое свое движение».)

writer opposes Hegel's rationalist spirit of the world (*Weltgeist*) to the irrational soul of the world, which is also incarnated in Sophia (who is not explicitly addressed here):

> Конечно, я ценил ум (без него скучно): но ни на какую степень его не любовался. / С умом – интересно; это – само собою. Но почему-то не привлекает и не восхищает (совсем другая категория).
>
> Чем же нас тянет Б.? Явно – не умом, не 'премудростью'. Чем же? Любованье мое всегда было на *душу*. Вот тут я смотрел и 'забывался' (как при музыке)... Душа – обворожительна (совсем другая категория). Тогда не тянет ли Б. мира 'обворожительностью'? Во всяком случае Он тянет душою, а не мудростью, Б. – *душа мира*, а – не *мировой разум* (совсем разница).
>
> *11 июля 1912.*[57]

[Of course I valued reason (one gets bored without it): but in no way did I adore it.

Reason makes things interesting; this is self-evident. But for some reason the mind does not attract or delight me (which is a totally different category).

How does G. attract us? Clearly neither with reason nor with 'wisdom'. How then? My adoration was always for the *soul*. Just here I looked and lost myself (as when one listens to music)...The soul is bewitching (it's a totally different category). Does G. attract the world, then, by a 'bewitching' quality? In any case, He attracts with the soul, not with wisdom – G. is the *soul of the world*, and not the *world's reason* (totally different concepts).[58]

11th July 1912.]

Once again Rozanov elaborated his vision of the relation between rationality and irrationality in a short text of the 1913 book *In Sakharna* (*V Sakharne*). He goes back to Strakhov and his work on natural philosophy *The World as a Whole*

---

57   Rozanov, Opavshie list'ia. Korob pervyi, 256.

58   One of his correspondents, the Moscow student Vera Mordvinova, wrote to him in a letter of 14th February 1915 showing the presence of the European origin of the notion of the irrational in early twentieth-century Russian culture: 'That truth, my Truth is not composed of irrational numbers, but of something different' (Та истина, моя Истина, не из иррационалных чисел составлена, а из другого'). See Rozanov, *Literaturnye izgnanniki. P.A. Florenskii, S. A Rachinskii*, Moscow: Respublika, St. Petersburg: Rostok, 2010, 903. In her opinion the truth of the world consists of the gentle behaviour of the male and the female turkey, breeding their eggs.

(*Mir kak tseloe*, SPb., 1872) and notes the observation that Strakhov did not explain, "why 'we are so opposed to rationalism'" (почему же мы враждуем против рационализма).[59] Here Rozanov states that Strakhov's nature brings death to all poetry, every picture and all virtue. In a way, Rozanov deconstructs Strakhov's rationalist model of nature, in which all that is natural becomes rational and disgusting. It does not breathe any more, it is a dead body, as it is in Rozanov's view primarily already in German culture (he refers to Schelling). In fact, argues Rozanov here, "nature is not rational" («природа не рациональна»[60]) although it contains rational parts.

However, in 1916 Rozanov adds to this miniature a commentary, in which he states that our brains are phallic and as such they are a source of rationalism *and* anti-rationalism, and that they are a source of irrationalism because rationalism tends to consider the sexual as an impure phenomenon. The mystical and religious explanations of the world and nature, on the other hand, in Rozanov's view bring light to the brain, seen as "phallic explanations" («фаллические объяснения»[61]), deriving from creation and life-giving. Thus phallic reason can save us from the trap of the dichotomy of rationalism and irrationalism.

The striving of every culture towards norms has to be and is compensated for by non-normative acts. We not only observe this in languages, but also in acts of thinking. The more rigid the rules of thinking become, the greater the need to counterbalance them.

So fifteen years after Rozanov had written down his most fundamental reasoning about unreason and almost a decade after his death, on 27th July 1927, the Russian poet Daniil Kharms, formerly a student at an electro-technical institute and an admirer of modern mathematics, wrote in his diary about his relationship with his beloved friend Esther Rusakova a sentence that proves the ongoing energy of irrationalism in Russian culture: "Во мне нет ценности для рационалистического ума". ("The rational mind has no value for me".)[62] This new type of irrationalism was part of Russian absurdism in the late 1920s and the 1930s. But that is another subject.[63]

---

59 Rozanov, *Sacharna*, 29.
60 Rozanov, *Sacharna*, 29.
61 Rozanov, *Sacharna*, 30.
62 http://www.klassika.ru/read.html?proza/harms/xarms_diaries.txt&page=2 (consulted 6.7.2011). Cf. Aleksandr Kobrinskii, *Daniil Kharms*. (Zhizn' zamechatel'nykh liudei), Moscow: Molodaia Gvardiia, 2008, 69. This maxim also shows the relevance of Rozanov's writing for the development of irrationalism in Russian culture of the twentieth century.
63 Until now there has been almost no research on the reception of Rozanov in the work of Daniil Kharms.

Bibliography

Abrochnov, Aleksandr Michailovich. 2006. *Sosushestvovanie i vzaimoperechody racional'nogo i irracional'nogo*, Nizhnii Novgorod: Izdatel'stvo NGU.

Belaia, Irina A. 2001. 'Buddizm kak teoreticheskii istochnik ucheniia o soznanii zhizni L.N. Tolstogo' in: *Eticheskii mysl'*, vol. 2, Moscow: IF RAN, 203–215.

Berdiaev, Nikolai 1990 'Tolstoi v russkoe revoliutsii' [1918] in: idem, *Dukhi russkoi revoljjfutsii*, Moscow: Izdatel'stvo Moskovskogo universiteta.

―――― 1998. 'Gibel' russkikh illiuzii' in: idem: *Dukhovnye osnovy russkoi revoliutsii: Opyty 1917–1918 gg.*, Saint Petersburg: RKhGI.

Blavatsky [i.e. von Hahn-Rottenstern], Helena Pavlovna 1895. *The Secret Doctrine: The Synthesis of Science, Religion, and Philosophy*, 2 vols. London ets.: The Theosophical Publishing Company. Reprint 1999, Pasadena: Theosophical University Press.

Blok, Aleksandr. 1997. 'Blagoslovljaju vse, chto bylo' in: idem, *Polnoe sobranie sochinenii i pisem v dvadcati tomakh*, vol 1, Moscow: Nauka, 96.

Bykov, A.V. 'Nravstvennoe uchenie i tvorchestvo L.N. Tolstogo v interpretatsii A.L. Volynskogo'. http://www.ksu.ru/miku/info/sob/konf_tolstoi/s22.htm (consulted 26.2.2010).

Camus, Albert. 1942. *Le mythe de Sisyphe. Essai sur l'absurde*, Paris: Les Éditions Gallimard.

Etkind, Aleksandr. 1998. *Chlyst. Sekty, literatura i revoljutsiia*, Moscow: NLO.

Fichte, Johann Gottlieb. 1910. *Werke: Auswahl in VI Bänden*, ed. Fritz Medicus, vol. 4, Leipzig: Fritz Eckardt.

Frassetto, Michael 2007. *Heretic lives: medieval heresy from Bogomil and the Cathars to Wyclif and Hus*, London: Profile Books.

Galkovskii, Dmitrii. 1997. *Beskonechnyi tupik*, Moscow: Samizdat.

―――― 2004. 'Devjatnadtsatyi vek. Sviatochnyi rasskaz Nr. 13' in: *Novyi mir*, 3, 89–97.

Kobrinskii, Aleksandr. 2008. *Daniil Kharms* (Zhizn' zamechatel'nykh liudei), Moscow: Molodaia Gvardiia.

Korsgaard, Christine. 1996. *The Sources of Normativity*, New York: Cambridge University Press.

Grübel, Rainer. 2001. 'Judenfreund – Judenfeind: Vasilij Rozanovs Judenbild: eine problematische ästhetische Imagologie mit aporetischem Sprung aus der Theorie in die Praxis' in: S. Mierau/F. Mierau (eds.), Pawel Florenski, *Werke in zehn Lieferungen* (Appendix 2) Berlin: Kontextverlag, 7–58.

―――― 2010. 'Gogoljeva glad – jelovnik dvadesetog stoleća. Gladovanje kao estetsko samouništenie' in: Jasmina Vojvodić (ed.), *Hrana od gladi do prejedanja*, Zagreb, 59–84.

―――― 2011. „Gordoe slovo: spravedlivost"' – „Ein stolzes Wort: Gerechtigkeit". Der Gerechtigkeitsdiskurs in Tolstojs Roman "Krieg und Frieden"' in: Holger Kuße /

Nikolaj Plotnikov (ed.), *Pravda. Diskurse der Gerechtigkeit in der russischen Ideengeschichte*, München: Verlag Otto Sagner 2011, 39–74.

—— 2012. 'Gogol's Hunger(n) – Eine Speisekarte des 20. Jahrhunderts' in: *Zeitschrift für Kulturwissenschaften*, 1, 147–166.

—— 2013a. 'Kamernyi nomadizm Vasiliia Rozanova i ego vospriiatie Ėduardom Limonovym. Rasshazyvanie edinstva sub"ekta v russkoi kul'ture' in: *Zeitschrift für Slavische Philologie*, 69, 1, 81–106.

—— 2013b. 'Existentialismus' in: Martin George a.o., eds., *Tolstoj als theologischer Denker und Kirchenkritiker*, Göttingen: Vandenhoeck & Rupprecht 2014.

Hanegraaff, Wouter J. (ed.) 2006. *Dictionary of Gnosis and Western Esotericism*, Leiden: Brill.

Hegel, Gottfried Wilhelm Friedrich. 1927. *Enzyklopädie der philosophischen Wissenschaften im Grundrisse 1830. Erster Teil. Die Wissenschaft der Logik,* idem, *Sämtliche Werke in 20 Bänden*, ed. Glockner, vol. 8, Stuttgart: Fromann.

Krusche, Gunter 1994. 'The Church between accommodation and refusal: The significance of the Lutheran doctrine of the "two kingdoms" for the Churches of the German Democratic Republic' in: *Religion, State and Society*, vol. 22, 3, 323–332.

Link, Jürgen. 2006. *Versuch über den Normalismus. Wie Normalität produziert wird*, Göttingen: Vandenhoeck & Rupprecht.

Lukács, Georg. 1988. *Die Zerstörung der Vernunft: Der Weg des Irrationalismus von Schelling zu Hitler*, Berlin: Aufbau Verlag.

Kropotkin, Peter. 1911. 'Tolstoy' in *Encyclopædia Britannica*, London.

Melton, Gordon (ed.) 2000. *Encyclopedia of Occultism & Parapsychology*, Farmington Hills: Thomson Gale.

Mondri, Genrietta 2000. 'Vasilii Rozanov, evrei i russkaia literatura' in: E. Kurganov / eadem (eds.), *Rozanov i evrei*, Saint Peterburg: Akademicheskii proekt, 155–254.

Müller, Hans-Martin 'Homiletik' in: Gerhard Krause, Gerhard Müller (eds.), *Theologische Realenzyklopädie*, Band 15, Berlin: Walter de Gruyter. 1986, 526–565.

Novgorodcev, Pavel, *Krizis sovremennogo pravosoznaniia*, Moscow: Tipografiia I.N. Kušnera & Co., 1909.

Rolf, Thomas. 1999. *Normalität. Ein philosophischer Grundbegriff des 20. Jahrhunderts*. München: Wilhelm Fink.

Rozanov, Vasilii. 1886. Rozanov, *O ponmanii. Opyt issledovaniia prirody, granits i vnutrennego stroeniia nauki kak cel'nogo znaniia*, Moscow: Tipografiia E. Lissnera i Iu. Romana. Reprint Moscow: Tanais 1994.

—— 1892. 'Ideia ratsional'nogo estestvoznania' in: *Russkij vestnik*, 8, 196–221. Reprinted in: idem, *Esteticheskoe ponimanie istorii*, Moscow; Respublika 2009, 114–132.

—— 1894. *Velikii inkvizitor Dostoevskogo*, Saint Petersburg: Tipografiia S.N. Nikolaeva. 1894. Reprinted in: idem, *Legenda o Velikom inkvizitore Dostoevskogo. Sobranie sochinenii*, vol. 7, Moscow: Respublika 1990.

――― 1903. *Semejnyj vopros*, vol. 1, Saint Petersburg: Tipografiia M. Merkuševa.

――― 1912. *L.N. Tolstoi i Russkaia Cerkov'*, Saint Petersburg: Tipografiia A.S. Suvorina.

――― 1914. *Apokalipsicheskaia sekta,* Saint Petersburg: Tipografiia Veisberga i Shunina.

――― 1990. 'Opavshie list'ia. Korob pervyi' in: idem, *O sebe i o zhizni svoei*, Moscow: Moskovskii rabochii, 1990, 196–330.

――― 2009. 'Novaia rabota o Tolstom i Dostoevskom' in: idem, *Iudaizm. Stat'i i ocherki*, Moscow: Respublika, Saint Petersburg: Rostok, 487–494.

――― 2010. *Literaturnye izgnanniki. P.A. Florenskij, S. A Račinskij,* Moscow: Respublika, Saint Petersburg: Rostok.

Rybakov, Boris A. 1993. *Strigol'niki: Russkie Gumanisty XIV stoletiia*, Moscow: Nauka.

Schlüchter, Anita. 2004. Zur Verteidigung des Rechts. Die Kritik an Tolstojs Rechtsnihilismus durch Juristen und Solov'ev. http://www.jfsl.de/publikationen/2004/Schluechter.htm. (consulted 1.11.2009).

Shestov, Lev 1900. *Dobro v uchenii gr. Tolstogo i F. Nitshe (Filosofiia i propoved')*, Saint Petersburg: Stasjulevich.

Singer, Marcus George. 2002. *The Ideal of a Rational Morality. Philosophical Compositions*, Oxford: Clarendon Press.

Singer, Peter (ed.), *A Companion to Ethics*. (Blackwell Companions to Philosophy) Oxford 1993.

Suda, Max Josef. 2006. *Die Ethik Martin Luthers*. Göttingen: Vandenhoeck & Ruprecht.

Tolstoi, Lev. 1957. 'Ispoved'. (A confession)' in: idem, *Polnoe sobranie sochinenii*, vol. 23, Moscow: Khudozhestvennaia literatura.

――― 1959. 'Voskresenie' in: idem, *Sobranie sochinenii v dvenadtsati tomakh*. Vol. 11, Moscow: Khudozhestvennaia literature, 1959.

Tolstoy, Lev 1987. *A Confession and Other Religious Writings*, trans. Jane Kentish, New York: Penguin Books.

――― 2002. 'A Confession' in: Donna T. Orwin (ed.), *The Cambridge Companion to Tolstoy*, Cambridge University Press.

Viatte, Auguste. 1928. *Les sources occultes du romantisme*, 2 vols. Paris: H. Champion.

Vivekananda, Svami. 1896. *Filosofkaia ioga. Lektsii o radzhi-ioge, ili Ovladenie vnutrennei pravdoi*, New York.

Volynskii, Akim. 1906. *Dostoevskii*, Saint Petersburg: Tipografiia Energiia.

Weber, Max. 1951. *Gesammelte Aufsätze zur Wissenschaftslehre*, Tübingen: J.C.B. Mohr.

Zenkovskij, Vasilij. 1958. *Aus der Geschichte der ästhetischen Ideen in Russland im 19. und 20. Jahrhundert*, The Hague: Mouton.

PART 3

The Silver Age

CHAPTER 13

From Neo-Kantian Theory of Cognition to Christian Intellectual Mysticism: Logical Voluntarism in Vladimir Solov'ev and Andrei Belyi

Henrieke Stahl

The Epistemology of Solov'ev and Belyi – A Comparison

This chapter will focus on the central epistemological concept presented in the later philosophical work of Vladimir Solov'ev in order to compare it to the gnoseology of Andrei Belyi. The epistemological ideas of the two philosophers are closely connected in terms of their roots in neo-Kantian theory of cognition as well as with regard to Belyi's reception of Solov'ev. Solov'ev develops his epistemology in his *Theoretical Philosophy* (1897–99; abbreviation: ThP), which remained a fragment consisting of only three essays intended to introduce Solov'ev's planned but – due his death in 1900 – unwritten epistemology and metaphysics.[1] Unlike Solov'ev's *Theoretical Philosophy*, Andrei Belyi's main philosophical work, his *History of Development of the Self-consciousness-soul* (1926–31, *Istoriia stanovleniia samosoznaiushchii dushi*, abbreviation: ISSD) has historically been unaccounted for.[2] Belyi's manuscript, which also remained

---

1 For detailed analysis of Solov'ev's *Theoretical Philosophy* (ThP) and a discussion of research on this topic, see my article: Henrieke Stahl, 'Wer ist Ich? Vladimir Solov'ev's "Theoretische Philosophie"' in Plotnikov, Nikolaj and Meike Siegfried, Jens Bonnemann (eds.) *Zwischen den Lebenswelten. Interkulturelle Profile der Phänomenologie*. (Syneidos. Deutsch-russische Studien zur Philosophie und Ideengeschichte. Herausgegeben von Alexander Haardt und Nikolaj Plotnikov. Band 3.) Berlin: LIT Verlag, 2012, 37–68.
2 Until up to now the work has only been available in printed extracts (the edition Andrei Belyi, *Dusha samosoznaiushchaia*. Ed. by E.I. Chistiakova, Moscow: Kanon, 1999 contains only part two of three parts) or fragmented handwritten copies. The manuscript was rediscovered in 2007 by the international research project under the direction of Monika Spivak (Andrei Belyi's Memorial Museum in Moscow) and me. We have found it in the unofficial part of the Belyi-archive in Russian State library in Moscow (fond № 25, 45/1 and 45/2). This project is dedicated to the publication, commentary and analysis of the manuscript and is sponsored by Deutsche Forschungsgemeinschaft (DFG) and the Russian Foundation for Humanities (RGNF) for the period 2006–2012. Recent publications on the ISSD in: Duda, Krzysztof and Teresa Obolevitch (eds.). 2010. *Symvol w kulturze rosyjskiej*. Kraków: Wydawnictwo WAM, pp.559–636; see also: Stahl, Henrieke (ed., 2011): *Andrei Belyi – filosof*.

unfinished, comprises more than 1,200 handwritten pages and is an example of symbolist cultural philosophy. In his treatise, Belyi analyses the evolution of European consciousness on the basis of its reflections on the humanities and natural sciences, especially on art, literature and philosophical as well as religious thought. Naturally, epistemology plays a fundamental role in Belyi's considerations.

Solov'ev's Reception of Neo-Kantianism in His Theoretical Philosophy

The roots of Solov'ev's epistemology, which can be traced back to neo-Kantianism, are still unexplored. The main reason for this can be seen in the fact that the renowned philosopher Aleksei Losev vehemently denied the existence of a connection between Solov'ev's *Theoretical Philosophy* and neo-Kantianism that, according to him, exceeded the connecting link to the fashionable terminology at the time.[3] However, Losev apparently had not gained insights about the quite varying trends within neo-Kantianism. He indeed is right in claiming that Solov'ev objected to Marburg neo-Kantianism, especially of the Cohen type,[4] popular above all in St Petersburg in the 1890s, whose 'logicism' considered thinking as a creative producing force. But neo-Kantianism shows two more schools whose epistemological ideas feature striking similarities to Solov'ev's *Theoretical Philosophy*: on the one hand, 'metaphysical neo-Kantianism', among whose representatives, according to the current state of research, are authors like Otto Liebmann (1840–1912), Johannes Volkelt (1848–1930), Gideon Spicker (1840–1912), but also Eduard von Hartmann (1842–1906);[5] on the other hand – especially taking up to Rudolf Hermann Lotze – the Southwest German school with Wilhelm Windelband and his pupil Heinrich Rickert. This article will demonstrate that Solov'ev intended to provide a firm basis on which to establish his metaphysics (to which he had planned the *Theoretical Philosophy* to be an introduction)

'Istoriia stanovleniia samosoznaiushchei dushi' i ee konteksty. Amsterdam. Special issue of Russian Literature. Vol. LXX (2011) I/II.

3 Aleksei Losev, *Vladimir Solov'ev i ego vremia*, Moscow: Molodaia gvardiia, 1990, 145, 146.
4 *Ibid.*
5 On metaphysical neo-Kantianism see: H. Schwaetzer: 'Subjektivistischer Transsubjektivismus'. In: Volkelt, Johannes: *Erfahrung und Denken. Kritische Grundlegung der Erkenntnistheorie*. Mit einer Einleitung und einem Personen- und Sachregister hrsg. von Harald Schwaetzer. Vorwort von Hans-Ludwig Ollig. Hildesheim u.a. 2002 (Texte zum frühen Neukantianismus. Hrsg. von Harald Schwaetzer. Bd. 3). IX–XLVI, IXff.

by laying the foundation of the *Theoretical Philosophy* in the scientifically respected epistemology of neo-Kantianism at the time and the attempt to overcome it.[6]

In particular, the main epistemological work of Johannes Volkelt, *Experience and Thought* (1886), which scholarship considers an 'exemplary document of the metaphysical neo-Kantianism',[7] features a high degree of affinity to Solov'ev's *Theoretical Philosophy*. The central ideas of the *Theoretical Philosophy* can be found preconceived in Volkelt. The fact that Volkelt, among the metaphysic neo-Kantians, 'was the only one who tried to tackle the basic aporias of metaphysical issues again and again with a strict cognitive scientific approach"[8] might have attracted Solov'ev's attention.

With their epistemologies, both philosophers strive for the same goal: the epistemologically verified justification of metaphysics. While Solov'ev wants to concretely develop his metaphysics from epistemology, Volkelt wants to legitimate the possibility of metaphysics on the whole. Both methodologically pose the "question on the last cognitive principles"[9] that is to be looked at by eliminating all metaphysical presuppositions,[10] i.e. they choose an approach of presuppositionlessness, which is therefore concerned with starting "at the very beginning".[11] "Via self-observation"[12] something indubitable is to be found that is of "absolute naturalness" or "undeniable certainty" as can be read in both analogously.[13] In regard to the style of the procedure this means that both to start off in the form of an autobiographical 'monologue'.[14]

For Solov'ev the actual investigation proceeds in three major steps. The first two steps, as just shown, for aim and method can be found preconceived in Volkelt, where they also play a crucial role. Solov'ev's third step, however, differs decisively from Volkelt. Let us now consider the first two steps.

---

6   Solov'ev, V.S., *Sobranie sochinenii V.S. Solov'eva*. Vol. 1–12. Sankt Petersburg (Reprint: Bruxelles 1966). Vol. Bd. x, 83, note 1 (Predislovie, in: Tri razgovora. 1899–1900).
7   Schwaetzer, Subjektivistischer Transsubjektivismus, XIII.
8   Schwaetzer, Subjektivistischer Transsubjektivismus, XII.
9   Volkelt, J. *Erfahrung und Denken. Kritische Grundlegung der Erkenntnistheorie*. Mit einer Einleitung und einem Personen- und Sachregister hrsg. von Harald Schwaetzer. Vorwort von Hans-Ludwig Ollig. Hildesheim u.a. 2002 (Texte zum frühen Neukantianismus. Hrsg. von Harald Schwaetzer. Bd. 3), 18.
10 *Ibid.* 43.
11 Solov'ev, ThP 764.
12 'Selbstbesinnung', cf. Volkelt, *Erfahrung und Denken*, 332.
13 Volkelt, *Erfahrung und Denken*, 27f.; Solov'ev, ThP 769.
14 Volkelt, *Erfahrung und Denken*, 29. Solov'ev, ThP 787.

Both philosophers start off with 'methodical doubt', in order to put themselves on a trial basis into the state of 'absolute scepticism'.[15] This procedure helps them find the first, as they assume, indubitable principle: the certainty of pure givenness of consciousness, of "absolute self-certainty of present consciousness",[16] also called "pure consciousness"[17] or "pure experience".[18] Thus Volkelt talks about the "knowledge of my own processes of consciousness as the only unquestionable certain knowledge",[19] and Solov'ev calls the "necessary certainty of the present consciousness" the "basic truth of philosophy".[20] This viewpoint means for both that within the givenness of consciousness, appearance and reality cannot be distinguished because differentiating them would already be a judgement. Therefore only given 'facts' may be talked about.[21] This also applies, as both point out, for the subject itself, that is both for the empirical subject with its contents of consciousness and for the formal entity of these contents that as "thought of the I"[22] accompanies the conceptions, the "logical" or "transcendental subject".[23] The subject must not require any substantiality from this point of view, neither in actual nor potential form,[24] but it is, as said by Hume, a "bundle" or a "collection of perceptions".[25] As Solov'ev puts it distinctively, Descartes' self-certain I could hence be signified, as a "usurper without a philosophical passport", as a relic from the "scholastic monk's cell".[26] Instead it must be spoken of as nothing but a "phenomenological subject".[27]

The result of this first step of investigation turns out to be exactly the same for both philosophers: "The initial condition for all philosophy" is "the cognition that our knowledge *as a start* does not reach anything more than our conceptions".[28] They state likewise that this givenness is not enough for

---

15 Volkelt, *Erfahrung und Denken,* S.63f.; Solov'ev, ThP 788.
16 Solov'ev, ThP 771.
17 Ibid.
18 Volkelt, *Erfahrung und Denken,* 51, 64ff.
19 Volkelt, *Erfahrung und Denken,* 53; see also p.55.
20 Cf. Solov'ev, ThP, 771.
21 Volkelt, *Erfahrung und Denken,* 59f.; Solov'ev, ThP 773.
22 Solov'ev, ThP 784.
23 Volkelt, *Erfahrung und Denken,* 86f.
24 *Ibid.* 86.
25 *Ibid.* 87f., see also 106. Solov'ev, ThP 793f.
26 Solov'ev, ThP 781f.
27 *Ibid.* 785.
28 Volkelt, J. *Immanuel Kants Erkenntnistheorie nach ihren Grundprincipien analysiert. Ein Beitrag zur Grundlegung der Erkenntnistheorie,* Leipzig 1879, 1. Compare with Solov'ev, ThP 797.

cognition, because even though there are plenty of 'facts' available their meaning is trivial.²⁹ From there arises the need for them to look for something within the facts of consciousness that is more than a fact to itself but in givenness is still certain as a factum.³⁰ The "trans-subjective cognitive principle"³¹ as Volkelt calls it, along with Solov'ev, is able to "transcend the boundaries of the present consciousness" and is at the same time a matter of fact and "more than a matter of fact".³² Both philosophers locate it in thinking as the second or logical certainty, named by Volkelt "logical necessity",³³ and by Solov'ev "certainty of reason" or "formal certainty".³⁴

The feature by which thinking is distinguished from all other facts in consciousness is the form of "generality"³⁵ that lays claim to objectivity or rather "objective"³⁶ or "trans-subjective validity".³⁷ Both emphasise likewise – explicitly distancing themselves from Hegel and in implicit differentiation from the Marburg neo-Kantianism – the pure formality and non-productivity of thinking, which never *produces* anything³⁸ but is only able to check the contents given to it from outside. By locating this second source of certainty, cognition is yet still impossible, so that a third step of investigation becomes necessary. This step, however, proceeds differently for both.

According to Solov'ev, cognition only becomes possible if the 'intention' (*zamysel*) for cognition is at hand which as a "creative *let there be* makes intellectual little worlds and worlds from the chaos of factual states of consciousness".³⁹ Among the plenitude of possible 'intentions', there is a special one and that as given fact of consciousness: the will to attain "the truth itself" or "according to its essence".⁴⁰ The particularity of this 'intention' is that it is not only 'certainty' given both in terms of content and according to its form but that its object itself is certain. This means that it represents a third certainty, because – as opposed to all other objects – it claims to have an absolute meaning and, therefore, is the only object which, because of its absolute character, is appropriate to the infinite form of thinking. It is because this

---

29   Volkelt, *Erfahrung und Denken*, 100. Solov'ev, ThP 771.
30   Volkelt, *Erfahrung und Denken*, 39. Solov'ev, ThP 797.
31   Volkelt, *Erfahrung und Denken*, 134.
32   Solov'ev, ThP 797. See also 801.
33   Cf. Volkelt, *Erfahrung und Denken*, 139f.
34   Solov'ev, ThP 797, 814.
35   Volkelt, *Erfahrung und Denken*, 79. Solov'ev, ThP 800.
36   Volkelt, *Erfahrung und Denken*, 187, 190. Solov'ev, ThP 815f.
37   Volkelt, *Erfahrung und Denken*, 368. Solov'ev, ThP 805.
38   Volkelt, *Erfahrung und Denken*, 199f. Solov'ev, ThP 807.
39   Solov'ev, ThP 818f.
40   *Ibid.* 820.

'intention' is in line with 'the' truth as such, that an absolute precedes all concrete unconditioned particular truths. According to Solov'ev the subject of cognition that has this intention can be characterised as "reason of truth in the process of formation".[41]

Only the feasibility of this 'intention' remains doubtful. But because this 'intention' is as such absolutely certain the sceptic has to "step aside and see what becomes of it".[42] With this 'third certainty' based on the first two "sources of certainty"[43] (factual presence of consciousness and logical certainty), Solov'ev thinks he has gained back the truth for cognition and thus to have opened the door to metaphysics as knowledge of transcendence. He implies his claim to have initiated a philosophical 'turn', in its significance similar to the Kantian 'Copernican turn'.[44]

Volkelt, on the contrary, does not leave the boundaries of a theory of certainty for the benefit of the truth. Nonetheless, a certain analogy to Solov'ev's 'intention' can be detected. According to Volkelt, thinking implies only a *claim* for objective 'validity' to which, in regard of the cognising subject, the 'belief' in this 'validity' of thinking corresponds. Therefore both sides are metaphysically primed: for the man of knowledge, a "mystical foundation of belief";[45] for cognition itself the "metaphysical basic presupposition" is to be assumed, so that "cognising subject and recognised object" go together somehow "in the well of being".[46] Volkelt, as opposed to Solov'ev, believes the objective meaning of thinking, i.e. its actual capacity for truth, to be incapable of proof but its assumption to be at best intersubjectively comprehensible.[47]

Volkelt's and Solov'ev's approaches have a basic assumption in common: the existence of a desire for truth as the driver for knowledge.[48] In contrast to Volkelt, however, Solov'ev thinks he is able to show this striving for truth as a third certainty and thus to break the spell that was put on the knowledge of truth by the "theorem of consciousness".[49] Certainly, the knowledge of truth is

---

41   Ibid. 820.
42   Ibid. 819.
43   J. Volkelt, *Die Quellen der menschlichen Gewissheit*. München 1906, 2f.
44   Solov'ev, ThP 822.
45   Volkelt, *Erfahrung und Denken*, 184.
46   Ibid. 201.
47   Ibid. 182.
48   Ibid. 133.
49   'Satz des Bewusstseins', cf. Karl Leonhard Reinhold, *Beiträge zur Berichtigung bisheriger Mißverständnisse der Philosophen. Zweiter Band, die Fundamente des philosophischen Wissens, der Metaphysik, Moral, moralischen Religion und Geschmackslehre betreffend.* Mit einer Einleitung und Anmerkungen hrsg. von Faustino Fabbianelli. Hamburg 2004, 43f.

thus bound to the will. The will turns the cognitive act into a striving for truth itself, i.e. for necessary or rather absolute truth; it stands as *zamysel,* literally 'behind the thought'. The knowledge of truth is, therefore, although caused *logically,* caused *voluntarily* in the end. With his approach that, in line with Belyi, could accurately be named 'logical voluntarism',[50] Solov'ev transfers Volkelt's 'theory of certainty' into a 'theory of truth'. The parallelism of the reasoning that only ends at this point suggests an understanding of Solov'ev's approach as an attempt to correct the epistemology of metaphysical neo-Kantianism that in the end still does not validate metaphysics.

With this correction, Solov'ev approaches another neo-Kantian epistemology, namely the Southwest German school among whose works are Windelband's *Preludes*. In this school logical assessment and its judgement are differentiated while the latter bestows demand for truth from the first.[51] Thus the primacy is shifted from theoretical to practical reason and thinking is classified as dependent on will,[52] that – if the will has the 'intention' to cognise the truth – grants the "intended thought" the "certain value" or rather "the value of truth".[53] Windelband here takes truth as that "which is valid without having to be", as the "ideal" or "true being' that is 'eternal-timeless'. It is not what is but what 'ought to be'.[54] It is obvious that Windelband's idea is not only the source for Solov'ev's distinction between the given (*dan*) and the posited (*zadan*), but also for the 'intention' (*zamysel*) that warrants the knowledge of truth. The findings of a similarity in a threefold determination of the subject also point in this direction: neither of the two philosophers place the true subject in an empiric or formal-theoretical field but it only finds itself when it "forgets" itself as an "individual", in order to gain possession of "the timeless valid purpose"[55] and thus to participate in eternity as "absolute truth", as Solov'ev suggests, or rather, as said by Windelband, "universality".[56]

Windelband, however, decidedly disapproved of the possibility of a justification of epistemology by presuppositionlessness, as was attempted in metaphysical neo-Kantianism. Instead, he postulated the necessity of assuming the

---

50 'Logicheskii volyuntarizm'. See Belyi, ISSD (manuscript), third part, chapter 'Poznanie i samopoznanie'.
51 Wilhelm Windelband, *Präludien*. Aufsätze und Reden zur Philosophie und ihrer Geschichte. Neunte, photo-mechanisch gedruckte Auflage. Band I und II. Tübingen 1924, I,31f.; 32f.
52 *Ibid.* II, 47; II, 57.
53 Cf. 'drive to truth', 'feeling of truth', 'pursuit for truth'. *Ibid.* II,56.
54 *Ibid.* II, 343.
55 *Ibid.* II, 343.
56 *Ibid.* II, 345.

three 'ideals' (Truth, Good and Beauty) for "our thinking, volition and feeling" as teleological "purpose" of all axioms, i.e. in their validity unprovable norms that can be presupposed.[57] From the very beginning Solov'ev structured his philosophy according to just this 'metaphysical triad' as equivalent to trinity.[58] However, in his *Theoretical Philosophy* he tried, with just this approach of presuppositionlessness, to logically state a reason for the will to truth.

Solov'ev's *Theoretical Philosophy* can thus be understood as an attempt at a double correction of two neo-Kantian models of knowledge, related in terms of their metaphysical orientation yet exclusive in regard to their premises: on the one hand, that of the neo-Kantian theory of certainty (Volkelt) that is transferred into a theory of truth in line with the Southwest German school (Windelband), and on the other hand, that of the SouthwestGerman philosophy of values (Windelband) whose postulation of truth is to be made logically justifiable by the theory of certainty as exemplarily constructed in Volkelt's philosophy. This double correction by Solov'ev aims to dissolve the paradox of legitimating cognition of transcendence in a transcendental way. Thus, the cognition of transcendence is transferred from a theoretical issue into a practical task whose redemption does not consist of a particular cognition's benefit but of the *experience* of the participation in truth itself.

The Mystical Turn of Epistemology in Solov'ev's Theoretical Philosophy

However, unlike with the neo-Kantian approaches, the subject's participation in truth or rather transcendence in Solov'ev's *Theoretical Philosophy* represents a mystical turn: *theory* of knowledge becomes mystical *practice*. *Theoretical Philosophy* is actually a mystical script that is to show a 'path to truth' via epistemology as experience of God *in concreto*. Allusions to the New Testament as well as religious and mystical contexts that form a coherent subtext in the *Theoretical Philosophy* confirm this assumption.

With 'absolute truth' and the third concept of subject Solov'ev thus revolves around the word of Christ: "I am the truth" ("I am the way, the truth, and the life" – John 14:6; King James Version). The knowledge of truth thus becomes an

---

57   *Ibid.* II, 111f.
58   Cf. H. Stahl, – „Erinnert ihr euch an das Bild des schönen Leibes?': Aspekte der Sophiologie Vladimir Solov'evs. In: Urs Heftrich/Gerhard Ressel (Hgg.): *Vladimir Solov'ev und Friedrich Nietzsche: eine deutsch-russische kulturelle Jahrhundertbilanz.* Frankfurt am Main et al. 2003, 341–370.

act of communion via cognition that immediately assimilates the logos and with it God, i.e. philosophical cognition in its essence is determined as spiritual communion. For Solov'ev cognition, as a result, contributes significantly to the *theosis* (*obozhenie*) or deification of man. By participating in Christ via cognition, the individual man of knowledge gains *immortality* as '*act*ualisation' of truth in the double sense of the word.[59]

Accordingly, Solov'ev calls this form of philosophising "philosophical action".[60] This construction points to the central form of orthodox prayer, the so-called "intellectual action" (*umnoe delanie*), better known as the "Jesus prayer", that aims for spiritual communion as the path to theosis.[61] The three bases of thinking emphasised in the *Theoretical Philosophy* ('memory', 'word', and 'intention') also have a mystical grounding. Through these, the *three mystical steps* that Solov'ev has distinguished ever since his early work are concealed: the pictorial step (spiritual vision), the word or sound-like step (spiritual hearing), and the step of the *unio mystica*.

In addition Solov'ev names the preparatory state of the step-path which we already find developed in his early work: the attainment of the "pure" or "absolute consciousness" via the purging of all conditional contents[62] and the concentration of thinking in itself that is to discover itself as absolute or rather unlimited or infinite.[63] In this epistemological context Solov'ev introduces an important term of mysticism, which is designated as a goal: liberation from – as Plato might put it – the 'dungeon' of the world of appearances or rather of the illusory subject consciousness.[64]

The *Theoretical Philosophy* can thus be considered as the attempt to develop a Christian intellectual mysticism that is epistemologically legitimated and that demands a scientific justification.

Belyi's Anthroposophic Transformation of Logical Voluntarism

In his later philosophical work, especially in the above mentioned *History of Development of* the *Self-consciousness-soul* (ISSD), Andrei Belyi develops a

---

59 Solov'ev, ThP 822.
60 'filosofskoe delanie', *ibid*. 829.
61 Cf. also Peter Ehlen, "'Impersonalismus' und die, 'werdende Vernunft der Wahrheit' in Solov'evs Spätphilosophie.,, In: *Studies in East European Thought* 51 (1999), 155–175, 164f.
62 Solov'ev, ThP 771.
63 *Ibid.*, 764.
64 *Ibid.*, 823.

Christian gnoseology related to Solov'ev's approach. Like Solov'ev, he also considers the driving force of will to cognition of truth to be the crucial basis for the connection with Christ. He displaces with reference to Rickert, the pupil of Windelband, the primacy from thinking to will.[65] The epistemological justification of Christian cognition of truth, however, proceeds differently for Belyi to Solov'ev and, because of that, leads to different consequences.

As a basis, Belyi takes the correction that Rudolf Steiner made to the neo-Kantian approach of presupposition and which therefore is also relevant for Solov'ev's *Theoretical Philosophy*. Steiner emphasises that also consciousness with its conceptions which Volkelt and other neo-Kantians take as the only certain given, would already imply a judgement and hence does not grant presuppositionlessness.[66] The only thing that precedes all that is possibly given is thinking itself and that as pure "mental action".[67] Every insight turns out to be a result or product of the process of thinking, even if it is closely intertwined with perception. Accordingly, Belyi emphasises that epistemology is to take presuppositionlessness as a basis which gives up all defined concepts[68] and is to be found only in the act of thinking itself.[69]

In this way, a certain quality is ascribed to thinking which Solov'ev challenges together with both the metaphysical and the Southwest German neo-Kantians but which was actually similarly assumed by the Marburg school: thinking is not form but creatively produces both form and content. The producing action of thinking is made possible by the act of volition, i.e. will is not *logical* reason of knowledge of truth any longer, but *psychological*.

---

65   Cf. Belyi, ISSD (manuscript), part 2, chapter 'Dusha samosoznaiushchaia'. Cf. on the concept of truth in the ISSD my article Stahl, *'Pravda – protsess opravdanija istiny v stile so-istin'*.

66   Cf. Rudolf Steiner, *Wahrheit und Wissenschaft. Vorspiel einer „Philosophie der Freiheit'*. (GA 3), Dornach/Schweiz: Rudolf Steiner Verlag 1980, 38, 39; *Einleitungen zu Goethes Naturwissenschaftlichen Schriften*. (GA 001), Dornach/Schweiz: Rudolf Steiner Verlag 1987, 159; *Grundlinien einer Erkenntnistheorie der Goetheschen Weltanschauung mit besonderer Rücksicht auf Schiller*. (GA 2), Dornach/Schweiz: Rudolf Steiner Verlag 2003, 36ff.; *Die Philosophie der Freiheit. Grundzüge einer modernen Weltanschauung*. (GA 4), Dornach/Schweiz: Rudolf Steiner Verlag 1995, 70; *Die Rätsel der Philosophie in ihrer Geschichte als Umriss dargestellt*. (GA 18), Dornach/Schweiz: Rudolf Steiner Verlag 1985, 479; *Philosophie und Anthroposophie. Gesammelte Aufsätze 1904–1923*. (GA 35), Dornach/Schweiz: Rudolf Steiner Verlag 1984, 313ff.

67   Steiner, Die Philosophie der Freiheit, 43f., 51ff.

68   Belyi, ISSD (manuscript), part III, chapter 'Poznanie i chuvstvo v samosoznanii'; part II, chapter 'Simvolizm'.

69   Belyi, 'O smysle poznaniia' (1916) (Nachdruck der Ausgabe: Peterburg: Ėpocha 1922.) in *Russian Language Specialities* (Russian Study Series Nr. 51). Chicago 1965. 35–51, 41.

This view, in regard to Belyi, leads to a concept of truth, reality and subject whose differences to Solov'ev's *Theoretical Philosophy* can only be briefly indicated here. In the act of thinking the difference between subject and object, of concepts and appearances, becomes annihilated[70] because they are products of thinking as such. Thus, in thinking as action itself a bridge is built to transcendence, then "cognition is," as Belyi writes "immanent in reality",[71] whereas reality is only present in the action of production and not in a created product. The symbolist writer understands the actual process of this cognitive form as the transformation of the epistemology into meditative practice whose peculiarities he describes according to the esoteric path of anthroposophy. According to Belyi, man finds logos as "not I but Christ inside me" (Gal. 2:20)[72] in the pure act of thinking, whereas the personal I is not to be lost but, via participation in logos, is turned into a creative "individual" that in the pure action of thinking together with truth also constitutes itself as "spiritual being". While Solov'ev in his "logical voluntarism" focuses on *voluntarism*, Belyi emphasises the *logical* element.

Conclusion

In their later works Solov'ev and Belyi develop an epistemology which is based on a critical reception of key concepts of the Metaphysical (Johannes Volkelt) and of the Southwestern school of neo-Kantianism (Heinrich Rickert, Wilhelm Windelband). Both Solov'ev and Belyi start from the idea of presuppositionlessness, which plays a central role in the epistemology of Volkelt. Based on corrections, they try to inaugurate a third 'Copernican turn' by showing scientifically that man's cognition is rooted in spiritual being. Each of them arrives in his own way at some kind of cognition, which is based on the primacy of practical reason, in accordance with a typical pattern of the South-Western school. Belyi called his epistemology "logical voluntarism". The way in which Belyi supports his theory differs substantially from Solov'ev's "logical voluntarism": the will is no longer understood as a *logical*, but only a *psychological* function, and thought becomes creative power. Therefore, Belyi's theory of cognition should rather be called "voluntaristic logicism".

The reason for this difference between Belyi and Solov'ev can be traced back to the epistemology of Rudolf Steiner and his correction of the idea of

---

70 Cf. Steiner, *Die Philosophie der Freiheit*, 60.
71 Belyi, 'O smysle poznaniia', 44.
72 Belyi, ISSD (manuscript), part II, chapter 'Dusha samosoznanaiushchaia'.

presuppositionlessness in neo-Kantianism, already accepted by Belyi in 1914. The reception of anthroposophy leads Belyi[73] to an epistemological *monism*, while Solov'ev sticks to a *dualism*, because his transgression into transcendence does not overcome the dichotomy of form and content in thought. In Solov'ev's work intellect is only form for the Logos, but cannot achieve its creative power.

In contrast to neo-Kantianism, both Russian philosophers aim at a transformation of theory of cognition into spiritual practice, which can be characterised as Christian intellectual mysticism culminating in communion with Christ via an act of cognition. Unlike Solov'ev who modernises the Orthodox tradition of the "Jesus prayer", Belyi opts for the esoteric path, developed by Steiner in his anthroposophy. Therefore, both thinkers transform the highest form of rational philosophy of their time, transcendental theory of cognition, into an intellectual mysticism as a path that leads to experience of transcendence.

Bibliography

Belyi, Andrei. 1999. *Dusha samosoznaiushchaia* (ed. E.I. Chistiakova). Moscow: Kanon.
—————— 1965. 'O smysle poznaniia' (1916) (Reprint of the edition: Peterburg: Ėpocha 1922.) in *Russian Language Specialities* (Russian Study Series Nr. 51). Chicago 1965: 35–51.
Duda, Krzysztof and Teresa Obolevitch (eds.). 2010. *Symvol w kulturze rosyjskiej*. Kraków: Wydawnictwo WAM.
Ehlen, Peter. 1999. '"Impersonalismus" und die „werdende Vernunft der Wahrheit" in Solov'evs Spätphilosophie' in *Studies in East European Thought* 51: 155–175.
Losev, Aleksei. 1990. *Vladimir Solov'ev i ego vremia*. Moscow: Molodaia gvardiia.
Reinhold, Karl Leonhard. 2004. *Beiträge zur Berichtigung bisheriger Mißverständnisse der Philosophen. Zweiter Band, die Fundamente des philosophischen Wissens, der Metaphysik, Moral, moralischen Religion und Geschmackslehre betreffend*. Mit einer Einleitung und Anmerkungen hrsg. von Faustino Fabbianelli. Hamburg.
Schwaetzer Harald. 2002. 'Subjektivistischer Transsubjektivismus' in Volkelt, Johannes: *Erfahrung und Denken. Kritische Grundlegung der Erkenntnistheorie*. Mit einer Einleitung und einem Personen- und Sachregister hrsg. von Harald Schwaetzer. Vorwort von Hans-Ludwig Ollig. Hildesheim u.a. (Texte zum frühen Neukantianismus. Hrsg. von Harald Schwaetzer. Bd. 3): IX–XLVI.

---

[73] Cf. Stahl-Schwaetzer, Renaissance des Rosenkreuzertums.

Solov'ev, Vladimir S. 1966. *Sobranie sochinenii V.S. Solov'eva*. Vol. 1–12. Sankt Petersburg (Reprint: Bruxelles 1966).

——— 1990. *Sočinenija v dvuch tomach*. Moscow.

Stahl-Schwaetzer, Henrieke. 2002. *Renaissance des Rosenkreuzertums. Initiation in Andrej Belyjs Romanen „Serebrjanyj golub'" und „Peterburg"*. (Trierer Abhandlungen zur Slavistik, herausgegeben von Gerhard Ressel. Band 3.). Frankfurt/M. et al.

——— [Stahl, Henrieke] (2003): '„Erinnert ihr euch an das Bild des schönen Leibes?": Aspekte der Sophiologie Vladimir Solov'evs' in: Heftrich, Urs and Gerhard Ressel (eds.) *Vladimir Solov'ev und Friedrich Nietzsche: eine deutsch-russische kulturelle Jahrhundertbilanz*. Frankfurt am Main et al.: 341–370.

——— (ed.) (2011): *Andrei Belyi – filosof. 'Istoriia stanovleniia samosoznaiushchei dushi' i ee konteksty*. Amsterdam. Special issue of Russian Literature. Vol. LXX (2011) I/II.

——— (2012): 'Wer ist Ich? Vladimir Solov'ev's "Theoretische Philosophie"' in Plotnikov, Nikolaj and Meike Siegfried, Jens Bonnemann (eds.) *Zwischen den Lebenswelten. Interkulturelle Profile der Phänomenologie*. (Syneidos. Deutsch-russische Studien zur Philosophie und Ideengeschichte. Herausgegeben von Alexander Haardt und Nikolaj Plotnikov. Band 3.) Berlin: LIT Verlag: 37–68.

Steiner, Rudolf. 1980. *Wahrheit und Wissenschaft. Vorspiel einer „Philosophie der Freiheit"*. (GA 3), Dornach/Schweiz: Rudolf Steiner Verlag.

——— 1984. *Philosophie und Anthroposophie. Gesammelte Aufsätze 1904–1923*. (GA 35), Dornach/Schweiz: Rudolf Steiner Verlag.

——— 1985. *Die Rätsel der Philosophie in ihrer Geschichte als Umriss dargestellt*. (GA 18), Dornach/Schweiz: Rudolf Steiner Verlag.

——— 1987. *Einleitungen zu Goethes Naturwissenschaftlichen Schriften*. (GA 001), Dornach/Schweiz: Rudolf Steiner Verlag.

——— 1995. *Die Philosophie der Freiheit. Grundzüge einer modernen Weltanschauung*. (GA 4), Dornach/Schweiz: Rudolf Steiner Verlag 1995.

——— 2003. *Grundlinien einer Erkenntnistheorie der Goetheschen Weltanschauung mit besonderer Rücksicht auf Schiller*. (GA 2), Dornach/Schweiz: Rudolf Steiner Verlag.

Volkelt, Johannes (1879): *Immanuel Kants Erkenntnistheorie nach ihren Grundprincipien analysiert. Ein Beitrag zur Grundlegung der Erkenntnistheorie*. Leipzig.

——— (1906): *Die Quellen der menschlichen Gewissheit*. München.

——— (2002): *Erfahrung und Denken. Kritische Grundlegung der Erkenntnistheorie*. Mit einer Einleitung und einem Personen- und Sachregister hrsg. von Harald Schwaetzer. Vorwort von Hans-Ludwig Ollig. Hildesheim u.a. (Texte zum frühen Neukantianismus. Hrsg. von Harald Schwaetzer. Bd. 3).

Windelband, Wilhelm. 1924. *Präludien. Aufsätze und Reden zur Philosophie und ihrer Geschichte*. Neunte, photo-mechanisch gedruckte Auflage. Band I und II. Tübingen.

CHAPTER 14

Aleksei Remizov's *Pliashushchii demon* – *tanets i slovo*: Cultural Memory, Dreams and Demons

Marilyn Schwinn Smith

> Сны, память и переписывание – может быть, три основные темы-аспекта ремизовского творчества, и часто не знаешь, где начинается одно и кончается другое.
>
> ('Dreams, memory and transcription are perhaps the three main themes and aspects of Remizov's work, and you often don't know where one ends and another begins.')
>
> MARKOV, 'Neizvestnyi pisatel' Remizov', 17

Demons, dreams and cultural memory – all categories verging on the irrational – freely intermingle and metamorphose, one into the other, across and within the chapters of Aleksei Remizov's *The Dancing Demon – Dance and the Word*.[1] A late work, *The Dancing Demon* draws on all of Remizov's previous writing. This writing is both prolific and diverse. It is not merely that Remizov worked in a variety of overlapping genres, but that his innovative practice nearly always defies generic boundaries. For Remizov rebels against boundaries, the very *sine qua non* of rational discourse, at every turn.

---

1   In the text, *Pliashushchii demon* will be referenced by its English title, *The Dancing Demon*, and page numbers will appear in the text. *Pliashushchii demon* does not appear in the recent, ten volume, *Collected Works*, A.M. Remizov, *Sobranie sochinenii*, ed. A.M. Gracheva, Moscow, 2000–2003. Jean-Claude Marcadé, "Remizovskie pis'mena", in *Aleksej Remizov. Approaches to a Protean Writer*, ed. Greta N. Slobin, Columbus, OH, 1986, 132n7, indicates that it is reprinted in *Russkaia Mysl'* No. 3556 (14 February 1985); *Pliashushchii demon* is included in A.M. Remizov, *Ogon' Veshchei*, ed. V.A. Chalmaev, Moscow, 1989, 231–300; Natalia Reznikova published a French translation of the first section of chapter I, "Rusaliia", titled "La Roussalia ou Rythme et mesure d'un russe", *La Revue de Culture Européene*, Paris, 1er-2ème trimester 1954, No. 9–10; The second section of Chapter III, "Pervopechatnik Ivan Fedorov" had previously appeared under the title "Knigopisets i shtanba. Pamiati pervopechatnika Ivana Fedorova", *Poslednie novosti*, Paris, 7 Juin 1934, No 4833 et 24 juin 1934, No. 4840; This latter section had also appeared in French translation in *Papyrus*, Paris, 31 juil., 30 sept., 31 oct. 1935, Nos. 185, 186 et 187. See Hélène Sinany, *Bibliographie des Oeuvres de Alexis Remizov*, Paris, 1978.

Cultural memory is the principal ethos of Remizov's writing. Examples predating *The Dancing Demon* include: *Sunwise* (*Posolon'* 1907), the pagan past of the Slavs; *Limonar'* (*Limonar'* 1908), the diversity of Russia's religious writing; *Russia in Letters* (*Rossiia v pis'mena* 1922), a catalogue of 'textual remnants of the Russian past',[2] *Russia in the Whirlwind* (*Vzvikhrennaia Rus'* 1927), an avant-garde chronicle of the revolutionary years. Dreams are the thematic focus of Remizov's literary-critical writing, published both in the periodic press and as separate books (*Ogon' Veshchei. Sny i predson'e* 1954). He recorded, published and illustrated his (and his wife's) dreams (*Martyn Zadeka. Sonnik* 1954).[3] Demons, harking back to the Greek *daimon* (local spirit), had become Remizov's 'friends and acquaintances' since his exposure to the world of folk belief during his years of exile in the Russian far north. They fill his works from the first decade of the twentieth century and emerge, notably in *The Dancing Demon*, as metaphor for the dynamism of earthly existence, for its animating and creative impulse.

When it appeared in 1949, *The Dancing Demon* was Remizov's first work published as an independent book since 1931. Given the economic climate, world war and Remizov's émigré status, difficulties with publishing are not altogether surprising. However, Remizov had been writing constantly, publishing in periodicals and continually sending out manuscripts, often hand-written, to publishers. When this first book in eighteen years appeared, it was produced in an elegant edition of 75 numbered copies on elaborately folded Arches paper and 400 copies on Helio-Alfa paper. The volume's material extravagance marks it as a collector's item. Its production may have been intended as a fundraiser for its impoverished author.

The first two, unnumbered, pages are an ornate calligraphic rendering of the book's preface, faced by a color reproduction of a Remizov collage in black and red, bordered in gold and brown. The central image is a partial profile in red, resembling Pushkin. Or, the profile may represent the *maecenas* of this private publication, Serge Lifar' – Diaghilev dancer and, later, ballet-master of the Paris Opera.[4] The sub-title is, after all, 'Dance and the Word'. The preface

---

2 Edward Manouelian, "From *Pis'ma* to *Pis'mena*: Ideological and Journalistic Contexts of Remizov's Documentary Project", *The Russian Review*, LV (January 1996), 2.

3 See Avril Pyman, "Petersburg Dreams", in *Aleksei Remizov. Approaches to a Protean Writer*, 51–112; Adrian Wanner, "Aleksei Remizov's Dreams: Surrealism *Avant la Lettre*", *The Russian Review* LVIII (October 1999), 599–614; Sandra Yates, "Remizov's Quest: Discerning the Dimension of Dream in *Ogon' Veshchei*", *Australian Slavonic and East European Studies*, IX/1 (1995), 1–29.

4 A.M. Gracheva, "Rukopisnye knigi", in A.M. Remizov, *Rukopisnye knigi. Iz raznykh moikh knig i na raznye sluchai. Gadan'e dannoe liudiam ot Burkhana-Mandzywhira. Kak nauchit'sia pisat',*

ILLUSTRATION 14.1 *Dancing Demon' by Aleksei Mikhailovich Remizov.*
IT IS THE FRONTISPIECE OF THE 1949 PARIS PUBLICATION (PUBLISHER NOT DESIGNATED) *PLIASHUSHCHII DEMON: TANETS I SLOVO.*

identifies Lifar' as the title's 'dancing demon': "Across all the centuries flashes the image of Lifar' – 'the dancing demon'. History from St. Sophia in Kiev even to the Paris Opera" (*The Dancing Demon*, unnumbered preface). In the text proper, Remizov states that seeing Lifar' perform as Icarus at the Paris Opera in 1936 had unlocked his memory, and enabled him to write the book:

> And how my memory flew open, through 'Icarus'. And I recalled Kiev, Ask'l'dov's grove. Green week, a blue peacock evening, the rusal'nyi procession with musicians. And that [one, blackened and grown,] under the enchantment of a demon [into a threatening], – And that one, swimming in the air above [our] heads – a black sinister light – Sergei Lifar'!

The profile is truncated to the shape of a flame. From the proximate position of the mouth emerges, swirling leftwards and upwards, a band of red merging, as a fold in its skirt, with a figure hovering – as a muse, an angel, a demon – with her arm raised above the human profile below. Beneath the image is Remizov's self-citation: "Only dreams open the door for me onto my magic fields: there, is bitter memory, illumined memory and song".

Closely related to *The Dancing Demon* is *Peterburgskii buerak* . Conceived the year *The Dancing Demon* was published (1949) though not published in full until 2003, *Peterburgskii buerak* has been described as an exposition of Remizov's "artistic credo".[5] The same is true of *The Dancing Demon*. They are both explicitly texts of cultural memory – of the history of dance and the word in Russia and of the Russian Silver Age, and employ dreams, *sny/snovideniia*, as the primary mode of knowledge. Together, they are summary accounts of

---

St. Petersburg, 2008, 14. N.V. Reznikova notes numerous acts of kindness and generosity on the part of Lifar' in her memoir about Remizov, *Ognennaia pamiat'. Vospominaniia o Aleksee Remizove*, Berkeley, CA, 1980, 96, 98, 101. Recalling in 1950 those who, over the years, had rescued his literary career, Remizov writes the following: 'P.B. Struve menia reabilitiroval, kak potom Lifar' – posle vosemnadtsatiletnego mordovorota – s 1931 po 1949 – izdaniem 'Pliashushchego demona. Po-russki menia ne izdavali, odin durak zametil "chto zh tut takogo, zhdut i piat'desiat let": s "Pliashushchego demona" moe imia snova poiavliaetsia na knizhnom rynke – chuvstvuiu sebia novichkom'. A.M. Remizov, *Vstrechi. Peterburgskii buerak*, Paris, 1981, 34. The reference to Lifar' is omitted from the manuscript used for the Russian edition, titled "Peterburgskii buerak", in Remizov, *Sobranie sochinenii*, X, Moscow, 2003, 196. Lifar' is recalled further in the "Diagilev" section of the 1981 edition of *Vstrechi*, 147–164; see also 259–272 in *Sobranie sochinenii*, X. For discussion of the two, differing editions, see A.M. Gracheva, "Basni, koshchuny i mirakli russkoi kul'tury ('Myshkina dudochka' i 'Peterburgskii buerak' Alekseia Remizova", in Remizov, *Sobranie sochinenii*, X, 418–430.

5 Gracheva, "Basni", 429.

Remizov's evolving relationship with the world of art. A meditation on the city's Silver Age culture and its afterlife, *Peterburgskii buerak* includes the central section of *The Dancing Demon*, 'Peterburgskaia rusaliia'. The incorporation of one text into another is symptomatic of Remizov's method across his career. He continuously re-wrote, re-cycled, re-organised and re-published his own work. This proclivity began early, as noted in a 1910 review: "Compare the first edition of *The Clock* and *The Pond* (1905 and 1907) with the texts of these novels in the *Collected Works* (1910) – practically no sentence has escaped change, and some pages are totally unrecognizable". Olga Raevskaia-Hughes makes a comparable point, noting that Remizov's memoir of his years in political exile (1896–1903), *Iveren'*, re-iterated pronouncements and views already known to readers from his earlier books.[6] *The Dancing Demon* is no different. It elegantly recapitulates many of Remizov's notions regarding the nature of reality, especially his rejection of rationalism. Much of what appears in *The Dancing Demon* reaches back to his 'birth' as an author during political exile in Russia's far north and his post-exile association with the Petersburg *miriskusniki* (1905–1921).[7] The demons, dreams and cultural memory of *The Dancing Demon* were already well-established categories, with which his readers were well familiar. *The Dancing Demon* brings these *topoi* together in a new formulation and may be read as its author's performative theory of art.[8]

Victor Terras describes *The Dancing Demon* as a "quaint vision of Russia's orgiastic past".[9] *The Dancing Demon* is "quaint", putting on bold display the knowledge, skill, and learning initiated during his post-exile association with the Petersburg academic world. Taking advantage of his wife's formal study in Old Russian literature, paleography and culture, Remizov had attended class with her and established informal relations with her professors and other

---

6   R. Ivanov-Razumnik, "Between 'Holy Russia' and 'a Monkey': The Work of Alexei Remizov", in *The Noise of Change: Russian Literature and the Critics (1891–1917)*, ed. and tr. Stanley R. Rabinowitz, Ann Arbor, 1986, 166; Olga Raevskaia-Hughes, "Volshebnaia skazka v knige A. Remizova *Iveren'*", in *Aleksej Remizov. Approaches to a Protean Writer*, Columbus, OH, 1986, 41.

7   Remizov frequented Viacheslav Ivanov's Tower, filled as it was with Ivanov's adumbration of Nietzsche's *Gay Science* and Wagner's *Gesamtkunstwerk*. With Aleksandr Blok, he visited the sectarian *Khlysty*. From Nikolai Evreinov, he heard about "survivals" of pagan seasonal celebrations among the peasantry. From Evgenii, he learned the ritual 'spring songs' of Russia's pagan antiquity. All these experiences echo through the pages of *The Dancing Demon*.

8   See Greta N. Slobin, "The Ethos of Performance in Remizov", *Canadian-American Slavic Studies*, XIX/4 (Winter 1985), 412–425.

9   Victor Terras, "The Twentieth Century: 1925–53", in *Cambridge History of Russian Literature*, ed. Charles A. Moser, New York, 1989, 518.

leading scholars.[10] It is "visionary", presenting as spectacle the unity of one man's personal life with his national life; and both, in the context of cosmic life. Peter Jensen employs the term "cosmocentricity", as opposed to "anthropocentricity", to better describe the modernist 'objectivity' characteristic of Remizov's prose. The categories of so-called realist texts, which include "its explanatory devices, such as motivation, indication of causal and temporal sequences [...] came to be neglected in the modernist text or was deliberately disrupted, since historical man was no longer regarded as the origin of anything like cosmos. On the contrary, in this type of text man is exposed to the world on an equal footing with animals and things".[11] Likewise, the vision of *The Dancing Demon* is not given to the "ordinarily-sighted", but to one held in the trance of ecstasy or dream. Contrasting Remizov as poet and Lev Shestov as philosopher, Avril Pyman finds the ground of their mutual understanding in their rejection of reason and affinity to irrationalism. She locates these characteristics in Remizov's dream-world, which she describes "as a release from bonds of causality and ratio, space and time".[12] The vision of "Russia's orgiastic past", resurrected in the text's eye-witness account of the history of Russian dance and the word, operates through dream. In this dream-world, man is "on an equal footing with animals and things", such things as demons.

The structure of *The Dancing Demon* complicates any attempt to assign the work any simple generic classification and warrants delineation. A twelve-sentence authorial introduction lays out the metaphysical context, in which the central player is the faculty of memory. Positing a 'trace' left by each human life to persist endlessly in time, Remizov asserts that the finite individual retains access to his ever-metamorphosing-through-time trace through memory. Remizov's own memory of dance and the word, from his various incarnations across the span of Russian cultural history, is narrated in the two framing chapters of *The Dancing Demon*: 'Rusaliia' and 'The Scribe – A Crow's Pen'. His finite, strictly biographical, memory is narrated in the central chapter, 'Petersburg Rusaliia'.

This abstract formulation of man's intermediate position between finitude and infinity re-iterates the contours of Remizov's cosmology known to his readers from decades of previous works. The difference here is that memory is foregrounded; in much of Remizov's earlier work, dreams or the folk imagination

---

10   See A.M. Gracheva, *Aleksei Remizov i drevnerusskaia kul'tura*, St. Petersburg, 2000, 76.
11   Peter Jensen, "Typological Remarks on Remizovs's Prose", in *Aleksej Remizov. Approaches to a Protean Writer*, 282–283.
12   Pyman, "Petersburg Dreams", 52, 57.

supply the primary vehicle for his conception of reality. Let us look, then, at what he says about memory:

Our eyes are curtained off, our knowledge is only passing (*mel'kom*). Dim memory lives in dreams and awakes during encounters – with people and with books. [...] I put down in writing my deep memory: – a record of my past in the XVI, XVII, XVIII centuries. I call it 'The Scribe – A Crow's Pen' after the instrument of my age-old labor. [...] An encounter with Lifar' stirred up my *rusal'nyi* memory. And from books, I narrate my past from the IX century.

Memory is dim, deep and *rusal'nyi*; further, it is implicitly opposed to both 'knowledge' (rational thought) and to ordinary, day-time sight (3-dimensional reality). The finite individual's infinite, time-and-space-defying experience of his ever-metamorphosing trace is, then, memory itself, and is located in dreams. The 'time-and-space-defying' quality of memory in *The Dancing Demon* is not unique to it, but is operative in much of his 'autobiographical' prose.[13] One held in the trance of ecstasy or dream is "extra-ordinarily-sighted", and like the muses, possesses the vision of, and remembers, all time. The intimate relation of memory to dream is re-iterated in the epigraph: "Only dreams open the door for me onto my magic fields: there, is bitter memory, illumined memory and song". It is probable that 'sleep-visions' is a more accurate translation of *snovideniia*. One can never overestimate word-play and etymology in Remizov's lexical choices. Consider, for example, the following formulation: 'V serebrianye niti snova vlomilis' tugie mysli dnia – son bez snoviden'ia' (*Vstrechi*, "Blok" 91).

A weakness in Terras's description is that it does not account for the historical reach of *The Dancing Demon*. *The Dancing Demon* elaborates a specific story about the history of Russian culture (the arts) from pre-historic (pagan) time to the present. In the opening to Chapter 2, '*Petersburg Rusaliia*', Remizov refers to an "unwritten history" (31) – a history of the *skomorokhi*. Personally, Remizov identified himself as a *skomorokh*, considered his art as *skomoroshee*, and *The Dancing Demon* is, implicitly, that unwritten history – the history of aboriginal, Russian *skomoroshaia kultura* and its evolution into the present-day arts. In 1978, Russell Zguta published a scholarly version of the same history. Zguta dismissed earlier theories about the origin and role of the *skomorokhi* in Russian culture as inadequate – based on fruitless literary and linguistic analyses rather than on the historical record. It would be interesting to know how Zguta might have evaluated Remizov's history. For the two men arrived at

---

13   See Olga Raevsky-Hughes, "Alexey Remizov's Later Autobiographical Prose", in *Autobiographical Statements in Twentieth-Century Russian Literature*, Princeton, 1990, 53–56.

comparable story lines – the one in a professional historical text, the other in an artistic text. In contra-distinction to the general view that the *skomorokhi* emerged only in the eleventh century and their craft was a foreign import, the underlying premise to Zguta's 'story' holds that the *skomorokhi* "were originally priests of the pagan religion of the Eastern Slavs", and "that were it not for [them] much of what is regarded as native in Russian culture might not have survived".[14]

Remizov was situated at the heart of those Silver Age figures who viewed the *skomorokhi* as the preservers of pre-Christian Russian culture, as preservers of those ancient practices which developed into the arts. In a short notice published in a 1915 issue of the journal *Muzyka*, Remizov outlines a 'story' similar to Zguta's, to explain how he came to name the ballet, for which he had been commissioned to write a libretto, *Rusaliia*. First, he offers a thumbnail history of *rusaliia*: the religious celebrations (*obriady*) of Russia's pagan past, conducted at appointed, seasonal periods were called *rusaliia*; with conversion to Christianity, the pagan gods, like so many demons, were banished; some fell to children as toys; the *rusal'nyi* ritual itself turned into a secular *igrishche-gul'bishche*. "And *rusaliia* became a dance, musical action, performed (played) by the 'gay people', – the *skomorokhi*'" ['*I stala rusaliia pliasovym myzykal'nym deistvom, a razygryvalas' ona "liud'mi veselymi", – skomorokhami'*]. Remizov concludes: "So, when I got to thinking by which name to call Liadov's ballet to my libretto, I found nothing better than to call it the old way, by our from-ancient-times Russian – *Rusalii*."[15]

Zguta asserts that his theory ran counter to accepted tradition. He was able to revise the history of the *skomorokhi* by turning to other kinds of records than the predominantly literary texts used by other scholars. How should Remizov have arrived at his theory? Zguta found precedence for his theory in Afanas'ev's *Poeticheskaiia vozzreniia slavian na prirodu* (1865) and later scholarly papers by Sobolevskii (1893) and Ponomarev (1897), a precedence that other scholars had not pursued.[16] These are most probably influential sources for Remizov's schema as well. Remizov's acceptance of many of Afanas'ev's views regarding Slavic folk culture is well-documented. He was probably familiar with Sobolevskii and Ponomarev as well. Among his personal friends, E.V. Anichkov and N.N. Evreinov were deeply interested in the *skomorokhi*. The correspondence among these men, even during emigration, is filled with references to

---

14   Russell Zguta, *Russian Minstrels. A History of the Skomorokhi*, Philadelphia, 1978, xiii.
15   A.M. Remizov, "A.M. Remizov o svoei Rusalii", *Muzyka*, No. 217, (4 April 1915), 226.
16   Zguta, *Russian Minstrels*, 2–3.

the *skomorokhi*.[17] In addition to their common theoretical orientation, Zguta and Remizov used many of the same sources. Remizov's framing chapters, on dance and on the word, contain sections individually dedicated to seminal cultural-historical moments; moments whose written records established them as the basic texts of Russian history and culture. These texts would inevitably be used by Zguta. They are, of course, the books referred to in *The Dancing Demon*'s preface. These moments would be well known to any Russian, whether reader or not of Remizov's texts. In *The Dancing Demon* these moments are given a totally idiosyncratic reading through the personal accounts of Remizov's narrator.

The crucial similarity between Zguta's and Remizov's stories is the presumption that the *skomorokhi* pre-date the cultural transformations consequent to such unquestionably foreign influences as: the conversion to Christianity; the introduction of the printing press or identifiably foreign literary and performance genres; that the *skomorokhi* represent (and preserve an ever-diminishing, though inextinguishable, trace of) native (not foreign) culture. No less important in both Zguta's and Remizov's stories is the portrait of progressive marginalisation and demonisation, whereby the 'new' replaces the 'old'. With Remizov, demonisation is literalised: the arts are demonic, demons preside over art. A second point of contact between Zguta and Remizov is their emphasis on the performative, rather than theological or doctrinal nature of the pre-Christian, native culture. When calling attention to children's toys as transmogrified pagan gods, Remizov's 1915 sketch of the evolution of *rusaliia* suggests a history of cultural transformation that can be reconstructed through attention to children's toys and games. Such a history adheres closely to the nineteenth-century anthropological theory of 'survivals' promulgated in England by E.B. Tylor and current throughout Europe and Russia at this time: 'survivals' of pagan religious practice exist in contemporary, primarily peasant, culture, as games, songs and toys.[18]

In an essay on performance, Greta Slobin focuses on Remizov's multiple modes of "transformation". She cites literary examples whereby he "becomes" Avvakum in one work, the medieval scribe who burned the first printing press in another, "or the legendary dancer Lifar and the spirit of dance in *Pliashushchii demon*".[19] The context of these remarks is Remizov's friendship with Evreinov

---

17   See, for example, Remizov's obituary for Evreinov, "Potikhon'ku, skomorokhi, igraite", in Remizov, *Sobranie sochineii*, x, 359–362.
18   For discussion of British theories in Russia, see Rachel Polonsky, *English Literature and the Russian Aesthetic Renaissance*, Cambridge, 1998, esp. Chapter 2.
19   Slobin, "Ethos of Performance", 422.

and their shared passion for theatre, for games and for the *skomorokhi*. 'Games' acquire a fundamental relevance to *The Dancing Demon*, when read as Remizov's 'theory of art'. Zguta documents the consistent use of the verb *igrat'*, 'to play', in connection with pagan practices, and the subsequent employment of the root **igr* in terms referring to the activities of the *skomorokhi*. He writes: "Sources such as the *Povest' vremennykh let* contain frequent references to *igrishcha* in the context of ritual games associated with the pagan cult of the ancient Slavs". Zguta's implicit analogy, when he writes: "As in ancient Greece, these games represent the earliest stage in the evolution of drama in Russia",[20] is based on the theory of the ritual origin of the arts, a theory that was just emerging at the time Remizov was working on his ballet and theorising about the history of *rusaliia*.[21] In Remizov's version: secularised into an *igrishche*, the *rusaliia* was performed (*razygryvalas'*) by *skomorokhi*.

Remizov's interest in pagan celebrations performed/played by the *skomorokhi* led him to group many works of differing genres (folk tales, drama, ballet) under an umbrella term, *rusaliia*. I would like to review this background to *The Dancing Demon*. Explaining in 1909 his re-workings of folk genres, Remizov wrote: "Working on this material I set myself the task of re-constructing the folk myth, fragments of which I recognised in surviving rituals, games, *koliadki*, superstitions, omens, proverbs, riddles, incantations and apocrypha. Thus were published my two books: *Posolon'* and *Limonar'* (1907)".[22] *Posolon'* was Remizov's first major publication of re-written folk tales. But as this letter makes clear, his material is less 'tales' than surviving fragments of native culture. The common application of the generic term 'tales' (*skazki*) to *Posolon'* reflects Remizov's transformation of fragments, of things said and done, into tales. We note that, even at this early date, Remizov has set himself the task of re-constructing something lost from native consciousness; a task akin to his remembering and narrating the lost history of the *skomorokhi*, the history of dance and the word.

Concurrently with work on *Posolon'*, Remizov's immersion in medieval and apocryphal literature resulted in three dramatic works: *Besovskoe deistvo*

---

20 Zguta, *Russian Minstrels*, 117–118.

21 For the origins of pagan games, and for the ritual origins of art, see in particular: Francis Cornford, "The Origin of the Olympic Games," Chapter VII in Jane Ellen Harrison, *Themis. A Study of the Social Origins of Greek Religion*. Cambridge: Cambridge University Press, 1912, 212–59; and Jane Ellen Harrison, *Ancient Art and Ritual*. London: Williams and Norgate, 1913, (Home University Library of Modern Knowledge). Remizov's friend, E.V. Anichkov, who wrote on Russian paganism and was familiar with British theory, may have kept Remizov up-to-date.

22 Remizov, "Pis'mo v redaktsiiu", in *Sobranie sochinenii*. II, 607.

(1907), *Tragediia o Iude printse Iskariotskom* (1908) and *Deistvo o Georgii Khrabrom* (1910). When these works were published in 1912, they were grouped under the inclusive title, *Rusal'nye deistva*. *Besovskoe deistvo* opened, with much scandal, at Vera Kommisarzhevskaia's St. Petersburg theatre on 4th December 1907, with scenery by M.V. Dobuzhinskii and music by M.A. Kuzmin. Remizov's recollections of the Kommissarzhevskaia production, also titled *Besovskoe deistvo*, constitute the fourth section of Chapter 2, 'Petersburg rusaliia', of *The Dancing Demon*. *Tragediia o Iude printse Iskariotskom* opened at the same theatre in February 1910. N.K. Rerikh's sketches for the scenery were published in both *Zolotoe Runo* and *Apollon*. *Deistvo o Georgii Khrabrom* was never produced. *Besovskoe deistvo* was based on ancient monuments from the Kiev-Pecherskii monastery and a spiritual song from Bezsonov's *Kaliki perekhozhie*, supplemented by reading in academic sources by I.N. Zhdanov, F.D. Batiushkov, N. Storozhenko and N.S. Tikhonravov. *Tragediia o Iude* was based on apocryphal legends published by I. Ia Porfir'ev, N.I. Kostomarov, A.I. Iatsimirskii, and text again from Bezsonov, together with folk songs, incantations, *koliadki*, *stariny* and lamentations. *Deistvo o Georgii Khrabrom* was based on a text published by A. Kirpichnikov and academic works by A.N. Veselovskii and A.V. Rystenko.[23]

Remizov's 1925 précis of the trilogy, in an English-language curriculum vitae, indicates his conceptual framework and is notable for both word choice and its depiction of the cycle's dramatic arc: "3 plays based on a song cycle. Demonical Tri-action/Besovskoe Trideistvo – one vast action. 1) Demonical action – the demons are not organised – they have tails, horns, hoofs 2) 'The Tragedy of Judas' – the human principle/the demons are only masked 3) 'George the Brave' – the collective principle/the demons are organized". The 'Autobiograph' gives additional production information: "Demonical action was staged in Petersburg by V.F. Kommissarjevskaya, 'Tragedy of Judas' in Moscow by F.F. Kommissarjevsky in the Theatre Workshop. 'George the Brave' planned for staging by P.P. Gaideboorov in the Travelling Theatre/Peredvizhnicheskii Teatr/ but never was realised and the opera of V.A. Senilov based on 'George the Brave' was never staged".[24]

The cosmological arc of the trilogy – chaos to order – is a prototype for the historical arc of *The Dancing Demon's* 'Rusaliia' chapter. Writing about both his ballet (*"rusaliia* became a dance, musical *deistvo"*) and his dramatic work, Remizov connects the term *deistvo* with *rusaliia*, as he will in *The Dancing*

---

23 Remizov, "Primechaniia" to *"Rusal'nye deistva"* in *Sochineniia*, VIII, St. Petersburg, 1912, 269–70, 284.

24 Remizov, "Autobiograph", Typescript in the Bakhmeteff Collection. Columbia University.

Demon. Earlier, I translated *deistvo* as 'action.' 'Play' is the generic translation. However, I feel that the emphasis of *deistvo* is on performance, while the emphasis of the English 'play' is on the written text. Remizov's own use of 'action' in his English-language précis of the *Rusal'nye deistva* implies that he had precisely the performative dimension of drama in mind. The translation as 'action' also is consonant with the dramatic theory and practice of Remizov's friend, N.N. Evreinov, who was deeply interested in peasant ritual performance. Andrei Malaev suggests 'ritual' or 'ceremony' as possible translations. The extended title, 'Besovskoe deistvo nad nekim muzhem', suggests that the 'action' being performed may be ritual.[25] As the *Rusal'nye deistva* had described a ritual-based arc, the cyclic agricultural calendar of seasonal ritual festivities (*obriady*) had organised *Posolon'* into four sections: *Vesna-Krasna, Leto Krasnoe, Osen' Temnaia* and *Zima Liutaia*. When writing about his ballet, Remizov gave Russian ritual practice a specific name: "the religious celebrations (*obriady*) of Russia's pagan past, conducted at appointed, seasonal periods were called *rusaliia*".

Remizov had begun work on the ballet by January 1911. The production never took place and Remizov eventually published the libretto in emigration.[26] His reminiscences of work on the ballet, like his reminiscences of work on *Besovskoe deistvo*, appear in the 'Petersburg *Rusaliia*' chapter of *The Dancing Demon*. When the libretto was published in 1923, it was titled for its protagonists, the adventurers Alalei and Leila of *K Moriu-Okeanu*. *K Moriu-Okeanu*, the second installment to his collection of re-written children's songs and games, was appended to *Posolon'* in its 2nd edition.[27] 'Alalei i Leila' (1913–1921) was combined with two newer works, 'Iasnia' (1916) and 'Gori-tsvet' (1915–1922). As he had done with his dramatic pieces from 1907–1910, Remizov grouped these libretti on publication under an umbrella title, *Rusaliia*. There is a clear trajectory from the re-written *obriady* of *Posolon'* through the dramatic pieces of *Rusal'nye deistva* and the libretti of *Rusaliia*, from the intention to re-construct a native mythology out the surviving fragments of a ceremonial/festival/ performance-based culture to the ever-metamorphosing trace of *rusaliia* in Chapter 1 of *The Dancing Demon*.

Remizov devotes the first section of the 'Rusaliia' chapter (9–29), also titled 'Rusaliia' (9–13), to an exposition of the genesis of all the 'lively' arts, as well as

---

25 Personal communication with the author (13.03.10).
26 I.F. Danilova, "Primechaniia" in Remizov, *Sobranie sochinenii* 11, 631, q.v. *Alalei*.
27 Remizov, *Sochineniia*, VI, St. Petersburg, 1912. For an analysis of the organisational shift from "dreams" to "tales," and from *obriady* to narrative in *K Moriu-Okeanu*, see Danilova, "Primechaniia", 620–626, esp. 624–625.

painting and writing, from a primordial *rusaliia*. Its first sentence reads: "*Tanets po-russki "plias" – pliasat' – pliasun – pliask'*". This sentence contains the narrative trajectory of the entire *Dancing Demon*: native Russian culture is so overlaid with foreign accretions that the very word for dance – *tanets* – is foreign (German: *Tanz*). One needs to be reminded of its Russian root(s) – *plias*. The first three paragraphs are a highly poeticised and playful riff on Russian words related to dance. The trajectory of these paragraphs grounds dance in rhythmic sound: the natural sounds of plashing water and wings flapping, and the human sounds of clapping, banging, pounding. Remizov next interprets: "'*Tanets – plias' znachit*' upward, spiral motion to the sound of plashing, banging".

The rhythmic sounds of natural and human activity generate dance – movement from the earth toward heaven. Or as Remizov states at the conclusion of the section: "*Tanets s zemli greet nebo*" [Dance warms heaven from the earth] (13). Dance, then, is primordial and essentially religious. It is grounded in physical reality, but is characterised by its inherent propensity to transcend. Fire is its analog in the natural world. This section traces an evolution, from basic sound into the arts – dance, music, song, the word; the process by which 'man became man' (9). This five-page section is a poetic exposition of the early twentieth-century anthropological theory that the arts arise out of ritual practice.[28] In the remaining six sections of 'Rusaliia', our narrator recounts his experiences during seminal moments (moments identifiable from medieval literature) in the historical transformation of this aboriginal ethos of dance.

Chapter 2, 'Petersburg Rusaliia' (29–60), bridges the framing chapters, recounting episodes from Remizov's actual life in Petersburg. Some sections consist of Remizov's reminiscences of work on the ballet and the dramatic works discussed earlier; others are devoted to specific literary figures with whom Remizov worked. The first section 'Kikimora' (31–7) picks up the story of the historical Remizov's work on the ballet libretto. But first, it re-iterates the foundational images of the 'Rusaliia' chapter. 'Rusaliia' had opened with the assertion that behind *tanets* stands *plias*. 'Petersburg *Rusaliia*' opens with a reprised (and familiar to us from his earlier writings) definition of *rusaliia*: "*pliasovoe muzykal'noe deistvo*" [a dance-music action] (31). We now learn more about its demonic ringleader (*konovod*), who led the revelers in the 'Kiev

---

[28] During the mid-1920s, Remizov worked closely with Jane Ellen Harrison, a leading figure among the Cambridge Ritualists. It is possible that through their collaborative work and close friendship, the ritual theory of art may have become more explicit in Remizov's conceptualisation of *rusaliia*. On this relationship, see Marilyn Schwinn Smith, "'Bergsonian Poetics' and the Beast: Jane Harrison's Translations from the Russian", *Translation and Literature*, XX (2011), 314–333.

1025-1035' section of Chapter 1. His name is Alazion: "demonic prince, demon of joy and 'pleasure', temptation of the church, ruin to the Christian soul" (31). He and his assistant demons of all kinds are the executors/performers of *rusaliia*.

Alazion had captured Remizov's imagination since at least 1915, when he is named in the *Muzyka* notice. He is named again in the preface to the 1923 book, *Rusaliia* and in the 'Kikimora' section. With all three namings, Remizov identifies his source and inspiration: St. Nifont, who names Alazion in his condemnation of *rusaliia*.[29] With the naming in *The Dancing Demon*, we can now look back through the text and recognise the riff of the work's opening section based on words from the Old Russian text of Nifont's sermon against the *rusaliia* rites of pagan Rus'. We can recognise Alazion not only as the ringleader of the pagan revels of the 'Kiev 1025-1035' section, as that very Alazion, who led the musicians against whom Nifont preached, but as the primordial and elemental force generating all the arts in the opening section of *The Dancing Demon*. Appearing now in the 'Kikimora' section of '*Petersburg Rusaliia*', time-tripping and shape-shifting like the narrator himself, Alazion appears, anachronistically, in twentieth-century St. Petersburg to preside over work on Remizov's ballet, *Alalei i Leila* – that same ballet about which Remizov wrote in 1915 for *Muzyka*, when he first names both Nifont and Alazion. Time, as a rational category for delineation, has utterly collapsed. As has any notion of a discrete or stable identity. All is in flux. All is porous.

Even the title of the section, 'Kikimora', is multiplicitous. As a figure of Russian folkloric demonology, Kikimora harkens from the world of Remizov's exile – the land of the midnight sun, as Remizov calls Ust-Sysolsk in his memoir about that period, *Iveren'*.[30] Kikimora belongs to the 'invisible' world, 'visible'

---

29   In the preface to his 1923 book, *Rusaliia*, Remizov cited as his source the *Izmaragd*, one of the many Old Russian manuscripts with which he may have become familiar through his acquaintance with Petersburg medievalists. The language used in the manuscript from the Vygoleksinsky monastery to describe Nifont's vision of Alazion and his band of musicians consists of a lexicon comparable to that of Remizov's riff and, presumably, is the same as Remizov's source manuscript. See the relevant passage of "Slovo Nifonta" in *Vygoleksinskii sbornik*, ed. S.I. Kotkov, Moscow, 1977, 108–112. Dimitri Obolensky cites a book by Remizov's close friend, the scholar of pagan Rus', E.V. Anichkov, (*Iazychestvo i drevniaia Rus'*, St. Petersburg, 1914, 190) as a source for a 'Legend of Saint Nifont', a legend which adheres closely to the text of the *Vygoleksinskii sbornik*. Dimitri Obolensky, "Popular Religion in Medieval Russia", in *Russia and Orthodoxy. Essays in honor of Georges Florovsky*, II, Paris: Mouton, 1975, 43–54, 51n16.

30   See Olga Raevsky-Hughes, "Alexey Remizov's Later Autobiographical Prose", in *Autobiographical Statements in Twentieth-Century Russian Literature*, ed. Jane Gary Harris, Princeton, 1990, 60.

to the extra-ordinarily sighted – to the 'folk' still immersed in a pagan consciousness, who 'see' spirits; to medieval saint, Nifont, who saw Alazion "with his own eyes"; and to the twentieth-century Remizov, who attributed his own visionary capacities to his biologically determined near-sightedness. 'Kikimora' also belongs to the historical world Remizov is resurrecting, the cultural world of Silver Age Russia, of its music and dance. The name resonates with the tone poem, 'Kikimora' by Anatoly Liadov, the composer who was to write the score for Remizov's libretto, *Alalei i Leila*, and with Remizov's own creation of Kikimora for the Diaghilev-Stravinsky ballet, *The Firebird*. And thence, back to Alazion, whose dancers and musicians are implicated in the actual ballets staged by Diaghilev's Ballets Russes and performed by his dancers, mostly notably by Lifar' – the 1936 incarnation of Alazion (as mentioned above).

I conclude with brief remarks about the final chapter. A second weakness of the characterisation of *The Dancing Demon* as a "quaint vision of Russia's orgiastic past" is that it alludes only to ecstatic dance. And for Remizov, the word also was ecstatic, as we learn from his late memoir, *Iveren'*. The metaphor of the dancing demon extends equally to the Word. Aleksandr Etkind's characterisation, including both of the title's terms, sets right the balance: "In *The Dancing Demon*, Remizov formed a unified line from Archpriest Avvakum to Serzh Lifar', and this is a dancing line".[31] While chapter one had included much literary interpretation, chapter three asserts the persistence of *skomoroshaia kultura*, so essential to *rusaliia*, in the transformation of the word. 'The Scribe – A Crow's Pen' parallels the historical reach of 'Rusaliia', narrating Remizov's scribal, *skomoroshaia rabota* (hence the crow, rather than peacock feather) at seminal moments in the history of the Russian, written word. As there is a direct line from 'Posolon" to 'Rusaliia', there exists a direct line from the 'documentary project' of *Rossiia v pis'menakh* (1922) to *Pisets – Voron'e Pero*. As Remizov set out to re-construct native myth through *Posolon'*, so he intended to resurrect 'popular memory' through *Rossiia v pis'menakh*. Edward Manouelian's article on Remizov's early 'documentary project', begun in 1914 and culminating in the 1922 book, *Rossiia v pis'menakh*, gives insight into the origins and meaning of Remizov's attention to scribal art and the preservation of the most quotidian printed material, stuff of the rubbish bin. Manouelian places Remizov's periodical publications that went into *Rossiia v pis'menakh* into the context of a late imperial "trend toward nostalgic historiography" and characterises the eventual book as telling "the story of a continuing encounter

---

31   Alexander Etkind, *Eros of the Impossible. The History of Psychoanalysis in Russia*, tr. Noah and Maria Rubins, Boulder, CO, 1997, 559.

with the textual remnants of the Russian past".[32] Manouelian's term "encounter" echoes precisely Remizov's assertion in *The Dancing Demon* that the cultural memory presented in this latter work, is activated by encounters with books or people. *Rossiia v pis'menakh* presents material Remizov found in the Rachinskii family archive in Kostroma: ranging from domestic and legal documents to books, inscriptions on pottery and gravestones, to catalogues of the contents of storage chests, between the years 1914, when the first publication appeared in the journal *Zavety*, and 1922 when the book was produced. These sources parallel the cultural 'fragments' on which *Posolon'* was based.

Parallels between *Peterburgskii buerak* and *The Dancing Demon* abound, as do the parallels between *The Dancing Demon* and *Iveren'*. One may posit that *The Dancing Demon* is a generative text for these later, major works of memoiristic prose. Where *Iveren'* grounds Remizov's birth as a writer in the fabulous world of the *volshebncia skazka* and *Peterburgskii buerak* grounds him in the historical milieu of the Silver Age, each world open to the other, *The Dancing Demon* combines both worlds more intimately – the fantastic chapters framing the central, historical chapter, history and magic interpenetrating them all. Alazion-Lifar', demonic prince of *The Dancing Demon*, the inextinguishable essence of *rusaliia*, appears, as does Woland in *The Master and Margarita*, like the return of the repressed.

The Dancing Demon is doubly relevant to an investigation of irrationalism in Russian culture. Its modernist technique, dispensing with the norms and conventions of realist chronology and mimesis, reflects Silver Age rapprochement with the irrational. Equally with its modernism, *The Dancing Demon* reflects Remizov's immersion in Russian antiquity. *The Dancing Demon* brings forward – as a psycho-analyst would bring forward from an archaic unconscious – the pre-Petrine (pre-Westernised, pre-rationalised) culture of the *skomorokhi* into the consciousness of the twentieth century.

Bibliography

Anichkov, E.V. 1914. *Iazychestvo i drevniaia Rus'*. St. Petersburg: Stasiulevich.
Danilova, I.F. 2000. "Primechaniia", in Remizov, A.M., *Sobranie sochineii*, II, 618–705.
Etkind, Alexander. 1997. *Eros of the Impossible. The History of Psychoanalysis in Russia*. tr. Noah and Maria Rubins. Boulder, CO: Westview Press.
Gracheva, A.M. 2000. *Aleksei Remizov i drevnerusskaia kul'tura*. St. Petersburg: Bulanin.

---

32 Edward Manouelian, "From *Pis'ma* to *Pis'mena*", 5, 2, 3.

―――― 2003. "Basni, koshchuny i mirakli russkoi kul'tury ('Myshkina dudochka' i 'Peterburgskii buerak' Alekseia Remizova)", in Remizov, *Sobranie sochinenii*, X, 418-430.

―――― 2008. "Rukopisnye knigi", in Remizov, A.M. *Rukopisnye knigi. Iz raznykh moikh knig i na raznye sluchai. Gadan'e dannoe liudiam ot Burkhana-Mandzywhira. Kak nauchit'sia pisat'*. St. Petersburg: Pushkinskii dom: 5-24.

Harrison, Jane Ellen. 1913. *Ancient Art and Ritual*. (Home University Library of Modern Knowledge) London: Williams and Norgate.

―――― 1912. *Themis. A Study of the Social Origins of Greek Religion*. Cambridge: Cambridge University Press.

Ivanov-Razumnik, R. 1986. "Between 'Holy Russia' and 'a Monkey': The Work of Alexei Remizov" (1910), in *The Noise of Change: Russian Literature and the Critics (1891-1917)*, ed. and tr. Stanley R. Rabinowitz. Ann Arbor: Ardis: 151-167.

Jensen, Peter Alberg. 1986. "Typological Remarks on Remizov's Prose", in Slobin (1986): 277-285.

Manouelian, Edward. 1996. "From *Pis'ma* to *Pis'mena*: Ideological and Journalistic Contexts of Remizov's Documentary Project", *The Russian Review* LV/1: 1-20.

Marcade, Jean-Claude. 1986. "Remizovskie pis'mena", in Slobin (1986): 121-134.

Markov, V. 1986. "Neizvestnyi pisatel' Remizov", in Slobin (1986): 13-18.

Obolensky, Dimitri. 1975. "Popular Religion in Medieval Russia", in *Russia and Orthodoxy. Essays in honor of Georges Florovsky*, II, Paris: Mouton,

Polonsky, Rachel. 1998. *English Literature and the Russian Aesthetic Renaissance*. Cambridge: Cambridge University Press.

Pyman, Avril. 1986. "Petersburg Dreams", in Slobin (1986): 51-112.

Raevskaia-Hughes, Olga. 1986. "Volshebnaia skazka v knige A. Remizova *Iveren*'", in Slobin (1986): 41-49.

―――― 1990. "Alexey Remizov's Later Autobiographical Prose", in *Autobiographical Statements in Twentieth-Century Russian Literature*, ed. Jane Gary Harris, (Studies of the Harriman Institute, Columbia University). Princeton: Princeton University Press: 52-65.

Remizov A. M. 1915. "A.M. Remizov o svoei 'Rusalii'", in *Muzika* No. 217. (4 April 1915). (Moscow). 226.

―――― s.d. "Autobiograph", Typescript in the Bakhmeteff Collection. Columbia University.

―――― 1989. *Ogon' Veshchei*, ed. V.A. Chalmaev. Moscow: Sovetskaia Rossiia, 1989.

―――― 2000. "Pis'mo v redaktsiiu", in *Sobranie sochinenii*, II, 607-610.

―――― 1949. *Pliashushchii demon*. Paris: s.n.

――――. "Potikhon'ku, skomorokhi, igraite", in *Vstrechi, 1981*; *Sobranie Sochineniia*, X, 2003, 359-362.

———— 1912. "Primechaniia", "*Rusal'nye deistva*", in *Sochineniia*. Vols. 1–8. St.Petersburg: Shipovnik-Sirin, 1910–1912, VIII, 269–70, 284 (Reprint: Munich 1971).

———— 2008. *Rukopisnye knigi. Iz raznykh moikh knig i na raznye sluchai. Gadan'e dannoe liudiam ot Burkhana-Mandzywhira. Kak nauchit'sia pisat'*. ed. Alla M. Gracheva. St. Petersburg: Pushkinskii dom.

———— 1923. *Rusaliia*. Berlin and Petersburg and Moscow: Grzhebin.

———— 1923. *Skazki russkogo naroda*. Berlin: Grzhebin.

———— 2000–2003. *Sobranie sochinenii*. Vols. 1–10, ed. A.M. Gracheva. Moscow: Russkaia kniga.

———— 1981. *Vstrechi. Peterburgskii buerak*. Paris: Lev.

Reznikova, N.V. 1980. *Ognennaia pamiat'. Vospominaniia o Aleksee Remizove*. In *Berkeley Slavic Specialities* (Modern Russian Literature and Culture. Studies and Texts 4). Berkeley, CA.

Sinany, Hélène. 1978. *Bibliographie des Oeuvres de Alexis Remizov*. Paris: Institut d'Études.

Smith, Marilyn Schwinn. 2011. "'Bergsonian Poetics' and the Beast: Jane Harrison's Translations from the Russian". *Translation and Literature*, XX, 314–333.

Slobin, Greta N. (ed.). 1986. *Aleksej Remizov: Approaches to a Protean Writer*. Columbus, OH: Slavica.

———— 1985. "The Ethos of Performance in Remizov", *Canadian-American Slavic Studies*, XIX/4: 412–425.

Terras, Victor. 1989. "The Twentieth Century: 1925–53", in *Cambridge History of Russian Literature*, ed. Charles A Moser. New York: Cambridge University Press: 458–519.

Vygoleksinskii sbornik. 1977. ed. S.I. Kotkov. Moscow: Nauka.

Wanner, Adrian. 1999. "Aleksei Remizov's Dreams: Surrealism *Avant la Lettre*", *The Russian Review* LVIII: 599–614.

Yates, Sandra. 1995. "Remizov's Quest: Discerning the Dimension of Dream in *Ogon' Veshchei*", *Australian Slavonic and East European Studies* IX/1: 1–29.

Zguta, Russell. 1978. *Russian Minstrels. A History of the Skomorokhi*. Philadelphia: University of Pennsylvania Press.

CHAPTER 15

Irrational Elements in Ivan Bunin's Short Story 'The Grammar of Love'

Ildikó Mária Rácz

The aim of the present study is not to discuss irrationalism as a philosophy but to analyse elements of a literary work that, although ostensibly realistic, turn out to involve a number of irrationalities. This analysis also provides an opportunity to examine the unique place occupied by Ivan Alekseevich Bunin (1870–1953) in the Russian literary and artistic world of the end of the nineteenth and beginning of the twentieth century. Research to date has principally explored his place in literary history and the structural elements of his short stories, finding in him a follower of Chekhovian realism and impressionism.

This essay argues that the rational-irrational dichotomy appears at various levels in the plot throughout Bunin's short story 'The Grammar of Love' (1915). This paper analyses the roles played by the irrational elements in this work and the levels at which they function. At the various structural levels of the work the most obtrusive is the chronotope. The artistic space depicted in Bunin's works is an inseparable part of their semantic message. The actions of the main character begin in a real outer place that changes gradually, becoming ever more bleak and schematic. We are, in effect, travelling in the inner consciousness, in the world of memories and imagination. Under the influence of the spatial projection of memories, the unfamiliar countryside suddenly becomes familiar as the location of Ivlev's youthful riding experiences. We read in the first part of the story that "*такого пути Ивлев не знал*"[1] ("Ivlev knew of no such road"[2]), then, not much later, Bunin continues: "*Ивлев вспомнил места, вспомнил, что не раз ездил тут в молодости верхом*" (301) ("…and suddenly Ivlev recalled the locality and remembered that as a youth he had often ridden in this area on horseback" (7)).

---

1 Ivan Bunin, *Sobranie sochinenii.* 9 vols. Edited by A.S. Miasnikov, B.S. Riurikov and A.T. Tvardovskii. Moscow. 1966. IV. 300. All the Russian citations are taken from this edition, with page number references in the text.
2 Ivan Bunin, *Night of Denial: Stories and Novellas.* Translated from the Russian and with notes and an afterword by Robert Bowie. Northwestern University Press. 2006. 6. All the English citations are taken from this edition, with page number references in the text.

Throughout the story, we tread on the narrow path bordering dreams and reality, that is, irrationality and rationality. Already at the beginning of the work, the narrator himself has already conjured up the lulling effects of the cadenced beating of the horses' hooves and the rhythmic tinkling of the troika's bells. The carriage driver is unhappy and melancholic, disinclined to engage in conversation. His passenger therefore surrenders himself to peaceful, purposeless contemplation, perhaps even to the type of sleep that occurs when the consciousness is dulled. Later, during the course of the journey, the unfamiliar countryside suddenly becomes familiar, conjuring up in Ivlev a dreamlike landscape, a scene that his conscious mind had guarded from his dreams and whose existence was therefore also tied to memories.

The author keeps the spatial-time modality under a veil of uncertainty – we never do find out whether Ivlev actually did ride on that land, since the rest of the countryside remains unfamiliar to him. The oscillating spatial-time modality is in elemental connection with the fact that Bunin shows every occurrence in his short story in diverse contexts, value perspectives and temporal viewpoints at the same time. As a result of the artistic portrayal of space, the richly detailed descriptions of nature one came to expect from Bunin are all increasingly absent; moreover, the outer landscape is completely cleared, "becoming ever more impoverished and more remote" (6). In 'The Grammar of Love', the changing spatial location reveals the time travel occurring in the depths of the protagonist's consciousness, and traces his process of self-recognition and self-interpretation to the end – just as in Bunin's other works of the 1910s, *Siblings* or *The Dreams of Chang*.

If we study the temporal structure of the short story, we find that, instead of the rationally categorised, linear recorded time, various planes of time alternate. There appear also, together with the narrator's objective present and the story's past, the concepts of timelessness, eternal life and the inner, experiential time of the conscious mind. If we try to reconstruct and organise chronologically what happens in the story, or arrange in a linear fashion the fabular causality line, the following story evolves:

> Twenty years before Ivlev's journey (marking this as the time we relate to), a chambermaid, Lushka, dies on the Khvoshinsky[3] estate, leaving her squire, who is madly in love with her, the gift of a young son.

---

3   In this paper we follow the transliteration of the names *Khvoshinsky* and *Khvoshino* used in the English translation (Robert Bowie, 2006) of the short story.

Ivlev is still a child when he first hears of this 'oddball' who had idolised his maid all his life. Influenced by the squire's obsessive love, he himself at a young age almost falls in love with the girl, who by that time has died long ago. On numerous occasions, he rides along the shores of the lake where the girl supposedly drowned.

Khvoshinsky dies in the winter of the year of Ivlev's travels. Ivlev arrives in Khvoshino in the summer, meets Lushka's son, checks out his old room and purchases the squire's heavily guarded book. Upon arriving on the estate, he becomes fascinated by the unfolding secret environment and feels that Lushka had lived and died a very long time ago. On his way home, he thinks only of Lushka and feels that this woman had now become a part of his entire future life.

Due to Bunin's artistic method of observation, his virtuoso prose style and the rapid changes in the time planes, the story's rational time structure becomes difficult to follow and is pushed into the background. Moreover, its measurable temporal boundaries become increasingly vague, suggesting the timelessness of the world of fables.

The characters in the short story are full of rational-irrational contradictions, making the reader wonder where the boundary between the comprehensible and the incomprehensible might be. An example is the main character in this story, the one-time estate owner, Khvoshinsky, whom, some critics have claimed, Bunin modelled on his grandfather, Nikolai Dmitreevich.[4] The story, in line with Bunin's other works, contains autobiographical aspects.[5] The author, when still young, had heard a confusing story from his father concerning a poor landowner in their neighbourhood who had lost his mind over his love for one of his serf girls. Khvoshinsky's character changes continually, depending on the person in the story who conjures him up or tries to explain for the reader his personality or behaviour. He is a central figure and yet it is never clear whether he had in reality lost his sanity or whether he had, as his son claimed, died with a sound mind. Only one thing is certain: that he kept the little book, *The Grammar of Love*, with him constantly, even going so far as to put it under his pillow at night.

Ivlev's travelling companion, the coach driver, is also an ambiguous character. At the beginning of the journey he is depicted as grouchy, uncommunicative and passive. Then, at one point during the course of their travels, he takes over the role of the leading figure, making decisions regarding the course they

---

4 See, e.g. Serge Kryzytski, *The Works of Ivan Bunin*. Mouton. The Hague. 1971. 116.
5 See Bunin, *Sob. soch.*, IX. 369.

should take. In fact, he determines the purpose of their entire journey and, while Ivlev is laid back, passive and introspective, becomes not only the driver of the *troika*, but also Ivlev's guide and helper. He is the one who diverts Ivlev from his original course onto another. He is familiar with his surroundings and their past, and with the people's stories and their souls. His character, like that of the fairy-tale peasant lad who overcomes obstacles, is also irrational. Even so, he is the one who tries to find a rational explanation for Khvoshinsky's story: "Нет, утопилась, – сказал малый. – Ну, только думается, он скорей всего от бедности от своей сошел с ума, а не от ней…" (301). ("No, she did, she drowned herself", said the lad. "Only they figure he most likely went crazy from being so poor, not on account of her" (7)).

The title of the story is also contradictory. Grammar describes a language system, a logically constructed, rational collection of rules. In contrast, love is an irrational force depicted, even in Greek-Roman mythologies, as coming upon men incomprehensibly and out of the control of the human mind and will; it is something imposed upon them by the gods (cf. Cupid's arrow). The lovesick landowner turns Lushka, previously his maid, into the lady of the house and her room into a hallowed place. He idolises her to the extreme and weaves fanciful dreams around her, whereas, in reality, she is quite homely. The cause and circumstances of Lushka's death are never really clarified – she drowned, drowned herself, or perhaps died suddenly, quite young, in some other way – no clear explanation is ever given in the short story.

In his works of the 1910s, Bunin describes love as an irrational, cosmic force which to the rational mind is just as incomprehensible as death or nature itself. Love itself is a secret, its subject puzzling, incomprehensible and its consequences unforeseeable – a fateful force, suddenly and unexpectedly coming upon a person, dominating and changing destinies. This passion, according to Bunin, is followed by devastation and tragedy, which the main hero experiences as either a loss or a punishment. It is always a life-altering, exceptional occurrence, which appears in his works of the 1920s as a force inherent in the unconscious.[6] In the stories of the 1910s, the main characters' tragedy is that of not understanding fatal love's basic characteristic: infinity. The cause of their destruction is not recognising that love as an infinite natural force cannot be realised within the finite boundaries of man.[7]

In 'The Grammar of Love' Bunin makes a parallel comparison between Khvoshinsky's *Codex of Love* and the eccentric squire's unusual behaviour:

---

6 Cf. Mitia's Love, Sunstroke, The Elagin Affair.
7 See N.M. Kucherovskii, *Ivan Bunin i ego prosa*. Tula. 1980. 207.

Любовь не есть простая эпизода в нашей жизни. (306)

(Love is no Mere Episode in our Lives (13)].
It follows us to the grave.)

Khvoshinsky idolised Lushka and wove crazy dreams about her all his life. After her death, he shut himself up in her room, and lived the rest of his life in its confines, never leaving it.

Разум наш противоречит сердцу и не убеждает оного. (306)

(Our Reason gainsays the Heart, but the Latter is not persuaded (13)).

По рассказам стариков-помещиков, сверстников Хвощинского, он когда-то слыл в уезде за редкого умницу. И вдруг свалилась на него эта любовь, эта Лушка, потом неожиданная смерть ее, – и все пошло прахом...(300)

(According to the stories of old-time landowners, the contemporaries of Khvoshinsky, at one time people in the province considered him a man of rare intelligence. But all at once he was stricken with this love, this Lushka; then came her sudden death and everything went to pieces (5–6))

Женщину мы обожаем за то, что она владычествует над нашей мечтой идеальной. (306)

(We worship Woman because She holds Dominion over our Ideal Dream (13)])

Lushka became Khvoshinsky's ideal whom he respected as wife and, even more, as a goddess:

выделялся и величиной и древностью образ в серебряной ризе, и на нем, желтея воском, как мертвым телом, лежали венчальные свечи в бледно-зеленых бантах. (303–304)

(Prominent among them, both for size and for antiquity, was an icon in a silver mounting; on top of it, all waxy yellow like dead flesh, lay some wedding candles tied with pale green bows (10)).

Тщеславие выбирает, истинная любовь не выбирает. – Женщина прекрасная должна занимать вторую ступень; первая принадлежит женщине милой. Сия-то делается владычицей нашего сердца: прежде нежели мы отдадим о ней отчет сами себе, сердце наше делается невольником любви навеки…(306)

Vainglory chooses, True Love never chooses. The Woman of Beauty is relegated to a secondary Station; first belongs to the Woman of Grace. She becomes the Sovereign of our Hearts; ere we ourselves take Cognizance, our Hearts have become Thralls of Love for All Time…(13).

Оттого, что этот чудак обоготворил ее, всю жизнь посвятил сумасшедшим мечтам о ней, я в молодости был почти влюблен в нее, воображал, думая о ней, бог знает что, хотя она, говорят, совсем нехороша была собой. (299)

(Because of the way that eccentric worshiped her and dedicated all his life to insane dreams of her, I was almost in love with her myself as a boy; God only knows what fancies came into my head when I thought about her, although they say she was certainly no beauty (5)).

The writer's conception of love that appeared first in this short story[8] was a determining factor in his artistry for several years. It was enriched with further significant nuances in the decades that followed.

I have mentioned above the fairy-tale parallel found in this short story and the similarity to the tales of its time structure in terms of its timelessness. The short story's fairy-tale quality can be explained by Vladimir Propp's theory of fairy-tale functions.[9] In his analysis of Russian fairy-tales, Propp differentiates the so-called *functions* from the plot and the motives, itemising the constant and sequentially determined contextual elements that play an important part in the course of the plot's development and determine the fairy-tale's structural framework.

Fairy-tales usually begin with: 'Once upon a time…' – a phrase referring to the set spatial-temporal structure showing that the story is not under the constraints of either space or time. The tale then usually continues with the hero travelling to a place for a period of time. Bunin's story begins with: "Некто Ивлев ехал однажды в начале июня в дальний край своего уезда" (298).

---

8   See V.N. Afanasiev, *I.A. Bunin. Ocherk tvorchestva*. Moscow. 1966. 231.
9   V. Ya. Propp, 'Volshebniie skazki' in *Russkaia skazka*. Leningrad. 1984. 173–201.

("One day in early June a certain Ivlev was travelling to a distant region of his province" [3]), with neither space nor time precisely determined, nor the main character concretely identified. Propp calls this function "temporal absence" which might be linked with "set on his way" or "search path". The reason for the journey might be the absence or lack of something, and the hero is either sent away or leaves on his own in order to find or bring home that thing. At the beginning of the fairy-tale all goes well, in marked contrast to the later misadventures or trials.

Bunin's short story also contains these elements, although the absence or lack is not knowingly manifested at the beginning. It is only later that the true purpose of the journey is made clear. Bunin makes skilful use of changes in weather to describe the contrast between the initial fortunate situation and the later difficulties. He writes: "Ехать сначала было приятно" (298), [The drive was pleasant at first (3)], then later:

> погода поскучнела, со всех сторон натянуло линючих туч и уже накрапывало [...] когда поехали дальше, дождь разошелся уже по-настоящему (299–300).
>
> The weather had turned bleaker, discoloured clouds had gathered on all sides, and now it was sprinkling [...] when they started off again, the rain came down in torrents (4–5).

A set structural element of the fairy-tale is the spatial structure built around two simultaneously existing worlds: one, the world that the protagonist leaves on embarking on his journey, and which the introductory words refer to; and the other, a world found far away both in space and time, where various difficulties have to be overcome in order to enter, since it is guarded by a witch or by similar characters in other versions of the fairy-tale. Entrance to this other world, where real space completely disappears and the irrational, fantastical world of fairy-tales exists, is through the witch's hut or other versions thereof, such as castles or mountains. The witch is not easily definable. She is a very complex character. She guards the entrance to the mysterious world, deciding who is worthy to enter. She continually puts the protagonists to the test and, when one succeeds, she takes on the role of giver by either handing him a magic tool or giving advice or directions. The meeting with her is an element registered beforehand, a part of the canonical unfolding of the plot. The witch's hut is where the dark forest begins and beyond which the other world opens up to where the hero intends to go.

In Bunin's story, Ivlev, the discoverer of an old secret, is also a hero in search of something. The spatial-temporal structure of the work results in the portrayal of two different simultaneously existing worlds – Ivlev's journey begins in the real outer dimension on a particular day in June, then leads into the past, into the land of memories, the inner fields of consciousness. The catalyst setting in motion the process of remembrance and, at the same time, the one guarding the world of secrets, is the Countess who, in Bunin's short story, assumes the role of the witch. When Ivlev passes the test, she takes on the role of giver and provides him various pieces of information directing him towards Khvoshino. Beyond the Countess's palace (a variant of the witch's hut), he finds himself on a strange road which leads him through a forest to Khvoshino, to the residence of the late landowner.

In the fairy-tale, the function of the helper is also set. The earliest, zoomorphic helper is the bird, a cult animal that transported the souls of the dead. Later on, this role was taken over by the winged horse whose main duties were to transport the hero from one world to the next. The helper may be anthropomorphic and extraordinary, with super-human physical capabilities, capable of anything, or else an all-knowing character who helps the protagonist by giving advice or through craftiness. In the fairy-tales, the hero with a helper is entirely passive; the helper takes over his obligations and even fights the enemy.

In 'The Grammar of Love', instead of Ivlev it is the "lad" who not only drives the carriage and cares for the horses, but also defines the route and the journey's purpose. He takes the hero to see the Countess, easily orients himself in surroundings unfamiliar to Ivlev, takes on the pack of angry dogs and, with the help of his horses, delivers his passenger to the Khvoshinsky estate so that he may obtain and take home the object of his search, the book of love. He also assumes the role of the all-knowing helper, for whom the animals are also companions, and beside whom, apart from when purchasing the Khvoshinsky book, Ivlev stays passive. Bunin remained true to the fairy-tale's structure here, too, since the role of acquiring, abducting or stealing the sought-after object and then returning home with it is always the function of the hero, while the helper may only advise as to the manner in which this might be achieved.

There is also one more essential archetypal element in fairy-tales which is also found in Bunin's short story: the role of the accidental. The structure of the fairy-tale is not based on logic. The accidental turn of events affords imagination the opportunity to flow freely, thus allowing the rational world to open its doors to the world of the fantastic and the irrational.

The references indicated in the short story take the reader into the world of superstition, interpretation of dreams and the esoteric. Among the books in Khvoshinsky's library, Ivlev finds the following obscure, old tomes: *The Accursed Demesne, The Morning Star and Nocturnal Daemons* and *The Latest Dream Book*. Demonic beliefs also appear on the plot level in the story focusing on Lushka's character, as well as in the accounts of her mysterious death. Bunin describes Lushka as a legendary and mysterious figure, who upon her death is revered even as a saint, whose necklace is guarded as a relic, and whose wedding candles receive a place on the icon shelf. Yet the only thing we know about her for certain is that she served as a maid in Khvoshinsky's household and that she died quite young and unexpectedly. The unwritten tradition has it that she drowned, moreover, that she intentionally drowned herself. In Slavic mythology[10] the girl who drowns herself is called an *utoplenitsa*; she later turns into a *rusalka*, a 'water fairy' or 'mermaid', who may appear to humans in the form of animals (for example, frogs or rats). The *utoplenitsa* drowns herself because of a broken heart, and the legends surrounding the *rusalka* also concern a very deep yearning for love.

Why might Lushka have drowned herself? We only know that for Khvoshinsky she did not stop existing following her death:

>...Лушкиному влиянию приписывал буквально все, что совершалось в мире: гроза заходит – это Лушка насылает грозу, объявлена война – значит, так Лушка решила, неурожай случился – не угодили мужики Лушке...(300)

>...he ascribed literally all phenomena in the world to Lushka's influence. If there was a thunderstorm, it was Lushka who had visited this affliction upon them; if war was declared, it meant Lushka had so decided; if the event of a crop failure, the peasants had incurred the displeasure of Lushka (6)].

Upon her death, Lushka became one with the universe's unpredictable and irrational forces, part of the cosmos, even as love itself. She became its equal and, having enclosed Ivlev within her powers, she entered his life forever.

By examining the intertextual relationships of Bunin's work, we can determine that citations have an important role both at the composition and at the fabular level, enriching and exposing the plot with new denotations. From 'The Last Death', a poem written by one of Bunin's favourite poets, Evgenii Baratynskii,[11] he copied the following first few sentences:

---

10 See A.N. Afanasiev, *Poeticheskie vozzreniia slavian na prirodu.* 3 vols. Moscow. 1995. II. 339.
11 Russian poet, short story writer, and essayist, who lived between 1800 and 1844. Baratynskii holds an important place among the poets who contributed to the Golden Age of Russian poetry. He is best known for his sensitive elegies dealing with loss and despair and for the personal, revelatory tone of his love poems. Baratynskii and his works were rediscovered

Есть бытие; но именем каким
Его назвать? Ни сон оно, ни бденье;
Меж них оно, и в человеке им
С безумием граничит разуменье. (304)

There is a state but by what name
shall it be called? Nor dream is it, nor wake,
it lies somewhere between. Through it the
mind's dementia may verge upon the truth (11)]

The enlightenment occurring at the fine line between the sound mind and madness, between "*son*" (dreaming) and "*bden'e*" (being awake) that Baratynskii alluded to in his poem, serves Bunin as explanation and justification for Khvoshinsky's fateful story. There is, then, an existence between the rational and the irrational, where the mind falls under the spell of inexplicable higher powers. The irrational natural forces found in the story, such as love even, or its embodiment in the form of a woman in the person of Lushka, "в какое-то экстатическое житие превратившей целую человеческую жизнь, которой, может, надлежало быть самой обыденной жизнью..." (304–305) [had transmuted a whole human life into some rapturous state of existence, a life destined to be most commonplace...(11)]. The short story's original title, *Nevol'nik lubvi*, that is, 'The Thrall of Love', also alluded to this obsessive condition.

The citations taken from the little book, *The Grammar of Love*, bought by Ivlev from Khvoshinsky's son have become part of the story's text. As discussed above, the rules of the *Codex of Love* accorded point by point with the eccentric landowner's behaviour, as described by Bunin. Khvoshinsky's own quatrain, together with the book it is found in, plays an accentuated role at the end of the short story, with its contents projecting back to the course of the entire story, thus, enlightening some previously 'hazy' situations.

That we are dealing with an existing book becomes evident from the notes the author wrote concerning the writing of the story:

Мой племянник, Коля Пушешников, большой любитель книг, редких особенно приятель многих московских букинистов, добыл где-то и подарил мне маленькую старинную книжечку под заглавием *Грамматика любви*

BUNIN, *Sob. soch.*, IX. 369.

---

at the end of the nineteenth century by the Russian Symbolist poets, and a complete edition of his works was published for the first time in the early twentieth century.

My nephew, Kolia Pusheshnikov, a book collector who especially likes old books and who has several friends who are antiquarian booksellers, acquired somewhere a small old book entitled *The Grammar of Love*, which he gave to me as a present][12]

In his short story, Bunin sets the book's publication in the nineteenth century. Literary historians, however (Vladislav Afanas'ev[13] among them), were of the opinion that the citations referred to were taken from an eighteenth century book. The reason for this was that the form and content of the citations drawn from the *Codex of Love*, and especially their linguistic terms, were very similar to those of the works written in the eighteenth century. Some commentators have also assumed that they were mere stylisations, that is, that Bunin here imitated the writing style of the eighteenth century.

It was Arlen Blum[14] who, on the basis of his bibliographical research, succeeded in finding the book described by Bunin and who published his discovery in *Nauka i zhizn* (*Science and Life*) in 1970. The book figuring in Bunin's short story was published in Moscow in 1831 under the title *The Grammar of Love, or the Art of Loving and of Being Loved in Return...the Work of Molière*. The question arose as to whether it really is the work of the great seventeenth-century French writer that we are dealing with here. Through further research, Blum discovered that the book's original author was the French writer Jules Demoliere, who lived between 1802 and 1877, and who under the pseudonym Moleri published the book entitled *Code de l'amour* to which Bunin alluded. The Russian version appeared in Moscow in 1831, a copy of which Kolia Pusheshnikov gave to Bunin as a present. We know nothing of the translator, only that he published under the alias "*SZ. S*". The book is indeed a "magnificent publication" and "full of witty anecdotes" just as Bunin described it. From Blum's article we learn that Bunin cites accurately from the book, though, for artistic effect he occasionally puts in close proximity to each other two statements that, in the original work, were found far apart and in different paragraphs. Stylistically, the book resembles the 'gallant' eighteenth-century works that were quite prevalent in the century previous to its publication.

---

12   Translation is mine.
13   See V.A. Afanasiev, *I.A. Bunin*, 233.
14   Arlen Blum is a bibliographer and academician who works at the St Petersburg Academy of Culture and has published a bibliographical "*Index librorum prohibitorum* of foreign authors (in Russian translation, 1917—1991)", which lists books by foreign authors that were banned after being published in Russian and removed from libraries.
(Online at: http://magazines.russ.ru/nlo/2008/92/su43.html).

In fairy-tales the realm of secrets can only be reached with the help of some kind of incantation. According to Bunin's story, this may be through books or having knowledge of the contents of a certain book. In his quest, Ivlev the hero comes upon a secret of the past and, in the course of his travels, falls under the spell of the irrational forces that ruled the sometime landowner Khvoshinsky's fate. This story, like Bunin's *The Dreams of Chang*, contains two truths. One is the truth of Khvoshinsky's environment: his neighbour, the countess or old friend, Pisarev, only know his figure and life story from the outside, and judge him rationally. The other is the truth of the traveller, Ivlev, who tries to understand Khvoshinsky's personality from the inside, in such a way that he almost identifies with him. Thus Ivlev's journey in search of the truth leads him into the irrational world: the outer spatial changes display a process occurring in the deep inner consciousness and memory. This timelessness conjures up the fairy-tale world, where the character of heroes is not altered and the early harmony is ultimately restored. By contrast, in Bunin's story the main hero goes through inner changes. The early harmony cannot be regained, since understanding the secret, Khvoshinsky's truth, entails the start of a type of new existence for Ivlev.

The central theme of the story is deciphering a secret which, in itself, is already irrational. Moreover, this is a secret that accompanies the protagonist throughout his entire life and whose roots can be traced back to his childhood (cf. *Mitia's Love*). The fluctuation of the interpretation process (the explanation of a secret) is illustrated by Bunin by changes in the weather, which is at times cloudy, indicating the dark side of consciousness, and at times clear, illustrating the conscious mind's enlightenment. At the beginning everything is covered by a haze, then the weather clouds over and only upon arrival at Khvoshinsky's estate, in Lushka's room, does the twilight sky clear. But it is not the secret that gets revealed; on the contrary, Ivlev falls under the secret's spell.

By analysing the structural levels of the composition, we find that two mental processes coincide in the short story. On the one hand, we try to expose and explore something irrational in a rational manner, and, on the other hand, the solution to the secret coincides with the protagonist's process of self-interpretation, the projection of which at the level of the plot is again twofold. On the one hand, there is the journey completed in the real outer dimension, and, on the other hand, we have the journey through time, arriving in the depths of the protagonist's memory. The purpose of his voyage, the act of understanding ("*razumen'e*"), cannot, according to Bunin, be realised simply through rational means, by knowing or interpreting Khvoshinsky's stories. For this, Ivlev must identify with the by now legendary world of past heroes possible only irrationally, through empathy and intuitive experience. It means that clear understanding – as Bunin alluded to it in citing Baratynskii's poem – cannot be attained either through a simple rational search for reasons, or by means of irrational identification only. It happens namely between the state of dreaming and of being awake, at the fine line bordering rational and irrational modes of cognition.

Bibliography

Primary References

Afanasiev, A.N. 1995. *Poeticheskie vozzreniia slavian na prirodu*. 3 vols. Moscow: Indrik.
Bunin, Ivan. 1966. *Grammatika liubvi* (eds. A.S. Miasnikov, B.S. Riurikov and A.T. Tvardovskii) (Sobranie sochinenii 9 vols. IV). Moscow: Khudozhestvennaia literatura.
Bunin, Ivan. 1966. *Proishozhdenie moikh rasskazov* (eds. A.S. Miasnikov, B.S. Riurikov and A.T. Tvardovskii) (Sobranie sochinenii 9 vols. IX). Moscow: Khudozhestvennaia literatura.
Bunin, Ivan. 2006. *The Grammar of Love* (tr. Robert Bowie) (Night of Denial: Stories and Novellas). Evanston: Northwestern University Press.
Propp, V. Ya. 1984. *Volshebniie skazki* (Russkaia skazka). Leningrad: LGU.

Secondary References

Afanasiev, V.N. 1966. *I. A. Bunin. Ocherk tvorchestva*. Moscow: Prosvescenie.
Blum, Arlen. 'Grammatika ljubvi'. Online at: http://magazines.russ.ru/nlo/2008/92/su43.html (consulted 13.03.2010).
Broitman, S. N, Magomedova, D.M. (eds). 2000. 'Ivan Bunin' in *Russkaia literatura rubezha vekov*. Moscow: IMLI RAN, Nasled'ie. I. vol. 540–585.
Dolgopolov, L.K. 1977. *Na rubezhe vekov: O russkoi literature konca XIX – nachala XX veka*. Leningrad: Sovjetskii pisatel'.
Drozda, M. 1987. 'Ivan Bunin and modernist poetics' in *Scottish Slavonic Review*. №8. 17–38.
Drozda, M. 1994. 'Narrativniie maski russkoi khudozhestvennoi prozi (ot Puskina do Belogo) I.A. Bunin' in *Russian Literature* (XXXV (III/IV) 1994). 465–483.
Iliin, I.A. 1959. *Tvorchestva I. Bunina* (O t'me i prosvetlenii. Kniga hudozhestvennoi kritiki. Bunin, Remizov, Shmelev). Munich.
Ioannisian, D.V. 1973. 'Priroda, vremia, chelovek u A.P. Chehova i I.A. Bunina' in *Russkaia literatura XX veka IV.vol. Tvorchestva Bunina*. Kaluga. 50–69.
Kryzytski, Serge. 1971. *The Works of Ivan Bunin*. Mouton: The Hague.
Kucherovskii, N.M. 1980. *Ivan Bunin i ego prosa*. Tula: Priokskoe.

Mikhailov, O.N. 1976. *Strogii talant. Ivan Bunin. Zhizn'. Sud'ba. Tvorchestvo.* Moscow: Sovremennik.

Polotskaia, E.A. 1974. 'Realizm Chehova i russkaia literatura kontsa XIX – nachala XX v. (Kuprin, Bunin, Andreiev)' in *Razvitie realizma v russkoi literature. III. vol.* Moscow: Nauka. 77–164.

Slivitskaia, O.V. 1974. 'Fabula-kompozitsiia-detal' buninskoi novelli' in *Buninskii sbornik.* Orel. 90–103.

PART 4

Russian Culture into the 20th Century and Beyond

∴

CHAPTER 16

Viewing Askance: Irrationalist Aspects in Russian Art from Fedotov to Malevich and into the Beyond

Jeremy Howard

Introduction

Applying pigment to canvas in order to express yourself is difficult to conceive of as intrinsically rational. Likewise the beliefs that an icon is miraculous by nature and that gates, doors and bargeboards carved with *sirin* nature spirit figures will protect those within from harm are hardly reasonable. Art, for all its being a sign of things, frequently involves the suspension of the cerebral and engages instead with superstition, faith, emotion and illusion. Pavel Fedotov's *Gamblers* (1852) and Kazimir Malevich's *Quadrilateral [Black Square]* (1914–15) are painted studies of altered states of consciousness. Despite their opposition to the circle, they are open-ended full-stops that are reductive meditations on life, death and emptiness. They can be seen as key visual markers on a chronological voyage into the 'super-real', the 'beyond-reason' and the 'uncanny otherworld' by Russian artists. Perhaps the journey was begun by the 7th–12th-century Chud makers of bronze animist ornaments and enjoined by Byzantinist fresco painters of Christian mythical views from 'Creation' to 'The Last Judgment' and beyond. Certainly it was taken into 'alternative' worldviews of the Pacific and Americas by Mikhail Tikhanov in the post-Napoleonic age and in the late twentieth century reached a form of postmodern expression in the performance and appropriation art of, for instance, Oleg Kulik.[1] The focus

---

1   Little has been written on Tikhanov (1789–1862), though numerous of his watercolours survive in the Museums of the Academy of Science and Academy of Arts, St Petersburg. His images of, for example Alaskan, Californian, Brazilian, Peruvian and Filippino life, often depict indigenous folk in ritual dress, with signs of their pagan religion, and sometimes smoking or drinking. He also includes signs of the encroachment of Russian imperial and western metropolitan culture into the native ways of life. The most detailed study of this remarkable artist is that of Leonid A. Shur, 'Khudozhnik-Puteshestvennik Mikhail Tikhanov', *Latinskaya Amerika*, 1974, 5, 163–180. See also, Jeremy Howard, *East European Art*, Oxford: Oxford University Press, 2006, 79–84. Tikhanov 'lost his mind' while returning to Russia in 1819, and thereafter was largely to be found in the psychiatric wing of St Petersburg's Obukhov Hospital. From 1822 to 1862 he was in the care of the Luchaninov family. A sign of his breakdown, which seems to have occurred about the time he was in The Philippines,

for this chapter, however, is on 'irrationalist' artistic developments of the second half of the nineteenth century, through to the second decade of the twentieth. For many these can be seen as a continuation of certain 'Gothic' trends which, despite popular and scholarly belief, held great sway in Russia and whose legacy was to be felt, if largely unacknowledged, in some of the most 'rational' and/or 'abstract' movements of the 1910s and 1920s (e.g. Popova's versions of Constructivism). They can also be interpreted as counterparts to 'realist' art and its apparent grounding in materialism, science and positivism. They are like visual, secular koans or mandalas, reflecting at once confusion and enlightenment, states of fey and becoming, mysterious sensations of space and light, and charting a voyage into emotional-meditative appreciations of experience.

ILLUSTRATION 16.1   *Montage of Kazimir Malevich, Quadrilateral [The Black Square], 1914–15, oil on canvas, 80.1 × 80.1*
TRETYAKOV GALLERY, MOSCOW, AND FRAGMENT FROM PAVEL FEDOTOV, THE GAMBLERS

---

can be seen, if one adopts a psychoanalytical reading, in what may have been his last work: *An Indian in Manila plucked off Mr Tikhanov's Hat by a Chinese Kiosk and Made Off* (1818–19, Museum of Academy of Arts, St Petersburg). Concerning Kulik (b. 1961), see note 20.

Fedotov's and Malevich's paintings offer rough, distinct positive-negative rectangles in rectangles. They do not detail or narrate. They do not contain a coherent plot or strictly definable message. Rather through their withdrawal from the usual props of visual topoi and tropes, they question the authority of intellectualism. This pictured undermining of the value of rationale, let alone conventional notions of knowledge and progress, proposes worldviews based on distinct forms of irrationalism. In fact the history of irrationalist art in Russia is a history of irrationalist diversity. For its concerns include studies (or anti-studies) of the so-called absurd, esoteric, fantastic, magical, ineffable, cosmic, naïve, emotional and iconoclastic, as well as of human folly, madness, chance, spontaneity and intuition.

Fedotov's Gamblers

While Fedotov's *Gamblers* defies straightforward reading, it can be considered an essay in the intrinsicality of human folly. As Tuchman has pointed out we seem bound to go through life dominated by forces addicted to folly, the power of which means the conducting of policy contrary to self-interest and likely to be self-defeating.[2] The painted representation of a nocturnal, shadowy scene of four mannequin-like gamblers by a dying artist incarcerated in a St Petersburg psychiatric hospital suggests a personal articulation of man's folly nature. Gambling may involve elements of calculated risk and significant amounts of knowledge, skill and reasoning, yet these are always subordinate to its quintessential quality of uncertainty. The gambler embroils themselves with questions of probability and chance, and often does so in the awareness that failure is more likely than success, that loss more likely than gain. 'Throwing caution to the wind', may, however, be rational, if not instinctively human, i.e. 'hoping against hope'. And someone in the gambling setup has worked things out rationally and will profit...

One of the figures in Fedotov's *Gamblers* stretches and faces askance at three blank pictures on the wall behind him. Kuznetsov has interpreted him as the winner and the man seated opposite the loser.[3] I have always thought (was it reasonable?), or perhaps more correctly felt, it more likely to be the other way round but am willing to concede that either view is possible. Irrespective

---

2   See Barbara Tuchman, *The March of Folly: From Troy to Vietnam*, New York: Ballantine, 1984 (or later editions).
3   See Erast Kuznetsov, *Pavel Fedotov*, Leningrad: Iskusstvo, 1990, 284 f.

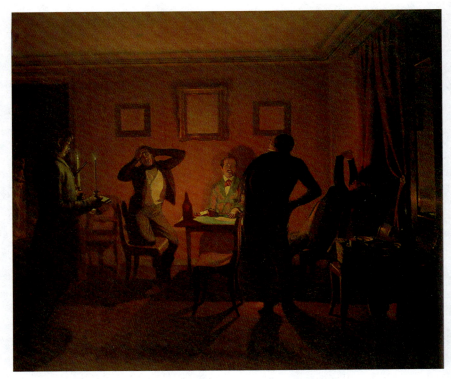

ILLUSTRATION 16.2   *Pavel Fedotov, The Gamblers, 1852, oil on canvas, 60.5 × 70.2*
MUSEUM OF RUSSIAN ART, KIEV

of which way of seeing is more correct, the eyes of the standing man seem not to see/look and we do not see his eyes. Similarly the 'pictures' are blanks – just three frames. The central one is elongated vertically (portrait-style) and comprises a gilded swept frame whose curvilinear outer edge surrounds an internal rectangle. It contains nothing. Rather, it contains colour: an orangey void that darkens slightly towards the top. The diffuse shadow around the upper half of the frame suggests it is suspended, despite lacking signs of how, at a slight angle from the wall. If it is a mirror it faces the viewer in the upper centre of the composition, yet is empty. In semblance of order the two 'pictures' either side of this central emptiness of enclosed abstract light are symmetrically positioned equidistant from it. Smaller than the centrepiece these 'pictures' are virtual squares within virtually square plain, dark frames. As such, and proportionally, they can be seen as counterparts to Malevich's *Quadrilateral*. Milner has pointed out how the latter is the result and expression of a spiritual search for a generating and dynamic world of geometric harmonies: in its "ikon-like quality" it is "an assertion of faith...a sign of revelation...a 'living royal infant'"... that "opened the door to a world parallel to our own".[4]

The reflected light that the squared frames contain is more muted and even than their grander neighbour with its pretensions to style and decoration. A further distinction to that more bulky and curvy form is that they appear flat and desubstantiated against the wall. The lower right rim of the right-hand nothing-picture is cut by the brow of the back-stretching dark silhouette of the tall man in unbuttoned frockcoat and high white collar. The visible sliver of his diagonally turned face is illuminated from below and has a yellowish poison glow. He might be parallel to the otherworld of the square but he appears incapable of seeing its door let alone opening it. Rather he disrupts its line and form, an intervention that breaks any potential sense of sacred harmony. Fedotov's rectangles of emptiness, unlike Malevich's, are testaments to both the vacuousness and pointless folly of human activity.

Very little is 'right' about the scene Fedotov reveals under the wall's non-scenes/empty mirror and around the stiff standing figure. Yet, on the face of it, all seems normal: is this not just a representation of a group of middle-class men playing cards in a well-proportioned and furnished room, attended by a candle-bearing servant? No. Perception and reality are questioned. No one looks at anyone else. No one looks. The tall mirror above the right-hand-side table with its empty plates and bottle reflects only a glimmer of light and the edge of another square frame. The apertures of window and door frame only darkness, their shroud-like qualities being enhanced by heavy curtains on the one hand and the apparition of a disproportionately small, blanched, feminine sculptural figure on the other.

The Gamblers is a study in anguish.[5] With its ghostly light emanating from a hidden source on the gaming table, the hand gestures of the players, the looming shadows, the sinister, shining, staring eye and cigar of the seated man, the absence of his legs and those of some chairs and tables, the scene is turned into a surreal performance of grotesque silhouette-mannequins. The leering seated man with his empty palm outstretched imploringly appears like a ventriloquist's

---

4 John Milner, *Kazimir Malevich and the Art of Geometry*, New Haven and London: Yale University Press, 1996, 127. In 2015 Tretyakov Gallery resarchers indicated that x-ray examination had revealed two other paintings and a partially-legible Russian inscription underneath the painted surface. The latter, apparently, toys with Alphonse Allais' 1882 painting of a black rectangle entitled 'Combat de nègres dans une cave, pendant la nuit'. The discoveries allow new layers of irrationalist readings of the work.

5 While Kuznetsov (op. cit.) provides valuable insights for reading Fedotov's *The Gamblers*, a pioneer in this regard is Dmitrii Sarab'ianov. See, for example, Sarab'ianov's *Pavel Andreevich Fedotov*, Leningrad: Khudozhnik RSFSR, 1985, 83 f., and D.V. Sarab'ianov, *Russian Art from Neoclassicism to the Avant-Garde*, London: Thames and Hudson, 1990, 92–93.

dummy. Is he then incapable of self-reflective thought? The problem is that he might also be something of a Fedotov self-portrait. In any case the effect is one of depersonalisation and tension. Of course Pushkin had written about the unbalancing, addictive power of gambling in *The Queen of Spades* (1834), Gogol had produced a play called *The Gamblers* (1842) in which only deceit and the Devil win, and the compulsive Dostoyevsky was to publish *The Gambler* in 1867. Furthermore, Fedotov's *Gamblers* is connected to Russian visual art, and folk art at that, by its similarities to the mid-eighteenth century *lubok* depicting *Paramoshka and Savoska playing Cards*. 'Chance' had it that this woodcut came into the public domain in 1852, the year Fedotov was working on *The Gamblers*, it being then that a good example moved from the Pogodin collection to the St Petersburg Public Library.[6] Here too there is a central gaming table. Both players appear as flattened, disfigured cutouts, face forward straight at the viewer and have a crooked dull gaze akin to the seated figure in Fedotov. Paramoshka, the winner, even bares his teeth and holds out his left hand in a pose not dissimilar to that of Fedotov's man. Behind them are apertures and frames, and while these are confusingly ambiguous in terms of space, they contain no art, being instead a leaded window and a board proclaiming Savoska's unhappy fate. They are divided from one another by three pillars. Savoska puts his right hand to his head, as the left player in Fedotov's *Gamblers*. Each player is supported by a stylised figure at their backs. The colour scheme is restricted and the light sources unclear. The ajar door, tree and balustrade in front of which stands the loser's apparently legless servant, mirror the room entrance in Fedotov, while the stove or ornate cupboard on the left in the *lubok* takes the reverse place of the large mirror and sidetable in *The Gamblers*.

But Fedotov's *Gamblers* is also about both the tragedy of his life and Russia in the mid-nineteenth century. Its creation coincides with a cholera epidemic and a new oppressive stage in the reign of Tsar Nicholas I, following the European revolutions of 1848. 'Thought' and 'education' were leading to disquiet and demands for a better, fairer life. Intellectuals were regarded with suspicion. The reactionaries called for suppression, closure of the universities (closure of minds) and the incarceration of 'subversives' and those associated with them. Carting the Petrashevskii circle of thinkers off to forced labour in Siberia for their socialist desire to transform the village commune from its feudal, enslaved, illiterate and 'dumb' state, was just one example of the regime's cruel folly. Its instinct to survive through control and expansion, while inevitably doomed, was to have profound effects on Fedotov, the former ensign in the regiment of Finnish Life-Guards and recipient of royal patronage. One of the problems was

---

6   See Alla Sytova, *The Lubok. Russian Folk Pictures. 17th to 19th Century*, Leningrad: Aurora, 1984, plate 33.

ILLUSTRATION 16.3　*Anon., Paramoshka and Savoska playing Cards, c. 1760s, coloured woodcut 29 × 33.1*
NATIONAL LIBRARY OF RUSSIA, ST PETERSBURG

that his paintings were being engraved by Evstafii Bernardskii, a graphic artist connected with Mikhail Petrashevskii's progressives, who had just produced illustrations for Gogol's *Dead Souls*. Although, after ten weeks in prison Bernardsky was cleared of any illegal activity, both he and Fedotov essentially became *personae non gratae*. As far as Fedotov was concerned this meant the loss of commissions, reduced circumstances and the onset of despondency, depression, and ultimately a declaration of insanity. Simultaneously he tore himself away from Julia Tarnovskaia, the young woman to whom he was betrothed and with whom he had been in love. In nervous turmoil, he wandered the Petersburg streets, was seen crying in cemeteries, apparently ordered a coffin and wound up in a mental asylum. In this state he painted *The Gamblers*. It was to be his last work. But it was not to be realised alone, for simultaneously he produced *Encore! Again Encore!*, (Tretyakov Gallery, Moscow) a bleak portrayal of the tedium of life. With its image of an officer in a claustrophobic, dimly lit yet stiflingly hot wooden hut, lying on his bed, ignoring his guitar and uniform while getting a dog to jump over a spear, this is a study in desperate, lonely 'killing time'. There is no reason to this life. A shadowy figure is half-hidden in the doorway. In both of these final paintings Fedotov's mind, 'soul' and society are disintegrating. He is 'Waiting for Godot'.

Repin's Ivans

Unlike Fedotov, Ilia Repin is rarely associated with hallucinatory art, madness or irrationalist trends. Rather he is more likely to be considered a realist, populist, materialist, converted nationalist and regime image-maker. Yet on many an occasion his work confronts the march of the intellect and deals with the pursuit of folly. He remains figurative, wedded to optical illusionism, mostly seeks anatomical correctness, is concerned with 'capturing the moment' and strives for technical mastery. Yet he avoids reaching conclusions, does not just hold up a mirror to reality, and his side-taking is ambiguous. Even a formal portrait of Tsar Nicholas II (of which he did several in the 1890s) leaves doubts about his sympathies, and, with the emperor in dress uniform looking diminutive, pensive, solitary and idle in strangely uncomfortable, cold and palatial settings, one has to wonder if he is not foreshadowing Tuchman's thoughts on leaders' enthrallment to policies of folly that will inevitably bring about their downfall. Certainly he had intimated the cruel ludicrousness of the Tsarist state of things in his celebrated early painting of *The Volga Bargehaulers* (1870–73) in which the bent gang of enslaved men toil like animals (their cognitive faculties reduced but not annihilated) as they pull the barge upstream while a steamer and sailboat slip easily off in the opposite direction. Was it irrational that such a work should have been sponsored by the state and that the President of the Academy of Arts, Grand Duke Vladimir Alexandrovich should have purchased it and hung it in the billiard room of his new palace on the Palace Embankment in St Petersburg?

While consistently enraptured by colour and vivacious young life, an inkling of which can be discerned in *Volga Bargehaulers*, Repin creates many 'approaching death' works, be they images of the ageing Tolstoi (from 1887–1909), the alcoholic Mussorgskii in his final hospital dressing gown (1881), revolutionaries awaiting execution (1880s), a duel scene (1896), a *Golgotha* (1922) with two crucified thieves and Christ's empty cross, or his most notorious history painting *Ivan the Terrible and his son Ivan 16 Nov 1581* (1882–5).[7] The latter

---

7 This painting has been the subject of much debate – both contemporary and historical, with recent commentators in English being led by Alison Hilton, who provides the most illuminating analysis in *The Art of Ilia Repin: Tradition and Innovation in Russian Realism*, PhD thesis, Columbia University, New York, 1979, 109 f. Possibly a little more accessible, and also very

ILLUSTRATION 16.4   *Ilia Repin, Ivan the Terrible and his Son Ivan, 16 November 1581, 1882–85, oil on canvas, 199.5 × 254*
TRETYAKOV GALLERY, MOSCOW

was huge (two by two-and-a-half metres), its scale helping to elicit the controversy it stirred upon exhibition at the thirteenth *Peredvizhniki* exhibition in 1885. It was purchased by Pavel Tretiakov and, after its censorship had been relaxed, hung in his Moscow gallery.

useful, particularly in terms of reaction, is David Jackson's account in *The Russian Vision. The Art of Ilya Repin*, Schoten: BAI, 2006, 85 f. More recently Kevin M.F. Platt has made a valuable deconstruction of the expressive import of the work in his *Terror and Greatness: Ivan and Peter as Russian Myths*, Cornell University Press, Ithaca and London, 2011, 111 f. and 164f, this being an extension of the interpretation given by Platt in , 'On Blood, Scandal, Renunciation, and Russian History. Il'ia Repin's *Ivan the Terrible and His Son Ivan*', in Marcus Levitt, Tatyana Novikov, eds., *Times of Trouble. Violence in Russian Literature and Culture*, Wisconsin: University of Wisconsin Press, 2007, 112–122. In Russian, one of the most detailed historical and critical accounts (particularly derived from an immersion in Russian Orthodoxy) in the post-Soviet period is Sergei Fomin, '"Kartina krovi", ili kak Il'ia Repin tsarevicha Ivana ubival', *Russkii vestnik*, 11.07.2007, 19.07.2007, 29.09.2007, 30.10.2007, 28.11.2007, 25.12.2007. See, for example, http://rusk.ru/st.php?idar=25141.

On the morning of 16th (29th) January 1913 a twenty-nine-year old, smartly dressed man entered the Tretyakov Gallery, gazed at the works in the Surikov room, then headed for Repin's *Ivan and Ivan* and slashed it three times with a knife. As he did so he cried, "Why the blood? Enough Blood, Down with Blood".[8] The man was Abram Balashov, son of a Moscow furniture manufacturer, an Old Believer and icon painter. The canvas was cut in its very centre, long lacerations carving downwards across the faces of the father and son. The *Niva* magazine (1913, 5, 96) carried a photograph of the cut parts of the painting and noted that *"fortunately* [my italics] the eyes of the Terrible and his son, with their remarkable expressiveness, remained untouched". After his arrest and medical examination, Balashov was declared mentally ill and removed to a Moscow psychiatric hospital. His treatment having run its course he was freed under a guarantee provided by his father.

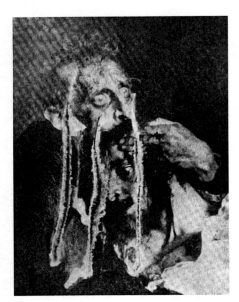

ILLUSTRATION 16.5
Abram Balashov and Ilia Repin. Fragment of slashed Ivan the Terrible and his Son Ivan, as reproduced in Niva, 5, 1913

---

8   Fourteen months later a similar 'irrational' art attack was perpetrated by Mary Richardson, this time in the National Gallery, London, against the naked, fleshy back of Velázquez's *Venus and the Mirror* (*The Rokeby Venus*), and in the rational cause of women's suffrage. For an extended analysis offering various interpretations of the attack on Repin's work (although with an erroneous date for the event), see Platt, op.cit. For a brief discussion of the *Ivan* slashing event and its impact, see Elizabeth Kridl Valkenier, *Ilya Repin and the World of Russian Art*, New York: Columbia University Press, 1990, 179–181.

So was Balashov's act one of iconoclasm, sheer vandalism, a paranoid mind or a combination of these? The adjectives Valkenier uses to describe the event and the unprecedented public furore it produced include "deranged", "vituperative", "indecorous" and "hysterical".[9] She does not give many clues as to the actual nature or appropriateness of these descriptors. Platt claims Balashov was "unhinged by psychosis" and that his "scandalous act of violence…set the Russian public reeling".[10] But by stabbing the painting did Balashov really commit an irrational act and was the public response one of mass hysteria? Some contemporaries, in the forefront of whom stood symbolist poet Maksimilian Voloshin, questioned this. Perhaps they were right. For all the violence, aggressiveness and tumult of the incident Balashov did not spill any actual blood but rather drew attention to what may be regarded itself as a sensationalist and false visualisation of a bloody killing and one which the artist had intended to entitle *Filicide* (until deciding it was politic to have a more emotionally neutral 'father, son and date' tag).[11] Balashov's slitting of *Ivan and Ivan* was premeditated. He was seen in the gallery on several occasions in the weeks leading up to his attack. He brought a knife. His act took place in the run-up to the elaborate 300th anniversary celebrations of rule by the Romanov dynasty. This, and his Old Believer icon painting background, suggests deliberate iconoclasm against something that profaned religious, and particularly Byzantine, prototype. The diagnosis of personality disorder may well have been correct, but Balashov was following his beliefs, and, simultaneously, following in a long tradition of art vandalism by those who considered the art they attacked as offensive, immoral, agitational, subversive, oppressive, etc. – i.e. opposed to their concept of order.

A famous precedent of such a direct action occurred in recent times, also against a Russian painting first exhibited in 1885, and by a 'religious fanatic'. This was the throwing of sulphuric acid at Vasilii Vereshchagin's *The Holy Family* and *Christ's Resurrection* while they were on display in Vienna. In this earlier case, the attack (which even led to his life being threatened) on the most 'rationalist' of Russian modern artists, the outspoken advocate of realism,

9   Valkenier, *Ilya Repin and the World of Russian Art*, 179, 225.
10 Platt, *Terror and Greatness*, 132.
11 The decision did not prevent Repin working on another version of the painting, for which he retained the original title, for the Moscow art collector, financier and Old Believer, Stepan Riabushinskii. Completed in 1909, *Filicide*, was created for Riabushinskii's new Moscow mansion built in the questionably 'anti-rationalist' Art Nouveau style by Franz Schechtel [Fedor Shekhtel] (see below). It is now in the Voronezh Regional Museum of Fine Arts.

was due to his representation of gospel subjects being deemed too worldly, too ethnographic, too documentarist and therefore devoid of divinity and blasphemous. He had been in Palestine and copied the landscape, the building and human types. His humanisation went too far for the Roman Catholic church of Austria. Shortly after Vereshchagin's exhibition had opened in November 1885, a much-publicised campaign to have the 'anti-religious' religious works removed was mounted by the new Archbishop of Vienna, Cardinal Cölestin Josef Ganglbauer. It was decreed that those who had seen such a 'perverse' rendering of Christ should, for three days, pray and repent, and then buy an indulgence from the church. The local press carried cartoons of the offending pictures being burned. It was no coincidence that an Austrian cleric, Father Geronimo Karvan, should, after several exploratory visits, arm himself with a bottle of acid hidden in his cassock, wait for a quiet moment in front of the Palestinian paintings and then 'frenziedly' throw the contents of the bottle at the paintings (damaging six in total).[12]

One of the distinctions between the Vereshchagin and the Repin damage acts was that Repin's was carried out by an artist, albeit a religious one. As such it could be regarded as a form of art intervention, with an element of performance. Balashov's (literally) incisive changing of the artwork meant a contribution to it. Some would say it even helped 'improve' it and certainly encouraged the debate about 'what is art' to move on in Russia, just at the time that the Futurists were, in highly controversial and revolutionary ways, doing likewise. As such the event was picked up by the avant-garde, Velimir Khlebnikov proselytising its effect in his declaration *Trumpet of Martians* (1916), with its call for a new universal order run by youthful, bold inventors. Even after the 1917 Revolution, in one of his last poems, 'Burliuk' (1921), Khlebnikov recalled how "[the] sticking of the knife into the heart of poor art...had been...more deeply made when carried out beautifully by Balashov".

More immediately, the vociferous polemic that followed the slicing of *Ivan and Ivan* was most provocatively stirred by a Futurist Debate organised in Moscow by the Jack of Diamonds arts society. Held in the Polytechnical Museum on 12th (25th) February 1913, the disputers included Voloshin and Burliuk (against the work) and Repin and the art teacher Dmitrii Shcherbinovskii (for). In what was an act of folly as far as his literary reputation was concerned, it was

---

12   The subsequent fate of the paintings is currently unknown to me. A black and white reproduction of *Holy Family* can be found in A.K. Lebedev, A.V. Solodovnikov, *V.V. Vereshchagin*, Leningrad: Khudozhnik RSFSR, 1987, 67, and Vahan Barooshian, *V.V. Vereshchagin. Artist at War*, Gainsville: University Press of Florida, 1993, 106.

Voloshin who made the most substantial contribution to the debate.[13] He argued that visitors to the Tretyakov Gallery had been subjected to almost three decades of offence when they gazed upon *Ivan and Ivan*; that the painting and the direction it stood for had led to a crippling state of trauma in Russian art; that the flawed and cheap appeal of the painting was base; that it had brought the attack upon itself; that Balashov was a victim of its contradictory feeble, naturalist impulse and exaggeratedly expressive, vulgar dramatism; and ultimately that Balashov had made an appropriate aesthetic statement given the gore of Repin's image. To cap it all, Voloshin, the freemason and idealist, claimed that his critique of the painting came from a commitment to the social good.

Voloshin brought to his defence the arguments of Theodor Landzert (1833–89), a professor of anatomy at the Military-Medical Academy in St Petersburg, who is still today known for his discoveries concerning the human skull. As early as 1885 Landzert had been called in to the Academy of Arts to denounce, through scientific analysis, *Ivan and Ivan*. He did so not least by indicating that the amount of blood spilling from the Tsarevich's cranium was impossible. Given the official condemnation of the painting when it was first shown, it is perhaps not difficult to surmise upon whose bidding Landzert made (and published) his conclusions. Oddly (irrationally?), for a medical scientist, he went far beyond a 'rational' deconstruction of Repin's work, entering instead into the realm of subjective appraisal of artistic merit:

> The artist has lapsed into caricature and inadmissible bad taste. Instead of the Tsar's face he has represented some kind of ape-like physiognomy... The artist has gone beyond the bounds in which artistic creativity should move. He has sacrificed artistic beauty to expressiveness but not achieved expressiveness. He has somehow not wanted to comprehend that through such a harsh and gross appeal to the feelings of the masses he destroys the seriousness and worth of the work as a whole.[14]

13　Voloshin's detailed lecture was widely reported and published in part his *O Repine*, Moscow, 1913, 59–64. For a contemporary review of the evening and its 'heated' nature, see Anon., 'Bubrovye Valety', *Russkoe Slovo*, 13 February 1913, 36, 5. For an analysis of Voloshin's position, see Platt, *Terror and Greatness*, 165 f.

14　F.P. Landtsert, 'Po povodu kartiny I.E. Repina "Ivan groznyi i ego syn, 16 noyabria 1581". Lektsiia chitannaia uchenikam Akademii kudhozhestv', *Vestnik izyashchnykh iskusstv*, St Petersburg, 1885, volume 3, 2, 201. Landzert had entered into the debate about the artistic representation of human character a year earlier, with an article entitled 'Physiognomics and Mimicry', published in the same Academy of Arts bulletin (vol. 2, 1884, 87 f.) According to Johannes Ranke, he had also claimed, and produced drawings to the effect, that the

Landzert was prone to artistic speculations and took issue with what he viewed as a growing and ill-fated tendency in European art to revel in human cruelty and baseness, something that leads to pretension, superficiality and an ill form of art: "These are not aesthetic but pathological works that bear witness to the absence in their authors, if not of talent then of some pure, virgin creative ability borne by a healthy and broadminded worldview".[15]

What Landzert overlooked was that Repin's *Ivan and Ivan* was an expression of agony, that it was a response both to Russian history and its times, and that agony had been a subject for art for centuries. Whatever Winckelmann and Lessing may have thought about the noble countenance of the Hellenistic sculpture of Laocoön, it is an expression of extreme suffering derived from torture and leading to death.[16] Further, images of Jesus' Passion and death are so widespread that they have spawned innumerable similar enactments of secular 'agony' subjects. In many respects Repin was following in this tradition. His attention on the two main actors, their disposition and relationship could be transferred from a scene depicting the Lamentation of Christ, and in particular, almost any Pietà since in this the dead and bloodied Jesus is usually held on the knee and cradled by the mournful Virgin Mary.[17] In addition, and as he admitted after his painting had been slashed, he was inspired by, and tried to recreate in painterly form, the powerful, irresistible effects that he had experienced listening to a performance of the 'Joy of Vengeance' movement of Rimskii-Korsakov's orientalist *Antar* symphonic suite, it being an allegro marked by raging crescendos.[18]

Simultaneously Repin acknowledged that he had painted *Ivan and Ivan* in a state of ever-intensifying terrible rapture and that his agitation coincided with that which gripped the Russian public after the assassination of Tsar Alexander II on 1 March 1881. He had attended the executions of the *People's Will* members associated with the regicide. He found it impossible to ignore the fact that Ivan IV's wrathful and crazed killing of his heir had taken place exactly three hundred years earlier and had been a 'Reform or Die!' signal that resulted not

---

Quaternary Engis Skull was comparable to 'a beautiful skull of an ancient Greek from the classical period of Athens' (Ranke, *Der Mensch*, Leipzig and Vienna: Verlag des Bibliographischen Institutes, 1890, 443, with illustration by Landzert on 438).

15 Landtsert, 204.
16 See Gotthold Ephraim Lessing, *Laocoon. An Essay upon the Limits of Painting and Poetry*, Boston: Little, Brown and Company, 1898, 1.
17 As an example, the *Pietà* (1876, Dallas Museum of Art) recently painted by the then popular French artist William-Adolphe Bouguereau bears some comparison with Repin's work.
18 See Igor Grabar', *Il'ia Efimovich Repin*, Moscow: Gosudarstvennoe izdatel'stvo izobrazitel'nykh iskusstv, I, 1937, 258.

only in a royal death but in the death of a regime. Landzert is right that Repin was pathological in his approach, but he was also extraordinarily careful and skilled in his composition, colour, light and focus. The intensity of pathos, madness and emotional awakening that he achieves is a complex combination of influences acting upon him, his ability to extrapolate elements from these influences for his own goals, and his sense of personal artistic identity. There is something of Rembrandt's spirit of tragedy as seen in *Return of the Prodigal Son* (c.1666–69) and of Mark Antokolskii's bronze of a 'ready to erupt' *Ivan the Terrible* (1870–71), both of which Repin had access to in St Petersburg since they were in The Hermitage.[19] But more than that, there is also a clear evocation of Goya's terrifying 'black' mural *Saturn devouring his Son* (1819–23), which had just been shown for the first time, in Paris at the Exposition Universelle of 1878. The Greek-Roman myth accords with the story of *Ivan and Ivan*, as does the concentration on the two figures, the highlights of gushing red blood and the glaring eyes of the mad father-murderer.[20]

---

19 Antokolskii's lifesize sculpture is of a frowning, compassionless despot hunched on his throne with his sceptre upright and threatening by his strained right hand. He appears sunken in blind thought, ready to unleash some awful act upon his people (or enemies). In contrast to the condemnation of Repin's 'awakened conscience' painting by the Holy Synod, Ministry of Interior and Tsar Alexander III, Antokolskii's grotesque *Ivan the Terrible* was greeted with wholesale approbation, gained the young Jewish sculptor the title of Academician and so delighted Alexander II and his sister Grand Princess Maria Nikolaevna, that the Tsar purchased it for the Hermitage for the enormous sum of 8000 roubles. How curious that the 'soft' Tsar Liberator, the one who had emancipated the serfs in 1861, should be so impressed by such an image of Tsarist tyranny and yet his reactionary son should have been so fearful of one which contained seeds of reconciliation and peace. Would Antokolskii's work have been so lauded if it had been created in the wake of March 1881 rather than a decade earlier? Fate, when it concerns human judgment, not least that of political masters and artists, has a fickle, if not irrational, finger.

20 It is worth noting in passing that the cannibalism and naked bestiality of the Goya can also be seen as akin to that expressed in Oleg Kulik's *Eclipse I* (1999), a digitally edited photograph (and 'highlight' of the *Berlin-Moskau/Moskva-Berlin 1950–2000* exhibition of 2004). Here a nude man depicted against a scene of snow, highrise blocks and cranes, holds aloft a red flag while having his legs grasped zoosexually by two dogs. The man's aghast facial expression is ambiguous. Kulik gained notoriety as a performance artist who adopted a dog 'persona', and who, as such, on occasion destroyed others' artworks. He claims he needs to go beyond the human condition and express canine anger and violence in order to bring attention to the quagmire and aloofness of contemporary culture. The head of the man in *Eclipse I*, similar to that of Ivan IV in *Ivan and Ivan*, is turned to the right, centrally positioned and has a gaze that stares beyond the canvas at nothing in particular.

For all Repin's frenzy then, his is a calculated picture of 'realisation' and lament. It can be claimed that he shows the moment when tyrannical Ivan comes to his senses recognising his crime and its implications. This then is a coming to terms with folly. Cradling the son he has mortally wounded during an argument, he pathetically attempts to stop the flow of blood and, as he looks towards the light, is about to call out for help. With Ivan unable to prevent the tsarevich's death Repin captures (for all his historical inaccuracies, orientalising and mythmaking) an absolutely key moment in Russian history and in the life of the 'terrible' Tsar. The personal story is rendered equally with the national one. For this moment was to be followed by Ivan 'losing' his mind in grief, jumping out of bed at night with heart-rending wails, announcing he no longer wanted to rule, and that he intended to enter a monastery. His decision was overturned by his Boyar council who announced that his younger son Fedor was mentally unfit to rule. Reassuming his rule as leader he was a changed man, sending vast alms to monasteries, making peace with the Poles and Swedes and returning territories to them, courting Queen Elizabeth of England and Lady Mary Hastings. All of this was too little too late, and Ivan himself died just over two years later. Repin's darkened chamber, with overturned 'throne', cast-aside sceptre, rumpled oriental carpets, and small high window upon whose chink of light Ivan turns his back, suggests this. As such it is a clarion call to those at the head of the Romanov house, which had eventually taken over after Ivan's fatal ending of Rurik dynastical rule, to 'come to their senses' over the state of things before the blood of their offspring would be on their hands and Russia would enter another catastrophic 'Times of Troubles'. If Repin's work can be seen, in hindsight, to contain this foresight it can also be read in terms of Tolstoi's current outspoken pacifism and demands not to kill. The calls of these leaders of Russia's literary and artistic worlds went unheeded.

If human history is the history of the irrational battling with the rational nowhere has this been more sweetly and disturbingly expressed than in Gogol's satirical *Diary of a Madman* (1835). Repin was drawn to its anti-hero Poprishchin from an early age, making a drawing of the lunatic lying in his bed while still a student (1870) and returning to him just as he began to formulate *Ivan and Ivan* in 1882. The later work has the hallmarks of his filicide painting, with the obsessed, hallucinating and crazed civil servant standing centrally in his dressing gown, bathed in (and scowling blindly at) light from an unknown source, surrounded by the dark interior of his asylum room and turning his back on the glimmer of light that is discernible as a small window in the top left corner.[21]

---

21 The painting actually shows the actor Vasilii Andreev-Burlak (1843–88), who had founded the Pushkin Theatre in Moscow in 1880 and adapted Gogol's short story for the stage.

ILLUSTRATION 16.6
Ilia Repin, Poprishchin. 'I'm really astonished the deputation's so slow in coming. Whatever could have held them up...', 1882, oil on canvas, 98 × 69
MUSEUM OF RUSSIAN ART, KIEV

Vrubel's Demons

Incarceration in a mental hospital has been a recurrent issue for modern Russian art, ever since institutionalised psychiatric care had 'taken off' in the early nineteenth century.[22] If around 1810 there had been fourteen asylums across Russia, by 1905 there were one hundred and twenty-eight (with 33,607 beds), plus a whole new range of private mental health clinics, in one of which (the new sanatorium of neuro-psychologist Dr Fedor Usoltsev in Moscow's

---

Theatrical performance helps explain the 'spotlighting' on Repin's madman and dramatism of the work as a whole. *Poprishchin* was bought by the industrialist Fedor Tereshchenko and is now in the National Museum of Russian Art, Kiev. Repin's painting shows remarkable similarities to Konstantin Shapiro's 1883 album of photographs of Andreev-Burlak in the role (State Historical Museum, Moscow), though the latter are tagged with clips of Poprishchin's absurd proclamations.

22 For an illuminating analysis of a February 1993 'performance'-experience of mental illness in Republican Psychiatric Hospital No. 1, Simferopol, Crimea, its semiological issues and subsequent reincarnation in exhibition form ('Crimania', MAK, Vienna, 1995) by Sergei Bugaev (Afrika) (b. 1966), see: Amy Bryzgel, *Performing the East: Performance Art in Russia, Latvia and Poland since 1980*, London: I.B. Tauris, 2013, 48 f.

ILLUSTRATION 16.7   *Mikhail Vrubel, Demon Downcast, 1902, oil on canvas, 139 × 387*
TRETYAKOV GALLERY, MOSCOW

Petrovskii Park) was a man considered by many to be the country's greatest living artist, Mikhail Vrubel (1856–1910). His last major work before he was diagnosed with tabes dorsalis and paralysis leading to dementia and sight-loss as a result of syphilis, was a monumental (four-metres wide) study of helpless torment, anguish and failure: *Demon Downcast* (1901–02).[23] He worked on it twenty hours a day and first showed it at the 'Exhibition of the 36 Artists' in Moscow...but only from the day before the exhibition closed (2nd February 1902). In March he took it to the fourth exhibition of *Mir Iskusstva* [The World of Art] in St Petersburg, reworking it even while it was on display. The painting received negative reviews and the Tretyakov Gallery refused to buy it owing to what its council considered flaws in draftsmanship and the non-fixing of its 'bronze' pigments. By April that year Vrubel was in the private clinic of psychiatrist Fedor Savei-Mogilevich before being moved to Moscow University Psychiatric Clinic in September. He spent the last four years of his life blind and in the newly built sanatorium for the 'neurological and mentally ill' of Dr Adolf Bari (5th Line of Vasil'evskii Ostrov, St Petersburg).

Vrubel's depiction of, and obsession with, the fallen 'superhuman' spirit is well known. It is worth recalling here that this is the folly of Lermontov's brooding, hopeless tyrant who, for all his intentions to overcome what he perceived as earthly injustices, has destroyed the one he is closest to (the beautiful Princess Tamara), and with her death contributed to his own cruel destiny. As such, while they may be deemed to belong to 'symbolist' and 'realist' trends respectively, Vrubel's *Demon* bears much in common with Repin's *Ivan and Ivan*. The demon is a crushed angel, a contorted and hybrid figure lying trapped

---

23   The Russian title is *Demon Poverzhennyi*. It is now, together with its great counterpart *Demon Seated*, in the Tretyakov Gallery.

on his-her flightless wings before an icy, craggy and desolate mountainscape. The eyes glare, seeing nothing but a realisation of futility. They are the central focal point of the composition. The canvas conveys a sense of powerlessness in the face of cosmic forces; it shows that suffering is pervasive and consuming, irrespective of attempts to overcome it. As such, *Demon Downcast* is both a personal statement and a warning of impending doom. While Repin may offer a glimmer of hope, for Vrubel the outlook is bleak, and inevitably so. His is the ultimate decadence, expressed both formally and in his non-resolution of his subject.

Vrubel's visual probing of the relationships of good and evil, mortal and immortal, real and illusory, had started in 1884–85. Then he had begun work painting and restoring icons and frescos, including the choir vault Pentecost fresco, at the medieval St Cyril's church in the grounds of Kiev's main psychiatric hospital. His infatuation with *The Demon* begins at this time. Subsequently he was asked to paint more monumental religious works, including Pietàs (for both the new St Vladimir's Cathedral and St Cyril's), but his watercolour sketches of the lamentation scene, which actually are quite riveting in their serene dolefulness, disappointed (himself as much as others). He was continually dissatisfied with his studies of demons, his unfinished *Flying Demon* (c. 1899) bearing particularly unhappy testament to his struggle. Yet I would argue that some of his illustrations to Lermontov's poem (from around 1890–91), his heads of demons and his *Demon Seated* (1890) are masterly, haunting visual definitions of irrationalism. Vrubel captures at once (without necessarily answering) contradictory questions of heavens and earth, east and west, suffering and injury, male and female, nobility and despair, terror and despair, ambivalence and certainty. Cast in the heights yet simultaneously low and spreading into our space *Demon Downcast* is the epitome of ambiguity, be that spatio-temporal, Nietzschean-Faustian, representational-abstract, or personal-universal. It was the ultimate expression of Vrubel's almost schizophrenic sense of being and becoming. The early, brooding *Demon Seated* with its taut muscular power emerging out from a complex arrangement of modulated, abstracted colour forms evolves then into a tragic and broken expression of non-religious prostration.[24]

Demon Downcast may have been Vrubel's last great canvas before the onset of his final physical and mental collapse, but it did not signal a diminishment in dedication to art, to probing visual expression. In 1904 he produced a series of

---

24   It is worth recalling here that while engaged with his demons Vrubel worked on Faustian subjects for the Morozov family homes in Moscow (most designed in Neo-Gothic style by Schechtel [Shekhtel']). *Demon Seated* is in the Tretyakov Gallery, Moscow.

portraits of patients and staff at Usoltsev's clinic, as well as a portrait of Usoltsev himself, and his spouse.[25] He also drew a whole cycle of pencil sketches entitled 'Insomnia', in which he depicts his dishevelled bed and plaids bundled in various states of untidiness and from different angles atop a bentwood chair.[26] With a febrile sense of transience, dark and light hatching, and quick, unstable fragmentariness, these capture, as much as his monumental *Demon Downcast*, Vrubel's disturbed psychological state. From this period too there are, besides a quantity of works on spiritual beings, numerous pencil sketch self-portraits, mainly frontal close-up heads with furrowed brows and disappearing eyes, as well as portraits of his wife, her eyes large and protruding.

Vrubel's condition was well known. Some voices called for his 'madness' not to be considered when judging the aesthetic merits of his works, maintaining, essentially, that the flaws in his character actually mirrored flaws in his technique and art as a whole.[27] Others recognised that his emotional volatility and trauma were, in those hypersensitive times, leading to innovative artworks that captured the *Zeitgeist* in a nuanced, special way. In this they saw that Vrubel was leading the Russian charge away from salon superficiality, stifling academicism and naturalist reliance on the physical. His psychiatrist, Doctor Usoltsev, provided firsthand insight into the relationship of Vrubel's psychological state and his art:

> ...this was an artist-creator with all his being, to the innermost recesses of his psychic makeup...creativity was like breathing for him... I saw him in extreme states of excitement and confusion...his feelings and thoughts carried away by his illness, his head spinning with the speed of ideas, when his bodily processes could not keep up with the vortex carrying them. And still he created. He covered the walls of his little house with fantastic, and,

---

25 For a revealing intepretation of one of the drawings of a patient, see Viacheslav P'etsukh, 'Puteshestvie po moey komnate', *Zhizn' zamechatel'nykh liudey*, Moscow: Globus, 2006, 187–188.

26 Now in the Russian Museum, St Petersburg.

27 Some warned that his illness should not be considered in the arguments for new trends in art. At the same time the vitriolic attacks on *Demon Downcast* signalled a new state of polarised invective for Russian art criticism. See, for example, Silen [Alfred Nurok], '*Novoe vremia* i Vrubel'', *Mir Iskusstva*, 1902, 7, 1–3. A year earlier in *Mir Iskusstva* (June 1901) Nurok had labelled Alessandro Rizzoni, an academic painter much valued by Vrubel, the worst living artist. Within months Rizzoni had committed suicide. As a result Vrubel himself began to rage against the critics, as seen in a 1902 letter to Savva Mamontov (published in E. Gomberg-Verzhbinskaia, Yu.N. Podkopaeva, *Vrubel'. Perepiska. Vospominaniia o khudozhnike*, Leningrad: Iskusstvo, 1976, 79–80).

it would seem, absurd lines and colours. From clay, and anything he could lay his hands on, he would make grotesque, absurd figures. But one only had to listen to him talk and to consider his words thoroughly and then the absurd would seem to disappear.... I studied Vrubel intensively for a long time and I consider that his art is not only completely normal but so strong and grounded that even his dreadful illness could not destroy it...as an artist he was extremely healthy, even as he was dying.[28]

Kulbin's Exhibitions

Such an understanding was followed by Nikolai Kulbin whose appearance on the stage of Russian art from the wings of the medical establishment coincided with Vrubel's move in the opposite direction. But rather than being a patient, and though he was frequently described as mad (or anarchic), Kulbin was a psychiatrist turned artist, art impresario and lecturer on art. At the opening of the joint Triangle and Wreath group exhibition which he had organised and which took place in St Petersburg two weeks before Vrubel died 1910, he gave a talk which was reported by the critic Vasilii Ianchevetskii in the following terms:

> He said: it would be wrong to think these artists cannot draw...they are all excellent artists...but they are dissatisfied with the contemporary rules and requirements for painting and are against all sugariness in art...they deny routine harmony, symmetry, anatomy...this does not mean the turning of the beautiful into the ugly. After all did not Vrubel in his numerous demons and other fantastic paintings continually break all the academic rules? And rather than rising up against beauty he strove to embody it by new means. It is possible to contravene all the academic rules, trying to cross to the so-called 'fourth dimension', trying to convey one's own inner, spiritual world. Thus the artist can sincerely represent on the canvas all that surrounds him as it appears to him.[29]

---

28   F.A. Usol'tsev, "Vrubel", *Russkoe Slovo*, 3 April 1910, republished in Gomberg-Verzhbinskaia, Podkopaeva, 289–290.

29   V. Ianch[evetskii]., 'Vystavka impressionistov 'Treugol'nik'', *Rossiia*, 24 March 1910, 1331, 4. Concerning Kulbin, see Jeremy Howard, *The Union of Youth. An Artists' Society of the Russian Avant-Garde*, Manchester and New York: Manchester University Press, 1992, particularly 8–40. See also Boris Kalaushin, ed., *Nikolai Kul'bin*, 1 and 2, St Petersburg: Apollon, 1994 and 1995, and Isabel Wünsche, The Organic School of the Russian Avant-Garde: Nature's Creative Principles, Farnham: Ashgate, 2015, 39 f.

ILLUSTRATION 16.8
Nikolai Kulbin, Self-Portrait, c. 1913–14

In October 1912, for the catalogue of Doctor Kulbin's one-man exhibition in St Petersburg, Sergei Gorodetskii published 'He Who is Given to Troubling the Waters', his tribute to the medic-artist:

> In every act of artistic influence there is a healing, and ever since Fechner we cannot comprehend catharsis without considering its psychological and physiological aspects. The ozone of life, which is breathed by the soul in tragedies, must, simultaneously be a unique massage of the nerves. Conversely, in every convalescence there is a sensation, similar to the sensation of artistic influence, if, of course he who heals is what he should be, i.e. a master of his art...
>
> The world represented in art is an unstable, barely perceptible, ever-changing and moving world. This is the battlefield between Subject and Object... It is this which is to be found in the creative work of Kulbin... In his art Kulbin is a fanatic. Fanaticism is always sincere. Sincerity is always persuasive.[30]

In his numerous talks and publications of the years 1908 to 1914 Kulbin proselytised "free" art, enthusing over "miracles and monsters in art", the "psychology

---

30   Sergei Gorodetskii, 'Tot komu dano vozmushchat' vodu', *Kul'bin*, St Petersburg: Obshchestvo intimnago teatra, 1912, 15 f.

of the artist", the "viewer in Purgatory", art as the revelation of invisible things, and the world being comprised of 'our' sensations.[31] In his scientific career he had, for many years, made psychophysical studies of human sensitivity, feeling and addiction. Impulse and instinct, conscious and mysterious processes of creativity, absorbed Kulbin. His appearance on the art scene encapsulated the pan-European age when "The irrational bubbled up, and met the rational, which fastened on it with glee...".[32]

Between 1908 and 1910 Kulbin organised three exhibitions in St Petersburg of the group of artists he variously called Triangle (*Treugol'nik*), The Impressionists, and the Art and Psychology Group. He backed up the shows with numerous performance-lectures and publications in which he essentially called for artists to "reflect their intimate experiences in psychological art, avoid everything that is preconceived, forced or deliberate, and love a single, free art and the new, because art is always new".[33] Virtually all of the works exhibited at the Triangle shows have been lost but descriptions survive, not least from contemporary reviews, and from these we can get a picture of the 'irrationalist' range displayed. Of particular significance here is the work of Boris Ferdinandov, Vasilii Nechaev and Aleksandr Gorodetskii. It is worth observing that Kulbin supplemented his 1910 show with 'The First Exhibition of Drawings and Signatures by Russian Writers', explaining in the catalogue: "When a writer takes charcoal or paints in his hands he creates something of worth. If he has not studied the techniques of painting then this will show in his drawing. But maybe what will also be reflected is the absence of academic conjuring and cliché? A discovery? Unconscious creativity? Spontaneity? Sometimes vice versa?"[34] Sixty-eight works by writers as diverse as Khlebnikov, Turgenev, Tolstoi, Solov'ev, Pushkin, Chekhov and Kuzmin were displayed.

In the first hall of Kulbin's first exhibition were shown nine paintings in two groups by the nineteen-year-old actor (and future theatre designer) Boris Ferdinandov (1889–1959). In the first group were Ferdinandov's *Subjective Experiences* and in the second his *Problems of Objective Essences*. Judging from the critical reaction, these were highly abstract works that comprised an early rejection of figuration for Russian art. While some saw them as "disarray" or more "decorative pattern than image of reality", others indicated how subjective the appreciation of the works could be, concluding that one work alone

---

31 See, for example, the extensive selection of Kulbin's articles and reviews of his public appearances in Kalaushin, *Nikolai Kul'bin*, 2, St Petersburg: Apollon, 1995.
32 A.S. Byatt, *The Children's Book*, London: Vintage, 2009, 484–485.
33 From I.Z., 'Lektsiia priv.-dots. N.I. Kul'bina' *Vilenskii kur'er*, 13 January 1910, 3.
34 N.I. Kul'bin, *Treugol'nik*, catalogue [1910], St Petersburg: Satirikon.

could be either a house or a wave with a seagull or a human portrait. Nikolai Kravchenko went furthest in condemnation:

> Ferdinandov's works depict absolutely nothing...a dirty mosaic in oil where form and idea have been totally forgotten. Titles like *Merriment through Dark Shadows* and *Joys of Grey: Dull Boredom* have nothing in common with the absurdities exhibited...which really only give cause for concern for the artist's sanity.[35]

While the negative appraisal of Ferdinandov had echoes of that which greeted Vrubel's *Demon Downcast*, the negativity helps the works be considered positively in terms of the "bubbling up" of the irrational in art at this time. However, a different reaction was to greet the artist who shared the first hall with Ferdinandov, Vasilii Nechaev (c.1876–?). Nechaev had lost his sight entirely about eleven years previously and had taken up painting, working mainly in pastels, in early 1907. He was to contribute to all Triangle exhibitions. He aimed to establish a world union of blind artists. In 1908 he showed eight pieces that were considered landscapes. Their appreciation saw them regarded as "very strong and tonally effective", having "a certain coloristic charm", being "naïve and fantastic", having "very beautiful colour spots".[36] Nechaev pinned down strips of plasticine on the canvas as outlines, selected colour by 'memory', applied paint by 'touch'. The results were regarded as reproductions of visual imagination and memory. 'Views' of hills, skies and plains dominated, be they the crimson peaks of *Bogatyr-Mountain*, *The Alps*, *The Ravine*, *The Dying Day*, *Clouds* or *Willow*. One critic (Konstantin L'dov) noted the significance of Nechaev for Kulbin's irrationalist 'vision': "A blind artist is not simply an astonishing thing: it is full of symbolic meaning and serves as a forewarning that the ensuing pictures at the exhibition, especially those of Triangle, the Art and Psychology group, are to be perceived not with external vision, but with what may be called an inner, spiritual sight".[37]

---

35 Nikolai Kravchenko, 'Vystavka sovremennykh techenii v iskusstve', *Novoe vremia*, 30 April 1908, 5.
36 See, for example, Kravchenko, 'Vystavka sovremennykh techenii'; K. L'dov [V.K. Rozenblium], 'Khudozhniki-Revoliutsionery', *Birzhevye Vedomosti*, 30 April 1908, 3–4; M.S. [Mariia Simonovich], 'Sovremennye napravleniia v iskusstve', *Rech'*, 9 May 1908, 2–3.
37 K. L'dov [V.K. Rozenblium], 'Khudozhniki-Revoliutsionery'. Nechaev had actually made his exhibition debut in September 1907, when he showed thirty pastels at the St Petersburg Artists' Club.

ILLUSTRATION 16.9
Aleksandr Gorodetskii, Illustration to Sergei Gorodetskii's poem, Intense Heat, 1906

A man who was extremely aesthetically gifted, talented and nervous, Aleksandr Gorodetskii was regarded by contemporaries as somewhat infantile, but it was quite likely because of this that he so acutely responded to the latest trends in art and so fully immersed himself in the bohemian art world of Petersburg.[38]

Gorodetskii (1886–1914) died after experimenting with narcotic drugs on New Year's Eve 1914. He had contributed to at least two of Kulbin's exhibitions (using the pseudonym of A. Gei) as well as to the 'Art in the Life of the Child' exhibition that took place in St Petersburg from December 1908 to January 1909. Besides his own work he showed his collection of seventy children's whistles and pipes from various regions of Russia, plus folk sculptures. His own exhibits were described by Vladimir Piast:

> The first work was called *Stain*, the second *Foetus* and the third and final one *Stain-Foetus*. All these were made of cotton wool which was then in fashion for filling the gaps in our northern windows between the months of September and May. While in the windows they were only white A. Gorodetskii painted them.[39]

He also showed *Mould* and a set of cambric *Wreathes* (White, Faded, Funeral and Lilac) designed as screens to shade lamps. None of his exhibits are known

---

38   Vladimir Enisherlov, 'Chelovek osveshchennym litsom. Zabytyi peterburgskii khudozhnik i poet nachala xx veka', *Nashe Nasledie*, 2003, 66. See http://nasledie-rus.ru/podshivka/6610.php, accessed 5.09.2011.

39   Vladimir Piast [Pestovskii], *Vstrechi*, Moscow: Federatsiia, 1929, 76.

to have survived. Their descriptions and titles suggest a radical overturning of rational, 'adult' 'high' art in favour of that celebrating naivety, chance, the unborn. Abstract fluid spillage and growth can be seen in his illustration to his brother Sergei's poem 'Intense Heat' (Znoi).[40]

Alogisms, Ontologisms

Through the exposure of artists like Gorodetskii, Nechaev and Ferdinandov to the Russian public, Kulbin surpassed the irrationalist expressivity of Fedotov, Repin and Vrubel, taking visual art on a new stage of its journey into non-reason. The gauntlet he threw down to the establishment and to the young generation was taken up by artists who became widely recognised as the foremost innovators in Russia in the second and third decades of the twentieth century. Their combination of a 'bubbling' irrationalism and a new sense of logic has been the source for numerous studies and retrospectives, each with their own 'rhyme and reason'. Those extended such honour include Pavel Filonov, with his nervous "analytical" and "flowering" art; Mikhail Matiushin, with his use of roots for sculpture, extended (parapsychological) vision based on Petr Uspenskii's ideas of higher dimensions, and synaesthetic experiments; Vladimir Markov [Voldemars Matvejs] with his broad ranging exploration of the creative process including an emphasis on the accidental, the dissonant, the non-constructive and illogical; and finally Malevich with his move into Suprematist other worlds via his alogist (*zaum*) invocation of superhuman awareness and the reductivist disappearance of the object in ["the impossible"] *Victory over the Sun*.[41]

Bibliography

Anon. 1913. 'Bubnovye Valety', *Russkoe Slovo*, 13 February, 36: 5.
Barooshian, Vahan. 1993. *V.V. Vereshchagin. Artist at War*, Gainsville: University Press of Florida.

---

40 Enisherlov, op. cit.
41 Concerning Malevich's alogism, Markov, see Jeremy Howard, Irena Buzinska, Z.S. Strother, Vladimir Markov and Russian Primitivism. A Charter for the Avant-Garde, Farnham: Ashgate, 2015. Concerning Malevich's alogism, see, for instance, Milner, *Kazimir Malevich*. For an introduction to all those mentioned, see Howard, *The Union of Youth*.

Bryzgel, Amy. 2013. *Performing the East: Performance Art in Russia, Latvia and Poland since 1980*, London: I.B. Tauris.
Byatt, A.S. 2009. *The Chilaren's Book*, London: Vintage, 2009.
Enisherlov, Vladimir. 2003. 'Chelovek osveshchennym litsom. Zabytyi peterburgskiy khudozhnik i poet nachala XX veka', *Nashe Nasledie*, 66. See http://nasledie-rus.ru/podshivka/6610.php, accessed 5.09.2011.
Fomin, Sergei. 2007. '"Kartina krovi", ili kak Il'ia Repin tsarevicha Ivana ubival', *Russkii vestnik*, 11.07.2007, 19.07.2007, 29.09.2007, 30.10.2007, 28.11.2007, 25.12.2007. See, for example, http://rusk.ru/st.php?idar=25141, accessed 30.11.2013.
Gomberg-Verzhbinskaia, E., Podkopaeva, Yu. N. 1976. *Vrubel'. Perepiska. Vospominaniia o khudozhnike*, Leningrad: Iskusstvo, 1976.
Gorodetskii, Sergei. 1912. 'Tot komu dano vozmushchat' vodu', *Kul'bin*, St Petersburg: Obshchestvo intimnago teatra.
Grabar', Igor. 1937. *Il'ia Efimovich Repin*, Moscow: Gosudarstvennoe izdatel'stvo izobrazitel'nykh iskusstv.
Hilton, Alison. 1979. *The Art of Ilia Repin: Tradition and Innovation in Russian Realism*, PhD thesis, Columbia University, New York.
Howard, Jeremy. 1992. *The Union of Youth. An Artists' Society of the Russian Avant-Garde*, Manchester and New York: Manchester University Press.
——— 2006. *East European Art*, Oxford: Oxford University Press.
Howard, Jeremy, Buzinska, I., Strother Z.S.2015. Vladimir Markov and Russian Primitivism. A Charter for the Avant-Garde, Farnham: Ashgate.
I.Z.. 1910. 'Lektsiia priv.-dots. N. I. Kul'bina' *Vilenskii kur'er*, 13 January: 3.
Jackson, David. 2006. *The Russian Vision. The Art of Ilya Repin*, Schoten: BAI.
Kalaushin, Boris (ed.). 1994 and 1995 . *Nikolai Kul'bin*, 1 and 2, St Petersburg: Apollon.
Kravchenko, Nikolai. 1908. 'Vystavka sovremennykh techenii v iskusstve', *Novoe vremia*, 30 April: 5.
Kul'bin, Nikolai. 1910. *Treugol'nik*, catalogue, St Petersburg: Satirikon.
Kuznetsov, Erast. 1990. *Pavel Fedotov*, Leningrad: Iskusstvo.
Landtsert, F.P. 1885. 'Po povodu kartiny I.E. Repina "Ivan groznyi i ego syn, 16 noyabria 1581". Lektsiia chitannaia uchenikam Akademii kudhozhestv', *Vestnik iziashchnykh iskusstv*, St Petersburg, 1885, volume 3, 2, 192–205.
L'dov, K. [V.K. Rozenblium]. 1908. 'Khudozhniki-Revoliutsionery', *Birzhevye Vedomosti*, 30 April: 3–4.
Lebedev, A.K., Solodovnikov, A.V. 1987. *V.V. Vereshchagin*, Leningrad: Khudozhnik RSFSR.
Lessing, Gotthold Ephraim. 1898. *Laocoon. An Essay upon the Limits of Painting and Poetry*, Boston: Little, Brown and Company.
Milner, John. 1996. *Kazimir Malevich and the Art of Geometry*, New Haven and London: Yale University Press.

P'etsukh, Viacheslav. 2006. *Zhizn' zamechatel'nykh liudei*, Moscow: Globus.

Platt, Kevin M.F. 2011. *Terror and Greatness: Ivan and Peter as Russian Myths*, Cornell University Press, Ithaca and London.

—————— 2006. 'On Blood, Scandal, Renunciation, and Russian History. Il'ia Repin's *Ivan the Terrible and His Son Ivan*', in Levitt, Marcus, Tatyana Novikov (eds.), *Times of Trouble. Violence in Russian Literature and Culture*, Wisconsin: University of Wisconsin Press, 2007: 112–122.

Piast [Pestovskii], Vladimir. 1929. *Vstrechi*, Moscow: Federatsiia.

Ranke, Johannes. 1890, *Der Mensch*, Leipzig and Vienna: Verlag des Bibliographischen Institutes.

M.S. [Simonovich, Mariia]. 1908. 'Sovremennye napravleniia v iskusstve', *Rech'*, 9 May: 2–3.

Sarabianov, D.V. 1990. *Russian Art from Neoclassicism to the Avant-Garde*, London: Thames and Hudson.

Sarabianov, Dmitry. 1985. *Pavel Andreevich Fedotov*, Leningrad: Khudozhnik RSFSR.

Shur, Leonid A. 1974. 'Khudozhnik-Puteshestvennik Mikhail Tikhanov', *Latinskaia Amerika*, 5: 163–180.

Silen [Alfred Nurok]. 1902. '*Novoe vremia* i Vrubel', *Mir Iskusstva*, 1902, 7: 1–3.

Sytova, Alla. 1984. *The Lubok. Russian Folk Pictures. 17th to 19th Century*, Leningrad: Aurora.

Tuchman, Barbara. 1984. *The March of Folly: From Troy to* Vietnam, New York: Ballantine.

Valkenier, Elizabeth Kridl. 1990. *Ilia Repin and the World of Russian Art*, New York: Columbia University Press, 1990.

Wünsche, Isabel. 2015. The Organic School of the Russian Avant-Garde: Nature's Creative Principles, Farnham: Ashgate.

Ianch[evetskii] V. 1910. 'Vystavka impressionistov 'Treugol'nik'', *Rossiia*, 24 March, 1331, 4.

CHAPTER 17

Symbols, Metaphors and Irrationalities in Twentieth-Century Music[1]

Alexander Ivashkin

Twenthieth-century music is both very rational and extremely irrational. On the one hand, very strict rational compositional techniques were established, especially in the serial way of composition and in the post-serial works by Boulez, Messiaen and Xenakis. On the other hand, many ideas by the twentieth-century composers were influenced by chance theory and indeterminacy, and have a symbolic context or hidden meanings, or use metaphoric language.

In his seminal book *Mimesis*, Erich Auerbach describes two major types of world culture, two types of utterance. One is direct, taking its origin in Ancient Greek culture, and the second is indirect, ambivalent, coming from the Old Testament texts and never having existed before.[2] As Auerbach writes:

The two styles (Homeric realism and Old Testament symbolism), in their opposition, represent basic types: on the one hand, fully externalised description, uniform illumination, uninterrupted connection, free expression, all events in the foreground, displaying unmistakable meanings, few elements of historical development and of psychological perspective; on the other hand, certain parts brought into high relief, other left obscure, abruptness, suggestive influence of the unexpressed, 'background' quality, multiplicity of meanings and the need for interpretation, universal-historical claims, development of the concept of the historically becoming, and preoccupation with the problematic.[3]

The secret meanings in music are in line with these very old traditions. 'Multilayeredness' in many different cultures has been naturally connected and historically related to the symbolic character of the church tradition. This tradition, in its turn, was the direct continuation of the older mysticism, and,

---

1 This work first appeared in Cataño, Rafael Jiménez and Yarza, Ignacio (Ed.). *Mimesi, Verità e Fiction*, Roma: Edusc, 2009, 69–87. The author is grateful to the original publishers for the permission to reprint the text in the current volume.
2 Erich Auerbach, *Mimesis. The Representation of Reality in Western Literature*, Princeton: Princeton University Press. 1974, 23.
3 Ibid.

most importantly, the tradition of Old Testament symbols, with their enigmatic meaning and necessity of 'interpretation'.

This latter type was inherited by the composers of the nineteenth and twentieth century, first by Gustav Mahler (1860–1911) and Charles Ives (1874–1954); later by Russian composers, including Alexander Scriabin (1872–1915), Dmitrii Shostakovich (1906–1975); composers of the Paris circle in the 1920s-1930s (see below); and later Galina Ustvolskaia (1919–2006), Alfred Schnittke (1934–1998), Sofia Gubaidulina (1931-) and Vladimir Martynov (1946-).

One of the greatest masterpieces of the twentieth century is the Sonata No 2 for piano 'Concord' by the American composer Charles Ives, who was often called "a businessman writing music on weekends". For many years, Ives had been a co-owner of a successful insurance company, Ives and Myrick in New York City. He was always reluctant to make a living by composing music. Music for him, as he often said, was "a metaphor of a human soul".

Ives worked on the sonata for many years (1909–1915). The published score of the Sonata in the first edition also included fragments from Ives' own *Essay before a Sonata* – his philosophical work, written as an extended commentary to the Sonata.[4] All his life Ives was very close to the transcendental American philosophy of Ralph Waldo Emerson, Henry Thoreau, and Nathaniel Hawthorne. *Nature* by Emerson and *Walden* by Thoreau were always two most important books for Ives – he read and quoted them almost constantly. The titles of the four movements of the Concord sonata are the names of Ives' favourite philosophers: Emerson, Hawthorne, Alcott and Thoreau. The full title of the Sonata is: 'Concord, Mass., 1845'. Concord is the name of a small town in New England, near Boston, where all the philosophers-transcendentalists lived in the mid-nineteenth century.[5]

Like Emerson and Thoreau, Ives considered music as a part of the spiritual language of Nature. "We would rather believe that music is beyond any analogy to word language", wrote Ives, "and that time is coming when it will develop possibilities inconceivable now – a language so transcendent that its heights and depths will be common to all mankind".[6] In his Sonata, Ives make an attempt to create a new, symbolic, esoteric musical language, with many references to past music history.

---

4   Charles Ives, *Essays before a Sonata, the Majority and other Writings*, New York: Norton, 1970.
5   Ives has never lived in Concord, however, he was born in Danbury, very close to Concord, and was spending more than half of each year in his country-house in West Redding, also in the same area of New England.
6   Ives, *Essays before a Sonata, the Majority and other Writings*, 8.

There are many symbols in the first movement, Emerson: one can hear modified the opening tune from Beethoven's Fifth Symphony (which Ives calls "a human-faith-melody"); J.S. Bach's monogram BACH; religious hymns by American composer Stephen Foster; an allusion from the Second Piano Sonata by Brahms; Ives's own monogram (C-H[B]-A-E = Charles Ives); the opening of Beethoven's Piano Sonata op.109; and J.S. Bach's chorale *Es ist genug*. Of course, all these quotations and symbols are never too direct. They rather form a very wide, surrealistic historical 'context' – very similar to James Joyce's novels written during the same period.

The second movement, Hawthorne, is a rather mystical, surreal Scherzo – very similar to Hawthorne's own novels and stories. As Ives wrote in his *Essays*, "The substance of Hawthorne is so dripping wet with the supernatural, the phantasmal, the mystical, so surcharged with adventures…It is not something that happens, but the way something happens…or something about the ghost of a man who never lived, or about something that never will happen, or something else that is not".[7] Still, one can hear motifs such as BACH, and allusions from Beethoven and Brahms' piano sonatas. In the middle of the movement Ives found an almost mystical effect of 'shining': part of the keyboard should be silently pressed with the ruler, which gives a special, shimmering effect, similar to the "mystical rainbow" chords in music written by Olivier Messiaen half a century later.

In the third, slow movement of the Sonata Ives presents a unique atmosphere of a family house. Here again one can hear religious hymn tunes melted together with Beethoven's 'Hammerklavier' Sonata motive and the monogram BACH. But the development of this movement – unlike the others – is slow and very clear – like the "sermons" or a prayer with many references. A lyrical mood dominates throughout, bringing again allusions from the music of the three 'great B's': Bach, Beethoven and Brahms.

The final movement of Concord is called Thoreau. It follows the meditative mood of Henry Thoreau's *Walden* – the book which he wrote living in a small cabin near the pond in Concord. There are no bar lines in the score – music flows like an improvisation, without any strict boundaries. It emerges from a morning mist, and dissolves into the sound of an evening church bell. Ives uses here all twelve tones – and the monogram BACH becomes just a part of this chromatic palette. As Ives writes about Thoreau, "His meditations, – are interrupted only by the faint sound of the Concord bell…He releases his more personal desires to her [Nature's] broader rhythm, to the harmony of her solitude".[8]

---

7   Ives, *Essays before a Sonata, the Majority and other Writings*, 42.
8   *Ibid.*, 68.

Ives' last, unfinished work was his *Universe Symphony* – a further development of his ideas expressed in the 'Concord Sonata' and in the *Essays before a Sonata*. He was planning to perform his *Universe Symphony* outside, somewhere in the hills of India or Tibet, with several orchestras playing in the different corners of the valleys. This symphony, a life-long work by Ives, was never finished and only left in sketches.

At approximately the same time, around 1914–1915, a very similar project called *Mystery* was planned by the Russian composer Alexander Scriabin. He too never finished this work, and it too was to be performed in outdoor gorges in Tibet or India. Scriabin and Ives meant for these two works to be performed in the same place, although they did not know anything about each other.

Scriabin, known for his theosophical ideas, had a very strong influence on Russian culture in the twentieth century. His ideas in many aspects were symbolic and very important as expressions of major issues of Russian culture in general. He said:

It is necessary to understand that the material of which our Universe is made, is our imagination, our creative idea, our desire, and therefore – in terms of the material there is no difference between the state of our mind we call 'a stone which we hold in our hands', and the other state of our mind called 'a dream'. A stone and a dream are made of the same matter and they are equally real. They only occupy different positions in our mind. The...stone is a psychological process which happens at present...A dream is a process in the future.[9]

Scriabin indeed managed to bring Nature and Culture closer to each other. His last finished orchestral piece, "Prometheus", was written for orchestra, chorus, piano solo and a "colour organ" (a special keyboard producing color beams at the time of the performance; Scriabin notated this instrument in detail in the score). The work was built on one particular chord (which was later called the "Prometheus Chord" – C, F#, Bb, E, A, D), which could be also seen as a scale (and was used by Scriabin as a mode in Prometheus). This scale is a part of a natural overtone row which always existed in the physical world. The Prometheus Chord is often called a "mystic chord" because Scriabin used it to build chords, melodies and harmonies, so expanding it into three-dimensional space. It also consists of many major elements heard and known in music history: a whole-tone scale, a series of fourths, a major triad, and an enhanced dominant chord. The mystic chord also combines the qualities of a medieval, Romantic and jazz harmonies – depending on its position.

---

9   "Russkie Propilei", quoted in Boris Asaf'ev (Igor Glebov), *De Musica*, Petrograd: Petrogradskaia Gosudarstvennaia Akademicheskaia Filarmoniia, 1923, 146.

Scriabin's idea of Mystery being performed in Tibet had a strong resonance in the so-called 'Eurasian' movement of the 1920s – 30s. A large group of composers, philosophers and writers who immigrated to Paris from the Soviet Russia wanted to see new Russian culture instead of standardised modern European culture. They saw Russian culture based on the tradition of Eastern mysticism, with an important spiritual mission.

In his recently published book *Evrasiiskoe uklonenie v muzyke 1920-1930-kh godov (Eurasian Inclination in the Music of the 1920s-1930s)*, Igor Vishnevetskii discusses Eurasian ideas in Russian culture in the early twentieth century.[10] Composers who left Russia – Sergei Prokofiev (1891–1953), Igor Stravinskii (1882–1971), Arthur Lourie (1891–1966), Vladimir Dukel'skii (1903–1969), Alexander Tcherepnine (1899–1977), Nikolai Obukhov (1892–1954) and Ivan Vyshnegradskii (1893–1979) – were based in Paris (and some of them later in the USA). The major idea of the Eurasian movement was to establish a new and correct identity for Russian music, which should be independent from Western 'modernism'. The theoretical foundation for these Eurasian ideas came mostly from Petr (Pierre) Souvchinskii (1892–1985) and Arthur Lourie. Lourie was convinced that "The artist, with the gift from God, had to replace a priest".[11]

Russia and Germany are the only two countries where one can find an exceptionally well-structured system of music schools, music colleges and conservatories. This system is non-existent in English-speaking countries such as the United Kingdom, United States, Australia and Canada, where music performance and composition are taught at universities, and well-established performance groups are often formed by semi-amateurs who were never systematically trained in performance (such as many various 'consorts' or chamber orchestras). It is probably not by chance that the two major totalitarian regimes of the twentieth century have produced and established the best systems of vocational musical and sport education.

It is also correct that since the 1900s it has been typical for Russian families to attend classical music concerts regularly (concert series tickets – called *abonement* – to be purchased in advance, are still very popular and sell extremely well; this is a practice unheard of in the Western classical music industry). Classical music, including its performance, was a part of the normal education, as were languages and sciences. You could find a piano in almost every flat in Moscow in Soviet times. The status of composers was therefore always supported by large audiences. That is why the 'prophetic', heroic,

---

10   See Igor Vishnevetskii, *Evraziiskoe Uklonenie v muzyke 1920–1930 godov*, Moscow: Novoe Literaturnoe Obozrenie, 2005.
11   *Ibid.*, 47.

Romantic profile of a composer, performer, writer, poet or painter was always the norm in Russia and in Germany. The need for a person with super-human qualities was always typical for Russian history – long before the Romantic age – starting with pagan 'witches' and 'wizards' in Russian tales and finishing with the idea of Russian monarchy. It still remains a norm in post-Soviet Russian culture, with its well-established hierarchy of names, for example, artists and politicians. Understanding history as a hagiography has always been a part of the Russian mentality.

The idea of Eurasia itself has deep roots in Russian history and can explain a constant search for something extra – or meta – in Russian culture and history. Already Vladimir Stasov (1824–1906), the key figure in nineteenth-century *narodnichestvo* (populism) and the person behind many of the ideas of 'The Five' composers group, surprisingly had seen these roots in Eastern cultures. *Byliny* (Russian folk stories similar to Homeric Odes) are most similar to Buddhist and Eastern prototypes, and in particular to the poetic creations of Eastern nations geographically close to Russia.[12]

At the time of the 1910s – 'the Silver Age', one of the highest points in Russian cultural history – Russian culture was very hermeneutic, trying to find and to establish its identity in the common roots of many various cultures and religions. Andrei Belyi published a book titled *Symbolism* (1910), in which he calls symbolism a mentality (*miroponimaniye*). In his dissertation *Stolp i utverzhdenie istiny* (*The Pillar and Ground of the Truth: An Essay in Orthodox Theodicy in Twelve Letters*), Pavel Floresnkii attempted to explain the equal importance of the rational and irrational, with a definite preference for the latter. As he wrote, "The rationalist says that the contradictions of the Bible (*sviashchennogo pisaniia*) prove their non-Divine nature; the mystic states that in the state of Lucidness [*Prosvetlenie*] the contradictions proves their Divine nature".[13] It may sound like a paradox, but the irrationalities and symbolism in Shostakovich's late music comes from the mentality of a Silver Age, saturated with the ideas and doctrines of the Orthodox faith.

From the 1920s to the 1930s, the young Shostakovich had already witnessed the birth of many of the most important aesthetic theories in Russia. This was

---

12   Vladimir Stasov, "Proiskhozhdenie russkikh bylin", 1894 (quoted in Vishnevetskii, *Evraziiskoe Uklonenie v muzyke 1920–1930 godov*, 31). Vishnevetskii finds more Stasov's statements on Eastern sources of Russian culture: Indian and Persian elements in Russian ornaments, and Turkic and Mongol elements in Russian *bylinas* (Vishnevetskii, 32 – 33). See also discussion of Eurasian ideas in Richard Taruskin, *Stravinskii and the Russian Traditions*, Oxford: Oxford University Press, 1996, 119–1136.

13   Pavel Florenskii, *Stolp i utverzhdenie istiny: Opyt pravoslavnoi teoditsei v dvenadtsati pis'makh*, Moscow, 1914, 504.

the time when Mikhail Bakhtin (1895–1975) started to formulate his theory of dialogue and chronotope, and published his seminal book *Problemy poetiki Dostoevskogo* (1929). At the same time Aleksei Losev (1893–1988) published his *Filosofia imeni* (*Philosophy of Name*, 1927) *Muzyka kak predmet logiki* (*Music as a subject for logic*, 1927), and *Dialektika mifa* (*Dialectics of a Myth*, 1930). In these books Losev established the hermeneutics of music, and the metaphorical meanings of just about everything in real life. It is not surprising that both Losev and Bakhtin were banned as "dangerous idealists" and spent many years in Stalin's camps, only able to return to normal research activities after Stalin's death. In the 1960s-1980s Losev published a fundamental work, *History of Poetics in Antiquity*, which was related to Aristotle's *Poetics*. In 1930 he wrote about myth very much in the style of Aristotle: "Any living organism is a myth... Personality is a myth not because it is a personality, but because it is formed and thought through a mythological mentality...Even not-living objects – blood, hair, heart... – also can be mythical...because they have been constructed from the point of view of a mythical mentality".[14]

Boris Asaf'ev (1884–1949) published his first articles and books related to his theory of the intonation and "energy" of music.[15] Furthermore, a book by the Swiss musicologist Ernst Kurth, *Romantische Harmonik und ihre Krise in Wagners Tristan*, was published in 1920 in Switzerland. It was not allowed to be translated into Russian until 1975, but nevertheless became quite well known between Russian musicians, especially after the publication of a Russian edition of Kurth's first book, *Grundlagen des linearen Kontrapunkts* (1917), in Russia in 1931 and edited by Asaf'ev. Already the very first paragraph of this second book by Kurth, speaks for itself. As he writes, "a harmony as a reflection of energies of a psyche...a reflection of something irrational".[16] And the book finishes with the rhetorical question "What is music?". Asaf'ev tried to answer this question two years later, in his article 'Value of Music', stating that "Music is a world of relations, a world of functional dependence with no room for materialism" [*muzyka – mir otnoshenii, mir funktsional'noi zavisimosti, v kotorom net mesta veshchnosti* – see Asaf'ev, 19].

---

14 Aleksei Losev, "Dialektika mifa", in Losev, *Iz Rannikh Proizvedenii*, Moscow: Pravda Publishers, 1990, 461.

15 It was much later, in 1948, when Asaf'ev betrayed many great Russian musicians, including Shostakovich, and took the line of the Soviet officialdom. Before that Asaf'ev's ideas were important for many Russian musicians, in particular for Shostakovich's creative work.

16 Ernst Kurth, *Romantische Harmonik und ihre Krise in Wagners Tristan*, Bern: P. Haupt, 1920.

Shostakovich's good friend, Boleslav Iavorskii (1877–1942), built his theory of 'modal rhythm' on similar ideas of music as a world of functional relations, on the basis of the energy of the interval of a triton, as a representative of the universal gravitation force in music. As he wrote, "Gravity in music is an expression of a life, and the sense of gravity is a sense of a life. Delaying the moment of a resolution is a delaying of death, and, at the same time, a prolongation of a sense of life"[17] – quite in line with Kurth's ideas in *Romantische Harmonik und ihre Krise in Wagners Tristan*! In other words, a typical example of an 'idealism' in music opposed to the official doctrine of 'Socialist Realism'. Shostakovich was well aware of the theory (Iavorskii published the first volume of his *Uprazhneniia v obrazovanii ladovogo ritma* [*Exercises in Modal Rhythm*] in 1915). Shostakovich was fascinated with Iavorskii's personality; twice he wanted to become his student – in 1925 and in 1938.[18] Iavorskii (who was also a popular professor of piano and performance practice) was researching symbolism in the music of J.S. Bach. His research results were never published, but it is very certain that Shostakovich knew Iavorskii's ideas – they had been presented at numerous seminars in Kiev (1916, 1917, 1919), Moscow (1924–25, 1927–28, 1938–41), and the last ones in Saratov (1941–42). Still unpublished, these ideas represent a system of musical and religious symbolism found in the keyboard compositions of Bach, mainly in his *Well-Tempered Clavier* and in his keyboard Suites. Iavorskii stated that "Sounding musical events, after the centuries of their development, have been transformed in Bach's music into organising structures bearing certain meaning, into symbols".[19] His explanation of the meaning of Bach's music was based on the fact that Bach used these symbolic elements (for example, well-known church chorales) in the themes of his fugues in the *Well-Tempered Clavier*.[20] Consequently, every interval and every ascending or descending passage does have a hidden meaning related to the original text of the chorale, which requires a certain knowledge and interpretation.

17   Iavorskii Archive (Glinka State Central Museum of Musical Culture, Moscow), 146/346/64.
18   His 66 letters to Iavorskii, recently published, show importance of Iavorskii's influence for Shostakovich, especially in 1925–26, before he met Ivan Sollertinskii (see Irina Bobykina (ed.), *Dmitri Shostakovich v pis'makh i dokumentakh*, Moscow: Glinka State Central Museum of Musical Culture, 2000, 18–145). "After meeting with Iavorskii my mentality has been changed completely", wrote Shostakovich in his letter to Lev Oborin in 1925 (see Bobykina, 9).
19   Iavorskii Archive, 146/4454.
20   Vera Nosina, *Simvolika muzyki Bakha*, Moscow: Klassika XX1, 2006, 11–20.

Losev, Bakhtin, Florenskii, Iavorskii, Asaf'ev and their theoretical ideas made a very important and significant impact on the mentality of Soviet composers and listeners, and on the meaning of music in Soviet society in general. Paradoxically, at the time when Socialist Realism was declared the official ideology for Soviet Art, the art itself was very much in the line with the ideas of early Christian symbolism.[21] Myth, mythological situations and symbols were important for hermeneutic art and for the closed society in Soviet Russia, and reflected the way Russian people saw life and its values. Myth and mythological symbols have been heavily used in the creation of Soviet socialist realism as well as in the rituals of party events. The overuse of German patterns in musical forms, such as the almost religious reliance on sonata allegro form in numerous Soviet compositions, shows the same deep influence of German Classical philosophy on Soviet mentality.[22] Partly this can be explained by compulsory studies of 'historical materialism' in all tertiary institutions, which (apart from compulsory Communist Party history studies) included relatively serious studies of German classical philosophy (actually, the only serious philosophical course in the standard programs of the Soviet School – thanks to Marx and Engels). Some compulsory books by Vladimir Lenin (such as his *Philosophical Notebooks*) also had relation to German philosophers.[23] Lenin's book, which Soviet people enjoyed reading at the time (since it included some fascinating quotes from otherwise unknown statements by European philosophers), was in fact a collection of his marginal, often quite rude comments, on the publications by leading European philosophers. Some most important ideas of classical German philosophy – like a syllogism – were really made a part of Soviet mentality through various sources, including classics of Marxism-Leninism.

Later on, in the 1960s-1980s, this influence of theoretical thought on creative processes continued, for example, in the publication of Bulgakov's and Platonov's novels in the late 1960s and in the books and lectures by Iuri Lotman. Philip Gershkovich, in the 1970s, became equally important for the Russian

---

21 'It may seem strange, but the views of [Andrei] Belyi at the time [1907] and views of the people in the Kremlin had much in common. They, like him, reject art for art's sake. Art for them is just a means 'to transform life'... Artists are 'engineers of souls' (Simon Morrison, *Russian Opera and the Symbolist Movement*, Berkeley: University of California Press, 2002, 310).

22 Boris Tishchenko in private conversation with the author in his St Petersburg home on the 17th February 2007 said that Sonata allegro is a universal structure which could be found in any good music.

23 He called some of them (Hegel, for instance) *'idealisticheskaia svoloch'* [a bastard-idealist].

intelligentsia in the time of Khrushchev and Brezhnev. All these theories reflected the flavour of the time, with its strong underground resistance to the primitive cultural politics of the official Soviet regime. The publication of Bulgakov's *The Master and Margarita* in its abridged (cut by Soviet censors) version in 1968, was like a bombshell; millions of people read it overnight. The novel was a very clear, simple demonstration of the typical duality of any reality, particularly Soviet life, with its ambivalence between vulgarity of everyday life and heights of spiritualism ever present in Russian history. This is why the novel immediately gained enormous popularity – and still remains at that level forty years on. Some 'right-wing' Soviet artists and critics stated that the novel gained such popularity because it openly offered to the Soviets a real and practical way of "collaborating with the Devil".[24]

"Art for art's sake may exist anywhere except in the Russian cultural tradition. In Russia this type of art is quickly obliterated from memory. Usually, our geniuses are summoned to share in our people's woes", wrote Alexander Solzhenitsyn in 1980s.[25] This statement was especially important for the music of Dmitrii Shostakovich, who, unlike his many contemporaries – Prokofiev, Rakhmaninov, Stravinskii – was destined to spend all his life in Soviet Russia. The important source for Shostakovich's spirituality was, surprisingly (and perhaps unconsciously), religion. His Mussorgskii-like music after 1936, with its rather austere diatonic palette, often sounds very similar to the music of Old Believers.

Shostakovich never wrote any music for church services (as this was impossible in Soviet Russia), but he was well aware of the practices of Russian church services, although he was not a church-goer. His widow, Irina Shostakovich, witnessed that Shostakovich was not a believer[26] but an atheist. However, he was educated in an old gymnasium, learnt the '*Zakon Bozhii*' (Basic Fundamentals of the Orthodox Religion – taught at schools before the October Revolution), and was undoubtedly familiar with Russian sacred tunes.[27]

---

24   Georgii Sviridov, *Muzyka kak sud'ba*, Moscow: Molodaia Gvardiia, 2002.

25   Private letter to Mstislav Rostropovich. The Rostropovich Archive in St. Petersburg, Russia.

26   Private conversation with the author at the Shostakovich Archive in Moscow, 14.02.07.

27   In 1973 Shostakovich was able to consult competently Benjamin Britten on Russian church tunes when Britten approached him in relation to the tune '*So Sviatymi Upokoi*' in his Solo Cello Suite No 3. As Britten wrote in his Preface to the Suite: 'I based this Suite on Russian themes: the first three tunes were taken from Chaikovskii's volumes of folk-song arrangements; the fourth, the '*Kontakion*' (Hymn for the Departed), from the English Hymnal. When I played the Suite through to Dmitri Shostakovich during our visit to Moscow he remarked that he had been brought up on a different version of the *Kontakion*'. (See Britten, *Three Suites for Cello*, London: Faber Music Limited, 1986, 35).

He learnt much through Mussorgskii's music that was directly inspired by Old Believers. Shostakovich's music after 1936 is largely based on the *obikhod* mode. Very effective and deeply religious, old tunes remained unidentified by Soviet officials since for them it looked and sounded like a folk music, music which belonged to the people, the music of Socialist realism.

The unique feature of Russian music in the 10th-17th centuries was that folk tunes were based on the same *Obikhod* (*Znamenny*) mode as church music (Old Believers' tunes). So 'folk' – in a broad sense – was always 'sacred' and 'sacred' was 'folk'.[28] This situation was only changed by Peter the Great in the late seventeenth century. One of the oldest folk tunes – No 1 in Balakirev's collection – 'Ne bylo vetru' ('There Was No Wind'), is a good example of such a tune sung in *obikhod* mode. This tune is very similar to the opening of Mussorgskii's Boris Godunov, the melody used and quoted by Shostakovich so many times.[29] We hear it in the Scherzo of his *Tenth Symphony* (1953), in the finale of his *Second Violoncello Concerto* (1966), in the *Ninth and Tenth String Quartets* (1964), in the 'Burlesque' of his *First Violin Concerto* (1948), at the beginning of his cantata *Execution of Stepan Razin* (1964) and in his *Unfinished String Quartet* (1963). It's not surprising that Shostakovich not only destroyed but literally burnt his Unfinished String Quartet, which had old church tunes in it. He was afraid that the real meaning of these tunes was too obvious.

Pavel Lamm's edition of the piano score of Mussorgskii's *Khovanshchina* shows an example of an Old Believers' prayer, which Mussorgskii knew. Stravinskii later used these tunes for his reconstruction of the finale of *Khovanshchina*. This tune was sung by a woman named *Praskovia Tsaritsa* (in Armenia, where many Old Believers – there called mollokane – still live now). Mussorgskii used this tune in the final scene of *Khovanshchina*. It too is in the *obikhod* mode and is very similar to the opening of *Boris Godunov*. Old Russian liturgical singing has been preserved in the community of Nekrassov Cossacks since the eighteenth century. There is a unique recording made in Russia in early 1990s by Professor Margarita Mazo of Ohio State University, USA.

The repetitive character of Shostakovich's music also has its roots in Russian religious music and its spiritual, almost fanatical and obsessive power. The Russian Orthodox Church Service is very long. Easter liturgy lasts all night and is a very repetitive service; you must repeat the same prayer time and again.

---

28 Anna Rudneva, *Russkoe narodnoe muzykal'noe tvorchestvo: Ocherki po teorii fol'klora*, Moscow: Kompozitor, 1994, 138–157.

29 Mussorgskii's tune (pointed out to me by Professor Margarita Mazo in 2006) is a folk song 'Gory, Gory Vorobiovskie' [Hills, Sparrow Hills]; nevertheless it is based on the *Obikhod* mode of old believers.

Shostakovich's long, slowly unfolding mature compositions after 1937 are influenced by this particular characteristic of the Orthodox liturgy.

There are stunning similarities in the repetitiveness of Russian Orthodox church service music with that of official Soviet rituals. Communist leaders themselves used this powerful tool to make their speeches and their meetings more convincing. It is well known that Lenin and Stalin were constantly returning to the same issues in their public speeches. Ritualistic repetitiveness was one of the major principles in Lenin's and especially Stalin's rhetoric. These 'ritualistic' principles, also important in pop music today, were very typical for Soviet mass-culture songs in the 1930s-1950s. Exploring this repetitiveness, Shostakovich was able to find new resources for his musical language – conveniently suitable for 'official' propaganda demands and for his own use, without any compromise in musical terms.

As opposed to Stravinskii's irregular rhythmical structures, Shostakovich's rhythm is deliberately regular. The most typical rhythmical pattern in his music is one crotchet, two quavers. This pattern can be easily found in almost any of his composition. Why is Shostakovich so repetitive rhythmically? Was he concerned with making his music in line with official demand of *'dostupnost'* – easy understandable? Interestingly enough, examples of Shostakovich's typical rhythmical patterns – a crotchet, two quavers – could be found in so-called Church *Azbukas* (syllabaries) of the eighteenth century. These books were designed to help learn the language, as well as prayers. Each character of the alphabet had to be presented in a very regular rhythmical way – a kind of old Russian rap. In both old Russian ABC books and in Shostakovich's music this regular, simple rhythm helps in understanding the basics of meaning, the foundations of a language. Shostakovich's repetitions are senseless in terms of logical or structural meaning.

The violinist Mark Lubotskii told me in 2004 that Shostakovich used to say to him: "You have to 'stomp' on the spot before you move elsewhere". Shostakovich often repeats the same pattern twice before moving ahead. Examples of this are numerous: the beginning of the *First Cello Concerto*, the First Movement of the *Fifteenth Symphony*, the Finale of the *Sixth symphony*. Any change always comes after the second attempt. This principle applies to rhythmical structure, motif development and the general structural patterns in Shostakovich's music.

This tradition is definitely related to the magic number 3 in Russian fairy tales as well as in Russian prayers. If the first attempt is unsuccessful, the third will definitely be a success. This very old Russian superstition has been part of the Russian mentality for many centuries. There are always three roads to choose from in Russian fairy tales. The Russian Orthodox *Molitvoslov* (Book of

Prayers) teaches us to repeat the same text of the prayer either three or seven times. You kiss your friends three times. You believe in the Trinity. You say "God loves number three". The same can be found much later in the superstitious numerology of Chaikovskii's (and Pushkin's) *Queen of Spades*: three – seven – ace (one). Shostakovich takes this three-based pattern everywhere. His music may seem rhythmically monotonous, but this is something taken from a genetic well of old Pagan and Christian religious roots. As in ritual, complexity comes out of simplicity. And as in ritual, the structure is often not important. Energy often comes out of a single primitive basic pattern that evolves by itself in an organic way like a genetic code.

Shostakovich's music does not have any religious context. However, it inherited the meaning of spiritual symbolism through Mahler's influence, the influence of Russian thinkers of the early twentieth-century, Mussorgskii idioms and the use of the "genetic well" of the *obikhod* mode. His "socialist realism" was in fact new, ritualistically coloured post-modernism. Paradoxically, Shostakovich, who was urged to make his language more realistic, managed to make it more ritualistic. Like Columbus, he discovered the new world and new recourses intuitively, and in an involuntary way, while he was being pushed in an opposite direction.

Galina Ustvolskaia's (1919–2006) official catalogue comprises only twenty-four works. Her style has remained consistent throughout her career. The works written in the 1940s sound almost exactly the same as her most recent works of the 1990s. Her music does not fit easily into any traditional categories of Western music. Ustvolskaia said that her music is not religious, but spiritual. She used hidden monograms in her music, often presenting the word 'Deus' in different spelling: In her *Fifth Piano Sonata* it is spelled D flat [Des] and presented by fanatically repeated single tone D flat. In the second movement of her *Composition No 1* for a group of instruments Deus is spelled like D – E – Es [E flat]. In *Composition No 2* the word *gastigo* (punishment) is spelled like G and A flat [As] and in *Composition No 3* she repeats the tone F sharp (fis) 7 times, hinting a word *fistula* (in Latin 'trumpet'), meaning the Seven Trumpets of the Last Judgment.

Numerous examples of symbolism, numerology and irrationalities can be found in the works of Alfred Schnittke and Sofia Gubaidulina. They are related to a well known European tradition of the use of the number alphabet. In many works by the poets and composers of the seventeenth century, the music text often needs to be deciphered. Thus, J.S. Bach often used his monogram BACH, sometimes in relation to the number 14 (shown in either rhythmical values or in the bar numbers) as follows: B = 2, A = 1, C = 3, H = 8.

It has been suggested by Friedrich Smend (the editor of Bach's *Complete Works* in the 1940s) that Bach used cabbalistic technique in many of his compositions. The latest research by Ruth Tatlow, in her book *Bach and the Riddle of the Number Alphabet*, does not corroborate this theory. She thinks that Bach wouldn't have used cabbalistic technique because of its assigned specific theological purposes.[30] "The possibility of Bach's use of magical number alphabets must be ruled out on the grounds of his reputation and character. Any active involvement in magic would have led to dismissal from his Leipzig post".[31] However, Bach definitely used the notes BACH for his monogram (in his last and unfinished work, *Die Kunst der Fuge*), and may also have used various number alphabets to place hidden messages in his works.

Alfred Schnittke (1934–1998) was once very interested in learning more about the issue of Bach and the cabbala, after the German musicologist Ulrich Siegele (who was the mentor of Ruth Tatlow and inspired her in writing the book mentioned above) showed him an example of Bach's hidden messages written in cabbalistic technique. Numerology and the technique of enciphered names was something which Schnittke used many times in his music. For example, his *Fourth Violin Concerto* is built on the monogram of Gidon Kremer, and his *Symphony No 3* is full of many hidden names of German composers (and allusions based on the styles of their compositions). Like Shostakovich, Schnittke also used the *obikhod* mode in many of his works (*Second String Quartet, Four Hymns*). His *Fourth Symphony* is a unique example in music history when the hymns of all four religions – Judaic, Orthodox, Catholic and Protestant – are brought together for reconciliation. One of the pages of his *Symphony No 2*, 'Missa Invisibile' visually presents a gigantic cross.

So too does Sofia Gubaidulina (born 1932) in her Violin Concerto *Offertorium* based on a Bach theme from *Das Musikalische Opfer* (Musical Offering). In her many compositions we find a constant use of numerology. Gubaidulina herself says it is the major principle for the structure of her works. Since the 1980s Gubaidulina has often used the Fibonacci series as major structural element in her music. The proportion and rhythmical profile of her compositions are related to very different but clear structural ideas (golden mean, Fibonacci series, monograms). The piece for violin and piano 'Dancer on the Tightrope' is built on certain proportions. "A tightrope dancer", says Gubaidulina, is "a metaphor for the opposition: life as risk, and art as flight into another

---

30   "Seventeenth- and Eighteenth-century cabbalistic *gematria* as an exegetical technique which employed the Hebrew or Greek milesian alphabet to gain a deeper insight into a word or verse from the Scriptures, and which was particularly useful in persuading Jews that Jesus was the Messiah". (See Ruth Tatlow, *Bach and the Riddle of the Number Alphabet*, Cambridge: Cambridge University Press, 1991, 127).

31   *Ibid.*

existence".³² The length of the violin's phrases (counted in crotchets) correspond to the Fibonacci series: 2 – 3 – 5 – 5 – 8 – 21 – 5 – 5 – 8. "The climax at the point of a golden mean is determined by the number 666 – a 'devilish number', a symbol of 'fear'. At the moment of a golden mean the fear is overcome".³³

In *Meditations on Bach Chorale* for harpsichord and string quintet (1993), Gubaidulina uses not a choral "Vor deinen Thron tret ich hiermit" (which is not Bach's own composition), but his *Choralvorspiel* (*Choral Prelude*), BWV 668, based on the chorale melody and printed in the Bach Edition. It is believed that Bach dictated this Prelude to his son-in-law just a few days before he died. Gubaidulina only borrows a melody of the chorale, as well as Bach's formal ideas and Bach's numeric proportions. Gubaidulina sees the numbers in Bach (and in her own music) as symbols, and as principles of natural proportions. So the structure of both Bach's and Gubaidulina's pieces is determined by the Fibonacci series. On a symbolic level, both composers use the same numbers of the beats:

14 = Bach
23 = J.Bach
32 = S.Bach
37 = Jesus Christus
41 = JS Bach
   = (32 + 41)
88 = 14 + 2 + 37
158 = Johann Sebastian Bach
48 = Sofia

Vladimir Martynov (born 1946) is even more radical. In his recently published book *End of Composers' Time* he accuses Giulio Caccini of destroying traditional meaning in arts in his *La nuove musiche* (1602). The new age, says Martynov, started not at the time of German classical philosophy, but much earlier, with this manifesto by Caccini. Since then music gradually fell into a slavery in favour of literature and of subjectivity. Ancient system of seven arts always listed music, along with geometry, arithmetic and astronomy, in one group (*quadrivium*), while grammar, rhetoric and dialectic formed a smaller group of *trivium*. Caccini's ideas changed the very fundamentals of music's nature. Music was simply taken out of *quadrivium* and put into *trivium*. Instead of discussing principles of cosmic and divine proportions, music degraded into

---

32 See Valentina Kholopova, *Sofia Gubaidulina: Putevoditel*, Moscow, 2001.
33 *Ibid.*

a simple art of rhetoric and of representation. The period of 'professional', 'authored' music, which started in the late sixteenth century in Florence, laid the foundation for at least four centuries of European music. It is now time, according to Martynov, to stop writing any professional music. The time given to the composers has expired. The only exception can be made for church service music. Otherwise music should be returned to the *quadrivium*.[34]

Russia has never created art for art's sake. The real content, the real tensions, are between words and sounds. In Dostoevskii's novels, the heroes are ideas, not people. More precisely, people are represented as the bearers of ideas. So, Russian art was always in *"quadrivium"*. According to Wassily Kandinsky's essay, "On the Spiritual in Art", all abstracts, figures, and single colors were considered symbolic, spiritual entities.

Russian music's development was much more intense in an atmosphere of harsh political pressure and social discomfort than it has been in more recent times, when Russians have the freedom to travel, bargain and sell. Fewer freedoms increased creativity, and, conversely, more freedom has diminished creativity. It never flourished under conditions of so-called total freedom. It has always been more productive in an atmosphere of social and political restriction. The long periods of social repression in Russian history produced music of great power and symbolic character with hidden levels of meaning, requiring investigation and interpretation. Much of Russian life and art is like an iceberg, much of it is hidden.

But the origins and roots of "hidden" meanings and metaphoric language in culture are deeper and older than just a political resistance and dissidence in the non-liberty situation of a communist regime. Christian responsibility often created a similar context of non-liberty in the past. Christian art, from its very beginning, was never an art of freedom. And there is no art for art's for a believer. With no political or social pressure, there is always a sense of a higher, hidden substance in symbolic art.

Russia inherited the spiritual traditions of early Christianity from the Byzantine Empire, which was The Second Rome. It is enough to compare mosaics in Ravenna, once a capital of the Eastern Roman Empire and in Kiev, the old capital of *Rus* until Russia was united under Moscow. They are the same.[35] Moscow was "The Third Rome". The line of history was clear and continuous.

Similarly continuous is the line between Aristotle and the spiritual mentality of the twentieth century. As Aristotle stated, "a poet should prefer probable

---

34 Vladimir Martynov, *Konets vremeni kompozitorov*, Moscow: Russkii put, 2002, 202.
35 It is also quite obvious on the mosaics in the St Clement's church in Rome.

impossibilities to improbable possibilities...once the irrational has been introduced and an air of likelihood imparted to it, we must accept it in spite of the absurdity".[36] This acceptance of "absurdity" or irrationalities was the key factor for the spiritual ideas of the generations to come. The admittance of irrationalities supported symbolism philosophically and was particularly important for twentieth-century art. A book by the Russian priest and philosopher Pavel Florenskii develops Aristotle's statement: "Common sense cannot explain certain things, and the major spiritual foundations are far beyond any carnal (*plotskoi*) pragmatism (*rassuditelnosti*). And therefore they could not be invented by a human being; they are Divine".[37]

Bibliography

Aristotle. 1996. *Poetics*. London: Penguin.

Asaf'ev, Boris (Igor Glebov). 1923. "Tsennost' muzyki", in *De Musica*. Petrograd: Petrogradskaia Gosudarstvennaia Akademicheskaia Filarmoniia.

——— 1923 "Process oformleniia zvuchashchego veshchestva", in *De Musica*. Petrograd: Petrogradskaia Gosudarstvennaia Akademicheskaia Filarmoniia.

Auerbach, Erich. 1974. *Mimesis. The Representation of Reality in Western Literature*. Princeton: Princeton University Press.

Bobykina, Irina (ed.). 2000. *Dmitri Shostakovich v pis'makh i dokumentakh*. Moscow: Glinka State Central Museum of Musical Culture.

Britten, Benjamin. 1986. *Three Suites for Cello*. London: Faber Music Limited.

Florenskii, Pavel. 1914. *Stolp i utverzhdenie istiny: Opyt pravoslavnoi teoditsei v dvenadtsati pis'makh*. Moscow: Put'.

Ivashkin, Alexander. 1991. *Charles Ives i muzyka XX veka*. Moscow: Sovetskii Kompozitor.

Ives, Charles. 1970. *Essays before a Sonata, the Majority and other Writings*. New York: Norton.

Valentina Kholopova. 2001. *Sofia Gubaidulina: Putevoditel*. Moscow: Kompozitor.

Kurth, Ernst. 1920. *Romantische Harmonik und ihre Krise in Wagners Tristan*. Bern: P. Haupt.

Losev, Aleksei. 1990. "Dialektika mifa", in *Iz rannikh proizvedenii*. Moscow: Pravda Publishers.

Martynov, Vladimir. 2002. *Konets vremeni kompozitorov*. Moscow: Russkii put'.

---

36 Aristotle, *Poetics*, chapter 24, translated with an introduction and notes by M. Heath, London: Penguin, 1996.

37 Florenskii, 504–505.

Morrison, Simon. 2002. *Russian Opera and the Symbolist Movement*. Berkeley: University of California Press.
Nosina, Vera. 2006. *Simvolika muzyki Bakha*. Moscow: Klassika XXı.
Rudneva, Anna. 1994. *Russkoe narodnoe muzykal'noe tvorchestvo: Ocherki po teorii fol'klora*. Moscow: Kompozitor.
Sviridov, Georgii. 2002. *Muzyka kak sud'ba*. Moscow: Molodaia Gvardiia.
Taruskin, Richard. 1996. *Stravinskii and the Russian Traditions*. Oxford: Oxford University Press.
Tatlow, Ruth. 1991. *Bach and the Riddle of the Number Alphabet*. Cambridge: Cambridge University Press.
Vishnevetskii, Igor'. 2005. *Evraziiskoe Uklonenie v muzyke 1920–1930 godov*. Moscow: Novoe Literaturnoe Obozrenie.

CHAPTER 18

The Irrational in Russian Cinema: A Short Course

Oleg Kovalov

> Secrets are not revealed. That's why they are secrets.
> P.I. CHAIKOVSKII

In his article 'The Ontology of the Photographic Image' André Bazin wrote that the cinematographer fundamentally needs the characteristic of being able to "embalm time".[1] Against one's will this very elegant formula is mixed with a certain frightening, sepulchral tincture: the expression "the mummy of time" itself cannot but remind one of the old horror films starring Boris Karloff. Therefore, probably, Andrei Tarkovskii in his article-manifesto 'Imprinted Time' (1967) gave a more merciful formula – cinematography, in his opinion, is the only one of the arts which creates a "matrix of real time".[2]

Surprisingly, the critic and art expert Vladimir Vasil'evich Stasov (1824 – 1906) came to a similar understanding of the nature of cinema in the nineteenth century, soon after he first saw so-called 'living pictures'. He had the reputation of a bellicose conservative. He called impressionists 'leperous' and feverishly unmasked all and every type of 'decadents'. It was indeed he who became an excited film viewer and enthusiast of the new art. It is easy, of course, to suggest that 'living photography' attracted him exclusively by the fact that it copied reality more exactly than usual photography – everything, it was said, as in real life, and not more than that. But, according to Stasov, a lot more came of cinema.

He described the Lumière clip in a letter to his brother of the 30th of May 1896 thus:

> ...купанье! [...] Голые тела от жары толпой суются в воду – что тут есть интересного, важного, красивого? Так вот нет же. Из всей этой ординарщины тут состраивается что-то такое и интересное, и важное, и красивое, что ничего не расскажешь из виденного.

---

1 See André Bazin, Hugh Gray, "The Ontology of the Photographic Image", *Film Quarterly*, Vol. 13, No. 4 (Summer, 1960), 4–9.
2 Andrei Tarkovskii, *Arkhivy, Dokumenty, Vospominaniia*, Moscow: Podkova, Eksmo-Press, 2002, 162.

[...bathing! [...] A crowd of naked bodies dipping into the water to escape the heat, what in this is interesting, important or beautiful? It turns out there is something, against all odds! From all this ordinariness something so interesting, important, beautiful emerges, that you can't say anything about what you've seen].[3]

With these words Stasov spread his arms in puzzlement and admiration after his first meeting with cinematography, at once seizing the most vital and valuable characteristics in the very phenomenon of depiction on screen.

Behind these apparently guileless sketches Stasov feels "something more", a certain quality for which there is not yet a name. It seems that the term 'cinegenius' is already on the tip of his tongue. The shots of "real cinema" seem to exude a certain irrational aura, which envelops a depiction of the most unprepossessing objects – a waste ground, a crooked fence or a factory chimney. It seems that it is precisely to these things, and not to normative beauty that the cine lens is attracted. Why is it that the ruin in cinema is more 'interesting' than a palace, and a non-professional, just the 'type' from real life, is more expressive than a People's Artiste? Why does a filmstrip 'love' one actor, and 'doesn't love' another, and this cannot be corrected by any kind of actor's talents? There are no distinct answers. A filmstrip, as it were, gets 'inspired' or charged with a certain energy by some personalities, but not by others, and that is as much of an explanation as there is.

It has become a legend by now how some of the first viewers of early cinema ran away in horror when the 'Lumière train' appeared to run straight into them from the screen. It is easy to suggest that they panicked only because of a naive assumption that a train would run over them. Is it not possible that there was another, different fear in addition to this one?

This is how Maksim Gor'kii, who had seen this innovation at the Nizhnii Novgorod trade fair in 1896, describes his first meeting with cinematography: "Yesterday I was in the kingdom of shadows. How terrifying it was to be there, if only you knew!"[4]

If Stasov was singing of the vital power of cinema, then precisely the same film by the Lumière brothers moved the young Gor'kii to almost mystical terror. "Ash-grey foliage", "the shadow-like figures of people" caused him to recall "visions, the damned" and "evil magicians, who have sent whole towns to sleep

---

3 "V.V. Stasov o kinematografii", Prepared for publication by A. Shifman, *Iskusstvo kino*, No. 3 (1957), 128.
4 "Gor'kii ob iskusstve", M.-L., 1940, 5, cited in N.M. Zorkaia, *Na rubezhe stoletii (U istokov massovgo iskusstva v Rossii 1900–1910 godov)*, Moscow: Nauka, 1976, 41.

with their enchantments". "It seems that before our eyes lay an evil joke of Merlin...".[5] Citing his articles, N. Zorkaia precisely defines the original characteristics of depiction on screen, which is able to raise up atavistic fears from the feeling of a meeting with another world: "the colourlessness, silence of the performance combined with the illusion of life and stormy, active and intense movement".[6]

The contrast of the reception of essentially the same film by two contemporaries is simply astonishing. It is clear, however, that each sees in them 'their own'. For Stasov, an adherent of spiritual health and realist art, the birth of cinema was the long-awaited guarantee of the coming triumph of a certain majestic "total realism". Gor'kii, as if moved by the instinct of an artist of the Silver Age with its sickly tendency towards otherness, as though it glanced at the other side of visible events, felt a mystical tremor.

Both these seemingly opposing points of view about the phenomenon of cinematography itself are in fact similar, in that both Stasov and Gor'kii at once saw in it something 'bigger' than an engineering achievement or even a new type of art. Straight away, they perceived cinematography as a phenomenon which was in a certain magical manner linked with the matter of existence – be it its mysterious other/outer side or the same kind of endlessness, but this time 'optimistic', painted in the bright tones of triumphant positivism. Stasov, like a true progressive of the nineteenth century, dreamed that film was capable of immortality "for the very greatest".[7]

Like the legendary Charon, cinematography is a mediator between two worlds, the world of the living and of the dead...it does not belong wholly to one or the other. The child of the Lumière brothers was perceived by the shrewd minds of humanitarian Russia in precisely such a metaphysical and not a technocratic aspect.

By convention, a work where certain 'fantastical' events, that do not occur in reality, are depicted, is itself called fantastical. But Tsvetan Todorov considered the true fantastic to be totally different kinds of artistic statements – those in which an initial cause of improbable events is simply missing, and is not even hinted at. The intricate storyline of such works allows a 'two-way' reading: that either all these extremely odd phenomena are caused by otherworldly powers, or they are of the most 'earthly' or prosaic origin, and their mystical background

---

5 N.M. Zorkaia, *Na rubezhe stoletii* (*U istokov massovgo iskusstva v Rossii 1900–1910 godov*), Moscow: Nauka, 1976, 42.

6 Ibid., p. 41.

7 "V.V. Stasov o kinematografii", p. 130.

is made by the confused, or extremely overheated imagination of one of the characters, usually a first-person narrator.[8]

"The fantastic", writes Todorov, "exists, while the reader hesitates",[9] with which key – mystical or positivistic – he must unlock the narrative. Any choice here leads to unambiguity, while 'ambiguity' provides them with a worrying uncertainty, which is, properly speaking, a trait of the truly 'fantastic' – not so much of the depicted events, as of the particularities of the perception of their depiction. With all the delicacy of such 'modernist' construction, it can, all the same, be noted that the number of such works, based on a plot of ambiguity, is extremely small. It is clear why: the general reader or viewer gets very annoyed when authors who have been teasing him by a certain mystery, in the end leave it unsolved, not answering the question of "what exactly happened then? And why tell a whole story when you yourself don't know what happened…?"

If one accepts the classification of Todorov, then it turns out that Andrei Tarkovskii's *Soliaris* (1972) and *Stalker* (1979), typically characterised as fantasy, are not. The supernatural powers, which control events, the 'rational' ocean or the room which fulfils desires, are presented in these films right away and appear as if they really exist. However, where are these powers hidden in *Zhertvoprinoshenie* (Switzerland-England, 1986) (*The Sacrifice*) by that very same Tarkovskii? A world war breaks out and Aleksandr, the hero of the film, pleads to the Creator to save unreasonable humanity. In the most unimaginable way a universal catastrophe is averted, and those close to Aleksandr, who were only just struck dumb by the terrible news, now do 'not remember' it at all. Does that mean that the Almighty, who has listened to the voice of one of the mortals, simply cancelled the end of the world? Or is it that there was in fact no war, and its beginning was just dreamt of by an exalted intellectual?…

In a rather paradoxical way, Todorov distinguished the substance of the fantastic as arising not from its external subject or from the material of the work, but exclusively from its reception. That is, from those 'hesitations' of the reader or viewer, who, having fallen into a zone of existential mysteries, helplessly tries to get to the world which assumes straight answers to all the most intricate questions. The fantastic in a work, Todorov suggested, exists only insofar as this duality of interpretation of the original plot – which excites the imagination of a viewer – continues; and it disappears at once, as soon as the 'receiving side' finds/establishes its position with respect to 'what really goes on', and

---

8 Tsvetan Todorov, *Vvedenie v fantasticheskuiu literaturu*, http://modernlib.ru/books/todorov_cvetan/vvedenie_v_fantasticheskuyu_literaturu/ (consulted 01.01.2012).

9 Todorov, *Vvedenie v fantasticheskuiu literaturu*.

with that – calms down.[10] It is clear that such a perception renders the work one-dimensional and uninteresting.

The 'Todorov Approach' to irrational subject matter is useful also when trying to distinguish the irrational in Russian cinema. Thus, to turn here to the material which in itself suggests the demonstration of fantastical occurrences is not very productive. Some cinematic images often represent the standard norm of the genre and no longer surprise anybody – thus elephants and witches fly across the sky in fairy tales, in comedies the most notional resolutions to plots are possible, and the most grotesque images (aliens) are as everyday in sci-fi as a yardman seen through the window. The structure of plots and the artistic solution of the majority of genre films are given, in essence, by their profoundly speculative and rational plot constructions. That means that there is simply nothing truly irrational in them – their irrationality is external rather than internal.

If, however, the film mystifies its audience with oddities which occur apparently against its generic or thematic nature, for example, fanciful rhythms, whims of tone, imaginative accents 'not in the right places' or an arrangement of narration that does not seem to suit what is going on, then there, in these hidden nooks and crannies, the deeply irrational is concealed.

To a large extent the irrational appears in material that seems far from being designed to provide a way out or a loophole to a transcendental dimension, but which is on the contrary intentionally 'earthly' or, it would seem, clearly propagandistic. The audience, who have been brought in to watch such an apparently innocent everyday or entirely industrial drama, or even a particularly ideological work about Soviet patriotism, the beloved party or the passionately adored leader, quite soon begin to experience a certain inner sense of discomfort. They cannot fail to sense that in the film everything is quite clear and correct, and yet there is something in it which is not 'quite right', something elusive which irritates and knocks their perception out of its conventional rut.

Therefore, when describing the phenomenon of the irrational in Russian cinema, one must leave aside the genres and storylines of those films where the fantastic is an element of the plot construction, that is, where it is a condition and even a subject of depiction. We will also avoid 'art (auteur) cinema', which gives a visible face to the world of deeply subjective ideas and interpretations of reality. The presence of irrational motifs and images here is too obvious – usually they constitute the artistic fabric itself of the work, where reality is inseparable from dreams, and the real world is inseparable from the imagined. Therefore in such films anything whatsoever can appear on the

---

10   See Todorov, *Vvedenie v fantasticheskuiu literaturu*.

screen before us, in any form: dreams, nightmares, and lyrical hallucinations are in 'art (auteur) cinema' as much of the norm as the witch on a broom is in the fairy tale, or a spaceship in sci-fi.

The reason why irrationality in art is indeed irrationality lies in its quality of being 'non-material', independent of the visible determinism of the rationally constructed plot. And therefore in its pure form this irrationality can be sensed in the films of those cinematic movements and thematic models which in principle did not intend to allow for this elusive substance.

In the 1910s, Russian cinema with great ease showed 'otherworldly' powers: young drowned girls with melancholy faces and unkempt hair emerged onto the screen from dark whirlpools, and the Enemy of humankind himself – adroit, smiling and charming – excelled in his perfect manners, artistically leading fragile souls into temptation. But the truly irrational was felt more acutely in those films, the material of which did not apparently suggest anything of the kind.

The 'school' of Evgenii Frantsevich Bauer (1867–1917) expressed this tendency. He was a director only in the last four years of his life, tragically cut short, but despite this, his cinematic innovations are countless. Behind the bulk of plastic inventions and the decorative refinements of Bauer's films, somehow such a 'small' feature as their content was usually overlooked. His films are normally considered 'aestheticised' melodramas, that is, melodramas, the native qualities of which were not simply highlighted by their director, but were polished by him to a highpoint of brilliance as an end in itself. Bauer, however, made his films without looking at genre canons and loved blowing up the stereotypes of standard perception.

Thus in her remarkable work *Na rubezhe stoletii* (1976) (*At the Turn of the Century*), Neia Markovna Zorkaia named the main archetype of the melodrama plots in early Russian cinema.[11] This archetype emerged in the Karamzin story *Bednaia Liza* (1792), which tells of a peasant girl who is seduced and then abandoned by the handsome nobleman Erast. As a result, her trusting heart is broken, and she drowns herself in a pond. The echo of this literary manifesto of Russian sentimentalism has rumbled across the wide, open spaces of Russian cinema, as many films have been constructed according to this model.

Following this archetype, the main heroine of these films is a beautiful, modest and poor girl, who is slightly burdened by the measured ordinariness of her existence and secretly dreams of a brighter, more romantic life. Unexpectedly, and in a most prosaic guise, a demon-tempter appears, as if born from these clearly indecorous ideas of hers. He leads the girl into those

---

11   See Zorkaia, *Na rubezhe stoletii*, 244–245.

spheres where people live wealthily, happily and in a carefree manner, and naturally, all sorts of exotic 'Erasts' are there. For the sake of such a sleek, superficial, worldly dandy, she leaves her respectable (if dull and a little boring, but still solid and habitable) little world and, her head turned, throws herself into the stormy waves of passion and the elements. But when her unfaithful chosen one 'lays his eyes' on another, the heroine comes back to her senses. She realises the false brilliance of wealth and, consumed by repentance for all the woe she has caused her former plain, but honest admirer, her abandoned children or her old mother, she 'runs to the pond', drinks poison or shoots herself with an elegant lady's pistol.

The plot formula, so loved by the Russian screen, is 'seduction and punishment'. Already in his first film, *Sumerki zhenskoi dushi* (1913) [*The Twilight of a Woman's Soul*] Bauer turns it inside out. The denominative 'Liza' lauded by the Russian melodrama was brought low by her poverty, whereas Bauer's heroine, the languid, elegant Vera, on the contrary, pines away in aristocratic salons, drawing rooms and boudoirs. These places are decorated by tropical plants and garlands of flowers, and Vera, like a rare exotic bird, languishes in these wonderful orangeries, as if they exude humid vapours. She is drawn to that simple, natural and real life, which the world of the poor for her embodies and generally, to poverty. This world is shown by Bauer not only without sentimental 'charitable' sweetening, but also without the compassion traditional in Russian culture. Here in his film, it is a world of cruel, cunning and dissipated urban scum, and contact with them is as fatal for Vera, as for the screen 'Liza' the entry was into the world of the rich.

The real whirlpool here is reality itself because it is unsteady, unrefined and so dangerous that it is from this reality that one should run away to the natural maelstrom. Russian cinema before the Revolution was generally seized by fear in the face of reality, and Evgenii Bauer expressed this wonderfully: "Life is more terrible than death", writes the graceful Giselle in elegant handwriting in her young lady's notebook in the film *Umiraiushchii lebed'* (1916) [*The Dying Swan*]. The ideal of other characters of Bauer is also beyond the borders of tangible existence, and in the figurative flesh of his films it is expressed in the compulsive motif of the passion of the characters for bodies and bodiless souls of dead girls who have not known earthly love. In the film *Posle smerti* (1915) (*After Death*), Life symbolically appears as a potbelly-aunt in little spectacles and an old cap, whereas Death is shown as a wonderful, attractive and melancholic young woman.

The sickly 'world of Bauer' is arranged around this concept, common to the era of decadence. However, as in the Todorov's example of embodiments of the 'irrational', it is impossible to pause on one or the other treatment of events shown in the programmatic films of the director. Are they called forth by the psychological pathologies of the heroes, or perhaps these characters, as in mystical plots, are play-things of invisible dark forces? Some of the plastic solutions of Bauer are so strange that they are simply not amenable to logical analysis.

His gigantic stage settings, reminiscent of aeroplane hangars, used even for chamber/intimate scenes, have become legendary. Thus in the film *Deti veka* (1915) (*Children of the Century*) there is a high glass wall, not of an exhibition pavilion, but of a gazebo, behind the fence of which a mysterious shine washes over the fluttering foliage of the garden, so the viewer, who is not accustomed to the wonders of the silver screen, at once notes: such gazebos simply 'don't exist'.

Bauer is the acknowledged exponent of the style 'Modern', and yet he depicted the urban landscapes as if he was verging towards a different aesthetic hardly known in Russia at that time. It seems that he was the first to bring to the screen those 'empty towns' reminiscent of the mysterious spaces of Giorgio de Chirico, the maître of 'metaphysical painting' – created, by the way, also in that first decade of the twentieth century. The unknown towns on his canvases, with the arches of galleries, ending in a sharp point of perspective, with monuments to unknown people, and mysterious towers of unknown purpose, all exude a sense of languishing, existential mystery. Not only emptied, dreamlike towns in Bauer's films, but also his plastic solutions of other interiors, resonate with Chirico's 'faceless' people, mysterious sculptures and painstakingly painted constructions of unknown purpose. Recall, for instance, the outlandish woman's bedroom from the film *Za shchast'em* (1915) (*For Happiness*), deprived of the slightest hint of comfort or intimacy and more reminiscent of a railway station waiting room; or the famous 'chequered' wall in the film *Korol' Parizha* (1917) (*The King of Paris*) in which an octagonal (!) window has been cut, through which one can see a fake city that looks like a mirage.

It is significant that the artist of these films was Lev Kuleshov, who himself later became a director and theorist, inventor of new principles of montage, creator of a legendary cinema school and generally, as his followers argue, of all Soviet cinematography. The status of innovator caused him to unmask unmercifully that screen routine, which 'the cinema of Tsarist Russia' surely symbolised for avant-garde youth. In reality though, Kuleshov's practice provided a firm 'bridge' between the aesthetic of the pre-Revolutionary screen and the principles of the Soviet avant-garde. Generally, it is deeply unproductive to cut the single body of living culture into its Russian and Soviet halves: it has been clear for a long time that the better works of the Soviet epoch emerged from the tradition of their predecessors, and the links and clashes between the two stages can be most diverse and paradoxical.

Rather unexpectedly, the internal rejection of reality as such is usual for conceptual works not just of the 'Bauer school', but also of the Soviet avant-garde. It emerged from the 'Russian Idea', which, according to Berdiaev, gave rise to the outlandish peculiarities of life in Russia. Public consciousness strived here to the promised future, where, it seemed, there was already erected a heaven for souls torn away from the captivity of grimy, tortuously imperfect reality. "The true kingdom is the City of Kitezh, under the lake", wrote Berdiaev.[12] From faith in the certainty of the existence of this City a logical conclusion emerged: reality, which by its grimaces blocks such a wonderful mirage, must be refuted, rejected, exploded.

The Soviet period, it seems, was obliged to break with the religious and philosophical systems of the 'accursed past', but instead it became the Golden Age for the 'Russian idea' which manifested itself where its appearance was least of all expected. The question about the links of this idea with the 'most important of the arts' was not even posed, since Soviet cinema was considered an ideologically sound child of socialist realism. Yet, in the stormy epoch of 'searching', cinema, like the other troops of the Russian avant-garde, was obsessed with cosmic projects for the remaking of reality, the creation on earth of a Temple of a luminous utopia, which only the new man of 'tomorrow's' would be worthy of entering.

The film *Bronenosets "Potemkin"* (Sergei Eisenstein, 1925) [Battleship Potemkin] opened with an incendiary quotation from Trotskii's work *Revoliutsiia v Rossii* [*Revolution in Russia*] (1909). Later, of course, the Soviet censor replaced this with a quotation from Lenin. But ideally it would have been more appropriate to open the film with the Gospel citation which is the epigraph to *Brat'ia Karamazovy* [*The Brothers Karamazov*]: "Truly, truly, I say to you, unless a grain of wheat falls into the earth and dies, it remains alone; but if it dies, it bears much fruit". (John 12:24). Eisenstein embodied here the idealistic concept of the path of the people, which was formed by the religious-messianic principle of the 'Russian idea' – rivers of sacrificial blood flowing for the sake of a sudden, rationally inexplicable jump forward to the harmonic world of universal brotherhood. The injured Vakulinchuk, dying, is hanged at the yard-arm – the canonical pose of the martyr-messiah, which overtly alluded to the

---

12 Nikolai Berdiaev, "Russkaia idea: Osnovnye problemy russkoi mysli kontsa XIX-nachala XX vekov", in *Russkaia idea: v krugu pisatelei i myslitelei russkogo zarubezhia, v 2 tomakh*, Moscow: Iskusstvo, 1994, vol. 2, 214.

association with Gospel imagery. This was at once noted by the critics of the twenties.

The film *Mat'* (*The Mother*) (Vsevolod Pudovkin, 1926), like Eisenstein's film, was hastily declared historico-revolutionary, but it also expressed the 'Russian idea', only by different means, skilfully cultivating it from the picture of everyday life and the analysis of human psychology. The screen depicted that under Tsarism workers lived in conditions worse than cattle, dividing their leisure hours between the taverns and the police station. This hopelessness was a condition of the transformation of life of the downtrodden and destitute Nilovna into a *zhitie*.[13] Passing through the forge of suffering, she and her revolutionary son were united, in order to perish together for the sake of a mirage of a new 'City of Kitezh' dawning over the thick mud of their suburb. This mirage was embodied by the vision of the crenellations of the Moscow Kremlin walls floating against each other. The moment of the happy unity is inevitably linked here with death, since it is absolute and in its highest triumph it aspires to nonexistence, liberating one from the unstable earthly fetters.

It is thus not accidental that artistic intuition forced Pudovkin to film the fate of Nilovna against the backdrop of the destruction of God's Temple. The achievement of this woman, who arises with the banner in the path of a mounted police charge, is devoid of practical meaning: this, like the martyrdom of a saint, is purely a spiritual act of sublime self-immolation. The characteristics of the realistic work did not contradict here the irrational meaning of conversion as such: faith is not cognised by reason, it is the fruit of momentary inspiration.

Some are certain today that cinema is a technological means to 'photograph' the work of good actors. But directors of the Soviet avant-garde least of all aspired to 'make cinema', that is to narrate more or less well-turned stories. Their aim was the visible embodiment of existential categories, such as Faith, Non-existence, Love, Death, Freedom, Birth, Sacrifice in the name of Resurrection and Universal Brotherhood, and they all, even Eros and Desire, had to appear on the screen in all the might of their eternal meaning, as it were, as if written in capital letters. The films in which this grandiose attempt was made had a reputation as models of historico-revolutionary works, but their links with social reality were relative: who in their right mind would study the history of the *kolkhoz* from the film *Zemlia* [*Land*] (1930) by Aleksandr Dovzhenko, and the storming of the Winter Palace from *Oktiabr'* [*October*] (1927) by Sergei Eisenstein?

---

13   *Vita*, i.e. Life of a Saint (trans. Ed.).

Operating purely on existential categories, the 'big cinema' of the avant-garde created its own cosmos, and the films were akin to certain cosmic bodies (similar to the 'nonfigurative' canvases of Kazimir Malevich, which he himself considered the offspring of things not made by hands), as if they were windows on to different spaces and a new reality. Such were indeed the films of the Soviet avant-garde: 'cosmic bodies' like the magical canvases of Malevich. They live outside the laws of traditional psychological realism and canons of propagandist art, and that is why even the most famous cinema texts so often remain 'unread'.

So *Arsenal* (1928) by Aleksandr Dovzhenko, is considered through inertia to be a film about class struggle, but an impartial view of this extremely cruel, uncomfortable (and in some ways unpleasant) work could see in it a variation on a theme of *Pliaska smerti* (Dance of Death). Usually the artist draws a variety of life events; here, by contrast, before the dumbfounded gaze of the viewer, a string of those various forms of death (from collective to individual) passes by, and, instead of a quiet expiry in one's bed, the cruel epoch of uprising and oppression is legitimised. Whereas life, on the contrary, is depicted here as a dull non-existence which is worse than any death. In a word, a truly philosophical treatise is depicted on the screen, created as a type of existential poem.

The semantic foundation of the film *Zemlia* is based not on pleas and slogans, but Eros and Thanatos, Death and Conception. Juicy, round apples which cover the whole screen, a ripening woman's womb, the whole cycle of existence from meetings amongst night-time dew and gleaming moonlight patches, to the exit to nothingness, depicted as a sweet immersion in slumber amongst the mounds of ripened fruit – this is Aleksandr Dovzhenko's ideology, and not the propaganda of tractors and *kolkhozy*.

Therefore, these famous shots, where after the death of Vasil' a naked young woman in despair rushes around the chamber, express not grief for her dead bridegroom, as he would have been, most likely, in a different – 'normal' – film, but grief that there is no-one to fertilise her yearning body. In the 'veneered' ending to the film, she is easily consoled by another, who is 'no worse' than the perished Vasil', and vitally, the generations must continue. In the worldview expressed in this film, a certain 'balance' is found – here someone leaves, another arrives – for Dovzhenko paints not private heroes with their tragedies and collisions of their lives, but the existential cosmos, where the human race itself is directed by the laws of the hive. What does the death of one small bee mean for the universal, eternal and great cosmic flow of the natural laws?

The intonation of the epic films of Dovzhenko is therefore twofold. On the one hand, we can conceive of the Revolution, depicted by him, as a great occurrence that matches those events which were sung by the Ancients in epics. On the other hand, in such a depiction of the social revolution – no more and no less – it is possible to see an apology for a certain unconscious, biological, almost animal principle, and this revolution itself can be perceived as an expression of a regrettable historical regression, and even as the result of the moral savagery of the population.

Eisenstein's film *General'naia liniia* (*The General Line*) (1929) was formally dedicated to the process of cooperation in the village, but while it was being filmed, 'nonstop collectivisation' was declared, and the director had to change the film's tone and title. However, even here, the visibly revealed characteristics of the national consciousness – prone to exalted meditations, and therefore always ready to fly away from the uncomfortable earthly firmament – in the final analysis take preference over the burning questions of the day.

In the real village where Marfa Lapkina lives there is darkness and dirt, whereas in the utopian village commune there are light buildings, fatted cattle and waterfalls of milk, which come down straight from the sky. The abundant future appears to Marfa only in a dream: reality and the ideal are indicatively separated by the director. But how can one enter the wonderful 'city of Kitezh'? The people know that the only way to the mirage is by a miracle. In Eisenstein's film the villager-worshippers ecstatically seek blessed rain from the heavens. Obviously, in the film this is declared as old-time savagery, while Marfa Lapkina knows a different recipe for happy abundance: it is a cream-separating unit. But the prosaic contraption is cunningly shot in the film as a magical, fairy tale accessory, like Aladdin's lamp, which can fulfil all your desires. A change of systems and of civilisations does not change the national consciousness with its tendency to passive mythmaking. Iosif Stalin recommended the film to be renamed *Staroe i novoe* (*The Old and the New*) which was what was agreed. In the title of the film, the accent was supposed to stand on the 'new' conquering the 'old'. However, the overall imagery of the film points instead to the powerlessness of the new to break an age-old psychological mind-set.

In the film *Entuziazm* (*Enthusiasm*) (Dziga Vertov, 1930) the documentary shots of a showcase church destruction are priceless. They provoked a liberal outcry on several occasions – here, it was said, a Soviet director lauds such barbarity – but the incredibly expressive artistic commentary that goes with it was completely overlooked. In fact, Vertov depicted this – seemingly dishonoured – bell tower, whose dome is removed and which is decorated with a plywood star, in majestic angles, filmed against the background of clouds dashing past with a whistle. A handmade needle seems to cut the space in half, it hovered across the centuries as a symbol of faith in general, denoted by various emblems.

Sometimes Party slogans and the most benevolent declarations, even quotations from the leaders, were quite clumsily introduced in the films of the Soviet avant-garde. The censors, however, could not help sensing that although everything seems correct, something here is not quite right... Thus, why, for example, in the film, *Tri pesni o Lenine* (*Three Songs about Lenin*) (1934) does Vertov so suspiciously sincerely mourn for the departed Il'ich? What is there to get so worked up about, if the Party is led by a reliable successor? But the fact of the matter was not that 'the wrong' leader was lauded here, but that the artistic variations on the theme of the 'Russian idea' in this film, as in many other works of the avant-garde, internally contradicted the imposter socialist mythology.

Vertov's film poured out meditative sorrow over a Messiah who had sacrificially abandoned a frail world for the sake of a reigning 'paradise for all', when the propaganda insisted that the way to a bright future lay in Stalin's Five Year Plans and the unflinching Stakhanovite movement. In the film, 'paradise' seemingly occurs of its own accord, through a sad indolence, the flowing of tears in a cold space. It, like a higher grace, is bought, begged from the echoing emptiness by the depth of sorrowful experiences, with which the peoples have literally irritated themselves here.

In the films of Aleksandr Dovzhenko there is much that cannot be subjected to rational analysis. Their plots are scarcely detectable, and some plot links, with magnificent disregard for conventional narrative logic, are simply omitted. Instead, the landscapes, panning shots, long shots and panoramas are so lengthy that it seems at times that the film consists only of them. Thus the action of the film *Aerograd* (*Aero-city*) (1935) suddenly pauses, in order to show a shot of a young Chukchi on skis, a beautiful external plotline, but one that goes 'nowhere'. By contrast with the skier who flies like an arrow across the taiga and the wintery wastes, the plot peacefully stays still.

In his diary, Dovzhenko himself wrote openly about this peculiarity of his films that can act as a key to the reception of their strangeness: "The dream is a form, a montage, a compositional method of expressing various interesting and extreme things and non-existent possibilities. For a time the border between sleep and waking is blurred".[14]

In this Dovzhenko is the direct descendent of his great compatriot, Nikolai Vasil'evich Gogol': "Woods, meadows, the sky, valleys, everything, it seemed, slept with their eyes open",[15] he described the land at night, seen from the

---

14   A. Dovzhenko, *Zacharovannaia Desna' Rasskazy. Iz zapisnykh knizhek*, Moscow: Sovetskii pisatel', 1964, 190.

15   This is a famous quotation from Nikolai Gogol's celebrated novella "Vii" (1835).

bird's eye view. And in the same way, with widening, unblinking eyes turned to a certain transcendence, the young men and women in Dovzhenko's *Zemlia* sit strangely spellbound, as though enchanted, and the dappled patches of moonlight wander across their detached faces.

In the bewitching rhythms and in the strangely viscous substance of his films, in the sense of certain irrational principles where they are least expected, not only a mytho-poetic perception of the world, but also a general surreal aura is expressed, in obvious or very hidden forms pervading the action. People in Dovzhenko's films every now and again seem to fall into a stupor, turning into 'living statues', and animals obtain the gift of speech. The horses in *Arsenal* gallop for such a long time, as if they are carrying the fallen hero not to his native village, but to the edge of the world. The mother of the dead worker in the film *Ivan* (*1932*), mad from grief, throws open the doors of innumerable bosses' offices an uncountable number of times: her movements are swift and yet it seems that she runs on the spot, not moving anywhere, just as in a horrible nightmare when, however hard you try, you cannot overcome a certain invisible barrier.

The action develops here as in a dream. Sometimes quickly, and not on account of any external dynamics, but because of gaps in the place of missing logical links, then with extreme, almost sick slowness. Instead of a particular event, a subtitle might come up, not one which explains the 'disappearing' circumstance of the plot, but one that expresses a certain declaration, as if sent to the cinema-hall straight from the bright future. Sometimes a retrospective cuts across the episode, made in an intentionally conditional key and clarifying things which had already seemed clear enough. That is why it is so difficult to retell the plots of Dovzhenko's films: the events in them are often deprived of their traditional motivations and the external links; therefore we remember not their causality, but the brightest fragments and screen images.

From this embodiment on the screen of the material of a dream, it is one step to research the subconscious, which is recognised as objective reality. One of the first examples of this was the strangest film made by Pudovkin (not understood by contemporaries) *Prostoi sluchai (A Simple Occurrence)* (*1930–1932*). Its story-line is intentionally simple. While his wife Mashen¢ka is away, the Red Army commander has an affair with another woman, but soon repents and returns to his family: after all he and Masha are military comrades in the Civil War. This circumstance is represented as the main reason to preserve the marriage, but within the framework of the film this did not work – indeed, if the new love interest of the commander had not been such so obviously a dolly, but a true member of the proletariat, then what? The social rhetoric was ceasing to serve as the universal magic wand for the director.

The triumphant victors, having defeated the old world, now clashed with a power which they were not able to overcome by the usual sword stroke and not do away with by a decree of VTsIK – the mighty biological principle which subjects powerfully and completely. Pudovkin, the master of the realist film-portrait, aimed at conveying in his film not the feelings of a private individual, but the very biology of processes which take place in the individual subconscious, and, as a result, to identify in every person the genetic traits of a certain generalised 'everyman'. The revelation of the screen was in a visible depiction of how at first an ill, and then a recovering, man perceived the world; and whether he was from the Red Army or from the White Guard was not important here.

The images of revolt or calls to revolution in the films of the 1920s exuded from the essence of the 'Russian idea' which formed their imagery. The final call of the metaphysical film *A Simple Occurrence* to strengthen the Red Army was absolutely absurd, because it did not follow from the ideas depicted on the screen about various, often foggy existential categories. This spoke of the crisis of the 'Russian idea', and of the fact that directors were gradually departing from it, admitting the invincibility/indestructibility of the precepts of life which did not want to succumb to wilful 'corrections'.

Generally, irrationality, with which avant-garde art was infected in the 1920s, with time is manifestly modified, shifting towards the strange. Vladimir Krichevskii, the contemporary scholar of artistic innovation, simply adores this quality. He shifts the most famous examples of the Soviet avant-garde – its subsequent 'visiting cards' – to one side, and moves to the centre strange, bizarre, even savage things which are not reminiscent of anything. This 'strangeness' generally serves for him as a higher value of a work. This characteristic slips away from analysis and interpretation and almost teases by the fact that for a time it can easily be seen as an artistic flaw or an accidental absurdity, and for a time, on the other hand, it is impossible to capture its essence and location.

Most acutely, the 'strange' reveals itself in banal and recycled material rather than in the extravagant and exceptional. For example, the external forms of Symbolism, Surrealism and abstract art are 'strange' enough in their own right, and therefore do not leave any room or cause for a certain 'additional' mystery that appears through what is depicted. Hence, according to a subtle observation of Krichevskii, "The strange is manifested with a special force and is received precisely as the strange in a figurative context, more or less transparent in its literary fulfilment".[16]

---

16   Vladimir Krichevskii, *Pechatnye Kartinki Revoliutsii,* Moscow: Publikatsiia № 3 izd-va "Tipoligon-AB", 2009, 68.

By the same token, from the early 1930s films began to appear which seemed to be shot according to the most ideologically sound, conformist material, but whose aesthetics sharply departed not only from the stereotypes of agitational films, but also, seemingly, from common sense.

Thus the film *Ledolom* (*Icebreaker*) (1931) has always been considered a humiliating failure by Boris Barnet: for some reason it was decided that he showed collectivisation 'incorrectly'. However, by depicting the destitute and violent life on the uninhabitable earth, squeezed by ice, it seems that in fact Barnet certainly depicted the godforsaken times of the extermination of the Russian village 'correctly' – as a horrific nightmare.

The film *Rvanye bashmaki* (*The Torn Shoes*) (Margarita Barskaia, 1933) narrated how class-conscious children of Germany helped the workers in their class struggle. Such an abstract could discourage all from going to the cinema, as it seemed that on the screen there would be presented something totally and hopelessly dreary about the loyal henchmen of the party and Komsomol. However, the first shots of the film are not simply surprising, but shocking. It looks as if they were filmed not during Stalin's Five Year Plans, but thirty years later, in the liberal time of various 'new waves' with their 'hidden cameras' and a cult of improvisation.

Barskaia, however, creatively fixes not improvisations on a theme, but various manifestations of 'individual unconscious'. These peculiar 'documents of behaviour' with unbelievable audacity are 'stuck in' here, as though in an avant-garde collage, in the most tentative and speculative dramatic structures. If an earlier cinema presented on the screen the image of children, even if wonderfully embodied, then Barskaia's film for the first time showed children per se, with the psychophysics of each individual child carefully captured. This artistic overtone, which does not seem too essential for the film's ideological import, in fact became that very ferment which served to radically rebuild its content.

In this film about class struggle basically two main 'classes' are depicted – the class of children and the class of grown-ups, in which side by side, and not in accordance with Marx, the workers and their masters develop. Whoever these characters of Barskaia were, she portrayed organically free children and fatally captive adults, imprisoned by conditions, conventionalities and by their social roles. It turned out that the children were much better and purer than their fathers, while official dogmas continually insisted that the older generation, idealised beyond limits, had the fundamental role of 'teachers of life' and ideological mentors.

The most interesting phenomenon of those years was the emergence of films infused with motifs of social utopianism. The directors of the films *Ivan*

(Aleksandr Dovzhenko, 1932), *Strogii iunosha* (*A Strict Youth*) (Abram Room, 1936), *Chudesnitsa* (*The Miracle Worker*)(Aleksandr Medvedkin, 1936), *Kolybel'naia* (*Cradle Song*) (Dziga Vertov, 1937) apparently lauded the 'radiant present', but the intonation of these films was so strange that it allowed the idea of a malevolent parodic quality of their luminous paintings, which stealthily acquired grotesque colours and sinister overtones.

The beginning of the century was the epoch of *Sturm und Drang* for the avant-garde movements. However, in the thirties, classical traditions and substantive depictions started to regain their ground. Soviet cinematography, which in the 1920s was intoxicated by the reckless recreation of reality, in the 1930s returned as if to a 'new integrity'. It exuded anxiety and expressed the fragility of deceptive stability, as had occurred in the 'neoclassicism' of Picasso. The same effect was caused by the film *Novaia Moskva* (*New* Moscow) (A. Medvedkin, 1938), which depicted the capital of the future, rebuilt in the spirit of Stalin's precepts. The city looked so freakish and dead that the film was banned.

The post-war 'Thaw' swiftly renewed the spiritual orientation of society: the idea of the 'cleansing of the banners' from the blood and dirt of Stalinism became a form of return to a certain unpolluted source. The centre of the films was now occupied not by the Leader, a party functionary or a 'cog' in the system, but by an idealist exuding the light of truth, in essence, a new saint.

The perceptive viewer was not deceived by the spiked helmet of Pavel Korchagin in the film of the same name (Aleksandr Alov, Vladimir Naumov, 1956). The passionate revolutionary was presented in it as a true martyr and spiritual warrior, carrying not peace but a sword to the stupefied people. In one of the shots, next to this fanatic with a fiery gaze, unmerciful to himself and to those close to him, appeared an image of the Saviour, quietly and sacrificially carrying His cross. But what corresponded better to this emblematic depiction was the image of another well-known hero of the 'Thaw': the gentle, internally honest Moscow lad who seemed also very distant from religion, Boris, played by Aleksei Batalov in the film *Letiat zhuravli* (*The Cranes are Flying*) (Mikhail Kalatozov, 1957).

The religious motifs, so obvious in Eisenstein and Tarkovskii, are not so obvious in Mikhail Kalatozov's work, probably because the aesthetics of his 'Thaw' films was reminiscent of the avant-garde *Sturm und Drang* of the boisterous twenties. Both he and his colleague, the brilliant cameraman Sergei Urusevskii, were the successors of this era. *Letiat zhuravli* is one of the most mysterious films of Soviet cinema. In the present public consciousness this film has a firm reputation as a 'secular' melodrama, yet at the same time it is one of the most sophisticated 'religious' cinematic texts.

The motifs of the canonical 'Way of the Cross' so subtly penetrate the plotline of 'Boris in the war' that we are not at once aware of them as allegorical – so skilfully do they hide in the cloak of an exclusively secular narrative. Thus sending him off to the front, Boris's grandmother blesses him with the sign of the cross. At first this seems a usual 'realist' gesture, for in Soviet cinema, the 'positive' character of the grandmother was still permitted at times to show a touching, forgivable backwardness. But in the context of the imagery of the Boris plotline, the symbolic parting wishes of the grandmother can be seen also as a direct 'conversion' of the hero, and as a sign of his involvement in sacred matters.

In the war, as shown in the film, not only does he not shoot even once, but in both episodes at the front, he actually saves injured people and carries them himself. At first, he takes the stretcher on his shoulder, and then carries the second soldier piggyback, his feet dragging in the thick mud, and to the sound of the whistling of bullets and fierce fighting on all sides. In order to make the symbolism of the episode more graphic, the foreground of this shot, filmed in motion, depicts a barbed-wire fence. When the camera pauses, one of the coils of the barbed wire, brought into close-up, looks like a crown of thorns.

In the film *Neotpravlennoe pis'mo* (*The Unsent Letter*) (Mikhail Kalatozov, 1959), the work of the geologist is also depicted as the sacrificial journey of an ascetic. The sequences where the geologist Sabinin in his long-hemmed coat wonders alone through grey stone boulders remind the viewer of the canonical subject 'Christ in the Wilderness', and one thinks here least about the search for mineral resources for the prosperity of the socialist Motherland. The log raft, on which the mortal body of Sabinin is virtually frozen with outstretched arms, is reminiscent of a crucifixion. He is carried straight to eternity and to spiritual immortality on the dark waters of the vast river.

As with painting, where after the canvas of Pablo Picasso *Avignon Girls* (1907) it became unthinkable to paint in the same way as before, so it was with cinema after the film *L'Avventura* (*The Adventure*) (Michelangelo Antonioni, Italy-France, 1960). It simply became unacceptable to follow strictly rational models of narrative on the screen. The 'absence of event', the key element of the poetics of Antonioni, provokes the fascinating rhythms of his films, such as meditative music, and the complete ignoring of stereotypical links between thoughts and actions, cause and effect, what is important and unimportant, and also, between sequences, parts and episodes. All this causes a general sense of existential inscrutability despite the fact of a seemingly strict objectivity of narration. Antonioni's characters are 'alone' not for personal, social or psychological reasons, but because they remain at one with the existential cosmos. What can be further, it seems, from both the dogmas of official art and from the light-hearted sentiments of the 'Thaw' than these existential conceptions? Nevertheless, the experience of the Italian maestro simply entered into the blood of Russian film-making.

It is logical when his intonations are sensed in the film *Deviat' dnei odnogo goda* (*Nine Days of One Year*) (Mikhail Romm, 1961). Indeed, in the depiction of physicists, whose milieu was perceived to embody intellectual relaxedness, and seemed to carry the aura of belonging to the mysteries of existence, the elements of modernist aesthetics as it were went without saying. In the film *Zastava Il'icha* (*The Il'ich Rules*) (Marlen Khutsiev, 1962) the usual gatherings with wine and music of the Moscow intellectual youth are shown in the same drawling rhythms and with the same moral condemnation as the sluggish and dreary 'orgies' in the villas of millionaires, in which the sleek characters of the Western screen, depraved by idleness, tend to waste their time. These sequences even seem to be enveloped in a light, barely perceptible parodic quality, and this mismatch of texture with the general tone of the narration causes ones to smile involuntarily.

The film *Nikogda* (*Never*) (Vladimir D'iachenko, Petr Todorovskii, 1962) depicts, in the same slow rhythms and with a lengthiness which cannot be motivated by anything except the directors' familiarity with the films of Antonioni, other gatherings – this time of young workers. And this looks even more parodic, especially when the meaningful dramatic pauses of characters who have nothing to talk about are filled with the sound of tape recordings of organ music.

Of course, meditating on the internal problems of the intelligentsia in *Iiul'skii dozhd'* (*July Rain*) (Marlen Khutsiev, 1966), it was natural, even if unconsciously so, to reproduce the intonation of the director who set the standard intonation for the depiction of this environment. But the film *Bol'shaia ruda* (*The Big Ore*) (Vasilii Ordynskii, 1964) portrayed not some sort of ideologically immature and unstable 'layer' of society, but 'our heroic working class' and, all the same, by its texture and mood, it was not so different from the film by Antonini *Il Grido* (*The Cry*) (1957), which depicted the spiritual restlessness of an Italian proletarian. How could one then refrain from a bitter sigh, "Something is rotten in the state of Denmark"?

This was all the more so, since the characters of the existential dramas became the director of a factory (*Nikogda*), a former military pilot (*Kryl'ia, Wings*) (Larisa Shepit'ko, 1966), the chair of the City Council (*Korotkie vstrechi, Short Meetings*, Kira Muratova, 1967). It turned out that, when confronted with suffering caused by the loneliness and impossibility of internal links with the people closest to them, their social roles turn to nothing and they themselves are not such wilful and brave managers as depicted by socialist realism. The process expanded and the screen showed that the symptoms of the main illnesses of the age had affected the top of society.

It was even more bizarre, and for dogmatists blasphemous, when the tones seemingly created for the depiction of the languishing of Western elites, exhausted from an abundance of free time, were superimposed on the material of the Great Patriotic War (Second World War), which was supposed to have an exclusively heroic colouring, lauding the comradeships of the front, and not the depressing statement of fatal disunity. Thus it is easy to detect Antonioni's influence in the scene from the film *Ivanovo detstvo* (*Ivan's Childhood*) (Andrei Tarkovskii, 1962) where the nurse Masha and the Lieutenant Kholin walk in a birch grove 'with a subtext'.

The fixation with the 'incommunicability' that the Italian master explored advanced on all fronts. Indeed, a huge number of Soviet animated films which were essentially small 'poems of loneliness', constituted an answer to the years of the 'pathos of collectivism'. With a great clarity this tendency was expressed a bit later, in the 'metaphysical' animation of the 1970s and in the works of Iurii Norshtein.

The emergence of all these pieces in a minor key, which were a complete change from the works of the 'Thaw' with their mood of high hopes, was not only completely natural, but was directly caused by the tendencies of cinematography of that same 'Thaw'. Soviet dogmatists usually linked the key films of the 'Thaw', such as *Letiat zhuravli* or *Ballada o soldate* (*Ballad of a Soldier*), (Grigorii Chukhrai, 1959), to socialist realism. However, in April 1962, Pier Paolo Pasolini used the term 'neo-romanticism' in relation to the new Soviet cinema.[17]

Indeed, the characters of these films were in conflict not so much with each other, with society or their era, as with the whole world order (which is usual for a 'normal' hero of a romantic work). If one makes the depiction of this resistance just slightly more acute, the links between the hero and the world become overstrung and simply break. It is at the point of designating this painful break where the 'world of Antonioni' inevitably emerges.

There was one more reason (and not the most metaphysical one) why films about the languishing life-style of well-groomed 'playboys' turned out to be internally consistent with the population, with those who had seen villas with swimming pools only on screen, and who knew of night clubs only from the clip 'Their (i.e. bourgeois) mores'. Maiia Turovskaia clarifies this point:

---

17   See N. Zorkaia, *Portrety*, Moscow: Iskusstvo, 1966, 274–275.

How did the generation of Sandro [the hero of the film *L'Avventura*, O.K.] [...] acquire a type of fatigue which [...] is not the same as personal fatigue? It was a fatigue from the past years of fascist oppression with its impersonalising of personality, from the necessity to switch to an intense intellectual effort of comprehension, from shooting and blood on the streets of Italian cities in [...] the days of war, and from the black market...From the death camps in which he was neither a prisoner, nor a guard, but whose very possibility of existence all over Europe overtaxes the emotional sphere of man...[18]

Sandro in the film is in his early thirties. One only needs to replace a few words in this extract from Turovskaia and one can see that the social experience of his generation exactly coincides with the experiences of subjects of that state power where the possibility to become a prisoner of the 'death camps', which never existed in Italy, was not the most tentative and which hugely overtaxed the emotional sphere of even the most ideologically reliable citizen.

The most irrational artist of the time of Perestroika was, of course, Evgenii Iufit. From the mid-1980s, when his 'tempestuous' short films appeared, he developed several persistent motifs on the screen. His characters were the forest, water, clouds melting in the sky and shrubbery at twilight. He was enchanted by his twilight, gloomy world, where the meditative enchantment with the world of nature is bizarrely woven together with carnival parody and black humour.

In his film *Ubitye molniei (Struck by Lightning)* (2002) the lyrical principle takes the upper hand. The director is enchanted here not only with the space of glades and forests, a cloud slowly moving over the horizon or the movement of currents on the surface of a river. Iufit was the first to film a city poetically – all these empty spaces through which, like Alice with her adventures through the looking-glass, a young girl wanders, as if out of Chirico's canvases. *Struck by Lightning* is a rare example of a spontaneous and consistent surrealism in contemporary Russian cinema.

Aleksandr Sokurov, it seems, is the last in a line of artists of Russian cinema whose entire object of reflection is existential values. Some representatives of 'auteur cinema' quite rationally construct their artistic worlds and cherish the elements of their personal and 'in-house/brand-name' mythology. And other, true metaphysics, seemingly simply 'photograph' those mirages that appear before their inner gaze. In the films of Sokurov, however – shot through a lens

---

18   Maiia Turovskaia, *Da i Net. O kino i teatre poslednego deciatiletiia,* Moscow, «Isskusstvo», 277–278.

which seems out of focus – distorted silhouettes of figures and objects are kept on the screen, as though with the last of their strength, by a fragile, 'smeared-out', shaking and seemingly vanishing contour.

A general point of discussion has been that Sokurov is obsessed with the theme of death. However, he does not always evoke in his work images of 'private' passing. Artists-mystics visibly construct pictures of a certain imagined alternative reality, but with regard to Sokurov this description is not very precise either. His cinematography concerns rather that twilight zone between life and nonexistence, though which, generally speaking, every one of us has already wandered alone. From film to film, and with surprising variety, Sokurov reproduces the very essence of (again) not the private, or individual, but a certain universal and all-embracing 'dream' per se.

Translated by Elizabeth Harrison and Olga Tabachnikova

Bibliography

Berdiaev, Nikolai. 1994. "Russkaia idea: Osnovnye problemy russkoi mysli kontsa XIX-nachala XX vekov", in *Russkaia idea: v krugu pisatelei i myslitelei russkogo zarubezhia, v 2 tomakh*, Moscow: Iskusstvo, vol. 2.

Dovzhenko, 1964. *'Zacharovannaia Desna'. Rasskazy. Iz zapisnykh knizhek*. Moscow: Sovetskii pisatel.

Turovskaia, Maiia. 1966. *Da i Net. O kino i teatre poslednego deciatiletiia*. Moscow: Isskusstvo.

Tarkovskii, Andrei. 2002. *Arkhivy, Dokumenty, Vospominaniia*. Moscow: Podkova, Eksmo-Press.

Todorov, Tsvetan. *Vvedenie v fantasticheskuiu literaturu*, http://modernlib.ru/books/todorov_cvetan/vvedenie_v_fantasticheskuyu_literaturu.

Krichevskii, Vladimir. 2009. *Pechatnye Kartinki Revoliutsii*. Moscow: Publikatsiia № 3 izd-va "Tipoligon-AB".

Shifman A. (prepared for publication). 1957. "V.V. Stasov o kinematografii" in *Iskusstvo kino*, 3: 127–141.

Zorkaia, Neia. 1966. *Portrety*. Moscow: Iskusstvo.

——— 1976. *Na rubezhe stoletii (U istokov massovgo iskusstva v Rossii 1900–1910 godov)*. Moscow: Nauka.

CHAPTER 19

The Rational and Irrational Standard: Russian Architecture as a Facet of Culture

Elena Kabkova and Olga Stukalova

What can be more rational than a building designed for a human being to live in and carry out his daily routines? Everything seems so thoroughly thought-through, down-to-earth and normal. It is no coincidence that the Latin word 'rational' means something based on reason, not contradictory to logic. But if one looks closely, the word *zdanie* (building) derives from the Old Russian verb *z'dati*,[1] which means 'to build, to raise', but, even earlier, from the word *z'd*, which means 'clay'.

It all seems to make sense: a building, a construction, clay (from which bricks or – as they were called in ancient times – plinths are made). But in the very sound of the word *z'd*, there is a feeling of unstable, fast-moving sliding, of falling and collapse. This series of associations somehow does not readily tie in with the rational idea of construction, with its aim of obtaining stability and peace. This duality, or even multi-layered quality, appears in Moscow architecture in all its manifestations, from buildings of high aesthetic taste and international cultural significance to common, everyday buildings constructed to fulfil the basic need 'to hold on through the night and then keep on standing up through the day, too'.

After a first glance at any of the maps of Moscow, the resemblance of the city's features to an outline of a wheel leaps straight out at one. Moreover, it is not a subtle, swift, light wheel, but a heavy, archaic, rough wooden wheel, which in its unstoppable movement grinds through everything that gets in its way. This impression is not as groundless as it might seem. In reality, everything built in Moscow that has failed to blend in with the general countenance of the city has at first provoked bewilderment or surprise from its inhabitants. Then, with the passing of time – sometimes quite quickly, sometimes after a great deal of time – it has been swallowed up by the city and ground down under that eternally moving wheel to become an organic part of the whole.

---

1   This word's etymology is investigated in: I.B. Levontina, *Dom, zdaniie, postroika, korpus* // in: Apresian Yu.D. *Novyi ob'iasnitel'nyi slovar' synonimov russkogo iazyka,* Moscow: Prospect, 1995, 179–184.

So it was with the seven buildings nicknamed Moscow's 'Seven Sisters' or 'Stalinskie vysotki' ('Stalin's High-rises'). Built in Moscow at the end of the 1940s and beginning of the 1950s,[2] they were at first perceived not as architectural monuments, but exclusively as monuments of a political era. In fact, one cannot call these constructions 'architecture' in the strict sense of the term, because architecture always consists in the blending of construction and space, whereas these buildings blend space and volume, something which is more characteristic of sculpture. The way in which the internal space of these 'high-rises' is organised makes it possible for them to be seen as peculiar 'termite mounds'. This internal space is in no way connected to the exterior of the building. Yet architecture, or rather not architecture, but these constructions fairly quickly grew to be part of the Moscow landscape, and these sharp-pointed silhouettes have become one of the characteristic symbols of the face of Moscow. The same did not occur with a similar building in Warsaw. That building did not blend into the cityscape, but remains to this day something foreign brought in from outside.

It is telling that such famous buildings of Moscow's architectural heritage as the Church of the Annunciation at Kolomenskoe or the Cathedral of the Virgin's Shroud on the Moat (the Cathedral of St Basil the Blessed) resemble sculpture, as their exteriors have a much more interesting, expressive and meaningful character than their inner space.[3] They were also built as commemorative constructions – the church at Kolomenskoe for the birth of Ivan IV, and St Basil's in honour of the taking of the city of Kazan'.

We would dare to suggest that such an irresistible striving for the external beauty of a building, even at the cost of functionality and utility, is one of the characteristic signs of Russian irrationalism in architecture. We find an interesting confirmation of this view in the work of Ivan Il'in, who, criticising Western European 'rational culture', notes that "on close inspection it turns out that at is basis lies a discipline of will, a concept of usefulness and a skilful organisation, not love, conscience or feeling".[4] From his point of view, in this abides the reason for the crisis of Western European culture, which 'is built as though from *stone and ice*. Here religion, art and science (apart from a few genius exceptions) are cold. Love can hamper the mind and the will; culture is

---

2 J.V. Stalin, *The Council of Ministers of the USSR "On the construction in Moscow high-rise buildings" from January 13, 1947 // Works,* Tver: Information and Publishing Center "Union", 2006. – Vol. 18, 430–432.

3 *Architectural Monuments of Moscow. Neighborhood of old Moscow.* Science editor A.I. Komech, Moscow, "Art-XXI Century", 2007.

4 I.A. Il'in, *Put' kochevidnosti*, Moscow: Respublika, 1993, 431, 295.

considered a matter namely of the will and the mind. To reveal the life of feelings appears childish, frivolous, or even ridiculous! Culture is a strict matter, and strictness is formal cold and cruel'.[5] Based on Il'in's conclusions, one can suppose that Russian aesthetic thought, on the contrary, strives primarily to be sensed in its objective content; it is a contemplative process based largely on intuition.[6]

Irrationalism is also manifest in the fact that the beauty of architectural constructions built through incredible toil often turns out to be partially unnecessary to the next generation, and is consequently abandoned and left to ruin. Moreover, this beauty begins to provoke aggression and a desire to destroy the building.

It is significant that the story of how Saint Basil's Cathedral was saved from destruction has something of the miraculous about it, namely, the personal bravery of the extraordinary Soviet architect and restorer Peter Dmitrievich Baranovskii. In 1936 the government decided to knock down the building, believing that it was hindering the traffic flow on Red Square.[7] It proposed to Baranovskii that he take the required measurements. He told the bureaucrats that destroying the cathedral was madness, and vowed to kill himself if it occurred. In the context of that bloody era, his reaction was completely irrational, and needless to say, Baranovskii was quickly arrested.[8] Nevertheless, the cathedral remains standing on Red Square.

The history of Moscow's architectural development is extremely dramatic, and the heat of passions surrounding it has only become more inflamed over the last century. The history of the destruction of Moscow's architectural heritage merits separate investigation.[9] It is a story of the struggle between scholars – historians, art historians, architects, journalists – and the city authorities. It has been known for a long time that a large number of constructions that had architectural and historical significance were excised from the

---

5 *Ibid.*, 295.

6 *Ibid.*, 298.

7 Andrew Mozhaev, *Red Square of Peter Baranovskii // Russian Loyalists*, Moscow, Tradition, 2010.

8 P. Baranovskii in conversation with S. Gavrilov called reason for his arrest as confrontation with the deputy chairman of the district executive committee demolition of Sukharev Tower in Moscow. Biography of Peter Baranovskii presented in the paper: Yu.A. Bychkov, *Life of Peter Baranovskii*, Moscow, Soviet Russia, 1991.

9 Investigations of this problem are presented in the works: *Keeper. Alexei Il'ich Komech and fate of Russian architecture* / N. Samover, Moscow, Arts – XXI Century, 2009. I.K. Kondratiev, *Grizzled old Moscow*, Moscow: AST: Keeper, 2008. B. Fedorov, K. Mikhailov, *Chronicle destruction of old Moscow: 1990–2006*, Moscow, 2006.

list of monuments which the state should have conserved. This process continues to this day, exacerbated by the efforts of badly educated, avaricious civil servants and unscrupulous builders.

Moscow is a mystical city literally built on a void: a long time ago the area was affected by karst processes, by which voids and pits in the earth's crust form. The city continues to live and develop by its own laws, often in spite of the obvious and against the laws of physics. Indeed, Moscow would not be Moscow if events had not taken place here that could be viewed as exceptions to the rule. Moscow's heavy wheel not only knocks together everything that falls into its sphere of influence, but also, contrary to expectations, carefully preserves some objects – those which by most appearances should not be able to survive in conditions created by the complex and dramatic events which have taken place in the history of the city.

As far back as at the end of the nineteenth century, Moscow's bourgeoisie actively cultivated irrationalism. This saw the appearance of a remarkable number of original commercial apartment buildings and mansions in the symbolist style. The style of these houses differed from their European equivalents through the addition of Russian 'epic' elements, which heightened the mystical mood that they evoked.

The period of the 'Russian Modern',[10] a style of art and architecture related to the Art Nouveau, coincided with a turning point in Russian history. Style was required not only to reflect the striving for art itself, but also the political, economic and social organisation of the world. The Russian Modern was an independent phenomenon born in the context of increasing interest in national culture. However, one cannot deny the Western European influence on Russian culture at the end of the nineteenth and early twentieth centuries, especially if one considers the breadth and variety of economic links and the cosmopolitan aspirations that existed at that time. Modernism valued individuality and almost all its creators were people of universal talent. Painters were simultaneously architects, sculptors, graphic artists, designers and interior decorators. They made many things with their hands, and the artist's touch was visible in everything they did – an essential feature of this style. Modern artists brought about the renaissance of mosaic and stained glass, and re-discovered wood, metal and ceramics. They strove to recreate the reality around them, bringing aesthetic content to all objects in man's surroundings.

Beauty seemed to be capable of changing not only the environment of human habitation, but also man himself. Architecture turned out to be the

---

10 M.B. Nashchokina, *Architects of Moscow Art Nouveau. Creative portraits.* – Edition 3. – Moscow, Giraffe, 2005.

very type of multifaceted, all-embracing artistic creation that allowed one to unite different art forms. It was thus able to reflect the Russian Modern's aspiration towards the synthesis of the arts. One could find shelter and harmonious unity under the roof of one building (in both the literal and figurative sense) in the combination of painting, decorative and other forms of applied arts, music, and literature. New architecture seemed to embody the boldest dreams. The house became a special model of the world, a place designed to give birth to various ideas. In this way, utopian dreams about the transformation of the world via art found their strongest reflection in architecture. This transformative aspiration secured an unusual heyday for architecture as a type of art.

The Moscow Modern produced a large number of splendid buildings and monuments.[11] Architectural constructions were given facades unlike anything seen before. Five movements in the development of the new style can be identified: neo-Russian, Gothic revival, international (also called irrational), rational and neo-classical.

The revolutionary idea of progressive social, industrial and technical development succeeded in uniting society. The Soviets sought to combine the values of the proletariat, as embodied by Bolshevism, with those of the global humanist cultural tradition, namely, the ideals of social justice, spiritual, social, material and economic progress. At the same time, the ideology of Bolshevism was essentially an ideology of modernism, innovation, industrialism, and in this lay the root of Bolshevism's non-acceptance of traditional culture. In the final analysis, the development of culture itself, its inner content, was forced into the tight framework of one-dimensional thought. The culture that was forming under the conditions of the new power was popular in essence and type, and 'Soviet' in form.

'New Culture' became, first and foremost, both the interpreter and the illustration of official ideology. However, it did not always conform to it. Popular culture is democratic. In the West, popular culture, owing to it its supranational, 'cosmopolitan' character, aimed to bring about the socialisation and enculturation of the individual within a market economy. This process was accompanied by the increased commercialisation of art. In the isolated land of the Soviets, popular culture also pursued the socialisation and the enculturation of the individual, causing him to break away (both willingly and under compulsion) from his former culture and enter a new socialist culture. Soviet culture came to embody society's entry into modernity.

---

11 M.V. Nashchokina, *Moscow Art Nouveau,* St. Petersburg, Kolo, 2011; E.A. Borisova, G. Yu. Sternin, *Russian Art Nouveau*. Album. – Moscow: Soviet Artist, 1990.

Culture needed to become the foundation of the new political and social structure. A special place was allocated to the nation's intelligentsia. They constituted the stratum between the working class and the labouring peasantry that, while working for its bread, also had to serve the working masses through the state. The Soviet system undertook the unrestrained politicisation of literature, art, philosophy and science, pushing all meaningful manifestations of culture to the edge of extinction. Traditional folk and religious culture were dealt a powerful blow, and social violence against culture became the norm.

As a result of cultural revolution and urbanisation – achieved in record short time – and the large-scale transfer of the population from village to town, an unstable and 'hybrid' culture arose. The commune model of the Russian peasantry lay at the foundations of Soviet culture. This was obviously a clear paradox. Being inimical to the peasantry, Stalinist ideology nevertheless took its inspiration from the Russian peasant experience. This experience was multifaceted. Cultural and social development and labour productivity were hampered by a range of factors: fear of social inequality in one's midst (which was channelled into envy of the possessions of one's rich neighbours), forced equalisation and shortages of basic necessities.

Citizens' mythological consciousness held back the formation of a culture founded on reason, an essential precondition for the development of science. By seeking to impose communality on society as a whole, the regime made it resemble a Russian peasant commune (*obshchina*),[12] with its indistinct social boundaries. An inevitable result of this process was the appearance of utopian ideals that hindered the individual's ability to navigate the complexities of the social sphere.

Naturally, Bolshevik ideology borrowed directly from the *obshchina* model, which made the system easy for the 'people' to understand and accept. Archaism and simplification became symbols of the era. Citizens were also taught to value highly the head of the party and the state in his role as the supreme leader. They were indoctrinated in the principle of integration into the collective to which man was held to belong, and to view inclusion in the system as a higher goal. The formulation of the Soviet mentality required the selection of positive inducements and powerful incentives, amongst which the strongest was fear. A unique experiment in the area of social psychology

---

12   Mental peculiarities of "community consciousness" is one of the most significant themes of Russian philosophy and culture. In particular, this problem is considered in M.M.Gromyko. For example: *The Russian village's world*, Moscow,1991; *Family and community in the traditional spiritual culture of Russian peasants XVIII–XIX centuries*, Moscow, 1989, and A. Gordon, *Type of management – Lifestyle – personality*, Moscow, 1993.

gave desirable results. Something was created that was officially named the moral-political unity of the Soviet people.

Soviet culture was distinctive for its wilful character, the commanding intonations of its lyrics, the intrusive didacticism of its prose, the gigantomania of its sculpture and the brutality of its architecture. All these features embodied the spirit of the times and the requirements of political and economic institutions. The Soviets developed a mechanism to subject culture to the requirements of ideology. The state set the standard of culture in such a way as to comply with its system. It stipulated the requirements for the classical canon and for bringing the people closer to the classics, but only as much as was necessary so that the culture of the masses remained at a primitive level. The authorities not only oppressed, persecuted and exiled the agents of culture. They also turned them into sycophants by suffocating them in delighted embraces and showering them with gold stars and prizes.

The negative underpinnings of socialist ideology that had been instrumental in the construction of the *Homo sovieticus* weakened after Stalin's death. The Third Party Programme, which was approved in 1961, advocated revitalising the shattered myth of Soviet man. At the heart of this programme lay the so-called 'Moral Codex of the Builders of Communism'.[13]

But life continued to change. The 1960s and subsequent years witnessed the appearance and development of a phenomenon new to the USSR – private life. The concept of private life was foreign until that period in the wide swathe of Russian culture. The concept developed at such a fast pace that it became a defensive reaction against the endless inquisition of the bodies of state power. From the 1960s, Russians' needs began increasingly to focus on the private sphere, to the detriment of the social sphere. If one adds to the idea of individual existence improvements in citizens' education and their increasing inclusion in the orbit of world events (albeit in a limited manner), the reasons why the cultural atmosphere changed become clear.

After the Twentieth Party Congress a tortuous process began to restore to society its memories, although they were still fragmentary and limited. At the end of the 1950s and the beginning of the 1960s, it was not history but literature and memoirs that were prioritised in efforts to reconstruct memories. However, from the second half of the 1960s, the process of memory restoration began to halt. This transformed the literati, who had been aspiring to the truth, into

---

[13] The text of this document can be found on the website: http://leftinmsu.narod.ru/polit_files/books/III_program_KPSS_files/III_program_KPSS.htm. Research on this problem: N. Barsukov, *Khrushchev Communist illusions* // Dialogue. 1991. №. 5; A.V. Pyzhikov, *Thaw: ideological innovations and projects (1953–1964)*, Moscow, 1998.

dissidents, or forced them to fall silent. A vacuum was created once again in society's perceptions of the past. Various phenomena emerged through which Russians sought to alleviate the pain inflicted by the loss of the national heritage and to understand the reasons for their sorrows. Chief among them were the increasing popularity of collecting icons, the rise to prominence of the 'village' theme in literature (known as the 'village prose' movement), and the many expeditions and individual journeys to the Russian North, which left a deep imprint on Dmitrii Likhachev's works.[14]

Despite the fact that in the last decades of Soviet power the picture appeared different, as though painted in softer tones, the position and function of culture were the same: to remain the servant of the political and socio-economic system governing society, and to obey it. If Soviet masses had shared Communist ideology after the victory of 1945, then by the beginning of the 1980s this faith had been seriously undermined. The intervening years had seen the destruction of the pyramid of power and its anthropological bases, such as unanimity, forced loyalty and public subjugation. The destruction of normative standards of social behaviour – that is, the standard normatively given by the 'Soviet man' concept – started in the upper pyramid of power and spread to its supporting structures. The intelligentsia, once supportive of the regime, began to advocate a model of Westernisation that was attractive to certain social groups. The masses had lost their illusions concerning the Soviet model and the sense of coercion that compelled them to profess adherence to it. However, none of this meant that Russians refrained from 'collective' values[15] or, for example, acquired alongside them those of the individualistic American cultural model. There remained the traditional Russian values of equality, fairness, solidarity and faith – everything that had constituted the heart of the Russian masses' cultural model.[16]

This complex and critical socio-cultural situation was brought about by dynamic and often contradictory modernising processes. Many names 'forgotten' by official ideology returned to national culture. There was an increase in interest in Russian and other national cultures' languages, literatures, traditions and customs. Artistic spheres broadened in scope and new types of organisations appeared, such as cultural and creative societies, theatres and ensembles. People's understanding of world culture changed.

14   D.S. Likhachev, *Russian culture*, Moscow, Arts, 2000.
15   Questions of "collective values" are investigated by M.B. Chernitskaia. For example: *Human Values in Russian and Western cultures* / / Culture and anticulture, Nizhnii Novgorod, 2003.
16   P. Weill, A. Genis, *6oth. World of Soviet man*, Moscow, New Literary Review, 1996.

In the present day Russians are once again having to face the irrational treatment of the best achievements of their national culture, in particular with regard to architecture. Many splendid buildings are now on the verge of destruction because for some reason they have not been listed for state protection. The most recent big scandal concerns a fire in an apartment house designed by Lev Kekushev.[17] The building had been neglected for a long time, and, according to some sources, had been illegally occupied by foreign workers from former Soviet republics.

We are also facing an uncontrolled, aggressive influx of various flows of information. The cultural sphere is under attack. Various cultural influences from a more intense and pressurised sphere of culture and information are forcing their way into a cultural vacuum. This entails the loss of that special place which Russian culture occupied and continues to occupy in the classic tradition and even in popular culture, as exemplified, for example, by the music of Rachmaninov, the Bolshoi Theatre, film adaptations of the works of Tolstoi and Dostoevskii, and the Soviet school of animation.

One type of popular culture – that dictated by the state – and the accompanying Soviet mentality are shifting to another popular culture constrained by another mentality. However, in any case, these cultures are practically synonymous in terms of their unifying and simplifying effect. Both play a role in shaping a common type of consumer, reader, viewer and listener. Every day these consumers are subjected to the impact of all sorts of *Simplemente Marias* and *Empires of Passion*.[18] Such culture can be the basis only of a non-national sense of a common bond.

But what is the difference between works of art and monuments of cultural heritage, are they not one and the same? The answer is no. Can one, for example, call the five-floor housing blocks of the period from 1959–63 model works of art – not masterpieces but simply works of art? Perhaps not, because in architectural terms these constructions – even without taking account of the primitive engineering – generally lack any kind of artistic or imaginative principles.

However, at the same time, these buildings are a very characteristic and interesting manifestation of the culture of the 1960s. The very simplicity of their construction says much about the historical situation of the period. At that time, the main task was to find a way to re-house large numbers of people living in overcrowded city centres in the shortest possible time and through an

---

17   M.V. Nashchokina, *Moscow architect Leo Kekushev*, St. Petersburg: Colo, 2012.
18   Translator's note: the authors refer to a Mexican soap opera from the 1980s. The second reference is to a Japanese horror film, *Empire of Passion* (1978), which in the UK is rated 18.

easily replicable project, without resorting to measures that could be considered too extreme. Consequently, the notorious five-floor blocks built under Khrushchev known as *khrushchoby* offer abundant historical and cultural information.[19]

On the one hand, these boxes, which are divided into meagre rabbit hutches, are symbols of a cruel, calculating rationalism. On the other hand, the extent to which they embody the rational goes beyond what can be considered reasonable to such an extent that it becomes not simply a question of strict bookkeeping, but a sort of 'accounting for every twenty and a half kopecks'. Although the conditions in these houses of cards were incredibly trying, people who were re-housed in them from a crowded basement thought that behind their little doors they could build their own world, in keeping with the times, and be free from life's burdens.

Let us recall a typical interior of one of these little flats from that period: meagre, humble 'utility furniture' (always two armchairs and a coffee table under a plastic lampshade), no carpets or antimacassars, a photograph of Hemingway on the wall, and a small bust of Nefertiti on the sideboard. This romantic, touching and extremely irrational environment was not conserved for long, but the irrationalism of the past was replaced by a new one that was also initially dressed up as reason and calculation.

Translated by Elizabeth Harrison

Bibliography

Architectural Monuments of Moscow. Neighborhood of old Moscow. Science editor A.I. Komech, 2007. Moscow, "Art-XXI Century".

Barsukov, Nikolai A. 1991. *Khrushchev Communist illusions* // Dialogue. №. 5.

Borisova Elena A., Sternin, Georgii Yu. 1990. *Russian Art Nouveau*. Album. – Moscow: Soviet Artist.

Bychkov, Iurii A. 1991. *Life of Peter Baranovskii,* Moscow, Soviet Russia.

Chernitskaia, Maia B. 2003. *Human Values in Russian and Western cultures* [:] Culture and anticulture, Nizhnii Novgorod.

Fedorov, Boris, Mikhailov, Konstantin. 2006. *Chronicle destruction of old Moscow: 1990–2006,* Moscow.

Gordon, Alexander V. 1993. *Type of management – Lifestyle – personality,* Moscow.

Gromyko, Marina M. 1991. *The Russian village's world*, Moscow.

---

19   Vita, Malygina, Khruschoba as a mirror of Russian democracy / / Ogonek, 2008.

Gromyko, Marina M. 1989. *Family and community in the traditional spiritual culture of Russian peasants XVIII–XIX centuries*, Moscow.

Il'in, Ivan A. 1993. *Put' k ochevidnosti*, Moscow: Respublika.

Kondratiev, Ivan K. 2008. *Grizzled old Moscow*, Moscow: AST: Keeper

Levontina, Irina B. 1995. *Dom, zdaniie, postroika, korpus* [:] Apresian Yu.D. *Novyi ob'iasnitel'nyi slovar' synonimov russkogo yazyka*, Moscow: Prospect.

Likhachev, Dmitrii S. 2000. Russian culture, Moscow, Arts.

Malygina, Vita. 2008. Khruschoba as a mirror of Russian democracy [:] Ogonek.

Moral Codex of the Builders of Communism [Text] // http://leftinmsu.narod.ru/polit_files/books/III_program_KPSS_files/III_program_KPSS.htm.

Mozhaev, Andrew. 2010. *Red Square of Peter Baranovskii // Russian Loyalists*, Moscow, Tradition.

PART 5

Soviet and Post-Soviet Literature

∴

CHAPTER 20

The Irrational in the Perception of Andrei Platonov's Characters

Kira Gordovich

When interpreting the irrational, scholars use the concepts of the unreal, the apparent and the ostensible. According to Yablokov, who compared Platonov and Nabokov, the world created by these writers is a "kingdom of ostensibility".[1]

Nosov describes Platonov's *Chevengur* as a novel about a "disappearing reality": "you may call *Chevengur* a novel about people losing reality";[2] "In Platonov's prose there is a peculiar balance between the real and the unreal that exists only in the imagination".[3] The researcher says that the writer uses this special situation to transform the artwork from the common, material world to the world of the imagination: "Literature turns into life though this life is unreal, based on endless dreams only [...] and if this is not an objective world then any fairy tale may turn into a true story, any fantasy is real and any dream may become reality...the picture of a collapsing society has turned into something like an epic poem about the fight of the human spirit... The share of playfulness in this "unreal world" created by Platonov is unquestionable."[4] Nosov sums it up with a quote from the novel: "...in the dream the same life continues though in a bare sense"[5]

Analysing the the writer's conception of life with those of his characters, Kornienko declares that in Platonov's opposition of "the conscious and the unconscious", the unconscious, intuitive and natural is always above the rational and reasonable, and that "the presence of the unconscious helps to understand the nature of the conscious".[6] Angela Livingston analyses the distinction between the ordinary and the transcendent and the characters' ability "to see

---

[1] Yablokov, E. 1999. '"Carstvo mnimosti" in the works of A. Platonov and V. Nabokov of the beginning of the 30-s', *Strana filosofov Andreia Platonova* (3): 339.
[2] Nosov, S. 1997. 'Gibel' dejstvitel'nosti (irratsionalizm v russkom modernistskom soznanii)', *Novyi zhurnal* (2): 184.
[3] Ibid., 186.
[4] Ibid., 187–90.
[5] Ibid., 191.
[6] Kornienko, N. 2003. 'Hudozhestvennaja funkcija oppozicii soznatel'noe-bessoznatel'noe v rasskaze "Reka Potudan'". *Strana filosofov Andreia Platonova* (5): 580.

what cannot be seen", which is quite characteristic of Platonov's texts.[7] Mikheev supports the same idea of the real world being substituted with the unreal: "Platonov reduces the real world to the minimum and devotes his story to the description of an apparent imaginary world".[8] This is achieved by shifting the major part of the story to the world of dreams where ordinary reality and the absurd mix well. In this context, the irrational world is not just imaginary but, in fact, absurd.

Unlike some researchers, who consider dreams in *Chevengur* as a "privilege" of the central characters, Mikheev presumes that Chevengur exists in the world of dreams as a reflection of total unconsciousness, as "a composition of all of Platonov's characters".[9] Similar speculation on the relationship between the real and the unreal can be found in the work of Dragunskaia. She interprets the unreal and irrational as something that is "beyond reality".[10] At the same time, she emphasises the loss of sense and the horrible nature of the things happening. If reality is life, then in this case it is substituted with dreams or theatre.

Khriashcheva's analysis of dreams in *Chevengur* is interesting. While pointing out "how thin the boundaries between dreams and reality in the novel are", she claims that it is Chevengur's dreams that reveal the author's perception of people and the world, that this is the sphere of the unconscious in which the writer combines "hypotheses, fantasy and miracles as a real opportunity".[11]

V'ugin devotes a great part of his book about Platonov to the poetics of dreams in *Chevengur*. He thinks that these are dreams that lead the reader away from the one-sided perception of the plot and determine the "inability to judge positively the degree of reality or unreality of the matter".[12] He says that "while solving the riddles of the dreams in *Chevengur*, the reader gains access to a meaning that is contrary to the depiction of historic events".[13]

---

7   Livingston, A. 2003. 'Gran' obydennogo i zapredel'nogo kak osnovnoj obraz v romane "Chevengur"'. *Strana filosofov Andreia Platonova* (5): 505.

8   Mikheev, M. 2001. 'Son, jav' ili utopiia. Eshhe odin kommentarii k "Chevenguru" Platonova'. *Logos* 1(27): 59.

9   *Ibid.*, 76.

10 Dragunskaia, L. 2008. 'Dva tipa snovidnosti – metafora sna i prezentatsiia sna' *Russkaiia antropologicheskaia shkola* (5): 373.

11 Khriashcheva, N. 2005. "Tonok son": k poetike snov v "Chevengure" *Strana filosofov Andreia Platonova* (6): 445.

12 V'ugin, V. 2004. *Andrei Platonov: poetika zagadki (ocherki stanovleniia i evoliutsii stilia)*. St Petersburg: 183.

13 *Ibid.*, 158.

V'ugin's article on Platonov's relationship with surrealism reveals both differences and similar methods and principles: "Platonov only approaches this nonsense, plays with it in all seriousness and uses it as a method, though he does not cross the line that would completely destroy the narration, in contrast to, for instance, Kharms".[14]

There are grounds to consider the characteristics of dreams in *Chevengur* in more detail and with references to the text. We have already mentioned the idea that everything that occurs in the novel happens in a dream. Equally, if we take into account the fact that the author repeatedly registers the moment of the character's dropping off to sleep, then this assumption seems wrong. Let us refer to Platonov's description of a dream and to the features that distinguish it from "actual", "real" life: "his thought disappeared as his consciousness turned in sleep";[15] "There is no transition from clear consciousness to dreaming: the exact same life continues in sleep, only in a bared form" (131); "people were healing the exhaustion of day's inner life through the strength of sleep" (172); "No one looks at sleeping people, but only they have real, beloved faces, for when awake the face of man is disfigured by memory, feeling, and need". (192). We cannot agree that Platonov depicts only the dreams of his central characters (Dvanov, Kopenkin, Chepurnyi) and that the background characters "do not have dreams". The point here is actually that at certain moments, sleeping is the state of everything and everyone in Chevengur. The surrounding nature (the air and earth) is asleep: "The earth slept bare and tormented, like a mother whose blankets have slipped to the floor" (158). "I was asleep and I had a dream. I saw all of Chevengur, like from the top of a tree" (215). "They could hear how the Komsomol had fallen into a burdensome sleep, without having completely left his frenzy" (191). "All the Bolsheviks of Chevengur were already lying on straw on the floor, muttering and smiling in unconscious dreams" (222). Chepurnyi "was probably participating in happy dreams at that moment" (156) and when Kopenkin saw him for the first time he was sleeping as well. Zakhar Pavlovich drowned himself in sleep. However, "His father lived sensibly and wisely in sleep, similar to his life in the day, and his face changed little at night" (192).

The sick boy in Chevengur also dies while sleeping. At first he drowns himself in a "cool and calm sleep" and then cries out because of a nightmare vision

---

14 V'ugin, V. 2008. "Sur-realii" Platonova: ot Bretona do Brodskogo (k probleme esteticheskoi identifikatsii pisatelia)', *Tvorchestvo Platonova: Issledovaniia i materialy:* p. 16.

15 Platonov, A. 1978. *Chevengur*, translated by Anthony Olcott, Ann Arbor: Ardis, p. 60. The quotations from the novel are taken from this edition; the page numbers are indicated in brackets in the text.

and the sensation of his mother giving pieces of his body to naked beggar women (245). The boy's mother also sees him alive for the last time in a dream.

All the dreams referred to above are important for the plot development, but they are not recurring dreams, whereas Platonov's central characters "are laid down to sleep" several times. It is interesting to compare both of Kopenkin's dreams. When he comes to Chevengur for the first time, the author points out that he "plunged into Chevengur as though into sleep feeling its quiet communism as a warm comfort all over his body" (241). Almost at the end, the reader sees Kopenkin sleeping "next to the walking road". His sleep is not calm at all – he is sniffing, screaming deliriously and crying offended: "You swine! Where is my horse? Where is my Proletarian Strength? You've poisoned him in the barn! You have deceived me with communism! I'll die his dreams" (321). It is in dreams that insights take place and revelations are pronounced.

At the beginning of the novel, Sasha Dvanov, when in difficult situations (for example, when he is leaving home or when Sonya is leaving), finds rescue in sleep: "...his thought disappeared as his consciousness turned in sleep, as a bird flies from a wheel as it begins to move" (60). His childhood dreams come back to him later and they help him feel "the warmth of consciousness in his head" (319).

Platonov often shows his characters acting involuntarily, both in dreams and in waking life, and their mind hinders rather than helps. Take, for instance, Zakhar Pavlovich's state when he watches Dvanov: "But Zakhar Pavlovich didn't say anything, although something simple, like joy, moved constantly within him – his mind, though, interfered with its expression" (41).

Dvanov may well think and realise what is going on better than anyone else. However, "no matter how much he read and thought, some kind of hollow place remained ever within him, an emptiness through which an undescribed and untold world passed like a startled wind " (43). Body and its state may become more important than emotions and thoughts: "Sasha felt a coldness within...there was something transparent, light and enormous...the void inside his body was expanding" (43). It is interesting that in Platonov's novel, machines (especially locomotives) are humanised: they possess souls and minds. And, just like people, they sometimes act "unconsciously": "The engine trembled from the pressure, waving its entire body, seeking an opportunity to throw itself down some bank, away from the force which was choking it and the speed it couldn't expend. ..." (51).

Platonov shows Dvanov's uncontrolled and unreal condition during his illness: "In minutes of consciousness Dvanov lay empty and dessicated; he could feel only his own skin, so he pressed himself to the bed, because it seemed to him he might fly off, like the light dry corpses of dead spiders". (59).

Platonov grants him the capacity for self-reflection but points out the dualism of his inner world. There are two people living in him simultaneously: an ordinary man and a spectator watching and registering actions and movements. The author uses the image of a doorman to characterise him: "But there is within man also a tiny spectator who takes part neither in action nor in suffering, and who is always cold-blooded and the same... This corner of man's consciousness is lit both day and night, like the doorman's room in a large building... While Dvanov walked and rode without memory, this spectator within him saw everything, but it never warned him and never helped him, not once. He lived parallel to Dvanov, but he wasn't Dvanov" (80).

Let us refer to the use of the concept words "casually" and "delirium" in the text. Both are connected to an evident switching-off of consciousness, of reasonable and rational thinking. Kopenkin's example is quite expressive: "suddenly upon him, by chance, but then the delirium of life as it continued enveloped his sudden wisdom in its warmth and he had again foreseen that he would soon ride into another country" (109). Knowledge and memories do not imply the ability to control them. Take, for example, Chepurnyi's "disordered memory": "Fragments of the world he had seen and events he had encountered floated in his head as though in a quiet lake, but they never united into a single whole, since for Chepurnyi they had neither connections nor living sense" (163). If a person is not of high intellectual development, then his body power is much stronger than the power of thoughts and emotions: "...He was tormented by some sort of black joy in his abundant body, and the Jap flung himself through the reeds into the clean river, where he could live out his own unclear, grieving passions" (177). He is unable to control himself, he has nobody "to rely on him with the feeling of comradeship": "If he could have embraced Klavdyusha immediately he could have freely waited another two or three days for communism, but he could no longer live as is, for his sense of comradeship had nothing to hold itself up" (198). The author points out the obviously doomed attempts to self-comprehension: "Occasionally Chepurnyi went into the main room of a hut, sat down in the preserved armchair, and sniffed tobacco, so that at least something would rustle and make noise for him" (204).

The author often registers the unconscious condition, mindlessness and uncontrollability, where instead of thoughts and human emotions, there are feelings and physiology: "'Piiusia, are you thinking?' Dvanov asked. 'Yes, I'm thinking', Piiusia immediately answered a little bit confused – he often forgot to think and was not thinking at the moment. 'I'm thinking too', Dvanov confided approvingly. By thought Dvanov intended not an idea, but rather the pleasure of continually imagining beloved objects" (283).

The failure of communism in Chevengur is depicted more effectively through the immersion of both characters and readers in the world of the irrational, rather than through attempting to describe the Bolsheviks' "achievements" satirically. The introduction of this irrational element into the characters greatly expands the possibility of depiction. In some cases, it reveals the obvious narrow-mindedness of an absolutely honest and selfless character (Chepurnyi). In other cases, the sphere of the unconscious emphasises the peculiarities of a spiritual and ideological search, as in the cases of Dvanov and Kopenkin. The background characters' images are important because of their entrancement with what is happening around them and their occasionally obvious slow thinking, which reflects the general chaos and mess.

Bibliography

Dragunskaia, L. 2008. 'Two types of dreaming – the metaphor of dream and the presentation of dream' *Russian anthropological school* (5): 366–375.

Khriashcheva, N. 2005. '"Thin dream": on the poetics of dreams in "Chevengur"' *Strana filosofov Andreia Platonova* (6): 442–449.

Kornienko, N. 2003. 'The artistic function of the opposition between the conscious and unconscious in the story "The River Potudan"' *Strana filosofov Andreia Platonova* (5): 579–581.

Livingston, A. 2003. 'The brink between ordinary and transcendent as a main image in "Chevengur"' *Strana filosofov Andreia Platonova* (5): 501–506.

Mikheev, M. 2001. 'Dream, reality or utopia. Another commentary to Platonov's "Chevengur"' *Logos* 1(27): 55–86.

Nosov, S. 1997. 'The death of reality (irrationalism in Russian modernistic consciousness)' *The New magazine* (2): 181–191.

Platonov, A. 2008. 1978. 'Chevengur' *Platonov. Chevengur*. Ann Arbor: Ardis.

Viugin, V. 2004. *Andrei Platonov: poetics of enigma (sketches on the style formation and evolution)*. SPb.

V'ugin, V. 2008. 'Platonov's "sur-realias": from Breton to Brodsky (on the problem of writer's aesthetic identification)' *Platonov's works: Research and materials:* 3–21.

Yablokov, E. 1999. '"The kingdom of ostensibility" in the works of A. Platonov and V. Nabokov of the beginning of the 30-s', *Strana filosofov Andreia Platonova* (3): 332–342.

CHAPTER 21

The Metaphysics of Numbers in the Eurasian Artistic Mentality: Viktor Pelevin's *The Dialectics of the Transition Period (From Nowhere to No Place)*

Liudmila Safronova

Subject to information overload in an increasingly complex world, modern man finds himself in a state of heightened anxiety. He is forced to expand his inner reality in order to accommodate the presence of an Other in whose image he can exist without the risk of confronting his own problems. If one extrapolates from observations of an individual's personal, invented mythology to phenomena within the subjective-objective sphere, it becomes apparent that the significance of this disintegration of a person's internal world lies in the removal of personal responsibility, which makes it possible to defer crucial decisions, or transfer the responsibility for them to others.

In literature, this type of character expresses himself through obsessive discourse and behaviour,[1] as manifested in a series of protective speech acts and life situations. This complicated system of repetitions is intended to bring about a kind of relaxation – the overcoming of psychological trauma in a series of stages and the elimination of the state of fear.[2] In Julia Kristeva's terminology, this process acquired the name 'renunciation': impulsive activity that is symptomatic of the person's fight against his impossible desires and which is directly connected to the basic mechanisms of artistic creation.

Somatic impulses, which come about through the person's suppression of manifestations of instinct, engender a specially rhythmicised network of repetitions, namely, an accumulation, repetition or concentration of certain morphemes or of isomorphic linguistic units and units of plot composition. This is also a source of aesthetic enjoyment (calming).[3] The semiotic structure of a literary text presupposes the suspension of meaning and frees the mental

---

[1] An obsession is defined as "the condition of being consumed by a single thought; a defensive operation or complicated series of actions that precipitate anxiety if they are not performed". Laplansh Zh., *Slovar' po psikhoanalizu*, Moscow, 1996, 237.

[2] A. Latynina, "Potom opiat' teper'". Online at: http://pelevin.nov.ru 22.02.2009.

[3] Zapadnoe literaturovedenie XX veka: Entsiklopediia, Moscow, 2004, 304–305.

space for the unconscious, from which the Other begins to speak.[4] Consequently, the neurotic belonging to the obsessive personality type becomes not only a character peculiar to contemporary society, but also a particularly successful feature of the poetics of the literary work with regard to reader reception (identification). Assigning to their works multiple tasks in this manner has become popular among postmodern writers.

An anankastic character is a person of an obsessive-compulsive personality suffering from a neurosis of obsessive conditions. He is pedantic and internally extremely orderly, tending to ritualise his own life, as well as to keep activity around him under his control. He usually fits easily into any social hierarchy, since he consciously limits his and others' freedom. He is characterised above all by a megalomaniac devotion to large numbers, a passion for various types of collecting (things, money, women and so on), and a distorted perception of reality.

Rudnev identifies a whole body of similar literary types whose biographical authors – whom he studies in parallel – are known to have suffered from an obsessive neurosis or who had an obsessive-compulsive character.[5] Taking this series of characters chronologically, one finds at the start Pushkin's anankastic characters: the covetous knight, Salieri, Silvio, Germann and Don Juan. Then Gogol' took from Pushkin the idea of portraying the anankastic money-grubber, creating Chichikov, the collector of dead souls, and Pliushkin, the gatherer of dead things. Naturally, Dostoevskii's old money-lender belongs to the same category, as do the obsessive, 'German-like' characters of Tolstoi (such as Karenin) and Andrei Belyi (Ableukhov); Vladimir Maiakovskii's enormous numbers, who were the 'heroes' of his poems and for whom he had a maniacal love; and Iurii Olesha's Kavalerov, the writer's main accountant and the embodiment of his personal creative credo ("not a single day without a line"), who pedantically calculated the age of almost all his acquaintances out of fear of his own death.

A further function of obsession is to bring about the cessation of entropy, time and death. In Rudnev's opinion, Kharms mastered this obsessive sedative vocational psychology particularly well. Aided by the poetics of obsessive repetitions, he incorporated in his children's 'bogeyman tales' various elements irrelevant to the plot that were ostensibly intended to retard the plot development but which, paradoxically, had the opposite effect, causing the children to

---

4 Iu. Kristeva [Julia Kristeva], *Sily uzhasa: Esse ob otvrashchenii* [= *Powers of Horror: An Essay on Abjection*] (tr. A. Kostikova), Khar′kov and St Petersburg, 2003.

5 V. Rudnev, *Metafizika futbola*, Moscow, 2001, 228–265 (the section "Obsessivnyi diskurs").

deny the reality of what was portrayed. Rudnev writes: "It is more likely that Kharms was influenced by [...] the general neo-mythological, pre-postmodern artistic paradigm of 1920s European culture, a paradigm that in effect does away with the idea of history as 'coming into being' and which, under the influence of the 'obsessive' philosophies of history of Nietzsche and Spengler, cultivates the eternal return".[6] And of course he relates the work of Sorokin to the same phenomenon. Sorokin himself "undergoes medical treatment" and "treats" his reader through his deconstruction of schizophrenic discourse and his poetics of cyclically recurring delirium. This amounts to a kind of obsessive defence against the nightmare of social realist reality, or even its idiosyncratic renunciation.

If examined using the same psychoanalytic technique, Pelevin's anankastic character from the novel with the programmatic obsessive title *Numbers: The Dialectics of the Transition Period (From Nowhere to No Place)* Stepa Mikhailov represents a faithful copy of the young Russian entrepreneur of the period in post-Soviet history characterised by the wild accumulation of capital. Mikhailov is a thrifty and yet mystically inclined financial expert – it is namely in contemporary reality that the communicative alarm signal "our money" finds its strongest expression.[7] He is also a textbook example of an obsessive neurotic with a typical 'programmer's' character, trapped vice-like between his own unconscious and the super-ego of the state machine, "between Freud and Feliks Dzerzhinskii", as the dedication to the novel declares. In the author's opinion, contraposition is one of the most effective means of promotion.

The accumulation of numbers is obsessive discourse's defining formal characteristic. Toporov examines the number as an image of peace in archaic cultures, ascribing to it the capacity periodically to bring about renewal in a cyclical scheme of development that serves to overcome destructive chaotic tendencies.[8] The neurotic character's fixation with numbers orders his inner world, functioning as a neurotic defence against his own instincts. Moreover, inner orderliness, harmony and self-confidence also defend him against desires that are destructive for the identity of the Other's desires. In Rudnev's formulation, the Other is initially the archaic divine being, the ancient analogue of the super-ego. Later, it is the 'other half' of the person, the fundamental object of

---

6   *Ibid.*
7   I. Milevich, "Kommunikativnyi signal trevogi: kognitivno-diskursnyi analiz mass-media", in *Kognitivnye stili kommunikatsii. Teorii i prikladnye modeli. Doklady mezhdunarodnoi konferentsii. 20–25 sentiabria 2004, Krym*, Simferopol': Partent, 2004, 120.
8   V. Toporov, "O chislovykh modeliakh v arkhaicheskikh tekstakh", *Struktura teksta*, Moscow, 1980, 5.

his desires and the most important object in the life of the Other. A traumatic situation is usually played out in contact with the Other with the aim of eliminating the identity of the Other's desires: "It was when Stepa Mikhailov began reading about and pondering over the differences between the sexes that the idea of making a pact with the number seven occurred to him" (p. 8).[9]

Kristeva observes that the neurotic's accumulation of the symbolic (in this case, numbers) serves to protect his identity, which threatens to destroy through chaos, first and foremost through the feminine, instinctive, natural element. The basic function of the number is administrative and organisational. Consequently, Mikhailov's union with the number in its role as the manager and master of the world serves as a psychological self-camouflage that delays his relations with the opposite sex, which can be stressful for a teenager.

As Liz Burbo, an American psychologist and teacher well known in the West, asserts: "Behind every emotion that we experience there lurks another emotion – fear".[10] However, according to Freud's hypothesis, an obsessive condition is associated with ideas concerning the "omnipotence of thought" and attempts to control reality – essentially, with a sort of religious *samizdat* that allows one to attain optimum harmonic contact and reconciliation with the world and with oneself.[11]

Affiliation and attachment to one's lucky number (while the hysteric weeps, the neurotic counts) facilitates the sedation of consciousness. It gives one the illusion of being able to put up an impenetrable defense against attacks; with every new calculation, one's anxiety reduces:

> Stepa had different types of sevens for different life events. For example, if he drew a large, hollow one that took up a whole page, it would protect him against older, stronger guys. Four well-formed sevens in the corners of the page would stop his rowdy neighbours in the ward sneaking around when it was quiet and hitting him over the head with a pillow or putting some disgusting thing right in front of his nose, as was their habit. [...] Since he invested all the fear that his soul generated on his relationship with numbers, Stepa had almost no fear of bandits. (8–23)

---

9   V. Pelevin, Dialektika Perehodnogo perioda iz Niotkuda v Nikuda: Izbrannye proizvedeniya. Moscow, 2003.

10 L. Burbo, *Emotsii, chuvstva i proshcheniie* [Emotions, Feelings and Forgiveness], tr. by S. Melishkevich, Kiev, Sofiia and Moscow, 2001, 13.

11 Z. Freud [Sigmund Freud], *Totem i tabu* [Totem and Taboo], Moscow, 1998, 93.

This kind of attachment leads to an even closer contact between the protagonist and the number/divine being, and produces the obsessive neurotic's irresistible yearning to make the plan of content correspond with the plan of expression. This yearning reveals the biographical-authorial obsessive syndrome in character description that is characteristic of Pelevin:

> If there were a person in Stepa's vicinity who knew of his secret, he would probably see a connection with the number 34 in Stepa's facial features. Stepa had a nose as straight as the back of a number four – during the era when schoolchildren still studied the Classics, these noses were called Greek. His round and slightly puffed-out cheeks resembled the two projections on a troika, and there was something of that troika in his little black moustache with its natural upward-curling ends. (17–18)

Pelevin's distinctive style employs manipulative techniques, including the mythology of numbers. It owes its success at the level of reader reception to its calculated artistic regulation and its isomorphism of form and content, a phenomenon analogous to the therapeutic identification with the symptom.

The world of numbers is a world of protective illusions that shield one from reality and defend one against its inevitably entropic processes. This world adapts itself anthropomorphically, adopting an appearance that is organically dichotomous and individualised: it takes on the guise of a particular person. The world is characterised by a natural division into friends and enemies, into happy, sunny numbers (Mikhailov chooses as his personal guardian-angel the number 34, the digits of which add up to 7) and reverse, unlucky, shadowy ones (the number 43 is an analogue of 13 in the collective unconscious), which are counteragents and the symbolic manifestation of all that oppresses the character's psyche. This artificially created world is called upon first and foremost to serve the unconscious, covering up its asocial impulses. Driven by the force of the dynamics of events, it becomes the feeling of fear, principally the fear of taking an uncertain step or of making an incorrect decision: "After all, a person works things out roughly, too, he counts and is scared of making a mistake. He hopes it will all work out all right...He thinks about his soul..." (190).

Only the dilettante believes that rationality decides everything in synergenetically developing reality, and Mikhailov considers logic and common sense no more than one-sided information exercises that only in retrospect are capable of producing an explanation for why counting all the way until the end is clearly unrealistic: "Then again there was a place in life for logic and common sense all the same. But they came into action not when you needed to take a decision, but when you'd already taken it" (22). That is why postmodernism is interested not in the result, which instils fear, but in the process, which has the effect of deferring the decision – and consequently also the punishment for the mistakes: "While performing these operations, Stepa felt an inner comfort that he had experienced only rarely in recent months. He didn't think about the end goal at all, just as if he were practising some kind of harmless hobby like using a fret saw" (154).

According to Freud, all these "innocent repetitions of infancy" (79) accentuate the neurotic's infantilism and return him to a state of primitive thought. During infancy, the presence of responsible guardians to make decisions on behalf of the child keeps him undivided psychologically and safe: "Stepa didn't just know the properties of the number 34; he had been in a special relationship with it since childhood. This was his most important secret" (97). One of the principal features of this condition is delayed personality formation, or, in postmodern literature, delayed character revelation. "Stepa transformed from a round-faced little boy to an equally round-faced young man, as if all the changes associated with becoming older amounted to inflating him with a pump and turning his facial hair upwards" (17). The lifestyle of the contemporary anankastic character who is unwilling to evolve constitutes a fairly successful form of psychological self-defence – a prerequisite for survival in a world that assails us with information overload.

Srakandaev (no. 43) --- imaginary counter-agents --- Stepa Mikhailov (no. 34)
      (donkey, hare, hamster)   (bear, wolf)
Mius (no. 52) ------------ actual counter-agents --- Stepa Mikhailov (no. 25)
    (Pokemon cat)   (Pokemon pig)[12]

For example, "donkey seven cents" Srakandaev, who "swindles" Mikhailov's bank later in the novel is also a copy of a wise old hare and "a cunning hamster who knows something that makes him senior not only to the fox, wolf and bear, but also to the naked, calculator-wielding Berezovskii" (132). On the one hand, the donkey is described as "powerful, very powerful". On the other hand, the reader is informed that "there was one animal he was scared of – a beast able to defeat him…Number 34 flashed through Stepa's mind and became the word 'wolf'" (192). The depiction of this initially natural hierarchy of totems anticipates the novel's next plot development, Mikhailov's murder of Srakandaev.

---

12   Since Stepa considers Srakandaev, his enemy, to be devoted to the number that is the opposite of the one that Stepa has chosen as his divinity, he does not notice the intrigues of his beloved, who is his real contestant and who eventually defeats him.

Textual allusions also anticipate the defeat of the protagonist (an archetypical embodiment of the Russian bear) in a treacherous plot against him hatched by the English woman Mius (the cat being an archetype of treachery). Within Pelevin's oeuvre there is a metanarrative context for this contrapositioning of characters, which is repeated many times in the novel at various textual levels. It echoes the confrontation portrayed in Pelevin's favourite Russian folk tale, 'The Cat and the Fox', on which he based his short novel *Omon Ra*. As Adibaeva states:

> As in the folk tale, in Pelevin's work the bear personifies a people that is simple and trusting but that becomes terrifying when angered. The cat symbolises something alien and unintelligible to the Russian forest-dwellers. It is not by chance that Pelevin chooses the surname Kissinger for the American who stops by: Russians call cats affectionately 'kis-kis' and 'kiska', and the cat is essentially a hunter. Moreover, in America there is a game that has a name similar to the surname Kissinger, 'kiss-in-the-ring', and which is almost the same as the game tag, which in Russian is called 'cats and mice'. In this way, we can see how the great big Russian bear in Pelevin's work transforms into the animal that Kissinger the cat pursues – the mouse.[13]

Yet again, Russia in Pelevin's conception metaphorically loses to the English-speaking West, as Balod observes:

> The novel contains many allegories and symbolic scenes. The treachery depicted in the work may be an allegory, for example, of the different periods in the relations between Russia and the West: at first we had the sweet-tasting propaganda concerning the benefits of Western civilisation; then the advocacy of *perestroika* and a new life, the promise of a land flowing with milk and honey; and then the finale: the same old deviousness.[14]

Almost all the main characters are classic examples of obsessive characters. Rudnev opines that the quantitative increase in obsessive personality types and their qualitative influence on the increase in society's well-being (in particular, the tangible 'victory' of the West within the technological sphere) are

---

13 Sh. Adibaeva, "Arkhetip ottsa v romane V. Pelevina *Omon Ra*", *Literaturnaia kritika: vchera, segodnia, zavtra*, Almaty, 2003, 30.

14 A. Balod, *Pelevin: dialektika i kritika*. Online at: http://lito.ru (15.03.2008).

natural consequences of universal biological processes. According to the hypothesis formulated by Ivanov in *Odd and Even Numbers: The Asymmetry of the Brain and Systems of Symbols*, there has been a steady increase in the left hemisphere of the human brain in recent times, an increase in the specific gravity of functions it performs and, consequently, an increase in the rate at which the rational element is coming to dominate culture. This, in turn, has accelerated the movement from complex figurative ideas towards discrete scientific ideas.[15] This purely biological fact may explains why postmodern poetics tend to combine artistic aspects with analytical, self-reflective ones.

All of Pelevin's characters exhibit the same set of symptoms, manifested in an obsessive vocabulary and delayed character revelation; Pelevin also delays the novel's plot development. This testifies to how extraordinarily widespread this compulsive symptom is: "Stepa gradually stopped considering himself abnormal" (18). Thrust into the post-industrial world, this Russian character's life is transformed into a "painstaking sifting through of options" (134), although his demands on reality remain fundamentally the same, as they are invariable. Mikhailov seeks peace and self-affirmation: "Breezes and engaging in communicating through rattle sounds always brought him calm and, most importantly, somehow filled him with the consciousness of his own rightness" (156). He wants free will but cannot obtain it, as he is cut from the same cloth as all other human beings, he shares their "Gestalt", their psychological axis, "what makes us what we are, regardless of volition and desire. It's sort of like there is something in the background imperceptibly hypnotising you" (208).

"Capital wants very little from us in exchange for all its gifts to humanity: it wants us to agree to forget ourselves and play simple, clear roles in the great theatre of life. [...] The meaning of life consists only in self-expression. But the only kind of selfhood that business can have is capital", asserts Zhora Srakandaev, an anankastic character with oral-anal symbolism inherent in both his first name and his surname (251–252). He is the perfect economic twin of Mikhailov, repeating the sinusoid of Mikhailov's obsessive character: "The figures indicate that in Srakandaev, just like in Stepa himself, a battle was being waged between good and evil and light and darkness, except that these eternal elements were flowing through someone else's heart along unknown courses" (190).

However, it is logical that the most intensely obsessive type, the obsessive leader of Pelevin's text, is not a Russian character but the English woman Mius, Mikhailov's beloved and his main assistant in the business world. She has no match in her stubbornness and perseverance in achieving her goals. Mikhailov is notably inferior to her with regard to competitiveness. If "Stepa didn't analyse

---

15   V.V. Ivanov, *Chet i nechet: Asimmetriia mozga i znakovykh sistem*, Moscow, 1978, 68.

his life but lived it" (21), then Mius is a cold and collected professional analyst, a philologist from London who is researching the folklore of Russian cities for pragmatic reasons, given that such study constitutes "the best business school". While Mikhailov loves, Mius plays at love; when Mikhailov is crying, Mius is counting his money. Mius's internal structure, the "secret book-keeping of her soul" (p. 77), functions like clockwork, never failing. She is able not only to calculate her own life precisely to a fraction of a percentage, but also to calculate the functioning of her partner's conscious and unconscious: "Mius understood well what was needed from a business person in Russia – to be a bit of a thief, a bit of a lawyer and a bit streetwise" (83).

It is Mius who is the first person to explain to Mikhailov clearly what is happening both in contemporary Russia and in him: "An infantile fool – that's who you are. Apart from those rare moments when I help you play at Pikacha, you're just a savage and a nonentity, do you understand?" (81). Mius gives Mikhailov lectures, controls his desires and forces him to play the roles she needs him to play: "'How many times do I need to tell you?' she said, 'all this Far Eastern crap doesn't work in the Occident! It's just an attempt to escape the problems of life...'" (p. 103). This is how Mius tries to turn Mikhailov off Zen, Buddhist philosophy and culture, to which Mikhailov, as a Eurasian, is especially attached because of the region's inherent semi-self-reflectiveness and semi-mysticism. As O. Shatalova contends in her article 'The Alchemical Marriage or "Eastern Art is a Terrorist Act"', "The East is the West's Other, it is a mystery that the West fears".[16]

Mius is no less mentally synthetic than the Eurasian Mikhailov, but the "cocktail of her features" is totally lacking the mystical element present in Mikhailov's; as a result, her multi-sidedness constitutes a vector of strength concentrated in a single point. The abstract component determining people's Russianness is present in Mius's genetics, which allows her to be a kind of internal intelligence officer in the world of Mikhailov's unconscious ("a psychologist is a spy", as Bakhtin recognised) while remaining free from the influence of "ancient Russian chaos", a Russian ethnic feature: "Despite speaking outstanding Russian (passed on to her by her émigré grandmother), Mius didn't consider herself Russian" (35).

Does this mean that it is the more obsessive person who emerges victorious? This idea is one of the hidden components driving the plot. Essentially, the novel is a description of the competition between the national unconscious, continental mentalities and physiological resources of the West and

---

16   O. Shatalova, "Alkhimicheskii brak po raschetu ili 'Iskusstvo vostoka – eto terakt'", Tamir (Almaty), 2004, 3 (13), 87.

Russia (considered to be a part of Eurasia): "You Russians are always going on about the West's lack of a spiritual side, about its unbridled materialism, and so on. But that's just because of the primitive poverty of your internal life" (80). According to the Kazakh philosopher Auezkhan Kodar, Russian philosophy, with the exception of a few of its representatives, is a variety of Eastern philosophy. And Eastern philosophy does not reorganise the world, it interacts with reality in a fundamentally different manner – it integrates itself into it.[17]

In psycho-physiological semiotics, for example, a particularly topical subject is the examination of the concept of genetic structures of the cerebrum as bases for a person's "supermemory", a long-term memory that has features peculiar to the individual's ethnicity. This conception takes account of essential differences in Europeans' and Easterners' ways of thinking: they differ fundamentally in the features of their memory, the structure of their dialogue and their perception. European thinking is convergent, it tends towards discrete logic. The European's thinking process is a stream of broken thoughts striving towards maximum specificity and unambiguity. This type of thinking is embodied in words that have a particularly concrete sense (for example, 'white', 'grey', 'unambiguous'), and is typical of a dominant left hemisphere. Eastern thinking is divergent: it is characterised by a consciousness and thoughts that diverge and are at variance with each other, and that therefore do not lend themselves to logical expression. Easterners' thinking is essentially continuous and metaphorical, colourful and ambiguous. The language of the Easterner is bright and poetic. Such figurative thinking is characteristic of a dominant right hemisphere.[18] That is why Mikhailov, a Eurasian possessing a mixed type of thinking, seems at first glance to be an inferior businessperson to the 'pure' European Mius.

In Pelevin's formulation, the condition for the 'victory' of the Western personality type over the Eurasian is also to be found in the former's psychological health, which has been conditioned by a correctly organised social way of life. As Mius says, "Our society strives to provide the consumer not only with cheap petrol but also with moral satisfaction from protesting against the way that petrol is obtained. We have heated debates on TV where various well-known Pharisees are unmasked, and this happens every time there's a war on. But everyone lives calmly side-by-side. But you guys, on the other hand, are always trying to get at each other's throats. And at the same time there are no TV

---

17 A. Kodar, *Interv'iu s samim soboi*, Tamyr (Almaty), 2004, 3 (13), 4.

18 L. Khromov, "Iskusstvo reklamy glazami psikhofiziologa", in L. Khromov, *Reklamnaia deiatel'nost': iskusstvo, teoriia, praktika*, Petrozavodsk, 1994.

debates, no protests, just trivia. Because your society's underdeveloped, understand?" (79–80).

Sysoeva observes in her article 'The Phraseology of Fear in Ukrainian, Russian and English' that the English have significantly fewer linguistic (and consequently also mental, according to Lacan) ways of conveying fear and anger than the Slavonic nations:

> Taking into consideration historical factors and the particular development of the languages among the nations by which they are spoken, there are significant differences in the frequency of use of the various thematic groups of the phraseological microsystem of "a person's emotions" in Ukrainian, Russian and English. The thematic groups conveying fear (100/90 units), alarm (59) and suffering (47) predominate in Ukrainian and Russian, while joy (64), pleasure (51) and amazement (38) predominate in English.[19]

As Russians, Zhora Srakandaev and Stepa Mikhailov lack a legal social outlet for their obsessions. Consequently, the obsessions exceed the characters' psychological breaking point and take on unhealthy, maniacal forms: they become "wicked". For example, a rumour circulates that Srakandaev "ordered" the murder of several people during the turbulent 1990s. Also, the particularly infantile Mikhailov kills an incalculable number of flies, attaching to this action a special ritual meaning:

> In order to ensure that their souls got to the correct address, every time he achieved a successful hit Stepa would repeatedly whisper a rhyme that had somehow composed itself in his head unbeknown to him: "Sem′ osin i sosen sem′, sem′ semerok nasovsem" [Seven asps and seven pines, seven sevens forever]. It wasn't exactly clear how many flies that calculation was telling you to send off towards the figure seven – was it seven times seven or seventy-seven? Stepa decided to opt for the second possibility and was already making his way up to the magic number when suddenly the hand of fate rendered the project redundant. (10)

---

19   M. Sysoeva, "Osobennosti funktionirovaniia frazeologizmov, oboznachaiushchikh emotsiiu strakha, v ukrainskom, russkom i angliiskom iazykakh", *Kognitivnye stili kommunikatsii. Teorii i prikladnye modeli. Doklady mezhdunarodnoi konferentsii. 20–25 sentiabria 2004*, 126.

Rudnev asserts that a tendency towards ritualisation (a form of rhythmicity) is a feature of the so-called 'Petersburg text' in Russian literature, the quintessential text of this type being Belyi's *Petersburg*. He also singles out as possessing these literary symptoms such therapeutic 'Petersburg texts' beloved by the Russian readership as those by Gogol', Dostoeskii and the Anglophile Nabokov during his Petersburg period; all these works are referred to in some way in *Numbers*. The origins of Petersburg's culture, especially its architecture, can be found German culture, which is quintessentially European. And Rudnev believes that the strict geometry, extreme regularity and ordered nature of the city's style also have an important influence on the ideological reserves of the 'Petersburg text'.

Like Nabokov, Mikhailov is an Anglophile, possessing the anankastic complex that is characteristic of West European culture. He is in love with the "economic" English language with its wealth of idioms and clichés, features that constitute the language's own particular forms of "therapeutic" repetition. And Mikhailov is absolutely crazy about things German. One reads in this fixation and in the endless returns to the German theme the Russians' global, collective trauma – an unconscious, instinctual national "supermemory" of one of the decisive moments in the Second World War, the gruelling Battle of Kursk of 1943 that was almost lost to the Germans and that saw the destruction of an enormous number of T-34 tanks.

Almost every day Mikhailov acts out this national trauma in the plot of his own life through placing the numbers 34 and 43 in opposition to each other. By endlessly repeating this unpleasant event, Mikhailov exhibits what Freud called the "death drive" and what postmodernists term the "death of the individual", as they believe that it simultaneously relieves one of both the burden of responsibility and the fear of death. One can also include within the system of repetitions specially engineered by Mikhailov his driving a German model of car that is slightly second-hand, a Mercedes *Gelandewagen* that has "replaced Gogol's flying troika". Moreover, he plans the decisive battle with Srakandaev, his financial enemy, in 'German' Petersburg. The city influences Pelevin's characters in a manner that is somewhat traditional in Russian literature, awakening in the unconscious of each of them a dark, forbidden, criminal side: "He had his usual Petersburg dreams – at first the clinging darkness that contained nothing, and then the cold fog that grew ever thicker and thicker" (198). It is at this point in the novel that the protagonist enters into the manic phase of his obsession and plans Srakandaev's murder.

The principal "mistake inherent in Russian fate" consists in the Eurasian's transitional character, which is not the classical compulsive personality type but a mixed one that fluctuates between hysteria and neurosis. According to

Pelevin, the percentage of hysteria in the Russian character (an indicator of how unbalanced and internally disordered a person is) determines the degree of his 'weakness'. For example, Srakandaev is closer to the hysterical personality type. Consequently, he is weaker than Mikhailov and is killed by him. Such are the "Dialectics of the Transitional Period".

Zhora Srakandaev	Stepa Mikhailov
"Srakandaev was reputed to be a patron of the fine arts and counted a number of Moscow bohemians among his friends". "Srakandaev collected the paintings of contemporary artists".	"Stepa despised bohemians: he thought that the main reason they existed was to relieve lawyers of their leisure time". "Stepa considered all of them without exception spiritual scam artists – and scam artists of an evil spirit, at that".
"Srakandaev spent his nights in elite night clubs".	"It was impossible to lure Stepa there".
"Srakandaev drove an Aston Martin – a 'Vanquish 12', just like James Bond. Only Bond didn't have a flashing light – but Srakandaev did".	"Stepa preferred a solidly patriotic 'Rusich V 700', which was based on the classic Gelandewagen. He had one of the first models from Stuttgart's Brabus Delivery Office for Russian Clients, and he was terribly proud of it, even though it wasn't new when he bought it".
"Srakandaev didn't like being driven: he liked driving himself".	"Stepa couldn't stand driving and got a chauffeur to do it for him".
"Srakandaev's office was located in a rather strange building – a half-ruined church [...]. The architect had restored it in a rather unusual manner such that, once completed, the building didn't look like a temple that had been restored, but like a strange hybrid, a modern construction built on ruins barely held up by steel braces".	"Stepa was envious: his own office, which was based in a highly respectably mansion, looked vulgar compared to this avant-garde chic".

If one follows Lotman's approach to the experience of art as a therapeutic method,[20] then Srakandaev appears to be "sicker" than Mikhailov. In the

---

20 Iu.M. Lotman, "Tekst v protsesse dvizheniia: avtor – auditoriia, zamysel – tekst", in Lotman, *Semiosfera*, St Petersburg, 2000, 208.

modern world it is the person who is more calculating and less impulsive who "wins". Speaking metaphorically and using Pelevin's examples, it is not the person who has the car with the hysterical flashing lights who survives, but the one who has the most robust and safest German mode of transport in the world. Indeed, according to Kristeva, the fears that overwhelm a person are connected in the first instance with the weakness of his symbolic system and the weak functioning of prohibition in his personality structure.[21]

In this sense, Mikhailov is far more vulnerable (hysterical and erratic) than Mius, who is able cold-bloodedly to feed off his love for her. The protagonist of *Numbers* "is capable of shedding a tear": "Stepa involuntarily emitted a physiological sound – something between a hiccup and a sob" (259). He is so sentimental that a flood of emotions can compel him to marry:

> In the evening they went to the Scandinavia restaurant for dinner. Mius usually dressed very simply but on this occasion she was wearing a striking dress that looked like a sleeveless raincoat. It really suited her. But over dinner Stepa noticed that her face had small wrinkles that he hadn't seen before. And the antennae on her head no longer seemed as elastic and long as before. It was strange, but these wrinkles filled his heart with such tenderness that he felt tears in his eyes. In order to prevent Mius from seeing them, he picked up an unfinished cigarette and went over to the balcony [...] *Oh...if everything works out all right...*Thinking about the task ahead, Stepa felt an overwhelming wave of fear. *If I can pull it all off, I'll marry her. I swear.*[22]

The ideal obsessive character, Mius, on the other hand, does not stray from the predetermined behaviour pattern of Pokemon 52 even once: "Pokemon Meowth, number 52. A nice little cat, that one. You'll laugh, but she looks like Mius Julianovna. The same arrows sticking up from her haircut – or is it from her fur? I'm not sure what to call it. She adores little round things. Wanders around the street at night picking up things people have dropped. If Meowth finds something round she can't stop playing with it right up until she falls asleep. She especially likes coins, which she collects as if they were treasure" (244). This is why the English woman manages to "sabotage Stepa's bank", robbing the Russian who loves her (acting on the principle that any kind of emotion weakens you, and love disarms you) by calculating with absolute precision the route by which to transfer all his "coins" to her own offshore account. The

---

21   Kristeva, *Sily uzhasa*.
22   Pelevin, pp. 155–156.

plot pattern pertaining to the protagonist's psychoanalytically predetermined defeat is played out in the novel through a metaphorical refrain, formulated this time in the succinct form of the advertising slogan "While Alpha is trying to outdo Beta and Beta is trying to outdo Alpha, Gamma-Bank is withdrawing your Delta" (120).

In *The Semantics of Numbers and Culture Type*, Lotman defines a similar model of the world (a closed, mythologically loop-backed model of the world – a world within a world) as a paradigmatic, actualising model of isomorphisms. The scholar summarises thus:

> It is namely a paradigmatic culture structure that possesses favourable conditions for the transformation of a number from an element of culture into its universal symbol. The isomorphism of the levels brings about a situation whereby the whole range of qualities takes on the character of quantitative degrees of one quality. This hierarchical and paradigmatic construction forms the basis for the reduction of elements of one level to a certain elementary set, and of other levels to their quantitative variation. Consequently, a number constitutes the most natural expression for the relationship of any concept to a corresponding semantic element.[23]

But in what do the particularities and pathos of the Eurasian character consist? Perhaps in the battle with the West, as Shatalova writes? "With an audacious anomaly that took it upon itself to consider itself the norm? The East is striving to become the mystical barrier to the West's expansion".[24] Mikhailov loses the financial fight because he does not follow the path that would help him become a victor in the capitalist game. He tries to bring order to a world that is collapsing right in front of his eyes, to restore that world and its integrity not through rigorous calculation and West European logic, but through the Eastern approach – through harnessing the healing power of myth. On the one hand, the hero believes that Christianity, the official confession of the Slavs, is a religion from which life has evaporated: "After reading the Bible as a child, an image formed in his mind of a cruel, vengeful tyrant for whom there is nothing nicer than the smell of burnt meat. Naturally, his distrust spread to all those who declared their affinity with this parochial goblin".[25] On the other hand, as a Eurasian, Mikhailov is physiologically incapable of becoming a vulgar atheist who recognises only the power of money. Just like a primitive person, the

---

23   Iu.M. Lotman, *Semantika chisla i tip kul'tury*, 432.
24   O. Shatalova, "Alkhimicheskii brak po raschetu ili 'Iskusstvo vostoka – eto terakt'", 88.
25   Pelevin, 29–30.

Eurasian repeats the Creation, creating his own person mythology and inventing his own individual god:

> Stepa felt the need to consult a kind of spiritual authority, a mediator between the chaos of life and the eternal order of the heavens. [...] He understood that the number 34 was a half-open door through which he could talk to the same force that was available to other people in an endless variety of forms, including ones that scared him with their ugliness. But within the religious marketplace there wasn't a single product that could satisfy his yearning for the miraculous better than associating with numbers.[26]

Mikhailov, a contemporary and relatively pragmatic Eurasian anankastic character, finds a more rational form of contact with his god. He rationalises and modernises mysterious, half-forgotten rituals, reviving technologies that had been used in ancient times to attain prosperity:

> Stepa knew that people used to sacrifice bulls to ancient gods by burning them on campfires. For several weeks he had been seriously considering setting fire to one of the cowsheds in the state farms near their country cottage. [...] Stepa changed his mind at the last minute. It was too big a project after all. But the petrol didn't go to waste. Stepa pilfered seven tins of canned beef from the house.[27]

Pelevin's hero introduces a personal meditative god, a unique, magical combination of figures – 34. The embodiment of his personal interests, this number gives him a sense of his own uniqueness, an essential quality for a person who wishes to assert himself and achieve superiority over others. It also provides him with more reliable protection against the actual evil that is directed at him personally, as a Eurasian. As Rudnev contends: "Since the Creation is regularly repeated in ritual, a temporal cyclisation takes place in the ritual-mythological consciousness, a cessation of time oriented towards the battle with the chaotic, entropic, profane time of total break-up – the break-up and disintegration of the body of primal man, whose stability and integrity ritual is called upon to support".[28] This is how the postmodern neurotic, and particularly Pelevin's Eurasian character, is able to fight both his own discretisation and the dispersive

---

26 Pelevin, 29–30.
27 Pelevin, 9.
28 V. Rudnev, *Obsessivnyi diskurs*, 258.

nature of the world around him. This, in turn, allows him to preserve what remains of his psychological health, since neurosis protects people from complete madness.

Freud identified this essential function of the obsessive character as indispensable in creating a personal "caricature of religion": "Like the majority of well-off Russians, Stepa was a shaman with eclectic interests".[29] Whether it is sorcery, northern shamanistic ritual, or Tibetan rituals, his individual religion essentially consists in seeking the ideal "attachment manoeuvre", the optimum means by which to merge with his favourite number and impersonate it in complicated real-life situations. This amounts to self-sacralisation, which is also a means of self-preservation and psychological self-defense. As Batai writes in his *Vnutrennii opyt* (*Inner Experience*), if the aim of mystical experience is to acquire some kind of knowledge, particularly knowledge of God, then after losing any sense of theological purpose the human being himself became the sole goal of and authority on inner experience.[30]

Through the psychological gates opened by religion, mystical experience enters the life of the modern anankastic mystic character. The trajectory of his fate depends not only on the "calculations of his mind" and the confused instruction of his reasoning, but also on his own particular irrational rules:

> the most real magic, which stronger than all the intellect's constructions [...] The era was so fundamentally absurd, and the economy and business were so dependent on God knows what, that any person making decisions on the basis of sober analysis was like a fool trying to skate during a storm.[31]

According to Prigozhin's conception of the structure of reality, the time needed for bifurcational clots and turning points in history to develop is impossible to predict. Yet one wants to look into the future. This is where the need for additional interpretations, the search for alternative versions to explain life, comes from.

Mikhailov perceives his enemies as acquiring a mystical aura:

> In the word "Srakandaev" Stepa clearly heard the word "sorok" (forty) in a slightly distorted form, and at the end of the word – as if to allay any remaining doubt – there stood the third letter of the Cyrillic alphabet

---

29 Pelevin, 30.
30 Zh. Batai, *Vnutrennii opyt*, St Petersburg, 1997, 111.
31 Pelevin, 28.

again. This triple evil was obvious, brazen, fat, self-satisfied, certain of its impunity – and did not even consider hiding itself. Stepa didn't need his enemy's corpse – he needed victory over the shadowy number 43.[32]

His choice of his beloved is associated with fateful signs. This involvement of forces "from beyond" reinforces the protagonist's positions: they inform him of an additional "mystical fearlessness".[33] However, primitive prayers, conspiracies and incantations (which are all kinds of obsessive 'calculations') help to overcome the collective neurosis. One might say that Pelevin uses his character as an example so as not to forget to teach his reader practical existentialism: "After all, now furnishing one's flat and furnishing one's soul are the same thing – they help with everything".[34]

This combination of mysticism and super-rationalism gives one the illusion that one rules the world and facilitates what Freud termed "the omnipotence of thought": "Stepa decided that the number seven in the singular possessed insufficient strength, and he set about covering page after page with tiny blue corners, feeling like a conqueror marshalling an army to conquer the world".[35] The protagonist believes that serving the god of numbers can solve all his problems. It turns out that the will-power, decisiveness, fearlessness, self-confidence and self-possession that he seeks do not originate as personal qualities: they are supplements to a number. Fortunately, the number is able to endow him with these qualities. A number offering patronage to a character "looks after" all his plans right up until he puts them into action. Moreover, the number selects an anthropomorphic vessel from which it will be convenient to rule the world. The number comes both to constitute and to drive the character's inner world, his "soul": "Once his doubts had gone, Stepa's life became simpler. The number 34 dictated to him all the steps he needed to undertake with iron necessity. [...] All his decisions were governed by two numbers, 34 and 43: the first one contained green, the second red".[36]

If Pelevin's previous novel, *Generation "П"*, insightfully depicts human beings as driven by their passion for money, then in *Numbers* the author "gets even deeper inside his characters' heads", revealing that is the person's fears that drive him, and that amassing money is only their psychological manifestation. Pelevin's hero almost guesses this, but then casts aside his own discovery

---

[32] Pelevin, 124.
[33] Pelevin, 158.
[34] Pelevin, 236.
[35] Pelevin, 9.
[36] Pelevin, 19, 27.

in a cowardly manner, not wishing to reflect on and therefore answer for his actions:

> Could it be that he was unconsciously arranging these misfortunes himself? The possibility did occur to him. Everything could be put down to autosuggestion. Only this explanation didn't explain anything, actually. Human existence, an acquaintance of Stepan's had told him, is nothing other than a séance of self-hypnosis in which the person is brought out of the trance by force. The word "autosuggestion" sounded scientific, but Stepa didn't study his life – he lived it. Whatever others might call it, the joy that filled his soul when fate sent him a 3 and a 4 in the required order was completely real for him. But then he had to pay with a heartrending melancholy that was just as real when the order of the figures was reversed.[37]

The author considers that this numerical picture of reality covering up a feeling of fear is present in everyone's conscious: it is the universal principle governing the structure of the human conscious and unconscious. In Rudnev's formulation, one out of every two contemporary people is an obsessive neurotic; he just does not know about it:

> As he observed his comrades at school, he began to notice that many of them attached significance to numbers, just like he did. But they didn't take responsibility for which numbers governed their lives, and they resembled a flock of sheep.[38]

It is logical to suppose that this psychological law applies to both the biographical and the implied author. Of course, Pelevin does not make any direct statements about his obsessions. On the other hand, the scholars Maria Koshel' and Il'ia Kukulin believe that *Numbers* is a "summarising text, ending with a literary apology and a personal aesthetic manifesto that explains why the novel was written. [...] It is a novel about how literary creativity gives order to Chaos".[39] The presence in the novel of Pelevin's signature question – a question that roams from text to text urging the reader to interpret fate as something imposed

---

37   Pelevin, 21.
38   Pelevin, 18.
39   M. Koshel' and I. Kukulin, "Viktor Pelevin. Dialektika Perekhodnogo Perioda iz Niotkuda v Nikuda: Izbrannye proizvedeniia", in *Novoe literaturnoe obozrenie*, 64 (2003).

from without and which therefore frees a person from any responsibility for his own life – completely gives away the identity of the author:

> Only one thing was unclear: who was it who gave the orders to the numbers themselves? [...] There was another question associated with the first, and this question often troubled his soul: if the world is ruled by numbers, who rules the numbers?[40]

Like the typical mystical American horror film (and Americans are also terrible pedants; theirs is a typical compulsive culture), where victory over supernatural forces always turns out to be false and is in principle impossible, Pelevin's novel *Numbers* ends with a transition to a new round of horrors and moves on to a new combination of figures that defend against them: "Nought point six or nought point nine? Back to school again, a whole *jihad* against a new..."[41] Material reality does not exhaust the picture of the world in Pelevin's work; indeed, it turns out to be sham and illusory. Pelevin casts great doubt on the idea that the European mentality, which has taken over most of the material world, will achieve victory over the Eurasians. In this way, the author's search for answers for his eternal questions regarding Eastern philosophy – which attests to the multifaceted nature of reality – is the only promising one:

> "I get it", Mius said. "This means that in the West bulls and pigs are born. And what about in Russia, who do they give birth to there?"
> "In Russia?" Stepa strained his memory. [...] "In Russia they give birth to defeated gods".[42]

Translated by Christopher Tooke

Bibliography

Adibaeva, Sh. 2003. "Arkhetip ottsa v romane V. Pelevina *Omon Ra*", in *Literaturnaia kritika: vchera, segodnia, zavtra*. Almaty: Iskander. 27–31.
Balod, A. *Pelevin: dialektika i kritika*. Online at: http://lito.ru 15.03.2008.
Batai, Zh. 1997. *Vnutrennii opyt* (tr. A. Fokin). St Petersburg: Aksioma; Mifril.

---

40 Pelevin, 147.
41 Pelevin, 264.
42 Pelevin, 109.

Burbo, L. 2001. *Emotsii, chuvstva i proshcheniie* [Emotions, Feelings and Forgiveness], tr. by S. Melishkevich. Kiev, Sofiia and Moscow: Gelios.

Freud, Z. [Sigmund Freud]. 1998. *Totem i tabu* [Totem and Taboo]. Moscow, Respublika.

Ivanov, V.V. 1978. *Chet i nechet: Asimmetriia mozga i znakovykh sistem*, Moscow: Sovetskoe radio.

Khromov, L. 1994. "Iskusstvo reklamy glazami psikhofiziologa", in L. Khromov, *Reklamnaia deiatel'nost': iskusstvo, teoriia, praktika*, Petrozavodsk: Irias. 58–64.

Kodar A. 2004. *Interv'iu s samim soboi*, Tamyr (Almaty), 3 (13), 4. 3–9.

Koshel M. and I. Kukulin. 2003. "Viktor Pelevin. Dialektika Perekhodnogo Perioda iz Niotkuda v Nikuda: Izbrannye proizvedeniia", in *Novoe literaturnoe obozrenie*, 64. 80–89.

Kristeva, Iu. [Julia Kristeva]. 2003. *Sily uzhasa: Esse ob otvrashchenii* [= *Powers of Horror: An Essay on Abjection*] (tr. A. Kostikova), Khar'kov and St Petersburg: Aletheia.

Laplansh, Zh. 1996. *Slovar' po psikhoanalizu*, Moscow: Vysshaia shkola.

Latynina, A. 2004. "Potom opiat' teper'". Online at: http://pelevin.nov.ru.

Lotman, Iu.M. 2000a. "Semantika chisla i tip kul'tury", in Lotman, *Semiosfera*, St Petersburg: Yazyki russkoi kul'tury. 430–434.

Lotman, Iu.M. 2000b. "Tekst v protsesse dvizheniia: avtor – auditoriia, zamysel – tekst", in Lotman, *Semiosfera*, St Petersburg: Yazyki russkoi kul'tury. 150–390

Milevich, I. 2004. "Kommunikativnyi signal trevogi: kognitivno-diskursnyi analiz mass-media", *Kognitivnye stili kommunikatsii. Teorii i prikladnye modeli. Doklady mezhdunarodnoi konferentsii. 20–25 sentiabria 2004*, Simferopol: Partent. 120–124.

Pelevin, V. 2003. *Dialektika Perekhodnogo perioda iz Niotkuda v Nikuda: Izbrannye proizvedeniia*. Moscow: Izd-vo Eksmo.

Rudnev, V. 2001. *Metafizika futbola*, Moscow: Agraf, 228–65.

Shatalova, O. 2004. "Alkhimicheskii brak po raschetu ili 'Iskusstvo vostoka – eto terakt'", Tamir: Almaty. 3 (13), 87. 83–89

Sysoeva, M. 2004. "Osobennosti funktionirovaniia frazeologizmov, oboznachaiushchikh emotsiiu strakha, v ukrainskom, russkom i angliiskom iazykakh", in *Kognitivnye stili kommunikatsii. Teorii i prikladnye modeli. Doklady mezhdunarodnoi konferentsii. 20–25 sentiabria 2004*, 124–127.

Toporov, V. 1980. "O chislovykh modeliakh v arkhaicheskikh tekstakh", in *Struktura teksta*. Moscow: Nauk, 3–58.

Zapadnoe literaturovedenie XX veka: Entsiklopediia, 2004. INION RAN. ed. A. Kurganova. Moscow: Intrada.

CHAPTER 22

"Questions to Which Reason Has No Answer": Iurii Mamleev's Irrationalism in European Context

Oliver Ready

Iurii Mamleev (1931–2015) has haunted Russian intellectual life for more than half a century: as the host of a now legendary circle of artists and intellectuals that met at his flat on Iuzhinskii Lane in 1960s Moscow, drawn there by his stories of madmen, cannibals and vampires; as a mystic with a specialist interest in Indian thought; as a prominent representative, in America and Paris, of the literary emigration of the 'third wave' in the 1970s and 80s; and, following his return to Moscow, as a magnet of post-Soviet culture. The otherworldly and perverse reality conjured by his fiction has left a permanent mark on Russian literature, albeit one that remains to be adequately evaluated by scholars.[1] The notion of a Mamleev school is sometimes invoked by critics,[2] whether to describe Mamleev's influence in *samizdat* culture or, more recently, among young writers participating in the Club of Metaphysical Realism with which he was prominently associated. Implying a genealogical link to the "fantastical realism" of Dostoevskii, metaphysical realism appears to have been Mamleev's preferred definition for the inimitable genre of his fiction.[3]

---

1 Interesting critical writing on Mamleev exists mainly in fragmentary form, and includes: Aleksandr Gol'dshtein, *Rasstavanie s Nartsissom: Opyty pominal'noi ritoriki*, Moscow, 1997, 277–301; Ulrich Schmid, 'Flowers of Evil: The Poetics of Monstrosity in Contemporary Russian Literature (Erofeev, Mamleev, Sokolov, Sorokin)', *Russian Literature*, 48 (2000), 205–22 (208–213); Eugene Gorny, 'The Negative World of Yuri Mamleev', online at <http://www.zhurnal.ru/staff/gorny/english/mamleev.htm> (consulted 26.11.2013); Tat'iana Goricheva, 'Krugi ada', *Kontinent*, 36 (1983), 382–385, and 'Pronzennye pustotoi', *Sintaksis*, 20 (1987), 196–199; Natal'ia Mazur, 'Kobob', *Literaturnoe Obozrenie*, 7 (1992), 76–80; I.P. Smirnov, 'Evoliutsiia chudovishchnosti (Mamleev i drugie)', *Novoe Literaturnoe Obozrenie*, 3 (1993), 303–7; and Mikhail Ryklin's analysis of the visual and symbolic aspects of Mamleev's world as a response to Stalinist terror, 'Tela terrora (tezisy k logike nasiliia)', in *Bakhtinskii sbornik*, eds D. Kuiundzhich and V.L. Makhlin, Moscow, 1990, 1, 60–76 (71–76).
2 See, for example, Iurii Mal'tsev, *Vol'naia russkaia literatura, 1955–1975*, Frankfurt, 1976, 116–20 (116).
3 See, for example, Mamleev, *Rossiia vechnaia*, Moscow, 2002, 283, and the author's preface to Mamleev, *Vechnyi dom: povest' i rasskazy*, Moscow, 1991, 3. Mamleev has evidently been

Mamleev's artistic originality (recognised by the award of the Andrei Bely Prize in 1991) is closely tied to the disturbing nature of his subject-matter. Goodness, compassion and love directed beyond the self – all traditional concerns of the Russian literary tradition – are virtually absent from his stories and novels. Instead, we find a grotesque world of death-fixated, solipsistic characters, who engage in all manner of atrocities in attempts to satisfy their morbid desires and curiosity. In the hands of Vladimir Sorokin, whom Mamleev undoubtedly influenced, the effect of similar catalogues of horrors is (to this reader at least) mechanical and literary: mere words on a page, as Sorokin has himself claimed on numerous occasions. By contrast, Mamleev's most accomplished work fully succeeds in implicating and affecting the reader. It also has a clear purpose, though one that is neither sentimental nor moral. Heaping up images of grotesquerie and cruelty, Mamleev paradoxically forces the reader to look beyond the human, beyond suffering and vicissitude, towards the mystical 'unknown' (*nevedomoe, neizvestnoe*). The intention, it seems, is to open a crack in the reader's perception of reality. As the critics Petr Vail' and Aleksandr Genis have noted, Mamleev's monotonous yet frequently compelling fiction is an "insistent attempt to convince us of the reality of the unreal".[4]

A concise illustration of this approach is provided by Mamleev's story 'The Magic Carpet', in which a mother abuses her three-year-old child for damaging her new rug (to the extent that the boy's hands need to be amputated) and then hangs herself. The metaphysical perspective is supplied by a feeble-minded relative, Maria, at the story's end:

> "There is nothing terrifying about this at all, nothing at all," she kept saying.
>
> But in her eyes some other, higher terror was reflected, a terror which, nevertheless, bore no relation at all either to this world or to what was happening. But for mortal beings, this dark, this terror, was perhaps light. And, separating itself from the bottomless horror in her eyes, this light cleansed everything around it.[5]

---

inspired by what he sees as as one of Dostoevskii's "revelations": that "the truth in Russia is fantastic by nature". *Rossiia vechnaia*, 38.

4 Petr Vail' and Aleksandr Genis, *Sovremennaia russkaia proza*, Ann Arbor, 1982, 167.

5 'Kover-samolet', in Mamleev, *Izbrannoe*, Moscow, 1993, 510–514 (514). Subsequent page references to this edition will be given in the main text. All translations are mine. Most of Mamleev's publications may also be read on-line as part of the Russian Virtual Library: <http://www.rvb.ru/mamleev> (consulted 26.11.2013).

This rather schematic passage barely communicates the unnerving effect of reading Mamleev, but it does offer a glimpse of the paradoxical nature of his metaphysics, in which the material, phenomenal world is perceived as absurd and unreal in comparison with the noumenal reality that is accessible, as we read in another story, "on the other side not of life, but of human consciousness" (468).

The passage cited also indicates the absolute centrality of the irrational in Mamleev's fiction, where it is those deprived of reason and ordinary "human consciousness" who act as vehicles for the author's apprehension of ultimate reality. Though in his essays and interviews Mamleev writes and speaks in a notably logical and lucid manner (however outlandish his premises), his stories and novels are densely populated with unhinged or schizophrenic characters whose behaviour and speech appears to mirror an underlying, authorial vision of metaphysical reality as illogical and disharmonic. This vision is set out most fully in Mamleev's main mystical tract, *The Fate of Being* (*Sud'ba bytiia*), which was written mainly before emigration, but published only in 1993. It includes extravagant hypotheses, presented as doctrines, about the "Trans-Abyss" which lies beyond God, and other abstractions. The paradoxical nature of this vision has been aptly summarised by Ulrich Schmid: "The different layers of Mamleev's cosmological model are like pieces of a puzzle which do not fit together. Absurdities occur on every level: Human beings exist, but they are not real [...] Mankind strives towards a God, who at the same time seeks his own destruction".[6]

For Mamleev, it seems, the real is not rational (as Hegel said) but thoroughly irrational, and the task of his crazy and monstrous characters is to "ask themselves questions to which reason has no answer".[7] In his fiction, the madman or fool (*bezumets*) thus becomes the only link between the illusory, mundane world and metaphysical reality. He or she is the person "possessed by invisible reality".[8] The fool's cousin, undoubtedly, is the figure of the writer himself, or "the man of Art", about whom Mamleev had the following to say in his essay 'Between Madness and Magic' (1987):

> The sphere of people of art is the divine sphere of creativity (in which, it seems, demons are helpless); their tool of cognition is not the *ratsio* ['ratio'] but intellectual intuition (similar to the "reason of angels", reason

---

6 Schmid, 'Flowers of Evil', 211.
7 Mamleev, *Rossiia vechnaia*, 290.
8 Iu. Mamleev, 'Mezhdu bezumiem i magiei', *Beseda*, 6 (1987), 178–184 (179).

which attains reality directly, "sees it", instead of coming to it by means of analysis, experience, etc.).[9]

Mamleev's fiction assumes a correspondingly hostile and satirical attitude towards the rationalism "of analysis, experience, etc.": reason, his stories suggest, does not offer a privileged path to an understanding of the truth and of ultimate reality; on the contrary, it impedes it. As such, Mamleev's irrationalism, with its emphasis on intuition, continues a major strand in Russian literature and thought that was further galvanised in the 1960s and early 1970s when Mamleev wrote much of his most important work. These years witnessed a powerful reaction in unofficial culture to the Soviet cult of reason and science, to Scientific Atheism (which by the 1960s had become a university course in its own right), and to the use of psychiatric hospitals as a means of repression, especially of writers and artists. Like Mamleev, Venedikt Erofeev, Iuz Aleshkovsky, Sasha Sokolov and numerous other *samizdat* writers all tended to take the side of those ostracised by the state and society as mad and foolish.[10]

Mamleev's irrationalism, however, is best seen as a response to the values not just of the Soviet Union but of post-Enlightenment modernity as a whole, and has drawn inspiration from foreign as well as native sources. As such, it can most fruitfully be explored in a broad European intellectual context, and I will suggest that it draws especially heavily on the ideas of the French philosopher and esotericist René Guénon (1886–1950), to whom Mamleev has often referred. The rejection of modernity and rationalism leads directly to a fascination with madness in Mamleev's short stories of the 1960s and 70s. We will see that his treatment of madness has much in common with that undertaken by intellectuals at the same time on the other side of the Berlin Wall. Like Michel Foucault in *Folie et déraison: Histoire de la folie à l'âge classique* (1961; known in English as *Madness and Civilisation: A History of Insanity in the Age of Reason*), Mamleev seeks to recover in the experience of the mad sacred and esoteric values lost to modernity, and locates them through imagery comparable to that traced in Foucault's portrayal of *folie* in the late-medieval West. Like R.D. Laing, he is sympathetic to "madness" and schizophrenia as responses to modern societies of "one-dimensional men". I have found no evidence in Mamleev's works of direct acquaintance with these thinkers, although the indirect transmission of their ideas is not to be discounted, given the eclectic and cosmopolitan interests of *samizdat* intellectuals, especially in Mamleev's circle. The parallels, in

---

9   Ibid., 178.
10 See, for example, Aleshkovskii's novella *Nikolai Nikolaevich* (written 1970), and Sasha Sokolov's novel *Shkola dlia durakov* (written 1972–1973).

any case, are interesting in themselves and mutually informative; they also reflect a Europe-wide critique of modernity that goes beyond considerations of political ideology.

I have chosen as the focus for discussion Mamleev's short stories from before his emigration in 1974, since it is here that the tension between rationalism and irrationalism, folly and wisdom, sanity and madness, is most apparent, and most interestingly articulated. His best-known novel *Shatuny* (written 1966–68) and *The Fate of Being* largely leave such tension behind, developing along lines that can perhaps only fully be understood by initiates in the various esoteric traditions (Indian as well as European) by which they are inspired. Mamleev's short fiction, by contrast, is relatively exoteric contrasting the excessive dependence on reason of materialist, modern man with the crazed behaviour of its eccentric protagonists. Before turning to these stories, however, we should briefly consider the autobiographical and intellectual context from which Mamleev's fiction first developed.

*

Mamleev's life before his emigration presents a model illustration of the kind of divided existence commonly (if not always accurately) associated with the Soviet cultural underground.[11] His father was a professor of psychiatry who was arrested in the 1940s and died in the Gulag, events which Mamleev's mother concealed from him until he was older. Warned off the study of literature and philosophy at university (because, in his words, "my inclinations were of a manifestly non-Marxist persuasion"),[12] he entered the Institute of Forestry. After graduating he became a teacher of mathematics at evening school, a job he held until his emigration. Yet in his fiction, as we will soon see, mathematicians and psychiatrists are often derided, both cast as prisoners of a limiting worldview.

Mamleev's unofficial existence centred around the salon he hosted at the flat which once belonged to his father. Among the visitors to Iuzhinskii Lane were writers (among them Eduard Limonov, Vladimir Bukovskii, and Venedikt

---

11 My information about Mamleev's biography is culled mainly from the long interviews Mamleev has given since the early 1990s (and in small part from my own interview with Mamleev in Moscow, April 2000). Perhaps the best interview was carried out in 1993 by Sergei Shepoval, 'Izobrazhenie zla ne est' zlo…', *Ural'skaia Nov'*, 1 (1998), available online at <http://magazines.russ.ru/urnov/1998/1/beseda1.html> (consulted 26.11.2013).

12 *Ibid.*

Erofeev), artists and assorted "wandering mystics".[13] In the post-Soviet era, the salon has undergone enthusiastic mythologisation. In an article of 1997, the Iuzhinskii gatherings were portrayed by the journalist Aleksei Chelnokov as occasions for excess of various kinds (alcoholic, narcotic, sexual). His account, along with that of the participant Igor' Dudinskii, emphasises that a fascination with the occult was matched by a conscious cult of craziness. This was the so-called "schizoid underground", which flourished under the slogan, "If a man's not done a stint in a loony bin, there must be something wrong with him".[14] Here, the identification with madness characteristic of late-Soviet underground culture was acted out in practice. Mamleev, according to the (doubtless fallible) memories of those present, liked to provoke others into crazy behaviour, then use the material for his stories.[15] He himself rejects the more lurid rumours associated with the Iuzhinskii crowd, recalling a symposium-like atmosphere of creative discussions and readings, and the "baring of souls" in a Dostoevskian manner.[16] He describes the attendees as "representatives of pure art", detached from political life (whether Soviet or dissident) and socio-political debates.[17]

Mamleev's writing does indeed reflect an urge to transcend socio-political and ideological considerations (which partly explains why the fundamental concerns of his prose changed so little across different decades and continents). Nevertheless, an image of total detachment from society and politics would be misleading. Aspects of the Soviet context are everywhere to be found in his pre-emigration fiction (notably, the communal flat as the setting of many of his stories),[18] while Soviet values appear to have exerted a deep-rooted

---

13   Mamleev, *Rossiia vechnaia*, 192.
14   Aleksei Chelnokov, 'Melkie i krupnye besy iz shizoidnogo podpol'ia', *Litsa*, 7 August 1997, online at < http://chelnokov-ac.livejournal.com/7987.html > (consulted 26.11.2013). See also Dudinskii's memoiristic article 'Chto takoe 'Moskovskaia ideiia'. Pervoe priblizhenie', online at <http://kolonna.mitin.com/archive/mjo6/dudinskij.shtml> (consulted 26.11.2013). Dudinskii notes that "Sadly, a full portrait of schizoid culture has not come down to us. Its creators were unworldly souls, who, naturally, were not at all concerned about the fate of their legacy [...] The only valuable source for studying the legacy of the 'schizoids' remains the work of Iurii Mamleev".
15   See Chelnokov, 'Melkie i krupnye besy'.
16   See Mamleev, *Rossiia vechnaia*, 191–192; and Mariia Efimova, 'O chudesnom i real'nom', *Nezavisimaia Gazeta*, 13 October 2005, online at <http://www.ng.ru/fakty/2005-10-13/2_mamleev.html > (consulted 26.11.2013).
17   Shepoval, 'Izobrazhenie zla'.
18   A stimulating analysis of the oppressive effects of the *kommunalka* on the psychology of Mamleev's characters is provided in Ryklin, 'Tela terrora', 73–76.

influence as an ideological antithesis. Beyond the enclosure of his social and intellectual circle lay the "spiritual vacuum" into which members of his generation were born in the 1930s and 40s. In his interviews, Mamleev returns repeatedly to the profound consequences of an initial experience of total atheism in fostering a sense of existential terror and a heightened consciousness of death: "The black atheism which we were offered gave rise to a sense of all-prevailing death".[19] Many within the intellectual elite of his generation, he wrote, "passed through a secret experience of 'death'", a process which had the positive effect of forcing him and others in his circle into a lucid and self-reliant spiritual quest.[20] The process also seems to have helped him identify the material for his fiction. In many respects, the concerns of the Mamleevan protagonist are the anti-image of Soviet values and ideology: against an optimistic propaganda of health and vitality, death; against collectivism and civic endeavour, solipsism; against atheism and materialism, an obsession with the metaphysical; against urbanisation, a yearning for the forest and country.[21] Given the long-standing association in Russian culture of militant atheism with militant rationalism, and, in the Marxist-Leninist tradition, of the countryside with backwardness, these last two sets of contrasts may be said to inform the most comprehensive inversion of Soviet values in Mamleev's fiction: madness in place of reason.

But if Mamleev's principle of inversion developed from local factors, it grew to encompass an even larger target: modern civilisation in general. The critique of the materialistic, rationalistic and anti-transcendental premises of Soviet ideology that is implicit in his fiction is only part of a wider rejection of a centuries-long process of spiritual and intellectual *involiutsiia* ('involution') in the Western world. In Mamleev's eyes, the West is currently in a state of "spiritual death", in which rationalism, scientism, widespread agnosticism and pseudo-religion have blunted the awareness of metaphysical reality that has underpinned all healthy spiritual traditions (such as that which survives in India).[22]

---

19 Dmitrii Ol'shanskii, 'Tri metafizicheskie Moskvy' [Interview with Mamleev], *Vremia MN*, 26 April 2002, 11.

20 Mamleev, 'Opyt vosstanovleniia', in *Antologiia gnozisa*, ed. A. Rovner, St Petersburg, 1994, 1, 25–27 (26).

21 In an article of 1979, Mamleev criticises the mentality "of our urbanised civilisation of the nineteenth and twentieth centuries"; see Mamleev *Rossiia vechnaia*, 262.

22 *Ibid.*, 240. For a caricature of pseudo-religiosity, see, *inter alia*, the key story of Mamleev's American cycle, 'Charli'; Mamleev, *Izbrannoe*, 602–620.

The primary model for this narrative appears to have been provided not by Dostoevskii (who might well have agreed with some if not all of its premises), but by Guénon, a Roman Catholic turned Sufi who drew on eclectic sources, notably the Vedas and the writings of Marsilio Ficino, in his attempts to identify a spiritual heritage, common to all the world's main religious traditions, which modernity had lost sight of in its quest for "progress". Guénon was cited as an authority in a number of Mamleev's most substantial interviews, and his singular influence on intellectuals of Mamleev's acquaintance is explicitly attested in *The Fate of Being*.[23] It would be mistaken to suggest that Mamleev's own worldview originated or fully coincided with that of Guénon, but it is clear that the discovery of Guénon led to a fertile meeting of minds. Guénonian "Traditionalism" made a profound impact on the Iuzhinskii circle, having been discovered by the poet and translator Evgenii Golovin in the Lenin Library in the early 1960s.[24] That this should have happened is less surprising than it might seem: the Iuzhinskii circle was deeply immersed in mystical, occult and esoteric literature of the medieval and modern West.

In *La crise du monde moderne* (1927) and *Le règne de la quantité et les signes des temps* (1945) Guénon elaborated to powerful effect the type of inversion of values found throughout Mamleev's writing. The modern Western world was, in his view, monstrous, "abnormal", ignorant and "mentally disturbed" in its very progressiveness and rationalism; its privileging of physics over metaphysics; and its self-satisfied agnosticism ("men glorying in their ignorance").[25] It was experiencing the Kali-Yuga, the 6,000-year period of decline that represents the fourth and final age of the Hindu cycle and that is itself characterised by inversion. The end of the Middle Ages marked the end of authentic Christianity and the point when the "tradition" had been broken.[26] The Renaissance and Reformation had, Guénon writes, "completed the rupture with the traditional

---

23 Mamleev, *Sud'ba bytiia*, online at <http://www.rvb.ru/mamleev/03philos/01sb/sb.htm> (consulted 26.11.2013), 5 (page reference corresponds to print-out); Mamleev, *Rossiia vechnaia*, 203–207; and the continuing references to the Tradition and Guénon in Mamleev's post-Soviet fiction, for example Mamleev, *Mir i khokhot*, Moscow, 2003, 72, 104.

24 Discussed in Mark Sedgwick, *Against the Modern World: Traditionalism and the Secret Intellectual History of the Twentieth Century*, Oxford, 2004, 221–240. Golovin (1938–2010) and the philosopher Geidar Dzhemal', with whom Mamleev collaborated on *Sud'ba bytiia*, have since brought Traditionalism into post-Soviet Russia's political mainstream, through the Neo-Eurasian movement associated with Aleksandr Dugin, who also attended the Iuzhinskii circle in later years.

25 René Guénon, *The Crisis of the Modern World*, trans. Marco Pallis and Richard Nicholson, London, 1962, 41.

26 Sedgwick, *Against the Modern World*, 28, 21.

spirit, the former in the domain of the arts and sciences, the latter in the sphere of religion itself". The legacy of this rupture would be individualism and rationalism; and, instead of "intellectual intuition", the fragmentation of knowledge and the victory of the "profane" point of view, with its advances in "practical applications of the kind which constitute the sole real superiority of modern civilization – hardly an enviable superiority, moreover, which by its development to the point of shifting every other preoccupation has only succeeded in endowing this civilization with the purely material character that makes of it a sheer monstrosity".[27] For Guénon, in Mamleev's approving précis, contemporary Western civilisation "has proved to be a hindrance to man's spiritual fulfilment because it is in the grip of the counter-tradition, in which all values are turned upside down, inverting the normal spiritual tradition".[28]

Mamleev's fiction echoes all these arguments strongly. In particular, the notion of an inverted spiritual norm translates for both writers into paradoxical evaluations of the intelligence of modern (Western) humanity. Its dominant species – atheist/agnostic, materialist and rationalist – is simply stupid, party to a process in which, Mamleev has said, "The cult of money, the cult of the everyday and mass culture will inevitably lead to the *idiotizatsiia* ['idiotisation'] of life".[29] The ordinary citizens to whom Mamleev's protagonists react may be described as "pathologically stupid" in the emptiness of their spiritual lives (525); it is the apparently crazy protagonist who, at least in his own eyes, is intelligent and spiritual.

For Guénon, modernity had mistaken reason, "a purely human and relative faculty", with "the highest part of intelligence", and had condemned itself to the rationalism "of which Descartes was the real originator", thus obscuring higher, divine forms of knowledge (the "intellectual intuition" to which Mamleev refers in his essay 'Between Madness and Magic').[30] Mamleev's hostility to rationalistic interpretations of being is similarly acute, leading him to claim that "philosophy is merely a rational attempt to understand that which cannot rationally be understood", and to suggest, in *The Fate of Being*, that the path to spiritual fulfilment involves turning Descartes' formula upside down: "I don't think, therefore I am".[31] In his fiction, the assault on reason (*razum*) expands into a frustration with the mind (*um*) per se. His characters are either in flight from thought – "The mind brings nothing but boredom" (636); "What in us is

---

27 Guénon, *Crisis*, 10.
28 Mamleev, *Rossiia vechnaia*, 207.
29 *Ibid.*, 208.
30 Guénon, *Crisis*, 53.
31 See Mamleev, *Rossiia vechnaia*, 211; *Sud'ba bytiia*, 29; and Schmid, 'Flowers of Evil', 209.

eternal? Not the mind" (168) – or are caricatured for their absurd obsessions with rationalistic, problem-solving pursuits, which are presented as deliberate attempts to avoid the essential questions. 'The Underside of Gauguin' ('Iznanka Gogena') begins with the mathematician Liubimov being informed by telegram that his father is dying: "Liubimov, dulled by sorrow, decided to set off, taking his wife Irina with him. In the train he chain-smoked and pondered the solution of a very fiddly geometrical problem" (418–419). Liubimov's father returns to the living as a vampire to haunt (and bite) his children. Unable to find a satisfactory "scientific explanation" for the occurrence, Liubimov starts reciting mathematical formulae (422); but even these incantations (recalling Gogol's story 'Vii') fail to ward off his father's reappearances, and the son never recovers from this intrusion of the supernatural onto a rationalistic worldview.

The allergy to Cartesian rationalism shared by Guénon and Mamleev is linked, in the latter's fiction, to a rejection of a dualist view of the mind and body. Those of Mamleev's characters not obsessed by mathematics and other putatively secondary and illusory forms of knowledge tend to resist any form of activity which exerts the mind more than the body. Frequently, we see them eating and thinking at the same time, or seeking the meaning of life in a part of their body, such as their throat or leg.[32] The Marxist belief in the unity of mind and body (requiring therefore a unified science)[33] is thus ironically mirrored and put at the service of a metaphysical rather than materialist doctrine. Other conventional Western dualist categories also fall by the wayside: good and evil, man and God. As Ulrich Schmid comments in his discussion of *The Fate of Being*: "Mamleev sees the fundamental task of every human being as the realization of God ('Bogorealizacija'). Man has to transform himself into what he really is: God".[34]

Of course, many connections also exist between Mamleev's irrationalism and his native literary tradition. Dostoevskii, whose *Notes from Underground* (1864) Mamleev acknowledges to have been a powerful influence, is a constant, tangible presence.[35] More generally, Mamleev's hostility to Descartes continues a long tradition in Russian literature and thought, one to which Andrei Platonov, to whom Mamleev feels a "strange kinship", also made an outstanding contribution.[36] Certainly, Mamleev's observations about Platonov's writing

---

32 See, for example, the stories 'Khoziain svoego gorla' and 'Vania Kirpichikov v vanne' in Mamleev, *Izbrannoe*, 503–9, discussed below.
33 See David Joravsky, *Russian Psychology: A Critical History*, Oxford, 1989, 264.
34 Schmid, 'Flowers of Evil', 209.
35 As Tat'iana Goricheva has suggested, both authors examine and criticise, in their different ways, a perceived excess of human consciousness; Goricheva, 'Krugi ada', 198.
36 Mamleev, *Rossiia vechnaia*, p. 284. "Descartes is an idiot! What thinks cannot exist" says Likhtenberg in Platonov's story 'Rubbish Wind' (written 1933); Andrei Platonov, *Vzyskanie*

are often equally applicable to his own: "Platonov's works describe a world that has fallen out of the rational universe, a world attained as the result of the higher 'disconnection' (*otkliuchennost'*) of his heroes and their link with primordial, yet majestic chaos".[37]

There is, however, a fundamental difference between Mamleev's critique of reason and the main line of Russian anti-rationalism. Mamleev notably eschews the value of (Christian) humility promoted variously by the Slavophiles, Dostoevskii, Platonov, and many of Mamleev's contemporaries (such as Venedikt Erofeev and Iuz Aleshkovskii). Behind all his writing stand the elitist principles and doctrine of his Guénonian mysticism, which affirms a hierarchy of spiritual knowledge and enlightenment. Mamleev is, one feels, in sympathy with the Indian image of the artist as Brahmin that he describes in 'Between Madness and Magic'.[38] His characters act "rightly" or "wrongly" to the extent that they achieve spiritual self-realisation. This achievement is made possible by knowledge of their potential, a knowledge which brings with it an inversion of conventional evaluations of wisdom and folly, sanity and madness. If there is any compassion to be found in Mamleev's writing, it is pity for humans' widespread ignorance about themselves, their "terrible dream of themselves as mortal (creaturely) beings".[39] Against this ignorance, Mamleev posits, as we have seen, a mystical plane of consciousness from which suffering and conflict appear as secondary, even negligible. This "higher level" was described by Guénon as one where the antimonies of ordinary life cease to exist;[40] it represents the permanent (and generally unfulfilled) aspiration of Mamleev's characters.

*

Turning now to a more detailed consideration of Mamleev's stories, and especially of their extraordinary imagery, we find complex and often paradoxical manifestations of the irrationalist position traced so far in this chapter. The broad-brush rejection of modernity and rationalism which Mamleev shares

---

pogibshikh, Moscow, 1995, 383. For an insightful discussion of the polemic with Descartes in Russian philosophy, see Lesley Chamberlain, *Motherland: A Philosophical History of Russia*, London, 2004, 138–164.

37 *Rossiia vechnaia*, 43. See also *ibid.*, 228–229, 253–256.
38 Mamleev, 'Mezhdu bezumiem i magiei', 178. In Guénon's view, the interpretation of the Tradition should be the task of the elite. The Reformation elicits his particular scorn, since by establishing freedom of enquiry Protestantism left interpretation "to the private judgement of individuals, even of the ignorant and incompetent"; Guénon, *Crisis*, 56–57.
39 Mamleev, *Sud'ba bytiia*, 4.
40 Guénon, *Crisis*, 29.

with Guénon issues in a striking contrast of modern and medieval tropes. The stories combine contemporary medical and psychiatric discourse, cited in a satirical and de-familiarising way, with a visual symbolic landscape that frequently recalls imagery of the late-medieval West. In particular, they revive the apocalyptic imagery of madness and death found by Foucault in the art and literature of the late Middle Ages, when madness became, in Foucault's phrase, "the *déjà-là* of death".[41]

In her centenary study of Mikhail Bakhtin, Caryl Emerson comments that "Mamleevian grotesquerie does indeed recall the Rabelaisian world that so disgusted [Aleksei] Losev and [Konstantin] Isupov with its incipient 'Satanism'".[42] There is, however, none of the cyclical vitality of Bakhtinian carnival in Mamleev's artistic and metaphysical vision. Here, all flesh is dead flesh: "the entire world is an enormous corpse" (*ves' mir – ogromnyi trup*), a character says in one of Mamleev's post-Soviet novels.[43] Closer to Mamleev's thought and imagination are the apocalyptic visions of late-medieval artists, notably Hieronymus Bosch. Like Bosch, Mamleev presents teeming and highly variegated canvases of human activity in which natural appetites appear to have been wholly distorted.[44] And like Bosch, Mamleev depicts hell; or, in James McConkey's more accurate observation, he depicts a world in which it is "as if Earth has become Hell without human awareness that such a transformation has taken place".[45] Mamleev describes the spirit trapped in flesh and illusion, in the anonymity of urban spaces perceived as merely the face of spiritual death: "Formally, this was called a space for communal living, but in fact it was a piling up of the dead with no exit to the beyond, like souls that had frozen over" (506). Hans Belting finds similar imagery in Bosch's Hell, commenting that "the window reflected in the cauldron [worn by the Prince of Hell] must surely be a metaphor for a room with no way out".[46]

On other occasions, Mamleev's scenes recall the Ship of Fools, medieval paintings of which by Bosch and others provided metaphors of damnation,

---

41   Michel Foucault, *Madness and Civilization*, trans. Richard Howard, London and New York, 2001, 13.
42   Caryl Emerson, *The First Hundred Years of Mikhail Bakhtin*, Princeton, 1997, 192.
43   Mamleev, *Bluzhdaiushchee vremia*, St Petersburg, 2001, 36.
44   Mamleev himself drew attention to the comparison between his art and that of Bosch; see Mamleev, *Rossiia vechnaia*, 269, and his preface to *Shatuny* for the Russian Virtual Library, <http://www.rvb.ru/mamleev/05comments/comments.htm> (consulted 26.11.2013).
45   James McConkey, [Review of Yuri Mamleyev, *The Sky Above Hell*], *Epoch*, 30 (1980), 93–94 (94).
46   Hans Belting, *The Garden of Earthly Delights*, Munich, 2002, 35.

illustrating, in Foucault's words, a "false happiness [that] is the diabolical triumph of the Antichrist; it is the End, already at hand".[47] Such a "triumph" is suggested by many of Mamleev's mass portraits of urban life. In 'Grey Days', the drunken, gluttonous, cacophonous and lustful bestiary of the Ship of Fools appears to have sailed into the "insane belly" (394) of Soviet communal life: "All sorts of half-drunk people dwell there. Lots of fatsos, with overhanging bellies and arses, men who are bald, foul-mouthed, lewd. And all manner of women" (393).

Echoes of the late-medieval imagery of madness are reinforced by the mystical significance attached to water in Mamleev's fiction and thought. A motif of his stories is the urge of his characters to submerge their consciousness in water, to dissolve any rational process. "Drown my head!" begs a girl who has committed suicide in the story of that name, terrifying the narrator with her insistent requests from beyond the grave (439–447); while in 'Vania Kirpichikov in the Bath' (503–506), bathing brings the mad protagonist to a mystical ecstasy which dissolves both his sense of physical selfhood and his mental processes ("not a single thought", 505).[48] Like the figure of the Poet described in 'Between Madness and Magic', Mamleev's characters yearn to be submerged by the "great dark waves of the Unknown" (or, from another essay, by the "true Ocean which 'surrounds' reality").[49]

Foucault's exploration of the ancient link "in the dreams of European man" between water and madness gives a rich context in which to place such imagery. In 'Stultifera Navis', the opening chapter of *Madness and Civilisation*, Foucault traces this link in all its ambivalence, arguing that the symbolic role of the madman on the cusp of the Renaissance replaced that of the leper, whose punishment was evidence that he had been chosen by God.[50] Discussing the historical precedents for the literary and artistic *topos* of the Ship of Fools, he asserts that in the Rhineland of fifteenth-century Germany the mad were regularly expelled from towns and handed over to boatmen, and speculates about the obscure paradoxical symbolism of this practice, which "haunted the imagination of the entire early Renaissance".[51] The sea to which the mad were

---

47 Foucault, *Madness and Civilization*, 19–20.
48 Mamleev's stories are typically drenched in fluids of all kinds, notably sexual and alcoholic. In the latter respect, they are very much of their time. Like vodka in Erofeev's *Moskva-Petushki* (1970), the abundance of beer in Mamleev's stories creates an atmosphere of universal foolishness, dissolving thought.
49 Mamleev, 'Mezhdu bezumiem i magiei', 184; Schmid, 'Flowers of Evil', 210.
50 Foucault, *Madness and Civilization*, 9 and 4.
51 *Ibid.*, 6–7. Foucault's factual claims about this practice have been questioned by historians; see for example Erik Midelfort, 'Madness and Civilisation in Early Modern Europe', in

consigned was a symbol both of confinement and liberation, of "unreason" and an otherworldly, esoteric wisdom ("those unknown highways which conceal so much strange knowledge"): "It is for the other world that the madman sets sail in his fools' boat; it is from the other world that he comes when he disembarks [...] He has his truth and his homeland only in that fruitless expanse between two countries that cannot belong to him".[52]

In 'Vania Kirpichikov in the Bath', Mamleev invests water with similar symbolic meaning, albeit with characteristic bathos: not the open seas, but a grubby tub in a communal flat, "with the bog next door and rats and roaches like tits on a beach" (503). Kirpichikov is given to spending inordinate amounts of time in the bath, taking with him a guitar and a bundle of filthy clothes. He describes how, sitting in the empty tub, he contemplates his body, sometimes trying to run away from it, sometimes trying to eat it. Only when he actually runs the water does he attain the mystical state he desires: "I've said already, for me, water's like God's own tears. When I sink my sinning flesh – this ol' body of mine – into that lovely warm space, it's like I'm no longer me" (505). The story recovers the same paradox between "social exclusion" and "spiritual reintegration" manifested, for Foucault, by the experience of the lepers and, subsequently, wandering madmen of Western Europe. Only by being cut off from his neighbours and society can Kirpichikov recover a sense of wholeness. For him, as in Foucault's reading water is an escape from the ordinary world, from secular values and authority, even if he is at the same time, like Foucault's madmen, its "prisoner":[53] "The dear water fences me off – all of me – from the world"; "They've called the police, but the dear water's fencing me off from every devil there is, for ever and always" (505). For Kirpichikov too, water is, in Foucault's phrase, "his truth and his homeland". A common source suggests itself: both writers were steeped in the mysticism of medieval Western Europe, where the soul was seen as a "skiff, abandoned on the infinite sea of desires" and could be "brought to port" only by the grace of God.[54] Dissolving reason, water defines the madman's privileged ("liminal")[55] position between worlds and reflects a mystery of explicitly divine origin: "The water – for me, it's like God's own tears:

After the Reformation: Essays in Honor of J.H. Hexter, ed. B.C. Malament, Philadelphia, 1980, 254.

52   Foucault, *Madness and Civilization*, 8–9.
53   Foucault, 9.
54   *Ibid.*, 10.
55   *Ibid.*, 8.

gentle but beyond understanding" (503). A neighbour, old Nastasia Vasil'evna, describes the tub as Kirpichikov's "no-God church" (*bezbozhnaia tserkov'*).[56]

*

In stark contrast to such imagery, the language of irrationalism and madness which Mamleev employs in his stories is distinctly modern. A liberal and apparently careless scattering of terminology from psychology, psychiatry and psychoanalysis helps define the absurdist outlines of Mamleevan reality, where human experience is so saturated in varieties of mental derangement that pathologies leak out onto inanimate surroundings. A staircase can have "schizophrenic" corners as it winds its way up to a communal flat, where every inhabitant has his own "psychopathology" (372); the windows of another urban dwelling express *idiotizm* (584).

Lacquering his stories with the discourse of psychology and psychiatry, Mamleev uses that language in a double-edged way. On the one hand, it is deployed to describe a contemporary, urban world that really is plagued by psychic disorder, with Mamleev drawing on his knowledge of psychiatric case-studies (gained in part from expertise within his own family, especially that of his aunt, a psychopathologist at the Kashchenko Hospital in Moscow).[57] On the other, it is used in highly ironic relation to the professionals who command it. Psychiatrists and psychoanalysts are the regular target of satirical barbs throughout Mamleev's fiction.[58] In 'Reflection', a story from his 'American' cycle, seventy-year-old Mary, about to die from cancer, is told by her psychoanalyst: "you've still got so much ahead of you: a whole three weeks. Live vigorously. Chase away negative thoughts and don't think about death" (598–599). Evidently, Mamleev's quarrel is not just with repressive Soviet psychiatry, but with the modern science of the mind *tout court*, which, he suggests (following Guénon) derives from a limited view of human experience and an ignorance of spiritual potential.[59] In 'Love Story', modern psychiatry is presented as a

---

56 Undoubtedly, Mamleev is also playing on the cultural trope of the traditional Russian bath-house (*bania*) as a place where sins are washed away. On this trope, see Daniel Rancour-Laferriere, *The Slave Soul of Russia: Moral Masochism and the Cult of Suffering*, New York, 1995, 183.

57 See Mamleev, *Rossiia vechnaia*, 281.

58 See, for example, Mamleev, *Izbrannoe*, 370–72, 375, 426.

59 It was Guénon, he has written, who "managed to give a complete account of the total profanity and spiritual ignorance of contemporary science, psychology, philosophy"; Mamleev, *Rossiia vechnaia*, 55.

debased science, infinitely inferior to esoteric mysticism (586); while psychoanalysis, Mamleev has said, appeals only to man's basest nature.[60]

The sciences of the mind enable Mamleev to focus his universal polemic against the pretensions of modern science, with its "mechanical, naïve, professorly" (496) efforts at rational explanation.[61] It is just such rationalism that Mamleev appears to find culpable for the psychic disorder of modernity. If the world has gone mad, it is because of an excess, not a lack, of reason, which has imposed artificial limitations on spiritual potential. Mamleev's infernal tableaux of cramped Muscovite dwellings (worthy descendants of the garrets of Dostoevskii's Petersburg) are the visible and metaphorical expression of this process. Confined by the fruits of "progress", free souls are turned into eccentrics and "schizos", while conformists flourish under the sign of materialism and stupidity. All of life has become a loony bin run by unimaginative, soulless, "impregnable 'logic'" (535). The only possible (if absurd) response to this situation, Mamleev's stories suggest, is more of the "disease" (madness) and less of the "cure".

In giving madness a voice, Mamleev's fiction fits squarely in the European tendency of his time that has often gone under the name of "anti-psychiatry", a term which is both reductive and misleading, given that some of the individuals prominently associated with it, such as R.D. Laing, were themselves psychiatrists, albeit of a highly nonconformist bent.[62] What the diverse thinkers associated with this tendency undeniably shared was an urgent wish to challenge what Foucault calls "the monologue of reason about madness"[63] and the power of clinicians. They were also connected by their hostility towards any scientistic, positivistic approach to the human subject. Instead of objectifying madness, they sought to give it its full subjective expression, in the belief that the "mad" knew and experienced things which men of "reason" did not. 'Vania Kirpichikov in the Bath' is one of many stories in Mamleev's oeuvre that echoes this position. Mamleev gives full rein to his protagonist's undoubted madness, while invoking the clinical perspective for satirical ends. Kirpichikov compares the bathroom where he carries out his amateur surgery to an "operating theatre" (503), mocks "the professors" and describes himself as "my own doc" (*sam sebe doctor*, 504), refusing to allow his "craziness" to be objectified and pathologised.

---

60   Author's interview with Mamleev in Moscow, April 2000.
61   The limitations of science are the topic of Mamleev's article, "Skazka kak realnost", in Mamleev, *Rossiia vechnaia*, 262–265.
62   The term was brought into common use by David Cooper, author of *Psychiatry and Antipsychiatry* (1967).
63   Foucault, *Madness and Civilization*, xii.

The cult of craziness expressed by Mamleev's stories (and the Iuzhinskii lifestyle in which many of them germinated) has a famous counterpart in the experiments which R.D. Laing carried out in the 1960s, notably as chairman of the Philadelphia Association in Kingsley Hall, where therapists saw it as their task, in Laing's words, "to follow and assist the movement of what is called 'an acute psychotic episode' instead of arresting it".[64] It is no surprise that when we turn to Laing's eloquent accounts and interpretations of schizophrenia, we find profound similarities with Mamleev's fiction, testifying both to the two authors' psychiatric expertise and to their shared empathy with the "mad" and "abnormal". Writing in the same period, both were fascinated with how, in Laing's words, "the cracked mind of the schizophrenic may *let in* light which does not enter the intact minds of many sane people whose minds are closed".[65] Both found in the experience of the 'mad' a mystical urge which is otherwise self-censored in a society that encourages the adaptation of, in Laing's expression, false selves to false realities. Our discussion so far suggests that Mamleev would subscribe to all of the following comments in Laing's preface of 1964 to *The Divided Self* (1959), including its implicit criticism of Freud: "Our civilization represses not only 'the instincts', not only sexuality, but any form of transcendence. [...] In the context of our present pervasive madness that we call normality, sanity, freedom, all our frames of reference are ambiguous and equivocal".[66]

Comparing *The Divided Self* with Mamleev's fiction, we can see how close the two men's interpretation of "madness" was in point of clinical detail as well. The availability of the schizophrenic to "other dimensions" issues in what Laing calls "ontological insecurity": a weak sense of the reality and identity of oneself and others.[67] This insecurity is characteristic of many of Mamleev's protagonists: "I feel like I'm a song-nail... Only who's going to knock me into the wall?" asks the 'Man Who Runs Like a Horse' in the story of the same name (470). At the same time, both authors are interested in how the schizophrenic mind defends its own perception of reality against that of others. Mamleev's madmen try to cling on to their selfhood and are as unwilling as Laing's to surrender themselves to the hateful, 'ordinary' other.

A clear illustration of this pattern is given in 'An Individualist's Notebook', one of Mamleev's most anthologised stories. It is a febrile, first-person account

---

64   Quoted in *Going Crazy: The radical therapy of R.D. Laing and others*, ed. H.M. Ruitenbeek, Toronto, 1972, 15.
65   R.D. Laing, *The Divided Self*, London, 1990, 27.
66   Ibid., 11.
67   Ibid., 39.

(indebted to Dostoevskii's *Notes from Underground*) of a man's inability to accommodate himself to society and his eventual separation from his wife, Zina. Mamleev establishes a characteristic contrast between the approximately but affectionately described madness of the narrator, with his "insanely-penetrative gaze" (524), "secret-mad little thoughts" (530), "schizophrenic rooms" (528), and the conformist idiocy of those who surround him, namely his wife's family. His in-laws, "respectable *inzhenery*" (that broad category of Soviet professional life), are said to typify nine-tenths of the world's population in their stupidity (525). Simply by finding himself in their company, the narrator feels that he is being "placed on their idiotic level" (526). Gradually recognising the gulf that separates him from his wife as well, he disappears into his "own worlds", eventually receiving visits (hallucinated or otherwise) from a guru who tries to goad him into further self-absorption: the mystical solipsism that is one of the major preoccupations of *The Fate of Being*.

"I have never known a schizophrenic who could say he was loved", writes Laing.[68] Mamleev's Individualist did once his love his wife, but now professes amazement at the fact: "How very astonishing – to love another person!" (524). So radically different are the perceptions of the "mad" and the "sane" that they are mutually exclusive, hence the loneliness of the schizophrenic. The way the Individualist expels Zina from his mind accords closely with the schizophrenic "technique" described by Laing as "petrification". The schizophrenic, Laing writes, often tries to deal with his dread of losing his fragile subjectivity, of becoming "no more than a thing in the world of the other", by petrifying the other in his mind and thus destroying him.[69] Correspondingly, the Individualist imagines Zina in his mind as a tree, a wall, or "a thing, a cup that can be broken without the slightest twinge in the heart" (531).[70] The clinical pattern observed by Laing is completed in Mamleev's story by the narrator's redirection of his affection towards himself: "But the ruder I became towards her, the tenderer I became towards myself… This tenderness reached such a pitch that I sought to break off with all that surrounded me" (531–532). In Laing's words, "To consume oneself by one's own love prevents the possibility of being consumed by another".[71]

Equally striking are the parallels between the two authors' representation of the schizophrenic in society. In 1967 Laing wrote of schizophrenia as being

---

68 Laing, *Divided Self*, 38.
69 Ibid., 46–52.
70 Compare also Vania Kirpichikov's mania for water with the technique of "engulfment" described by Laing in *Divided Self*, 43–5.
71 Ibid., p.51. See also Mamleev's similar story 'Tenderness' in Mamleev, *Izbrannoe*, 403–407.

"a special strategy that the patient invents in order to live an unliveable situation".[72] For Laing, society was maximally culpable in the distress of the "patient". Lionel Trilling accurately summarised the plight of Laing's patients as follows:

> The malignant influence which he fails to withstand commonly masks itself in benevolence, yet its true nature is easily detected, for it is always the same thing, a pressure exerted by society through the agency of the family. It is the family which is directly responsible for the ontological break, the "divided self" of schizophrenia [...] We may put it that Laing construes schizophrenia as the patient's response to the parental imposition of inauthenticity.[73]

The "family" in 'An Individualist's Notebook' is that of the narrator's in-laws, with whom the couple lived for a brief period after their marriage (524–527). The situation was indeed "unliveable": "I was completely unable not only to argue with them, but even to talk to them" (526). The narrator perceives the family's outward shows of "benevolence" (their polite, but suspicious questioning of him) as an affront to his personal dignity, and their idiocy and materialism as a threat. The ways by which he tries to protect himself from their contaminating, "malignant influence" and inauthenticity are identified as deliberate strategies (his *politika*, 527): first he tries to say nothing but to conform in his actions, then, when this fails, he decides to defend himself from his in-laws by answering their questions with meaningless sounds.

In the final part of the story, the Individualist has withdrawn completely from living people, devoting himself to the contemplation of death, watching funerals and sometimes pushing through to kiss the corpses (537). For him, death is on the one hand his childhood "terror", cruel and "atheistic" (in a passage that closely echoes Mamleev's own comments in interview, cited earlier); on the other, it is the "secret which no one could kill" (534). The rejection of empty modernity and the embrace of death and the metaphysical are emphatically spelled out:

> Life was so dark in its hopelessness and materialism, its bestial stupidity and clarity, that Death – the sole Great Secret to be seen and felt by all, a secret, moreover, that hit you smack in the face – was a true oasis amidst this torrent of decrees, oatmeal, televisions and impregnable "logic". (535)

---

72   R.D. Laing, *The Politics of Experience*, Harmondsworth, 1967, 115.
73   Lionel Trilling, *Sincerity and Authenticity*, Oxford, 1972, 159–161.

Here, as for Vania Kirpichikov (whose cleansing rituals take him "way beyond the grave"), madness is once again tied to death in a connection recalling the image of pre-modern *folie* given by Foucault (madness as "the *déjà-là* of death"). Like Mamleev, Foucault similarly speaks of the mystical space of "the Great Secret" putatively abandoned by European culture since Shakespeare and Cervantes.[74] Scholarly and rationalist explanations of death are derided by the Individualist: it is inaccessible to the language of "theories, books, dissertations" (534) Only a sustained experience of mental ecstasy at its threshold makes possible a solution to "the riddle of life, the riddle of oneself" (536).

*

Following his return from emigration, Mamleev was increasingly preoccupied with the "special path" of Russian culture and spirituality (a position for which he finds support in the ideas of Guénon).[75] This chapter would suggest, however, that the irrationalism at the heart of Mamleev's writing is not to be interpreted solely through the prism of Russian exceptionalism. In fact, the distinctive elements of the Russian irrationalist tradition – such as the role of the *iurodivyi* or Russian holy fool; the relationship between the intelligentsia and the people; Russian Orthodox values of humility and self-abasement – play a fairly minor role in Mamleev's fiction. Its anti-modern, anti-scientistic, mystical thrust and its polemic with modern psychiatric practice and psychoanalysis are instead part of a broader European tendency by which it is informed and by which it may be illuminated. Indeed, there are other strong parallels to be explored between Mamleev's writing and contemporaneous European irrationalist literature and thought, notably Deleuze and Guattari's *Capitalisme et schizophréni: L'Anti-Oedipe* (1972), which also puts forward an anti-clinical, anti-Freudian model of schizophrenia and continues Laing and Foucault's critique of the way "psychiatric practice" has made the schizophrenic a "sort of rag": "this schizo who sought to remain at that unbearable point where the mind touches matter and lives its every intensity, consumes it".[76]

The question poses itself: how has Mamleev distinctively *contributed* to what we might call this recent European monologue of madness about reason? To answer this would require another article and a different critical approach; a few suggestions can, however, be offered. Mamleev's extravagant mystical

---

74 Foucault, *Madness and Civilization*, 28, 18.
75 Mamleev, *Rossiia vechnaia*, 210.
76 Gilles Deleuze and Félix Guattari, *Anti-Oedipus. Capitalism and schizophrenia*, trans. Robert Hurley, Mark Seem, and Helen R. Lane, London, 2004, 21.

philosophy seems unlikely to stand the test of time. His fiction, by contrast, can be deeply affecting, through its imagery (as Mamleev has emphasised: "an image goes deeper than an idea"),[77] its language and its style. The key influence here is undoubtedly Dostoevskii. Mamleev's style is in some respects almost offensively sub-Dostoevskian. The Individualist's notebook begins with the phrase "What a nasty little brat I really am" (*poganen'kii vse-taki ia chelovechishko*), a pastiche of the Underground Man's opening salvo ("I am a sick man... I am an angry man"). The voice of the Individualist is ugly, the style unappealing, and so too the personality behind it. Moreover the speaker, like Dostoevskii's Underground Man, Marmeladov or other protagonists, mocks himself and his own obsessions (his mysticism and solipsism). Yet his is the only voice we are given, and our defences are eventually worn down, while the imprecision of expression so characteristic of Mamleev's irrationalist fiction (with its abundance of absurd diminutives and incongruously hyphenated nouns) also exerts a peculiarly disorienting charm. We risk taking the speaker more seriously than he takes himself. Like Dostoevskii, Mamleev evidently wishes, in Malcolm Jones's phrase, "to drive the reader crazy",[78] and in this he occasionally succeeds no less than his master. A detailed analysis of how he does so is very much in order.

Bibliography

Belting, Hans. 2002. *The Garden of Earthly Delights*. Munich: Prestel.

Chamberlain, Lesley. 2004. *Motherland: A Philosophical History of Russia*. London: Atlantic.

Chelnokov, Aleksei. 1997. 'Melkie i krupnye besy iz shizoidnogo podpol'ia'. <http://chelnokov-ac.livejournal.com/7987.html>.

Deleuze, Gilles, and Félix Guattari. 2004. *Anti-Oedipus. Capitalism and Schizophrenia*, trans. Robert Hurley, Mark Seem, and Helen R. Lane. London: Continuum.

Dudinskii, Igor'. s.d. 'Chto takoe "Moskovskaia ideiia". Pervoe priblizhenie'. <http://kolonna.mitin.com/archive/mj06/dudinskij.shtml>.

Efimova, Mariia. 2005. 'O chudesnom i real'nom'. <http://www.ng.ru/fakty/2005-10-13/2_mamleev.html >.

Emerson, Caryl. 1997. *The First Hundred Years of Mikhail Bakhtin*. Princeton: Princeton University Press.

---

[77] Mamleev, *Sud'ba bytiia*, 3.
[78] See Malcolm Jones, *Dostoyevsky after Bakhtin: Readings in Dostoyevsky's Fantastic Realism*, Cambridge, 1990, 113–146.

Foucault, Michel. 2001. *Madness and Civilization*, abridged and trans. Richard Howard. London: Routledge.

Gol'dshtein, Aleksandr. 1997. *Rasstavanie s Nartsissom: Opyty pominal'noi ritoriki*. Moscow: Novoe Literaturnoe Obozrenie.

Goricheva, Tat'iana. 1983. 'Krugi ada' in *Kontinent* 36: 382–385.

———. 1987. 'Pronzennye pustotoi' in *Sintaksis* 20: 196–199.

Gorny, Eugene. s.d. 'The Negative World of Yury Mamleev'. <http://www.zhurnal.ru/staff/gorny/english/mamleev.htm>.

Guénon, René. 1962. *The Crisis of the Modern World*, trans. Marco Pallis and Richard Nicholson. London: Luzac.

Jones, Malcolm. 1990. *Dostoyevsky after Bakhtin: Readings in Dostoyevsky's Fantastic Realism*. Cambridge: Cambridge University Press.

Joravsky, David. 1989. *Russian Psychology: A Critical History*. Oxford: Oxford University Press.

Laing, R.D. 1967. *The Politics of Experience*. Harmondsworth: Penguin.

———. 1990. *The Divided Self*. London: Penguin.

Mal'tsev, Iurii. 1976. *Vol'naia russkaia literatura, 1955–1975*. Frankfurt/Main: Posev.

Mamleev, Iurii. 1987. 'Mezhdu bezumiem i magiei' in *Beseda* 6: 178–184.

———. 1991. *Vechnyi dom: povest' i rasskazy*. Moscow: Khudozhestvennaia Literatura.

———. 1993. *Izbrannoe*. Moscow: Terra.

———. 1994. 'Opyt vosstanovleniia' in A. Rovner (ed.) *Antologiia gnozisa* 1. St Petersburg: Medusa: 25–27.

———. 2001. *Bluzhdaiushchee vremia*. St Petersburg: Limbus.

———. 2002. *Rossiia vechnaia*. Moscow: AiF-Print.

———. 2003. *Mir i khokhot*. Moscow: Vagrius.

———. s.d. *Sud'ba bytiia*. <http://www.rvb.ru/mamleev/03philos/01sb/sb.htm>.

Mazur, Natal'ia. 1992. 'Kobob' in *Literaturnoe Obozrenie* 7: 76–80.

McConkey, James. 1980 [Review of Yuri Mamleyev, *The Sky Above Hell*] in *Epoch* 30: 93–94.

Midelfort, Erik. 1980. 'Madness and Civilisation in Early Modern Europe', in B.C. Malament (ed.) *After the Reformation: Essays in Honor of J.H. Hexter*. Philadelphia: University of Pennsylvania Press.

Ol'shanskii, Dmitrii. 2002. 'Tri metafizicheskie Moskvy' in *Vremia MN*: 11 (26 April 2002).

Platonov, Andrei. 1995. *Vzyskanie pogibshikh*. Moscow: Shkola-Press.

Rancour-Laferriere. 1995. *The Slave Soul of Russia: Moral Masochism and the Cult of Suffering*. New York: New York University Press.

Ruitenbeck, H.M. (ed). 1972. *Going Crazy: The Radical Therapy of R.D. Laing and Others*. Toronto: Bantam.

Ryklin, Mikhail. 1990. 'Tela terrora (tezisy k logike nasiliia)' in D. Kuiundzhich and V.L. Makhlin (eds) *Bakhtinskii sbornik* 1. Moscow: Prometei: 60–76.

Schmid, Ulrich. 2000. 'Flowers of Evil: The Poetics of Monstrosity in Contemporary Russian Literature (Erofeev, Mamleev, Sokolov, Sorokin)' in *Russian Literature* 48: 205–222.

Sedgwick, Mark. 2004. *Against the Modern World: Traditionalism and the Secret Intellectual History of the Twentieth Century*. Oxford: Oxford University Press.

Shepoval, Sergei. 1998. 'Izobrazhenie zla ne est' zlo...'. <http://magazines.russ.ru/urnov/1998/1/beseda1.html>.

Smirnov, I.P. 1993. 'Evoliutsiia chudovishchnosti (Mamleev i drugie)' in *Novoe Literaturnoe Obozrenie* 3: 303–307.

Trilling, Lionel. 1972. *Sincerity and Authenticity*. Oxford: Oxford University Press.

Vail' Petr, and Aleksandr Genis. 1982. *Sovremennaia russkaia proza*. Ann Arbor: Ermitazh.

CHAPTER 23

Vladimir Sorokin and the Return of History

David Gillespie

In Solzhenitsyn's *V kruge pervom* (*The First Circle*, 1968), the young diplomat Innokentii Volodin engages in conversation with the budding writer Galakhov on the role of literature and the status of the writer in society. In a speech since regarded as reflecting Solzhenitsyn's own credo, Volodin explains: "After all, a writer is a mentor to others, this has surely always been understood? A great writer is, sorry for my audacity, as I lower my voice, something of a second government. That is why no regime has ever loved great writers, only insignificant ones".[1]

Solzhenitsyn famously stood up to the Soviet authorities in the 1960s and 1970s before his exile in 1974, accusing them of peddling "the lie as a form of existence" and "the continuing basis of life", and thus of undermining and destroying bonds between people.[2] As in the nineteenth century, the writer was the nation's moral guide and teacher, reminding it of fundamental truths and immutable values.

When the work of Vladimir Sorokin began to be published in the early 1990s, it was equated with the 'shock therapy' to which the economy and country as a whole were subjected after the collapse of the Soviet Union.[3] Certainly, the style and themes of Sorokin's prose were qualitatively different from anything that had been published in Russia before. By way of summary, the subject-matter of Sorokin's early works include murder, mayhem, indiscriminate slaughter, cannibalism, sexual deviance and abuse, coprophagy, mutilation, torture, sadism, masochism, sexual explicitness that often crosses over into pornography, all rendered in an idiom and style that becomes increasingly deranged and nonsensical before the narrative and the text either ends abruptly, or collapses in on itself. In these works Sorokin challenged the reader's sensibilities – aesthetic, moral, linguistic and cultural – at the same time throwing down the gauntlet to the hallowed status of Russian literature itself. Sorokin was declaring the death of Russian literature as a moral force in a

---

1 Alexander Solzhenitsyn, *V kruge pervom,* in A. Solzhenitsyn, *Sobranie sochinenii,* Posev, Frankfurt, 1970, IV, 503.
2 Alexander Solzhenitsyn, *The Gulag Archipelago 2, 1918–1956; Parts III-IV,* trans. Thomas P. Whitney, Collins/Fontana, London, 1975, 628, 630.
3 Robert Porter, *Russia's Alternative Prose,* Berg, Oxford, 1994, 38–42.

society where the ruled were tyrannised by the rulers, where the political structure of the country was divided into masters and lackeys, despots and playthings, the cynical and the duped. That structure, it was assumed, had been swept away with the new 'democratic' government and civic norms that emerged from the chaos of 1991; literature could become as 'normal' as in Western Europe, where there are different markets for different genres, and literature is for enjoyment and perhaps personal uplift, but no longer needed as a 'second government'.

This is not to suggest that Vladimir Sorokin is a Solzhenitsyn for a new age. Sorokin remains a writer addressing first and foremost his fellow-countrymen, cruelly and vividly dissecting the falseness and hypocrisies of the previous regime, but does not assume the self-acclaimed status as spokesman for his generation, nor is he elevated by his admirers into some latter-day prophet. Sorokin remains a writer of fiction, whose creative trajectory demonstrates evolution from the abstract to the specific, from satire to engagement, and from a rationalist discourse on totalitarianism to a fatalistic, perhaps irrational, embrace of the finality of Russian history.

Ochered' (*The Queue*, 1985) remains a startlingly innovative work that consists of dialogue only, with no narrative or even named characters, that also distils the entire Soviet experience into one long, seemingly never-ending queue, and one that people join not knowing what is actually on sale (if anything). *Tridsataia liubov' Mariny* (*The Thirtieth Love of Marina*, 1987) is an explicitly sexual journey of the eponymous Marina from abused adolescent to lesbian adult and finally to fully committed Communist, and is the first work of Russian literature where a male author depicts the female orgasm (in detail). In *Serdtsa chetyrekh* (*Four Stout Hearts*, 1993) Sorokin parodies to grotesque excess the new post-Soviet gangster thriller genre, with multiple blood-spattered shoot-outs and gratuitous sexual encounters. The work bears the same title as a very popular Soviet romantic comedy film from 1940. The gruesome violence of Sorokin's text has nothing in common with the innocent charm of the 1940 film, but its extreme violence offers a pointed and subversive commentary to the artificial innocence on parade in the film.

I would argue that it is this work that marks the 'later' period of Sorokin's work. The four central characters of *Serdtsa chetyrekh* are people set apart from and above their environment; they cheerfully remain untouched until the finale while inflicting mayhem all around. In these works published in the immediate aftermath of the collapse of the USSR Sorokin delights in the new-found freedoms. The human body is tortured and dismembered, language is mutilated, sex becomes grotesque, basic bodily functions given an importance not usually accorded to them in a literary text. Russian life and literature become not just parodies, but travesties of their former selves. Sorokin moves beyond merely challenging the reader to turn the page and read on amidst a morass of butchery, pornography, excreta and linguistic chaos. Seemingly paradoxically, he also embraces fully the Russian literary mission: literature is important because it tells the truth.

In *Serdtsa chetyrkh* Sorokin also assumes a social stance beloved of Russian writers. The novel's surface narrative may relate to the lawlessness and criminality of the early 1990s, but its title is a clear indication to a Russian reader that society accepted violence as the norm in Stalin's time. The 'norm', of course, is the daily lot of ordinary people, the excrement that is a literalised symbol of the lies and injustices the population is force-fed by authority. Sorokin's anti-Soviet stance is in full display in the novel of that name, *Norma* (*The Norm*, 1994), which also contains allusions to the work of Vasilii Grossman and Andrei Platonov in its harrowing depiction of the destruction of people under the Soviet experiment, and to the poetry of Boris Pasternak and Anna Akhmatova. That is not to say that the literary canon is sacrosanct: in *Roman* (*Novel*, 1994) he destabilises and then deconstructs Russian literature's ethical identity.

The internal contradiction of Sorokin's early writings, its irrational core, lies in the fact that he denies the importance of literature by defacing the text and metaphorically spitting in the face of the author as guide and prophet. Yet Sorokin is also aware of his own status as writer, one who through his writings brings to the reader truths not otherwise perceived.

In a recent interview with *Der Spiegel* Sorokin claims that he remained stubbornly "apolitical" until only a few years ago. "As a storyteller, I was influenced by the Moscow underground, where it was common to be apolitical. [...] This was one of our favourite anecdotes: as German troops marched into Paris, Picasso sat there and drew an apple. That was our attitude – you must sit there and draw your apple, no matter what happens around you. I held fast to that principle until I was fifty. Now the citizen in me has come to life".[4]

Sorokin's new civic-mindedness is clearly aimed at what he sees as the "destruction" and "collapse" of Russia under the current regime. At the age of

---

4   Quoted in Ellen Barry, 'From a Novelist, Shock Treatment for Mother Russia', *The New York Times*, 29 April 2011. I have written on Sorokin's 'apolitical' prose elsewhere: see 'Sex, violence and the video nasty: the ferocious prose of Vladimir Sorokin', *Essays in Poetics*, 22 (1997), 158–75; 'Vladimir Sorokin and the Norm', in Arnold McMillin (ed.), *Reconstructing the Canon: Russian Writing in the 1980s*, Harwood Academic Publishers, Amsterdam: 2000, 299–309.

fifty Sorokin decides that he must join the ranks of Russian writers who believe that their writings will change things. In the early 1990s, by way of contrast, Sorokin would claim that his writings were simply "words on paper" and that as such there could be no "ethical aspect" of what he was writing.[5]

Sorokin's engagement with Russian history can be traced to his most controversial work, *Goluboe salo* (*Blue Lard*, 1999). Three years after its publication it was 'sued' in a Moscow court for its 'pornographic' content. That content was the graphic description of homosexual sex between Nikita Khrushchev and Iosif Stalin. Khrushchev's penetration of the *vozhd'* (leader) is a metaphor for his attack on Stalin's crimes and "violations of socialist legality" in 1956. In *Goluboe salo* for the first time in Sorokin's writing pornography and explicit sex have a political significance.

The central premise of *Den' oprichnika* (*Day of the Oprichnik*, 2006) is brilliant in its simplicity. In the near future, Russia is ruled by an oppressive autocrat whose main arm of government is the *oprichniki,* the secret police of Ivan the Terrible's time. Furthermore, the very title is reminiscent of another classic story of resistance to tyranny, Alexander Solzhenitsyn's *Odin den' Ivana Denisovicha* ('One Day in the Life of Ivan Denisovich', 1962). If in previous works Sorokin re-imagined and re-worked themes and motifs from Russian literature of the nineteenth and twentieth centuries, in *Den' oprichnika* he self-consciously references the Dystopian traditions of Russian literature, most notably Evgenii Zamiatin's *My* (*We,* 1921).

Sorokin's view of Russia's future is as bleak as Zamiatin's vision of the Soviet Union's, though much more violent. In 2028 Russia is surrounded by a Great Wall that separates it from Europe and China, and is ruled by a Sovereign (cf. Zamiatin's 'Benefactor') after the Red and White Troubles of the Soviet and immediate post-Soviet past. Zamiatin's Single State was also instituted after a war that destroyed most of the population. The Sovereign's *oprichniki* very much resemble the Benefactor's Guardians in their ruthless persecution of sedition. There, however, the resemblance ends, because whereas Zamiatin's novel is narrated by the rebel engineer D-503, Sorokin's 'hero' is Danilo Khomiaga, a highly-placed *oprichnik.* If Zamiatin's Single State was ruled as a scientifically rational society guaranteeing 'mathematically infallible happiness', then Sorokin's rulers regard themselves as above the rest of the nation in their patriotic fervour; indeed, as Khomiaga muses, standing in the Kremlin's Uspenskii Cathedral clutching a candle, the Sovereign would not be able to reign without their support.

---

5 Vladimir Sorokin, 'Tekst kak narkotik', in Vladimir Sorokin, *Sbornik rasskazov,* Russlit, Moscow, 1992, 120.

Sorokin posits a picture of Russia in 2028 that is essentially identical to that of Ivan the Terrible, despite new forms of communication and transport that enable the *oprichniki* to carry out their work with such efficiency, such as mobile phones and Mercedes cars. As Stephen Kotkin has noted in a review of the English translation, the *oprichniki* resemble the 'siloviki' of modern Russia, who 'lord over not just the richest private citizens but also other parts of the state'.[6] As in today's Russia, anyone, no matter how rich and eminent, can become a victim of State 'justice', graphically exemplified in the novel's opening pages which see the execution of a rich merchant, the gang rape of his wife and the despatch of the children to an orphanage where they will be raised as "honest citizens of a great country" (28).

The *oprichniki* are (literally) men "set apart", they answer only to the Sovereign and with his blessing hold the power of life or death over everyone else. They are similar to the fair-haired, blue-eyed tribe in *Trilogiia Led* (*Ice Trilogy*, 2004–5) who form the chosen elite of a totalitarian state (some may even see a reference to the physical features of Vladimir Putin). Russia's power structure is strictly vertical, and when anyone of importance loses favour or protection, no mercy is shown. As they perform sexually grotesque and masochistic rituals they reference the dance of the *oprichniki* in Eisenstein's film *Ivan Groznyi* ('Ivan the Terrible', 1944–46'): Гойда! Гойда! Жги! Жги! Жги!' (217). In *Trilogiia* ordinary humans are simply 'meat' to be destroyed over the decades in their search for greater meaning. In Sorokin's Russia of the future, just as in the actual Russia of the present, people do not matter, they are playthings in the lifestyle of those who have chosen themselves to be in power.

Den' oprichnika offers a vision of Russian history not as cyclical – a return to autocratic tyranny – but rather as terminal. The work shows that Sorokin has evolved from *laissez faire* apoliticism to a more aware and conscious stance that lies squarely in the Russian tradition. Sorokin finds himself in glorious company: Lev Tolstoi angered the government and Church with his outraged attack on the corruption of the criminal justice system in *Voskresen'e* (*Resurrection*, 1899), and Alexander Solzhenitsyn was arrested and deported from the Soviet Union in 1974 after the publication abroad of the first volume of *Arkhipelag GULag* (*The Gulag Archipelago*, 3 vols, 1973–76). With his equation of the government of 2028 and that of Ivan the Terrible, is Sorokin claiming his lineage, as the great dissident Russian writer of the twenty-first century?

Sorokin has foregrounded an aspect of Russian life that is consistent from the time of Ivan the Terrible to the present day: the individual has no rights, he

---

6   Stephen Kotkin, 'A Dystopian Tale of Russia's Future', *The New York Times*, 11 March 2011.

is not bound to society by any moral or collective bonds, he is alone and at the mercy of the state. Nadezhda Mandel'shtam articulated this 'sickness' as the essence of the Soviet state:

> The loss of 'self' leads either to self-effacement (as in my case) or to blatant individualism with its extremes of egocentrism and self-assertiveness. The outward signs may differ, but it is the same sickness: the atrophy of true personality. And the cause is the same in both cases, namely, the severing of all social bonds. The question is: how did it happen? We saw it come about in front of our very eyes. All intermediate social links, such as the family, one's circle of friends, class, society itself – each abruptly disappeared, leaving every one of us to stand alone before the mysterious force embodied in the State, with its powers of life and death. In ordinary parlance, this was summed up in the word 'Lubianka'.[7]

By drawing a parallel between two historical periods as united by a common form of government, Sorokin affirms the finality of Russian history. Violence was the dominant feature of Ivan the Terrible's reign, just as it was in the Soviet period, and for Sorokin it also defines the present regime. Violence derives from a feeling of strength and power over others, and the 'new' Russia flexes its muscles before the rest of the world. The Russia of *Den' oprichnika* and *Sakharnyi Kreml'* is cut off from the rest of the world by the Great Russian Wall; it is simultaneously a fortress and a prison.

Sorokin's writing not only abolishes past taboos and demolishes all notions of authority, it also does not offer any renewal or regeneration. It is the end of things. Doctor Garin in *Metel'* (*The Snowstorm*, 2010) does not reach his destination and does not succeed in vaccinating the local population from a deadly epidemic, so we are left to wonder whether the epidemic will spread and destroy civilisation as a whole. Roman in *Roman* kills everyone and at the same time kills Russian literature. The 'stout-hearted four' all die, achieving nothing but their own grisly deaths. All of European history is ultimately reduced to one historically irrefutable fact: a month in Dachau is ontologically very different from a month in the country à la Turgenev. For Sorokin, this is where European history comes to an end.

The Russian national emblem is the two-headed eagle, where one head looks east the other west. In the twenty-first century Sorokin's Russian eagle definitively turns away from the West and looks East, towards China. In *Den'*

---

7   Nadezhda Mandelshtam, *Hope Abandoned: A Memoir*, trans. Max Hayward, Harmondsworth, Penguin Books, 1976 (18–19).

oprichnika China is Russia's major geo-political rival as the author seemingly grants the wishes of the ruling classes in Russia to denigrate and destroy America and Europe. In *Metel'* Garin does not reach his goal because of the continuing snowstorm, and is rescued from freezing to death by Chinamen. In Alexander Zel'dovich's film *Mishen'* (Target, 2011), co-scripted by Sorokin, Russian customs officials reap financial rewards as a transit country for huge tracks travelling between Europe and China (also a major theme in *Den' oprichnika*).[8]

With the increasing prevalence of Chinese words and phrases in Sorokin's texts, it becomes clear that the Chinese influence for Sorokin is assuming greater significance, though not necessarily positive. China offers the opportunity both for corruption and power-play: Russian border guards in *Mishen'* struggle to keep out the masses of illegal Chinese immigrants trying to cross the border in a parody of a computer shoot-'em-up game. The USA barely gets a mention in Sorokin's works. But as ever with Sorokin, it remains unclear whether he is affirming the importance of the East to Russia's economic and political future, or poking fun at his government's derision of all things American.

Mishen' provides an interesting development on Sorokin's picture of Russia in the near future. Although there are no *oprichniki*, and we do not know who or which party is in power, the Russia of 2020 is stable, its population content with a constant diet of mind-numbingly banal TV shows. There are, as in *Serdtsa chetyrekh,* four main characters who travel to a former military site in the Altai where cosmic particles have been collected and which apparently prevent people from growing old. Their dream therefore is never-ending youth, and to conquer death itself. But on their return to Moscow, seemingly rejuvenated, their individual personalities come to the fore, and they rebel against their everyday, monotonous existence. But tragedy awaits them all. Russia does not allow its citizens freedom of will, or to transgress beyond the permissible.

Sorokin works within a clearly-defined Russian eschatological tradition which declares the end of all things, without delineating a beginning of anything new. The mindset of finality is one he shares with several prominent

---

8   The director of *Mishen',* Alexander Zel'dovich (whose previous film, the 2000 film *Moskva*, was also scripted by Sorokin), is positively gushing about the Chinese national character: 'But in general a very good feeling remains of China. The Chinese know what they're doing. They have, in contrast to us, a mission, they are developing. When you are there, then it becomes very noticeable – people have a sense of tomorrow. Maybe they can't see it, but it is there, that tomorrow. And they are creating it'. See Alexander Zel'dovich, 'Ne stat' geran'iu', *Iskusstvo kino* (2011:3), 23–31 (30).

Russian cultural commentators. The satirist Evgenii Popov writes from the stance of the disempowered, the once hallowed status of the Russian writer who now struggles to makes ends meet, and his recent works are laced with bitter irony and lacerating satire. Though not aimed specifically at the government of the day, Popov's ire is directed at policies that have pauperised whole swathes of the population. Popov's writings reflect the end of the old regime, but do not embrace the new. The film-maker Alexander Sokurov avoids direct social commentary but shows a similar concern for the end of things. In films such as *Mat' i syn* (Mother and Son, 1997) and *Russkii kovcheg* (Russian Ark, 2003) his camera moves slowly across faces and paintings, the cinematic gaze focused on the beauty of the natural world and of artistic achievement. *Mat' i syn* and its companion piece *Otets i syn* (Father and Son, 2003) are about the end of things: a dying mother is looked after in her last moments by her son; a father and son take leave of each other as the son prepares to leave for army service, thus symbolically leaving behind his childhood. Beauty is corrupted by history, however, and Sokurov's films *Molokh* (1999), *Telets* (2000) and *Solntse* (2004) are about the men who changed history for the worst: Lenin, Hitler and Emperor Hirohito, respectively. These are studies not of power or men taking critical decisions that fundamentally affect the course of twentieth century history, but rather of men in their vulnerable, personal moments, human beings rather than historical characters. For Sorokin the 'end' is usually accompanied by violence or catastrophe, Sokurov allows the viewer to contemplate the end of beauty and art more sedately. But both these very different artists view post-Soviet society not as a new beginning for Russia, but rather as the end of the world they once knew.

Sorokin's ferocious onslaught against current political power in Russia continues unabated in *Sakharnyi Kreml'* (*The Sugary Kremlin*, 2008), where Russia in the near future is still governed in the manner of Ivan the Terrible. The Sovereign showers gifts on his people ('the children of Russia') from out of the sky as a symbol of his munificence. These gifts are in the form of sugar models of the Kremlin, which, in order to demonstrate loyalty, the population must lick. Such physical participation as an affirmation of political obedience is the modern counterpart of the Soviet government's encouragement of 'the norm' in *Norma*. The key difference is that whereas the Soviet government peddled filth and everyone had to swallow it, the 'new' government bestows gifts that the population is meant to find palatable, though the falseness of these gifts is evident. Whether it be shit or sugar, Sorokin's literalisation of the motifs of governance and control remains the dominant narrative strategy.

Sorokin's evolution from 'paper' to 'politics' can also be seen in his treatment of the motif of food. Very often, especially in the early short stories and novels, the human body is the food source, both the flesh and its excrement. Such details are intended above all to shock and repel the reader, and in *Mesiats v Dakhau* to damn totalitarianism, both Nazi and Soviet. Thus, when the author/narrator visits the notorious prison camp his account of cannibalism brings the two ideologies closer in a ferocious parody of a popular Soviet war poem: 'Жри меня, и я вернусь/только очень жри'.[9]

The devouring of people by the totalitarian machine is an image Sorokin returns to time and again. The collection of short stories *Pir* (*The Feast*, 2001) is built around cooking and eating, and the human body is again an absurd metaphor. But in post-Soviet Russia the human body becomes a commodity. In *Mishen'* the TV host Mitia pours his own blood into a wine glass and offers it up in front of a live audience to the politician and businessman who call for 'new blood' to regenerate the country. Rapacious consumption morphs into vampirism and becomes the abiding motif of Russia in 2020, a country where the super-rich have everything and want only to remain young and not lose their corporeal vitality.

Just as Russian history does not develop, neither does its literature. In *Den' oprichnika* the clairvoyant Praskov'ia Mamontovna cheerfully consigns Dostoevskii's *Idiot* (*The Idiot*) and Tolstoi's *Anna Karenina* to the flames, and at the end of *Mishen'* Zoia, the wife of Viktor, a government minister, throws herself under a train in despair at the collapse of her affair with Nikolai the border guard and amateur jockey (cf Vronskii). The final image from *Mishen'* is of a Russia in 2020 where the beggars and destitute invited to the table transform it into a debauch, and consciously and deliberately subvert and ruin all that they were supposed to celebrate. With its explicit reference to Luis Buñuel's 1961 film *Viridiana*, this final scene also encapsulates Sorokin's vision of the Russian soul as above all vindictive and destructive. Incapable of anything constructive, and deprived through centuries of pillage and violation of grace or munificence, it knows only brutality. The *narod* finally gets its vengeance. The major change for Russia in the post-Soviet period is that the *oprichniki* have taken over the stable, intent only on power but not management.

Is it really the case that Sorokin now waits for the likes of Khomiaga and Okhlop to arrest him and take him away to the Liubianka in the early hours, in time-honoured Stalinist tradition? Solzhenitsyn recounts how he prepared himself for arrest following the publication abroad of *GULag Arkhipelag*. Certainly, after the furore of the 'arrest' of *Goluboe salo* in 2002 Sorokin feared persecution, if not from the authorities then certainly from the shady pro-Putin

---

9 The 1992 edition of *Mesiats v Dakhau* is the culmination of Sorokin's 'anti-book' phase, as it contains no publication details, or even page numbers.

youth movement 'Idushchie vmeste' ('Moving together'), and he and his wife spent some time in Estonia.

The trajectory of Sorokin in post-Soviet Russia can be seen as a synecdoche of the passage of cultural history over twenty years or so. Back in August 1991 Evgenii Evtushenko published a poem about freedom and hope for the future, explicitly citing Pushkin and Tolstoi as the inspiration for the 'new' Russia that would emerge in the wake of the collapse of the Soviet Union.[10] Sorokin's negation of the importance of literature and the 'word' flew in the face of such romanticism, but destiny, it would seem, has come full circle. No longer simple a writer of "words on paper", Sorokin has understood the importance of history, and the Russian writer's place and role in it. His voice rails against conformity, corruption, tyranny and injustice. *Plus ça change…*

Irrationalism has tended to prefer the 'natural' to the 'rational', the importance of feeling and instinct as opposed to the power of reason. In Sorokin's recent work Russia reveals itself to be defiantly un-European, lacking a linear and logical historical trajectory, moving not forward but backwards, repeating its mistakes of the past and reverting to historical type. The result can only be disaster, and indeed, his 2013 novel *Telluriia* (*Tellurium*) shows Russia and Western Europe in post-apocalyptic meltdown.

The novel is set some time after 2028, with major European cities ravaged and destroyed after a momentous war with the Taliban, and Russia divided into regional republics (the 'Baikal Republic' and the 'United States of the Urals', for instance). 'Muscovy' is ruled by 'Orthodox Communists', with the trusted *oprichniks* enforcing law and order.[11] The novel consists of fifty chapters, all of them featuring different characters, viewpoints, styles and themes and none of them linked, with a fair sprinkling of the usual Sorokin motifs of extreme violence and graphic sex (interestingly, the book edition comes with a 18+ certificate stamped on its cover). The 'Tellurium' of the title is both the name of the Republic where peace and harmony exist, and the substance hammered into the head to provide hallucogenic tranquillity and strength.

In this novel 'the West' no longer exists as a political entity or force, and history and time itself seem to have stopped for Russia. In the texts of the 'new' Sorokin, the denial of history and politics, as in his youthful "words on paper", has been replaced by a strident politicised engagement with the powers-that-be, and a call to resist the return of Ivan the Terrible, his *oprichniks* and the

---

10   E. Evtushenko, '19 avgusta', *Literaturnaia gazeta*, 22 August 1991; for discussion, se A.D.P. Briggs, 'Russia's Muse on the Barricades: Yevtushenko's *August 19*', *Rusistika* 4 (December 1991), 26–29.

11   Vladimir Sorokin, *Telluriia. Roman*, Moscow: AST, 2013, 76.

sugar-coated lies and criminality of the Kremlin.[12] In Solzhenitsyn's terms Sorokin may not yet be a "great writer", but he is certainly not an "insignificant" one for the Russia of the early twenty-first century.

Bibliography

Abasheva, Marina. 2012. 'Sorokin nulevykh: V prostranstve mifov o natsional'noi identichnosti', in *Vestnik Permskogo Universiteta: Rossiiskaia i Zarubezhnaia Filologiia*, 1 (17): 2002–09.

Barry, Ellen. 2011. 'From a Novelist, Shock Treatment for Mother Russia', in *The New York Times*, 29 April 2011.

Briggs, A.D.P. 1991. 'Russia's Muse on the Barricades: Yevtushenko's *August 19*', in *Rusistika* 4:26–29.

Evtushenko, Evgenii. 1991. '19 avgusta', in *Literaturnaia gazeta*, 22 August 1991.

Gillespie, David. 1997. 'Sex, Violence and the Video Nasty: The Ferocious Prose of Vladimir Sorokin', in *Essays in Poetics*, 22, 158–75.

——— 2000. 'Vladimir Sorokin and the Norm', in A. McMillin (ed.), *Reconstructing the Canon: Russian Writing in the 1980s*. Amsterdam: Harwood Academic Publishers.

Kotkin, Stephen. 2011. 'A Dystopian Tale of Russia's Future', in *The New York Times*, 11 March 2011.

Kucherskaia, Maia. 2013. '"Telluria": Vladimir Sorokin opisal postapokalipticheskii mir', in www.vedomosti.ru/lifestyle/print/2013/10/21/1770841.

Mandelshtam, Nadezhda. 1976. *Hope Abandoned: A Memoir*, trans. Max Hayward. Harmondsworth: Penguin Books.

Paramonov, Boris, and Genis, Alexander. 2013. '"Telluriia" Sorokna', in www.svoboda.org/articleprintview/25187148.html.

Porter, Robert. 1994. *Russia's Alternative Prose*. Oxford: Berg.

---

12   Maksim Marusenkov asserts that Sorokin 'is not only the central figure of Russian postmodern literature, but also the major writer of the absurd in Russian literature'. See Maksim Marusenkov, *Absurdistskie tendentsii v tvorchestve V.G. Sorokina* (Avtoreferat dissertatsii na soiskanie uchenoi stepeni kandidata filologicheskikh nauk), Moscow, 2010, p. 20. For further discussion of Sorokin and the historical theme, see M.P. Abasheva, 'Sorokin nulevykh: V prostranstve mifov o natsional'noi identichnosti', *Vestnik Permskogo universiteta: Rossiiskaia i zarubezhnaia filologiia*, 1 (17), 2012, 2002–09, and A.V. Shcherbenok, 'Sorokin, travma i russkaia istoriia', *ib.*, 210–14. For discussion of *Telluriia* see, for example, Boris Paramonov and Alexander Genis, '"Telluriia" Sorokina', www.svoboda.org/articleprintview/25187148.html (consulted 10.03.2014), and Maia Kucherskaia, '"Telluria": Vladimir Sorokin opisal postapokalipticheskii mir', www.vedomosti.ru/lifestyle/print/2013/10/21/1770841 (consulted 10.03.2014).

Shcherbenok, A.V. 2012. 'Sorokin, travma i russkaia istoriia', in *Vestnik Permskogo Universiteta: Rossiiskaia i Zarubezhnaia Filologiia*, 1 (17): 210–14.

Solzhenitsyn, Alexander. 1970. *V kruge pervom*, in A. Solzhenitsyn, *Sobranie sochinenii*, vol. IV. Frankfurt: Posev.

────── 1975. *The Gulag Archipelago 2, 1918–1956; An Experiment in Literary Investigation, Parts III–IV,* trans. Thomas P. Whitney. London: Collins/Fontana.

Sorokin, Vladimir. 1994. *Roman,* Moscow: Obscura Viti and Tri Kita.

────── 1994. *Norma,* Moscow: Obscura Viti and Tri Kita.

────── 1994. 'Serdtsa chetyrekh', in *Konets veka,* ed. Alexander Nikitishin.

────── 1995. *Tridsataia liubov' Mariny,* Moscow: izd. R. Elinina.

────── 1995. *Ochered',* Paris: Sintaksis.

────── 1999. *Goluboe salo,* Moscow: Ad Marginem.

────── 2000. *Pir,* Moscow: Ad Marginem.

────── 2008. *Sakharnyi Kreml',* Moscow: AST; Astrel'.

────── 2009. *Den' oprichnika,* Moscow: "Zakharov".

────── 2010. *Metel',* Moscow: AST; Astrel'.

────── 2013. *Telluriia,* Moscow: AST.

Screenplays

────── 2000. *Moskva* ('Moscow'), co-written with Alexander Zel'dovich.

────── 2002. *Kopeika* ('The Kopeck'), co-written with Ivan Dykhovichnyi.

────── 2005. *4,* written by Vladimir Sorokin.

────── 2001. *Mishen'* ('Target'), co-written with Alexander Zel'dovich.

Zel'dovich, Alexander. 2011. 'Ne stat' geran'iu', in *Iskusstvo kino* 3:23–31.

Index

Abasheva, M.P.   529
Abrochnov, A.M.   314, 334
Adibaeva, Sh.   481, 494
Afanas'ev, Vladislav   380
Afrika (pseudonym of Bugaev, Sergei)   403
Agapkina, Tatiana   196, 201
Aikhenval'd, Iulii   241, 257
Akhmatova, Anna   12, 45
Akhutin, Anatolii   4, 5, 45, 94 112, 202
Albov, V.P.   281, 286, 308
Alcott   416
Aldanov, Mark   142
Aleksandrova, B.   241
Alekseev, M.P.   250, 257
Alekseevskii, Mikhail   201
Aleksievich, Svetlana   152, 153
Aleshkovskii, Iuz   499, 506
Alexander I, Tsar   314
Alexander II, Tsar   124, 128
Alexander II, Tsar   400, 401
Alexander III, Tsar   401
Allais, Alphonse   391
Alov A. P.   449
Amfiteatrov, A.   66
Amosov, Iurii   23
Andreeva, I.V.   137, 138, 157
Andreeva, Maria Fedorovna   142
Andreev-Burlak, Vasilii   402, 403
Anichkov, D. S.   16, 54
Anichkov, E. V.   359, 361, 365, 367, 536
Annenkov, P.   320
Annenskii, Innokentii   245, 257
Antokolskii, Mark   401
Antonioni M. P.   450
Apresyan, Yu. D.   455
Argunova, V. N.   8, 45
Aristotle   9, 16, 79, 87, 88, 261, 295, 304, 421, 430, 431
Asaf'ev, Boris   418, 421, 423, 431
Auerbach, Erich   3, 36, 415, 431
Aurelius, Marcus   261, 297
Averintsev, S.S.   91
Avilova, Lidiia   297
Avvakum   1, 360, 366
Azarkovich, T.   71

Bach, J. S.   36, 417, 422, 427, 428, 429, 432
Baiburin, Al'bert   195, 201
Bakhtin, Mikhail   96, 111, 287, 293–296, 298–303, 309, 310, 421, 423, 483, 496, 507, 516, 517
Bakunin, Mikhail   210
Balashov, Abram   xii, 35, 396
Balbiani, Valentine   89
Balod, A.   481, 494
Bamford, Christopher   107, 112
Baranova-Shestova, Natalie   231, 239, 269, 304, 309
Baranovskii, P.D.   456, 457
Barantsevich, K. S.   280, 286, 301
Baratynskii, Evgenii   34, 378, 379, 382
Bari, Adolf   404
Barnet, B. P.   448
Barry, Ellen   521, 529
Barskaia, M. P.   448
Barsov, E.V.   84, 92
Barsukov, N.   461, 464
Basil of Caesarea   85
Batai, Zh.   491, 494
Batalov, A. P.   449
Baudelaire, Ch.   314
Bauer, Evgenii   38, 438, 439, 441
Bazanov, V.G.   220
Bazin, A. P.   433
Beckett, Samuel   193
Belaia, I.A.   328, 334
Belinskii, Vissarion Grigor'evich   14, 20, 45, 56, 58, 70, 96, 101, 102, 103, 111, 112, 267, 309
Belting, Hans   507, 516
Belyi, Andrei   xviii , 31–32, 47, 62–63, 70, 270, 309, 339–340, 345, 347–351, 420, 423, 476, 486
Berdiaev, Nikolai Alexandrovich   xiv, 9, 20, 45, 95, 228–229, 237, 280, 441, 454
Berezovskii, B.   480
Berlin, Isaiah   4, 46, 65, 66, 121, 259, 262, 263, 265–268, 293, 294, 303, 307, 309, 310
Bernardskii, Evstafii   393
Bezhetsky   280
Bibler, Vladimir Solomonovich   109, 110, 111, 112

Bitov, Andrei   278, 305, 309
Blavatskaia, E.P. (Blavatsky, H.P.)   317
Blok, A.   63, 70, 316, 317, 334
Blum, Arlen   380
Bobykina, Irina   422, 431
Bocharov, S. G.   300, 309
Bodrova-Gogenmos, Tatiana   309
Bogatyrev, A.P.   155, 157
Bogatyrev, Petr   198, 201
Bohr, Niels   218
Bonetskaia, Natalia   294, 309
Borisova, Elena A.   459, 464
Borovoi, A.   209
Borts, A.   87, 92
Bosch, Hieronymus   43, 44, 507
Bouguereau, William-Adolphe   400
Boulez, Messiaen   415
Brafman, Iakov Aleksandrovich   115–116
Brant S.   87, 92
Brezhnev, Leonid   424
Briggs, A.D.P.   528, 529
Brilliantov, A. I.   7, 45
Britten, Benjamin   424, 431
Briusov, Valerii   62, 63, 67, 70
Broda, M.   51, 52, 53, 70
Brodsky, Joseph   5, 9, 15, 37, 45, 47, 270, 288, 298, 301, 309, 312
Bryzgel, Amy   403
Buber, Martin   295, 301
Buckle, H. T.   59
Bukovskii, Vladimir   500
Bulgakov, Mikhail   15, 46, 193
Bulgakov, S.   53, 135, 136, 153, 157, 204, 219, 280, 300
Bunin, Ivan   xvii, 33, 34, 370–383
Buonarroti, Michelangelo   89
Burbo, L.   478, 494
Burliuk, David   398
Buslayev, F.I.   73, 92
Byatt, A. S.   35, 45
Bychkov Yu. A.   457, 464
Bykov, A.V.   314, 334
Bykov, Dmitrii   9, 23, 45
Byzov, Leontii   147, 148, 157

Cabanis, P.   59
Cabet, Etienne   27, 205, 206, 207, 219
Caccini, Giulio   429
Camus, Albert   xvi, 28, 224, 235–240, 270, 274, 277, 291, 309, 315

Chaadaev, Petr   9, 16, 21, 55, 57, 161,162, 163, 164, 173, 174, 186, 188, 189
Chaikovskii, Petr   424, 427
Chamberlain, Lesley   506, 516
Chandler, E.   296, 311
Chandler, R.   296, 311
Charbonnel, Victor.   225, 239
Chekhov, Aleksandr   287, 290, 291, 297
Chekhov, Anton   xv, xvi, xix, 13, 30, 45, 66, 69, 70, 144, 157, 204, 220, 241, 258, 260, 261, 269–312, 317, 409
Chekhova, Maria   291
Chelnokov, Aleksei   501, 516
Cherepanova, Ol'ga   194, 201
Chernaia, L.   53, 70
Chernitskaia, M.B.   460, 464
Chernyshevskii, Nikolai   17, 56, 57, 66, 68, 70, 207
Chesnokova, V. (see Kasianova)
Chumakova, Tatiana   xiii, 18, 19, 26, 72, 306
Chirico, G. P.   440, 453
Chudakov, Aleksandr   271, 309
Chukhrai, G. P.   452
Churchill, Winston   24, 47
Clark, Katerina   36
Clayton, Douglas   293, 309
Clement of Alexandria   81
Climacus, Johannes   99, 100
Cohen, Hermann   340
Comte, A.   55
Cooper, David   511
Corbin, Henry Clarke   20, 106, 107, 112
Cornwell, Neil   15, 45
Cross, S.H.   81, 92
Custine, Marquis de   9
Cyril of Beloozero (Kirill Belozerskii)   73, 76, 86

D'iachenko, V. P.   451
Dal', Vladimir   199, 202
Damm, C. T.   262, 263
Daniil, metropolitan   88
Danilevskii, Nikolai   203
Darling, David J.   4, 46
Darwin, Charles   12
Davison, Ray   239
De Lazari, A.   51, 71
De Maistre, Joseph   161, 188
Deleuze, Gilles   29, 253, 256, 257, 515, 516

INDEX 533

Delumeau J. 86, 92
Dement'ev, Victor 154, 157
Descartes, René ('Cartesian') 4, 99, 101, 105, 236, 238, 261, 264, 504, 505, 506
Desjarden, Paul 231
Diakonov, Gennadii 295, 296, 309
Dmitrieva, R.P. 87, 92
Dobroliubov, Nikolai 17, 56, 57
Doherty, Justin 218, 219
Dombrovskii, Iurii 291, 309
Donaldson J. 81, 92
Donne, John 258, 310
Dostoevskii, Fedor Mikhailovich (see also Dostoevsky, Fyodor and Dostoyevsky, Fedor) 1, 3, 10, 27, 28, 32, 35, 43, 44, 52, 65, 69, 70, 115, 119, 120, 123–125, 130–133, 143, 167, 175, 179, 189, 193, 203–241, 265–267, 272–274, 276, 288, 289, 292, 301, 302, 305, 307, 310, 311, 322, 330, 331, 335, 336, 392, 421, 430, 463, 476, 486, 496, 497, 501, 503, 505, 506, 511, 513, 516, 527
Dovlatov, Sergei 308, 310
Dovzhenko, A. P. 38, 442, 443, 445, 449
Dragunskaia, L. 470, 474
Dudinskii, Igor' 501, 516
Dugin, Aleksandr 503
Dukel'skii, Vladimir 419
Durkin, Andrew 294, 297, 299, 310
Dzerzhinskii, F. 477
Dzhemal', Geidar 503

Edwards, T.R.N. 15, 46
Efimova, Mariia 501, 516
Egorov, B. 55
Eisenstein, S. P. 38, 441, 442, 449
Ekshtut, Semen 144, 145, 158
Elizabeth I, Queen 402
Elliger, W. 328
Emerson, Caryl 294, 310, 507, 516
Emerson, Ralph Waldo 416, 417
Enfantin, B.P. 208, 219
Engels, Friedrich 423
Eremin, I.P. 82, 92
Ern, Vladimir Frantsevich 111, 112
Erofeev, Venedikt 193, 496, 499, 501, 506, 508, 518
Erofeev, Viktor 222, 240, 280, 281, 302, 310
Etkind, A. 321, 324
Euripides 43

Evdokimova, Svetlana 274, 277, 283, 310
Evreinov, N. N. 365, 359, 360, 363
Evtushenko, Evgenii 528, 529

Faure, Élie. 28, 227, 240
Fedorov, Boris 464
Fedorov, Nikolai Fedorovich 94
Fedotov, Pavel xii, 35, 36, 388–394
Ferdinandov, Boris 35, 409, 412
Ferreira, M.J. 100, 112
Fet, A.A. 322
Feuerbach, Ludwig 215–218
Fichte, Johann Gottlieb 7, 314, 224
Ficino, Marsilio 503
Finke, Michael 251, 257
Flaubert, Gustav 224
Florenskii, Pavel 94, 104, 105, 108, 109, 313, 327, 332, 420, 423, 431
Fomin, Sergei 395
Foster, Stephen 417
Foucault, Michel 42, 43, 499, 507, 508, 509, 511, 515, 517
Fourier, Charles 205, 207, 208, 219
Frank, Joseph 295, 300, 310
Frank, Semen 17, 18, 27, 46, 203, 217, 218, 219, 221
Freiberg, L.I. 74, 92
Freud, Sigmund (also Freid, Zigmund) 253, 257, 317, 331, 477, 478, 480, 486, 491, 492, 495, 512, 515
Fridlender, G.M. 220

Gachev, Georgii 9, 46
Galen 75, 79
Galkovskii, Dmitrii 7, 8, 17, 20, 46, 258, 310, 316, 334
Gandhi, M. 328
Ganglbauer, Cardinal Cölestin Josef 398
Garnett, Constance 194, 202, 215, 216, 219, 292, 309
Gartman, Nikolai 219
Gates, Bill 143
Gavriushin, N.K. 81, 92
Gazdanov, Gaito 218, 219
Genis, Aleksandr (Alexander) 462, 497, 518, 529
Gennady of Novgorod 87
Gennep, Arnold van 194
George, M. 325, 335
Gershenzon, Mikhail 10, 46

Gide, André   16, 28, 226, 228, 240
Gideon   340
Gill, Christopher   97, 112
Gillespie, David   xiii, 14, 44, 45, 519, 529
Glaz'ev, Sergei   154, 155, 158
Glebov, Igor   418, 431
Goethe, Johann Wolfgang von   259, 261, 266, 273, 310
Gogol, Nikolai   vii, xiii, 14, 21, 26, 33, 35, 45, 58, 161, 175–182, 185, 186, 188, 193–202, 316 , 317, 334, 335, 393, 402, 476, 486
Goldenberg, Arkadii   xiii, 26, 27, 33, 193
Gol'dshtein, Aleksandr   496, 517
Golovin, Evgenii   503
Golubeva, S. N.   301, 311
Goncharov, I.   60, 64, 65, 67, 70
Goncourt, Edmond and Jules de   10, 46
Gordon, A.   460, 464
Gordovich, Kira   xiii, 39, 40, 469
Gorenshtein, Fridrikh   15, 283, 288, 310
Goricheva, Tat'iana   496, 505, 517
Gorkii, Maksim (Gor'kii, Maxim)   142, 291, 296, 310, 317, 434, 435
Gorny, Eugene   496, 517
Gorodetskii, Aleksandr   xii, 35, 409, 411
Gorodetskii, Sergei   408, 412
Gorshkov, M.K.138
Goya, Francisco   401
Grabar', Igor   400, 413
Granzhar, A.   250
Gregory of Nyssa   72
Gregory of Sinai   74
Gregory Palamas   76
Griboedov, Aleksandr   14, 64, 70
Grigorovich, Dmitrii   13, 45, 273
Gromyko, M. M.   460, 464–465
Grossman, Vasilii   24, 24, 46
Grübel, R.   xiv, 8, 30–32, 296, 313, 317, 325, 328, 330, 334
Guattari, Félix   515, 516
Gubaidulina, Sofia   36, 416, 427, 428, 429, 431
Gubskii, Je.   71
Guénon, René   42, 43, 499, 503, 504, 505, 506, 507, 510, 515, 517
Gurevich, A. Ia.   84, 90
Gurevich, Liubov   271, 310
Guseinov, Abdusalam   287, 310

Halpérine-Kaminsky, E.   225, 231, 233–234, 239

Hamann, Johann Georg   4, 29, 30, 45, 46
Hannay, A.   103
Hardy, Henry   29, 46, 259, 310
Harrison, Elizabeth   xiv, 1, 10, 21, 70, 157, 160, 257, 454, 464
Harrison, Victoria S.   100, 112
Hartmann, Eduard von   340
Hastings, Lady Mary   402
Hawthorne, Nathaniel   416, 417
Hecker, Max   266, 310
Hegel, Georg Wilhelm Friedrich   7, 17, 19, 20, 56, 97, 98, 99, 101, 102, 105, 106, 112–114, 209, 260, 314, 316, 332, 335, 343, 423, 498
Heidegger, Martin   20, 105, 106, 107, 111
Helvétius, C.   54, 55
Hemmings, F.W.J.   240
Henkel, Arthur   4, 46
Hilarion, Metropolitan of Kiev   81, 86
Hilbert, David   4
Hilton, Alison   394
Hippocrates   75
Hirohito, Emperor   526
Hitler, Adolf   313, 526
Howard, Jeremy   xiv, 5, 34–36, 387, 407, 412, 413
Howard, Richard   43
Hume, David   265
Husserl, Edmund   219, 260

Ianchevetskii, Vasilii   407, 414
Iavorskii, Boleslav   422, 423
Ignatius of Loyola   172, 173, 188
Il'ichev, Georgii   139, 146, 158
Il'in, Ivan   136, 158, 456, 465, 457
Ionesco, Eugène   193
Iosif Volotski (Joseph of Volotsk/Volokolamsk)   88
Ippolitov, S. S.   241
Iskander, Fazil   3, 22, 46, 268, 284, 291, 310
Iufit, E. P.   453
Ivan IV (Ivan the Terrible, Tsar)   18, 35, 72, 394, 456
Ivan, Tsarevich   394
Ivanov, V.V.   482, 495
Ivashkin, Alexander   xv, 3, 36, 37, 415, 431
Ives, Charles   416, 417, 418, 431

Jackson, David   395
James P. Scanlan   294, 310

Jesus Christ   32, 73, 75, 76, 80, 81, 83, 91, 161, 173, 286, 319, 320, 324, 347, 350, 400, 428, 429
John Cassian the Roman   77
John Climacus   73
John Damascene   88
John of the Ladder   73
John the Sinaite   73
Jones, Malcolm   44, 46, 516, 517
Joravsky, David   505, 517
Jung, Carl Gustav   26, 29, 193, 245, 257

Kabkova, Elena   xv, 38, 39, 455
Kafka, Franz   193
Kalatozov, M. P.   449
Kandinsky, Wassily   430
Kant, Emmanuel (Immanuel)   7, 17, 19, 55, 94, 97, 104–106, 110, 112, 113, 209, 229, 230, 236, 237, 259, 260, 265, 293, 294, 311, 314, 323, 342, 344, 351
Karamzin, Nikolai   38
Karlinsky, Simon   272–274, 278, 280, 282, 284, 286, 288–290, 292, 310
Karloff, B. P.   433
Karpenko, Aleksandr   197, 202
Karvan, Father Geronimo   398
Kasianova (the pen-name of V. Chesnokova)   140, 141, 153, 158
Kataev, Vladimir   260, 261, 310
Katz, M.   266, 310
Kaufmann, Walter   223, 240
Kazin, Aleksandr   148, 158
Kekushev, Lev   463
Kent, Leonard J.   194, 202
Kentish, Jane   265, 310
Kharms, D.   15, 193, 315, 333, 334, 471, 474, 476, 477
Khlebnikov, Velimir   398, 409
Kholopova, Valentina   429, 431
Khomiakov, Aleksei   7, 16, 56, 163, 164, 165, 166, 167, 188
Khriashcheva, N.   470, 474
Khromov, L.   484, 495
Khrushchev, Nikita   424, 464, 522
Khutsiev, M. P.   451
Kibalnik, Sergei   xv, xvii, 14, 17, 18, 27–29, 174, 203–205, 220
Kierkegaard, Søren   99, 100, 101, 102, 105, 112, 237, 260, 261, 267, 269, 311

Kireevskii, Ivan   7, 10, 16, 46, 56, 58, 98, 100, 101, 102, 104, 105, 107, 163, 164, 188, 322
Kirill (Patriarch of Moscow and All Russia)   153, 159
Kirill of Turov (Kirill Turovsky)   82
Kirk, Irina.   237, 240
Kissinger, G.   481
Kliment Smoliatich   79
Knabe, G.S.   242, 256, 257
Knipper, Olga   277
Kobrinskii, A.   333
Kodar, A.   484, 495
Kolesov, V.V.   82
Komech, A.I.   456–457, 464
Kondratiev, I.K.   457, 465
Korableva, G.   71
Koriagina, T.I.   157, 159
Kornienko, N.   469, 474
Korolenko, Georgii   280
Koshel', M.   493, 495
Koteliansky, S. S.   11, 46
Kotkin, Stephen   523, 529
Kovalov, Oleg   xvi, 37, 38, 433
Kozel'skii (Kozelskii), Ia. P.   16, 54
Kozlovskii, Petr   173
Krafft-Ebing   250
Krasnikov, Nikita   141, 158
Krasnoshchekova, E.   67,71
Krause, G.   328, 335
Kravchenko, Nikolai   410
Kremer, Gidon   428
Krestovskii, Vsevolod Vladimirovich   22–24, 115, 119–128, 131
Krichevskii, V. P.   447, 454
Kristeva, J.   475, 476, 478, 488, 495
Krivonos, Vladislav   195, 202
Kropotkin, P.   319, 335
Krüdener, B.B.J. von   314
Krusche, G.   328, 335
Kryzhanovskaia, Vera Ivanovna   22, 24, 126–131
Kukulin, I.   493, 495
Kulbin, Nikolai   xii, 35, 407, 412
Kuleshov, L. P.   440
Kulik, Oleg   387, 401
Kuprin, Aleksandr   300, 301, 311
Kurth, Ernst   421, 422, 431
Kushchevskii, I.   68
Kuße, H.   328, 334
Kuzmin, Mikhail   409

Kuznetsov, Erast   389
Kuznetsov, S.   70
Kuzovkin, A.   157,159

L'dov, Konstantin (pseudonym of Vitold-Konstantin Rozenblium)   410
L'vov, Dmitrii   153, 154, 155, 158
Laing, R.D.   42, 43, 499, 511, 512, 513, 514, 515, 517
Lambert, E.E   248
Lamm, Pavel   425
Landzert, Theodor   399
Laplansh, Zh.   475, 495
Latynina, Alla   222–223, 240, 475, 495
Lawrence, D. H.   307
Lazarev, Adolf   304
Leibnitz, 4, 261
Lektorskii, V.   219, 220
Lenin, Vladimir   423, 426, 526
Leonhard, Karl   344, 350
Leontiev (Shcheglov)   280, 286, 288
Lermontov, Mikhail   35, 404, 405
Lesevich, V.   60, 71
Leskov, Nikolai   14
Lessing, Gotthold Ephraim   400
Leviash, I.   51, 70
Lévinas, Emmanuel   110, 113
Levinton, Georgii   195, 201
Levkievskaia, Elena   195, 202
Levontina, I.V.   455, 465
Lévy-Brühl, Lucien   201
Liadov, A.   359, 366
Liebmann, Otto   340
Lifar', Serge (Serzh)   353, 355, 358, 360, 366, 367
Likhachev, Dmitrii   25, 26, 46, 157, 158, 462
Limonov, Eduard   500
Link, J.   315, 335
Litvinov, Ivy   290, 309
Livak, Leonid   227–229, 235, 240
Livingston, A.   296, 311, 469, 474
Lomonosov, M.   16, 54
Lomunov, K.N.   223
Lopatin, Lev Mikhailovich   94, 113
Lorie, S.   257
Losev, Aleksei   xviii, 18, 20, 46, 60, 61, 71, 95, 104, 113, 340, 350, 421, 423, 431, 507
Lotman, Iurii   5, 6, 46, 487, 489, 495
Lotze, Rudolf Hermann   340
Lourie, Arthur   419

Lubkin, Aleksandr Stepanovich   97
Lubotskii, Mark   426
Lukács, G.   313, 335
Lunin, Mikhail   161, 173
Lutchenko, V.   71
Luther, M.   261, 328
Lynn, R.   158

Mahler, Gustav   416, 427
Maiakovskii, V.   476
Maimin, E.   55
Makarov, Valerii   154, 158
Maksim Grek (Maximus the Greek)   90
Malevanskii, Archimandrite (Bishop) Sil'vestr   101, 113
Malevich, Kazimir   xii, 35, 387, 412, 443
Mal'tsev, Iurii   496, 517
Malygina, Vita   464, 465
Mamleev, Iurii   27, 42–44, 156, 159, 496, 497, 498, 499, 500, 501, 502, 503, 504, 505, 506, 507, 508, 509, 510, 511, 512, 513, 514, 515, 516, 517, 518.
Mamontov, Savva   406
Mandel'shtam, Nadezhda   524
Mann, Iurii   195, 202
Marcadé, Jean-Claude   229, 235.
Marcel, Gabriel Honore   235
Maria Nikolaevna, Grand Princess   401
Marino, G.D.   103
Markov, Vladimir [pseudonym of Matvejs, Voldemars]   412
Martin, Eva   307, 310
Martynov, Vladimir   416, 429, 430, 431
Marusenkov, Maksim   529
Marx, Karl   218, 423
Mashevskii, Aleksei   278, 284, 285, 286, 287, 311
Matiushin, Mikhail   412
Matlaw, Ralph E.   309
Matvejs, Voldemars (see Markov, Vladimir)
Maurice, Charles   225, 231, 233–234, 239
Maxim Ispovednik (St Maxim the Confessor or Maximus the Confessor)   7, 46, 86
Mazo, Margarita   425
Mazur, Natal'ia   496, 517
McCabe, Alexander   xvi, 3, 27, 28, 222
McConkey, James   507, 517
McMillin, Arnold   521, 529
Mechnikov, I.   56
Medici, Giuliano   89

INDEX

Medovoi, M.   55
Medvedkin, A. P.   449
Meerson-Aksenov, Mikhail Georgievich (cited as Meerson)   104, 106, 113
Mel'nik, V.   61, 71
Melanchthon, Ph.   328
Mendeleev, D.   56
Merezhkovskii Dmitrii   62, 241, 228, 257, 269, 271, 309, 311, 312
Messiaen, Oliver   415, 417
Midelfort, Erik   508, 517
Mierau, F. and S.   330, 334
Mikeshina, L.A.   219, 220
Mikhailov, K.   457, 464
Mikhailovskii, N.   66
Mikheev, M.   470, 474
Milevich, I.   477, 495
Miliukov, Aleksandr   205, 220
Mill, John Stuart   59, 138, 158
Miller, Orest   205
Milner, John   390, 391
Milosz, Czeslaw   261, 262, 304, 311
Mirlikiiskii, Nikolai   200, 202
Miroliubov, Viktor   274, 280
Mkrtchian, G.M.   147, 158
Mondry, G.   330
Montesquieu, Ch.   54
Morino, Gordon   240
Morozov family   405
Morozov, Igor'   197, 202
Morozov, Savva   142, 143, 158
Morrison, Simon   423, 432
Mozhaev, Andrew   457, 465
Müller, G.   328, 335
Muratova, K. P.   451
Mure, Geoffrey Reginald Gilchrist   102, 113
Mussorgskii, Modest   36, 394, 424, 425, 427
Nabokov, Vladimir   201, 469, 474, 486
Nashchokina, M.B.   458–459, 463
Naumov, V. P.   449
Nazirov, Romain   211, 220
Nechaev, Vasilii   35, 409–10, 412
Nefertiti   464
Nekrasov, N.   64
Nelidova, L.F.   248, 257
Nemeth, Thomas   97, 113
Nemschemeyer, Judith   12, 45
Nevskaia, Lidiia   198, 202
Nicholas I, Tsar   392

Nicholas II, Tsar   394
Niekerk, Carl   251, 257
Nietzsche, Friedrich   3, 29, 41, 204, 226, 228, 231, 237, 240, 242, 261, 265, 269, 279, 288, 302, 305, 311, 314, 346, 351, 356, 405, 477
Nil Sorsky (Nilus of Sora)   73, 74, 75, 76, 77, 78, 80
Nilus, Sergei Aleksandrovich   117–118, 121
Norshtein, Iurii   452
Nosina, Vera   422, 432
Nosov, S.   469, 474
Novgorodtsev, Pavel   210, 220, 328
Nurok, Alfred (see Silen)
Nuzov, Vladimir   152, 158

Obukhov, Nikolai   419
Odesskaia, Margarita   xvi, 3, 28–30, 34, 241
Odoevskii, V.   16, 55, 66, 67, 71
Olaszek, Barbara xvi, 3, 15–18, 51, 57, 59, 65, 71
Olesha, Iurii   476
Ol'shanskii, Dmitrii   502, 517
Onassis, Aristotle   149
Ordynskii, V. P.   451
Orlov, Ivan   282
Orwin, D.T.   323, 336
Osor'ina, Uliania   83, 93
Otverzhennyi, Nikolai   208, 209, 211, 212, 214
Ovid   254
Ovsianiko-Kulikovskii, D.   59, 71

Panfilova, T.V.   151, 159
Paperno, I.   68, 71
Papernyi, Vladimir   302, 303, 311
Paramonov, Boris   529
Pascal, Blez   261, 237, 304
Pasternak, Boris   1, 46, 521
Paul, apostle   18, 72, 89
Peace, Richard   2, 46
Pecherin, Vladimir   177, 178, 188
Pelevin, Viktor   xv, xvii, 40–42, 193, 475, 477, 478, 479, 481, 482, 484, 487–489, 490–495
Peredol'skii, V.V.   331
Pessard, Hector   225, 240
Petrashevskii, Mikhail   204, 208, 214, 220, 392–393
Petrushevskaia, Liudmila   15
Petrushevskii, D.M.   219

Piast, Vladimir   411
Piatigorskii, A.M.   323
Picasso, Pablo   450, 521
Pilniak, 15
Pilon, Germain   89
Piron, Geneviève   230, 240
Pisarev, Dmitrii   16, 17, 56, 57, 58, 59, 71
Pisemskii, A.   68
Pius IX, Pope   160
Plato   3, 16, 43, 51, 88, 108, 218, 229, 284, 347
Platonov, Andrei   39, 40, 43, 295, 296, 311. 469, 470, 471, 472, 473, 474, 505, 506, 517, 521
Platt, Kevin M.F.   395
Pleshcheev, A. N.   282, 286
Plotinus   261
Plotnikov, N.   328, 335
Pogodin, M.P.   88
Poincare, Henri   301, 311
Polani, Karl   134, 135, 159
Poliakov, Sergei Aleksandrovich   140
Poltoratskii, N.T.   230
Poluboiarinova, L.N.   251, 257
Pomialovskii, N.   68
Pontmartin, Armand de   225, 240
Pontriagin, L. S.   301, 311
Porfiriev, I.Ia.   85, 92
Porter, Robert   519, 529
Porus, V.N.   107, 108, 113, 219, 220
Praxiteles   242
Prigozhin, I.   491
Prilepin, Zakhar   9, 46
Prokofiev, Sergei   419, 424
Propp, Vladimir   193, 375, 376
Przebinda, G.   57, 71
Pudovkin V. P.   38, 442
Pushkin, Aleksandr (Alexander)   xiv, xix, 9–11, 14, 15, 21, 26, 35, 46, 47, 161, 162, 168, 170, 172, 173, 174, 175, 179, 180, 182, 186, 187, 189, 392, 409, 427, 476, 528
Putin, Vladimir   523, 527
Pyzhikov, A.V.   461

Rachinski, S. A.   313, 327, 332
Rachmaninov, S.   463
Rácz, Ildikó Mária   xvii, 33, 34, 370
Radishchev, A.   16, 54, 55
Radlov, E.L.   103
Rancour-Laferriere, Daniel   510, 517
Ranke, Johannes   399

Rasmussen, A.M.   105, 113
Rayfield, Donald   197, 198, 199, 200, 202
Ready, Oliver   xvii, 27, 42–45, 496
Reeder, Roberta   12, 45
Rembrandt   401
Remizov, Aleksei   xii, xviii, 32–34
Repin, Ilia   xii, 35, 36, 394, 404–405, 412
Riabushinskii, Stepan   397
Ricardo, David   134
Richardson, Mary   396
Rickert, Heinrich   32, 340, 348–349
Rimskii-Korsakov, Nikolai   400
Rizzoni, Alessandro   406
Roberts, A.   81, 92
Roberts, R.C.   103, 113
Rolf, Th.   315, 335
Romm, M. P.   451
Room, A. P.   449
Rousseau, J.-J.   54, 321, 323
Rozanov, Vasilii   14, 19, 26, 31, 95, 104, 114, 136, 159, 313–338, 241, 269, 307, 309, 311, 312
Rozenblium, Vitold-Konstantin (see L'dov, Konstantin)
Rudnev, V.   476, 477, 486, 490, 493
Rudneva, Anna   425, 432
Rybakov, B.A.   319, 336
Ryklin, Mikhail   496, 501, 517

Saburova, T.   53, 71
Sacher-Mazoch, von Leopold   29, 249–251, 253, 257
Safronova, Liudmila   xvii, 37, 40–42, 475
Saint-Simon, Claude-Henri   205, 208, 219
Sakulin, P.   55, 71
Saltykov-Shchedrin, Mikhail   15
Samover, N.   457
Sarab'ianov, Dmitrii   391
Sartre, Jean-Paul   xvi, 28, 30, 105, 113. 235–238, 240
Savei-Mogilevich, Fedor   404
Savinova, E.   69, 71
Savodnik, V.   209, 220
Sazonova (Smirnova-Sazonova), S. I.   280, 282, 283
Schechtel, Franz (Shekhtel, Fedor)   397, 405
Schelling, Friedrich   7, 17, 55, 100, 101, 313, 318, 333, 335
Schiller, F.   255
Schloezer, Boris de   xix, 28, 228, 231–234, 240

INDEX

Schmemann, Alexander (see also Shmeman, Aleksandr)   82
Schmid, Ulrich   496, 498, 504, 505, 508, 518
Schnittke, Alfred   xv, 36, 416, 427, 428
Schopenhauer, Arthur   261, 269
Scott, Walter   172, 179, 189
Scriabin, Alexander   36, 416, 418, 419
Sebastien, K.   227
Sechenov, I.   56
Sedgwick, Mark   503, 518
Seeley, Frank   10
Senderovich, Savely   260, 269, 311
Shakespeare, William   102, 291, 313
Shapiro, Konstantin   403
Shatalova, O.   483, 489, 495
Shatskaia, Nina   145, 159
Shchedrina, T.   219
Shcheglov (see Leontiev)
Shcherbinovskii, Dmitrii   398
Shchukin, V.   56, 71
Sheller-Mikhailov, A.   68
Shemiakin, John   258
Shepit'ko, L. P.   451
Shepoval, Sergei   500, 501, 518
Sherbowitz-Wetz, O.P.   81, 92
Shestov, Lev   xvi, xix, 1, 3–5, 11, 27–30, 36, 42, 43, 45–47, 107, 113, 200–204, 219, 220, 224, 228, 229–232, 234–241, 256–277, 279–281, 283, 285–289, 292, 293, 301–312, 322, 325, 336, 357
Shimizu, Takashi   212
Shmeman, Aleksandr (see also Schmemann, Alexander)   271, 312
Shmid, Ul'rikh   228
Shostakovich, Dmitrii   36, 416, 420, 421, 422, 424, 425, 426, 427, 428, 431
Shostakovich, Irina   424
Shpet, Gustav   95, 107, 108, 109, 113, 219, 220
Shukshin, Vasilii   15
Shuvalov, I.   54
Shvarts, Elena   260, 311
Siegele, Ulrich   428
Silen (pseudonym of Alfred Nurok), 406
Singer, M.G.   314, 336
Singer, P.   328, 336
Skaftymov, Aleksandr   210, 211, 220, 297, 312
Skovoroda, Grigorii   1, 111, 112
Sleptsova, Irina   197, 202
Sluchevskii, K.   67
Smend, Friedrich   427

Smirnov, I.P.   496, 518
Smirnova, A.   258, 280
Smirnova, Elena   199, 202
Smirnova-Sazonova (see Sazonova)
Smith, Adam   134
Smith, Marilyn   xvii, 32–34, 352, 364, 369
Smith, Oliver   xviii, 14, 19, 20, 32, 94, 103, 109, 113
Sobennikov, Anatolii   260, 261, 277, 293, 294, 309, 310, 312
Socrates ['Socratic principle']   100
Sokolov, Sasha   496, 499, 518
Sokurov, Alexander   453, 454, 526
Solov'ev, S.M.   113
Solov'ev, Vladimir   xviii, 8, 17, 20, 31, 32, 60, 61, 63, 71, 85, 92, 97, 103, 105, 109–111, 113, 151, 167, 189, 318, 328, 336, 339–351, 409
Solovei, T.   151, 159
Solovei, V.   151, 159
Solzhenitsyn, Aleksandr (Alexander)   23, 424, 519, 520, 522, 523, 527, 529, 530
Sorokin, Vladimir   xiii, 44, 45, 477, 496, 497, 518
Sorskii, Nil   19
Souvtchinskii, Petr (Pierre)   419
Spengler, O.   477
Spinoza   4, 261
St. Nifont   365, 366
Stahl, Henrieke   xviii, 31, 32, 47, 339, 346, 348, 350, 351
Stalin, Iosif (Joseph)   456, 461, 521, 522, 527
Staniukovich, K.   68
Stankievich (Stankiewicz), N.   17, 55
Stasov, Vladimir   420, 433, 434, 435, 454
Steiner, Rudolf   32, 348–351
Stepanov, Andrei   270, 275, 281, 287, 308, 309, 312
Sternin, Georgii   459, 464
Stirner, Max   27, 208–219
Storm, Theodor   249
Strakhov, N.   330, 332, 333
Stravinskii, Igor   419, 420, 424, 425, 426, 432
Stukalova, Olga   xviii, 38, 39, 455
Suarès, André   227, 240
Suda, M.J.   328, 336
Sukhikh, I. N.   270, 281, 308, 309
Surikov, Vasilii   396
Suvorin, Aleksei   205, 250, 272, 273, 278–280, 282, 284, 289, 290, 292, 306, 307
Svetlov, Mikhail   152

Sviridov, Georgii   424, 432
Swiderski, Edward M.   111, 113
Symeon the New Theologian   78
Sysoeva, M.   485, 495
Sytova, Alla   392

Tabachnikova, Olga   xix, 1, 29, 47, 157, 258, 269–271, 274, 275, 298, 309–312, 454
Tarkovskii, Andrei   433, 436, 449, 452, 454
Tarnas, P.   51, 71
Tarnovskaia, Julia   393
Taruskin, Richard   420, 432
Tatlow, Ruth   428, 432
Taylor, Mark C.   110
Tcherepnine, Alexander   419
Tereshchenko, Fedor   403
Tertullian   318
Thomas à Kempis   161
Thoreau, Henry   328, 416, 417
Tiapkov, S. N.   8, 45
Tikhanov, Mikhail   387, 388
Tikhonov, V. A.   280
Timiriazev, K.   56
Tiutchev, Fedor   1, 21, 47, 64, 96, 113, 182, 183–189, 302, 312
Todorov, Tsvetan   37, 435, 436, 437, 439, 451, 454
Todorovskii, Petr   451
Tolstaia, S. M.   194, 195, 202
Tolstaia, T.   258
Tolstoi, Lev Nikolaevich   31, 35, 66, 69, 104, 144, 145, 200, 203, 224, 225, 241, 260, 276, 289, 302, 312, 313–338, 394, 409, 463, 476, 523, 527, 528
Tooke, Christopher   xix, 21–24, 115, 201, 494
Toporov, V.   477, 495
Tretiakov, Pavel   395
Trilling, Lionel   514, 518
Tristram, Ph.   87
Troitsky, Artemii   80, 83
Trubetskoi, Evgenii Nikolaevich   105, 106, 108, 109, 113
Trubetskoi, Nikolai   211
Tsvetaeva, Marina   301
Tuchman, Barbara   389, 394
Turgenev, Ivan   xvii, 10, 28, 29, 34, 65, 67, 70, 204, 241–254, 256, 257, 409

Turovskaia, M. P.   452, 453
Twain, Mark   211
Tylor, E. B.   360

Urusevskii, S. P.   449
Usacheva, Valeriia   200, 202
Usoltsev, Fedor   403, 406
Uspenskii, Boris   200, 202
Uspenskii, Petr   412
Ustvolskaia, Galina   416, 427
Uvarov, A.S.   88, 89, 90

Vail', Petr   497, 518
Valkenier, Elizabeth Kridl   396, 397
Vampilov, Aleksandr   15
Vandebilt, Cornelius   148
Velázquez, Diego   396
Vereshchagin, Vasilii   397, 398
Vertov, D. P.   38, 444, 445, 449
Vetlovskaia, Valentina   204, 220
Viardot, Pauline   29, 241, 246, 248, 249
Viazemskii, P.   64
Vinogradova, Liudmila   196, 197, 198, 199, 201, 202
Vinokurova, Natalia   xix, 25, 26, 134
Vishnevetskii, Igor   419, 420, 432
Vladimir Alexandrovich, Grand Duke   394
Vladimir, Great Prince   81, 86
Vogüé, E.-M.   224, 225, 227, 239, 240
Volkelt, Johannes   32, 340–346, 348–351
Volkonskii, V.A.   157, 159
Voloshin, Maksimilian   397
Voltaire   54, 56, 59, 261, 279, 280
Volynskii, A.L.   314, 322, 336
Vrubel, Mikhail   xii, 35, 36, 404, 412
V'ugin, V.   470, 471, 474
Vvedenskii, Aleksandr   97, 114, 315
Vysheslavtsev, Boris   218, 220
Vyshnegradskii, Ivan   419

Wagner, 421, 422, 431
Walicki, A.   55, 71
Weber, Max   135, 153, 314, 336
Weill, P.   462
West, J.   97, 114
Winckelmann, Johann Joachim   400
Windelband, Wilhelm   32, 340, 345–346, 348–349, 351

Wood, Allen W.   97, 114
Wood, James   277, 312

Xenakis   415

Yablokov, E.   469, 474

Zaitzev, Boris   241, 249
Zamiatin, Evgenii   15, 522

Zel'dovich, Alexander   525, 530
Zenkovskii (Zen'kovskii), Vasilii   7, 47, 61, 71, 258, 260, 312, 317, 318
Zhakkar, Zhan-Filipp   228, 240
Zheimo, B.   68, 71
Zhikhareva, T.   322
Zhukovskii, Vasilii   241, 249, 257
Zola, Emil   224
Zorkaia N. P.   434, 435, 438, 452, 454

Printed in the United States
By Bookmasters